Best Places
to Stay in
New England

Laura & Scott
603-224-9116

Hampton Inn

8496 9891

515 ~~South Street~~
S. Concord St.

603-224-5322

D0775995

The Best Places to Stay Series

Best Places to Stay in America's Cities
Kenneth Hale-Wehmann, Editor

Best Places to Stay in Asia
Jerome E. Klein

Best Places to Stay in California
Anne E. Wright

Best Places to Stay in the Caribbean
Bill Jamison and Cheryl Alters Jamison

Best Places to Stay in Florida
Christine Davidson

Best Places to Stay in Hawaii
Kimberly Grant

Best Places to Stay in Mexico
Bill Jamison and Cheryl Alters Jamison

Best Places to Stay in the Mid-Atlantic States
Dana Nadel Foley

Best Places to Stay in the Midwest
John Monaghan

Best Places to Stay in New England
Christina Tree and Kimberly Grant

Best Places to Stay in the Pacific Northwest
Marilyn McFarlane

Best Places to Stay in the Rockies
Roger Cox

Best Places to Stay in the South
Carol Timblin

Best Places to Stay in the Southwest
Anne E. Wright

Best Places to Stay in New England

Christina Tree and Kimberly Grant

Bruce Shaw, Editorial Director

Seventh Edition

HOUGHTON MIFFLIN COMPANY
BOSTON • NEW YORK

For information about permission to reproduce selections from this book,
write to Permissions, Houghton Mifflin Company, 215 Park Avenue South,
New York, New York 10003.

Seventh Edition

ISSN: 1048-5449
ISBN: 0-395-86936-6

Printed in the United States of America

Maps by Charles Bahne
Design by Robert Overholtzer

This book was prepared in conjunction with Harvard Common Press.

QUM 10 9 8 7 6 5 4 3 2 1

To L.M. Otero
*   — K.G.*

To Liam, Timothy, and Christopher Davis,
Three of the best sons anywhere
*   — C.T.*

We would like to thank Bruce Shaw
for his continuing interest and support

Contents

Introduction

This isn't simply a guide to inns and/or B&Bs. While it describes the crème de la crème of inns and B&Bs (we've selected 275 from the more than 800 we visited), it also presents the full gamut of places to stay in New England — from grand old resorts to working farms, from spas to ski resorts to windjammers, from some of the most expensive places to some of the best bargains.

Some of our suggestions are well known, but many are found in no other guidebook. We have personally checked each of the places included and tried to describe them with as few adjectives and as much detail as possible. We decide what to include based on merit, not money. In contrast to the policy of most lodging guides, there is no charge for inclusion, no "processing fee," and no requirement to resell our book.

We have included available web sites in this edition and encourage readers to use the Internet to check the visuals of places their considering. We feel confident, however, that, as the amount of material on lodging continues to flood the market via the Intertnet and paid listings books, unbiased, consumer-geared guides such as this — based on a real knowledge of what's out there — will only increase in value.

The organization of Best Places to Stay has been radically altered over the years. In the first four editions, places were grouped by their nature. Now they are arranged by region and town, making it easier to see the choices available in each area.

Still, we recognize that many people, especially those within easy striking distance of New England, are less interested in a specific destination than in the kind of place they want to visit. For one trip, it may be a place to take the family; for another, to get away as a couple or to be alone at a spa or fishing lodge. To that end, we categorize places within each region at the start of each chapter and for the entire region in the "What's What" appendix. You might want to flip right to "What's What" for an overall look at "family finds," "romantic getaways," for places to which you will feel comfortable traveling solo, or for places that will accept your pet.

Obviously our criteria differ when judging the best city hotels and the best farms. Our primary standards are cleanliness, the palpable presence of a host (be it a manager or owner), and a conviction that we would like to stay in that place for more than one night. But most of all we look for an ingredient we can only call "soul." Some places have it, but many more don't. We have done our very best to provide you with accurate and up-to-date information. Inevitably, certain information changes quickly. We try to include places where the ownership is stable and long-term, but if you find the innkeeper has changed when making a reservation, listen to your instincts when talking with the new owner. Our reviews reflect the personality and presence of the innkeepers we met, and we can't speak for the quality of a place when the ownership has changed.

Before making a reservation, we suggest that you make a list of the four or five points that most concern you when you travel and make them clear to the person taking your reservation. If money is important, be sure you know what your room rate will be, tax and gratuity included. If noise bothers you, ask for a quiet room. If a double bed won't do, ask for a queen-size bed. We have found over and over again that we get what we ask for.

We are proud of *Best Places to Stay in New England*. It's the most comprehensive description of outstanding lodging places in this region. Please let us know what you think.

We would like to thank Bruce Shaw for his role as the book's co-creator and as the publisher who has parlayed Best Places into a series that now includes thirteen books.

DEFINITIONS OF CATEGORIES

Bed-and-Breakfasts

Many lodging places use the terms "inns" and "bed-and-breakfast" interchangeably. We use the term B&B to refer to a place that serves breakfast rather than breakfast and dinner. Many of these lodgings are every bit as handsome and professionally operated as the places we describe as inns. The hosts, however, tend to sit down after breakfast and talk with their guests. A minority make you feel as though you're staying in someone's home. With every edition, shared baths are becoming less common.

City Stops

New England's major cities all offer a far broader choice of lodging — from bed-and-breakfasts to luxury hotels — than they did just a few years ago. Many cater to business travelers during the week and may provide services like fax machines, computer hookups, and secretaries. For weekend lodging at large hotels, be sure to inquire about the myriad special packages designed to lure leisue travelers. The hotel rates we print are "rack rates," intended to serve as a relative guide. With a bit of luck, you'll never have to pay these prices. You'll frequently have to add the cost of parking, however. Smaller establishments have firm prices.

Family Finds

Beginning in the mid-19th century, taking in summer people was seen as a way to help farm families make ends meet — much as it is today with the farms we have described. Our other Family Finds range from fairly pricey resorts owned by and geared to families, like the Tyler Place on Lake Champlain and Oakland House on the Maine coast, to cottages and ski resorts, condo complexes, and family-geared inns.

Gourmet Getaways

Entire books have been devoted to "gourmet getaways," but our recommendations feature inns and places to stay where the quality of the guest rooms matches the cuisine. The range of culinary expertise in New England rivals that found anyplace in the country — from classical French to nouvelle to new American. To avoid disappointment on Saturday night, book dinner reservations along with your room. Furthermore, some inns offer a very limited or set menu; be sure to inquire if you don't eat meat, for instance. If you wish to plan your stay around the chef, be sure it is not his or her night off.

Grand Resorts

The grand dames of New England innkeeping are all rather large, fairly formal, and extremely inviting. Unfortunately, less than a dozen of the hundreds of 19th-century grand hotels in this region have survived. Look for them along the Maine coast and in the White Mountains. A half-dozen fairly new resorts, scattered throughout New England, emulate the dignity and opulence of the Gilded Era.

Inns

The country inns we've selected range from 18th-century taverns to a number of spacious summer homes that have been converted to inns. Each is very different, but in all of them the innkeeper makes you feel genuinely welcome and both breakfast and dinner are served.

Island Getaways

New England has thousands of miles of coastline and dozens of large and small islands just a short ferry ride away from the bustle of the mainland. Something in everyone craves a periodic escape to an island — be it a beach-fringed resort island like Martha's Vineyard or Nantucket or small, unspoiled outposts like Monhegan or Vinalhaven. When making reservations to the smaller islands, ask the innkeeper about the ferry schedule.

Romantic Getaways

These are the places we think of when we want to be completely alone with someone we like in a beautiful place. Some innkeepers pamper guests with candlelit rooms, chocolates on the bed, whirlpool baths, and luxurious furnishings. Others simply provide a means to enjoy the natural beauty of the surroundings. Either way, we generally include places to stay that are large enough so that you can disappear and no one will notice. While it seems like every inn and bed-and-breakfast has something they call a honeymoon suite, we've included only the really special places.

Spas and Fitness Centers

The spa spectrum is narrower than a few editions ago, but we trust this trend will reverse. Included are places designed to provide not only relaxation but increasing energy and physical well being.

Sports Resorts and Wilderness Retreats

From wilderness fishing camps to the region's best self-contained ski resorts, this category is not only for the sports enthusiast but for families in search of a healthy, away-from-it-all experience--be it llama trekking, mountain biking, whitewater rafting, sculling, running, or skiing. We have included a number of classic old Maine "camps" (a central lodge in which meals are served, surrounded by cottages), many dating back more than a century.

Definition of Terms

Innkeeper: We intentionally use different terms to describe the caretaker of a property: innkeeper, host, manager, and owner, for instance. Each conveys a different relationship to the place and is intended to alert you to its nature.

Rates/Meals: The terms that we occasionally use to describe meals are MAP (Modified American Plan), which includes breakfast and dinner, and EP (European Plan), an elegant way to say that no meals are included in the rates. Don't be put off by the seemingly high MAP rates until you stop to add the price of dinner for two to the price of a room by itself. B&B (Bed-and-Breakfast) means that breakfast is included, while AP (American Plan) rates include three meals a day.

Rates: There's more to the jargon of room rates, and we have tried our best to avoid it. Generally our prices indicate the cost of a room shared by two people. When the price for a single room is significantly less, we have noted the rate. (It is often just $10 less.) Otherwise, we note instances where the price of the room changes with the number of people in it, as in cottages or condos. Many seemingly expensive resorts, in particular, offer a wide variety of packages that make them competitive with smaller lodgings. We cannot begin to cite each one; be sure to ask about the different options when you reserve. Nor can we cite the litany of rates for each different season, each different month, each different holiday period. In general, we quote high-season rates, but keep in mind that they are sometimes slashed by half in the off-season.

Included: The term refers to which meals are included in the price of the room. It may also tell you whether other meals are available, although not included in the rates.

Minimum stay: Many places now require that you stay a minimum of two or three nights on weekends during their busiest periods. For some establishments, this policy is only enforced (or preferred) with reservations; for others it is always firm. Certainly, places will take guests for one night when they have openings.

Added: There is also the little-noted detail of room and meals tax, which is inescapable. It varies from state to state, and in Massachusetts, within the state. We never add it to the rates but cite the percentage and leave you to do the arithmetic. In addition, a number of places also add a service charge or a gratuity (tip), which can run as high as 18 percent, adding a very substantial amount to your final bill.

Payment: Cash and traveler's checks are accepted everywhere, and personal checks, almost everywhere. Regarding credit cards, we simply note "All major ones" to indicate that the basic ones — American Express, MasterCard, and Visa — are accepted. If one card in particular is not accepted, we note the cards that are.

About the Authors

Christina Tree, who has been the book's co-author since its inception, has written more than one thousand articles about New England for the *Boston Globe* in the past twenty-eight years and continues to contribute to the paper's Sunday Travel section on a regular basis. She also co-authors *Maine, An Explorer's Guide; Vermont, An Explorer's Guide; New Hampshire, An Explorer's Guide;* and *Massachusetts Beyond Boston and Cape Cod, An Explorer's Guide.* She has also served as the editorial consultant and chief contributor to the *Berlitz Travellers Guide to New England.* In 1991 she was the first travel writer to receive the annual award of the New England Innkeepers Association. In 1995 she received the Lila Wallace Reader's Digest fellowship to research 19th-century tourism patterns at the New England Antiquarian Society, and in 1997 she received the President's Award from the Maine Publicity Bureau.

Kimberly Grant began her association with Best Places in 1984 as a field researcher for Vermont and became a full-fledged co-author for the third edition. In addition to authoring *Cape Cod and the Islands, An Explorer's Guide;, Best Places to Stay In Hawaii;* and co-authoring *Lonely Planet New England,* Kim is the general editor and photographer for the *Insight Guide to New England.* She has also contributed to a number of national guidebook series, including the *Berlitz Traveller's Guide to New England* and *Fodor's Boston.* She logs more than 25,000 miles a year traveling around New England. When she's not staying in "Best Places," she enjoys the anonymity of wilderness campgrounds and big city hotels. Based in Boston, she is also a widely published photographer.

The authors welcome your thoughtful suggestions, observations, and recommendations. They may be reached directly via e-mail:
    kgrantfoto@aol.com
    ctree@worldnet.att.net

January 1998

New England

Maine

Vermont

New Hampshire

Massachusetts

Connecticut

Rhode Island

Belne '87

Connecticut

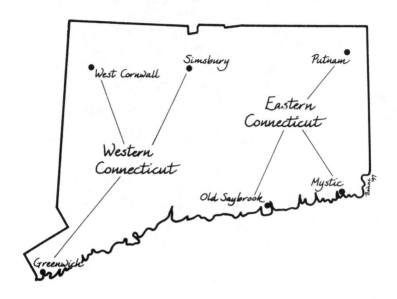

Western Connecticut

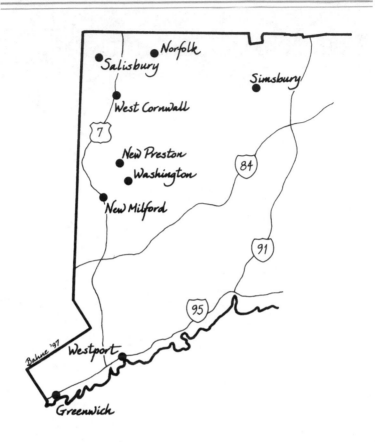

Best Bed-and-Breakfasts

Norfolk
Manor House, 17
Simsbury
Merrywood Bed & Breakfast, 21
West Cornwall
Hilltop Haven Bed & Breakfast, 27

Best Gourmet Getaways

Greenwich
The Homestead Inn, 11
New Preston
Boulders Inn on Lake Waramaug, 15
Washington
The Mayflower Inn, 23

Best Inns

Greenwich
The Homestead Inn, 11
New Preston
Boulders Inn on Lake Waramaug, 15
Salisbury
Under Mountain Inn, 19

Best Romantic Getaways

New Preston
Boulders Inn on Lake Waramaug, 15
Washington
The Mayflower Inn, 23
Westport
The Inn at National Hall, 25

Connecticut is a New England anomaly. To some it's a bit like New Jersey, a state you drive through on your way to somewhere else. To others it's a treasury of old New England in modern dress, with so much to offer that there's no reason to go farther.

Steeped in history and tradition (not for nothing is the Constitution State called the Land of Steady Habits), it's also contemporary and trendy. Nowhere is the ambivalence more pronounced than in Connecticut's western reaches, the regions bordering New York that serve, for many, as the gateway to New England.

You may know that Connecticut leads the country in per-capita income, that Hartford is the insurance capital of the nation, that Fairfield County is the home to more Fortune 500 companies — and their executives — than anyplace except New York City. But did you know that the state's modern facade masks backroad byways, lovely lakes, meandering rivers, covered bridges, 17th-century houses, Colonial villages, and historic seaports — all in an area so compact that no point is more than a two hours' drive from any other?

If you enter Connecticut from the southwest, be sure to stray from I-95, or you'll think you're still in metropolitan New York rather than the domain of the Connecticut Yankee. The Merritt Parkway, for instance, is a far more scenic route and introduces you to the rolling, wooded terrain that lies ahead and all around.

As you drive along the Fairfield County gold coast, pause in **Greenwich** to ogle palatial estates, both old and new. Take in the latest avant-garde art installation at the Bruce Museum. In the glittering city of **Stamford,** shop in the enormous, enclosed Stamford Town Center, or browse through the galleries and boutiques of South Norwalk, which is gradually living up to its nickname, SoNo. **Norwalk** boasts a 50-room Victorian château, the Lockwood-Mathews Mansion. **Westport,** just east of Norwalk, offers dining and shopping in a lovely riverside town.

Head inland on Route 7 to the sylvan hills and fancy homes of New Canaan. Drive on to Ridgefield, as imposing a Colonial Connecticut town as you'll find within an easy drive of New York City. The 1772 Keeler Tavern, which is now a house museum, paved the way for contemporary inns and restaurants of distinction, and the Aldrich Museum of Contemporary Art blends nicely with the gracious old homes that line Main Street.

Thirty minutes northeast is Hartford, which offers much more than insurance companies. Visit the Wadsworth Atheneum, the nation's oldest continually operating public art museum. You may want to duck into the capitol and Old State House, but if you have only a few minutes, don't miss the Mark Twain House and the Harriet Beecher Stowe House next door.

Just south of Hartford are historic houses in Old Wethersfield and Newington. North of Hartford, wander through the underground caves where prisoners were kept during the 1700s at the

Old New-Gate Prison and Copper Mine. West of Hartford, the primary attraction in **Simsbury** is the Massacoh Plantation, a complex of buildings depicting 300 years of local heritage.

Upcountry from Fairfield County is Connecticut's northwest corner — the "Quiet Corner," as many a travel writer have described it. Secluded it is, and you'll be surprised that such an area remains so rustic, remote, and unspoiled. Here, the Litchfield Hills face the better-known Berkshires and yield more public land and state parks than any other section of southern New England.

Dense forests, steep hills, and rushing rivers shape the landscape. Kent and Cornwall are rugged and outdoorsy, the perfect foils for the late Yankee artist-author Eric Sloane and his museum collection of Early Americana. The towns share the glories of the Housatonic River, still crossed by covered bridges (there are two in **West Cornwall**). Sharon and Salisbury are sedate and sophisticated, havens for the good life as lived by noted residents and weekenders alike. **Lake Waramaug (New Preston)**, with its alpine setting and hills covered with vineyards, is Brigadoon revisited. All is quaint and quiet in charming **Norfolk,** the scene of a fine summer chamber music festival, as well as in Riverton, where reproduction Hitchcock chairs are made. In **Washington** you'll find the outstanding Institute for American Indian Studies.

The county seat is Litchfield, a National Historic Landmark. This quintessential 18th-century New England village, perched on the crest of a long ridge, shelters a wealth of history (the nation's first law school, the birthplace of Harriet Beecher Stowe) and natural attractions (White Flower Farm — a horticulturist's delight).

Greenwich

The Homestead Inn

420 Field Point Road
Greenwich, CT 06830
203-869-7500
Fax: 203-869-7500

> A refined country inn an
> hour from Manhattan

Innkeepers: Lessie Davison and Nancy Smith. **Accommodations:** 23 rooms (all with private bath), 6 suites. **Rates:** $130–$195 per couple; $92 single. **Included:** Continental breakfast; all meals served except lunch on weekends. **Minimum stay:** None. **Added:** 12% tax. **Credit cards accepted:** All major ones. **Children:** Welcome. **Pets:** Not accepted. **Smoking:** Permitted. **Handicap access:** No. **Open:** Year-round.

➤ **The chef is famous for his soups and Sunday brunch, but don't overlook hors d'oeuvres like French country pâté, warmed oysters with caviar, or a pot of snails with Pernod.**

Less than a mile from Interstate 95, the Homestead is on a quiet rural road in an exclusive, residential neighborhood. This inn serves as a great example of what talent, energy, vision, money, and location can produce. Who could ask for more than impeccable service, elegant dining, and well-appointed rooms? Certainly not the midweek business people relaxing on the front lawn before dinner or New Yorkers away for a weekend or any traveler who enjoys the finer things in life.

When the main 18th-century building (converted to an inn in the mid-1800s) was purchased by the present innkeepers in 1979, it was in a state of total collapse. Onlookers were skeptical, suggesting that the residents of Greenwich would rather dine in the city than in their own backyard. But the inn was lovingly restored and its restaurant, La Grange, is an award-winner.

There are two dining areas: the glassed-in porch, which is particularly nice on a sunny day for breakfast or lunch, and the main dining room, which, with its original exposed beams, was formerly a barn. In the dining room the tables are well spaced and set with fine china and crystal. In the evening, crystal oil lamps and soft outdoor lighting add a romantic touch. As you'd expect, the perfectly balanced wine list is extensive.

The classical French cuisine is superb and has been awarded the highest ratings by the *New York Times*. The Homestead's chef, Jacques Thiebeault, made his mark in two very well-known New York restaurants — Le Cirque and Le Cygne. Duck with black currant sauce and wild rice, rack of lamb, and medallions of lobster in a creamy wine sauce are a few recommended entrées.

There isn't much common space indoors, but you can enjoy the fireplace in the backgammon room. Outdoors, you can enjoy a glass of lemonade on white wicker settees on the front porch.

All of the guest rooms are delightfully decorated and furnished. Each is a corner room or has a private porch. The wallpapers and fabrics are luxurious, and some of the furnishings are priceless antiques. Each room offers plush bathrobes, electric blankets, and TVs. The Robin Suite is so named because, in the process of stripping away six layers of wallpaper, delicate stencils of robins dating from 1860 were discovered. The late-19th-century Independence House next door, with a double-hung outdoor porch, has eight lovely rooms with modern baths and fine carpeting. The General's Suite, with the best bathroom in the inn, is located here. The private cottage has a suite and two bedrooms.

The Continental breakfast consists of good strong coffee and mini muffins; a more extensive selection is available for an extra charge.

New Milford

The Homestead Inn

5 Elm Street
New Milford, CT 06776
860-354-4080
Fax: 860-354-7046

> **B&B and motel-style rooms that are a good value**

Proprietors: Rolf and Peggy Hammer. **Accommodations:** 14 rooms (all with private bath), 1 suite. **Rates:** $78–$101 per couple, $140 in suite. **Included:** Expanded Continental breakfast. **Minimum stay:** 2 nights on weekends, May through October. **Added:** 12% tax. **Credit cards accepted:** All major ones. **Children:** Welcome, $6–$10 additional in same room with parents. **Pets:** Not accepted. **Smoking:** Limited to certain guest rooms. **Handicap access:** No. **Open:** Year-round.

➤ **It's nice to have a moderately priced place to recommend as a base for exploring the Litchfield Hills area.**

In 1985, when the Hammers purchased this two-building complex near the center of New Milford, it had had a previous life as a rather nondescript hotel and restaurant. After spending considerable time and talent on it, they replaced the restaurant with motel-style rooms and renovated the rooms in the Victorian house. It's a remarkable transformation. Rolf and Peggy, whose hospitality skills are finely honed, are active in innkeeping associations.

The guest rooms all have a telephone, TV, a desk with good lighting, and air conditioning. Rooms in the main house are decorated with antiques and reproduction pieces. Most have had a recent coat of paint and wallpaper and are bright and cheery. Room 25 (a corner room) is a favorite, as is Room 1 on the first floor, which can accommodate four people. In the Treadwell House, a former restaurant, the rooms are more uniform and look like motel rooms, albeit pleasant ones. Although they have drop ceilings, they also have perky window treatments and nice carpeting. A few rooms can be connected to accommodate a family of four.

In the summer, window boxes brighten the tidy buildings on the small plot of land. The main house has a common room with a fireplace, a piano, couches, and a few chairs. A Continental breakfast buffet is served here at a trestle table. Wicker furniture fills the small, enclosed front porch that is covered with indoor-outdoor carpeting.

The Homestead Inn is a good place for travelers to stop on their way to northern New England or as a base for exploring the lovely Litchfield Hills area. On weekdays, the place fills up with business travelers.

New Preston

Boulders Inn on Lake Waramaug

Route 45
New Preston, CT 06777
860-868-0541
800-552-6853
Fax: 860-868-1925
boulders@bouldersinn.com
www.bouldersinn.com

> **A romantic retreat with fine dining**

Innkeepers: Ulla and Kees Adema. **General manager:** Kevin Martin. **Accommodations:** 7 rooms (all with private bath), 2 suites, 8 cottages. **Rates:** $250–$350 per couple, MAP from May through October and all weekends throughout the year; $200–$250 off-season mid-week; B&B rates $50 less and subject to availability on weekends. **Included:** Varies with rates; lunch available in summer and October. **Minimum stay:** 3 nights on summer and October weekends (otherwise a $50 surcharge will be added). **Added:** 12% tax, 15% service charge. **Credit cards accepted:** All major ones. **Children:** Lodging by special arrangement. **Pets:** Not accepted. **Smoking:** Permitted in some areas. **Handicap access:** Yes. **Open:** Year-round.

➤ **Across the street from Lake Waramaug, the inn has a private lakefront beach, floating dock, and a narrow lawn (hidden from the road by trees) set with lounge chairs and umbrellas. Head over to the old-fashioned boat house for a game of Ping-Pong on a foggy day, or take a rowboat, canoe, or paddleboat onto the lake.**

The Ademas preside over this country-elegant inn, a first-class operation intent on providing guests the ultimate in service (without being obsequious we might add). This gracious inn has it all: a scenic lakeside location, excellent cuisine, and luxurious accommodations.

The Shingle-style main house, with massive boulders flanking each end, was built in 1895 and became an inn in the late 1940s. Most guest rooms here — with lovely antiques, wall-to-wall carpeting, and hundred-year-old quilts — have lake views. In fact, even the smallest room (with a four-poster wrought-iron bed) has a small outdoor deck with a lake view. All rooms are sophisticated and stylish, low-key but tony. The bathrooms are sparkling white, with pristine fixtures.

The three rooms in the adjacent carriage house, built in a style that is compatible with the main inn, feature stone fireplaces. They are tastefully furnished with French and traditional antiques. (Of the Carriage House rooms, we like C-1 the best.) Those desiring more privacy should reserve one of the cottage rooms — each has its own deck. Recently renovated, some have two-person Jacuzzis and each has a freestanding fireplace with an unlimited supply of wood. North and South Gem have the best lake views. Many cottages have two bedrooms, perfect for a family. Like the rest of the accommodations, each has a fresh feel with ultra-white walls.

The focal point of the inn's living room is an expanse of windows that allow unrestricted views of the lake and lush perennial gardens (which Ulla deftly tends). Both this room and an adjoining TV den have fireplaces. Sunsets are spectacular from any of the wing chairs and overstuffed couches.

Dining at the Boulders is taken very seriously: the *New York Times* has rated it with three well-deserved stars. In warm weather, request a table on the terrace overlooking the lake. (House guests get preferential seating.) Inside, most tables have a view of the lake, but the view is particularly good from the octagonal addition.

The regional American menu, with nightly specials, is eclectic and changes seasonally. Chef David Anderson presides. On our last visit we sampled sweet strawberry soup and an outstanding bouillabaisse. The pink salmon — simply but artfully presented — was stuffed with shredded leeks and served on a bed of spinach. Fresh herbs are plucked from the inn's garden. The inn's ever-expanding wine cellar is stocked with more than 4,500 bottles.

Breakfast consists of a buffet of baked goods (perhaps walnut scones and lemon poppy seed muffins), juices, fruit, and a choice of two entrées (perhaps a ham and cheese omelet or cinnamon French toast). Eggs are always available in any style.

Hikers enjoy climbing Pinnacle Mountain, just behind the inn. The inn has loaner bicycles and guests can use the tennis court next door. With all its fireplaces, the Boulders is also a romantic place to retreat for a winter weekend. Antiquing in New Preston and surrounding villages is popular year-round.

Norfolk

Manor House

P.O. Box 447
Maple Avenue
Norfolk, CT 06058
860-542-5690
Fax: 860-542-5690

> **A Tudor mansion with romantic Victorian overtones**

Innkeepers: Diane and Hank Tremblay. **Accommodations:** 9 rooms, 1 suite (all with private bath). **Rates:** $110–$190 per couple. **Included:** Full breakfast. **Minimum stay:** 2 nights on weekends; policy relaxed as the weekend in question approaches. **Added:** 12% tax. **Credit cards accepted:** All major ones. **Children:** Over age 12 welcome; $20 additional person in room. **Pets:** Not accepted. **Smoking:** Not permitted. **Handicap access:** No. **Open:** Year-round.

➤ **While you're in the area don't miss the Hillside Gardens, with five acres of perennial gardens surrounding a 1780s farmhouse. It's one of the few private residential gardens in America open to visitors.**

Owners since 1984, Diane and Hank Tremblay have earned the title of veteran innkeepers; you'll be well cared for. Not content to rest on the inn's already considerable merits, their continuous upgrades are impressive. Since the Tremblays also run a bed-and-breakfast reservation agency, they have their fingers on the pulse of the industry.

The Manor House, an 1898 gray stucco Tudor home with English overtones, was built by Charles Spofford, the man who designed the London subway system. The house, encircled by a stone wall and dominated by a big stone entrance, is situated on five acres of well-tended fields, lawn, perennial gardens, and raspberry bushes.

With strains of classical music wafting through the house and tea set out in the informal bar, the inn is immediately inviting. The grand, open entryway has rich cherry paneling, while the living room has a beamed ceiling and a six-foot-long baronial fireplace. It's very warm and cozy, furnished with a nod toward the arts and crafts movement. Stained glass windows (a gift from Louis Tiffany to the original owners) and Moroccan rugs add even more warmth. There are plenty of comfortable arm and wing chairs, couches, and Oriental carpets. Game boards, magazines, and lots of area information lend a homey feel to the common areas. An informal glassed-in porch, furnished with white wicker, is cozy — thanks to the addition of a gas fireplace — even when there is a blanket of snow outside.

Diane's collections of Victoriana, art, and English antiques are placed carefully around the house. All the guest rooms are individually decorated and many feature fireplaces (gas or wood, for which there is an additional charge) and private decks. The Morgan Room has a balcony overlooking the lawn and a private antique elevator that still works, while the Country French Room has a skylight and a two-person soaking tub. The Spofford Room has a fireplace, balcony, and a king-size canopy bed with ornately carved rails taken from an old ship. The English Room, quite secluded at the end of the hall, is equipped with a two-person Jacuzzi. Those on a budget will appreciate knowing that the three smaller rooms are all very nice. On the third floor, the Victorian Room is spacious and private. The only drawback to this room pertains to showering: the curtain in the Jacuzzi leaves little room for maneuvering.

On our last visit, a simple breakfast of fresh fruit, muffins, and scrambled eggs (or fruit pancakes if you prefer) was served on china at three formally set tables. You can also request breakfast in bed, or on the porch or lawn. In any event, be on the lookout for deer in the backyard, possibly munching on Hank's tomato plants or fallen apples. There are also beehives behind the house that Hank raids for honey for your morning toast.

Guests are free to use the extensive collection of 78-rpm records, compact discs, and to thumb through old books by Connecticut publishers. Depending on the season, the inn can arrange for a private carriage, hay, or sleigh ride. Norfolk is the summer home of the Yale Music School; try to coordinate an overnight with a chamber music concert under the stars.

Salisbury

Under Mountain Inn

482 Undermountain Road
(Route 41)
Salisbury, CT 06068
860-435-0242
Fax: 860-435-2379

A chef-owned country inn with British overtones

Innkeepers: Marged and Peter Higginson. **Accommodations:** 7 rooms (all with private bath). **Rates:** $170–$195 per couple, MAP; multiple-night packages. **Included:** Full breakfast and dinner. **Minimum stay:** 2 nights on weekends. **Added:** 12% tax, 7% service. **Credit cards accepted:** MasterCard, Visa. **Children:** Over age 6 welcome. **Pets:** Not accepted. **Smoking:** Not permitted in guest rooms. **Handicap access:** No. **Open:** Year-round.

➤ **The inn is just 35 minutes from Tanglewood, but it feels as if its across the Atlantic.**

On a rural road, across from a picturesque horse farm and riding center, the Under Mountain Inn is a delightfully homespun place. The house was built in the early 1700s, and retains its Colonial architectural integrity. For example, during the inn renovation, the Higginsons discovered in the attic the wide paneling now used in the dark and cozy pub. The rebellious colonial owner had probably hidden it there rather than turn it over to the King of England, as the law then required.

Despite the Colonial structure, the inn has a decidedly British ambiance: Marged's heritage is Welsh and Peter is from England. You can peruse a copy of the *Manchester Guardian* in the large front parlor or any number of books and magazines about all things British. Furthermore, Samuel Smith beer from Lancashire is on draught in the pub; the video library contains a large selection of British comedies, sitcoms, and movies.

As for the air-conditioned guest rooms, we particularly like the two brightest and largest rooms in the front of the house. Another room has two double beds that can accommodate a family or two couples traveling together. Covent Garden boasts a bathroom as big as the bedroom. Every room has a decanter of sherry.

The three Colonial-style dining rooms are intimate and warm, each with a roaring fireplace, simple wooden tables, and worn Oriental carpets over wood floors. Local art graces the walls. We always like dining with chef-owners, and Peter is no exception. Peter always offers a choice of fish, fowl, and flesh entrées (on our last visit it was scrod, roast Cornish hen, and steak and kidney pie); on Saturdays you'll find a lamb dish on the menu. The inn accepts outside diners on weekends, but on weekdays, house guests have the dining rooms all to themselves. For dinner on really quiet nights, the Higginsons will set up wing chairs and a private table in front of the fireplace in the small parlor.

A full English breakfast is served on alternate mornings. If you're only staying one night, hopefully you'll get lucky. In warm weather, the front porch wicker and rockers beckon. In cooler weather, you'll enjoy afternoon tea, complete with English tea service.

Since the innkeepers chambermaid their own rooms, the inn is closed after breakfast until 2:00 P.M. (Don't even think about checking in early!) The Litchfield Hills area offers an abundance of activities, depending on the season: hiking, biking, antiquing, vineyard touring, and even skiing.

Simsbury

Merrywood Bed & Breakfast

100 Hartford Road (Route 185)
Simsbury, CT 06070
860-651-1785
Fax: 860-651-8273
mfmarti@compuserve.com

> **A world-class B&B, hosted by world travelers**

Innkeepers: Mike and Gerlinde Marti. **Accommodations:** 2 rooms (both with private bath), 2 suites. **Rates:** $110, $140, $200 per couple; $20 each additional person. **Included:** Full breakfast. **Minimum stay:** None. **Added:** 12% tax. **Credit cards accepted:** All major ones. **Children:** Not appropriate. **Pets:** Not accepted. **Smoking:** Not permitted. **Handicap access:** No. **Open:** Year-round.

➤ **Merrywood combines the best qualities of a small, personalized bed-and-breakfast with the privacy and amenities found in five-star hotels. This is most keenly experienced at breakfast.**

This gracious Colonial Revival brick house, secluded within a 5-acre pine grove, is a well-kept secret. The Martis purchased the house in 1991, elegantly renovated it, and opened it as a B&B in late 1994. Since the Martis have traveled extensively, they know what travelers appreciate and they take great pride in providing it.

The common space is creatively furnished and decorated with pieces garnered during the Martis' world travels, from museum decommissions, and local auctions. This is one of the most tactile places we've encountered. Gerlinde collects textiles and is an antiques dealer, so the house is a showcase for one-of-a-kind pieces. The living room showcases a collection of wooden shoes, ceremonial Indian robes, and hats from the Far East. Little notes describing the pieces are usually tucked into the antiques. Sofas, tables, and chairs are draped with kilims, carpets, and tapestries. You won't have a hard time finding a comfortable nook to settle in. The sun porch is inviting, but then again, so is the library. French doors lead from one room to another. Light opera or classical music wafts through the manse.

Guest rooms are outfitted with slippers and robes, fine toiletries, air conditioning, television, and VCR. There are movies to choose from on the bookshelf. The Empire room is named for its period furnishings, while the Victorian room features a lace canopy bed. The private bathroom of Victorian is outside the room, but the Martis have rigged up an aesthetic and functional solution. The two-room suite, furnished with European antiques, has a kitchenette and small sauna. Rent this if it's available. On special occasions (with a two-night minimum), the Martis rent their own spacious suite. It features Far Eastern decor, subtle lighting, a solarium-like bedroom area, and a bathroom with an oversized steam shower with multiple heads and a whirlpool tub. They leave no trace of themselves behind, and while we're not completely comfortable with the idea of innkeepers being displaced, we highly recommend this room.

Breakfast is a treat, arguably the best within a hundred miles. You choose the hour (between 6:00 and 10:00 A.M.) and the place (in the library, on the porch, or in the formal dining room). Wherever you dine, you'll be served on the Marti's collection of antique china and porcelain. No two settings are alike. Make your selection the night before: perhaps a special egg dish like a "sea legs omelet," with tomato, crabmeat, and an onion and wine sauce, or pancakes — thin and light, with blueberries or bananas. Coffee aficionados take note: espresso and cappuccino are offered. The presentation is special.

The already manicured grounds continue as a work in progress. With each new season, new formal and informal gardens are carved out, benches added, stone walls created. Plan to spend some time outdoors.

If you have the time and inclination, afternoon tea can be as gracious an affair as you like, and may include cucumber finger sandwiches.

There's plenty to do in this neck of the woods: hiking, biking, ice skating, hot air ballooning. Hike to the top of Talcott Mountain, just a half-mile from Merrywood, for what many consider to be the best view in Connecticut. The Farmington River also provides fishing, tubing, and canoeing.

Washington

The Mayflower Inn

Route 47
Washington, CT 06793
860-868-9466
Fax: 860-868-1497

A luxurious country hotel with elegant dining

General manager: John Trevenen. **Accommodations:** 25 rooms and suites (all with private bath). **Rates:** $240–$395 per couple in rooms, $400–$580 in suites. **Included:** All meals available. **Minimum stay:** 2 nights on weekends; 3 nights on holidays. **Added:** 12% tax. **Credit cards accepted:** All major ones. **Children:** Over age 12 welcome. **Pets:** Not accepted. **Smoking:** Not permitted in guest rooms. **Handicap access:** No. **Open:** Year-round.

➤ **Local lore has it that one night in May of 1933, Eleanor Roosevelt drove up to the Mayflower in her Buick Roadster, checked in unexpectedly, and spent a quiet night alone. Now, as then, the Mayflower offers an impeccable setting where late-20th-century notables come for a discreet retreat.**

This Relais & Chateau property is deserving of all the accolades reaped upon it. Reminiscent of great French auberges and English country-house hotels, the inn has been meticulously decorated and boasts impeccable service.

Constructed originally as a boys' school in 1894, this cluster of buildings on 28 acres served as an inn from 1920 to the late 1980s. It was in a deep state of disrepair when the current owners, part-time Washington residents, purchased it in 1990. Instead of renovating it (it was too far gone), they tore it down and started from scratch. After two years and an undisclosed sum of money — *voilá* — a first-class country hotel appeared.

The approach to the house sets the stage. Drive beside a pond down a long curving driveway, past old stone walls, specimen trees, century-old rhododendrons, and through wooded acres to reach the centerpiece main house. Clad in shingles and clapboard, the three-story gambrel-roofed house shares the spotlight with two other guest houses, a teahouse, and a pool and bathhouse. The grand, wraparound wicker-furnished front porch overlooks the grounds.

Sumptuous paneling in both living rooms complements the Persian and Oriental carpets on hardwood floors. Many of the antiques were purchased specifically for the house on European shopping extravaganzas. (All the king-size four-poster beds were made specifically for the Mayflower in England.) Handsome appointments include floor-to-ceiling bookcases (filled with well-worn leather-bound volumes) and gilt-framed 18th- and 19th-century oil paintings. Floral tapestry upholstery, chintz drapes, and leather chairs would make Ralph Lauren feel quite at home.

The 28,000-square-foot house boasts a two-story lobby and wide corridors leading up to the guest rooms. Each room is decorated with its own color palette and contains a mix of antique and reproduction furnishings. Some have a fireplace or balcony; all have Frette linens and spacious marble-filled bathrooms with mahogany wainscoting. As you might imagine, you won't go wrong with any room.

The dining room is sophisticated and spacious, overlooking woodlands, lawn, and formal gardens. Among the highly recommended dishes served on Limoges china are ragout of white asparagus for an appetizer, and duck comfit with a warm salad of mixed mushrooms and Parmesan toast as a main course. The menu changes seasonally. A tempting selection of desserts or after-dinner drinks in the piano bar will please most palates.

The teahouse is set up for conferences and the inn has a private dining room as well. Above the terraced hillside is a heated pool and a tennis court with an Omni surface. In addition to a state-of-the-art fitness room, the inn also offers a wide variety of massages as well as aromatherapy and facials. Also for the body are nearby walking and hiking trails.

Westport

The Inn at National Hall

2 Post Road West
Westport, CT 06880
203-221-1351
800-628-4255
Fax: 203-221-0276

A luxurious, exquisite, and whimsical jewel

General manager: Keith Halford. **Accommodations:** 15 rooms and suites (all with private bath). **Rates:** $195–$395 per couple in rooms, $395–$525 in suites from June through November; midweek rates less. **Included:** Continental breakfast; lunch and dinner available. **Minimum stay:** 2 nights on weekends from June through November. **Added:** 12% tax. **Credit cards accepted:** All major ones. **Children:** Cot and crib available. **Pets:** Not accepted. **Smoking:** Not permitted. **Handicap access:** No. **Open:** Year-round.

➤ **Built in 1893, this building once housed Westport's first bank, a shirt shop, a newspaper, and a furniture store. After five years were spent gutting, renovating, and decorating it, it reopened as an elegant hotel on its 100th anniversary in 1993.**

This red brick Italianate structure, a Relais & Chateaux property, is an eastern seaboard jewel modeled after Europe's best manor houses. (It certainly spiffs up the restored waterfront boardwalk along the Saugatuck River!) To say that the elite hotel offers luxuriously appointed rooms is to understate the matter. Rarely matched in New England, these rooms must be seen to be appreciated — they are stunning.

The management is very protective of guests' privacy. After the doorman is assured of your reservation, you are escorted up to the second-floor lobby and greeted by name or announced. Immediately you are in another world — more genteel than the one you left, even in tony Westport. The elevator, which looks like a well-stocked library, will not be your last encounter with fanciful *trompe l'oeil* works.

Each guest room is exquisite, a work of art, and in fact contains many works of art. The interior designer reaps more yards of praise than fabrics used in each guest room. Although the least expensive rooms are smaller, they are just as meticulously done. All rooms have stenciled or *trompe l'oeil* walls; most have canopy beds enveloped with lush fabrics. Many rooms have river views. The Waterford Room, in particular, has a prime view and is quite large.

Some rooms, like the Henny Penny Suite, boast two-story living areas with 18-foot ceilings and oversize windows with sumptuous drapery. In these rooms the loft bedroom overlooks a cozy living room. The Indra Room, a large corner room, is particularly spectacular. The spacious Equestrian Suite has a fireplace, kitchenette, a whirlpool, and separate living room and bedroom. All the guest rooms have cable TV, a VCR, and a refrigerator with complimentary nonalcoholic beverages. Bathroom amenities are top-notch.

A Continental breakfast is served in the drawing room, where there is also a well-stocked honor bar. Early morning coffee and the newspaper can be brought to your room. The restaurant at National Hall, off the ground floor lobby, offers riverside dining and a French- and Italian-inspired menu. Room service is available around the clock.

Only one hour from Manhattan, the inn caters to New Yorkers on weekends, businesspeople, and sophisticated travelers from around the world.

West Cornwall

Hilltop Haven Bed & Breakfast

175 Dibble Hill Road
West Cornwall, CT 06796
860-672-6871
Fax: 860-672-6871
www.abbington.com/hilltop/hilltop.html

An unusual and old-fashioned B&B

Innkeeper: Everett Van Dorn. **Accommodations:** 3 rooms. **Rates:** $112–$160 per couple. **Included:** Full breakfast. **Minimum stay:** Roughly 2 nights; 3 nights on national holidays. **Added:** 12% tax. **Credit cards accepted:** None; personal checks accepted. **Children:** Over age 14 welcome. **Pets:** Not accepted. **Smoking:** Not permitted. **Handicap access:** No. **Open:** Year-round.

➤ **The nearby Cornwall Inn is surprisingly good and well regarded.**

Head through the covered bridge, beyond an enchanting New England village, and up a long private road to Hilltop Haven. The B&B, a homey stone and wood house, provides a real escape for urbanites. (New Yorkers favor this place, so you should reserve early if it sounds like your kind of place.) From the spacious terrace, you can often see for 75 miles across to the Catskills. This is one of the best views from a B&B we know of.

This small house, in Everett's family since 1930, is set on 63 forested acres. There are two focal points: the stone library and a flagstone terrace set with Bentwood chairs. The stone library, which has the feel of a remote and quaint mountain lodge, a raised ceiling, exposed beams, and windows on three sides, is magnificent. The room is furnished with some fine antiques as well as older pieces draped in makeshift slip covers, worn Oriental rugs, and an eclectic assortment of books and things. In the winter, you'll end up in a rocking chair in front of the five-foot-wide stone fireplace. If you stay in the winter, come with another couple, since we can't imagine wanting to enjoy the small space with strangers. Everett offers sherry in the evenings.

The shaded terrace, surrounded by tall pines, hemlocks, and oaks, overlooks the Housatonic River and surrounding foothills. It's an idyllic place to have an afternoon drink, watch the splendid display of fall foliage, or listen to crickets on a warm summer night. Other common spaces are filled to the brim with family mementos, knickknacks, and collectibles. If you prefer open, airy interior spaces, this place is not for you. Musicians appreciate the 1937 Kranich & Bach baby grand piano, although it is wedged between a bit of this and that.

Each paneled bedroom in the guest wing is comfortable although not fancy, with air conditioning. One is furnished simply with a double sleigh bed, reading lamps over the bed, and a sitting-writing area that looks out toward the woods. The other has a vintage double brass bed. Both have private lines and answering machines. Everett has set up each room with a coffee pot, all ready to turn on when you get up in the morning. (Since breakfast isn't served until 10:00, you'll appreciate this.)

Everett is a charmingly eccentric and endearing character. He enthusiastically presents the late-morning meal to guests at individual tables in the stone library or on the terrace. After a few leisurely cups of coffee or tea, you'll get a fruit course followed by one of Everett's unusual specialties, like shrimp-cheese strata or a vegetable quiche (with green beans on our last visit) with crème brûlée or Grand Marnier French toast. (Tell Everett ahead of time if you don't want a touch of alcohol in the morning!) The meal is served on family Stafforshire china with etched crystal water glasses.

In picturesque West Cornwall Village and nearby Cornwall Village, you'll also find an old general store, fine 18th- and 19th-century houses, a little village green, an old train station, craft shops, a great bookstore, and a historic red covered bridge across the Housatonic. The Northeast Audubon Center, with 11 miles of trails on 700 acres, is a 15-minute drive from Hilltop. The Appalachian Trail crosses the hills immediately facing the house, a 5-minute drive away.

Eastern Connecticut

Best Bed-and-Breakfasts

East Haddam
Bishopgate Inn, 35
Mystic
House of 1833 Bed & Breakfast, 41
Pomfret
Cobbscroft, 46
Putnam
Fellshaw Tavern, 47

Best Gourmet Getaways

Chester
The Inn at Chester, 34
Ivoryton
Copper Beech Inn, 37
Old Lyme
Bee & Thistle Inn, 43

Head south from Hartford, down along the Connecticut River to Middletown and on to **East Haddam,** where the stage of the ornate Victorian Goodspeed Opera House is filled from April through December with American musicals and where theater-goers sip champagne on a riverfront balcony.

The actor William Gillette's medieval castle, now a state park, stands guard on a hill in neighboring Hadlyme, which is linked to the opposite shore by the Chester Car Ferry, a service that originated in 1769; it gives you a brief sense of what it felt like to travel on this old river highway. Just downriver is Essex, a noted yachting center from which the first American warship was launched in the Revolution. It also offers the Connecticut River Museum and the Valley Railroad, which has excursions that connect with one of the area's several river cruises.

Two fine old towns flank the broad mouth of the Connecticut River. **Old Lyme,** on the eastern bank, is still known as the place American Impressionists gathered at the turn of the century under the auspices of Florence Griswold, whose handsome home is now a museum of note. Across the river in **Old Saybrook,** both residents and visitors can fish and stroll at Saybrook Point, the point at which New England's longest river empties into Connecticut Sound.

The shoreline west of Old Saybrook to New Haven and east to New London holds Connecticut's best beaches, most of them private. The largest and most beautiful of those open to the public is Hammonasset Beach State Park, in **Madison.** It includes 930 acres of woods, marshes, and meadows for birding and walking as well as a two-mile expanse of sand. This area is also studded with 18th-century and even some 17th-century historic house museums; the most interesting is the stone home Henry Whitefield built of local granite in Guilford in 1640. In Branford the Shore Line Trolley Museum offers an hour-long ride through salt marshes and woods, and from Stony Creek an excursion boat cruises among the Thimble Islands. New Haven, the cultural and commercial center of the shoreline, is the home of Yale University and its two outstanding art museums: the Yale University Art Gallery and the Yale Center for British Art.

Following the shoreline east from the Connecticut River, you reach bustling New London and Groton, twin cities straddling the Thames River. This is navy and submarine territory, where the nuclear submarine *U.S.S. Nautilus* is on view. The U.S. Coast Guard Academy stands on a hilltop across the river from the U.S. Naval Submarine Base, the nation's largest. In New London, the Shaw Mansion, built of granite in 1756, and Monte Cristo, the gingerbread summer cottage that was Eugene O'Neill's boyhood home, are both worth a visit.

The shore's prime attraction, however, is in **Mystic,** just to the east. Mystic Seaport encompasses 17 acres of ships and maritime memorabilia in a re-created 19th-century seafaring village. With the Mystic Marinelife Aquarium and Old Mystic Village shopping complex nearby, Mystic is the state's leading tourist destination by far.

On either side of Mystic are the waterfront villages of Noank and Stonington, which retain the look and feeling of past centuries. Off the beaten path and bypassed by time, they seem a world apart from their contemporary neighbors.

Along I-395 just south of the Massachusetts line is Connecticut's "Quiet Corner," far removed from the usual tourist traffic, where you find classic old New England towns such as Putney, **Pomfret,** and Woodstock.

Chester

The Inn at Chester

318 West Main Street (Route 148)
Chester, CT 06412
860-526-9541
800-949-STAY
Fax: 860-526-4387

| A motor inn with a B&B feel |

Innkeeper: Deborah Moore. **Accommodations:** 42 rooms, 1 suite. **Rates:** $105–$185 per room, $215 per suite. **Included:** Continental breakfast. **Minimum stay:** 2 days on holiday weekends. **Added:** 12% tax. **Credit cards accepted:** All major ones. **Children:** Welcome. **Pets:** Accepted. **Smoking:** Permitted. **Handicap access:** Yes. **Open:** Year-round.

➤ **The inn has a host of resort-style facilities, including a well-equipped exercise room, tennis courts, loaner bicycles, and a bocci court.**

For us, Schedar sums up The Inn at Chester. Schedar is a cat who we first met in the inn elevator. She entered on the first floor and exited on the second, regally leading the way to our room. Only later did we discover that she had been found as a worse-for-the-wear stray in the parking lot a few days before the inn's reopening. Deborah Moore adopted her the same way she does every guest. (Schedar now has company in the form of a retriever named Bacchus.) Deborah's a Chester native who graduated from Colby College and the Maine Maritime Academy, and who then served for nine years as second mate on an oil tanker.

It's amazing what a difference an energetic, personable innkeeper can make, even in a property as large as this inn, a vintage 1770s farmhouse attached to an old barn that has been converted into a restaurant. "It's not that different from a ship," Moore notes, explaining that there is always a crisis in some unexpected corner — a challenge she obviously thrives on. The 42 guest rooms are in two new wings; we prefer East wing rooms.

The simple motel-style rooms are furnished in reproduction antiques with an eye to comfort. No two are the same but all have air conditioning, TVs , and phones. King-size and canopy rooms have additional amenities and are worth the slight increase in price. You may wish to inquire about the Parmelle Homestead with three bedrooms, two sitting rooms, a kitchenette, private dining room, and three fireplaces. It's perfect for a family or group traveling together.

The Post and Beam dining room is as attractive as its name suggests, with a sun porch overlooking a quiet pond. At lunch you might try the duck and chicken pie. The New American dinner menu might include appetizers like smoked salmon sausage or mushroom strudel. Entrées could be a fresh herb risotto cake with Madeira morel sauce or medallions of beef with Gorgonzola. For the past few years, The Post and Beam has been highly rated by *Connecticut* magazine for such fancy desserts as chocolate cigars or the inn's signature orange crème brûlée. Try the sampler.

Dunk's Landing serves lighter (quicker and cheaper, too) fare in an informal setting. A very light Continental breakfast buffet is set out; in warm weather, there are a few outdoor tables.

Four miles from town on a rural, wooded state road, the inn is surrounded by state forest with miles of trails for walking and jogging. The Gentleman's Parlor features a library, pool table, darts, and other games. While it seems a million miles from everywhere, the inn is actually an easy ride from outstanding summer theater and river cruises on the lower reach of the Connecticut River, as well as Hammonasset State Beach in Madison.

East Haddam

Bishopgate Inn

Goodspeed Landing
P.O. Box 290
East Haddam, CT 06423
860-873-1677
Fax: 860-873-3898
ctkagel@bishopsgate.com

A hidden Colonial-style B&B

Innkeepers: The Kagel family: Jane and Colin (Sr.), Lisa and Colin (Jr.) **Accommodations:** 5 rooms (all with private bath), 1 suite. **Rates:** $95–$115 per couple for rooms, $140 for the suite. **Included:** Full breakfast. **Minimum stay:** 2 days on holiday weekends. **Added:** 12% tax. **Credit cards accepted:** MasterCard, Visa. **Children:** Well-behaved children welcome. **Pets:** Possibly accepted. **Smoking:** Not permitted. **Handicap access:** Yes. **Open:** Year-round.

➤ **A stone's throw from the Goodspeed Opera House, the Bishopgate Inn offers authentic Colonial rooms with modern amenities.**

East Haddam is a Connecticut River town clustered around the Goodspeed Opera House, a steamboat Gothic theater that is unquestionably the most picturesque playhouse in New England. Also one of the best, the opera house is known for the quality of its American musicals — both classics and Broadway tryouts — which play from mid-April to mid-December. The Bishopgate Inn is just a short uphill walk from the theater.

This vintage 1818 home has a few drawbacks (what small B&Bs don't?), but the hospitality is gracious and the rooms well-appointed. We also love the working fireplaces that feed into the center chimney. Four of the guest rooms have working Rumford fireplaces and all have air conditioning. They have all been carefully furnished with antiques, and the beds have feather beds and comforters that make for a good night's sleep. The Director's Suite is fabulous, with a cathedral ceiling, a private balcony overlooking the garden, a separate dressing area, and a dry sauna. The cheery living room contains a sofa, armchairs, and rocking chairs grouped around the Colonial-style hearth. There's also a sitting room upstairs with plenty of reading material. Both are comfortable but on the small side.

A full breakfast, which on out last visit included a nice plate of fruit, toast, and egg strata, is served at one table. When the house is full, guests may have to wait in the living room (quite comfy) to be seated. The Kagels are planning an atrium-like extension off the colonial dining room to address that issue.

Lisa is a very good cook, and with 48-hours notice, she can make dinner for you, to be served in your room or at the candlelit dining room table. You can discuss entrée preferences with her, but how she cooks your entrée and what she pairs with it for appetizers will depend on what she finds fresh at the market. Trust her; it's moderately priced. The only drawback to enjoying your romantic dinner in the dining room is that when other guests return to the inn they have to walk past you to get to their rooms. One way to avoid this is to have dinner served in your room, in front of the fire, perhaps. This works, but it can be a bit stressful for Lisa since she can't see how quickly or slowly you're eating. Having said this, all the guests who take her up on the offer seem to be quite pleased.

Theater aside, this lower reach of the Connecticut River is fascinating country. Gillette Castle, river cruises, the rail excursion, and museums are all nearby, and Mystic Seaport is only 25 miles away.

Ivoryton

Copper Beech Inn

Main Street
Ivoryton, CT 06442
860-767-0330
Fax: 860-767-7840

Exceptional French country-style cuisine from a traditional inn

Innkeepers: Sally and Eldon Senner. **Accommodations:** 13 rooms (all with private bath). **Rates:** $105–$175 per couple; weeknight upgrades. **Included:** Continental breakfast; dinner served. **Minimum stay:** 2 nights on weekends. **Added:** 12% tax. **Credit cards accepted:** All major ones. **Children:** Over age 10 welcome. **Pets:** Not accepted. **Smoking:** Restricted. **Handicap access:** No. **Open:** Year-round.

➤ **The Copper Beech Inn is widely respected along the Connecticut shoreline for the superior quality of its formal dining. It consistently receives rave reviews.**

This handsome white clapboard inn, located in the quiet village of Ivoryton, is shaded by a huge beech tree and surrounded by gardens. The inn serves fine food, of which some say is the best in Connecticut. Not prone to exaggeration, we'd rate it solidly in the state's top five.

Let's get right to the point: it would be foolish to stay here without enjoying the outstanding food. On our last visit, which still lingers in our minds, we started with a colorfully layered tower of grilled portobello mushrooms, summer squash, and tomato dressed with a light basil-infused olive oil. A pheasant sausage with a tropical fruit chutney glaze is also a favorite. Moving on to the main attraction, we devoured (we admit it) a fillet of salmon sautéed in a crisp crust of thinly sliced potato, complemented by a roasted sweet red pepper sauce. Wow! Vegetarians will be particularly delighted by the flavorful "plat de legumes." (Even non-vegetarians order it!) Fortunately the best desserts are also the lightest. We recommend the fresh sorbets made with champagne or the fruit ice creams served in a pastry tulip with a vanilla custard crème sauce. They are made, like everything here, from scratch. No first-class dining experience would be complete without knowledgeable and perfectly attentive service. Kudos to the whole staff and to executive chef Robert Celetano, who came on board in early 1997.

In addition to the regular menu, a prix fixe menu ($32) with three entrée choices is offered to guests ordering before 6:30 (except Saturday and Sunday). A Sunday brunch ($25) is also locally popular. Since 1994, Copper Beach has received the *Wine Spectator* award of excellence for its wine list. A meal here is a perfect end to any day and is a favorite of local residents celebrating special occasions.

The three formal dining rooms, in which fresh flowers abound, are furnished with reproduction Queen Anne, Chippendale, and Empire furniture, with the tables placed a generous distance from one another. White linen, sterling silver, candles, hand-blown goblets, and fine china grace each table. The atmosphere is elegant yet warm and inviting. Before dinner, guests can enjoy a drink in the conservatory, which, as well as overlooking lush gardens, wraps around the northeast corner of the main house. The Senners have also added an antiques gallery that specializes in Oriental porcelain.

Four of the guest rooms are upstairs in the main house, and nine are in the carriage house behind the garden. The rooms in the main house are gracious, with floral wallpaper, wicker and antiques, white ruffled curtains, and comforters. The baths have fine old fixtures, like clawfoot tubs. The bath in Room 2 is one of the finest (and largest) we've seen. The largest and brightest room is the combination bedroom/sitting area upstairs at the front of the house. It has a brass canopy bed, a crystal chandelier, a sofa in front of the fireplace, and a grand bay window overlooking the beech tree. The Carriage House is set back behind the garden and its rooms are generally larger, with exposed beams and cathedral ceilings on the second floor; each has a whirlpool bath, TV, and deck.

Besides the outstanding cuisine, the aspect that most impresses us about this inn is the obvious pride innkeepers Eldon and Sally Senner exhibit. They care about their guest's enjoyment and spend much of their day at the antique desk in the reception hall greeting guests and helping them plan daily river cruises, outings to nearby beaches and to the excursion railway and shops in Essex, and securing tickets to the three nearby theaters.

Madison

Madison Beach Hotel

94 West Wharf Road
Exit 61 on I-95
Madison, CT 06443
203-245-1404
Fax: 203-245-0410

A beachside summer motel

Innkeepers: Mr. and Mrs. Henry M. Cooney, Mr. and Mrs. Roben P. Bagdasrian. **Accommodations:** 35 rooms (all with private bath), 6 suites. **Rates:** $85–$225 per couple from May through October; less off-season. **Included:** Continental breakfast. **Minimum stay:** 2 nights on weekends in season. **Added:** 12% tax. **Credit cards accepted:** All major ones. **Children:** Welcome; under age 5, free; cribs free, cots $10. **Pets:** Not accepted. **Smoking:** Permitted. **Handicap access:** Yes. **Open:** March through December.

➤ **These beachside rooms have private balconies overlooking the Connecticut Sound in Madison, a colonial town and toney old summer resort with ample public space for beach walking and birdwatching.**

The Madison Beach Hotel, built around the turn of the century and renovated with modern rooms, is a rare survivor of Connecticut's old wooden Sound-side hotels. There are now only 35 spacious rooms (reduced from 52), each with a bath and a water view. The annex contains three Victorian-style rooms, all with glimpses of the water from behind the inn.

The beach itself is not too large, but it has character, curving to a rocky point and backed by beach grass. Like the Connecticut Sound, it seems to change with the hour and season. This particular strip belongs to the hotel, but a few steps away is the town's West Wharf, a favorite fishing place with its own small beach overlooking a line of beachside cottages and the grand old Madison Beach Club.

While the most reasonably priced, first-floor rooms look onto the front porch (which runs the length of the hotel), the second-, third-, and fourth-floor rooms each have a private patch of the upper porch. Most rooms lack closets (there are corner racks instead) but otherwise offer all the comfort of a summer beach motel. The furnishings include refinished oak dressers from the old hotel, bamboo and wicker headboards and chairs, desks, and shell-shaped brass bedside reading lights. Each has cable TV and air conditioning. It's the kind of place where you won't worry about tracking in a bit of sand. The second rooms of the suites are small but inviting spaces with sinks, fridges, and tables (no stoves). Our favorite is number 40, a corner suite on the top floor with water views on two sides.

The hotel/motel-style lobby is filled with white wicker that's bright and comfortable enough to tempt you to sit a spell and watch the stream of beachgoers in summer or just gaze out at the sea in winter. The porch beyond is lined with rockers from the hotel's previous life. One thoughtful touch: Trays are provided so that guests may enjoy their morning snack of muffins, coffee, and juice on their private balconies.

The Wharf Bar and Restaurant is in a separate wing from the guest rooms. The luncheon menu ranges from BLTs to soft-shell crab; the dinner menu, from fried seafood to lobster thermidor. There are also half a dozen more restaurants of every caliber within a mile or two.

The town of Madison actually offers the lion's share of publicly accessible Connecticut beachfront. Hammonasset State Beach is a great place to walk and birdwatch as well as swim. This is a low-key, private kind of resort town with a classic Colonial common, a line of stores on Main Street, and a dozen blocks of summer mansions and cottages in an assortment of architectural styles, many with water views. This is the only place to stay on the beach.

Mystic

House of 1833 Bed & Breakfast

72 North Stonington Road
Old Mystic, CT 06355
860-536-6325
800-FOR-1833
www.visitmystic.com

An elegant and comfortable B&B

Innkeepers: Carol and Matt Nolan. **Accommodations:** 5 rooms (all with private bath). **Rates:** $95–$205 per couple; special packages available. **Included:** Full breakfast. **Minimum stay:** 2 nights on weekends. **Added:** 12% tax. **Credit cards accepted:** MasterCard, Visa. **Children:** Welcome midweek. **Pets:** Not accepted. **Smoking:** Not permitted. **Handicap access:** No. **Open:** Year-round.

➤ **This small bed-and-breakfast has a lot of facilities that even larger places don't: a Har Tru tennis court with loaner racquets and balls, 18-speed bicycles, and a large, landscaped pool. It's a delightful find.**

Far enough from the bustle of Mystic and the Seaport, yet close enough to provide easy access, the House of 1833 is a welcome addition to the lodging scene in these parts. Converted to a B&B in 1994, the imposing Greek Revival mansion sits on three acres in a largely residential neighborhood.

You'll notice one of the house's most dramatic features as soon as you walk in the front door: a graceful curved staircase lined with a mural of 19th-century Old Mystic. The B&B has plenty of common space, all with dramatic 11-foot ceilings. The formal double parlor features a marble fireplace as well as a pump organ, baby grand piano, and a 19th-century chandelier. Despite the formality and elegance, on our recent visit there was a pile of son Alex's toys in the corner. This is not a pretentious place. In fact, it is one of the nicest — all around — in the state.

As for the guest rooms, they are all very nicely appointed, spacious, and very different from one another. Four have a fireplace and one has a woodstove. We're partial to the secluded first-floor

Peach Room. The bathroom is huge, designed so that when you get overheated from the Jacuzzi you can hop into the oversized shower. In warm weather you'll appreciate the Peach Room's private porch overlooking the backyard. On the second floor, the large Oak Room is the least expensive because its bathroom, although private, is across the hall. The third-floor Cupola Room, with peaked ceilings, is the most private. It boasts a queen canopy bed, double whirlpool, and access to the rooftop cupola, which is perfect for daydreaming, wine sipping, or composing quiet thoughts.

A two-course breakfast featuring, perhaps, French toast or quiche is served at 9:00 A.M. at one long table. Matt, who used to make his living as a musician, often plays the piano for guests.

Steamboat Inn

73 Steamboat Wharf
Mystic, CT 05355
860-536-8300
Fax: 860-536-9528

> **Waterside elegance and luxury in the heart of Mystic**

Innkeeper: Diana Stadtmiller. **Accommodations:** 10 rooms (all with private bath). **Rates:** $150–$275 May through September; $95–195 November through March. **Included:** Continental breakfast. **Minimum stay:** 2 nights on weekends. **Added:** 12% tax. **Credit cards accepted:** All major ones. **Children:** Welcome, free for up to 2 children, age 16 or less. **Pets:** Not accepted. **Smoking:** Not permitted. **Handicap access:** No. **Open:** Year-round.

➤   **Handy to Mystic Seaport and Mystic Marinelife Aquarium, the Steamboat Inn boasts water views, whirlpool baths, and easy access to village shops, restaurants, and boat excursions.**

These are the most luxurious digs in the area, right on the Mystic River next to the drawbridge. The same developers who turned this old warehouse into a restaurant decided that it would make an even better inn. They were right. We continue to be impressed by this intimate hotel every time we visit.

The Steamboat Inn has just ten rooms, but what rooms! Each one has a sitting area and a view of the water ("Mystic" has the best view), a whirlpool bath, a phone, and a TV hidden in a cupboard. Six of the ten have a wood-burning fireplace. Four larger demi-suites on the dock have kitchenettes and large bathrooms with double-size whirlpools. All the rooms are tastefully decorated, unfussy yet plush in appointments and fabrics. The Marie Gilbert room has a cathedral ceiling.

A light breakfast is served in the attractive upstairs gathering room, where guests can sit and read or visit at any time. Since the only drawbacks to downtown Mystic are the parking and traffic, it's nice to be within walking distance of dozens of shops, restaurants, and the exceptional Art Association Gallery. A variety of excursion boats are also based here, and in the summer a trolley connects this area with Mystic Seaport and the Aquarium.

Old Lyme

Bee & Thistle Inn

100 Lyme Street
Old Lyme, CT 06371
860-434-1667
800-622-4946
Fax: 860-434-3402

| An excellent dining spot that is also a full-service inn |

Innkeepers: Bob and Penny Nelson. **Accommodations:** 11 doubles (all with private bath), 1 cottage. **Rates:** Rooms: $75–$155 per couple; cottage: $210. **Included:** Continental breakfast with cottage; all meals are served (no lunch and dinner Tuesday). **Minimum stay:** None. **Added:** 12% tax. **Credit cards accepted:** All major ones. **Children:** Over age 12. **Pets:** Not allowed. **Smoking:** Restricted. **Handicap access:** No. **Open:** Year-round except two weeks in January.

➤ **The food is highly rated, the garden is beautiful, and the riverside cottage is a hidden gem.**

Dating from 1756, the Bee & Thistle is a hip-roofed mansion with a Palladian window above its entrance. It offers fine food served graciously, attractive common rooms filled with country collectibles and flowers (both real and artificial), pleasant guest rooms, and an exceptional cottage with a private dock.

This is a popular local place to lunch and dine out. Don't be misled into thinking that the food will parallel the inn's Colonial atmosphere: the cuisine is decidedly contemporary. The soups at lunch are excellent, as are the reasonably priced entrées. Dinner, served by candlelight, might begin with wild mushroom lasagna or oysters with a mignonette sauce and smoked salmon. Entrées are as far reaching as loin of pork served on a bourbon apple coulis with brown bread to roasted Idaho trout wrapped in bacon and served on caramelized balsamic-glazed onions. (Entrées are priced at $20–$29.) The wine list is good, and wine by the glass comes in a very large glass.

In the evening, the two common rooms invite you to relax. Each has a fireplace and furnishings from the early 1900s. Guests can have breakfast in their rooms, on a sunlit porch hung with Penny's collection of baskets, or before the fire in the Colonial gold dining room.

The cottage has its own kitchen and a living room with a fireplace, as well as decks and a dock. On past visits, our favorite guest rooms have been numbers 1 and 2; the former is spacious, with a canopy bed and private bath. We can't tell you much more than that about the rooms. On our last visit the proprietors said, by way of an employee, that the inn is always full and that it is never possible to see rooms. It may be difficult to get a room here. We hope readers will write to tell us of their experiences.

The inn is set on five acres with an English garden and views of the Lieutenant River. Mystic Seaport and the Goodspeed Opera House are among the nearby attractions, and the Florence Griswold Museum with its American Impressionist paintings is a few doors down the street.

Old Saybrook

Saybrook Point Inn & Spa

2 Bridge Street
Old Saybrook, CT 05475
860-395-2000
800-243-0212
Fax: 860-388-1504
saybrook@snet.net
www.saybrook.com

**A luxurious small hotel
with spa facilities**

General manager: Norman Mael. **Accommodations:** 62 rooms. **Rates:** $179–$275 per room, $329–$449 per suite from late May through November; less off-season. **Included:** No meals; all meals available at Terra Mar Grille. **Minimum stay:** 2 nights on summer weekends. **Added:** 12% tax. **Credit cards accepted:** All major ones. **Children:** Welcome; under age 12, free in parent's room. **Pets:** Not accepted. **Smoking:** Restricted. **Handicap access:** Yes. **Open:** Year-round.

➤ **On the premises are health and fitness facilities, indoor and outdoor pools, and a spa with treatments including massages, facials, and aromatherapy.**

Saybrook Point is for those who want to be as close to the water as possible. The inn, set right on the water, is at the mouth of the Connecticut River on Long Island Sound. The setting is picture-perfect, complete with sailboats docked at the marina and lovely sunrises.

The formal lobby sets the tone with marble floors, crystal chandeliers, hand-loomed rugs, and potted plants. The guest rooms are all large, with spacious bathrooms and dressing areas. Most also have sitting areas, a balcony, a fireplace, and a wet bar. Ask for a room overlooking the water rather than the parking lot. Hotel-style amenities include plush terry cloth robes, hair dryers, and nightly turndown. You may wish to inquire about the lighthouse apartment surrounded by water; it is available for in-season weekly stays.

The Terra Mar Grille (named for the old hotel that the new building replaced), might just as well be on a small cruise ship, with its curved glass wall maximizing the water views. All meals are served here. You can lunch on a tuna salad sandwich and dine on roasted vegetable and seafood lasagna or veal loin. The inspired and eclectic dishes lean towards New American and northern Italian. Room service is available. Sunday brunch ($22 per person) is popular and the offerings quite extensive.

Saybrook Point pampers you in style. Facilities include a state-of-the-art exercise room with a view of the water, indoor and outdoor pools, a steam room, and Jacuzzi. For an extra fee, spa services include massage, manicures, facials, and aromatherapy. Although there is no beach, the area offers plenty to do. The Point itself is a place to fish, bird, or to bicycle along the cottage-lined shore as it curves from the mouth of the river up along Connecticut Sound. You are also near public beaches and Essex.

Pomfret

Cobbscroft

349 Pomfret Street (Route 169)
P.O. Box 104
Pomfret, CT 06258
860-928-5560

> **A B&B with good art and great breakfasts**

Innkeepers: Janet and Tom McCobb. **Accommodations:** 3 rooms (all with private bath), 1 suite. **Rates:** $75–$90; 10% less for 3 days or more. **Included:** Full breakfast. **Minimum stay:** None. **Added:** 12% tax. **Credit cards accepted:** MasterCard, Visa. **Children:** Over age 12 welcome, in suite. **Pets:** Not accepted. **Smoking:** Not permitted. **Handicap access:** No. **Open:** Year-round.

➤   **Tom McCobb is a watercolorist specializing in New England landscapes. You will find his paintings and those of his friends throughout the house.**

Pomfret is one of several handsome old towns in Connecticut's Quiet Corner that became summer retreats for wealthy New Yorkers in the late 19th century. Cobbscroft is an inviting white clapboard house that has been an inn since 1985. Located across the street from the prestigious Pomfret School, the inn is a favorite of visiting parents. The rooms have a homey richness: the library has many shelves of books (as well as a TV), and the living room displays Tom's art. We were impressed by the quality, quantity, and variety of the art — all of it for sale.

The downstairs suite — a double and single room sharing a bath — is ideal for a family. The three upstairs rooms, however, are strictly for adults. These are wonderful spaces with antiques and special touches. The large bridal suite boasts a fireplace and is very bright, thanks to windows on three sides.

Breakfast is Janet's art. Her specialty is hot apple crisp, but her palette includes croissants and a number of elegant egg dishes. There is always a choice of a sweet or savory entrée.

This is the kind of place where you tend to linger after breakfast or gather for afternoon tea. In the evening, the McCobbs steer guests to a variety of restaurants, and welcome them back with an after-dinner drink in the living room.

Pomfret's sights range from windows by Louis Tiffany (a native of nearby Killingly) in Christ Church to the short hiking trail in Mashamoquet Brook State Park, which leads through the woods to a den where the young Israel Putnam is said to have killed the area's last she-wolf before he went on to conquer Bunker Hill.

Putnam

Fellshaw Tavern

Five Mile River Road (at Route 44)
Putnam, CT 06260
860-928-3467

An 18th-century tavern renovated into a comfortable, rural B&B

Innkeeper: Herb Kinsman. **Accommodations:** 2 rooms (both with private bath). **Rate:** $72. **Included:** Full breakfast. **Minimum stay:** None. **Added:** 12% tax. **Credit cards:** Not accepted. **Children:** Welcome. **Pets:** Not accepted. **Smoking:** Not permitted. **Handicap access:** Yes. **Open:** Year-round.

➤ **Herb Kinsman has reverently restored and expanded this historic old house with an eye to the comfort of his guests. It's lovely.**

Named for General Israel Putnam of Bunker Hill fame, Putnam is a little dot of a place that was probably better known in the 1700s than it is today. The original 18th-century tavern once hosted the famous general. Now a tranquil B&B, set back from a rural road on three acres behind a low stone wall, Fellshaw Tavern provides every comfort.

The house has been carefully refitted with many beautiful pieces collected by the Kinsmans; an amazing number were built by Herb. His skill is apparent in the fine black walnut grandfather clock in the formal dining room and a number of chairs and cabinets, as well as the handsome front door. "I don't sit down much," Herb observes as you wonder how one man could do so much to one house.

On a recent visit, we found a large new Federal living room with crown and dentil molding and an arched alcove around the fireplace and windows, some of stained glass and some of which are mullioned. If you use the back door, you'll enter by the sun room, whose windows overlook the garden, and where breakfast is usually served. In the kitchen, china and crystal are stored in a Dutch kas that dates from 1670. In the winter, the dining room is warmed by a fireplace. (There are a total of 6 fireplaces in the house.)

Of the three first-floor parlors, one has a sophisticated sound system and an assortment of rare Oriental rugs. An adjacent TV room with a low, paneled ceiling has another fireplace, a Winthrop desk crafted by Herb, and lots of books. Both guest rooms upstairs are spacious and charming, with four-poster beds, antique furnishings, interesting art, and fireplaces. A cozy, oak-paneled upstairs study offers guests yet another space to watch TV or read.

This is one of the most scenic and quiet corners of the state. Just off I-395, Putnam is convenient for exploring Sturbridge Village in Massachusetts. It's also near the picture-perfect villages of Woodstock and Pomfret, with its prep schools and lovely stone and brick churches. But you may want to sit and relax amidst Herb's extensive and elaborate rock garden.

Maine

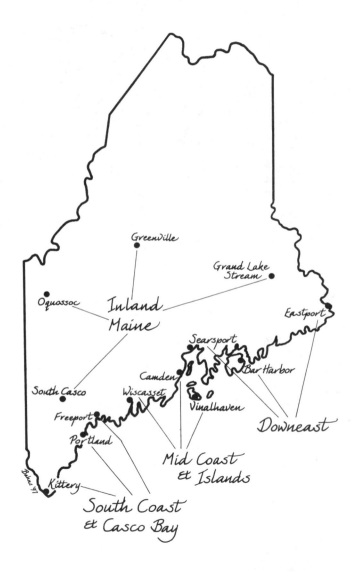

Greenville

Grand Lake
Stream

Oquossoc

Inland
Maine

Eastport

Searsport

Bar Harbor

Camden

South Casco

Wiscasset

Vinalhaven

Freeport

Downeast

Portland

Mid Coast
& Islands

Baker '97

Kittery

South Coast
& Casco Bay

South Coast and Casco Bay

Bailey Island
Driftwood Inn and Cottages, 57
Freeport
Atlantic Seal Bed & Breakfast, 58
Kennebunkport Area
Bufflehead Cove, 60
The Captain Lord Mansion, 61
The Colony Hotel, 63
The Inn at Harbor Head, 64
Kennebunkport Inn, 66
Maine Stay Inn and Cottages, 68
Tides Inn By-The-Sea, 69
White Barn Inn, 70
Kittery
Gundalow Inn, 72
Ogunquit
The Cliff House, 74
The Dunes on the Waterfront, 76
Sparhawk Resort, 77
The Trellis House, 78
Portland Area
The Danforth, 79
Inn by the Sea, 81
Pomegranate Inn, 82
Portland Regency, 84
Prouts Neck
Black Point Inn, 85
South Harpswell
Harpswell Inn B&B, 87
York Harbor
Dockside Guest Quarters, 89
Inn at Harmon Park, 64
Tanglewood Hall, 92

Best Beachside Places

Kennebunkport
  Tides Inn By-The-Sea, 69
Ogunquit
  The Dunes on the Waterfront, 76
Portland
  Inn by the Sea, 81

Best Bed and Breakfasts

Freeport
  Atlantic Seal Bed & Breakfast, 58
Kennebunkport Area
  Bufflehead Cove, 60
  The Captain Lord Mansion, 61
  The Inn at Harbor Head, 64
  Maine Stay Inn and Cottages, 68
Kittery
  Gundalow Inn, 72
Ogunquit
  The Trellis House, 78
Portland Area
  Pomegranate Inn, 82
South Harpswell
  Harpswell Inn B&B, 87
York Harbor
  Inn at Harmon Park, 64
  Tanglewood Hall, 92

Best Family Finds

Bailey Island
  Driftwood Inn and Cottages, 57
York Harbo
  Dockside Guest Quarters, 89
Kennebunkport
  Maine Stay Inn and Cottages, 68
Ogunquit
  The Dunes on the Waterfront, 76

Best Gourmet Getaway

Kennebunkport
  White Barn Inn, 70

Best Grand Resorts

Kennebunkport Area
  The Colony Hotel, 63
Ogunquit
  The Cliff House, 74
Portland Area
  Black Point Inn, 85

Best Inns

Kennebunkport Area
  Kennebunkport Inn, 66
  Tides Inn By-The-Sea, 69
Portland Area
  Black Point Inn, 85
York Harbor
  Dockside Guest Quarters, 89

Best Romantic Getaways

Kennebunkport Area
  Bufflehead Cove, 60
  The Captain Lord Mansion, 61
  White Barn Inn, 70
York Harbor
  Tanglewood Hall, 92
Portland Area
  Inn by the Sea, 81
  Pomegranate Inn, 82

The very mention of Maine conjures up the image of a rockbound coast, and that's what most visitors come to see. Many people try to see too much in their allotted time. While the distance from Kittery (on the New Hampshire border) to Eastport (facing Canada) is just 225 miles as the crow flies, it is more than 3,500 miles as the coastline tacks and jibs its way in and out of coves, inlets, reaches, and bays. In order to experience the true essence of Maine, it is far better to settle on one particular swatch of shoreline and to explore it thoroughly than to spend your vacation on Route 1.

From the moment you cross the Piscataqua River (Maine's southern border), you are in the real Maine. York, the first exit on I-95 after the Maine Publicity Bureau's information center (worth a stop), is one of Maine's earliest settlements and still retains its vintage 1719 gaol, billed as the oldest surviving public building of the English colonies. Half a dozen beautiful old buildings in the village are open to the public, as is the shore path that travels east from Sewall's Bridge to the Wiggly Bridge and by the handsome Victorian houses in **York Harbor.**

Ogunquit, a dozen miles up Route 1, is famed for its splendid, 3-mile-long, dune-backed beach; you'll even find some relatively warm water in the tidal river, also rimmed by beach. Ogunquit is also known for its ocean path (the Marginal Way), for the much painted Perkins Cove, and for one of the country's oldest summer theaters.

In **Kennebunkport,** summer life revolves around Dock Square, a group of old riverside buildings now filled with shops, restaurants, and galleries. Inns trail off down Ocean Avenue, following the river to the rocky shoreline, which is rimmed by another path and a spectacular road leading to the fishing community at Cape Porpoise and to smooth Goose Rocks Beach beyond.

Portland, Maine's largest and most sophisticated city, is a livable, likable community with a pervasive sense of the sea, an outstanding art museum, and a delightful assortment of shops, galleries, and restaurants packed into a five-block Victorian area known as the Old Port.

In the warm summer months, no visit to Portland is complete without a trip into Casco Bay to visit one of the many islands, which include Peaks (just a 15-minute ferry ride from Customs House Wharf) and Chebeague, farther down the bay. A variety of boats offer excursions.

While it's not far across Casco Bay to **Bailey Island** (Casco Bay Lines offers summer excursions), it takes most visitors at least a day to get there by land because they stop in **Freeport** and discover that, in addition to being the home of New England's most unusual department store, L.L. Bean, the town harbors more than one hundred other retail stores and outlets. Brunswick is also an interesting town; be sure to see the paintings by Winslow Homer (who lived and worked at Prouts Neck) in the Bowdoin College Museum of Art.

East of Portland, the coast is characterized by long, fingerlike peninsulas. The first of these is actually a collection of three narrow land fingers and several bridge-linked islands stretching seaward from Brunswick, defining the eastern rim of Casco Bay. Collectively they form the town of **Harpswell,** better known as the Harpswells because they include so many rivers, points, and islands, the most famous of which is **Bailey Island,** which is widely known for its seafood restaurants.

Bailey Island

Driftwood Inn and Cottages

Bailey Island, ME 04003
207-833-5461

A fading breed of seaside retreats in operation since the 1920s

Owners/managers: Mr. and Mrs. Charles Conrad. **Accommodations:** 19 doubles, 7 singles (shared baths), 6 housekeeping cottages. **Rates:** $65–$70 per couple EP, $45 single EP; $345 per couple per week MAP; cottages: $475 per week for 2, $550 per week for 4. **Included:** Varies with meal plan. **Minimum stay:** No. **Added:** 7% tax. **Credit cards accepted:** None. **Children:** Welcome, half price under age 12. **Pets:** Only in cottages. **Smoking:** Permitted. **Handicap access:** No. **Open:** June to mid-October.

➤ **On the tip of a peninsula, the Driftwood offers an isolated, old Maine feel that's rare these days.**

The Driftwood Inn is a weathered, shingled complex perched at the edge of the sea. Meals are served in an open-timbered dining room, where every table has a view of the water. Accommodations are sparc and simple, typifying the way Maine seaside rooms have always been. Each of the three guest houses has its own common rooms. The bedrooms, with unfinished wood walls and sinks, are on the small side, but they are all neat. In many of them you can hear the waves crashing against the rocks. The most dramatically sited, Driftwood Cottage (with many twin-bedded rooms), is perched on the edge of the rocky shoreline. It has both an enclosed and an open porch. Many of the rooms in Pleasant Place, which is set back from the water a bit, have new bathrooms. Of the cottages, we highly recommend the few that have been recently renovated; they're quite nice.

For a bit of activity, you can float in the safety of a saltwater swimming pool as waves crash all around you. And you can walk along the shoreline, up a wonderful old path called the Giant Stairs.

The Driftwood is near the tip of Bailey Island, now linked by a series of bridges to the peninsula south of Brunswick. Bailey Island is known for its restaurants and for its boat excursions, which range from deep-sea fishing expeditions to the ferry into Portland.

Freeport

Atlantic Seal Bed & Breakfast

25 Main Street
P.O. Box 146
South Freeport, ME 04078
207-865-6112

| A salty B&B by the bay

Innkeeper: Captain Thomas Ring. **Accommodations:** 3 rooms (all with private bath). **Rates:** $95–$135; less from December through April. **Included:** Full breakfast. **Minimum stay:** No. **Added:** 7% tax. **Credit cards accepted:** None.

Children: Over age 7. **Pets:** Not permitted. **Smoking:** Permitted only on back deck. **Handicap access:** No. **Open:** Year-round.

➤ **This clapboard Cape-style house is filled with a sense of the sea.**

Our advice would be to shop but not sleep in Freeport were it not for the Atlantic Seal Bed & Breakfast. Admittedly, there are a dozen pleasant places to stay within a 10-minute drive of L.L. Bean and Freeport's 100-plus other stores and outlets. Having shopped till you dropped, however, you might want to stay somewhere that reminds you why you really came to coastal Maine. Although the Atlantic Seal seems many miles from the crowds of downtown Freeport, it's just a 5-minute drive, overlooking water filled with pleasure crafts and working boats.

This snug, circa 1850 clapboard Cape-style house is filled with a sense of the sea. Thomas Ring, a licensed mariner who works on a tug boat for six months a year, is descended from a long line of Maine sea captains. (Note the two Civil War–era maritime licenses hanging by the back door, one from his father's and one from his mother's family.) The living room is a sunny, inviting room (with a fireplace) that's furnished with family antiques. A painting of a clipper ship, the *Governor Goodwin*, in which a cousin of Tom's grandfather sailed to China, hangs above the mantel, and a ship's model sits in the parlor window overlooking the tidal Harraseeket River. In fact, the antiques on the mantle occupy the exact same place they did forty years ago.

The three guest rooms vary, but all have low ceilings common to a house of this period and homemade quilts or down comforters. The Dash, a large, sunny room with three windows overlooking the harbor, has a private whirlpool bath, a large separate shower, two beds (a queen and a double), and cable TV. Heart's Desire has window seats looking out on the water, a queen-size poster bed, and a Rumford fireplace. Glen, the smallest room (also with a view of the water) has a queen bed and a Jacuzzi.

Breakfast may be soufflé-style featherbed eggs (a combination of cheese, milk, and bread) or blueberry pancakes, and there's always cereal, usually with fresh fruit. The meal is served at a mahogany table set simply with silver and china. Tom won't mind if you pass through the kitchen and his quarters to enjoy your morning coffee on the small back porch facing the harbor.

Guests can use the B&B's dock and rowboat. For lunch, walk down the road to the Harraseeket Lunch & Lobster Co., on the Freeport Town Wharf. It's one of the best places in Maine for a crabmeat roll, a fish sandwich, or a full lobster feed.

Kennebunkport Area

Note: The Kennebunks constitute one of the few areas in New England with so many exceptional inns that it seems unfair to select just a few as if these were the only we could enthusiastically recommend.

Bufflehead Cove

Off Route 35
P.O. Box 499
Kennebunkport, ME 04046
207-967-3879
www.dbanet.com/bcove

A romantic, riverside hideaway

Innkeepers: Harriet and Jim Gott. **Accommodations:** 5 rooms (all with private bath), 1 suite. **Rates:** $135–$250 per couple; $190 suite; less off-season. **Included:** Full breakfast. **Minimum stay:** 2 nights on weekends. **Added:** 7% tax. **Credit cards accepted:** MasterCard, Visa. **Children:** Over age 10 welcome. **Pets:** Not accepted. **Smoking:** Not permitted indoors. **Handicap access:** No. **Open:** May through December; other months vary.

➤   **Harriet and Jim Gott maintain a gracious B&B on a quiet cove of the Kennebunk River; few settings are more tranquil.**

Hidden at the end of a long drive and overlooking the tidal reach of the Kennebunk River, this turn-of-the-century summer home is airy and spacious. The grounds are soothing, the lawn broad, and the gardens lush. It's a South Coast gem. And it's often filled weeks in advance by those hoping others won't find out about it.

On our last visit, on a warm summer afternoon, the broad front porch was full of couples conversing over wine and cheese. One guest was asleep on the hammock at the river's edge, while two others were down on a little deck also by the river. The view from the porch is of a quiet cove, a haven in the fall for bufflehead ducks. There are also porches on the side of the house and a wraparound porch on the back of the house.

The Dutch Colonial gray shingle house has large living room windows to let in the light and river view. In the winter you can enjoy the view from deep window seats and comfortable chairs by the fire.

The rooms range from comfortable to exceptional — from the Teal Room, with a hand-painted flower design on the walls, to the Balcony Room (a favorite), with a queen-size brass bed, antique armoire, and wicker-furnished balcony. The L-shaped Garden Studio in back has a sitting area, a separate entrance, and a patio. The Cove Suite, with two wicker-filled rooms separated by a bathroom, features stenciling, a cove view, and a private balcony. With an extra bed, it's a good bet for families.

The most impressive room is Hideaway, in an adjacent cottage. The very large, romantic two-room suite has a gas fireplace that separates the living room and bedroom. The room also features a Jacuzzi, king-size bed, private deck, and lots of windows.

An impressive breakfast is served in the low-beamed, paneled dining room: fresh orange juice and, quite possibly, ginger-poached pears in English custard sauce, apple-stuffed French toast, and maple-glazed sausage.

Harriet, a native of nearby Cape Porpoise, and Jim, a commercial fisherman, have raised their four children here. They are familiar with most aspects of this intriguing community. It's difficult to believe that Dock Square, Kennebunkport's bustling tourist hub, is just downriver.

The Captain Lord Mansion

P.O. Box 800
Kennebunkport, ME 04046
207-967-3141
Fax: 207-967-3172
captain@biddeford.com
www.captainlord.com

| **A romantic landmark** |

Innkeepers: Bev Davis and Rick Litchfield. **Accommodations:** 16 rooms (all with private bath). **Rates:** Late May through October, $149–$249; $349 per couple for The Captain's Suite; less off-season. **Included:** Breakfast. **Minimum stay:** 2 nights on weekends. **Added:** 7% tax. **Credit cards accepted:** Discover, MasterCard, Visa. **Children:** Over age 6. **Pets:** Not accepted. **Smoking:** Not permitted. **Handicap access:** No. **Open:** Year-round.

➤ **The house, built in 1812, has many unusual features all in pristine condition: a four-story spiral staircase, a three-story suspended elliptical staircase, double Indian shutters, blown-glass windows,** *trompe l'oeil*

painted doors, original pumpkin pine wide floorboards, and 18-foot bay windows with curved sashes.

With its striking widow's walk and other classic architectural features, the Captain Lord is one of the best-known buildings on Maine's South Coast. Thanks to the warm and helpful innkeepers who have overseen the manse since 1978, it's also a genuinely pleasant place to stay. Photo albums in the gathering room document the restoration of the house. The cupola offers grand views of Kennebunkport.

Common rooms are attractive and inviting, but the bedrooms are equally well designed for lounging: each has at least two chairs and sometimes a sofa. Second-floor rooms are unusually large. Six rooms in the front of the house overlook a landscaped lawn and provide a glimpse of the Kennebunk River. Each is meticulously decorated with Colonial reproduction wallpaper, stenciling, an antique four-poster bed with a firm mattress, lace canopies, thick carpeting, and luxurious linens. Fourteen rooms have gas fireplaces, and the furniture is arranged to take best advantage of the hearth. Before reserving, you may want to request the color brochure insert that has color photos of most rooms.

Renovated in 1997, the Captain's Suite, on the first floor, now features a suite-sized bath. Seriously. It's divided in two: one part features a marble shower and ten-jet hydro massager, an antique pedestal sink, a bidet, and heated marble-tiled floor; and the second, a double whirlpool tub, mood lights, two sinks, a TV and VCR, wall-to-wall carpet, a gas fireplace, and exercise equipment. The bedroom features a king-size canopy bed.

Breakfast is served family-style in the modern country kitchen. Seven kinds of muffins and a daily hot special — maybe a cheese strata, waffles, or quiche — are served along with yogurt with fresh fruit. Sunday breakfast is special, with sticky buns, quiche, and English porridge.

The Colony Hotel

Ocean Avenue and Kings Road
Kennebunkport, ME 04046
207-967-3331
800-552-2363
Fax: 207-967-8738
colony@cybertours.com
www.cybertours.com/colony/home.html

An old-fashioned coastal resort

Manager: Justina Boughton. **Accommodations:** 135 rooms (all with private bath), 4 suites. **Rates:** July through early September: $199–$309 per couple, MAP; off-season: $109–$179 per couple, B&B. **Included:** Varies with meal plan; all facilities. **Minimum stay:** 2 days on weekends and holidays. **Added:** 7% tax, $12 service charge, 18% gratuity on meals and beverages. **Credit cards accepted:** All major ones. **Children:** Welcome; $30 per day, age 4 and under; $40 per day, age 5 and older. **Pets:** $22 per day. **Smoking:** Not permitted except in Marine Room porch. **Handicap access:** 9 rooms. **Open:** Mid-May to mid-October.

➤ **One of New England's last grand, family-owned seaside hotels.**

The Colony Hotel, which stands on the site of the first hotel in Kennebunkport, is one of the last New England coastal resorts still maintained in a grand manner. Built in 1914, the three-story white clapboard building sits on a rise at the point where the Kennebunk River meets the Atlantic Ocean.

There is an old, formal check-in desk in the comfortable lobby and a vast, pine-paneled dining room with chandeliers and paintings by Maine artists. The immense menu changes daily. Modified American Plan guests can have lobster for dinner and for breakfast (there's usually a lobster omelette or pancakes with creamed lobster sauce). A band plays during the Sunday jazz brunch and then moves to the gazebo to entertain guests at the pool.

The main hotel has wide halls and airy, nicely furnished rooms. All of the guest rooms have phones; most are decorated with Maine seascapes. The motel-like East House units have twin beds and TVs, as do the knotty pine rooms at the Galland and Florence houses.

In addition to its own swatch of beach, the hotel maintains a large, heated saltwater pool (where lunch is served) for those who can't bear Maine's low ocean temperatures. There is access to tennis and golf at nearby clubs; a putting green is on the premises.

Guests usually spend some time rocking on the wide verandah and walking along Parsons Way, a path above the rocks. It's a pleasant mile-long hike up Ocean Avenue into Dock Square, the busy hub of Kennebunkport, with more than its share of boutiques, art galleries, and restaurants. Guests tend to walk one way and take the trolley-on-wheels the other.

Out on this end of Ocean Avenue, the bustle of the village seems far away, and the beauty of the ocean dominates. The resort is its own ordered world of manicured lawns, splendid gardens, well-mannered guests (many of whom have been returning year after year), and ample staff. Jackets are requested for dinner, of course, and many guests dress formally on Saturday evening. Dance music and cocktails are offered in the Marine Room. Social events include putting tournaments, visiting lecturers, entertainers, hiking, and lobster cruises.

The Inn at Harbor Head

41 Pier Road, Cape Porpoise
Kennebunkport, ME 04046
207-967-5564
Fax: 207-967-5564
www.innsandouts.com/property/inn-harbor-at-head

Romantic B&B rooms with a view

Innkeepers: Joan and Dave Sutter. **Accommodations:** 3 rooms (all with private bath), 2 suites. **Rates:** $180–$275 per couple from late May to late October; $95–$195 off-season. **Included:** Full breakfast. **Minimum stay:** 2 nights on weekends. **Added:** 7% tax. **Credit cards accepted:** MasterCard, Visa. **Children:** Over age 12 welcome. **Pets:** Not accepted. **Smoking:** Not permitted. **Handicap access:** No. **Open:** Year-round except November.

➤   **This B&B is a pleasant bike ride to the heart of Kennebunkport in one direction and to Goose Rocks Beach in the other.**

The Kennebunkport area has dozens of inns and B&Bs, a number with water views, but none with a harbor view like this. The rambling shingle home overlooks Cape Porpoise Harbor, just 2½ miles from Kennebunkport. From the backyard the lawn slopes down to the head of the harbor (hence the inn's name), which rises and empties with the tides. Joan and Dave have lived here since 1972 and operated it as a B&B since 1984.

Guest rooms have a cocoon-like feel. To a guest who commented on the amount of objects adorning the walls and surfaces, Joan observed, "I turned my closets into bathrooms and I had to put all that good stuff somewhere!" Joan used to sculpt and her interesting pieces are scattered throughout the inn; her seascapes dot the walls.

Not surprisingly, our favorite rooms (Summer and Garden) have the best water views. The bright Summer Suite feels quite private and features a gas fireplace, small balcony, and whirlpool tub. The Garden Room has French doors leading to a private balcony with a view. We like the Japanese influence in the small Garden Room. The Harbor Suite features both a gas fireplace and balcony, as well as a *trompe l'oeil* mural and pencil-post bed with a fishnet canopy. Even the smallest room, the Ocean Room (without a view, despite its name), is lovely, with a mahogany plantation bed. Rooms have either air conditioning or ceiling paddle fans. None of the rooms share walls with other rooms, and thus feel very private.

The common space includes a terrace as well as two sitting rooms (one with a fireplace and water views). Guests can also use the dock. Beach passes and towels are provided for nearby Goose Rocks Beach. Afternoon tea or wine and cheese is served outdoors in good weather.

A full breakfast, accompanied by classical music, is served at 8:30 A.M. sharp at one long, formally set table. On a recent visit, one tardy couple was called to the table with a bell. The meal is quite an affair, one of the coast's fanciest. (Joan wouldn't even allow us to pour our own coffee.) The dining room is filled with pewter, crystal, and stenciling. On our last visit, we thoroughly enjoyed freshly squeezed juice, watermelon with fresh ginger slices presented on a giant hosta leaf, and thick French toast topped with hordes of raspberries and peaches and a luscious plum sauce.

For dinner, you can walk to a fine restaurant at the end of the road. The ever-thoughtful Sutters also equip guests with flashlights for the walk home.

Kennebunkport Inn

Dock Square, P.O. Box 111
Kennebunkport, ME 04046
207-967-2621
800-248-2621
Fax: 207-967-3705

A village inn in the heart of Dock Square

Innkeepers: Rick and Martha Griffin. **Accommodations:** 34 rooms (14 in the inn, 20 in the River House; all with private bath). **Rates:** $70–$189 per couple, EP; in-season MAP and multiple-night packages also available. **Included:** No meals unless part of package. **Minimum stay:** 3 nights on summer and holiday weekends; 2 nights on spring and fall weekends. **Added:** 7% tax. **Credit cards accepted:** All major ones. **Children:** $12 each additional person in room. **Pets:** Not accepted. **Smoking:** Permitted in cocktail lounge. **Handicap access:** No. **Open:** Rooms, year-round. Restaurant open daily from mid-May to late October and for Continental breakfast the rest of the year.

➤ **The inn is steps from the town's shops and restaurants but provides a quiet retreat from the hubbub.**

The white clapboard inn is set back from the noise and traffic, but it's within steps of Dock Square, the shops and two-lane drawbridge that form the heart of Kennebunkport. This is a real plus, given the lack of free parking in the square. Built in 1899 as a private mansion, the Kennebunkport Inn has been substantially enlarged several times in the more than 60 years it's been an inn. It has the ambiance of a small European hotel, with a locally respected dining room, a handsome and lively bar, and comfortable rooms.

Rick and Martha Griffin have owned the Kennebunkport Inn since 1979. Both have degrees in hotel administration; Martha's interest is the dining room and Rick is the man up front — a hospitable, helpful host. They take their jobs seriously and are almost always within call.

The rooms vary in size, but they are all decorated with real or reproduction antiques and have TVs, phones, and air conditioning. Several have views of the tidal Kennebunk River, and one has a fireplace.

The popular bar is dark and friendly, with a huge old bar, green hooded lights, and live entertainment (usually piano music) every evening in the summer. There is also a pool wedged between the inn and motel-like annex.

If you opt for the MAP rate, you'll dine in the candlelit dining rooms, which are open to the public. Entrées usually include the inn's signature Kennebunkport bouillabaisse (one serving is enough for two), pesto-crusted salmon and grilled swordfish with a warm lobster and corn salsa. The wine list includes over 150 carefully chosen labels in a wide price range. While dinner is impressive, it's nice not to be locked into an MAP rate because Kennebunkport offers dozens of restaurants. Multiple-night packages include a cruise on a lobster boat.

The Maine Stay Inn and Cottages

34 Maine Street
P.O. Box 500A
Kennebunkport, ME 04046
207-967-2117
800-950-2117
Fax: 207-967-8757
innkeeper@mainestayinn.com
www.mainestay.inn.com

Both gracious and family-geared

Innkeepers: Carol and Lindsay Copeland. **Accommodations:** 6 rooms in house (including 2 suites), 9 cottages. **Rates:** $85 (non-fireplace, low season); $225 (largest fireplace suite, high season). **Included:** Breakfast and afternoon tea. **Minimum stay:** 2 nights on weekends, 3 on holiday weekends in cottages. **Added:** 7 % tax. **Credit cards accepted:** Visa, American Express, MasterCard. **Children:** Age 6 and up in the main house; under age 4 is free, special rates up to age 18. **Pets:** Not accepted. **Smoking:** Not permitted. **Handicap access:** No. **Open:** Year-round

➤ **One of the few attractive places for families to stay that is within walking distance of Dock Square.**

What you notice first at The Maine Stay are the large cupola and porch, but what really sets it apart from other mansions and B&Bs in Kennebunkport's historic district are the 11 cottages behind the mansion. Carol and Lindsay have done a truly amazing job of transforming these formerly basic units into appealing, family-geared spaces — five with fireplaces, all but one with efficiency kitchens.

Room 1 is actually a great space for a couple, with a queen bed, a separate sitting room, and a wood-burning fireplace. The four rooms and two suites within the inn are definitely geared toward couples. The first-floor suite is downright elegant with its own spacious living room, complete with wood-burning fireplace. An upstairs suite has a gas-burning hearth.

A full breakfast is served in the inn's dining room: maybe blueberry blintzes or apricot scones. Cottage guests can opt to have breakfast delivered in a basket. All guests can enjoy full use of the attractive living room and wraparound porch. Carol and Lindsay Copeland are warm hosts, who are delighted to help guests make the most of their stay.

The Tides Inn By-The-Sea

R.R. 2 252, Goose Rocks Beach
Kennebunkport, ME 04046
207-967-3757

Steps from a superb beach

Hosts: Marie Henriksen and Kristin Blomberg. **Accommodations:** 22 rooms and one housekeeping apartment in the inn; 2 suites, 3 condo-style units (up to 6 people) in Tides Too, a modern annex next door on the beach. Inquire about housekeeping apartments around the corner. **Rates:** Rooms: $165–$225; Condos: $2,000–$2,500 per week; off-season by the day; 10% off if payment for a week's stay is received before March 31. **Included:** No meals. **Added:** 7% tax. **Credit cards accepted:** Visa, MasterCard, American Express. **Children:** Family rooms accommodating up to 4 are $195; $20 for additional children. **Pets:** Limited to Tides Too and apartments. **Smoking:** Only in pub. **Handicap access:** Apartments. **Open:** Mid-May to mid-October.

➤ **A small, very Victorian inn that was built by Maine's foremost Shingle-style architect, John Calvin Stevens, this is one of the area's best kept secrets.**

Several miles from Kennebunkport Village, this classic little Victorian summer hotel sits right across from Goose Rocks, the area's best beach: silvery, long, wide, and firm enough for running.

Built in 1899 by John Calvin Stevens, a Maine architect known for whimsical designs and detailing, The Tides Inn features a central peaked gable, an upstairs as well as downstairs porch, and bay windows. Guest rooms are on the small side but with views (it's worth the extra charge for a water view!) that expands the soul.

Marie Henriksen bought and began restoring the inn in 1972 and now runs it jointly with daughter Kristin Blomberg. The two women are a cheerful, effective pair who obviously have an eye for preserving both the simplicity and whimsy of this summer haven. Don't be surprised to find Teddy Roosevelt charging up a staircase wall (the Rough Rider is numbered, as is Sir Arthur Conan Doyle, among past guests) or Emma, the inn's original proprietor, sitting at the upright piano in the parlor.

A word of warning about Emma: She *is* around. Occasionally guests feel themselves tucked into bed, or notice small things moved around by invisible hands. This summer, in Emma's honor, the dining room was renamed the Belvidere (her name for the hotel) Room.

The dinning room is known locally as one of the very best places to eat in this restaurant-studded resort area. Specialties include lobster and roasted corn chowder, oysters baked with creamed leeks, smoked bacon and corn bread crumbs (for starters), and both seafood and exotic meat entrées (buffalo meat is daily). Breakfast (also open to the public) includes Emma's French toast and Teddy R's MacMuffin.

White Barn Inn

P.O. Box 560C
Beach Street
Kennebunkport, ME 04046
207-967-2321
Fax: 207-967-1100
innkeeper@whitebarninn.com
www.whitebarninn.com

A deservedly prestigious Relais et Chateaux property with innovative regional cuisine

Owner: Laurie Bongiorno. **Manager:** Jonathan Wise. **Accommodations:** 18 rooms (all with private bath), 7 suites, 1 cottage. **Rates:** $150–$400 per couple in-season; off-season packages. **Included:** Expanded continental breakfast; dinner available (make reservations). **Minimum stay:** 2 nights on weekends and 3 nights on holidays. **Added:** 7% tax. **Credit cards accepted:** All major ones. **Children:** Welcome. **Pets:** Not accepted. **Smoking:** Not permitted. **Handicap access:** No. **Open:** Year-round.

➤ **AAA awarded the restaurant its much-coveted (and rarely achieved) five diamonds; the guest rooms garnered four diamonds. If you're going to splurge, do it here. You will not be disappointed.**

The combination of luxurious guest rooms, outstanding cuisine, and black-tie service at the White Barn Inn is arguably unmatched in New England. This complex of clapboard buildings, dating to the 19th century, has taken in guests since the turn of the century — but never in the style it does these days.

A truly world-class dining experience unfolds in a converted post-and-beam barn. The rustically paneled dining rooms have highly polished original floorboards and still-visible hayloft and stalls. You dine by the glow of candlelight, with fresh flowers gracing tables beautifully set with linen and fine china. Chairs are brocaded. One end of the barn has been opened up with floor-to-ceiling windows, while the upper floors of the open barn are filled with Down East antiques. It's all quite elegant as a perceptive waitstaff attends to your every need. Owner Laurie Bongiorno (who purchased the inn in 1988) oversees the dining room.

Chef Jonathan Cartwright, who came to the White Barn Inn in 1995, combines a New American sensibility with classical European influences while highlighting regional ingredients. He says that "care with the sauces is what makes the dream come true on the plate." Indeed, your dreams will come true with every bite. Lobster is featured in two of the inn's signature dishes: spring rolls and fettucine with Cognac butter sauce. In addition to seafood purchased from local fishermen, Cartwright also prepares Maine-grown poultry and game, and he's particularly fond of lamb. The $58-per-person, four-course prix fixe menu changes weekly. The piano music is a lovely accompaniment.

Guest rooms are lavishly appointed with antiques and coordinated designer wall coverings and rich fabrics. Carriage House suites each have a fireplace, spacious sitting area, four-poster king-size bed, and a large marble bathroom with a whirlpool bath. Gatehouse rooms feature sleigh beds, fireplaces, and small private decks. All rooms have thick terrycloth robes and fine toiletries. Rooms in the main inn are the smallest. On arrival you'll find mineral water, fresh flowers, and fruit. Turndown service also includes a little something extra from the chef.

Common space is limited to a Colonial-style living room with fireplace and a smaller, less formal room with television, books, and games. The breakfast room boasts a chandelier, chintz curtains, and tin ceiling.

It's only a 5-minute walk into town from here, but the inn offers complimentary bicycles to explore farther afield. The inn also has a pool.

Kittery

Gundalow Inn

6 Water Street
Kittery, ME 03904
207-439-4040

| A quiet B&B near the water |

Innkeepers: Cevia and George Rosol. **Accommodations:** 6 rooms (all with private bath). **Rates:** $110–$125 per couple from mid-May through October; $20 each additional person in room. **Included:** Full breakfast. **Minimum stay:** 2 nights involving a Saturday. **Added:** 7% tax. **Credit cards accepted:** Master-Card, Visa. **Children:** Over age 15 welcome; younger children by prior arrangement. **Pets:** Not accepted. **Smoking:** Not permitted. **Handicap access:** No. **Open:** Year-round.

➤ **The inn is an unexpected gem, a handsome hub from which to explore both Portsmouth, New Hampshire, and Maine's South Coast.**

This 1890s brick house, just off the village green in Kittery, is across the street from the Piscataqua River and the bridge that spans it. The bridge leads to the oldest neighborhoods of Portsmouth, New Hampshire, including Strawberry Banke. It's also across from Warren's Lobster House, a dining landmark with a 1940s decor and an extensive seafood menu.

Location aside, however, the Gundalow is simply a great B&B. The kitchen, with open shelves and state-of-the-art stove, now forms the heart of the home. The living room retains its hominess with a baby grand piano, attractive couches, plenty of reading material (including four or five newspapers), and puzzles. There's another sitting room upstairs. A small front porch has rockers, while the screened-in flagstone porch remains a cool refuge throughout the summer.

The guest rooms have been carefully crafted to maximize the views. (Four of the six rooms have some sort of water view.) Our favorite is Royal George, with its skylight view of Portsmouth; but, if you like clawfoot tubs, it's a toss-up with Alice. Valdora is a bright corner room.

For breakfast you'll be served fresh fruit juice, a fruit course like blueberry-lemon soup, scones, meat or fish, and some kind of egg or pancake dish.

A gundalow, incidentally, is the shallow-bottomed sailing scow that served as the workhorse of the Piscataqua River for more than two hundred years, before the advent of steam. There is a replica in the sunny breakfast room, beyond the kitchen.

Ogunquit

The Cliff House

P.O. Box 2274
Shore Road
Ogunquit, ME 03907
207-361-1000
Fax: 207-361-2122
cliffhouse@maine.com
www.cliffhousemaine.com

A resort sited dramatically on a rocky promontory

Owner/manager: Kathryn Weare. **Accommodations:** 162 rooms and 2 suites from mid-April to late October; 104 rooms the balance of season. **Rates:** $115–$210 per couple in rooms; packages available. **Included:** No meals, but breakfast and dinner available; additionally, lunch is served in the summer. **Minimum stay:** 2 nights on weekends from mid-July to early September; 3 nights on holidays. **Added:** 7% tax; $1 per person, per day for housekeeping. **Credit cards accepted:** American Express and Discover for reservations; all major ones on premises. **Children:** Welcome; under 3, no charge; $15 per extra child in room. **Pets:** Not accepted. **Smoking:** Permitted. **Handicap access:** Yes. **Open:** Late March through December.

➤ **Officially, the Cliff House is in York. But it's actually closer to Perkins Cove and to the beach, shops, and restaurants in the village of Ogunquit than to any of the villages in York.**

The mansard-roofed Cliffscape Building, opened in 1990, is now the centerpiece of this 90-acre seaside resort, which, perched on Bald Head Cliff, is one of the most dramatically sited hotels on the

Maine coast. The multi-tiered lobby and dining room take full advantage of the ocean view. Billed as the oldest family-operated resort on the East Coast, it's also made one of the most impressive comebacks of any New England resort. And it's all the work of Kathryn Weare, a great-granddaughter worthy of Elsie Jane Weare, the indomitable lady who opened the Cliff House in 1872.

Back in the 1860s, when the Boston & Maine Railroad announced its spur line to York, Elsie Jane persuaded her husband, a sea captain, to invest all their money in Bald Hill Cliff, the most grand promontory on Maine's sandy South Coast. Her brother built the hotel with wood from the family lots and milled in their own sawmill. The clean rooms, fine food, fresh air, and locale — all for $6 a week — soon lured the well-heeled families from Philadelphia, New York, and Boston.

The resort maintained its status throughout the 1920s and 1930s, but during World War II it was drafted as a radar station. When the Weares were permitted to return, the property was so damaged that a discouraged Charles Weare placed an ad in a 1946 *Wall Street Journal*: "For sale. 144 rooms. 90 acres, over 2500 ft. ocean frontage for just $50,000." Luckily for us, he had no takers. So Charles turned the property over to his son Maurice, who went with the times and shaved off the top two floors of the original inn to create the resort motel that existed until 1990 when it passed to Kathryn.

So it happens that this once "grand old resort" is now a new resort. The oldest rooms are now large motel units in the Ledges and Cliff Top buildings. The second-floor Ledges rooms feel more spacious with their peaked ceilings. (But the porches are not private like they are in the main hotel.) The 1870s Captain's House, which retains its original cupola, is used for special functions. Newer rooms, furnished in an old-fashioned style, all have an oceanview balcony. Frontal oceanview rooms cost the same as those rooms with an oblique ocean view, so you know which ones to ask for. (Since groups are often booked here, reserve early for the best views.) Three corner rooms with frontal views are 525, 537, and 512. Hotel extras include a fitness center, sauna, whirlpool, indoor pool, outdoor pool, and tennis.

Kathryn takes particular pride in the design of the dining room (which overlooks Bald Head Cliff) and its seafood specialties like lobster hazelnut sauté. Light fare is served on the Ocean Terrace, an open space with a splendid view of the cliffs below. Jackets are preferred at dinnertime.

The Dunes on the Waterfront

Route 1, P.O. Box 917
Ogunquit, ME 03907
207-646-2612
888-295-3863
info@Dunesmotel.com

Beachside cottages in Ogunquit

Owners: The Perkins family. **Accommodations:** 36 units, including 19 cottages. **Rates:** In-season (mid-June to Labor Day): $84–$145 per unit; off-season: $65–$100. **Minimum stay:** In-season: 3 nights in motel units, 1 week in smaller cottages, 2 weeks in two-bedroom cottages. **Included:** Daily maid service, in-room coffee. **Added:** 7% tax. **Credit cards accepted:** MasterCard, Visa. **Children:** Welcome. **Pets:** Not accepted. **Smoking:** Permitted. **Open:** May through October.

➤ **The Dunes is a rare "motor court," an almost vanished breed of cottage once plentiful along coastal Route 1.**

The Dunes dates from the 1930s, an era in which hundreds of such motor courts — the forerunners of motels — opened along Route 1. This one has remained in the same family and has always been the finest of its kind. It's still one of the nicest places in Ogunquit, one of the most popular of Maine's South Coast resorts.

The location is unbeatable: It is set right on the tidal Ogunquit River with a view beyond of the high sand dunes on Ogunquit Beach. You enter from busy Route 1, but the cottages are set well back on twelve grassy acres — a priceless oasis amid the build-up all around it. The grounds include a small "sitting" beach, a swimming dock, and rowboats. At high tide you can row across to the main beach, and at low tide it's an easy wade to the three-mile strand for which others pay steep parking fees and have to walk a ways to reach this remote spot. There's also a pool with views of the dunes.

This is a great place for families. Children tend to meet each other around shuffleboard and croquet, and at the swimming pool and swings. The older cottages are the most in demand: white with green trim, pine walls inside and a screened porch outside, and many with water views. Some one- and two-bedroom units have a combination living room and bedroom with a fireplace. All have air conditioning and TV.

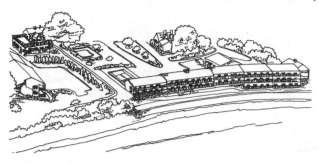

Sparhawk Resort

Shore Road
P.O. Box 936
Ogunquit, ME 03907
207-646-5562

A resort motor inn with a view

Innkeeper: Blaine Moores. **Accommodations:** 51 rooms, 27 suites, 4 apartments. **Rates:** $140–$160 for motel units and suites, $160–$220 for apartments (weekly rentals). **Included:** Continental breakfast. **Minimum stay:** 1 week, July 4–August 21. **Added:** 7% tax. **Credit cards accepted:** All major ones; discount for cash or traveler's check. **Children:** Welcome. **Pets:** Not accepted. **Smoking:** Restricted. **Handicap access:** 7 rooms. **Open:** Mid-April through late October.

➤ **Still the best address in Ogunquit**

The Sparhawk is an attractive motor inn that replaced a grand old shingled summer hotel in the 1960s. The site is superb. Most rooms in the complex are set back from the hubbub of Shore Road, and the 50 motel units, each with a balcony, overlook the entrance to the Ogunquit River and down the length of Ogunquit Beach. You are also a very short walk from the village shops and the Marginal Way, the shore path to Perkins Cove. In addition, 20 motel units in the Ireland House (with balconies overlooking the beach) have combination living room–bedroom suites. The Barbara Dean, a neighboring house on Shore Road, offers seven suites and three apartments.

Activities on the well-tended grounds include swimming in the large heated pool, tennis, shuffleboard, and croquet.

The Trellis House

2 Beachmere Place
P.O. Box 2229
Ogunquit, ME 03907
207-646-7909
1-800-681-7909
www.trellishouse.com

| A gem of a bed-and-breakfast |

Innkeepers: Pat and Jerry Houlihan. **Accommodations:** 3 rooms in house, 1 garden cottage, 4 rooms in carriage house. **Rates:** $95–$120 in-season, $65–$95 off-season. **Included:** Full breakfast. **Minimum stay:** Two nights on weekends, May through October. **Added:** 7% tax. **Credit cards accepted:** MasterCard, Visa, American Express, Discover. **Children:** Over age 12. **Pets:** Not accepted. **Smoking:** Not permitted. **Open:** Most of the year.

➤   **The Trellis House is within walking distance of Oqunquit Beach, the Marginal Way, and Perkins Cove.**

This shingled, turn-of-the-century summer cottage is sited just off Shore Road in a spot that, while not right on the water, is both tranquil and handy to every desirable corner of the resort.

Walk a few hundred yards in one direction and you are on one of the most appealing stretches of the Marginal Way — the shore path that winds around the rocky headland and into Perkins Cove, where shops and restaurants cluster around a picturesque mooring for pleasure and fishing boats. Walk down Shore Road and you are quickly in the middle of the village, or follow the Marginal Way to the village and cut across a footbridge to the beach. You can park your car when you arrive at the inn and need never battle the summer traffic or pay the steep parking fees that bedevil this otherwise delightful resort.

The Trellis House offers tasteful, comfortable common areas, including a wraparound screened porch on which breakfast is served in nice weather. Off-season guests also appreciate the seating around the living room hearth.

Upstairs are three guest rooms, all with private baths, one with a water view. The most romantic room is the one-room garden cottage. Jerry Houlihan's pride — given how its creation absorbed all his energy during the winter of 1996 — is the carriage house, containing four rooms, three of which have gas fireplaces.

Breakfast is a serious business that might include fruit compote and zucchini pie, or maybe apple-cinnamon French toast and sausage.

Portland Area

The Danforth

163 Danforth Street
Portland, ME 04102
207-879-8755
800-991-6557
Fax: 207-879-8754

> **A Federal mansion three blocks from the Old Port**

Proprietor: Barbara Hathaway. **Accommodations:** 8 rooms (all with private bath), 2 suites, 1 efficiency. **Rates:** $115–$185 per couple from late May through October; $95–$165 off-season; corporate rates. **Included:** Full breakfast. **Minimum stay:** 2 nights on most weekends and holidays. **Added:** 7% tax. **Credit cards accepted:** All major ones. **Children:** Well-behaved children welcome. **Pets:** Accepted. **Smoking:** Not permitted. **Handicap access:** No. **Open:** Year-round.

➤ **In 1997, The Danforth acquired a brownstone across the street. The open-floor-plan efficiency apartment is perfect for longer stays or for those seeking more privacy. It boasts two fireplaces, a full kitchen, and Oriental carpets over shiny hardwood floors. It sleeps three people and has access to a side yard.**

The graceful Federal-style brick mansion was built in 1823 for Joseph Holt Ingraham, a wealthy Portland benefactor who laid out Main Street. The 21-room mansion served for a time as a girl's boarding school before it was sold as a private home and remodeled by John Calvin Stevens at the turn of the century. Colonial Revival details include Baccarat crystal doorknobs, elaborate moldings, bowed walls to accommodate radiators, carved mantles for most of the dozen fireplaces, and shuttered windows. For fifty years (until Barbara purchased it) the house served as a rectory for the Catholic church next door.

This is the kind of hostelry for guests who do not require much innkeeper pampering. Although Barbara is constantly improving and attending to the property, she generally leaves guests to themselves unless they need help. There are common areas on every floor, including a comfortable front parlor, a second-floor sitting room that serves as an entryway for a porch ringed with flower boxes (we like to read the morning paper with a cup of coffee here), and a third-floor sitting room that was a work in progress on our last visit. Sometime during your stay, head up to the Italianate cupola at dusk for a view of the city and downstairs to an oak-paneled billiard room.

Each guest room has a queen-size bed, sitting area, television, air conditioning, desk, phone, and computer modem port. (Barbara gets a lot of business travelers.) Most of the spacious rooms have a wood-burning fireplace. The two rooms that don't (numbers 5 and 6) are smaller and can be connected as a family suite. All of the bathrooms have been upgraded and renovated nicely. We particularly like the large corner rooms on the second floor with their 10-foot ceilings.

Though there are two dining rooms, we like the sunny, glass-enclosed porch. It is set with a bountiful help-yourself buffet, including plenty of fresh fruit and an extensive selection of really tasty baked goods like raisin scones with lots of cinnamon. Barbara's "Maine Morning" breakfasts might include peach cobbler, a breakfast "wrap" made with tortillas, and perhaps a potato side dish.

Inn by the Sea

40 Bowery Beach Road (Route 77)
Cape Elizabeth, ME 04107
207-799-3134
800-888-4287 (outside Maine)
Fax: 207-799-4779
inmaine@aol.com
www.inbythesea.com

> **Elegant suites on the beach**

Owner: Maureen McQuade. **Accommodations:** 43 suites. **Rates:** $215–$390 per couple from July to early September; $110–$220 off-season. **Included:** All meals available. **Minimum stay:** 2 nights on weekends. **Added:** 7% tax, 3% service. **Credit cards accepted:** All major ones. **Children:** Welcome. **Pets:** Accepted. **Smoking:** Not permitted in inn. **Handicap access:** Some rooms. **Open:** Year-round.

➤ **This luxury beach resort is just 15 minutes from Portland.**

Inn by the Sea, a 15-minute drive from downtown Portland, overlooks the Atlantic Ocean at Crescent Beach. The complex, although reminiscent of turn-of-the century seaside resorts, was actually built in 1986. The shingled buildings with gables, eaves, and hundreds of windows belie the contemporary amenities and services provided.

All of the spacious units — one- and two-bedroom garden suites, loft suites, and cottages — vary. But all have a pretty combination living and dining area, full kitchen, TVs and VCRs, and a patio or porch overlooking the ocean. They are furnished with reproduction cherry antiques, chintz upholstered chairs, wicker, and down comforters. The cottages, connected in a townhouse arrangement, are away from the main inn. Beach house units, perfect for family gatherings, are generally larger, with woodstoves and full ocean views.

The Audubon Dining Room, named for the famed naturalist whose hand-colored prints are featured throughout the main inn, overlooks the great expanses of lawn and ocean. The menu features Maine seafood dishes and excellent New American cuisine. Its open for breakfast and dinner; in the summer, lunch and afternoon snacks are served at the poolside café.

The lushly landscaped grounds are often used as a backdrop for weddings and receptions. Summer evenings are magical here, with soft lighting throughout the grounds. Facilities include a small heated pool, a lighted tennis court, croquet, biking, and trails for walking and jogging. The inn's boardwalk leads guests across the salt marsh to Crescent Beach State Park. Portland Headlight and its museum are just down the road. Guests enjoy privileges at a nearby private golf club.

Pomegranate Inn

49 Neal Street
Portland, ME 04102
207-772-1006
800-356-0408
Fax: 207-773-4426

> **Perhaps the most artful small hotel in New England**

Owner: Isabel Smiles. **Manager:** Ann Baldwin. **Accommodations:** 8 rooms (all with private bath), 1 suite. **Rates:** $135 per couple in rooms and $165 in suite from late May through October; $95–$125 off-season. **Included:** Full breakfast. **Minimum stay:** 2 nights on weekends in season; 3 nights on holidays. **Added:** 7% tax. **Credit cards accepted:** All major ones. **Children:** Over age 16 welcome. **Pets:** Not allowed. **Smoking:** Not permitted. **Handicap access:** Yes. **Open:** Year-round.

➤ **This mansion in Portland's Western Promenade neighborhood proves that operating and decorating a B&B can be an art form.**

This 1888 Italianate mansion is a visual feast, a celebration of color, patterns, textures, and moods. If you're visiting Portland's Museum of Art, you'd be well advised to stay at the Pomegranate Inn so that you can surround yourself with art before and after museum hours. Isabel Smiles's artistic sensibilities come from her years as an interior designer and as co-owner of an antiques business in Greenwich, Connecticut. The inn is a showpiece for her talents.

For nine months before the inn opened in 1989, a Portland artist lived at the house, painting (and signing) seven of the guest rooms. (Look again — the walls are painted, not wallpapered.) Isabel's daughter did all the faux marbling in the house, including the four classical columns that separate the living and dining rooms. With double front doors, high ceilings, and lofty common rooms, the architecture provides just the right backdrop for the modern art that covers every inch of the common space. A gallery guide may well be in order.

Heading upstairs, you pass a checkerboard-style landing and a series of intaglio prints on the brash yellow and orange walls. The sophisticated guest rooms are decorated in a comfortable, high-style. Small touches range from the whimsical to the avant-garde. All have telephone, television, and air conditioning; many have gas fireplaces. Most of the guest rooms are off the long, narrow hallway, with recessed lighting. Isabel's husband, Alan, was a linen dealer from Belfast, Ireland, and the bedding is some of the most luxurious we've found.

Room 2 has a fluffy down comforter and multiple pillows on a king-size bed. Even the small television, on a graceful pedestal, poses as a piece of art. The walls in #3 have been painted with bouquets of large wildflowers that complement the wine and mauve Chinese rug. Room 4 is large, with bow windows and four-poster twin beds, and #6 has rose-striped walls with coordinated bedding. The smaller #5 has watercolors in the bathroom and delicate clusters of irises all over the walls. All the bathrooms have new tiling and porcelain sinks. Rooms in the Carriage House are particularly private; we especially like Room 7, with a lushly landscaped patio.

Upon arriving, guests are offered mineral water or tea, which can be taken in the small, cozy, third-floor sitting room or in the living room. Breakfast might be a choice of poached eggs, broiled tomatoes, or French toast. French doors lead from the breakfast room to the pretty garden.

Portland Regency

20 Milk Street
Portland, ME 04101
207-774-4200
800-727-3436
Fax: 207-775-2150
www.theregency.com

> A former armory in the
> heart of the Old Port

General manager: Anne DeRepentigny. **Accommodations:** 87 rooms, 8 suites. **Rates:** $149–$269 per room; packages available in the spring and late fall. **Parking:** $5 overnight, valet. **Restaurants:** Serve all three meals. **Included:** Coffee at your door with wake-up call. **Added:** 7% tax. **Credit cards accepted:** All major ones. **Children:** Under age 18, free in parents room; no charge for crib. **Pets:** Accepted by arrangement. **Smoking:** Rooms available for non-smokers. **Handicap access:** 1 room. **Open:** Year-round.

> ➤ **The Regency combines the amenities of a small, full-service hotel with a bustling location.**

The Regency sits smack in the middle of Portland's restored waterfront, the Old Port, five square blocks of intriguing shops, galleries, and restaurants. The building itself is a century-old armory, its exterior intact.

Despite its name, this is not a member of a chain and nothing about it is cookie-cutter. In fact, no two rooms are exactly the same shape, carved as they have been from the preexisting armory. The former officers' quarters — with fireplaces and long, leaded windows — are quite grand but the skylit rooms under the sloping roofline are also charming, with such architectural features as arched, small-paned windows. All are nicely appointed, with Colonial reproductions and flowery chintz fabrics, honor bars, and telephones in the bathroom as well as the bedroom. Color TVs are sequestered in armoires and the morning weather report is provided. Request a harbor view.

Of the hotel's two restaurants we prefer the less formal Armory Lounge with its pleasant square, sit-up bar and library ambiance (open 11:30 A.M. to 11:30 P.M).

The Regency also has one of Portland's most extensive health clubs, with Nautilus equipment, aerobics classes, sauna, steam rooms, and whirlpool. The reasonably priced valet parking is also a real plus in this very popular part of Portland. Other niceties include complimentary wake-up coffee and a courtesy van to the airport.

Prouts Neck

Black Point Inn

510 Black Point Road
Prouts Neck, ME 04074
207-883-4126
800-258-0003
Fax: 207-883-9976
bpi@nlis.com
www.blackpointinn.com

> **A grand old seaside resort with an equally grand setting**

Owner: Eric Cianchette. **Accommodations:** 68 rooms (all with private bath), 12 suites. **Rates:** $290–$450 per couple from June through October, MAP; $160–$450 per couple off-season. **Included:** Varies with meal plan. **Minimum stay:** 3 nights in July and August, otherwise 2 nights. **Added:** 7% tax, 15% service charge. **Credit cards accepted:** All major ones. **Children:** Over age 8 in summer; all welcome other times. **Pets:** Not accepted. **Smoking:** Permitted. **Handicap access:** Yes. **Open:** Early May to mid-December.

➤ **At the same time that the Black Point Inn conveys a sense of a slower-paced, more dignified era, it has also joined the 21st century with a new spa.**

Black Point Inn is an 1870s resort on an isolated peninsula only 20 minutes from Portland. Beautifully maintained, it has excellent service, first-rate facilities, and outstanding views that extend down the South Coast and across to open ocean. The peninsula itself offers wonderful walking and bird-watching. (The inner part of the peninsula is a bird sanctuary.) In fact, practically the only de rigeur activity is walking the spectacular Cliff Walk. It heads around the rocky promontory of Prouts Neck, and past the house where Winslow Homer painted many of his seascapes. To enjoy it fully, allow a couple of hours and bring a lunch or teatime picnic.

Back at the inn, spacious common rooms set the tone, with ample fireside seating in the dark-beamed living room, a grand piano in the music room, and comfortable leather club chairs in the cocktail lounge. Green wicker rockers on the porch overlook well-tended grounds that slope to the expansive beach beyond. Fortunately the sun sets in this direction. An inside porch makes rainy days palatable.

Outdoor activities are legion and a great draw. The heated salt-water pool overlooks a rocky beach, and you can swim or sun on two sandy beaches. There is also an indoor freshwater pool, Jacuzzi, and a health center with exercise equipment. Golf and fourteen tennis courts are available at the Prouts Neck Country Club, while boating is available at the Prouts Neck Yacht Club, both just down the road. Loaner bicycles are ready and waiting.

One thing that sets this place apart is its headlong march into the 21st century. In 1998 the resort added 12 oceanfront suites and a state-of-the-art spa. Throughout the resort, the large bedrooms are furnished in Colonial Beals rock maple or mahogany. The white crewel bedspreads and Colonial print papers emphasize tradition, but only to a point — all the rooms are air-conditioned, with television, telephone, and turn-down service. Be sure to ask for a room with a view.

Throughout your stay, you eat at your own, assigned table. Tea is served every afternoon as well. Lunch may be served poolside, weather permitting. A hot and cold buffet can include chowder, chicken pot pie, and lobster as well as hot dogs and hamburgers. Dinner, a more formal affair, gives you a chance to dress up. The five-course meal must appeal to long-time 90-year-old returnees as well as younger families creating their own new traditions, so don't expect anything too out of the ordinary. A lobster dish is always offered in addition to other local, old-fashioned staples. We particularly like the smaller dining room overlooking the rose garden.

Call ahead if you plan to come off-season or you may find yourself sharing the common areas with a hundred business people, all talking shop. A London taxi whisks guests to the airport and into Portland's Old Port.

Note: As we went to press, the inn had changed hands.

South Harpswell

Harpswell Inn B&B

141 Lookout Point Road
South Harpswell, ME 04079
207-833-5509
800-843-5509
www.gwl.net/-harpswel

> A convenient waterside
> B&B

Innkeepers: Susan and Bill Menz. **Accommodations:** 12 rooms (5 with private bath), 3 suites. **Rates:** $59–$116 per couple in rooms; $135–$150 per couple in suites; $16 for extra person. **Included:** Full breakfast. **Added:** 7% tax. **Credit cards accepted:** Visa, MasterCard. **Children:** Over age 10. **Pets:** Not accepted. **Smoking:** Not permitted. **Handicap access:** No. **Open:** Year-round.

➤ **Susan and Bill Menz have lived in many places, including Hawaii and Texas, and collected antiques and souvenirs along the way, so the house is filled with many interesting pieces. Bill's forebears actually helped settle nearby Phippsburg in the 17th century.**

Over the decades, the inn has served visitors under a number of names and is now a gracious bed-and-breakfast. The kitchen and dining room date from 1761, when they served as the cook house for the Lookout Point Shipyard across the way. In 1850 the building was expanded into the present three-story white clapboard house, which still has a bell on top for calling workers to lunch. (Go ahead and ring it.)

Guests enter through the carpeted living room, with its big hearth and windows overlooking Middle Bay. The space feels like a neighbor's living room, with its homey touches like framed family photographs as well as many interesting antiques. There's also a dining room and large porch, as well as Adirondack chairs on the lawn.

The guest rooms vary widely and come with and without private baths and water views. When the private baths were refurbished, soaking tubs were added. All rooms are decorated with a different theme — the Lilac Room, the Longfellow Room (Longfellow attended nearby Bowdoin College), the Bowdoin Room (so did Bill), and the Texas Room. The bilevel Sunset Suite, formerly the innkeeper's quarters, can certainly accommodate three comfortably.

In 1995 Susan and Bill added two 800-square-foot suites. Converted from the former barn, the tastefully furnished suites feature cathedral ceilings, decks, and antique and reproduction furniture. Both can sleep three people. One has a better water view and benefits from early morning sun.

Handy to Portland, to Brunswick's museums, and to all the shopping in Freeport, the Harpswells are quiet havens geared to the water. Unspoiled by rampant commercialism, they seem many miles farther Downeast than they really are. Bike or drive down to Potts Point, and be sure to try the chowder at the Dolphin Marina. You'll enjoy watching the lobstermen haul in their catch across the street from the inn. When the tide is in, guests can swim or sun on the inn's dock and float.

York Harbor

Dockside Guest Quarters

P.O. Box 205
Harris Island Road
York, ME 03909
207-363-2868
800-270-1977
Fax: 207-363-1977
dockside@docksidegg.com

A seaside inn and cottages

Innkeepers: The Lusty family. **Accommodations:** 6 cottage apartments/studios, 15 doubles (13 with private bath). **Rates:** Late June to early September: $108–$150 per couple in cottage apartment/studio; $98.50 in rooms with private bath; off-season packages. **Included:** "Continental plus" breakfast for $3 per person; all meals available. **Minimum stay:** 2 days, July through September. **Added:** 7% tax. **Credit cards accepted:** MasterCard, Visa. **Children:** Welcome; no charge for children under 12 in suites and studios. **Pets:** Not accepted. **Smoking:** No. **Handicap access:** No. **Open:** May through October and on Fridays and Saturdays the rest of the year.

➤ **The Lusty family has operated Dockside Guest Quarters since 1953 with an easy, distinctly salty hospitality.**

People often drive hundreds of miles farther up the Maine coast to find what is here at Dockside: peace and quiet and outstanding views of the picturesque harbor and coastline. The secluded inn is on a private island-like peninsula.

The Guest Quarters comprise the "Maine House" and several multi-unit cottage buildings. The Maine House has five bedrooms with painted pine floors and simple country decor. Second-floor rooms share a common deck that offers spectacular water views. The sunny, contemporary cottages are strung along the shoreline, with decks and comfortable chairs for lounging.

The living room in the Maine House is decorated with period antiques. Ship models, paintings of clipper ships, early marine prints and lithographs, scrimshaw, and books on nautical and Maine subjects abound. The innkeepers have printed up their own Boat Watchers Guide to help identify passing boats.

The Dockside Restaurant is popular, but it is far enough from the inn not to disturb the guests' sense of privacy. Of course, it also overlooks the water, and the menu is primarily seafood, although roast duckling is a specialty of the house. Cocktails are available.

Breakfast is served buffet style in the Maine House and in fine weather can be enjoyed outside. Seven acres of meticulously planted grounds provide lots of room for enjoying the view from old wooden chairs. Toward the north is the yacht basin; to the east is the sea. Numerous lawn games, bicycles, and rental boats are also available. David Lusty and his son, Eric, frequently take guests on motorboat excursions though York Harbor and nearby waters; both of them hold Coast Guard licenses.

Inn at Harmon Park

415 York Street, Box 495
York Harbor, Maine 03911
207-363-1031
Fax: 207-351-2948
santal@gwi.net
yorkme.org/inns/harmonpark.html

| **Affordable luxury** |

Innkeeper: Sue Antal. **Accommodations:** 4 rooms, 1 suite (all private bath). **Rates:** $79–$109 per couple, less off-season. **Included:** Full breakfast. **Minimum stay:** 2 days on weekends. **Added:** 7% tax. **Credit cards accepted:** No. **Children:** Age 12 and over. **Pets:** Not accepted. **Smoking:** Not permitted. **Handicap access:** No. **Open:** Year-round.

➤ **A relaxed retreat, the inn is within steps of a tranquil harbor.**

This shingled Victorian house, set in the dignified 19th-century resort village of York Harbor, is airy in the summer and cozy in cold weather — a welcoming retreat at any time of the year. Host Sue Antal encourages guests to walk York Harbor's Shore Path, following it either to the beach or along the river, across the Wiggly Bridge and into Steedman Woods.

Sue welcomes visitors in the living room of her family home, where they will find comfortable seating, books, and a frequently lit hearth. Sooner or later, however, most guests usually find their way back into the kitchen/work space and those who bring their own kayak can usually convince her to go paddling. Emma, Sue's golden retriever, comes on most expeditions.

The four guest rooms and one suite (with working fireplace) are all nicely furnished but vary substantially in size. Room diaries are filled with thanks to Sue for her unusual hospitality and sound suggestions for enjoying the immediate area — which includes several historic houses and buildings in York (Maine's oldest community) and the neighboring communities of York Beach and Ogunquit.

Breakfast is served on the sun porch at tables set with fresh flowers.

Tanglewood Hall

611 York Street
P.O. Box 12
York Harbor, ME 03911
207-363-7577

A harbor hideaway

Innkeepers: Jean Dyer and Michael Stotts. **Accommodations:** 2 rooms, 1 suite. **Rates:** $90 per room, $120 for the suite. **Included:** Full breakfast. **Minimum stay:** 2 nights on weekends and holidays. **Added:** 7% tax. **Credit cards accepted:** All major cards. **Children:** Not appropriate. **Pets:** Not accepted. **Smoking:** Not permitted. **Handicap access:** No. **Open:** Memorial Day through October.

➤ **Tanglewood Hall is a bandleader's quiet space.**

One of those magnificent shingle summer "cottages" that York Harbor is known for, Tanglewood is hidden away on the shore side of Route 1A. A romantic retreat, its natural elegance is enhanced both by its furnishings and the hospitality of its hosts.

Artist Winslow Homer is said to have been a guest here around the turn of the century, and in a later era Tanglewood Hall was the summer home of band leader Tommy Dorsey and his brother Jimmy. In 1994 it was selected as the York Historical Society's Decorator Show House, meaning that each room was professionally decorated — from hand-painted detailing to the themed rooms as they presently exist.

The York Harbor Suite is by far the largest space, featuring a queen-sized four-poster bed, a fireplace, and its own conservatory. The Tommy Dorsey Room is the smallest but still has a sitting space and a four-poster bed. Our favorite is the Winslow Homer Room, a former library with a total sense of privacy.

The downstairs rooms are exceptionally attractive, especially the dining room where guests tend to linger over very full breakfasts served at the long pine table.

Mid-Coast Maine and the Islands

Boothbay Harbor Area
Brunswick
Camden
Ilseboro
Monhegan Island
New Harbor
Pemaquid Point
Rockport/Rockland
Sebasco Estates
Tenants Harbor
Vinalhaven
Wiscasset

Best Bed-and-Breakfasts

Boothbay Harbor Area
Albonegon Inn, 98
Five Gables Inn, 100
Hogden Island Inn, 101
Brunswick
Brunswick Bed & Breakfast, 104
Camden
The Hawthorn, 105
Maine Stay, 107
Windward House, 109

Best Family Finds

Boothbay Harbor Area
Albonegon Inn, 98
New Harbor
The Gosnold Arms, 113
Sebasco Estates
Sebasco Harbor Resort, 122

Best Gourmet Getaway

Wiscasset
Squire Tarbox Inn, 127

Best Resorts

Boothbay Harbor Area
Spruce Point Inn, 102
Sebasco Estates
Sebasco Harbor Resort, 122

Best Inns

Pemaquid Point
The Bradley Inn, 115

Best Romantic Getaway

In the days of the steamboats, the tips of Maine's peninsulas were far more accessible than they are today. Travelers simply boarded a boat one evening in Boston and disembarked at Popham Point or Georgetown, at Boothbay Harbor (still a lively resort), and at New Harbor and Pemaquid Point.

Today, the mainstream traffic hugs Route 1, leaving the old resort villages to cater to the relatively small number of tourists willing to drive the narrow, winding peninsula roads and to the yachts that still sail in. Most visitors stop only in Portland, then **Boothbay Harbor,** then **Camden.**

An unusually appealing village backed by mountains, Camden attracted many wealthy summer people during the steamboat era. Several elaborate 19th-century summer homes are now B&Bs, as are many of the handsome old sea captain's and merchant's homes in the Historic District. Its lively yachting harbor, surrounded by shops and restaurants, is the departure point for several excursion boats and half a dozen windjammers.

A half-dozen more windjammers are based in nearby **Rockland.** For enterprising travelers who lack their own yacht, there are the Maine windjammers — two-masted schooners, some of which are a hundred years old and more (in part), and others that are replicas of the vessels that once plied this coast by the thousands. Today's windjammers carry between 20 and 38 passengers and sail Penobscot Bay on three- and five-day cruises. Each evening they put into beautiful, relatively untouristed ports like Castine and Stonington or moor in island harbors.

Of all the Maine islands, **Monhegan** is, many agree, the most beautiful and certainly the most hospitable. Barely a mile square, it offers paths along its high cliffs as well as through tall pine woods and along stony beaches. Long a summer artist's colony, it also offers many galleries and a few places to stay. You can take a day trip to Monhegan from Boothbay Harbor, but those who want to stay more than a day or two prefer to park in Port Clyde, a small land's end village, from which the mailboat Laura B serves Monhegan year-round. Few other islands offer inns or B&Bs. The exceptions are the old granite-quarrying community of **Vinalhaven** and exclusive **Islesboro** and North Haven.

Boothbay Harbor Area

Albonegon Inn

Capitol Island, ME 04538
207-633-2521

An authentic period piece on Boothbay Harbor

Innkeepers: Kim and Bob Peckham. **Accommodations:** 14 rooms (3 with shared bath), 3 cottages. **Rates:** $73–$123 per couple, $54 single. **Included:** Continental breakfast. **Minimum stay:** 2 nights on holiday weekends. **Added:** 7% tax. **Credit cards accepted:** None accepted. **Children:** $10 per extra person. **Pets:** Not accepted. **Smoking:** Not permitted. **Handicap access:** Some rooms. **Open:** Late May to mid-October.

➤ **Rock away on a porch overlooking harbor islands, lobster boats, and tidal pools.**

"Determinedly old-fashioned," boasts the brochure, and it's true. Built in the 1880s, Capitol Island remains virtually unchanged. Just four miles from the village of Boothbay Harbor, it is small and private, reached by a one-lane causeway. There are only 40 or so houses on the island, and most of them have been in the same family for more than a hundred years. Kim spent her summers on the island as a youngster, and her great-grandfather stayed at the Albonegon in the 1890s; his signature is in the guest register.

Preserving the inn's Old Maine ambiance is obviously a labor of love for the Peckhams. The summer's profits are visibly reinvested in maintaining the inn.

The guest rooms, upstairs, are furnished simply. Room 23, a corner room with great views of the ocean, is one of the best even though it has twin beds. From the bed in Room 35 you can lie on your side and watch a lobsterman setting his traps. A deck on the second floor affords peaceful views.

Because this place was built as, rather than converted to, an inn, the shared bath system works well; each room has a sink and there are half and full baths for every few rooms.

Three rooms with private bath are housed in outbuildings. One is a tiny bungalow named Barnacle and the others — Periwinkle and Starfish — can be rented separately or together.

The inn's living room, bright with many picture windows, is filled with comfortable mismatched furniture. A Continental breakfast with wild blueberry muffins is served in the many windowed dining room. Off the dining room is a long porch, seemingly suspended over the water; take your coffee out to one of the rocking chairs. Guests are welcome to grill their own steaks or burgers right here if they would rather not tear themselves away from the incredible view at sunset. Additional diversions include tennis and two small beaches. Boats may be rented.

Five Gables Inn

Murray Hill Road
P.O. Box 335
East Boothbay, ME 04544
207-633-4551
800-451-5048
fivegables@wiscasset.net
www.maineguide.com/boothbay/5gables

> A romantic B&B
> overlooking a small harbor

Innkeepers: Mike and De Kennedy. **Accommodations:** 16 rooms (all with private bath). **Rates:** $90–$160 per room. **Included:** Buffet breakfast. **Minimum stay:** None. **Added:** 7% tax. **Credit cards accepted:** MasterCard, Visa. **Children:** Over age 8. **Pets:** Not accepted. **Smoking:** Not permitted inside. **Handicap access:** No. **Open:** Mid-May to October.

➤ **Still one of Maine's active boat-building communities, East Boothbay is now a shade off the tourist track. There are two moorings in the bay for guests arriving by boat.**

Sited on a quiet, waterside byway, this venerable old inn has been substantially renovated within the past decade. The whole five-gabled facade is smartly painted, the long front verandah perfectly plumb, and the period detailing highlighted. A fireplace warms the large combination living and breakfast room (with high-gloss, light pine floors), where wing chairs and well-chosen antiques and collectibles have been carefully mixed.

Five guest rooms have fireplaces and all have baths, tasteful carpeting, good reproduction pieces, and interesting art. All overlook the water. Room 14 is one of the largest rooms, and number 8, with three windows, is particularly bright. The rooms in the four smaller gables, the least expensive in the house, are very appealing as well. We especially like Rooms 11 and 12 with their colorful window seats and pillows. Mike has crafted some great built-in touches, ranging from beds to bookshelves. Room 2 is exceptional.

Ninety-nine percent of De and Mike's guests are couples, and the atmosphere is low-key romantic, relaxed, with a sense of quiet comfort inside and out. There's space to sit in the garden and a dock leads to the water.

Mike is a graduate of the CIA (Culinary Institute of America) and breakfast, served in front of the large picture windows or out on the porch overlooking the bay, might include mushroom crust quiche along with fresh fruit and breads, muffins, granola, and musli.

Hogden Island Inn

Barter's Island Road
P.O. Box 492
Boothbay, ME 04571
207-633-7474

> **A waterside B&B with pool**

Innkeepers: Sydney and Joe Klenk. **Accommodations:** 6 rooms (all with private bath). **Rates:** $80–$102 per couple. **Included:** Full breakfast. **Minimum stay:** None. **Added:** 7% tax. **Credit cards accepted:** None. **Children:** Over age 12 welcome. **Pets:** Not accepted. **Smoking:** Not permitted indoors. **Handicap access:** No. **Open:** Year-round.

➤   **This small B&B boasts a landscaped chlorine-free pool with crystal-clear swimming. In addition, a 19-acre nature preserve, located on the next island over, is just one mile from the B&B.**

This restored sea captain's house, down a quiet country road on the way to a tranquil cove, offers the best of two worlds. The bustle of Boothbay Harbor is just a five-minute drive away, yet you can walk out the front door to your own little cove. It's an unpretentious place with old-fashioned hospitable hosts.

The Klenks opened this circa 1800 house as a B&B in 1990. The guest rooms are all sunny and bright. Room 2 is a favorite for its wicker chairs in front of picture windows. We also like the two queen-bedded rooms in the front of the house with bay windows. Rooms 5 and 6 share a deck and a view. Although bathrooms are on the smallish side, they all have new fixtures.

At breakfast, Sydney introduces guests to each other as they settle in at two tables. She may offer quiche with bacon on the side or something sweet like waffles. Fruit, granola, and muffins are always included.

The living room, complete with gas fireplace, is comfortable — the kind of place where you'll feel right at home. There's also a television, VCR, books, and games. From one of the front porch rockers, you can watch the sunset.

Spruce Point Inn

Boothbay Harbor, ME 04538
207-633-4152
800-553-0289
Fax: 207-633-7138
thepoint@sprucepoint.inn.com
www.sprucepoint.inn.com

A resort on the ocean

Owners: Joseph Paolillo and Angelo DiGiulian. **Accommodations:** 60 hotel rooms, 16 suites, 7 cottages, and 5 condominiums; 2 "downtown annex" condo units. **Rates:** $95–$132 per person in a room, $132–$198 in a suite, $376–$532 per cottage accommodating four, $242–$532 EP for the two- and three-bedroom Oceanhouse Conomdiniums. **Included (except where noted):** Full breakfast and dinner; special children's rates. **Minimum stay:** 2 nights on weekends in August. **Added:** 7% tax, 15% service charge. **Credit cards accepted:** MasterCard, Visa. **Children:** Free under age 4; ages 4–15, $10 if not participating in a meal plan ($20 extra for children's MAP, $49 for full MAP). **Pets:** Only in the Fisherman's Porch oceanview cottage. **Smoking:** Permitted in lounge. **Handicap access:** Yes. **Open:** Late May to late October.

➤ **After a substantial renovation, the inn has a gracious and luxurious new spirit. What hasn't changed are the wooded trails along the inn's extensive coastline. All provide views of the outer harbor, the islands, yacht club sailboat races, lobster boats, and the ferries.**

Spruce Point is a sprawling resort at the end of a 100-acre wooded peninsula at the entrance to Boothbay Harbor. It offers all activities imaginable, many rooms with spectacular views, good and abundant food, and excellent service by a young and energetic staff.

The resort began early in this century as a hunting lodge, later evolved into a tea house, then a summer boarding house, and in the 1950s and 1960s blossomed as a full-facility resort, attracting many prominent guests. A lot of the current families have been returning ever since and multigenerational gatherings are common.

Just eight guest rooms are in the main inn; the rest, in one- and two-bedroom cottages, are clustered on the landscaped grounds near the inn, while some are oceanfront. Gradually these mostly 1950s cottages are being replaced by modern, condo-style structures such as Evergreen Lodge (new in 1997). Perhaps as a reaction to the cottages, the new rooms are huge, with whirlpool soaking tubs in large bathrooms and decks overlooking the water.

There are also four two-story condominiums (each accommodating four to six people) with kitchen, living room with fireplace, porch and deck, but no water view.

All the common rooms are in the main inn, which has a relaxed feeling to it. A large living room has a view of the ocean and islands; a TV room and a study are nice for reading and writing letters; and the recreation room provides options at night and on rainy days. The dining room is framed with a wide view of the ocean on one side, flower gardens, a terrace, and spruces on the other.

Facilities include a solar-heated freshwater pool, a saltwater pool and whirlpool on the ocean, two clay tennis courts, three shuffleboard courts, croquet courts, and a private pier. Sailing and fishing are at your fingertips. A golf course is just a short drive away. The inn's minivan takes guests to and from Boothbay Harbor.

While there is no special program for children, an activity center near the freshwater pool is well stocked with games, and both games and movies are provided in the library during dinner. Families with young children are encouraged to dine in the informal Patriot's Room rather than in the main dining room. Babysitters are on call. In July and August both the formal and informal dining rooms are closed on Tuesday nights for a clambake on Sunset Point.

Room rates vary with the season, as well as with the size and view of the ocean. Most rooms have a telephone and cable TV, and almost every room has a porch. Suites have fireplaces and kitchenettes. Furnishings are Colonial Downeast — sturdy and comfortable. Inquire about the three- and six-day package rates.

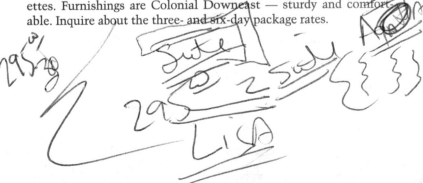

Brunswick

Brunswick Bed & Breakfast

165 Park Row
Brunswick, ME 04011
207-729-4914
800-299-4914
Fax: 207-725-1759
brunsbb@ime.net
www.ime.net/~brunswickbb

Easy elegance

Innkeepers: Steve and Mercie Normand. **Accommodations:** 7 rooms (all with bath); carriage house unit in summer. **Rates:** $87–$127; carriage house: $107 per night, $500 per week. **Included:** Full breakfast. **Added:** 7% tax. **Credit cards accepted:** MasterCard, Visa. **Children:** Welcome; free in room with parents. **Pets:** Not accepted. **Smoking:** Not permitted. **Handicap access:** No. **Open:** Year-round.

➤ **This is the B&B you would hope to find in Maine's premier college town.**

Brunswick's Maine Street is unusually wide and at its head is a broad, shady park lined with suitably substantial homes, among which is this mid-1800s Greek Revival house set behind a tidy picket fence and banked in flowers and tall old trees. A porch runs the entire face of the house, and above are triple-hung, floor-to-ceiling windows with matching shutters.

Steve and Mercie Normand have clearly separated the family and guest parts of the house, but because they do adjoin, either innkeeper is almost always on hand. Steve is an architect and Mercie makes the many handsome quilts that grace both beds and walls.

Common space is more than ample, consisting of twin parlors with those marvelous windows overlooking the mall. Guest rooms are larger than most, some with working fireplaces (Duraflame logs) and sitting areas; most have private baths. Each is distinctively colored and decorated in antiques and wicker.

The breakfast we sampled featured perfect pancakes served with blueberries, strawberries, and melon. Baked egg dishes and blueberry strussel French toast are among other frequent offerings.

Brunswick is a great side trip while enroute Down East. Right off Route 1, it's handy to the Freeport outlets and to the quiet coves within the peninsulas that stretch south into Casco Bay. Home of Bowdoin College and its museums, Brunswick is also a culturally rich town. Don't miss the Joshua L. Chamberlain Museum up the street, (Thanks to the Ken Burns's Civil War series, the entire country now seems to know about this Bowdoin College professor who became a Battle of Gettysburg hero), or the town's outstanding art galleries and restaurants. In summer, Brunswick is also home of music and theater festivals and early in August it's the site of the Maine Festival of the Arts.

Camden

Route 1 is the only route through town. As hard as innkeepers try to insulate their guests from traffic noises (and they do!), it's diffi-cult to escape the traffic. Although Camden boasts one of Maine's most picturesque harbors and an equally quaint shopping district, if you long for a night's sleep punctuated by owls hooting, perhaps you should visit Camden on a daytrip. Regardless, the first thing to do on arrival in Camden is to climb or drive to the top of Mount Battie for a spectacular view of Penobscot Bay.

The Hawthorn

9 High Street (Route 1)
Camden, ME 04843
207-236-8842
Fax: 207-236-6181
hawthorn@midcoast.com
www.midcoast.com/~hawthorn

An airy Victorian B&B

Innkeepers: Patricia and Nicholas Wharton. **Accommodations:** 10 rooms (all with private bath). **Rates:** $80–$185 per couple; $35 per additional person. **Included:** Full breakfast. **Minimum stay:** None. **Added:** 7% tax. **Credit cards ac cepted:** All major ones. **Children:** Over age 12 welcome. **Pets:** Not accepted. **Smoking:** Not permitted. **Handicap access:** No. **Open:** March to mid-January.

➤ **Through a clearing in the trees on the back lawn there's a "key-hole view" of one of Maine's most photogenic harbors. You can also reach the harbor and village through this back door — a kind of secret passageway.**

This spacious and elegant Victorian house came highly recommended by a respected local innkeeper, so we knew it had to be good. Sure enough — it's a gem. The Whartons came onto the scene in late 1995 and quickly distinguished The Hawthorne as a topnotch place.

It's a toss up as to which rooms we like better: those in the adjacent carriage house or those in the main inn. We'll let you decide. In the main house, reached by a wide, open staircase, are six rooms. Of these, Jillian's Suite is lovely, with a sitting room separated by French doors and five sets of windows. Regency has a view of the backyard and the harbor beyond. Turret, in the front of the house and facing Route 1, is quieter in the winter when the storm windows provide extra insulation from the traffic. It can sleep three people and the bow windows are appealing. And although Rose is smaller, it's charming, with bright floral wallpaper and a backyard harbor view. (Relative to the other rooms, ground-floor rooms are less desirable but they are also less expensive.) Thankfully, none of the rooms are overly fussy.

Carriage house rooms are more uniformly quiet and generally more countryish in decor. Each has a television, VCR, a set of sliding doors that open onto a private deck, and a harbor view. Most have a Jacuzzi; Broughman has a gas fireplace as well as a Jacuzzi and four-poster bed. Watney is the coziest, with a sleigh bed. If you plan an extended stay, choose spacious Cabriolet. In a nod to modernity and luxury, each room has a phone and robes.

Breakfast is part self-serve buffet and part served entrée. Perhaps the main event will be a crab strata with roasted red bell pepper sauce or grilled polenta or a tomato and onion tart. Count on it to be good. In warm weather guests enjoy eating on the private back porch; in cool weather the dining room is bright and sunny, warmed by a fireplace when it's really chilly.

The whole place has a casually elegant feel, including the two parlors that open onto one another. The Whartons attract an active crowd in their mid-20s to their mid-40s. The reason Patricia and Nicholas "speak kinda funny" (according to Patricia) is that they're Texan transplants (Nicholas by way of Britain).

Maine Stay

22 High Street (Route 1)
Camden, ME 04843
207-236-9636
Fax: 207-236-0621
mainstay@midcoast.com
www.mainestay.com

| **A convivial B&B** |

Innkeepers: Peter and Donny Smith and Diana Robson. **Accommodations:** 8 rooms (6 with private bath). **Rates:** $75–$140 per couple from June through October; $40 each additional person; $60–$100 off-season; also, off-season winter workshops. **Included:** Full breakfast. **Minimum stay:** None. **Added:** 7% tax. **Credit cards accepted:** All major ones. **Children:** Over age 8 welcome. **Pets:** Not accepted. **Smoking:** Not permitted. **Handicap access:** No. **Open:** Year-round.

➤ **These three innkeepers believe their job entails providing good conversation, companionship, and information as well as a hearty meal and a comfortable bed. They may even entertain you with three-part harmony (they are barber shop singers), a bosun's pipe, and a few jokes over breakfast.**

A few blocks from the harbor and village center, this classic Greek Revival house with an attached carriage house and four-story barn is one of 61 properties on the National Register of Historic Places in this predominantly residential Historic District.

In addition to innkeeper enthusiasm, a few other features come to mind immediately. The place is immaculate, there is incredible attention to detail, the innkeepers continually upgrade the inn without making it fussy, and they churn out reams of information from their computer database on area activities, recipes, and trip routes. Peter, a highly organized former navy captain, runs a tight ship with his wife and her identical twin, Diana. The place is in tip-top shape.

The common rooms include two comfortable living rooms, where a fire is always laid, and a den with a TV and VCR. But it's not uncommon for guests to congregate around the Queen Atlantic wood and coal stove in the kitchen. Afternoon tea or sherry can be enjoyed inside or in the backyard, which Peter is constantly enlarging and landscaping and where a trail to the top of Mount Battie begins.

The most private Carriage House room features a queen-size bed, window seat, woodstove, and glass doors opening onto the room's own garden patio. It's much coveted and includes morning coffee and paper that is delivered outside your door. The very comfortable and highly recommended Clark Suite is well-laid out, with the sitting room on the front side of the house and the bedroom on the quieter back side.

On our last visit, Peter had plans to convert two rooms on the third floor into a nice two-room suite. Although it won't be done until 1999, rest assured that these folks will complete it with precision, creativity, and a keen eye toward making your stay a comfortable one. (They don't have to be innkeepers to make a living, they just really love it.)

Breakfast is an event at the Maine Stay. Coffee is ready long before 8:30 A.M., when Peter announces breakfast, occasionally with his bosun's pipe. Served on Ainsley or Spode china with Simon Pierce or Waterford crystal at one long harvest table, the breakfasts in summer are buffets every two out of three days. The main course may be an egg casserole or cheese-stuffed French toast. Guests who miss breakfast are offered scrambled eggs, omelets, or simple pancakes or waffles. In the winter, when there are fewer guests, breakfasts are more complex: perhaps a soufflé or a fluffy omelet served in a cast-iron pan. A beautiful Samurai chest and an Amish pie safe, some of Peter's acquisitions from his seafaring days, grace the dining room.

Windward House

6 High Street (Route 1)
Camden, ME 04843
207-236-9656
Fax: 207-230-0433
windward@coastalmaine.com
www.windwardhouse.com

> **A romantic B&B**

Innkeepers: Sandy and Tim LaPlante. **Accommodations:** 8 rooms (all with private bath). **Rates:** $100–$170 per couple from mid-May through December; $85–$115 off-season. **Included:** Full breakfast. **Minimum stay:** None. **Added:** 7% tax. **Credit cards accepted:** MasterCard and Visa. **Children:** Over age 12 welcome. **Pets:** Not accepted. **Smoking:** Not permitted. **Handicap access:** No. **Open:** Year-round.

➤ **As with the other places we recommend in Camden, you can walk into town from here and avoid the summer traffic pile-ups.**

Sandy and Tim purchased this house in late 1995 and immediately set about gussying it up with lace, canopy beds, and a few stuffed rabbits or bears here and there. It's readily apparent that the innkeepers pay attention to the B&B, love their "work," and enjoy having guests who appreciate the place.

The 1854 Greek Revival house is in pristine condition, right down to the hardwood floors, elaborate moldings, and chair rails. Guests enjoy the back porch, a comfortable living room with soapstone fireplace, a casual game room, and a library where sherry and flavored coffees are offered with afternoon treats.

Of the guest rooms, many people gravitate to the Carriage and Garden rooms, which offer the privacy of separate entrances. The Carriage room has a country-fresh feel, done in summery blues and whites. A canopy bed and gas fireplace are the focal points, along with an antique hutch overflowing with lacey objects. The bathroom is oversized with a separate soaking tub. We like the Garden room, in the back of the house. It is less fussy than the others and features cathedral ceilings, a gas fireplace, and a maple cannonball bed.

Back in the main house, skylit Nest is tucked under the eaves on the third floor, while Brass is a quiet rear corner room that can accommodate an additional person. Trisha Romance is a romantic hideaway, as is Mount Battie, Sandy's personal favorite. All beds, by the way, have fine linens.

Breakfast is served at individual tables and might include the B&B's signature "featherbed eggs," or peaches-and-cream French toast. In season, plates are garnished with edible flowers.

Islesboro

Dark Harbor House

Box 185
Islesboro, ME 04848
207-734-6669

A small, elegant inn on a quiet island

Proprietor: Mathew Skinner. **Accommodations:** 8 rooms, 2 suites (all with private bath). **Rates:** $105–$245 per couple. **Included:** Full breakfast; dinner not included but also served. **Minimum stay:** 2 nights on some holiday weekends. **Added:** 7% tax. **Credit cards accepted:** MasterCard, Visa. **Children:** Not appropriate but negotiable. **Pets:** Not accepted. **Smoking:** Not permitted. **Handicap access:** No. **Open:** Mid-May through late October.

➤ **Islesboro is known for its summer mansions and for Dark Harbor, an unusually warm, calm pool of sea water. Dark Harbor House is a summer mansion beside this pool.**

Hedged from the water by its grounds and tall yews, Dark Harbor House is on a narrow neck of land between a cove and the protected, pool-like inlet of Dark Harbor. This house is one of those wonderfully airy summer mansions from the 1890s, with large windows, spacious rooms, and a wide entrance hall with a sweeping double staircase.

Matthew Skinner seems more like the master of this house than an innkeeper. He obviously relished the job of decorating it, filling the rooms with splendid 19th-century antiques, including high four-poster, sleigh, and iron beds. Five rooms have fireplaces, and four have French doors that open onto balconies or a porch. There are also two suites. Some of the bathrooms retain their original clawfoot tubs — the deepest, fanciest ones we have ever seen — and a pull-chain toilet with marble details.

The living room is suitably summery, with large windows, a sisal rug, and a glass door opening onto a porch. It overlooks a sloping lawn that's big enough for a good game of touch football.

Guests usually meet in the gracious library or living room for drinks before dinner. Dinner is served in the oval dining room, which holds eight tables and is open to the public (the chef has a strong island following). Entrées may be grilled salmon or quail with grapes or baked stuffed lobster with island spices; desserts usually include baked banana and mango-rum meringue.

A woodland path leads to the beach and dock in Ames Cove, with views over the harbor to the Camden Hills. Bicycles may be rented from the inn for exploring along the narrow, seaside roads. Day sails on a schooner or picnics on smaller, uninhabited islands can be arranged. On misty or rainy days, the house itself is warmed by fireplaces; it offers a wide selection of books, magazines, puzzles, and games.

Islesboro is a large, 10-mile-long string bean of an island just three miles offshore. The summer home of the rich and famous, the island is accessible by car ferry from Lincolnville Beach, north of Camden.

Monhegan Island

Shining Sails

Box 346
Monhegan Island, Maine 04852
207-596-0041
(Office Hours: 9:30–1:00)
Fax: 207-596-7166

A snug waterside B&B

Innkeepers: John and Winnie Murdock. **Accommodations:** 3 rooms (all private baths), 4 efficiencies. **Rates:** May through Columbus Day: $70–$95 per night for rooms, $80–$115 per night for apartments; weekly rates and off-season rates. **Included:** Continental breakfast in high season. **Minimum stay:** None. **Added:** 7% tax. **Credit cards accepted:** All major ones. **Children:** Welcome; $5 extra per night over age 5. **Pets:** Not accepted. **Smoking:** No. **Handicap access:** No. **Open:** Year-round.

➤ **An island getaway with mainland comforts**

This waterside home at the end of the village offers all the comforts of a mainland B&B with an unbeatable location. On a beautiful day it really doesn't matter where you stay on Monhegan — given the beauty of the cliff and woods paths. But when the fog sets in or a nor'easter strikes, there is no more comfortable haven on the island than this attractive shingled home with its water view and inviting common room with a fire glowing in the Franklin stove.

Monhegan really demands more than a couple days (given the fact you spend one day getting there and another getting back) and it doesn't take long to realize the advantage of having kitchen facilities — the better to cook the lobster and fish that's readily available. Shining Sails is one of several island properties that offer efficiency units but the only one that includes Continental breakfast, a great convenience (eliminating the need to buy milk, juice, coffee, and other staples) that provides an opportunity to meet fellow guests.

Breakfast usually includes muffins and bagels, juice, cereals, and fresh fruit. The two most desirable rooms have water views, as do the two 1-bedroom apartments. All have private baths and are furnished tastefully. Guests can also enjoy the front and back gardens, which include lawn furniture, picnic tables, and cooking facilities. Inquire about other island rental cottages available for a weekend, a week, or longer.

New Harbor

The Gosnold Arms

HC 61
P.O. Box 161
Northside Road
New Harbor, ME 04554
207-677-3727
407-575-9549 (winter)
Fax: 207-677-2662
www.gosnold.com

> Rooms and cottages on one of Maine's most picturesque harbors

Owner/operators: The Phinney family. **Accommodations:** 11 rooms (all with private bath), 14 cottages. **Rates:** $79–$134 per couple; less before July and after Labor Day; $75 for single, $15 for an additional person in the room. **Included:** Full breakfast. **Minimum stay:** 1 week in cottages on the water in July and August. **Added:** 7% tax. **Credit cards accepted:** MasterCard, Visa. **Children:** Welcome. **Pets:** Not accepted. **Smoking:** Permitted. **Handicap access:** No. **Open:** Mid-May through mid-October (the restaurant opens Memorial Day weekend).

➤ **Shaws and the New Harbor Co-op, two of Maine's best-known and least-expensive lobster restaurants, are a short walk away. The inn's restaurant also offers good Down East cooking.**

Just across the road from the harbor, this friendly, family-run inn has been welcoming guests since 1925. Nothing fancy, this is a rambling, white clapboard house with a long, inviting porch, an attached barn, and cottages scattered over a landscaped lawn.

The rooms, most with harbor views, have been fitted into the barn, above a gathering room with a huge fireplace. They have natural, unstained pine walls, attractive furnishings, firm mattresses, and private baths. There are also 14 cottages, some with fireplaces. Be sure to ask for one with a good view of the water.

On the water, the Wharf House has three separate units. Grey Cottage is particularly nice, with a fireplace and separate bedroom and living room. Next to the cottages is a large deck, where guests can sit and watch all the activity in the harbor.

The glassed-in dining porch in the main inn also overlooks the harbor. Dinner entrées include steak, roast beef, Maine lobster dishes, and fresh fish cooked many ways. Homemade desserts top off the meal. The fact that rates are not MAP is, however, a plus on this particular peninsula, studded as it is with some of the best lobster pounds in Maine.

From June through October, the Hardy III departs daily from New Harbor to visit Monhegan Island or to watch seals and puffins. We highly recommend this trip. You might want to consider spending a night or two on Monhegan and one or two here, allowing enough time to explore nearby Round Pond and Pemaquid Beach.

Pemaquid Point

The Bradley Inn

Route 130, HC 61
361 Pemaquid Point
New Harbor, ME 04554
207-677-2105
Fax: 207-677-3367

> **A full-service inn two miles from a picturesque lighthouse**

Innkeepers: Beth and Warren Busteed. **Accommodations:** 12 inn rooms (all with private bath), 3 carriage house rooms, 1 cottage. **Rates:** $110–$195 per couple in season. **Included:** Continental breakfast. **Minimum stay:** 2 nights on weekends from June to September; 3 nights on holiday weekends. **Added:** 7% tax. **Credit cards accepted:** All major ones. **Children:** Well-behaved children welcome. **Pets:** Not accepted. **Smoking:** Not permitted in guest rooms. **Handicap access:** No. **Open:** Year-round.

> ➤ **From here you can take a day trip to Monhegan Island, explore the tide pools of the nearby Rachel Carson Salt Pond, or use one of the inn's loaner bicycles to ride to the lighthouse. Or just stay around the inn and play croquet.**

In the summer of 1997 the Bradley Inn received what it has long needed: enthusiastic, hands-on owners. Warren comes from an innkeeping family — his parents put Vermont's Windham Hill Inn on the map in its early days.

On a rural road just two miles from one of the most photographed and painted lighthouses in the state, the inn is picturesque in its own right. Lovely gardens, a gazebo, and an artfully sculpted lawn accentuate the turn-of-the-century house.

Off the lobby, the comfortable living room hosts a piano player on summer weekends (otherwise it's piped-in classical music). A cozy bar, crammed with seafaring memorabilia, echoes the nautical motif of the common areas. Seafarers will feel at home among the antique model ships, nautical charts, and paintings of white-capped waves.

The inn's restaurant, aptly named Ships, focuses its attention on lobster and seafood, but other dishes are also available. (We were unable to sample the cuisine for this edition, so feel free to drop us a line to let us know how you think things are going in the kitchen.) The two dining rooms are romantic, with fresh flowers and candles on each table.

The guest rooms are spacious; some have cathedral ceilings. Room 305 is a large corner room. Room 202 is also large, with a slight water view. All the rooms have telephones. White-tiled bathrooms have shiny new fixtures. Some rooms on the second and third floor have views of John's Bay, beyond a small cluster of houses behind the backyard. On the first floor, two rooms can be connected for a family or couples who are traveling together. Though these are the oldest guest rooms in the house, with slate floors or the original floorboards, they have new bathrooms.

One of the best values lies in the renovated carriage house next door. Sparsely decorated with Early American reproductions, the second-floor room is quite open and airy. It has cathedral ceilings, a brand-new kitchen, a sleeping loft, and a picture window overlooking the gardens and gazebo. The entire two-story house can sleep eight people.

The Bradley Inn also rents a cottage, which is more in the style of an old Maine retreat. On our last visit, the innkeepers had begun to make it a bit more charming. Fresh white paint lends a summery feel and the fireplace is used on chilly evenings.

Rockport/Rockland

Capt. Lindsey House Inn

5 Lindsey Street
Rockland, ME 04841
207-596-7950
800-523-2145
Fax: 207-236-0585
kebarnes@midcoast.com
www.midcoast.com/-kebarnes/

A downtown inn within walking distance of the Farnsworth Museum, art galleries, and tall ships

Innkeepers: The Barnes family. **Accommodations:** 9 rooms (all with private baths). **Rates:** $95–$160; less off-season. **Included:** Continental breakfast and afternoon tea. **Minimum stay:** Weekends in summer only. **Added:** 7% tax. **Credit cards accepted:** Visa, MasterCard, and Discover. **Children:** Over age 10. **Pets:** Not accepted. **Smoking:** Not permitted. **Handicap access:** Yes. **Open:** Year-round.

➤ **Unexpected luxury in the middle of a workaday seaport**

From the exterior, this ocher-colored brick building, just off Main Street, looks like the office building it was until the mid-1990s. Inside, however, it has been restored to its original use — and then some. Built originally in 1837 by John Lindsey as one of Rockland's first inns, the inn is once more both a comfortable haven and a link to sailing vessels.

Both sailing captains, Ken and Ellen Barnes have lovingly restored the interior, much as they have their vintage 1871 passenger schooner, *Stephen Taber*, and the sardine carrier that's now motor yacht, *Pauline*.

The living room, with its fireplace and garden windows, is richly paneled, and the breakfast room is walled in Scottish oak. A separate library is shelved in books you might actually like to read and the desk offers a computer port.

The guest rooms are each individually furnished in a variety of periods (#4 is art deco). All have good reading lights and are equipped with air conditioning, phones, TVs in enclosed cabinets, and baths with hair dryers.

Next door is the Waterworks Restaurant, a low-slung extension of the inn that served as a garage during the many decades in which the inn building housed the offices and labs of the Camden-Rockland Water Company. It's now a popular dining and drinking spot (divided into an informal tavern and a more formal dining room) that features a large and varied menu and blackboard specials (open daily for lunch and dinner).

Windjammer passengers are particularly welcome here, whether they are sailing out on the *Taber* or on any of the other schooners that offer two- and six-day cruises from Rockland out through Penobscot Bay. Inquire about special discounts offered to passengers on the eve or return of a cruise. Pickup service is also offered from the airport, and if you come by bus to board a schooner, you can simply walk down the street from the stop to the inn.

Rockland itself is an increasingly interesting destination for art lovers. The Farnswoth Art Museum offers an exceptional collection of Maine landscape art, including many by three generations of Wyeths. The number of surrounding galleries grows every year. From the inn you can also board ferries to Vinalhaven and North Haven and take advantage of several harbor-based excursions.

Maine Windjammers

The Maine Windjammer Association
(represents 11 vessels)
P.O. Box 1144
Rockport, ME 04856
800-807-WIND
windjam@acadia.net
www.midcoast.com/~sailmwa

Sail away for many a day

North End Shipyard (represents 3
vessels, including the *American
Eagle*, pictured here)
P.O. Box 482
Rockland, ME 04841
800-648-4544
Schooner@midcoast.com
www.midcaost.com/~schooner.

Schooner *Stephen Taber*
Windjammer Wharf
Rockland, ME 04841
207-596-6528
800-999-7352

Accommodations: 170 cabins in several configurations (1 to 4 bunks) on 13 two-masted schooners, 1 three-masted schooner. **Rates:** 3-day sails: $350–$450; 6-day sails: $625–$745 per person. **Included:** All meals, tax. **Credit cards accepted:** All major ones. **Children:** Over age 15 on the Windjammer Association vessels (negotiable), except for the Timberwind, which offers special family cruises that accept age 5 and up. Of the North End Shipyard vessels, the *Heritage* and *Eagle* both accept children age 12 and up, and the *Isaac H. Evans* will accept family members age 8 and up. **Pets:** Not accepted. **Smoking:**

Restricted. **Handicap access:** No. **Sailings:** Memorial Day weekend to Columbus Day weekend.

➤ **The windjammers sail to a Maine you simply cannot reach by car, foot, or ferry.**

The sting of a salt breeze and the warmth of the sun, the scent of pine trees and the aroma of blueberry pie from a woodstove. For windjammer passengers, Maine isn't seen through a windshield or from an inn's window. You taste, feel, smell, and savor the essence of coastal Maine.

Of course, it doesn't happen overnight. You arrive on Sunday evening and nervously eye the two to three dozen strangers with whom you'll be sharing a week under sail. On Monday morning you cast off — in more ways than one. Wearing old jeans and sneakers (the uniform of the windjammer fleet), you help haul a line, watch the tall sails fill, and feel the rhythmic pull of the schooner as it gets under way. You pick up a book but never get into it. There's too much to see — islands all around. You simply steep in life on Penobscot Bay. As the wind and sun drop, the schooner eases into a hidden harbor.

Supper is hearty Yankee fare, maybe fish chowder and beef stew with plenty of fresh cornbread, served on the long tables of the galley. One evening, there is usually a clambake on a deserted island. After supper, the vessel's yawl is available for a foray into a quiet village. As the moon rises, there is singing and yarn-swapping back onboard.

By Wednesday, the days begin to blur. The sailors watch cormorants, spot a minke whale, and see eagles circling over island nests. The weather changes constantly, and occasional fog, even rain, is all part of the week's adventure. On Saturday morning a sadness settles over the boat. Sundays, strangers are now friends. No one wants to leave.

Choosing a vessel is the most difficult part of a windjammer vacation. All fourteen vessels are proud and trim, with their own followings. All share the distinction of being among the few dozen schooners currently plying a coast that once saw literally thousands of their prototypes.

Some windjammers are new vessels, built on the lines of the old coastal schooners. Others, although substantially rebuilt over the years, date from the 19th century.

The *Stephen Taber* and the *Lewis R. French* were originally launched in 1871, and both the *Grace Bailey* and the *Isaac H. Evans* date from the 1880s. The *J&E Riggin*, *Mercantile*, *Roseway*,

Adventure, American Eagle, Timberwind, and *Nathaniel Bow-ditch* have all been sailing since at least the 1930s. The *Mary Day* was launched in 1962, the steel-hulled *Angelique* in 1980, and *Heritage* in 1983. The largest windjammer, the three-masted *Victory Chimes,* served with the fleet for thirty-five years before an interlude on the Great Lakes.

Each schooner is as individual as its history, and the captains are hardly interchangeable. (Most of the windjammers have been built or restored by their captain or captains — some are married couples.) Most of the vessels now offer hot showers and cabin sinks. All offer comfortable bunks and cozy, well-heated gathering spaces as well as wide, gleaming decks. They range from 64 to 170 feet long and carry anywhere from 20 to 44 passengers. In a drizzle, an awning shelters the forward part of the deck, permitting plenty of space to sip coffee and play cards or Scrabble. Captains claim as many repeats from wet as dry weeks.

While all the windjammers offer a very similar experience they vary enough in amenities and atmosphere to make it worth your while — using their three toll-free information numbers — to ask the following questions, if they matter to you:

What is the bunk arrangement? Most vessels offer a choice of single, double, and twin bunks. Cabins for a family or group of three and four exist.

How about hot water? Most schooners now offer hot showers but check. Most also offer running water in each cabin.

Where are the heads (marine toilets) in relation to your cabin?

Is the lobster feast on an island? Most, but not all, are.

What is cabin ventilation? Some vessels offer cabins with portholes or windows that open.

What is the rule about children? On some vessels children have to be at least 16, on others 10, but several schooners schedule special family cruises with activities and other programs geared to children.

Is smoking allowed? It is not allowed on several schooners.

Can you bring a sleeping bag on deck? On warm starry nights you may want to.

Is there a library of local lore? Many, but not all, schooners have inviting reading corners, well stocked with maritime and Maine lore.

Is there music or other evening entertainment? Again, yes on some schooners (the *Stephen Taber* is best known for this) but not on others. The *American Eagle*'s Captain John Foss reads out loud from the ship's large library of maritime lore every evening.

How involved can you get with sailing the schooner? It varies. On most schooners passengers are invited to help hoist sails and steer; some even permit climbing in the rigging. But check. Many, but not all, vessels also carry sailing skiffs that passengers can use when the schooner is anchored.

What's the extent of weatherproof common space? It varies widely.

How many passengers will be aboard? Most schooners carry somewhere between 20 and 30 passengers — but, in our experience, the numbers make surprisingly little difference.

Sebasco Estates

Sebasco Harbor Resort

Sebasco Estates, ME 04565
207-389-1161
800-225-3819
Fax: 207-389-2004
info@sebasco.com
www.sebasco.com

> **An oceanfront family resort that is also great for groups**

Owners: Bob Smith. **Residential manager:** Rick Paige. **Accommodations:** 57 rooms (all with private bath), 22 1- to 6-bedroom cottages. **Rates:** $174–$244 per couple in rooms from July 4 through August; $140–$224 in the off-season; $40 per additional adult; $20 per additional child over 12; packages also available. **Included:** Full breakfast and dinner. **Attire:** Jackets encouraged in dining room at dinner. **Minimum stay:** None, but preference given to weeklong stays. **Added:** 7% tax, 15% service. **Credit cards accepted:** All major ones. **Children:** Over age 12 welcome. **Pets:** Not accepted. **Smoking:** Not permitted. **Handicap access:** Yes. **Open:** Mid-May through October.

➤ **The resort boasts the state's largest saltwater pool. It's situated right on the ocean, too!**

Set on 600 acres, Sebasco Harbor Estates has a new lease on life thanks to an infusion of capital and the vision of a new owner. It's exciting to see freshly restored accommodations, upgraded facilities, and an energetic staff ready to please and to show off the improvements.

The main lodge, reminiscent of old summer hotels with a big foyer, features nice, simple rooms. One quarter of the rooms overlook the golf course, while others overlook a tranquil freshwater lily pond. Many of the wooded waterfront cottages are quite large, but since all were occupied on our recent visit we can't give firsthand recommendations on which are better. On water's edge, rooms in the completely renovated Lighthouse are quite popular. Pebble Cottage, set inland, is also a winner and features a Jacuzzi. All rooms have cable television.

Cottages range from a 1 bedroom/1 bathroom all the way up to a 10 bedroom/10 bathroom that's perfect for a family reunion or group retreat. About a third of the cottages, though, are 2 bedrooms/2 bathrooms.

As for the meals, the weekly outdoor blueberry pancake breakfasts are newly "legendary," as are Tuesday lunchtime lobster picnics. As of this writing, plans were afoot to relocate the main dining room to the waterfront. We're sure the setting will be dramatic.

Facilities and scheduled activities, including a morning program for 3- to 7-year-olds, are extensive. A typical summer Saturday lineup might go like this: Start with a poolside breakfast, then send the kids off on a scenic harbor cruise that often includes seal sightings, get some free golf instruction for yourself or compete in a champagne putting contest, bring the entire gang to the innkeeper's reception, and end up at an evening comedy program. Or do nothing at all.

The grounds are lushly landscaped with blooming gardens and manicured lawns. Active types will enjoy a 9-hole golf course, two all-weather courts, an outdoor pool, an indoor health club for rainy days, and a children's playground. There's also canoeing on the lake and birdwatching.

Tenants Harbor

East Wind Inn and Meeting House

P.O. Box 149
Tenants Harbor, ME 04860
207-372-6366
800-241-VIEW
Fax: 207-372-6320
info@eastwindinn.com
eastwindinn.com

> **An inn with very good food at water's edge**

Innkeeper: Tim Watts. **Accommodations:** 20 rooms (13 with private bath), 2 suites, 4 apartments. **Rates (mid-June to early September):** $82–$120 per couple in rooms; $150–$260 in suites and apartments. **Included:** Full breakfast; dinner also served. **Minimum stay:** Two nights in suites and apartments. **Added:** 7% tax. **Credit cards accepted:** Major credit cards. **Children:** Over age 12. **Pets:** Accepted. **Smoking:** Permitted. **Handicap access:** No. **Open:** April through November.

➤ **The inn's wraparound deck offers beautiful harbor views. A friendship sloop often docks here and you might want to combine a stay at the inn with a sail. Inquire at the inn.**

The East Wind Inn is on beautiful Tenants Harbor, a picture-perfect Maine fishing village. From the wharf or the inn's wraparound deck, furnished with plenty of comfortable chairs and rockers, there's a prime view of the commercial and pleasure boating activities of the harbor. Friendship sloops often dock here for the night.

The East Wind consists of the main inn, a renovated sea captain's house (the Meeting House), and the Wheeler Cottage. The rooms in the inn and Meeting House are furnished simply with period antiques such as oak bureaus, Victorian side chairs, and brass beds. Many of them have terrific views of the harbor. Be sure to request a room with a view; that's why you're here. Both buildings have comfortable living rooms with televisions, books, magazines, and unpretentious furniture. Although Meeting House rooms are further from the water, they are a bit larger. The Wheeler Cottage (whose rooms are also simply furnished) offers more private accommodations, some with decks.

As for the dining, on a recent visit chef David Cooke had just come aboard and was turning out some very good dishes, including many featured Maine specialties ($12–$16.50). The fish chowder was light and flavorful — nothing but big chunks of fish and potatoes. A combo plate of baked haddock and crab cakes, one of the most popular dishes, was complemented by excellent horseradish mashed potatoes. An in-house pastry chef prepares all the breads and desserts. The strawberry rhubarb pie (Tim's favorite and ours too) would have made our grandmothers proud. Be sure to request a window table.

What East Wind really excels at is value. The rooms are simple and tidy, the food very good, and the location prime. Gent, the black Labrador, seems to make friends with everyone.

Places like this are disappearing along coastal Maine. You'll slow down a bit by staying here.

Vinalhaven

Fox Island Inn

P.O. Box 451
Carver Street
Vinalhaven, ME 04863
207-863-2122
904-425-5095 (off-season)
Gailrei@juno.com

> An island haven that's
> simple and relaxing — a
> good place to come alone

Innkeeper: Gail Reinertsen. **Accommodations:** 5 doubles, 1 single (most with shared bath). **Rates:** $50–$65 per couple, $40 single, $115 for the suite. **Included:** Buffet breakfast. **Credit cards accepted:** None. **Children:** 10 and above. **Pets:** Not allowed. **Smoking:** Permitted on enclosed porch only. **Handicap access:** No. **Open:** June through September.

➤ **Vinalhaven is an 8-mile-long island that's accessible by frequent car ferries.**

A restored, century-old town house near the library, this friendly B&B is just a 10-minute walk from the ferry. Gail Reinertsen is an affable, helpful host who helps guests locate walking paths and abandoned quarries. Best of all, she offers complimentary bikes, the obvious solution to dealing with the logistics of getting your car off and on the ferry, which can be exactly the kind of headache you are trying to escape when you come to a place like Vinalhaven.

The Fox Island Inn offers an unusually inviting and comfortable living room, well stocked with books. The kitchen is reserved for guest use, and a breakfast of homemade breads, muffins, scones, and granola is set out here every morning. Guest rooms are simple and most baths are shared. Two second-floor rooms can be combined into a suite.

An 8-mile-long island that's accessible by frequent car ferries from Rockland, Vinalhaven still has a serious fishing fleet. Carver's Harbor, where the ferry docks, is a funky, faded Victorian village dating from the era in which it was one of the chief sources of granite in the East.

While well-known artists congregate here and summer visitors now outnumber residents five to one, it still feels (and looks) like the locals are in charge. Once out of town, roads are heavily wooded and houses are hidden away down long drives. Therefore you'll need some help locating the nature preserves, berrying spots, and swimming holes. Gail is a marathoner and has plenty of tips on how and where to jog. This is the type of place where you'll enjoy reading, writing, and simply rocking on the porch — it's also the type of place you'll want to come back to.

Wiscasset

The Squire Tarbox Inn

P.O. Box 1181
Westport Island
Wiscasset, ME 04578
207-882-7693
Fax: 207-882-7107
squire@wiscasset.net

> **Quiet, country simplicity
> with fine dining**

Innkeepers: Bill and Karen Mitman. **Accommodations:** 11 rooms (all with private bath). **Rates:** $159–$220 per couple MAP; $105–$166 per couple B&B, from mid-July through October. **Included:** Full breakfast and dinner. **Minimum stay:** 2 nights on weekends in season. **Added:** 7% tax, 12% service charge. **Credit cards accepted:** All major ones. **Children:** Over age 14 welcome. **Pets:** Not accepted. **Smoking:** Permitted only on deck. **Handicap access:** No. **Open:** Mid-May to late October.

➤ **Karen and Bill's dairy goats are their pride and joy, and they'll gladly introduce each to you by name. The morning and evening milkings are a great time to get to know them. The Nubian goats produce enough milk to allow the Mitman's to make enough cheese to serve the inn and sustain a mail-order business.**

Down a country road on a quiet peninsula, eight miles from Route 1, the Squire Tarbox is a carefully restored classic Colonial farmhouse on a working farm. It doesn't get more authentic than this. The food is wonderful here and the living simple. If you're searching for peace and rest, you'll find it here. It's hard to believe you're within 45 minutes of coastal harbors, beaches, antiques shops, and lobster shacks.

There are plenty of comfortable living rooms, sitting rooms, and fireplaces that invite guests to socialize. There's also a music room with a player piano and a large screened-in back porch; camaraderie develops naturally.

All the guest rooms are restful, tastefully decorated, and well maintained. Colorful handmade quilts cover some of the beds. The four largest rooms are in the front of the main house. All are furnished with country colonial antiques and highly recommended. (Of these, we prefer the mustard-colored room.)

In the adjoining 1820 barn, there are seven small, less formal rooms carved out of the converted barn. Exposed beams and low ceilings create cozy spaces. Two rooms we particularly like have their own entrances and porches. Although rooms have a country feel, there are no frills or ruffles here! The open living room in the former barn has a woodstove, a good selection of coffee table books, and an eclectic ensemble of sofas and chairs.

The dining room, dating from 1763, is in the low-beamed portion of the house, with a brick and beam fireplace and a beehive oven. As a first course, guests mingle as they sample various farm-made goat cheeses served in front of the fire. There is an honor bar. A typical five-course, candlelit meal may include paté en croute with a rhubarb and peach chutney, an apple and pecan salad garnished with daylilies, whey buns, garlic and herb scallops with wild rice and sautéed vegetables, and to top it off, strawberry shortcake made with lovely nutmeg biscuits. The menu is set ahead of time, so inform the innkeepers if you have any dietary restrictions.

Breakfast is presented as a bountiful spread from which you help yourself. On our last visit, individual quiches were laid out, along with lots of mixed fruits, granolas, and an array of breads.

Karen and Bill have been here since 1983, so they've long since figured out how to create that perfect mix of informality, congeniality, and graciousness. They are soft-spoken folks who relish the life they've created and enjoy providing an atmosphere in which guests can find solitude. To that end, one corner of one barn has been turned into a small nature study center. There's also a swing hanging from high in the rafters where guests have been found well into the night. A path through the woods leads to a saltwater inlet and a screened porch furnished with binoculars, two chairs, bug repellent, and a birding book. A little dock anchors a rowboat for guests' use.

Down East Maine

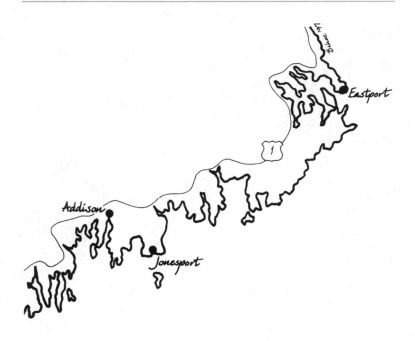

Best Bed-and-Breakfasts

Best Family Finds

Best Gourmet Getaways

Best Inns

Best Romantic Getaways

Southwest Harbor
  Lindenwood Inn, 173
Stonington
  Inn on the Harbor, 177
Sunset
  Goose Cove Lodge, 179

Down East is a nautical term referring to the way Maine's coastal winds blow dependably from the southwest, easing sailing vessels ever "down" (actually northeast) along the coast. While the shops and restaurants on Route 1 begin calling themselves Down East almost as soon as you cross the state line, the term really only applies to the coast north of Camden and, for purists, north of Bar Harbor.

North of Camden, Route 1 follows Penobscot Bay as it narrows to meet the Penobscot River. Many ships have been launched from this area, especially around **Searsport** and **Stockton Springs.** Searsport, the home of the Penobscot Marine Museum, once boasted more sea captains than any town its size, which explains the 19th-century mansions in town, many now B&Bs.

The Blue Hill Peninsula, which defines the eastern rim of Penobscot Bay, is one of the most rewarding to explore. It harbors no resort towns, just the proud old Tory town of **Castine,** the arty enclaves of **Blue Hill** and **Deer Isle,** the fishing village of **Stonington,** and myriad small coves and rolling meadows in between. Artists, musicians, and craftspeople are scattered through this area, and there's really nothing to do except hike on Cape Rosier or Isle au Haut, gallery hop, and attend evening concerts. You can also dine exceptionally well, and the choice of lodging, while limited, is outstanding.

Maine's most famous island is Mount Desert, home of **Bar Harbor** and Acadia National Park. The island is conveniently linked to the mainland by bridge and is webbed with roads for touring by car, trails for exploring on horseback, and 120 miles of biking paths. The summer people of the Gilded Era donated the core of Mount Desert to establish Acadia National Park, which draws more than four million visitors a year. A number of former mansions survive in and around the village of Bar Harbor as well as in quieter parts of the island, like **Northeast** and **Southwest** harbors.

The most dramatic aspect of Mount Desert is its mountains — seventeen rounded, pink, granite humps rising from the sea like giant bubbles. While you can circle and climb them, their amazing profiles are elusive. They are best viewed either from the west, from the lovely Blue Hill peninsula, or, more spectacularly, from the only truly beautiful stretch of Route 1 — as it continues Down East, by the **Hancock** peninsula, curving with the coast toward Winter Harbor and the stray scrap of Acadia National Park on Schoodic Point.

Beyond the island you enter Washington County, as Down East as you can get in this country. The harbors are filled with lobster boats and trawlers instead of pleasure craft, and both the light and the lay of the land change: open blueberry barrens are plentiful and the sky appears vast and never ending.

Here you can explore the Maine you thought disappeared decades ago: the Maine of blueberry pickers, clam diggers, logging outposts, and Indian reservations.

It's worth straying off Route 1 down through Columbia Falls (the Ruggles House here, built in 1818, is one of the most elegant Federal mansions in all New England) and **Addison** to **Jonesport,** a fishing and lobstering town. Don't miss the exceptional nature preserve on nearby Wass Island.

In Machias, the vintage 1770 Burnham Tavern is a museum dedicated to publicizing the first naval victory of the Revolution (in June 1775, Machias men captured a British man-of-war). Machias is, however, better known for its many restaurants, and its August blueberry festival. Most visitors who get this far continue on to see Quoddy Light in Lubec and then over the bridge to Franklin D. Roosevelt's onetime summer home on Campobello Island.

Both Lubec and **Eastport** claim to be the easternmost town in the country and both also share an end-of-the-world feel. The world does not end here, however. From Passamaquoddy Bay a pleasant ferry ride can ease you back and forth between the U.S. and Canada.

Addison

Pleasant Bay Bed & Breakfast

P.O. Box 222
West Side Road
Addison, ME 04606
207-483-4490
Fax: 207-483-4653
pleasantbay@nemaine.com
www.newmaine.com/pleasantbay

A seaside B&B on a 110-acre working llama farm

Innkeepers: Leon and Joan Yeaton. **Accommodations:** 3 rooms (1 with private bath), 1 apartment. **Rates:** $45–$70, $10 per extra guest over 2. **Included:** Full breakfast; optional llama walking. **Added:** 7% tax. **Credit cards accepted:** MasterCard, Visa. **Children:** Welcome; free under age 2. **Pets:** Not accepted. **Smoking:** Restricted. **Handicap access:** No. **Open:** Year-round.

➤ **The Yeatons are delighted to help plan itineraries — maybe a jaunt to Grand Manan Island, biking around Campobello Island, or hiking on Grand Wass.**

This is a 110-acre working llama farm, and guests are invited to stroll along the wooded trails down to the bay, either with or without llamas.

After raising six children and a number of llamas in New Hampshire, Leon and Joan Yeaton cleared this land and built themselves a large, especially well-designed home with many windows and a deck overlooking the tidal Pleasant River.

Dinner is available November to April by prior arrangement; in summer the area offers a variety of dining options.

Upstairs in the house three guest rooms all have water views; there is also an apartment, available by the month, above the barn. For most visitors this is the kind of house they have only dreamt of building — the large living room with fireplace cum dining room flows into the kitchen — and to share it is a rare pleasure, especially with such genuinely hospitable hosts.

In addition to the llamas, resident animals include several goats and a number of dogs and cats. A mooring is provided for guests who might want to come by boat. Seal watching, birding (including puffin-watching excursions), sea kayaking, and hiking are popular local pastimes.

Bar Harbor

Bar Harbor, the gateway to Acadia National Park and Mount Desert Island (linked by bridge to the mainland), is one of the most popular resort areas in Maine. Nowhere else in New England do the mountains sweep down to the ocean as dramatically as here. If you want to stay at one of the places we recommend, reserve as early as possible. If the B&Bs we recommend are fully booked, you can safely rely on recommendations from the innkeepers we list here. Quite often, when there is no vacancy in Bar Harbor, there are rooms available elsewhere on Mount Desert (see Northeast Harbor and Southwest Harbor). Furthermore, consider staying in the area at least three days in order to take advantage of the wealth of outdoor activities. Acadia, with over 120 miles of trails, is well suited to biking and hiking, as well as touring by auto.

Breakwater 1904

45 Hancock Street
Bar Harbor, ME 04609
207-288-2313
800-238-6309
Fax: 207-288-2377
breakwater@acadia.net
www.acadia.net/breakwater1904

A small luxury mansion on Frenchman Bay

Manager: Margaret Eden. **Accommodations:** 6 rooms (all with private bath), 2 apartments. **Rates:** $195–$330 per couple in season; $1,200–$1,500 weekly for apartments. **Included:** Full breakfast, evening hors d'oeuvres. **Minimum stay:** 2 nights may apply in season. **Added:** 7% tax. **Credit cards accepted:** All major ones. **Children:** Over age 12 welcome. **Pets:** Not accepted. **Smoking:** Not permitted. **Handicap access:** In one apartment. **Open:** Mid-April through mid-November.

➤ **The mansion is a few minute's walk from downtown, via the scenic Shore Path, yet delightfully away from all the bustle.**

In a resort town filled with dozens of turn-of-the-century "summer cottages," a mansion has to be pretty magnificent to stand out. Breakwater does. Situated on four acres along the shores of Frenchman Bay, the English Tudor mansion was brought back to life in the early 1990s. It boasts 39 rooms, 11-foot-high ceilings, 11 working fireplaces, and oak and birch floors throughout.

When the house was built in 1904 for the great-grandson of John Jacob Astor, life was carefree for the Bar Harbor social circle. Today, guests are encouraged by an unobtrusive manager to live like these turn-of-the-century, high-society folks: "Relax, put your feet up, make the house your own."

There are only six guest bedrooms, which leaves a lot of common space. The great living hall features a Steinway, a fireplace flanked by overstuffed couches, a Tabriz carpet, and two sets of French doors leading to a verandah. Wander down the expansive lawn and the ocean from here. The library boasts a mahogany billiard table that matches the wainscoting, bookcases, and table-height billiard chairs. From the library, a secret staircase leads to Mr. Kane's chambers above. (Mr. Kane, a former owner, was an insomniac, and with this passageway he could go straight to the billiard room without waking anyone.) The second floor has another large sitting room and oceanfront verandah.

Most of the spacious (to say the least) guest rooms have ocean views. Mrs. Alsop's chambers feature a settee, fireplace, and high king-size bed. Mr. Kane's chambers have a partial water view, fireplace, and sleigh bed. On the third floor, the nursery has an annex that can accommodate a third person.

The former carriage house has been converted into two large and tasteful apartments. Although there are none of the B&B amenities here, each has a fully-equipped kitchen, telephone, cable television, and can sleep from four to six people.

As for the food, in addition to muffins and the like, one hot breakfast entrée is offered. It is served on the verandah (weather permitting) or at a magnificent 16-foot-long oak table that seats 18 people. Sweets and beverages are available in the butler's pantry all day; help yourself. Afternoon tea includes scones and biscuits. An array of light hors d'oeuvres (like baked artichoke dip and puff pastries) are served in the parlor during the social hour.

Inn at Canoe Point

Box 216
Bar Harbor, ME 04609
207-288-9511
Fax: 207-288-2870

> **A romantic and sophisticated seaside B&B**

Innkeepers: Tom and Nancy Cervelli. **Accommodations:** 4 rooms and 1 suite (all with private bath). **Rates:** $135–$245 per couple from late May through October, $80–$150 off-season. **Included:** Full breakfast. **Minimum stay:** None. **Added:** 7% tax. **Credit cards accepted:** Visa, MasterCard, Discover. **Children:** Not appropriate for younger children. **Pets:** Not accepted. **Smoking:** Not permitted. **Handicap access:** No. **Open:** Year-round.

➤ **You'll want to spend as much time as possible on the deck perched over the rocky coast. Watching the sailboats drift by and listening to water splash on the rocks, you'll hardly remember that one of New England's most popular resort towns is just two miles away.**

Tasteful and romantic, sophisticated yet accessible, the Inn at Canoe Point has a stunning location, a few rooms, and lots of peace and quiet. Adirondack chairs have been placed at key shoreline vantage points — all the better for enjoying the views. Veteran area innkeepers Tom and Nancy purchased the property in mid-1996 because they, too, appreciated the magnificent location.

Off the busy road heading into Bar Harbor, through several acres of woods toward the water, stands this hundred-year-old Tudor timber and stone house. The focal point of the inn is the Ocean Room, which boasts a granite fireplace and overlooks the spectacular rocky coastline. Its windows reveal 180 degrees of woods and water. The oatmeal- and beige-colored room doubles as the breakfast room. Carpeting and classical music muffle conversations. A full breakfast, served at simple wooden tables for four, may include eggs Benedict or lemon French toast with blueberry sauce.

The guest rooms, with down comforters, double pillows, thick robes, fresh flowers, and a decanter of port, are in keeping with the stylish, understated atmosphere. The Master Suite, with an ocean view, has a fireplace and French doors leading to a sitting room with a fainting couch. The Master Suite and Anchor Room share a deck overlooking the water. We also like the Garden Room (formerly the potting room), surrounded on three sides by windows that open onto woods and ocean. (It feels like you're sleeping outdoors.) Up a steep set of steps, the two-room Garret Suite encompasses the entire third floor and has an unobstructed ocean view from the bed. There's plenty of space to spread out here (with a sofa bed, the room can sleep three). Portside is small but handsome, with a side view of the water and rocky beach.

Make reservations as early as possible; the inn and this location are a gem, and people know it. Of course, there are always last-minute cancellations and occasional openings (in mid-March!). Even if it's cold and rainy outside, this is a great place to read and daydream for a weekend.

Manor House Inn

106 West Street
Bar Harbor, ME 04609
207-288-3759
800-437-0088

**A centrally located
Victorian B&B with
cottages**

Innkeeper: Mac Noyes. **Accommodations:** 14 rooms (all with private bath), 2 cottages. **Rates:** $89–$175 per couple from mid-June to mid-October; $55–$135 in the off-season. **Included:** Full buffet breakfast. **Minimum stay:** 2 nights in July, August, and September. **Added:** 7% tax. **Credit cards accepted:** All major ones. **Children:** Not appropriate under age 10. **Pets:** Not accepted. **Smoking:** Not permitted. **Handicap access:** No. **Open:** April through mid-November.

➤ **There isn't a single room we would hesitate to recommend. Mac, a hands-on innkeeper, pays meticulous attention to detail and keeps all the rooms freshly updated.**

The 1887 Manor House, which is on the National Register of Historic Places, feels like a Victorian country inn. Most of the guest rooms, furnished with Victorian pieces, are large enough to accommodate large carved headboards. Lace curtains, brass bathroom fittings, and marble-topped night tables with bright reading lamps are standard. Many rooms have marble sinks; four have fireplaces.

We particularly like the Master Bedroom, with a massive antique bed and an alcove for reading or writing, and Room 7, tucked away on the top floor with a little sitting room — the blue and white tones are soothing. If you're tired of frilly rooms, Room 6 (in bur gundy and green) is lovely and breezy, with bay windows on three sides. Room 5 is delightfully large and features an oak bedstead.

The Chauffeur's Cottage, with a bedroom and two suites filled with antiques, offers more privacy than the main inn. The large two-room honeymoon suite has peaked ceilings, a fireplace, and porch. Two contemporary cottages overlooking the gardens were tastefully renovated in 1995. Cozy and private, each has a gas fireplace, peaked ceilings, and a television.

Back in the inn, you'll find unusual woodwork (such as a cherry banister and stair spindles) throughout the house. One of the parlor fireplace mantels was reassembled from more than fifty pieces. The lovely parlor has been restored with flowered wallpaper, wall sconces, lacey curtains, wood floors, upholstered chairs, antiques, and an Atlantic potbelly stove.

For breakfast, guests help themselves to fruit salad, apple pancakes with cider sauce, and cranberry bread from the pantry. Sit at the communal dining room table or use a tray table set up at one of the comfy living room chairs. We prefer eating breakfast on the wraparound porch, decked out with wicker and hanging plants. For those taking the early morning ferry to the Canadian Maritimes, Mac will prepare a box breakfast.

Although the inn lacks water views, it does have several pretty gardens visible from many bedrooms and common rooms. You'll enjoy flowers blooming from mid-April to mid-November.

We like how the inn is large enough so that you may be anonymous (if you choose to be) yet small enough so it is easy to strike up a conversation with other guests.

Nannau-Seaside Bed & Breakfast

P.O. Box 710
Lower Main Street
Bar Harbor, ME 04609
207-288-5575

| **A graciously understated cottage on the edge of Acadia National Park** |

Innkeepers: Vikki and Ron Evers. **Accommodations:** 4 rooms and 1 suite (all with private bath). **Rates:** $95–$145 per couple. **Included:** Full breakfast. **Minimum stay:** 2 nights. **Added:** 7% tax. **Credit cards accepted:** MasterCard, Visa. **Children:** "Above the age of reason." **Pets:** Not accepted. **Smoking:** Not permitted. **Handicap access:** No. **Open:** May through October and on long winter weekends.

➤   This 1904 Shingle-style summer estate is about a mile out of town and surrounded by acres of woods. We can't think of a better place to watch the sun rise — except maybe on nearby Cadillac Mountain; but the beach at Nannau is much more private (and closer!).

There are many reasons to come to Bar Harbor: views of the mighty Atlantic Ocean, famous storybook "cottages," and Acadia National Park. Staying at Nannau satisfies all of these and much more. It's rare to find a place so immediately inviting. We've spent many an hour sitting on Nannau's rocky beach, watching the tide come in, listening to the woods wake up, and appreciating how lucky we are to know about this place. As soon as we drive down the long driveway, a sense of peace washes over us.

Nannau is decorated in an eclectic style, with a predominance of English Aesthetic furnishings. William Morris turn-of-the-century fabrics and floral wallpapers are warm and soothing. Magazines and books are stacked neatly everywhere. The Oriental rugs on the wooden floors lend a comfortable, homey feeling. Drapery is sumptuous. Both of the spacious living rooms have overstuffed armchairs and couches, the kind you sink into and never want to leave. (The feather cushions seem to be "plumped" all the time!) On chilly evenings, a fire blazes in the fireplace, around which guests often gather to converse. French doors lead to a floor-to-ceiling screened-in porch with green wicker chairs and lots of plants. It feels like an extension of the woods. A croquet court lies beyond.

Two guest rooms on the second floor have fireplaces, sitting areas, and lovely views of the water; at night the yellow room has a nice, warm feel to it. The bathrooms have marble sinks and clawfoot tubs, most with European-style hand-held shower nozzles. The somewhat smaller guest rooms on the third floor are still spacious enough for a sitting area, a writing table in front of the window, and a queen-size bed. Luxuriously thick towels, soft linens, down comforters, and meticulously kept bathrooms complete the picture.

The elegantly inviting dining room has deep burgundy wallpaper, full-length drapes, and crisp table linens. On a recent visit, Vikki whipped up a tomato and Parmesan frittata and Ron baked French bread. And as you'd imagine, they squeeze oranges for juice and roast their own flavorful coffee beans.

When Vikki and Ron added a garden surrounded by a granite wall, it looked as though it had been there for a century. As with everything else at Nannau, it's lovely.

Ullikana Bed & Breakfast

16 The Field
Bar Harbor, ME 04609
207-288-9552

A centrally located, gracious B&B with truly gourmet breakfasts

Innkeepers: Hèléne Harton and Roy Kasindorf. **Accommodations:** 10 rooms (all with private bath). **Rates:** $115–$195 per couple in season. **Included:** Full breakfast. **Minimum stay:** None. **Added:** 7% tax. **Credit cards accepted:** MasterCard, Visa. **Children:** Not appropriate for children under 8; $20 each additional person in the same room. **Pets:** Not accepted. **Smoking:** Not permitted. **Handicap access:** No. **Open:** Early May to late October.

➤   **On our last visit, Hèléne's multi-course lineup featured an explosion of fruit: cold raspberry soup with a scoop of sorbet and fresh blueberries, warm strawberry muffins, and as a main dish, thin slices of apple baked into a popover.**

In-town locations are often fraught with noise and traffic problems. Not so with Ullikana, which feels delightfully secluded even though it's literally steps from the center of town and the harbor. But it's not just the location that makes Ullikana stand out. It's the innkeeper's warm personalities and sense of style that have turned this elegant 1885 Tudor-style mansion into a choice destination.

When Hèléne and Roy purchased the house in 1990, the basement and attic were filled with furniture that many people would have thrown out. But Hèléne has a knack for transforming raggedy old pieces into coveted treasures. The guest rooms, all of which we recommend, are filled with such pieces. We particularly like Audrey's room, which is whimsical and airy with cathedral ceilings. Parts of the room are also tucked under the eaves, which creates a secret hideaway feel. (From the soaking tub you can see the distant islands.) Rooms 3 and 5 are quite spacious (well suited to longer stays), each with a fireplace. The former has a sitting area and a French provincial bed; the latter has the feel of the countryside and a private porch. Room 6, also quite large, boasts a private deck. Room 7 is tucked away under eaves on the third floor, complete with a cozy sitting area.

The four least expensive guest rooms are smaller, but still charming. And although the Library Room is off of the living room and front porch, we still like it because (among other reasons) on a quiet night you'll feel as if the living room is all yours. The room features a fireplace, an iron bed, and French doors leading to the porch. Although the house has beautiful dark woodwork, it still feels bright and airy, with painted floors and high ceilings. White walls highlight Hèléne and Roy's art collection.

Breakfast is a real treat — in fact, it's one of the best in New England. Two of Hèléne's dozen or so specialties include apple crêpes and lemon soufflé pancakes with a warm berry sauce. The dining room is warmly decorated with kilim carpets, a woodstove, and cacti. In warm weather breakfast is served on the patio at individual tables with harbor views. A fountain trickles in the background.

Conversation both at breakfast and over afternoon refreshments is usually quite animated, a testimony to the gracious atmosphere created by Roy and Hèléne. They know Acadia National Park quite well and are happy to offer suggestions on how best to enjoy it. The living room, by the way, is delightfully inviting: bright yellow walls, a fireplace, paintings and puppets, original artwork, and natural wicker furniture. Tea is set out in the evenings.

Blue Hill

Blue Hill is one of Maine's most tranquil villages, known for its musicians and craftspeople. On the surface, the town and peninsula may appear rather sleepy, but scratch the surface and you'll find a veritable mine of studios, galleries, and buildings on the National Historical Register. (See also Deer Isle, Sunset, and Stonington at the tip of the peninsula.)

Blue Hill Farm Country Inn

Route 15
P.O. Box 437
Blue Hill, ME 04614
207-374-5126

| A country farmhouse B&B |

Innkeepers: Jim and Marcia Schatz. **Accommodations:** 14 rooms (7 with private bath). **Rates:** $75–$90 per couple from June through October, $10 less for single. **Included:** Expanded Continental breakfast. **Added:** 7% tax. **Credit cards accepted:** MasterCard, Visa. **Children:** Over age 12 welcome. **Pets:** Not accepted. **Smoking:** Not permitted. **Handicap access:** No. **Open:** Year-round.

➤ **The barn, with soaring rafters, woodstove, and dozens of comfortable chairs, has been transformed into a very comfortable living room.**

Two miles from "downtown" Blue Hill and 11 miles off Route 1, this pleasant farmhouse B&B is well placed for exploring much of Maine's most interesting coastline, from Castine to Bar Harbor. Behind the inn, there are 48 acres of woods, brooks, and trails that double as cross-country trails.

The inn is part farmhouse, part barn. Let's start with the barn, which Jim and Marcia have transformed into an unusually welcoming space. It's large and open, serving as both a living and breakfast room. This is where you'll spend most of your indoor time, since most of the guest rooms are small. Upstairs in the barn, there are seven nicely decorated guest rooms with iron beds and barnboard walls. Each has a modern bathroom. Of these, "D" and "E" are brighter corner rooms and "D" overlooks the garden and goat paddock.

The atmosphere in the farmhouse, which rambles off an old-fashioned kitchen, is very different: downstairs are small sitting rooms with sofas, one of which has a woodstove. The rooms upstairs, which share a bath and include one appealing single, are old-fashioned with quilts and braided rugs. The largest room, "I", can handle a four-poster bed.

On a recent visit, breakfast consisted of fresh-squeezed juice, baked apples, homemade granola, cereals, and muffins. The Schatzes are obviously attuned to the unusual wealth of the Blue Hill area's art, music, and crafts. In the summer, chamber music is performed frequently in the barn, and the check-in desk is lined with local products (walls throughout display the work of area artists).

The Blue Hill Inn

P.O. Box 403
Union Street
Blue Hill, ME 04614
207-374-2844
800-826-7415
Fax: 207-374-2829
bluhilin@downeast.net

A traditional inn known for its five-course, candlelit dinners

Innkeepers: Mary and Don Hartley. **Accommodations:** 10 rooms (all with private bath), 1 suite, 1 apartment. **Rates:** $160–$225 MAP from June to mid-October; B&B rate also available; apartment $160–$220. **Included:** Full breakfast, dinner (served Wednesday through Sunday). **Minimum stay:** 2 days on busy weekends. **Added:** 7% tax, 15% service charge. **Credit cards accepted:** MasterCard, Visa. **Children:** Over age 13. **Pets:** Not allowed. **Smoking:** Not permitted. **Handicap access:** In the apartment. **Open:** Mid-May through November.

➤ **The tasteful apartment next door (formerly the innkeeper's quarters) is perfect for longer stays and for older families. The open floor plan features**

a four-poster canopy bed, fireplace, living room, and cathedral ceilings. There is also a complete kitchen (stocked with cookbooks!) and private deck with barbecue grill.

Just up the hill from the village center and surrounded by a residential neighborhood, this brick-ended and clapboard double home has been welcoming guests since 1840. (The two front entrances, so the story goes, provided separate access for men and women way back when.) Mary and Don, genuinely hospitable hosts, have been welcoming guests since 1987. Old house lovers will appreciate the six-over-six shuttered windows, the many chimneys, and wide pumpkin floorboards.

Most guest rooms are surprisingly large. Some have sitting areas with writing desks, and three have fireplaces; all are comfortably and simply furnished with an eye to creating space for more than sleeping. One favorite is actually next to the front door: Room 10 is a warm corner room that features a sitting area, working fireplace, large Oriental carpet, and a very nice bathroom. Also recommended is room 8, which is large, with windows on three sides and a four-poster cherry bed. We weren't able to see room 4, but guests tell us that it is also a preferred choice. Although room 7 is the smallest, with little natural light, this third-floor room can accommodate an additional person under the eaves.

The two living rooms have low beams and are comfortably furnished with antiques. One serves as more of a reception room for guests who enjoy socializing over pre-dinner cocktails and cheese and crackers. The other has seating around a well-used hearth. Mary and Don frequently offer wine-tasting dinners, so you can trust their advice on matching wine with meals. You may opt, as we did, to select your wine before dinner and sip it with the snacks.

The five-course dinner, served by candlelight at white-clothed tables, is a good value. (If you choose not to dine at the inn, $20 per person is subtracted from your room rate.) Dinner begins at 7:00 and the menu changes nightly. On our last visit we all began with a light and flaky leek and chèvre puff pastry, followed by a refreshing grapefruit campari ice. The choice of two dinner entrées that night was between rack of lamb and lobster buerre blanc. Both were good choices. A mixed green salad followed, and the evening was topped with chocolate gâteau. While you're at dinner, some staff members are busy with turndown service and replacing used towels.

At breakfast you'll be presented with several entrée choices, including perhaps an omelet with spinach and brie or amaretto

French toast with almonds and raisins. As if that weren't enough, we were also given a fruit plate, popovers, and poppy seed cake.

The inn also offers packages that include an overnight on a schooner, sailing charters, and kayak trips. Or combine a visit with bluegrass concerts and chamber music. Don't forget about those wine dinner weekends in the shoulder seasons.

John Peters Inn

Peters Point
Blue Hill, ME 04614
207-374-2116
www.johnpetersinn.com

A romantic waterside retreat with outstanding breakfasts

Innkeepers: Rick and Barbara Seeger. **Accommodations:** 14 rooms (all with private bath). **Rates:** $105–$165 per couple. **Included:** Full breakfast. **Minimum stay:** None. **Added:** 7% tax. **Credit cards accepted:** MasterCard, Visa. **Children:** Over age 12 welcome. **Pets:** Not accepted. **Smoking:** Restricted. **Handicap access:** No. **Open:** May through October.

➤ **An expansive, comfortable B&B that you won't want to leave; in fact, most guests come and stay for days and days.**

As soon as you drive through the gates to the John Peters Inn, you'll be struck by its setting. Crowning the lawns and meadows that sweep down to the water is an 1815 white-columned mansion that more evokes the antebellum South than the coast of Maine. Arrive early enough to walk through the fields down to the rocky shore before dinner or, wake early enough the next morning to take a cup of coffee down to the water's edge and pebbly cove.

The guest rooms are unusually spacious and the kind you'd enjoy spending an entire afternoon in if it rains. Several have sofas and tables, and nine have fireplaces. The premier suite in the main house has a large private deck, king bed, water view, and wet bar. The Brooklyn suite is another hands-down favorite; it can accommodate four people. Both the large "Castine" and "Surry" rooms boast six windows. "Penobscot" is in the 1810 section of the house; it's delightfully old-fashioned and features a working fireplace and water views. Other special touches include line-dried linens (changed daily) and fresh flowers.

The rooms in the adjacent Carriage House offer complete privacy, each with a private deck. Many have kitchens and fireplaces and make a great haven for extended stays.

Even though the guest rooms invite long-term lounging, the common rooms vie for equal attention. There's a grand piano in the living room, where chamber music groups sometimes perform. A beautiful, unusual Oriental rug covers the floor before an often-used fireplace. The covered front porch has Adirondack chairs that face the expansive view.

Barbara calls her meals fantasy breakfasts, for they seem to include all the treats people dream of on a visit to Maine. The pièce de résistance is a lobster omelet garnished with lobster claws to make it look like the critter. But there are many other indulgences like a crabmeat omelet or poached eggs with asparagus. The meal starts with strong coffee, fresh-squeezed juice, and a choice of fresh berries with cream or cantaloupe with strawberry sorbet. Breakfast is served on the glassed-in porch. It's all quite refined and relaxed, one of the top ten breakfast experiences along coastal New England. The table is set with lovely china, crystal, and silverware, and classical music accompanies the meal. The Seegers' engaging Welsh terrier, Doc (DisObedient Canine), has been known to show up to earn a few treats with his antics.

The inn also offers a canoe, dory, or 16-foot Widgeon for guest's use. And at some point, too, you'll want to stretch your muscles in the small outdoor pool. Barbara and Rick have been welcoming guests since 1984 and do a great job making guests feel at home.

Brooksville

Bucks Harbor Inn

South Brooksville, ME 04617
207-326-8660
Fax: 207-326-0730

A seaside inn off the beaten track

Innkeepers: Peter and Ann Ebeling. **Accommodations:** 6 rooms, 1 suite (all shared baths). **Rates:** $65 per couple, $50 single, $75 for suite. **Included:** Full breakfast. **Minimum stay:** None. **Added:** 7% tax. **Credit cards accepted:** MasterCard, Visa. **Children:** Welcome. **Pets:** Sometimes accepted off-season. **Smoking:** Discouraged. **Handicap access:** No. **Open:** Year-round.

➤ **The atmosphere in Bucks Harbor is reminiscent of the late 1800s to 1930s, when vacationers arrived by steamer from New York and Boston and settled in for months at one of the two large summer hotels.**

Bucks Harbor is one of the most beautiful little byways along the Maine coast. The present inn was built in 1901 as an annex to one of those elaborate but long-vanished hostelries and looks more like a Maine farmhouse, the type with a mansard roof and attached barn in the back. The rooms are simple and sunny, drenched in light and the fresh feel of the sea. The suite, which has one large room with a queen-size bed and another smaller room with a single bed, is a wonderful deal for a family.

Downstairs there's a double living room, a dining room (open to the public), and a glass-faced breakfast room. Another sitting room is on the third floor.

The moderately priced Landing Restaurant next door offers water views and good food, and nearby Blue Hill is known for its fine dining options. On Saturdays, November to April, when many local restaurants (including the Landing) close, the inn serves Saturday night dinners.

The nearly circular harbor is now a quiet backwater favored by yachts. An old shingle yacht club overlooks it. The picturesque hamlet of South Brooksville has changed remarkably little since Robert McClosky described it in the children's book *One Morning in Maine*. The general store is a classic and a craft store or two are within walking distance. Hiking trails are nearby in the Holbrook Island Sanctuary and day sails are frequently available from the dock.

Oakland House

RR 1, Box 400
Brooksville, ME 04617
207-359-8521
800-359-RELAX
www.acadia.net/oaklandhse

An old family resort that just keeps getting better

Innkeepers: Jim and Sally Littlefield. **Accommodations:** 15 cottages, 10 rooms (7 with private bath) at Shore Oaks. **Rates:** Mid-June through Labor Day: Cottages, $910–$1,498 per couple per week MAP; rooms, $112–$172 per couple per day MAP, $51–$115 single. Before mid-June and from mid-September until late October, B&B rates in rooms are $51–$115 per couple and $355–$450 per week in cottages. Inquire about various discounts. **Included in MAP Rates:** Breakfast and dinner. **Minimum stay:** Not in the inn; one week during high season in cottages. **Added:** 7% tax, 15% service charge. **Credit cards accepted:** None. **Children:** All ages in cottages; sliding rates. **Pets:** Dogs accepted in some cottages. **Smoking:** Restricted. **Handicap access:** No. **Open:** Early May through late October.

➤ **Ocean and lake swimming, tidal pools, rowboats, hiking trails, lawn games, video movies in the barn, grand water vistas, and fabulous food are all part of a week's stay.**

Oakland House opened its doors in 1889 for guests who arrived at its landing on the Eastern Steamship Line. The already century-old farmhouse had been remodeled for these guests by Nanny and Gramp Herrick with new furniture that had also arrived by steamship. Much of it was cottage-style and is still in use today — host Jim Littlefield is Nanny and Gramp's great-grandson.

Today the centerpiece mansard-roofed hotel houses only the dining rooms, common rooms, and staff. Families stay in one of the 15 cottages scattered along the shore. Most have fireplaces, additional heat, and full kitchens or kitchenettes, and the cottages are scarcely visible from each other. Each is different: one was once an ice house; one has old clawfoot tubs; and many have tongue-and-groove pine paneling milled from trees cut on the property.

Single guests and couples stay in the newly renovated, vintage 1907 Mission-style Shore Oaks Seaside Inn, which offers a living room with a stone fireplace, library, and waterside front porch. Breakfast is served in its own dining room. This is truly a magical place with its appealing interior spaces and serene view of Eggemoggin Reach.

In all, Oakland House enjoys a mile of frontage on Eggemoggin Reach — a major thoroughfare for vessels sailing "Down East" from Rockland. On most Mondays or Tuesdays you can watch a dozen or so Windjammers parade by. Saltwater bathing and activities on the lake's beach are particularly popular. There's also badminton, croquet, and many scenic trails for hiking. The inn will arrange for sailing and deep-sea fishing.

Tables in the Oakland House dining rooms are set with white tablecloths and the atmosphere is old-fashioned, but in the past two years food has undergone a profound transformation — from plain Maine cooking to the ambitious culinary creations by classically trained chefs, featuring, of course, fresh produce, local seafood, and from-scratch desserts. Your dinner might begin with Eggemoggin mussels steamed in Chardonnay and garlic, followed by Greek egg and melon soup, a salad with feta and catamara olives, and a choice of pan-seared native tuna steak served with green Japanese horseradish or grilled duck breast with honey-glazed pears. Top this off with strawberry shortcake on a biscuit made from the inn's century-old recipe. Fare deserving of fine wines, 1997 marked the first season in the inn's 109-year history that wine and beer was served in the dining room.

The inn is well situated for exploring both the Blue Hill peninsula and Deer Isle and Isle au Haut, and staff are helpful with arranging whale watching and other expeditions. But the property is beautiful and offers so many great experiences for children that most families will want to stay put.

Castine

The Castine Inn

Main Street
P.O. Box 41
Castine, ME 04421
207-326-4365
Fax: 207-326-4570
relax@castineinn.com
www.castineinn.com

> **A village inn with gourmet cuisine**

Innkeepers: Tom and Amy Gutow. **Accommodations:** 17 rooms (all with private bath), 3 suites. **Rates:** Mid-June to mid-October: $85–$135 per couple in rooms and $150 for four people in suites. **Included:** Full breakfast; dinner also served. **Minimum stay:** 2 nights in July and August. **Added:** 7% tax. **Credit cards accepted:** MasterCard, Visa. **Children:** Over age 5 welcome. **Pets:** Not accepted. **Smoking:** Not permitted indoors or outdoors. **Handicap access:** No. **Open:** May through December.

➤ **Trained in New York and Paris, chef-owner Tom Gutow's focus is on local ingredients, creatively prepared and artfully presented. Desserts — perhaps a heavenly flourless chocolate cake draped with fromage blanc and a raspberry sauce — are exquisite.**

With its elm-shaded streets, varied architecture, and deep-water harbor, Castine is one of Maine's prettiest and least touristed coastal villages. It was an important trading port and military outpost from the 17th through the 19th century, when it became a posh resort town.

The Castine Inn, built in 1898, is a three-story summer inn with open, airy common rooms. The living room has comfortable period furniture, and guests gather here around the fire for drinks, coffee, or a board game. What you notice most are the paintings: fine contemporary local artwork is on loan from the McGrath-Dunham Gallery. Older seascapes and paintings of the harbor have graced the inn for years. The focal point of the dining room is a four-wall mural painted by a former owner that depicts scenes of Castine. Actual views of the town and harbor beyond complement the painting.

The broad verandah, with plenty of chairs and tables, overlooks well-landscaped perennial gardens, paths, benches, and arbors, where a series of summer concerts is held. The village slopes away from it downhill to the harbor.

The guest rooms are spotlessly clean and very simply furnished. When Tom and Amy purchased the inn in 1997, their primary focus was on the kitchen and cuisine. Rooms will be renovated and upgraded in time. In any event, request a room with a harbor view.

The inn's current focus is on serving fine cuisine, and that they do. Chef-owner Tom Gutow has already developed a following. (Even if you don't stay here, try to eat here.) Prior to his arrival, the inn was known for two specialties, which Tom had to continue offering or face mutiny: moist crab cakes with mustard sauce made from local crabmeat and chicken and leek pot pie. Early into Tom's tenure he had already hit his stride. We sampled a couple of his recent creations, including ginger-cured salmon with pickled ginger vinaigrette (a lovely pairing of flavors) and a large serving of pan-roasted wild striped bass with spicy celery root puree. Homemade biscuits, rather than rolls, were a nice touch. The wine list is well-priced and balanced; the wine is served at just the right temperature.

Breakfast is also a treat. Choices may include apple bread French toast, corned beef hash with a poached egg, and sage and Maine goat cheese omelet. In warm weather, dine on the harborview porch.

Deer Isle

Pilgrim's Inn

Deer Isle, ME 04627
207-348-6615
Fax: 207-348-7769
pilgrims@acadia.net
www.pilgrimsinn.com

> A country-elegant landmark
> inn with fine cuisine

Innkeepers: Dud and Jean Hendrick. **Accommodations:** 13 rooms (10 with private bath), 2 1-bedroom cottages. **Rates:** $150–$215 per couple in July and August; EP rates available. **Included:** Full breakfast, extensive afternoon hors d'ouevres, and dinner. **Minimum stay:** None. **Added:** 7% tax, 15% service charge. **Credit cards accepted:** MasterCard, Visa. **Children:** Over age 10. **Pets:** Not accepted. **Smoking:** Not permitted. **Handicap access:** No. **Open:** Mid-May to mid-October.

➤ **Two new carriage house apartments are bigger than most New York City studios! Each features a living room with TV, cast-iron stove, kitchenette and dining area, as well as a separate bedroom. The deck overlooks the harbor and meadows that reach down to the mill pond. It's a difficult choice between these and the inn rooms.**

This inn has it all, in understated abundance: fine food, lovely rooms, unpretentious innkeepers, and a tranquil location. You'll want to spend a few days here in order to relax as well as explore.

The gambrel-roofed structure is a gem. It was built in 1793 by Squire Ignatius Haskell for his wife. Haskell owned a successful sawmill and wanted to live near his business, but Mrs. Haskell was used to the comforts of Newburyport and demanded a civilized home. The house was built in Newburyport and shipped up to Deer Isle. The Hendricks purchased the inn in 1982 and are responsible for the restorative atmosphere that we experience today.

The inn has four very comfortable living rooms. You'll immediately be drawn into the warmth and authenticity of all these rooms. On the main floor, one is furnished with Colonial as well as simple Victorian pieces and the other is a large, homey library. Head downstairs to reach the two rooms that serve as a bar for the adjoining dining room. The focal points here are the massive Colonial fireplaces with Dutch ovens. There is attractive pottery, crafts, and local artwork throughout.

There isn't a bad guest room in the house! All are cheerful rooms, pristinely decorated. Room 5, in particular, is a favorite with its water views, four-poster bed, and hardwood floors. Room 6 is particularly spacious. Even the smallest room (#12) is sweet and cozy. Colonial colors have been chosen throughout and braided and Oriental rugs cover the beautifully refinished floors. Flowered curtains, comforters, and quilts are lovely. The triple sheeting is luxurious. All the rooms have either a view of the harbor across the road or the mill pond out back.

Cocktails and an extensive array of tasty hors d'oeuvres are served at 6:00 P.M., followed by dinner at 7:00 in the restored barn. (It can easily be argued that the hors d'oeuvres served here are the best in northern New England.) On a recent visit, the dinner menu went like this: To start we had crabmeat wrapped in phyllo with a light champagne lobster sauce. Then a fresh seasonal green salad and a honey-lemon whole wheat sourdough bread accompanied a hickory-grilled tenderloin of chicken with savory roasted summer vegetables. And an exquisitely simple blackberry tart provided a sublime finale. Even if you can't stay, make it a point to eat here. It's $30 per person and well worth it.

For breakfast we had the difficult choice of either mushroom and dill roulade or orange ginger French toast — yet another reason to stay for a few days!

Deer Isle, home to the internationally renowned Haystack School of Crafts, perhaps represents the greatest concentration of artists and craftspeople per capita in all Maine. (There is an extensive selection of crafts for sale in a gift barn on the inn's property.) The innkeepers can point you to specific galleries and artists worth checking out. Deer Isle is also a working fishing island so you'll see plenty of pickup trucks heading to and from the pier in the morning. As for activities, kayaking is great in these parts, as are hiking and biking (the inn has loaner bicycles). The inn prepares the best box lunches in the area.

Eastport

Weston House

26 Boynton Street
Eastport, ME 04631
207-853-2907
800-853-2907

An unusually historic,
comfortable B&B

Innkeepers: Jett and John Peterson. **Accommodations:** 5 rooms (shared baths). **Rates:** $60–$75 per couple, $50 for a small single. **Included:** Full breakfast. **Minimum stay:** None. **Added:** 7% tax. **Credit cards accepted:** None. **Children:** Welcome if well behaved; cots, $15. **Pets:** Not accepted. **Smoking:** Restricted. **Handicap access:** No. **Open:** Year-round.

➤ **Eastport is about as Down East as you can get, in feel as well as geography.**

There is a haunting, end-of-the-road quality to the brick 19th-century storefronts along Water Street in Eastport, and you don't expect to find a B&B as elegant as Weston House just up the hill.

Built in 1810 by a Harvard graduate who became a local politician, this classic white Federal house offers large second-floor guest rooms with antiques and bay views; one room has a fireplace. Our favorite is the Audubon Room, where John James Audubon stayed on his way to Labrador in 1833.

Breakfast may include pancakes with hot apricot syrup laced with apricot brandy, fresh muffins and coddled eggs, or smoked salmon and scrambled eggs with blueberry muffins.

There's a formal parlor with wing chairs and Oriental rugs and a comfortable back room with books and a TV.

Jett and John are gracious hosts who delight in their guests' surprise at the beauty of this little-touristed area. In the off-season they serve afternoon tea and sherry. Dinner and a picnic lunch can be arranged. The gardens are more beautiful every time we visit — another place to relax.

Eastport, incidentally, is not the end of the road by a long shot. In the summer, a small car ferry plies between the towns of Cannery Wharf and Deer Island in the middle of Passamaquoddy Bay, from which a free Canadian ferry transports you the rest of the way to New Brunswick. It's one of the most enjoyable, least known ferry crossings in North America; you can spend the night in the Canadian resort town of St. Andrews and drive back around the bay to Calais, Maine.

Hancock

Crocker House Country Inn

Hancock Point Road
Hancock, ME 04640
207-422-6806
Fax: 207-422-3105
www.maineguide.com/downeast/crocker

> **A coastal country inn**

Innkeeper: Richard Malaby. **Accommodations**: 11 inn rooms (all with private bath), 2 in the carriage house. **Rates**: $100–$130 per couple in August, $90–120 from mid-June through July and September 1 through mid-October, $75–90 the rest of the year. **Included**: Full breakfast; dinner also served. **Minimum stay**: None. **Added**: 7% tax. **Credit cards accepted**: All major ones. **Children**: Cot, breakfast: $8. **Pets**: Well-behaved pets welcome. **Smoking**: Restricted. **Handicap access**: No. **Open**: May to New Year's Eve.

➤ **The inn is only 250 yards from the water, and there's a pretty 25-minute walk around the point. It's also possible to come by sea; request a mooring.**

A half-hour's drive north of Bar Harbor and 10 miles or so down a peninsula, Hancock Point is very quiet and private. It's an old summer community with an octagonal library, a summer chapel, the second smallest post office in the country, and four clay tennis courts. The nearby dock is kept up by the Hancock Point Village Improvement Society.

The Crocker House, built in 1884 as an annex to one of the large (now vanished) hotels on the point, has been beautifully refurbished inside and out. Baths have been upgraded or added; they are nicely done with natural woods. This past year, all double beds were replaced with kings and queens, and new linens, drapes, arm-chairs, and wall hangings were added. Guests will find hand sten-ciling, shampoo in the baths, and chocolates by the bed.

Our favorite rooms are number 10 (which gets good morning light), done in light blue with a light carpet, and number 9, awash in mushroom and tan colors with a skylight in the bathroom. The carriage house also offers two guest rooms and a hot tub and com-mon room.

The common rooms include a couple of comfortable living rooms off the reception area and bar, which serves both guests and the public.

Dining is important here, and dinner is a several-course affair. Appetizers may include cream of mussel soup or pâté mousse truf-fle. The entrées may include poached salmon Florentine, Crocker House scallops, lobster, or rack of lamb. Sunday brunch is a pro-duction, featuring brandied French toast, steak and eggs, and a Cromlet (Crocker House omelette). Dinner entrées run $16.95 to $21.95.

Richard has established a strong reputation for his restaurant locally as well as a following among guests who have visited since 1980. Though there is plenty to see and do nearby, the Crocker House is the kind of place where you usually want to stay within walking and bicycling distance.

Le Domaine Restaurant and Inn

Route 1
P.O. Box 496
Hancock, ME 04604
207-422-3395
207-422-3916
800-554-8498
Fax: 207-422-2316
ledomaine@acadia.net

> A genuine French auberge ranked among New England's top restaurants

Proprietor/chef: Nicole Purslow. **Accommodations:** 7 rooms (all with private bath). **Rates:** $200 per couple, $125 single. **Included:** Continental breakfast and dinner. **Minimum stay:** 2 nights on busy weekends. **Added:** 7% tax, 15% service charge. **Credit cards accepted:** All major ones. **Children:** Over age 5. **Pets:** Not allowed. **Smoking:** Not permitted in dining room. **Handicap access:** No. **Open:** Late May to late October.

➤ **The people who live and summer up here revere Le Domaine as their special place to eat out. And while the emphasis is on the food, there are also mountains to climb; sea excursions; 100 acres, including gardens, to explore; and oceanside drives to fill the day.**

This unpretentious house on Route 1 offers some real surprises. A shade off the tourist trail, beyond the turnoff for Bar Harbor, Hancock is beautiful coastal country, its peninsulas studded with old estates and summer homes.

Your day begins with flaky croissants, café au lait, and fresh fruit and juices served in bed, on your own porch, or in the sun porch overlooking the garden. In the evening, dinner is served on white linen tablecloths in the intimate dining room — with maps of French Departments, pictures, and a large fireplace at one end — or on the screened porch overlooking the gardens. The menu features nouvelle cuisine, and the traditional French dishes — such as escalope de saumon l'oseille, lapin aux pruneaux, choux de Savoie farcié, and coquilles St. Jacques — are masterfully prepared. For dessert you might try the bread pudding, a dish found in all good Maine diners but not in the way Nicole prepares it: with cream and orange-flavored sugar syrup sauce, the raisins drenched in Cognac.

The inn's common space includes a sitting area with white wicker furniture (a waiting area for the restaurant) and a full bar with four stools (also a reception area).

The upstairs rooms are simply decorated with built-in desks and cabinets, thick carpeting, a hundred or so books and magazines, fresh fruit and flowers, and bath soaps (as well as a split of champagne for returning guests). Our favorite room is Rosemary, with its own balcony and a locally crafted potter's sink.

Nicole Purslow came to Maine during World War II with her parents, who had to flee from their inn in Les Baux after it was learned that they had been hiding Jews. After working with her mother at Le Domaine, Nicole attended the Cordon Bleu in Paris and served an apprenticeship in Switzerland before returning to Maine. She routinely returns to France each year when the inn is closed to renew her joi de vivre and wine cellar (which averages 5,000 bottles).

Harborside

Hiram Blake Camp

Harborside P.O. Box 59
Blake's Point
Cape Rosier, ME 04642
207-326-4951

A classic old family resort

Manager: Deborah Venno Ludlow. **Accommodations:** 15 cottages. **Rates:** July–August (per week, MAP): $500–$750 plus $165 extra per adult, $115 per child; $365 for single room with bath. Off-season (per week, EP): $350–$550. **Included:** Two meals in July and August. **Minimum stay:** 1 week. **Added:** 7% tax. **Credit cards accepted:** None. **Children:** Very welcome. **Pets:** Accepted. **Smoking:** Permitted. **Handicap access:** No. **Open:** June through September.

➤ **Picnics are held weekly (weather permitting) at Holbrook Island Sanctuary; they always include lobster, chocolate cake, and watermelon.**

Here is an old-fashioned family camp, run by the children, grand-children, and great-grandchildren of Captain Hiram Blake, who founded it in 1916. But it isn't for everybody. It's well off the beaten track, at the tip of a peninsula that encompasses a wildlife sanctuary. The weathered cottages are squirreled away in a quiet cove in the upper reaches of Penobscot Bay; guests tend to stay put.

All the cottages are within 200 feet of the bay, washed with the special light and smell of the sea. There are six one-bedroom cottages, five with two bedrooms, three with three, and one single-person unit. Each has a bath, a porch, a kitchen where guests can prepare lunch, and a living room with a woodstove; some have fireplaces, too. Dinners, which include soup, juice, salad, and dessert, are traditional homemade Down East fare; lobster is available at any meal.

A pebble beach on the property is fine for swimming, and small sailboats and rowboats are available. Hiking trails have been marked on the camp's 100 acres, and there are more trails in nearby Holbrook Island Sanctuary. For rainy days, a recreation room has table tennis, books, and puzzles. The dining room also doubles as a library, with thousands of books ingeniously filed away by category in its ceiling.

Although the camp is open from June through September, meals are served only in July and August. Reunions and small, informal conferences are welcome in the off-season.

Jonesport

Tootsie's Bed and Breakfast

R.F.D. 1
P.O. Box 252
Jonesport, ME 04694
207-497-5414

| The biggest bargain in Maine |

Innkeeper: Charlotte Beal. **Accommodations:** 3 rooms (with shared baths). **Rates:** $40 per couple, $25 single occupancy. **Included:** Full breakfast. **Minimum stay:** None. **Added:** 7% tax. **Credit cards accepted:** None. **Children:** $5 extra for 1 or 2 in same room. **Pets:** Possible. **Smoking:** Permitted. **Handicap access:** No. **Open:** Year-round.

➤ **Jonesport is a genuine fishing and lobstering village connected to Beals Island, which is linked, in turn, to Great Wass Island, where you can walk for hours through pine forest and along the rocky shore.**

This was the first bed-and-breakfast in Washington County, and it's still one of the best bargains in Maine. Washington County is the large swatch of Maine that lies Downeast from Bar Harbor, and it is reminiscent of the more southerly (or westerly) parts of Maine twenty to fifty years ago. The bridge between Jonesport and Beals Island is rumored to have been built low enough to exclude sailing yachts.

Charlotte Beal (called "Tootsie" by her grandchildren) lives near the water in the kind of Maine house that looks small from the outside but swells when you get inside. It's also so spotless and neat that surfaces shine. "Guests tell us that staying here is like going to Grandma's," Charlotte says, "and I consider that quite a compliment!" One guest room has a double bed, one has twins, and one has a double and a twin.

Northeast Harbor

The Asticou Inn

Route 3
Northeast Harbor, ME 04662
207-276-3344
800-258-3373
Fax: 207-276-3373
asticou@acadia.net
www.acadia.net/asticou

| A dignified, grand old resort |

Manager: Joseph Joy. **Accommodations:** 46 rooms (19 are suites, and all have a private bath) divided between the main inn, Cranberry Lodge, two traditional cottages, and 6 Topsiders (contemporary waterside units). **High Season (July and August) Rates:** $200–$349 per couple MAP; $166–$282 EP; Shoulder seasons: $120–$279 MAP, $86–$212 EP. **Included:** Continental breakfast and dinner are served at Cranberry Lodge in shoulder season when main dining room is closed. **Minimum stay:** 2 nights in high season. **Added:** 7% tax, 15% service charge. **Credit cards accepted:** MasterCard, Visa. **Children:** Welcome. **Pets:** Not accepted. **Smoking:** Permitted on the deck. **Handicap access:** No. **Open:** Main inn from mid-May to mid-October.

➤ **The meals feature Down East favorites. A lavish seafood and roast beef buffet — which includes lobster and a huge selection of salads and pastries — is offered every Thursday night, followed by dancing to a live band. Afternoon tea on the deck overlooking the harbor is particularly nice.**

This vintage 1883 inn has traditionally catered to a distinguished clientele and continues to serve loyal guests who return year after year. The atmosphere remains one of low-key luxury, quiet and dignified. The mood has, however, lightened in recent years. Bellmen are now dressed less formally, and visitors in shorts are welcome to come in and look around, maybe stay for lunch — which is now served on the deck overlooking the harbor until 5:00 P.M.

The main lobby is dominated by a large Oriental carpet and a large fireplace — where a fire is always crackling — with wing chairs on either side. The traditional living room has a fireplace and terrific views down to Northeast Harbor; a bar offers the same views. An enclosed porch for playing cards and watching TV is a popular spot at night. An ample porch runs the length of the inn, and affords a view of the formal gardens and the harbor.

The guest rooms are of moderate size and are simply furnished. Some rooms have bay windows overlooking the harbor; most have white iron beds and white wicker. Room 33 is particularly nice, with a triple bay window, ocean views, and a sitting room. Room 25 is a bright corner room with a bay window.

The contemporary Topsider units offer more privacy. Rooms 101 and 102 have the best harbor views. These rooms are good for families or couples traveling together; each has its own deck, a water view, and a limited kitchenette. In Blue Spruce Cottage, Room 304 (large, with a nice view of the harbor) gives you the feeling of being in a tree house. Room 301 is very large, with a parlor, king-size bed, private deck, kitchenette, and dining area. Across the street, in Cranberry Lodge, one room has a private porch.

The inn's flower arrangements are taken from its own cutting beds. Within an easy stroll is the peaceful and contemplative Asticou azalea garden. Also not to be missed are the wonderful Thuya Gardens, formal and tucked away, reached through the Asticou terraces.

Harbourside Inn

Northeast Harbor, ME 04662
207-276-3272

| An 1888 Shingle-style B&B furnished with exquisite taste |

Innkeepers: Gerrie Sweet and her family. **Accommodations:** 11 rooms and 3 suites (all with private bath). **August Rates:** $90–$125 per couple in rooms, $150–$175 per couple in suites. **Included:** Continental breakfast. **Minimum stay:** 2 nights. **Added:** 7% tax. **Credit cards accepted:** None. **Children:** Over age 12. **Pets:** Not accepted. **Smoking:** Not permitted. **Handicap access:** Yes. **Open:** Mid-June to mid-September.

➤ **The tag line on Maine's tourism literature reads "Maine, the way life should be." Harbourside's brochure, if it wasn't so low-key, would read "Innkeeping, the way it should be."**

If you want a tranquil and authentic inn experience, this is the place. If you want a spectacular ocean view, you'll have to go elsewhere. The brochure is honest: when the inn was built, the clear expanse between the harbor and the inn was under one ownership.

But when the property changed hands, cottages were built that obstructed the inn's views. In addition, trees that were mere saplings in 1888, when the inn was established, are now very tall.

The Sweets purchased the inn in 1977 from a woman intent on selling only to Maine residents. She was looking for buyers who would maintain the property in the "true" Maine spirit. The Sweets have been true to their word; and they've never needed to visit another inn for inspiration. They are down-to-earth folks, avid gardeners who pick their own nasturtium seeds, knowledgeable hikers (trails are just out their back door), and genuinely hospitable and gracious innkeepers.

There are two buildings on the premises, one for the innkeepers and one for the guests. The rooms in the three-story Shingle-style house remain old-fashioned but cheerful, and are meticulously maintained. Every time we return to Harbourside, we're delighted to recall how wonderful these rooms are. All but one room on the first and second floors have wood-burning fireplaces. Upon arriving, you will find that your fire has been laid, with extra wood piled by the hearth. Every room has at least two chairs so that guests can relax by the fire.

The three suites are well priced and well suited to families or those on longer stays. One of these suites has a glassed-in sun porch with a cathedral ceiling. Up among the treetops, Room 7 boasts two sitting rooms, a fireplace, and a Gustav Stickley area carpet. Room 4 has a semi-private entrance and an 1870 iron and brass queen-size bed. Some rooms have small but fully equipped kitchenettes.

A Continental breakfast is served on a bright sun porch furnished with antique white wicker. Enjoy your coffee and blueberry muffins (more blueberry than muffin — the batter is just a vehicle for the berries) on the porch, in the comfortable living room near the fireplace, or retreat to your room.

Searsport

The Homeport Inn

P.O. Box 647
Route 1
Searsport, ME 04974
207-548-2259
800-742-5814
Fax: 508-443-6682

> **The best in the Route 1
> lineup of Searsport B&Bs**

Innkeepers: Dr. and Mrs. George Johnson. **Accommodations:** 10 rooms (7 with private bath), 3 cottages. **Rates:** $55–$85 per couple, $35–$40 single, $20 per extra person in room; $600 per week for cottage; off-season rates, November to April. **Included:** Full breakfast. **Minimum stay:** None. **Added:** 7% tax. **Credit cards accepted:** All major ones. **Children:** Under age 14 in parents room, $6 extra; no children under age 3. **Pets:** Not accepted. **Smoking:** Restricted. **Handicap access:** No. **Open:** Year-round.

➤ **Searsport claims to be the antiques capital of the state. The shops lining Route 1 range from flea markets to elegant homes filled with outstanding furniture.**

Back in the days when Searsport sent more men out on the high seas than any other coastal port, its ship captains made a handsome living in the China trade. On their return, they built elegant houses and filled them with the objets d'art that they had found on their voyages.

The Homeport Inn is a beautifully preserved reminder of those times. Set behind a white picket fence right on Route 1 and topped with a distinctive cupola, it was built in the 1860s by a Captain Nichols. Today, George and Edith Johnson have recaptured the opulence of that era in gracious rooms filled with Oriental rugs, antique furniture, and an understated refinement.

A number of old captains' homes in Searsport are now B&Bs, but this remains our favorite; it has continuously expanded and improved under the Johnsons' care, and it is on the water side of Route 1, with grounds sweeping down to the ocean's edge.

Some of the guest rooms are in the front part of the original house; others are in the converted carriage house wing. In winter, the Johnsons close off part of the house, but the carriage house rooms, with their southern exposure, are sunny retreats with views of the bay.

Searsport has antiques shops galore as well as a major marine museum. This is a good place to stop if you're taking the scenic route to Bar Harbor. It's also a good place to relax for a few days and simply explore. The inn rents bicycles to its guests.

Southwest Harbor

The Claremont

Claremont Road
Southwest Harbor, ME 04679
207-244-5036
800-244-5036
Fax: 207-244-3512
www.acadia.net/claremont

> **A regal old resort with a superb location**

Owner: Gertrude McCue. **Manager:** John Madeira, Jr. **Accommodations:** 24 rooms in the hotel; 5 rooms, 1 suite in Phillips House; 12 cottages. **Rates:** July through Labor Day: $120 per couple B&B, $195 MAP, $112 single B&B room $163 MAP. Cottages: $153–$183 per night for cottages accommodating 1–4; $1,250 for Dirigo house, accommodating 6; less in June and September/October; still less late May to mid-June in the Phillips and Clark houses. **Minimum stay:** 3 days for cottages. **Added:** 7% tax, 15% service charge for lodging. **Credit cards accepted:** None. **Children:** Welcome; inquire about special rates. **Pets:** Not accepted. **Smoking:** Not permitted in the hotel. **Handicap access:** Some rooms. **Open:** Mid-June to mid-October in hotel; late May to late October in cottages.

➤   **The hotel's setting is spectacular, outstripping that of every other public lodging on Mount Desert. From a rocker on the porch, a broad-armed wooden chair on the lawn, or the boathouse, you can look from Cadillac**

Mountain across Somes Sound to the beautiful waterfront estates in Northeast Harbor.

Soft reds color the water below and the sky above the high, rounded mountains. Pines are inky black against the reds and sea birds whirl around outgoing lobster boats. This is the dawn view from the bed in The Claremont's room #207, Mount Desert Island's oldest hotel (which is, of course, on the National Register of Historic Places). It occupies a point near the entrance to Somes Sound, the long, fjord-like arm of water that divides the island almost in half.

More guests wax lyrical about the Claremont than any other New England inn we know. It has the grace and dignity but not the size of an 1880s grand hotel. It is small enough to be personal and the atmosphere is friendly and relaxed. Families feel welcome. This is, moreover, one of those rare places where you can spend your entire vacation on the grounds and still take in some of New England's most beautiful scenery. With binoculars, you can clearly see all the lobster boats, sailboats, and yachts that ply these waters.

The resort includes the four-story wooden hotel with its dining room — a beautifully designed add-on that replaced a large old wing — as well as the adjacent Phillips House and a variety of cottages, most scattered along the shore.

All rooms in the four-story hotel have been recently replumbed and rewired, equipped with phones and furnished in refinished cottage furniture and wicker. Guests are greeted with fresh bouquets of wildflowers. By all means request a water view but be aware that with it comes the MAP rate (B&B is available only for the landside rooms). Phillips House has generally larger guest rooms, a lovely living room with a large hearth, and a broad, wraparound verandah.

The cottages vary widely from rustic log cottages with stone fireplaces to some contemporary designs. They all have living rooms with fireplaces and decks. Some are right on the water, while others have water views. Ask for a complete description when reserving and be sure to request a water view.

The Claremont's common rooms include a reception area with a fireplace, a game room lined with bookshelves, and a living room with a TV. Wood floors gleam around the Oriental carpets. The dining room was designed so that every table has a view of the water. Jackets are required for men at dinner, but the atmosphere is laid-back, not stuffy. The food ranges from good to very good, with an emphasis on fresh fish and the menu offers more than a half dozen choices. You might begin with Maine mussels steamed in white wine, garlic, and shallots, finished with dill cream and fresh tomato or maybe a pesto and sundried tomato torte. Following this might be fresh salmon fillet with smoked salmon and horseradish that is wrapped and baked in rice paper and served with smoked seafood vinaigrette or maybe an 8-ounce club sirloin served with morel, chanterelle, and shitake mushrooms and sauce espagnole. In addition to the regular selection, wines by the glass are offered, keyed to the night's menu.

Clay tennis courts, badminton, and water sports, as well as bicycles are available, but the sport for which The Claremont is known far and wide is croquet. The Claremont Croquet Classic in August attracts top players from throughout the country and marks the social highpoint of the season in Southwest Harbor. Guests can participate or sip a drink on the verandah and watch the action.

Current owner Gertrude McCue's family has been summering on Mount Desert since 1871. Her grandfather discovered the island while still at Harvard and later, as Episcopal archbishop of Massachusetts, he built a "cottage" in Bar Harbor and was among the men to first discuss the idea of preserving much of Mount Desert as a park. Thirty years ago the McCues salvaged The Claremont from probable destruction and dedicated themselves to preserving its special spirit as well as look. Inquire about the Thursday evening lecture series on thought-provoking subjects.

Lindenwood Inn

118 Clark Point Road
P.O. Box 1328
Southwest Harbor, ME 04679
207-244-5335
800-307-5335
lindenwoodinn@acadia.net
www.acadia.net/lindenwood

> **A gourmet getaway with contemporary rooms**

Innkeepers: Herb Zahn and Jim King. **Accommodations:** 14 rooms (all with private bath), 3 suites, 3 housekeeping units, 3 cottages. **Rates (July through early September):** $85–$135 per couple in rooms; $95–$195 in suites; $1,085–$1,295 weekly in cottages for up to 4; less off-season. **Included:** Full breakfast with rooms. **Minimum stay:** Preference given to 3-night stays in July and August. **Added:** 7% tax. **Credit cards accepted:** All major ones. **Children:** Welcome in cottages. **Pets:** Not accepted. **Smoking:** Permitted on decks and porches only. **Handicap access:** No. **Open:** April through October.

> ➤ **The penthouse suite features a private rooftop deck with its own hot tub and panoramic harbor views.**

Lindenwood isn't your typical Down East–style bed-and-breakfast. Although it's a former turn-of-the-century sea captain's house, it melds historic elements with contemporary furnishings and an eclectic art collection. After years of overexposure to Laura Ashley this and Ralph Lauren that, it's fun to come across a place with its own sense of style.

Your first hint of something out of the ordinary comes in the two small living rooms, which serve as a check-in area for the inn and restaurant. Both are accented with primitive figurines, carvings, and masks, many of which were collected in Australia and Mexico.

The character of the guest rooms at Lindenwood changes from building to building, but we can make some generalizations.

Rooms are alternately bold with splashes of color or subdued with shades of gray. Halogen reading lamps are exceedingly functional, while collections of seashells and stones add touches of whimsy. Contemporary furnishings create clean lines, but the guest rooms retain a warm feel with down comforters and soft fabrics. All are light and airy.

Many rooms have private balconies or water views; a couple of rooms have both. About half have gas fireplaces. Housekeeping suites have televisions, fully equipped kitchens, and a pull-out couch that can accommodate an extra person. These are particularly well suited to families. Rooms across the street tend to be a bit more private since there isn't the traffic associated with the restaurant. This house has its own living room.

The two-bedroom contemporary guest cottage has a full galley kitchen, private deck, and a living room with a harbor view. It can sleep four. The other two cottages are smaller and without water views.

Dinner is not included in the room rate, but the inn's restaurant is among the best in the area. On a recent visit we feasted on mesclun greens with Maine goat cheese, Japanese maki sushi rolls, pan-seared salmon served with a saffron beurre blanc and Julienne vegetables. (Portions are large.) Although we didn't have room for the fresh blueberry pie, we forced ourselves and were glad we did. The wine offerings are smart, and the espresso rich. Aficionados will appreciate the French press pots. Like many bistro-like dining rooms, the tables are close together and the music is jazzy. All in all, it is well worth it. Do dine here.

In addition to muffins and fruit, you'll have an entrée choice (if you arrive before 9:00 A.M.) of perhaps herb omelets or French toast with blueberry sauce.

Stockton Springs

The Hichborn Inn

P.O. Box 115
Church Street
Stockton Springs, ME 04981
207-567-4183
800-346-1522

**A B&B with friendly hosts
and ghosts**

Innkeepers: Nancy and Bruce Suppes. **Accommodations:** 4 rooms (2 with private bath). **Rates:** $60–$95, less off-season. **Minimum stay:** None. **Added:** 7% tax. **Credit cards accepted:** None. **Children:** Not appropriate. **Pets:** Not accepted. **Smoking:** Not permitted. **Handicap access:** No. **Open:** Year-round.

➤ **Nancy, a Maine native, perpetuates the Down East tradition of a seaman's wife taking in guests (Bruce is an engineer on supertankers).**

This stately Italianate mansion sits in a quiet old shipbuilding village that's now bypassed by Route 1. The house is a beauty, the most elaborate one in town, complete with a Palladian window and widow's walk. It was built by a prolific shipbuilder, N. G. Hichborn. The house remained in the family until 1939, preserved by his two daughters. The Suppeses claim that the house is still visited by friendly ghosts.

Common rooms include a comfortable "gent's parlor," a music room, and an elegant library. Breakfast is served either in the restored dining room or on the sun porch.

The guest rooms vary in size. Our favorite is the Harriet Room, with a glimpse of the water. Nancy brings a cup of coffee with your wake-up call.

Stockton Springs is on the Penobscot River. It's just beyond Searsport, the home of the Penobscot Marine Museum as well as many antiques shops, and is a good place to stop on the way to Bar Harbor and points farther Down East.

Sullivan

Island View Inn

HCR 34, Box 24
Route 1
Sullivan Harbor, ME 04664
207-422-3031
lph@acadia.net

> **A seaside B&B with a
> spectacular view**

Innkeepers: Sarah and Evelyn Joost. **Accommodations:** 6 rooms (all with private bath). **Rates (July through mid-September):** $60–$90 per couple, otherwise: $55–$80; $10 for each extra person. **Included:** Full breakfast. **Minimum stay:** None. **Added:** 7% tax. **Credit cards accepted:** MasterCard, Visa, Discover. **Children:** Welcome. **Pets:** Accepted. **Smoking:** Not permitted in guest rooms. **Handicap access:** No. **Open:** Late May to mid-October.

> ➤   **Island View offers spectacular scenery, a private beach, a convenient location, and pancakes for Sunday breakfast.**

Even if the Island View wasn't idyllically situated — with splendid views of Frenchman Bay and the dome-shaped mountains on Mount Desert — and even if it didn't offer a private beach, or wasn't a convenient place to stop on the way to maritime Canada (right off Route 1, 30 minutes north of Bar Harbor), it would still be worth staying here.

This large, gracious, turn-of-the-century summer "cottage" is a two-story gray shingle structure with blue and yellow trim. Exposed dark woods, a moose head on the wall, and a stone hearth create the feeling of a big open lodge on the first floor. The dining room, where a breakfast of eggs (served a variety of ways) or French toast topped with seasonal berries is served, is a bit more formal. Since 1985, when the Joosts bought the inn, Sundays are traditionally pancake mornings. The countrified guest rooms, some with water views, are decorated with unpretentious antiques.

Set far enough back from Route 1 so that traffic noise is not a problem, the inn also has a nice wraparound porch. Schoodic Point, part of Acadia National Park, is just 30 minutes east and has its own rewarding mountain to climb; the views are spectacular from the shores here. Guests have access to a canoe and rowboat.

Stonington

Inn on the Harbor

Main Street
Stonington, ME 04681
207-367-2420
800-942-2420
Fax: 207-367-5165

> **Stonington is a picture-perfect working harbor at the tip of Deer Isle, where the picture-taking is remarkable.**

Proprietor: Christina Shipps. **Innkeeper:** Janet Snowden. **Accommodations:** 14 rooms (all with private bath). **Rates:** $100–$125 per couple. **Included:** Continental breakfast. **Minimum stay:** None **Added:** 7% tax. **Credit cards accepted:** All major ones. **Children:** Over age 12 welcome. **Pets:** Not accepted. **Smoking:** Permitted on deck only. **Handicap access:** Yes. **Open:** Early April through New Year's Day.

Those of you who remember the Captain's Quarters will certainly appreciate the current incarnation of this building, now known as the Inn on the Harbor. New Yorker Christina Shipps, whose aunt and uncle have lived in Stonington for years, recently "found her spot in the universe, and this is it." She purchased the property in late 1995, spent the next nine months completely renovating it with the aid of local craftspeople, and opened for business in June 1996.

The inn sits right on Main Street, but your focus will naturally be on the water. Ten of the rooms have water views (rooms on the second floor have better views because they sit slightly higher than the fish pier across the way). All are furnished in a sophisticated style, with overstuffed furniture and nice bedding. Some rooms can accommodate a third person, and most have a sofa or arm chairs well positioned in front of the bay windows.

Here are a few specifics about the rooms, all named for wind-jammers. We like the privacy of Heritage, which boasts a particularly nice view of the outer islands and a fireplace made of local granite. For the rooms with fireplaces, you may help yourself to wood from the shed. (There's no extra charge like at some inns.) American Eagle has a small but full kitchen for those who are staying longer, while Timber Wind has a particularly fresh and summery feel. Stephen Taber, a cottage-style room that used to be a barber shop, features the original tin walls and ceilings. Its private deck faces the water. Of the villageside rooms, Isaac Evans is the most spacious.

High tide comes right up to the deck, which is ringed with flower boxes and potted trees. There is also a second-floor deck from which there are slightly better views. Remember that this is a working harbor, so in addition to seeing lobster boats, you will probably hear the rumble of their motors, too. Fog rolls in (this is Maine after all), but so do spectacular windjammers, the magnificent sailing vessels of yesteryear.

A breakfast buffet of fruit, yogurt, and homemade granola, muffins, and breads are set out for guests. In warm weather, you'll be on the waterfront deck. But on cooler days, the fireplace will warm you in the glassed-in dining room. There is no other common space, but that's okay since many guests will want to enjoy the view from the comfort and privacy of their rooms. In the afternoon, guests return to the inn for wine and cheese. From 11:00 A.M. to 4:30 P.M. the deck is open to the public for a limited but delicious selection of soup and lobster rolls. The inn also serves the best espresso in these parts.

In the off-season these rooms are well suited to those who want to hole up for a long weekend.

Sunset

Goose Cove Lodge

Sunset, ME 04683
207-348-2508
Fax: 207-348-2624
goosecove@hypernet.com
www.hypernet.com/goosecove.html

> **The Maine you dream about but seldom find**

Innkeepers: Joanne and Dom Parisi. **Accommodations:** 13 cottages, 11 rooms; all with private bath; 2 new cabins (3-person minimum). **Rates:** High season (last weekend in June until the Saturday after Labor Day weekend): $82–$107 per person MAP. Off-season B&B: $90–$138 per couple; MAP rates also available but not imposed in the off-season; special rates for children. Cabins (3-person minimum): $170 B&B, $410 MAP. **Included:** Meals, depending on plan; use of kayaks and bicycles. **Minimum stay:** 2-night minimum in season; request a week in cabins during high season, but possible to stay a shorter time. **Added:** 7% tax, 15% service. **Credit cards accepted:** MasterCard, Visa, Discover, American Express. **Children:** Welcome. Evening program provided in-season, babysitting for infants, nature walks, crafts programs. **Pets:** Not accepted. **Smoking:** Not permitted in the Main Lodge. **Handicap access:** In dining room and 1 guest room. **Open:** May 15 to late October.

➤ **Creature comforts in a fir forest overlooking Penobscot Bay**

Windows everywhere command a spread of island-dotted Penobscot Bay, a constant invitation to go kayaking, sailing, swimming, or walking along the smooth granite ledges and beach. And when the fog rolls in, there are dozens of nearby art and artisan studios to visit, if you can tear yourself away from your own granite-faced hearth or the hearth in the comfortable, book-stocked common room of the Main Lodge.

Until 1992, Goose Cove Lodge was a far more spartan place, geared primarily to birders, botanists, and their families. Joanne and Dom Parisi have retained the rustic feel and sense of place but have brightened the resort with well-chosen art, quilts, hooked rugs, and attractive fabrics. They have also hired a chef whose fame has spread throughout the region.

Breakfast might feature potato latkes with sweet pepper relish and crème fraîche, poached eggs and avocado with tomato on toasted cornbread with cheddar béchamel, or frizzled ham and watercress and baked egg in a dilled crêpe nest with smoked salmon and chèvre. Friday night always features lobster, and one Saturday night we dined on potato and horseradish-crusted salmon fillet with chive and pink peppercorn buerre blanc, served with fresh asparagus and greens. Dessert was a chocolate almond terrine with a trio of sauces. Dinner for outside guests is $33. Goose Cove has a liquor license and wine is served. Since the 1997 addition of a large waterview deck, lunch is also served.

Guests are invited to congregate for cocktails and hors d'oeuvres at 6:00 P.M. and frequently team up for dinner, although there is no pressure to join others. Children are given a special menu and eat in a dining area that is supervised by counselors who also provide entertainment. After-dinner concerts or talks by local artisans or a lobsterman are also routine events.

You might want to pack a flashlight if you happen to book one of the more secluded cottages (we recommend Bunchberry) because, despite the stars, it's surprising how inky black that after-dinner walk through the firs can be. Seven of the cottages are widely scattered, each hidden deep in the pines, but all have views of the water. Each has a pine-paneled living room with fireplace, kitchenette, deck, and a varying number of bedrooms, sleeping from four to six. Four cottages attached to the lodge also have water views and either fireplaces or Franklin stoves, and there are two suites (sleeping four to six) in the Main Lodge itself, one with and one without a view. Each room or suite is different, and those in the East Annex and North Annex are also attractive. Be sure to request a fireplace or Franklin stove and water view. In 1997 two architect-designed family-sized cabins were added, each with massive fireplaces, kitchens, cathedral ceilings, and French windows opening onto decks — one cabin accommodates six and the other, eight. Both are winterized and available year-round.

Goose Cove is situated at the end of its own mile-and-a-half road but is less than 15 minutes from Stonington, a picturesque old granite quarrying and lobstering village. Stonington is a departure point for the mail boat to Isle au Haut, which features hiking trails that are considered among the most beautiful in Acadia National Park.

Deer Isle, thanks to a causeway, is an extension of the Blue Hill Peninsula, but Stonington is more than 40 miles south of Route 1. In other words, this is not exactly a convenient hub from which to explore the coast. But that's not what this resort is about. Many guests never leave the property — except at low tide, when they can walk across the sandbar to the Barred Island nature preserve.

Inland Maine

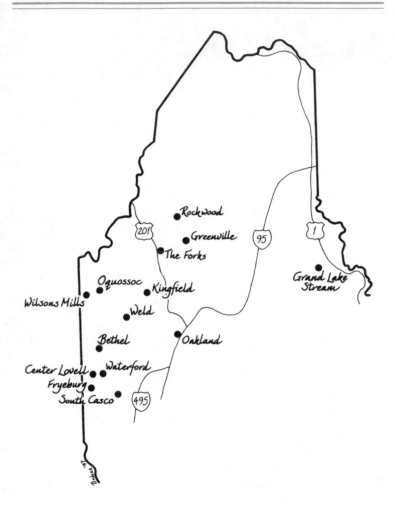

Best Bed-and-Breakfast

Fryeburg
Admiral Peary House, 193

Best Family Finds

The Forks
Northern Outdoors, 191
Oakland
Bear Spring Camps, 202
Oquossoc
Bald Mountain Camps, 203
Rockwood
The Birches, 205
South Casco
Migis Lodge, 207

Best Gourmet Getaways

Greenville
The Greenville Inn, 197
Kingfield
The Herbert Hotel, 200
Waterford
Lake House, 209

Best Grand Resorts

Bethel
Bethel Inn & Country Club, 186
South Casco
Migis Lodge, 207

Best Romantic Getaways

Greenville
The Lodge at Moosehead, 198

Best Sports Resorts and Wilderness Retreats

Bethel
The Telemark Inn, 188
The Forks
Northern Outdoors, 191
Grand Lake Stream
Weatherby's, the Fisherman's Resort, 195
Oquossoc
Bald Mountain Camps, 203
Rockwood
The Birches, 205
Weld
Kawanhee Inn, 211
Wilsons Mills
Bosebuck Mountain Camps, 213

Inland Maine is the single most underrated piece of New England. Its image is fir-covered and flat, but its ranges are actually as high as Vermont's Green Mountains and they rise from literally thousands of lakes.

The lakes begin with Sebago Lake, just west of Portland, stretching westward in a thin chain to Bridgton, a friendly old village with (relatively) warm-water beaches. Deep, clear Kezar Lake and small Keoka Lake are just to the north. Another popular route from Portland to western Maine is Route 26 (leave the Maine Turnpike at Gray), which climbs quickly into the hills, passing the country's last working Shaker community, at Sabbathday Lake, on the way to the old resort village of **Bethel.**

Bethel began as a summer resort, when it was a stop on the Grand Trunk rail line, but thanks to Sunday River, one of New England's most popular ski resorts, and to several excellent cross-country touring centers, it is now as much a winter ski resort as a summer golf, hiking, and mountain biking mecca. From here it is a beautiful ride via Mexico and Route 17 north to Rangeley, which is as much a region as a town, spotted with large lakes ringed by high mountains.

Much of this mountain and lake region is more remote today than it was in the days of rail. A century ago, New Yorkers could take an overnight train to **Greenville,** for instance, then board a steamer for the islands and points along the shore of mighty **Moosehead Lake,** the largest of all Maine's inland waters. In the North Woods, the lure for most urban gentlemen was and remains fishing. Many of the "sports lodges," classic Maine log lodges and cabins, survive. The most remote ones are found in the Rangeley region and around Moosehead.

Maine's North Woods cover more than six million acres of privately owned timberland bordered on two sides (the sides vary) by Canada. In recent years skiing and, even more recently, whitewater rafting have enticed many people to this area, especially around **The Forks,** at the junction of the Kennebec and Dead rivers. The big ski area here is Sugarloaf, in the steep Carrabassett Valley, once threaded by a narrow-gauge lumber railroad. **Kingfield,** at the base of this valley, still retains some of the opulence of its old lumber baron mansions and hotel.

Bethel

Bethel Inn & Country Club

Village Common
Bethel, ME 04217
207-824-2175
800-654-0125
Fax: 207-824-2233
connorsa@nxi.com

| A grand old resort in the mountains |

Owner: Dick Rasor. **General managers:** Bill White and Allen Connors. **Accommodations:** 57 rooms in the inn and guest houses; 40 1- and 2-bedroom townhouses. **Rates:** $198–$378 per couple, MAP in summer; $138–$300 per couple in winter; many packages available. **Included:** Breakfast and dinner, MAP; all facilities. **Added:** 7% tax, 18% gratuity on food. **Credit cards accepted:** All major ones. **Children:** Age 11 and under, free in parents room; meal plan for $15 per day. **Pets:** Accepted with advance notice. **Smoking:** Permitted. **Handicap access:** Some rooms. **Open:** Year-round.

➤ **Gracious yet comfortable as an old shoe, the Bethel Inn caters to golfers and skiers, both downhill and cross-country.**

When the Bethel Inn was built in 1913, most guests arrived by train from Boston and points south. The inn has always appealed to golfers, and the championship 18-hole golf course and golf school is still the big summertime draw.

In the 1980s nearby Sunday River grew from a local ski hill to a major resort, providing a focal point for winter travelers to the region. The inn has 28 kilometers of its own groomed ski trails, with rental equipment, lessons, and guided tours. An outdoor pool is well heated so you can swim under the stars, even on frosty nights. Year-round, children and teens quickly find their way to the recreation building, which also houses a fitness room, two saunas, and a Jacuzzi.

The inn itself is a rambling yellow clapboard building in the center of a fine old Maine town on the eastern fringe of the White Mountains. The parlor and lobby has a comfortable feel to it — not too elegant, not too dowdy. On the ground floor, the dark Mill Brook Tavern is usually a lively gathering place, and sometimes features live entertainment. Luncheons and lighter dinner fare are served at the poolside lounge next door.

The large dining room has a cheery hearth, a Steinway piano that is played during dinner, fresh flowers on the tables, and a view of the hills through picture windows. You can dine on the verandah, with views over the golf course and cross-country trails. Traditional Continental and New England fare usually includes a choice of a half-dozen entrées. Service is friendly and the kitchen staff is happy to a accommodate a special request to grill a piece of salmon, for instance, instead of preparing it in a butter sauce. We always ask for a double portion of vegetables since the portions are small.

All of the guest rooms have phones and cable TV, and some have fireplaces. They are modestly furnished; some could use a bit of freshening up. The bathrooms, though completely adequate, are 1950s-style. In the main inn, the larger rooms overlook the golf course, unlike the snug ones originally intended for chauffeurs and maids. Each annex has its own living room, making them ideal for small groups or couples traveling together. One- and two-bedroom, bi-level townhouse condominiums on the golf course are a good choice for families, since you can use all the inn's facilities but still do your own cooking if you want to.

In the summer there is canoeing, sailing, and swimming from the inn's private lake house on Songo Pond. The log cabin is woefully underutilized, so you may have it to yourself, which is especially nice for a swim at dusk. There is also tennis, golf, and mountain biking on a web of surrounding roads and on the lift-accessible trails at Sunday River. The nearby White Mountains and the Mahoosuc Range both offer outstanding hiking, and Bethel itself is good for strolling and shopping at any time of year.

The Telemark Inn

RFD 2
P.O. Box 800
Bethel, ME 04217
207-836-2703
www.maineguide.com/bethel/telemark

| **A wilderness retreat for llama lovers, ikers, and cross-country skiers** |

Innkeeper: Steve Crone. **Accommodations:** 5 rooms, sharing 2 baths. **Rates:** Spring through fall (includes lodging, meals, llama trekking, canoeing, mountain biking, hiking, and swimming) 3-day rate: $399 per adult, $265 per child; five days: $595 per adult, $425 per child. Winter weekend packages (includes lodging, meals, ski trail passes, ice skating, a sleigh ride, and teepee party): $220 per adult, $170 per child; inquire about overnight llama treks, group and midweek winter rates. **Included:** Full breakfast with rooms; all meals with packages. **Minimum stay:** 2 nights on winter weekends. **Added:** 7% tax. **Credit cards accepted:** All major ones. **Children:** Welcome, special rates for treks. **Pets:** Not accepted (but see skijoring) . **Smoking:** Permitted on porch. **Handicap access:** No. **Open:** Year-round except April.

> **At night the stars are very near and bright.**

Llama trekking and wildlife education or cross-country skiing, snowshoeing, or skijoring — depending on the season — is the big reason to visit Telemark Farm, formerly a millionaire's retreat deep in the forest on the eastern fringe of the White Mountains. Although the inn is only a dozen miles from Bethel, it seems as isolated as any sporting camp in the North Woods. Three miles up a private road, it has its own generator for electricity.

Surrounded by National Forest, the inn's remote location is ideal. There is ample grazing space for the 16 llamas — and miles of wooded trails for you to explore. Overnight and longer treks are into the little-visited Caribou Speckled Wilderness part of the White Mountains National Forest.

Steve Crone, an athlete and outdoorsman, was the first person in New England to offer llama treks. On a trek, you lead rather than ride your llama — a sure-footed, amiable animal who carries your luggage, food, and camping equipment. A remote teepee is frequently used for camping and three-day treks usually include a day of hiking and or canoeing.

In the winter, this is one of a relatively few New England country inns to offer reliable snow cover on its cross-country trail system. Unusually high and wooded, the trails are 15 feet wide and give access to a virtually unlimited backcountry trail system in the White Mountain National Forest. Sleigh riding and skating on the inn's pond (by kerosene light) are also part of the winter scene.

An avid skijorer (racing on skis behind a dog team), Steve enjoys sharing his passion for this sport with guests and offers training sessions for those who would like to train their own dogs to draw them along on skis.

Although Steve doesn't advertise it, it's also possible to simply stay at the Telemark Inn and not stray from its long front porch — from which the only sounds you hear are bird calls and llama neighs. The inn itself is handsomely rustic, with paneled walls and ceilings and hardwood floors. A fireplace warms both the living and dining room.

Breakfast is served on the porch or at the large round cherrywood table. One of the surviving pieces of "rustic" furniture built for this house by its original owner, it seems to rise organically in wedges from the center of the dining room. Don't expect antiques and private baths, but the guest rooms are attractive and each room has a sink in it. One has bunks beds, perfect for children.

Breakfast might be a fresh rhubarb crêpe, with rhubarb harvested from the inn's substantial herb and vegetable garden — the inn tries to be as self-sustaining as possible. But you won't be eating nuts and berries for dinner if you are on a trek either.

Center Lovell

Quisisana

Center Lovell, ME 04016
207-925-3500
914-833-0293 off-season
Fax: 207-925-1004

A lakeside resort for music
lovers

Innkeeper: Jane Orans. **Accommodations:** For 150 people in 2 lodges and for 38 people in 1-, 2-, and 3-bedroom cottages. **Rates:** $200–$300 per couple. Pre-season: $180–$220 (rehearsals, fewer performances). **Included:** All 3 meals, facilities, concerts. **Minimum stay:** 1 week in season. **Added:** 7% tax. **Credit cards accepted:** None. **Children:** Welcome; $80 when sharing parent's room; early dinner seating. **Pets:** Not accepted. **Smoking:** Not in buildings. **Handicap access:** No. **Open:** Mid-June through late August.

➤ **Quisisana means "a place where one heals oneself," and we would add "through music." Even without music this place would be special — it is a traditional lodge with dozens of cottages on one of Maine's deepest, purest lakes.**

This is unquestionably a music haven. It was founded in 1917 as a place for musicians to play together for their own entertainment. In fact, Vladimir Horowitz had his own Steinway delivered here so he could practice before returning to the stage in 1962. Today, the 47-acre compound employs more than seventy students from the country's top conservatories each year. By day they work in the kitchen, dining room, and as housekeepers. By night they perform — from chamber music and one-act operas to musical theater and concert arias — in the wood-frame Music Hall overlooking the lake. Milk and cookies or some other snacks usually follow the lakeside performances.

The pine-paneled cottages vary in size and proximity to the lake. There seems to be a pecking order, with regulars getting the beach units (some units have a waiting list of years). But all the units we've seen are crisp and nicely furnished and have screened porches. Mosquito repellent, which comes in handy in June, is left in the cottages. Staff keep the refrigerators stocked with spring water and ice. After a few days of performing and serving guests, a nice rapport develops between the staff and guests. Antique street lamps light the way between lakeside and wooded cottages and the communal buildings.

The beach is soft and curves to a grassy point with plenty of places to sit. One waterfront area is quite social (New York accents abound); on our last visit, there were very few people on the other part of the beach. Rowboats, Sunfish, kayaks, and sailboats are all available, as are three clay tennis courts. There is a supervised children's game room for rainy days.

The white frame central lodge with green shutters includes a bright, comfortable sitting room with children's toys and a big fireplace. The open-beamed dining room is a space you won't mind sitting in three times a day — at white-draped tables topped with fresh flowers and small water puzzles to placate a fidgety small fry (adults love them, too). At breakfast time, you make your selections for lunch and dinner. The 25-person kitchen gets rave reviews from guests; the Sunday evening buffet is particularly popular.

The Forks

Northern Outdoors

Route 201
P.O. Box 100
The Forks, ME 04985
207-663-4466
800-765-7238
Fax: 207-663-2244
www.NorthernOutdoors.com

| A whitewater rafting resort

Hosts: Wayne and Suzanne Hockmeyer. **Accommodations:** 7 cabins, 4 lodge rooms, 10 lodgominiums, 30 cabin tents, 60 campsites. **Rates:** $8–$60 per person; rafting, $79 extra; 2-day packages include rafting, extras. **Included:** No meals in the basic rate. **Added:** 7% tax. **Credit cards accepted:** Discover, MasterCard, Visa. **Children:** Under age 15, half price for lodging and rafting. **Pets:** Not accepted. **Smoking:** Not permitted in main lodge. **Handicap access:** Yes. **Open:** Cabins, lodge rooms, and logdominiums open in November, January, February, and March for snowmobiling as well as from May to mid-October for rafting.

➤ **Word spread quickly of the wildest, most dependable rafting ride in the country (water releases take place every day spring through fall). So many competitors were vying for river time that the sport became state regulated.**

Wayne and Suzie Hockmeyer were the first rafters on the Kennebec River, and their Northern Outdoors is still the biggest rafting outfit in Maine. Their resort center is attractive: an open-timbered building with high ceilings, a huge hearth, comfortable seating, a cheerful dining room, a bar, a pool, a private lake, platform tennis, a hot tub, and microbrewery. Rock climbing, fishing, and mountain biking are also available. Ninety-foot-high Moxie Falls is also nearby.

Halfway between Portland and Quebec City, the Forks, as its name suggests, is at the confluence of the Kennebec and the Dead rivers. Pictures of the long-gone 100-room hotel built in 1860 in the middle of this tiny village, along with photos of old logging camps (Suzie's grandfather owned one), decorate the dining room walls at Northern Outdoors.

Maine's whitewater rafting industry dates from a spring day in 1976 when Wayne Hockmeyer happened onto isolated Kennebec Gorge and sensed its appeal. (Rafting was already big on the Colorado River and in West Virginia.) He secured a raft and talked eight bear hunters into coming along for the ride. What a ride! Below Central Maine Power's Harris Hydroelectric Station, they found themselves shooting water releases that have since been measured at up to 8,000 cubic feet per second. Hockmeyer had seen the movie *River of No Return* and knew enough to position himself at the back of the raft. Good thing since the fishing guide and his hunters were generally out of control for much of the 12 miles. Hockmeyer, however, knew a good thing, especially when log drives on the Kennebec were outlawed later that same year. He bought a secondhand cattle truck and herded clients to the put-in spot, just below Harris Dam.

Lodging options at Northern Outdoors include campsites, cabin tents, cabins, lodge rooms with private baths, and attractive log-dominiums (cedar-sided units with a kitchenette, dining area, living room, and space to sleep five).

Fryeburg

Admiral Peary House

9 Elm Street
Fryeburg, ME 04037
207-935-3365
800-237-8080
Fax: 207-935-3365
admpeary@nxi.com
www.mountwashingtonvalley.com/admiralpearyhouse

> **A small B&B on the edge of
> the White Mountains**

Innkeepers: Nancy and Ed Greenberg. **Accommodations:** 5 rooms (all with private bath). **Rates:** $98–$118 per couple in season; $70–$80 per couple in winter, by reservation only; 10% discount year-round for 5 nights or more. **Included:** Full breakfast. **Added:** 7% tax. **Credit cards accepted:** American Express, MasterCard, Visa. **Children:** Not appropriate. **Pets:** Not accepted. **Smoking:** Not permitted. **Handicap access:** No. **Open:** Year-round.

➤   **We search for places that just feel "right" when you walk in the front door; the Admiral Peary House is one of those places.**

The house is named for the famous Arctic explorer, Admiral Peary, who lived here with his mother before he began surveying the Panama Canal. The Greenbergs opened it as a B&B in 1989 and they offer plenty of room for guests to spread out. The large house really feels like two separate houses because the original barn has been converted and connected to the main house. You'll notice elements of the former barn in the beamed living room in the back of the house. It's informal, with weathered barnboard walls and a large brick fireplace. It has a TV, a raised billiard table, and closets that hide games, a stereo system, and a small refrigerator with complimentary sodas. The living room and library in the front of the house are more formal and quiet, perfect for reading. Summer guests like to settle into wicker chairs on the large screened-in porch with its view of bird feeders.

Each guest room has a sitting area, wall-to-wall carpeting, air conditioning, and a tastefully remodeled bathroom. Each is quite soothing to the senses; not one is overdone. The North Pole room, the most spacious, has a king-size brass bed and mountain views. Another favorite is "The Jo," a cozy room with sloping ceilings. Henson boasts a double shower, while Pathfinder has its own screened-in porch furnished with wicker.

Full breakfasts are served at one long table in the country-style kitchen, where in the winter a woodstove is stoked nonstop. The morning of our last visit, breakfast included three homemade breads, a fruit cup, and stuffed French toast with a side order of sausage. You can always fix yourself a cup of tea throughout the day; afternoon beverages are offered as well.

You can relax on the deck overlooking a deep backyard, play billiards in the living room, or soak in the outdoor hot tub. The Greenbergs are both tennis pros who are proud of their well-maintained clay tennis court; they offer tennis lessons or sessions with their ball machine. They also have loaner bikes.

There's plenty to keep you busy in the area. The B&B is located one block from the center of town. Several canoe outfitters can set you up for a trip down the Saco River. Or you can enjoy the river at the town-maintained beach, which has a float. North Conway outlet shops are just 15 minutes away.

Grand Lake Stream

Weatherby's, the Fisherman's Resort

Grand Lake Stream, ME 04637
207-796-5558
207-237-2911 in winter
Fax: 207-796-5558
weather@somtel.com
www.weatherbys.com

> **A sporting camp for serious fishermen**

Innkeepers: Charlene and Ken Sassi. **Accommodations:** 16 units in 15 cottages (all with private bath). **Rates:** $170 per couple, MAP, $110 single; family rates available. **Included:** Breakfast and dinner; lunch also served. **Minimum stay:** None. **Added:** 7% tax, 15% service charge. **Credit cards accepted:** Master-Card, Visa. **Children:** Under age 12, $50 per day. **Pets:** Not accepted. **Smoking:** Not permitted in dining room. **Handicap access:** Some rooms. **Open:** May to October.

➤ **Weatherby's and Grand Lake Stream are names known to fishermen throughout the country.**

Weatherby's is right by Grand Lake Stream, the small river that connects West Grand Lake with Big Lake. The rambling white clapboard lodge has a spacious living room with a piano, a TV, and a hearth. Guests gather here in the evening to trade fishing stories. The dining room is homey and the meals better than down home: fish chowder and lobster stew, native turkey and berries, and plenty of fresh breads, pies, and cookies. Box lunches are available for a small charge.

Each cottage is slightly different, but most are made of log, with screened porches, a bath, and a Franklin stove or fireplace. There is daily housekeeping, and Ken and Charlene (who have owned the camp since the 1970s) are right there if you need or want anything. Fishing is what this place is about. Grand Lake Stream is one of the most famous fishing spots in the country, known for landlocked salmon, smallmouth bass, perch, pickerel, and lake trout. Fishing guides ($125 per day) and rental boats ($36 per day) are available. Those who don't fish come to swim, bird watch (more than a hundred species can be found in the area), hike, and generally unwind in this remote stretch of the Maine woods. Children are welcome and usually love it. Inquire about fly-fishing schools.

Greenville

The big draws in Greenville are moose-watching, fishing, hiking, whitewater rafting, and boating. But Greenville is also the largest seaplane base in New England, the jump-off spot for more remote North Woods lakes and camps.

The Greenville Inn

Norris Street
P.O. Box 1194
Greenville, ME 04441
207-695-2206
888-695-6000
Fax: 207-695-2206
gvlinn@moosehead.net
www.maineguide.com/moosehead/greenvilleinn

A gourmet getaway overlooking New England's largest lake

Innkeepers: Elfie, Michael, and Susie Schnetzer. **Accommodations:** 5 rooms (all with private bath), 1 suite, 6 cottages. **Rates:** $115–$148 per couple in rooms, $185–$195 per couple in suite from late June to mid-October; $ $20 each additional person. **Included:** Breakfast buffet; dinner is additional. **Added:** 7% tax. **Credit cards accepted:** MasterCard, Visa, Discover. **Minimum stay:** None. **Children:** Over age 7 welcome. **Pets:** Not accepted. **Smoking:** Not permitted. **Handicap access:** None. **Open:** Year-round.

➤ **This lumber baron's mansion is one of the most magnificent structures in New England.**

This elegant Victorian mansion is not what you expect to find at the foot of Moosehead Lake. It also provides the best dining in this neck of the North Woods.

This is a true lumber baron's mansion, built around 1885, with rich mahogany, cherry and oak paneling, embossed walls, stained glass windows, working fireplaces (with magnificent carved mantles), and an immense leaded-glass window depicting a single spruce tree. It took 10 years to complete the country retreat.

Each of the six second-floor bedrooms is different; you might request one with a working fireplace and/or lake view. The master suite is a stunner and features a spacious bathroom with antique fixtures. A more rustic Carriage House suite (with woodstove and TV) is good for families, as are the six one-room cottages. Four of these cottages were newly built with French doors opening to lake and mountain views; two older cottages also enjoy the same view.

We can think of few places more pleasant to sit than on the inn's front porch, looking up the length of New England's largest lake and across to the mountains. Nor can we think of more pleasant places to dine than in this inn's handsome dining rooms, set with crisp linens, heavy silver, and crystal. Chef Susie Schnetzer's menu may feature escargot, grilled lamb chops, a choice of well-dressed fish dishes, or Rahmnschnitzel (a veal cutlet with mushroom cream sauce). Offerings change with the season. The dessert menu features Austrian pastries.

The Lodge at Moosehead

P.O. Box 1175
Lily Bay Road
Greenville, ME 04441
207-695-4400
Fax: 207-695-2281

A luxurious retreat, à la elegant rustication

Innkeeper: Roger Cauchi. **Accommodations:** 11 rooms (all with private bath). **Rates:** $165–$350 per couple from late May through October; $165–$350 per couple, MAP, off-season. **Included:** Full breakfast in season; breakfast and dinner off-season. **Minimum stay:** 2 nights in season. **Added:** 7% tax. **Credit cards accepted:** MasterCard, Visa, Discover. **Children:** Not appropriate. **Pets:** Not accepted. **Smoking:** Not permitted. **Handicap access:** Some rooms. **Open:** Year-round except April.

➤ **Travel industry veteran Roger Cauchi has created the ultimate romantic getaway.**

This airy, Shingle-style lodge overlooking Moosehead Lake has been transformed into the most luxurious retreat in inland Maine.

Each guest room features a bed sculpted by local woodcarver Joe Bolf that is really a work of art — a four-poster with each of its posts a totem pole, another with bears climbing the posts, yet another with two larger-than-life mooseheads nuzzling each other. The beds set the themes for the rooms, four of which have lake views. The fifth, the Trout Room, compensates with fabric-covered walls patterned with hooks and flies to match the brightly painted wooden trout leaping up the bed's four posters and around the bathroom mirrors.

In 1997 Cauchi created three new "retreat suites." Of these, the Allagash and Baxter suites have swaying beds suspended from the ceiling; Katahdin's distinctive bed is highlighted by a twig and antler canopy. They are large rooms with sliding glass doors that open onto lake views and a patio. Each can accommodate a third person on the sofa bed.

Almost needless to say, the bathrooms all have whirlpool baths and each room has a gas fireplace, craftily encased in a rustic mantel with a TV and VCR sequestered in the cabinet above.

Like the guest rooms, the spacious Great Room and smaller common rooms are a whimsical mix of rustic twig furniture and formal, brightly upholstered armchairs, couches, and antiques. The dining room is almost too big (restaurant-sized) but, like everything in the inn, it's nicely furnished and features large sliding glass panels overlooking the lake. A combination buffet and full breakfast is served in season.

In winter, guests meet over evening cocktails, but otherwise the social atmosphere is very low-key and couple-oriented. Roger is delighted to help arrange any expeditions or services desired. Trail bikes, canoes, snow shoes, and skis can all be delivered to the inn.

Kingfield

The Herbert Hotel

P.O. Box 67
Kingfield, ME 04947
207-265-2000
800-843-4372
herbert@somtel.com
www.byme.com/the herbert

A city-style hotel in the North Woods

Owner: Bud Dick. **Accommodations:** 31 rooms, 4 suites (all with private bath). **Rates:** $80–$100 per couple in winter, $110–$140 for 2- or 3-room suite that sleeps 4 or 6 in winter, from $59 per couple in summer. Inquire about midweek packages. **Included:** Continental breakfast in summer, full breakfast in winter. **Minimum stay:** 2 nights during some periods. **Added:** 7% tax. **Credit cards accepted:** All major ones. **Children:** Welcome. **Pets:** Welcome if well trained. **Smoking:** Not permitted in dining room. **Handicap access:** No. **Open:** Year-round.

➤ **Billed as a palace in the wilderness when it opened in 1918, the Herbert still fills the bill.**

This three-story columned hotel in the center of town has been nicely restored. It was built in 1917–1918 for Herbert Wing, a prominent lawyer, judge, and member of the Maine House of Representatives. Some say it was built so that Wing, who was thinking about running for governor, would have a place to entertain notables. It was the first hotel north of Boston where diners could receive a telephone call at their table. In addition, it was one of the first houses to be electrified when it was built (note the brass lighting fixtures).

Throughout the building, the floors are native white oak and Italian marble. There is a grand piano in the somewhat stately lobby, an abundance of polished oak, and plenty of places to relax. Just so you don't forget you're in North Country, a moose head hangs above the hearth, while the living rooms center column displays a stuffed bobcat and a deer head.

In the intimate, candlelit dining room, fresh flowers grace the table, even in January. The gilded-style room glistens with cut glass, brass, and crystal ceiling fans. With one or two hiatuses, chef

Peter Freyer has been cooking here since the early 1980s, when owner Bud Dick took the helm. Freyer offers a number of specials each night, but prime rib is always popular. Thursday and Sunday night specials are quite enticing: the tab runs $14 to $16 for two people. The Herbert boasts an extensive and reasonably priced wine list. Many guests take their morning coffee to the second-floor verandah overlooking the town's main intersection.

The guest rooms are fresh and furnished with comfortable antiques. Many have Jacuzzis and brass beds. The basement houses a sauna and a hot tub with a moose head depicted in tile above it. On our last visit, one of the waitresses was also a masseuse; check to see if she is still there.

Once a prosperous lumbering center, Kingfield is now a handsome town with a decent selection of shops and restaurants. It's a long way from anywhere but Sugarloaf USA. In summer, the Stanley Museum is open, and the Sugarloaf golf course offers a challenge. Inquire about special midweek winter rates that include a lift ticket.

Oakland

Bear Spring Camps

Route 2
RR3, Box 9900
Oakland, ME 04963
207-397-2341

| **Unbeatable value plus good fishing** |

Managers: Ron and Peg Churchill. **Accommodations:** 32 cottages. **Rates:** $450 (for 2 people) to $1,600 (for 8) per week; less in May, June, and September. **Included:** All meals. **Minimum stay:** A week in July and August. **Added:** 7% tax. **Credit cards accepted:** None. **Children:** Under age 3, $25; ages 3–8, $80; over age 9, $165 (weekly). **Pets:** Not allowed. **Smoking:** Permitted. **Handicap access:** Yes. **Open:** Mid-May through September.

➤ **In Maine, lakeside cottages are known as "camps."**

The Belgrade Lakes are just north of Augusta, in rolling farm country generally known as mid-Maine. It's an area that doesn't promote itself much because it doesn't have to; most visitors have been coming for generations. The same is true for Bear Spring Camps. This gem of a family resort has 80 to 90 percent repeat business. Each cottage is right on Great Lake and has its own boat. This is because, as the brochure notes, "we know that many of our guests want to go fishing as soon as they arrive."

Serious fishermen come in May for trout and salmon, and in July there is still bass. In the summer most fishermen bring their families, who play tennis and lawn games and, of course, swim (the lake bottom is sandy). Sailboat and motorboat rentals are also available.

The cabins have fireplaces as well as gas heat. (Even in sunny weather, that extra blanket on the bed comes in handy.) It's the kind of place where, if something is missing, the cabin boy will fetch it in a jiffy; there is daily maid service.

The main lodge is an overgrown farmhouse, and the feeling, in contrast to that of most Maine camps, is very open, with many acres of clipped lawn. All the meals are served in the spacious dining room, and a box lunch is always available for those who want to go on an expedition. There are plenty of books and games in the main lodge for rainy days.

Oquossoc

Bald Mountain Camps

P.O. Box 332
Oquossoc, ME 04964
207-864-3671

A century-old sporting camp

Innkeeper: Stephen Philbrick. **Accommodations:** 15 cabins. **Rates:** $100 per person; less for children. **Included:** All meals. **Added:** 7% tax. **Credit cards accepted:** None. **Minimum stay:** 1 week in July and August, not necessarily Saturday to Saturday. **Children:** Welcome. **Pets:** Accepted if well behaved. **Handicap access:** No. **Open:** Mid-May to late September.

➤ **Bald Mountain is one of Maine's most accessible old-style sporting camps.**

Right on Mooselookmeguntic Lake and easy to reach, this classic, old-fashioned sporting camp exudes the kind of hospitality found only under long-term ownership. Built in 1897, it's been in Stephens family since 1940. Aside from the addition of electricity and picture windows (overlooking the lake), little in the dining room or living-room-cum-lobby has changed.

Each of the lakefront cottages has a porch and rocking chairs. Each unit has its own living room with a solid old brick fireplace and two to four bedrooms.

Guests do here what they've done for more than a century: fish. Fishing for trout and landlocked salmon is the big lure (aluminum boats with 6-hp motors rent for $60 a day). A variety of boats, from canoes to sailboats, are available.

Mooselookmeguntic is one of the largest of the seven Rangeley Lakes, and it's not difficult to spend an entire day out on the lake. Waterskiing is also an option. On land, hiking and moose-watching are popular pastimes. Bald Mountain Camps offers a sandy beach for swimming, a clay tennis court, shuffleboard, a children's playground, and horseshoes. Golf is nearby. For rainy days, there are cards and plenty of games to play in front of the fireplace.

Rockwood

The Birches

P.O. Box 81
Rockwood, ME 04478
207-534-7305
800-825-9453
wwld@aol.com
www.birches.com

**A classic North Woods
resort**

Innkeepers: The Willard family. **Accommodations:** 4 rooms, 15 cabins, 12 cabin tents. **Rates:** $55–$75 per person per room, B&B; $650–950 per week per cabin (sleeping up to 6 adults) in season; $426–$650 off-season; $17 per person per day in cabin tent; MAP, AP, and rafting packages also available. **Included:** B&B where indicated; EP in cottages. **Minimum stay:** None. **Added:** 7% tax. **Credit cards accepted:** All major ones. **Children:** Welcome, half price under age 11. **Pets:** Accepted. **Smoking:** Restricted in lodge rooms. **Handicap access:** Some rooms. **Open:** Year-round.

➤ **The hand-hewn log cabins are within sound of loons and sight of Mount Kineo, a dramatic cliff at the narrows of New England's largest lake.**

The Willard family has turned this classic 1930s hunting and fishing lodge into one of the most comfortable, family-geared resorts in the North Woods. It sits on its own 11,000 acres at the most scenic point on all of Moosehead Lake, with views of Mount Kineo and its dramatic cliff. Once you've arrived, you won't need (or want) to leave.

The hand-hewn log cabins are strung along the lake under tall, slender trees. In addition to a porch, each cabin has a Franklin stove or fireplace in the sitting room, a bath with a hot shower, and from one to three bedrooms. Some cabins have kitchens, but guests can also opt for the Full American Plan (FAP) — three substantial meals and housekeeping service. Four rooms upstairs (with shared bath) in the lodge are nicely designed, with balconies overlooking the lake. In the summer "cabin tents" (platform tents with camp beds), located near the marina and scattered through the woods, are a bargain.

The rustic timber lodge is the focus of social life at The Birches. It houses an open-beamed, pine-paneled dining room (with an Indian canoe hanging in its rafters and large windows overlooking the lake), a sitting room with a hearth, and a lobby with a trout pool. Maps, guidebooks, mosquito repellent, and other useful items are sold in the lobby, where you can also learn about boat rentals, rafting trips, and wilderness guides. Hearty meals feature traditional American fare.

In winter, The Birches runs a ski touring center, with rentals, instruction, snowshoes, and guided treks through the wilderness. Guides for ice fishing trips are also available. In summer, Wilderness Expeditions, a whitewater firm operating out of The Birches, arranges trips on various rivers and offers private instruction, guide service, and equipment rentals. They can also arrange horseback riding.

The Birches rents motorboats, windsurfers, canoes, kayaks, and sailboats, which can be launched from its private dock. A hot tub and sauna are just behind the lodge. Whatever time of year you come, you will want to paddle, motor, or ski over to Mount Kineo. A hiking path leads to the top of the cliff.

Rockwood, a small fishing and hunting outpost, is just a quick trip down the dirt road, and you can easily travel south to Greenville or Jackman or north on lumber company roads for lunch at a classic North Woods lumberman's oasis, Pittston Farm. Frequent boats also shuttle across the narrows to hiking paths, a golf course, and other facilities on Mt. Kineo. Inquire about Moose-watching cruises, kayaking the route Thoreau traveled to Northeast Carry, and about archeological programs.

South Casco

Migis Lodge

P.O. Box 40
South Casco, ME 04077
207-655-4524
Fax: 207-655-2054

**A first-rate, landmark
lakeside resort for families
and couples**

Innkeepers: Tim and Joan Porta. **Accommodations:** 7 lodge rooms (all with private bath) and 29 cottages (1–4 bedrooms). **Rates:** $125–$190 per person in cottages; $80–$115 per person in lodge. **Included:** All three meals, facilities. **Minimum stay:** Preference is given to weekly stays, but there are always shorter openings. **Added:** 7% tax, 15% gratuity. **Credit cards accepted:** None. **Children:** Welcome, with special rates. **Pets:** Not accepted. **Smoking:** Not permitted in dining room. **Handicap access:** Two cottages. **Open:** Mid-June to mid-October.

➤ **Forget the usual picture that comes to mind when you hear of cottages and cabins in Maine. These are a real treat — the kind you would relish even if it rained for your entire stay.**

Just two hours from Boston and 30 minutes from Portland, you may never want to leave Migis Lodge once you arrive. Over the past few years, the hands-on owners have invested almost $4 million in upgrading the property. And although infusion of capital doesn't guarantee success, in this case, we can think of few better places to spend a week's vacation. The resort combines the best of rustic elegance, great food, and plentiful activities.

The 1916 lodge is set on 100 piney acres with 2,000 feet of shorefront on a quiet section of Sebago Lake. The compound can easily absorb the 125 or so guests that spread out here. Upon arrival, you are escorted to your cottage, nestled in the trees and nicely separated from its neighbors.

A few guest rooms are available in the main lodge — the focal point of activity. Even on summer mornings there is usually a fire blazing in the homey living room. There are plenty of books, magazines, a game closet, and a television. Before and after dinner, guests tend to congregate for cocktails on the flagstone terrace, taking in sunset views over the lake and mountains.

Meals are served in the large dining room (jackets are required for men at dinner), which also has spectacular mountain and lake views. The food is bountiful and excellent; everything is homemade. There is an exceptional Saturday night buffet; on a recent visit we sampled practically everything and found all of it outstanding. Other traditions include complimentary cocktail parties, Sunday morning breakfast cookouts next to the lake, and Wednesday night steak roasts on a private island. Amiable college students make up the staff, and Lorraine, the dining room hostess since 1950, oversees them.

All of the one- and two-level cottages have been recently renovated and feel quite spiffy, spacious, and bright. Each cottage has a living room with fireplace, cable television, pine walls, and a wet bar. All but one has a view of the lake. (The one without a view compensates with a large screened-in porch with cathedral ceiling.) Handmade quilts, fresh flowers, and a porch furnished with rockers make the cabins feel quite homey. Each bedroom has its own full bath, and many of the master bedrooms have their own private balconies. Maid service, ice, and firewood are provided daily.

Most guests spend their time on the waterfront, which has many docks and two sand beaches. As you'd expect, there's great swimming, sailing, water skiing, canoeing, and fishing. Migis also has three Har-Tru tennis courts, two shuffleboard courts, a fitness center, horseshoes, marked trails for hiking and nature walks, a 35-foot Chris Craft for scenic lake cruises, a recreation center with table tennis and a pool table, and movies. Some folks, however, do nothing more strenuous than sunning, reading, taking a sauna, and enjoying the setting.

Waterford

Lake House

Routes 35 and 37
Waterford, ME 04088
207-583-4182
800-223-4182
Fax: 207-583-6078
www.virtualcities.com

> **A gourmet getaway in a picture-perfect village**

Innkeeper: Michael Myers. **Accommodations:** 3 rooms (all with private bath), 1 suite, 1 cottage. **Rates:** $140–$185 per couple, MAP; $84–$130 per couple, B&B; weekly rates for cottage; enticing packages and discounts for extended stays. **Included:** Varies with meal plan. **Minimum stay:** At times; a week is requested for the cottage. **Added:** 7% tax. **Credit cards accepted:** All major ones. **Children:** Over age 6 welcome. **Pets:** Not accepted. **Smoking:** Not permitted. **Handicap access:** No. **Open:** Year-round, but restaurant closed April and November.

> ➤ **Delightfully off the beaten path, this is an unpretentious inn with fine food and comfortable accommodations that are also a good value.**

In a village where the only other commercial ventures are a general store and a real estate office, the inn is an eye-catcher with its double porch. Townspeople were delighted when Myers purchased the inn in 1984 and began to renovate it. It sparked a renaissance of sorts in the village of Waterford Flat, spurring others to spruce up their own white clapboard houses. There are twenty-one village buildings listed on the National Historic Register, including the inn's gazebo, which Michael refurbished in 1995.

The former 1790s stagecoach stop and tavern have been lovingly restored and the former ballroom converted into a 600-square-foot suite. Michael designed an ingenious bathroom area for the former ballroom — with a clawfoot bathtub, hidden behind a screen, on a platform dais. The mint green room retains the raised, curved ceiling and receives good cross-ventilation from eight windows. Another suite has country furnishings and a separate library/reading room. "Waterford South" has twin beds, oak furniture, and access to the upper porch from which you can savor slow village life. "Waterford North" boasts Empire furnishings. Behind the inn,

Dudley House is a romantic little bungalow with cathedral ceilings and a screened porch. In late 1997 Michael planned to add two new spacious rooms above the barn; both will have access to their own "rec room."

Downstairs are a comfortable sitting room and two popular public dining rooms. One dining room is decorated with a collection of antique winemaking instruments and corkscrews. Both are set with linen and candles. Breakfast, available only to guests, is served at 9:00 A.M. on the screened-in porch, where guests are usually entertained by hummingbirds.

Dinner, prepared by Michael and an assistant, is excellent. From the well-rounded menu you might start with melt-in-your-mouth ravioli (a different filling each night) and move on to roast duck (a popular mainstay) served in a blackberry and wine sauce. Caesar salads are prepared right at the table. As you'd expect, all the baking (try the parfait pie or a flaming dessert) is done on premises. Seasonal fruit pies are always a good bet. An excellent cappuccino tops off the evening. The wine list is extensive and well priced, with more than one hundred selections. Ask about the wintertime wine-tasting dinners.

Waterford is a quiet pocket of Maine's Western Lakes region, a gem of a village on the shore of small Keoka Lake. In warm weather, you can swim at the beach just across the street, canoe, and sail. You can hike up Mount Tirem, which rises abruptly from the village, or tackle longer trails in the nearby Maine White Mountain National Forest. In the winter, it is possible to cross-country ski right around the inn. Groomed trails and downhill skiing are available nearby in Bridgton, or at Sunday River in Bethel.

Weld

Kawanhee Inn

Route 142, Lake Webb
Weld, ME 04285
207-585-2000
Maineinn@somtel.com
www.lakeinn.com

| **A Maine lakes classic**

Winter address:
7 High Street
Farmington, ME 04938
207-778-3809

Innkeepers: Sturges Butler and Marti Strunk. **Accommodations:** 9 rooms (5 with private bath), 1 suite, 11 cabins for 27. **Rates:** Rooms: $75–$100 per couple in high season; before mid-June and after September 1, $60–$95. Cabins: $450–$650 per week in high season; off-season, $115–$160 per night. **Included:** All meals are available from June through early September only. **Minimum stay:** 1 week in high season in cottages, Sunday to Sunday rentals. **Added:** 7% tax, 15% service. **Credit cards accepted:** MasterCard, Visa. **Children:** Welcome. **Pets:** Off-season and in one cabin in summer. **Smoking:** Not permitted in the lodge. **Handicap access:** One cabin. **Open:** May through mid-October.

➤   **Set on the brow of a hill overlooking Lake Webb, this Maine lodge has plenty of space for both rainy- and sunny-day activities.**

The Kawanhee Inn is in Maine's Rangeley Lakes district, off a rural road in a pine forest. It is dramatically set on a ledge with lawns sloping down to a shimmering lake ringed by mountains. The cabins either line the lakeshore below or have a view of the lake.

A huge central fireplace is the focal point of the rustic, open-beamed, pine-paneled living room. Thick birch trees serve as pillars for a room filled with cushioned rockers and chairs, a pool table, reading materials, and games. It opens onto the porch, lined with chairs and rockers overlooking the lake. The check-in desk resembles a counter in a general store, stocked with local maps and souvenirs and usually staffed by Marti, who obviously enjoys helping guests with nearby hikes and explorations.

Breakfast and dinner are served in the large, old-fashioned dining room. In most weather, the prized tables are on the screened verandah, which has water views, but from any of a dozen tables you can watch the sun slip into the lake. (*Kawanhee,* by the way, means "sunset" in Abenaki.) Fresh fish, steaks, crisp salads, and warm breads are the house specialties; try crab cakes for an appetizer. The dinner menu is priced from $8 to $19. Prime rib and lobster are offered on Friday and Saturday evenings, and Tuesday evenings feature two-for-one dinners. Guests often enjoy their dessert and coffee on the porch or have a nightcap under the moose head in the living room. After dark, guests study the star-studded sky with a telescope.

The upstairs rooms vary in size and have been recently upgraded with added insulation and baths. They are rustic but comfortable. Room 20 and a suite at the end of the hall are both large enough for families. Request a water view.

Unquestionably, however, it is the cabins that make this place. Each has a screened porch, camp chairs and tables, a stone fireplace, a roomy bedroom, and a bath. The five two-bedroom cottages all have kitchens, and Pine Lodge, which sleeps five, has a washer and dryer. Repeat guests get first dibs on cabins, which are held for them until January. You'll have the best luck at getting a cabin if you call in January or February for a summertime reservation. There are occasional "holes" in the reservations, so you may be able to get a cabin for less than a week.

The inn has a private beach and dock and canoes. Fishing, boating, sailing, long walks, all-day hikes to nearby Tumbledown or Bald Mountain or Mount Blue, and panning for gold on the nearby Swift River are all popular. Moose-watching is best done in the early morning. The inn prepares box lunches for day trips.

Wilsons Mills

Bosebuck Mountain Camps

P.O. Box 30
Route 16
Wilsons Mills, ME 03579
207-243-2945
207-486-3238 in winter

A wilderness retreat in the Rangeley Lakes region

Owner/operator: Tom Rideout. **Accommodations:** 11 cabins, each accommodating 2 to 6 people. **Rates:** $73–$78 per person per night; family rates and packages in summer. **Included:** All meals. **Minimum stay:** None. **Added:** 7% tax. **Credit cards accepted:** MasterCard, Visa. **Children:** Welcome. **Pets:** Accepted. **Smoking:** Permitted. **Handicap access:** No. **Open:** May 10 through November.

➤ **Aziscohos Lake has native brook trout and landlocked salmon, and by all accounts the fishing is tremendous.**

Bosebuck is in the middle of a 200,000-acre tract of land 15 miles from the nearest paved road. You have to drive down a dirt and gravel road to get to the camps or fly in from Rangeley with Mountain Air (call for rates: 207-864-5307). With the exception of a few camps that are accessible only by plane, this is one of the most remote places to stay in New England.

Most people come here for the excellent fishing and hunting and to enjoy the friendly, energetic, and extremely knowledgeable innkeeper. The accommodations are rustic, and although the cabins have indoor plumbing and showers, they are small and are meant for only one thing: sleep. The rest of your time is spent fishing or hunting or chatting in the lodge, decorated with heavy oak furniture. The kitchen serves an abundance of food and will happily cook your catch for any meal. A chambermaid makes your bed, and a dockhand helps you with boats and the fish you decide to keep.

Send for Bosebuck's pamphlet "Fishing at Bosebuck" for an excellent description of fishing opportunities. Grouse hunting is available on a limited basis in the fall, and trophy whitetailed deer hunting is offered in November. Those who wish to engage in deliberate inactivity can sit on the lodge's front porch, enjoying the tranquil view of the dock and lake, or go swimming or hiking.

It is imperative to make reservations at Bosebuck; someone must be there to unlock the gate about a mile from the camp. Call from the phone on Route 16 before heading down the dirt road.

Massachusetts

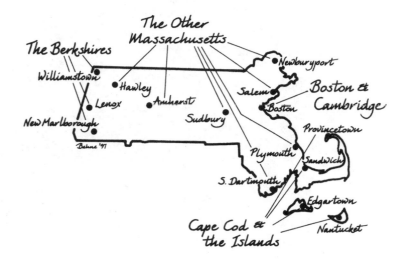

The Other
Massachusetts

The Berkshires

Williamstown

Hawley

Lenox

New Marlborough

Amherst

Sudbury

Behne '97

Newburyport

Salem

Boston

Boston &
Cambridge

Provincetown

Plymouth

Sandwich

S. Dartmouth

Edgartown

Nantucket

Cape Cod &
the Islands

Boston and Cambridge

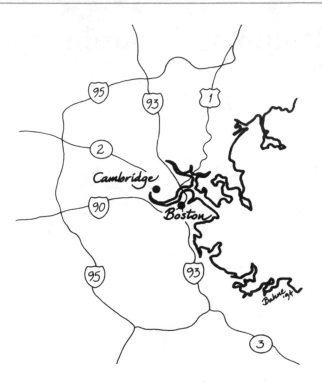

Best Bed-and-Breakfasts

Boston
Clarendon Square Bed & Breakfast, 226
Eliot and Pickett Houses, 229
Cambridge
The Mary Prentiss Inn, 247

Best Family Finds

Boston
The Four Seasons, 233
Hotel Meridien, 235
The Ritz Carlton, 241
Cambridge
Royal Sonesta Hotel, 249

Best Gourmet Getaways

Boston
Boston Harbor Hotel at Rowes Wharf, 224
The Four Seasons, 233
Hotel Meridien, 235
The Regal Bostonian Hotel, 239
Cambridge
The Charles Hotel, 243

Best Spas

Boston
Boston Harbor Hotel at Rowes Wharf, 224
The Four Seasons, 233
Cambridge
The Charles Hotel, 243

For many people, Massachusetts is **Boston.** The state capital is, after all, one of the country's most beautiful cities and invites exploration. Visitors stroll along the historic Freedom Trail (a self-guided walking tour of Revolutionary-era sites within the Boston National Historical Park), stopping along the way to dine and shop at Faneuil Hall/Quincy Marketplace, and pausing for cappuccino and cannoli in the North End. Although at its best in warm weather — when sidewalk cafés appear and excursion boats circle the harbor — Boston is a city of fine art and science museums, dozens of colleges and universities, outstanding winter concerts, and the country's original First Night, a celebration of the arts on New Year's Eve.

The T (short for MBTA, the Massachusetts Bay Transportation Authority), America's oldest underground public transit system, links the waterfront museums, shops, and restaurants with Boston Common and the downtown department stores (you can walk right from the subway station into Filene's Basement). The T also connects Back Bay's hotels and shops with the many attractions across the river in Cambridge.

Cambridge, Boston's sister city across the Charles River, is known chiefly as the home of Harvard University and the Massachusetts Institute of Technology (MIT); both offer museums and tours. Don't miss Harvard Square, a lively shopping, dining, and people-watching scene with an amazing variety of bookstores.

Boston is a city of neighborhoods, each with its own attractions. Plan your day's outing to cover one neighborhood in the morning and another in the afternoon.

Downtown comprises the Financial District, Beacon Hill, the North End, and the Waterfront. Don't miss Boston Common, the oldest public common in America and the beginning of the Freedom Trail; the Old State House and Old Granary Burying Ground; Faneuil Hall and Quincy Marketplace; and Beacon Hill, with its 19th-century houses, picturesque Acorn and Chestnut streets, the antiques stores on Charles Street, and the African Meeting House.

On the other side of Beacon Hill and the Common is Back Bay, which includes the Public Garden, the nation's oldest botanical garden, and its famed summertime swan boats, as well as elegant residential streets such as Commonwealth Avenue, artsy and fashionable shops on Newbury Street, and Copley Square Plaza. Around Copley Square is the Boston Public Library, the John Hancock Tower and its Observatory (which offers panoramic views of the city), and Trinity Church, widely considered Henry Hobson Richardson's crowning achievement. At the western end of Boylston Street, near Massachusetts Avenue, stop by the Institute of Contemporary Art.

At the lively Waterfront, there are excursion boats departing for the harbor islands and whalewatching, the New England Aquarium, the Children's Museum, and the Computer Museum, the only museum of its kind in the world. Encircled by the Waterfront is the North End (little Italy) with its cafés and restaurants, the historic Paul Revere House, Old North Church, and Copps Hill Cemetery (which looks toward Charlestown's *U.S.S. Constitution* — Old Ironsides — and the Bunker Hill Monument).

The Charles River offers ample opportunities for recreation — community sailing, jogging or strolling, and picnicking on its banks. The Museum of Science, its Planetarium, and the Omni Theater (a four-story wraparound screen that makes you feel as if you're inside the scene you're watching) are at one end of the Charles River Basin.

On the other side of the city is the Fenway, home of the Boston Red Sox and Fenway Park, the Museum of Fine Arts, and the Isabella Stewart Gardner Museum, an elaborate Venetian palazzo housing one woman's collection of treasures and art.

Boston

The lodging market is tight in Boston, especially for the less expensive rooms, so make reservations as soon as possible. All of the major hotels we include are excellent, so you'll want to base your choice primarily on location and price. Be sure to ask for corporate rates and about weekend packages, which tend to offer savings or added value.

When making reservations, request a room to your specifications: away from the elevator and ice machine, with a particular view, etc. Don't hesitate to request a room change (right away) if it isn't to your satisfaction. If you haven't requested a specific room, ask to be upgraded (or moved to a recently renovated room) for no additional charge. If you're traveling as a family, give them your children's names since many hotels will greet children with special gifts. And finally, ask to be introduced to the front desk manager so that there is someone who is invested in ensuring your visit is a good one.

The Bed & Breakfast Agency of Boston

47 Commercial Street
Boston, MA 02110
617-720-3540
800-248-9262
Fax: 617-523-5761

Although we're not in the habit of recommending B&B agencies (we think you buy this book because we have already searched out the best places to stay), we do want to make an exception here. This agency has listings for a 100 or so rooms in desirable locations. This guide cannot afford to devote space to a Victorian town house that rents one room, but this is what the agency specializes in. There are also atypical accommodations, like on a docked boat on the harborfront or a waterfront loft. Expect to pay about $80–$150 for a double room.

Boston Harbor Hotel at Rowes Wharf

70 Rowes Wharf on Atlantic Avenue
Boston, MA 02110
617-439-7000
800-752-7077
Fax: 617-330-9450
bhhsales@bhh.com
www.bhh.com

> **A luxury harborfront hotel with excellent dining**

Managing director: François-Laurent Nivaud. **Accommodations:** 202 rooms and 28 suites. **Rates:** $225–$470 in rooms; $355–$1,600 in suites; weekend packages. **Parking:** $23 overnight with unlimited in and out privileges; included with weekend packages. **Restaurant:** Open for all three meals. **Added:** 9.7% tax. **Credit cards accepted:** All major ones. **Children:** Under age 18, free in parent's room. **Pets:** Accepted. **Smoking:** Restricted. **Handicap access:** Yes. **Open:** Year-round.

➤ **A water shuttle whisks you from Logan Airport to the hotel in seven stress-free minutes. It provides the most impressive approach to the revitalized waterfront. Boston Harbor is, after all, one of the most vital working harbors in the country.**

Boston's most architecturally impressive luxury hotel is part of the Rowes Wharf harbor complex, which includes offices, residences, shops, parking, and a marina. The 16-story red brick building opened in 1987. The elegant structure, with a dramatic 80-foot arch and copper-domed rotunda, was called "a triumph of urban design" by the *New York Times*. Come for the view alone.

No expense has been spared inside, either. Marble floors, fabric-covered walls, ornate woodwork, and tapestry-style carpeting create warm, small-scale public spaces. A complete renovation of public space was completed in mid-1998. Antique navigational maps and museum-quality art grace the walls and contribute to the feel of an elegant private club, much like the great small hotels of London. A high employee-guest ratio produces excellent service, service that is more down-to-earth (though still professional and attentive) than other luxury hotels.

The rooms have sweeping views of either the harbor (watch the sunrise through practically floor-to-ceiling windows) or the city skyline. We prefer water views, but note that some are partially blocked by a brick ventilation unit. (Make sure not to get one of these.) Guest rooms occupy the top eight floors. Each room is decorated with flowered fabrics and chintzes, crystal lamps, and Chippendale furniture, and reflects Boston's historic ties to the harbor and world trade. Fresh flowers, plush bath-robes, umbrellas, a minibar, three telephones in each room, and windows that open are all standard. The hotel offers 24-hour room service. Because of the pyramid-nature of the architecture, guest rooms get slightly smaller as you go higher up.

The highly acclaimed and elegant Rowes Wharf Restaurant offers sweeping views of the harbor. Request a window table. Under the stewardship of Executive Chef Daniel Bruce, the menu offers a fresh take on regional American cuisine and seafood. You will not be disappointed. The menu changes seasonally, but breakfast always includes "red flannel hash," a hearty old-fashioned mainstay of beets, beef, and potatoes.

In late 1997 Café Intrigue opened, and we're thankful for it already. Serving meals from 6 A.M. to midnight in a casually elegant setting that spills on to the harborfront café (in summer only), the café is a great place to share a few dishes with friends or have a light, creative, somewhat internationally inspired meal at a very moderate price. You'll probably eat here more than once. (We have.) The Rowes Wharf Bar, also serving lunch and dinner, has become a meeting spot for professionals waiting for the commuter ferry.

From January to mid-April, the hotel hosts a popular wine festival, which includes a series of 40 dinners and receptions. Frenchman François-Laurent Nivaud, the hotel's managing director, grew up surrounded by wine and has a keen interest in raising the American consciousness in relation to wine; he established the festival in 1990.

The 10,000-square-foot Health Club and Spa is the most spacious facility in Boston. It boasts a 60-foot lap pool, whirlpool, sauna, steam room, and massage, exercise, and treatment rooms. It combines the ambiance of a classic European spa with the latest in training facilities and personalized nutrition, health, and beauty programs. A light spa menu is available poolside. A complimentary Continental breakfast for all hotel guests is available in the morning.

Whether you arrive from South Station (Amtrak) or the Southeast Expressway (autos), the location couldn't be more convenient. In case you haven't heard, Boston's "Big Dig" is a massive public works project to depress the Central Artery. Much of the work is going on right in front of the hotel, but the hotel has gone to great lengths (quite successfully, too) to lessen the impact on travelers. Once inside, you'll barely know that the multi-billion-dollar project exists. The hotel is within easy walking distance of the Aquarium, Faneuil Hall Marketplace, the North End, the Tea Party Ship, and the Computer and Children's museums.

Clarendon Square Bed & Breakfast

81 Warren Avenue
Boston, MA 02116
617-536-2229
www.cimarron.net/usa/ma/cs.html

A small, urbane B&B in a
hip neighborhood

Innkeepers: Stephen Gross and Michael Selbst. **Accommodations:** 3 rooms (all with private bath). **Rates:** $110–$150 per couple, $110 in winter. **Included:** Expanded Continental breakfast. **Minimum stay:** 2 nights. **Added:** 9.7% tax. **Credit cards accepted:** MasterCard, Visa. **Children:** Welcome with well-behaved parents. **Pets:** Not accepted. **Smoking:** Permitted on deck only. **Handicap access:** No. **Open:** Year-round.

➤ **The B&B is within walking distance of many of Boston's best restaurants and cafés, including Hammersley's Bistro.**

Located on a quiet residential street in the country's largest historic Victorian district, the South End, Clarendon Square Bed & Breakfast is Boston's best bed-and-breakfast. In recent years, as the neighborhood has gentrified, the South End has become one of Boston's most fashionable. The location is convenient to Back Bay, Newbury Street, the theater district, and Copley Square.

This town house dates to 1885 and had fallen into a state of disrepair before Stephen and Michael spent a full year renovating it in 1994. The B&B was refurbished with great care to preserve the detailing and was decorated with a sure designer's touch. It is urbane and sophisticated but warm and inviting, too. A dramatically open entry sets the tone. A curved staircase leads up to the second floor and a large bouquet graces the foyer's single table.

As for the guest rooms, we like the Yellow Room on the first floor the best. The ceilings are higher and the entryway feels like an extension of the guest room. Heavy velvet curtains can be pulled across the French doors to maintain privacy. Its bathroom is unusual: Italian marble wainscoting, French limestone floors, a silver leaf barrel-vaulted ceiling, and a hand-forged iron and porcelain wash basin. The Parchment Room is named for the parchment painted walls. This room is on the ground floor (though it does not feel dark like most ground-floor rooms) in the rear of the house and features a marble bath and a two-person double-headed shower. Since there is room for only one chair, you'll probably be lounging or watching TV from your bed. The other ground-floor guest room has a private front entrance, a queen bed draped overhead with silk taffeta, a sleep sofa, and glazed walls. All rooms have cable television, telephones with data ports, and fine toiletries.

The living room is airy and runs the length and width of the town house. Decorated with warm tones and clean lines, it features parquet floors, built-in bookcases, and recessed lighting. It's easy to imagine sipping an evening brandy by the fireplace in cooler months and lingering over the Sunday paper when the room is drenched with morning sunlight. In warmer months guests often relax on the small deck, dotted with flowering plants and jasmine, overlooking other South End town houses. Spending a bit of time on the deck will make you feel like a real insider.

Clarendon Square Bed & Breakfast offers a self-serve Continental breakfast consisting of fruit, sticky buns, dry cereal, juice, and yogurt.

The Eliot

370 Commonwealth Avenue
Boston, MA 02215
617-267-1607
800-443-5468
Fax: 617-536-9114
HotelEliot@aol.com
www.BostBest.com

A European-style suite hotel

Managing director: Dora Z. Ullian. **Accommodations:** 95 one- and two-bedroom suites. **Rates:** $225–$265 for one-bedroom, $375–$450 for two-bedroom; inquire about a few "regular" rooms. **Parking:** Bellman will park at nearby garage. **Restaurant:** Open for breakfast, dinner, and Sunday brunch. **Added:** 9.7% tax. **Credit cards accepted:** All major ones. **Children:** Welcome, under age 16 free in parent's room. **Pets:** Small ones accepted. **Smoking:** Three smoking floors. **Handicap access:** Yes. **Open:** Year-round.

➤ **Descendants of Charles Eliot, one of Harvard University's most re-nowned presidents, built the hotel in 1925 next to the Harvard Club. The brick buildings resemble one another architecturally and share an ornate black iron fence, a hallmark of old Back Bay.**

The Eliot is a gem. From the small, elegant lobby to the typical two-room suites — furnished in English chintz, Queen Anne mahogany, and adorned with botanical prints — the atmosphere is of a small elegant London hotel. But the prices represent the best hotel values in the Hub. The only difference between pricier hotels in Boston and the Eliot is that the Eliot lacks banquet rooms, multiple bars, and any significant public areas. This saves you money, but you'll find the rooms quite similar.

At the turn of the century, the Back Bay had many similar hotels, all now vanished or converted to dormitories or condos. Timing was initially against the Eliot. The last of its genre to be built, it never quite caught on and floundered during the Depression. By 1939, when Nathan Ullian purchased the nine-story property, it was a seedy "residential" hotel. It's been in the family ever since. But since 1990 it has been closely overseen by Arthur and Dora Ullian, who have resurrected it with the conviction that its time has come.

Each suite is comprised of a bedroom and a sitting room separated by French doors. The sitting room includes a desk, fax machine, a wet bar, a couch that converts to a queen-size bed, and a kitchenette with a microwave, and mini-bar. Bathrooms, although small, are dressed with Italian marble walls. Amenities include two televisions, plush terry robes, complimentary shoe shine service, and irons and ironing boards in the rooms. We prefer rooms that face Commonwealth or Massachusetts avenues rather than an interior room. Light sleepers will definitely want an interior room. Corner rooms end in "04."

In mid-1997 Clio opened to exceptional reviews. Contemporary, imaginative California cuisine with light but intense flavors is featured under the direction of chef Ken Oringer, graduate of the Culinary Institute of America. The elegant place has the feel of a European supper club and the noise level is subdued. Brilliant and sublime are adjectives that come to mind when thinking about Ken's food. Although the menu is laden with meat (short ribs are a specialty), we thoroughly enjoyed seared day boat scallops with parsley root, fried parsley and ossetra caviar before moving onto caramelized swordfish "au poivre" with a vegetable confetti. The flavors are intense and the presentation a work of art.

At breakfast, order á la carte or head for the buffet ($15 per person).

At the corner of Massachusetts and Commonwealth avenues, the Eliot is a short walk from Symphony Hall, the Hynes Convention Center, and a subway stop that connects all parts of Boston and Cambridge.

Eliot and Pickett Houses

25 Beacon Street
Boston, MA 02108-2800
617-248-8707
Fax: 617-742-1364
p&e@uua.org

| **Town houses adjacent to the State House** |

Manager: Darrin Morda. **Accommodations:** 20 rooms (18 with private bath). **Rates:** $85–$120 per couple, $140 for 4 people. **Included:** Make your own full breakfast. **Minimum stay:** None. **Added:** Tax is already included. **Credit cards accepted:** MasterCard, Visa. **Children:** Welcome, free under age 12 in parent's room. **Pets:** Not accepted. **Smoking:** Not permitted. **Handicap access:** Yes. **Open:** Year-round.

➤ **The kitchen is always open and the refrigerator stocked for you to make a meal.**

Tucked away on prestigious, leafy Beacon Hill, these two connected town houses are right next to the State House and across from Boston Common, and steps away from the historic Freedom Trail

Unlike a B&B, no one will know when you come and go. Unlike hotels, there is a parlor with a piano, a television and VCR. You'll also find a common iron and ironing board on the second floor and that the house is sometimes used as a base for high school groups visiting Boston. (On our last visit, a well-behaved group occupied most of the house.) Unlike any other accommodation we recommend, you make your own breakfast (eggs, juice, bagels, cereal, and the like) from a well-stocked refrigerator. Staff members will do the dishes. Guests are also welcomed to prepare lunch or dinner if they want, too.

As for the guest rooms, there is relatively little price difference between small and large rooms. All are furnished modestly with reproduction period antiques. Except for the top floor, ceilings are high and rooms spacious. (Rooms on the top floor are cozier; of these, we like room 405, with blue wallpaper and two dormer windows.) All rooms are carpeted and have either a queen bed or two double beds. Room 306 has two four-poster beds and a view from the deck, while room 201 has a view of otherwise hidden Beacon Hill gardens.

The building has a wooden and wrought-iron deck where guests relax and take in the view — the Park Street Church steeple, the Common, and the State House. Fortunately, unlike most of Beacon Hill, the buildings here aren't right on top of each other; the large deck gets plenty of light. It's particularly restful on weekends when there is less commercial traffic in the area.

Fairmont Copley Plaza Hotel

Copley Square
138 St. James Avenue
Boston, MA 02116
617-267-5300
800-527-4727
Fax: 617-267-7668
www.fairmont.com

> **Boston's grande dame in
> the Back Bay**

General manager: John Unwin. **Accommodations:** 318 rooms and 61 suites. **Rates:** $359–$409 in rooms; $680 in suites. **Parking:** $24 overnight, with in and out privileges. **Restaurants:** Open for all three meals. **Added:** 9.7% tax. **Credit cards accepted:** All major ones. **Children:** Under age 18, free in parent's room. **Pets:** Small pets welcome. **Smoking:** Nonsmoking rooms available. **Handicap access:** Yes. **Open:** Year-round.

➤ **Service has perked up since Fairmont took over. If you go out for an early morning jog, don't be surprised to see the doorman waiting for you with a fresh towel and bottle of Evian water.**

It seems only fitting that Fairmont Hotels, purveyors of the country's grandest properties, would purchase this venerable hotel. In late 1996 they immediately embarked on a complete renovation program with a "goal to restore it, not to change things." The magnificent architectural landmark, which dates from 1912, closely resembles New York's Fairmont Plaza both physically and in atmosphere. It's Boston's most palatial hotel, with exterior French and Venetian Renaissance elements.

The public spaces in the Fairmont Copley Plaza represent the true heart of Boston's Back Bay. Its 5,000-square-foot Edwardian marble lobby has a frescoed blue sky ceiling and its ballroom is the most grand. Ornate architectural details are almost taken for granted. All the gold leaf — and there's quite a bit of it — has been touched up.

Over 9½ miles of new drapery fabric was used during the guest room refurbishing. The guest rooms all have vintage 1912 mirrored closets and wall detailing as well as tasteful carpeting and reproduction furniture, mini-bars, marble bathrooms, and luxurious robes. Guests may choose from a variety of room layouts. Many "superior" rooms are actually two-room suites, with daybeds that fold out for children. The hotel also supplies cribs with cuddly stuffed animals, television with special cable channels for children, and a special children's guide to museums, events, and restaurants. Rooms that face Trinity Church get morning sun. About 100 or so rooms have two double beds and wooden shuttered windows with no real view.

As for dining, the Oak Room is a classic steakhouse housed in what many consider one of the grandest hotel dining rooms around. Drapes are opulent, the paneling intricately carved, and the crystal chandelier sparkling. The traditional menu features high-quality, thick, and simply prepared steaks and chops. The kitchen also offers a few requisite fish entrées, which appear almost as an afterthought. Nestled among the seafood appetizers, though, is a clear standout: a cold seafood platter (enough for four people). Order vegetables on the side; the smashed potatoes are great.

In recognition of changing times, the Oak Bar features martinis and a vast humidor of cigars. The raw bar is excellent. The room is richly paneled and dimly lit, with deep leather seats, evoking the feel of an exclusive private club. Copley's offers slightly less formal and less expensive dining on slightly more creative pairings with Mediterranean and New England flair.

Beyond the hotel lies Copley Square, the centerpiece of Boston's Back Bay neighborhood, with blocks of brownstone town houses and the city's smartest galleries and shops. The John Hancock Tower, Boston's highest building at 60 stories, is next door; head to its rooftop observatory for a birds-eye view.

The Four Seasons

200 Boylston Street
Boston, MA 02116
617-338-4400
800-332-3442
Fax: 617-423-2251
www.fshr.com

New England's only five-diamond hotel and restaurant

General manager: Robin A. Brown. **Accommodations:** 288 rooms, 63 suites. **Rates:** $375–$495 in rooms; $535–$3,050 in 1- and 2-bedroom suites; weekend and summer rates available from $249 per night (from $199 over summer holiday weekends). **Parking:** $22 overnight. **Restaurants:** Aujourd'hui open for breakfast and dinner; The Bristol open for lunch, afternoon tea, and dinner. **Added:** 9.7% tax. **Credit cards accepted:** All major ones. **Children:** Special programs; under age 18 free in parent's room. **Pets:** Accepted with prior approval; special pet menu. **Smoking:** One floor for smokers. **Handicap access:** Yes. **Open:** Year-round.

➤ **The Bristol Lounge features a decadent, old-world Viennese dessert buffet on Friday and Saturday evenings. For $7 per person you can choose two desserts (and unlimited chocolate-dipped strawberries) from more than a dozen luscious treats. As you sip your decaf cappuccino, a fine jazz combo plays softly in the background. The after-theater crowd adores this place, so try to arrive before 10:30 P.M.**

Less formal and much newer (1985) than the Ritz, the Four Seasons is also more welcoming, less stuffy. The atmosphere is coolly contemporary despite the crystal chandelier in the porte cochere and the grand staircase.

The Four Seasons excels because of its seamless attention to details and service. Note the lighting in the marble lobby: it's masterful. There isn't a seat or spot that's not perfectly lit. Furthermore, it's electronically controlled and adapts to the time of day and changing seasons.

With a warm assurance that he is happy to see you, the doorman whisks your luggage away. The bellhop carefully outlines all the facilities, which include a spectacular eighth-floor pool (with a view of Beacon Hill and the Public Garden and "disposable paper bathing suits" in case you forgot yours) and a full spa with amenities. Other services include 24-hour room service, a knowledgeable concierge, overnight shoeshine, one-hour pressing, a courtesy town car, and valet. In fact, we never encountered a staff member who wasn't eager to pamper us, to know if we were enjoying ourselves.

Service at the hotel is, in a word, superb. And isn't that what you're paying for — personal attention that isn't overbearing? After all, there's only so much a hotel can do with bedding. (Rest assured, though, that the Four Seasons takes bedding to the ultimate, too.) The majority of guests agree: the Four Seasons Boston consistently ranks at the top of worldwide polls.

If you want to stay here, do it right and book a room overlooking the Public Garden. Although there are more expensive rooms, a Four Seasons Executive Suite is as luxurious as you need to go: the bedroom is separated by French doors from an elegant sitting room with a table by the window (perfect for breakfast). Of course, there's a wet bar, fresh flowers, bottled water, windows that open, and a marble bathroom with a hair dryer, terry robe (in children's sizes, too), and fine toiletries. As you'd expect, rooms are exquisitely furnished.

Aujourd'hui is one of our two favorite Boston dining rooms. It boasts a terrifically loyal following who rely on its consistency, warm service, elegance, and sumptuous atmosphere. It is spacious, richly paneled in oak, and decorated with beveled mirrors, oil paintings, and old prints. A contemporary American cuisine is presented by Executive Chef David Fritchey, who joined this Four Seasons in late 1995. Dishes are refined and delicate, very subtly (sometimes too subtly) flavored.

On our last visit we indulged in the tasting menu ($70 per person; the vegetarian is $52 per person), featuring six masterfully presented dishes, each deftly described. A Grand Marnier soufflé, ordered at the beginning of the three-hour meal, provided a sublime finale. The combination of luxurious ambiance, artful food, and solicitous service makes for an exquisite dining experience. Request a table with a view of the Public Garden.

In the attractive Bristol Lounge off the lobby, a less expensive menu is available for both lunch and dinner. The burgers win awards here. Intimate seating arrangements, a fireplace, and afternoon and evening jazz make this a coveted meeting spot.

With the exception of Aujourd'hui, the hotel is comfortably informal. Even children and pets are made welcome. The hotel has anticipated every need a parent or child could think of: babysitters and videotapes are available to amuse youngsters, who can eat in their room while their parents dine in style. And as for the family pet, if you bring them along, the hotel will spoil them so much that you may never hear the end of it.

The Four Seasons is within walking distance of both the Back Bay and downtown shopping districts.

Hotel Meridien

250 Franklin Street
Boston, MA 02110
617-451-1900
800-543-4300
Fax: 617-423-2844
meridien@lemeridien.com
www.lemeridien.com

> **Outstanding French cuisine with impeccable service**

Manager: Serge Denis. **Accommodations:** 304 rooms, 22 suites. **Rates:** $305-$375 in rooms; $475-$1300 in suites; weekend rates available from $189. Parking: $13 weekends, $26 weekdays. Restaurants: Julien open for lunch and dinner; Cafe Fleuri open for all three meals and Sunday brunch. **Added:** 9.7% tax. **Credit cards accepted:** All major ones. **Children:** Welcome; additional children's room is $89. **Pets:** Small animals accommodated. **Smoking:** Seven floors for nonsmokers. **Handicap access:** Yes. **Open:** Year-round.

➤ **The lavish Sunday brunch buffet — the best in Boston — is wonderfully overwhelming. For $41 per person, you can choose from eight food stations, with many dishes made-to-order: omelets, crêpes, desserts, sushi, stir fry, spa cuisine, and seafood.**

Hotel Meridien is housed in Boston's former Federal Reserve Bank, a 1920s Renaissance Revival structure of granite and limestone modeled on a Roman palazzo. It opened as a hotel in 1981 after three more floors and a glass mansard roof had been added, as well as a six-story atrium and sloping glass walls in many guest rooms. Despite its size, it conveys the ambiance of a small European hotel.

When it was purchased in mid-1997 by Hong Kong investors, the price set an all-time record for the Boston market, a sure sign of how tight the city's occupancy rate is.

Each of the guest rooms, all light and modern, were refurbished during an extensive $5.5 million renovation in 1995. Because most of them were carved from former office space, they come in more than 150 different sizes and shapes. Lanvin toiletries, roses in the bathroom, chocolate truffles, slippers, and tomorrow's weather forecast are among the niceties. Bathrooms are of marble and granite. Rooms also have live plants, mini-bars, sofas, radios, bathroom scales, hair dryers, and telephones. Many of the suites are loft suites with a bathroom on each floor. About one-third of the rooms have sloped glass windows, and many have ceilings that are 16 feet high. Our favorite rooms overlook the loveliest small park in the city, Post Office Square.

With 20-foot vaulted ceilings edged in gold leaf, Julien is one of the most stylish and gracious dining rooms in the city. It has the feel of a very elegant courtyard with plushly upholstered wing chairs. The food is a perfect blend of contemporary and traditional French fare, overseen by Chef Dominique Rizzo. The service is impeccable and the waitstaff talented, friendly, and knowledgeable.

On our last visit, a puff pastry arrived unannounced, followed by a remarkably light fresh pea soup with lobster essence. A main course of venison with wild mushrooms, spaetzle, and a compote of fruit soared, as did the chocolate truffle (and crème brûlée that arrived unannounced). Hotel guests receive 25 percent off the food portion of lunch or dinner at Julien, an offer you shouldn't pass up. Hotel guests can also take advantage of the weekday business lunch for $26.

The award-winning Julien Lounge is a truly luxurious space with coffered ceilings and N. C. Wyeth murals on paneled walls. Since the mid-1980s, classically trained Jeffery Moore has played the piano here.

The less formal Café Fleuri, housed in a soaring atrium, is the perfect setting for morning croissants, the renowned Sunday buffet brunch, light dinners, and the all-you-can-eat, decidedly decadent Saturday Chocolate Bar Dessert Buffet. It's offered from September through May for $15.50 per adult, half price for children. A few of the 25 exotic selections might include chocolate mint roulade, Grand Marnier mousse, and chocolate orange brioche.

Families weekending at the Meridien will find milk and cookies upon check-in, an array of toys and games from the concierge, and a special food section ("Kid's Corner") at the buffet brunch. These are just a few of the amenities included.

Guests can enjoy Le Club Meridien, a third-floor sports facility with a lap pool, a Jacuzzi, aerobic exercise equipment, and a sauna.

The Meridien has an unusually large staff (330 for 326 rooms), and you can't help but notice. In the heart of the Financial District, the hotel caters to businesspeople during the week, but on weekends, tourists account for half of the clientele. The hotel is just two blocks from Faneuil Hall and the waterfront.

Newbury Guest House

261 Newbury Street
Boston, MA 02116
617-437-7666
Fax: 617-262-4243

Good value on a tony street

Owner: Nubar Hagopian. **Accommodations:** 32 rooms (all with private bath). **Rates:** $95–$130 per couple; $10 parking. **Included:** Continental breakfast. **Minimum stay:** 2–3 nights on weekends and special events. **Added:** 9.7% tax. **Credit cards accepted:** All major ones. **Children:** Welcome. **Pets:** Not accepted. **Smoking:** Permitted. **Handicap access:** Yes. **Open:** Year-round.

➤ **There are a dozen restaurants on this block of Newbury Street alone!**

Built as a private residence in 1882 in Boston's most fashionable neighborhood, these three brick and brownstone buildings offer perhaps the best value in Boston. Reserve early; many people know a good thing when they see it and repeat business is high. Newbury Guest House offers a rare combination: the price is right, the location is even better, the property is historic. What more could you want? As the manager said to us, "The sum of the whole is worth more than the parts."

Although guest rooms are not as ornate as they once were, still visible are 19th-century details like plaster ceilings, carved mantles, and bay windows. Furnishings are relatively modest but all the right reproduction pieces are there: reading chairs and lamps, perhaps a sleigh bed if you're lucky, a love seat, and a table. There's plenty of space to spread out. A Continental breakfast buffet is laid out in the lobby/living room.

Rooms have televisions mounted on the wall and have either central air conditioning or an individual thermostat. And even though the rooms are all quite similar, that won't keep us from recommending a specific room: room 209. We like its ornate marble mantle, original woodwork and wainscoting, hardwood floors, and a set of tables and chairs overlooking Newbury Street. Or you may wish to ask for one of the eight "Bay Window Rooms," which allow sunlight from three directions. Rooms on the second floor have higher ceilings than rooms on higher floors, and thus feel more spacious. Rooms on the fourth floor were former servants' quarters and are a bit smaller. One of the bigger decisions you'll have to make is whether you want to face bustling Newbury Street or the big and open back parking lot, which tends to be quieter.

There are only 10 parking spaces for 32 rooms, so you'll want to reserve one early.

The Regal Bostonian Hotel

Faneuil Hall Marketplace
Boston, MA 02109
617-523-3600
800-343-0922
Fax: 617-523-2454
www.regal-hotels.com/boston

A small luxury hotel next to Faneuil Hall

Managing director: Robert Rivers. **Accommodations:** 140 rooms, 12 suites. **Rates:** $245–$375 in rooms; $500–$775 in 1- and 2-bedroom suites; less in January, February, and March; weekend packages include breakfast. **Parking:** $22 overnight. **Restaurant:** Open for all three meals. **Added:** 9.7% tax. **Credit cards accepted:** All major ones. **Children:** Under age 12, free in parent's room. **Pets:** Not accepted. **Smoking:** One floor available for nonsmokers. **Handicap access:** Yes. **Open:** Year-round.

➤ **Over the years the kitchen has spawned some of the city's most creative chefs, including Jasper White, Lydia Shire, Gordon Hammersley, and Tony Ambrose. Michael Taylor is now in charge, and if history is a guide, you'll want to keep an eye out for him.**

The Bostonian, as much a sophisticated inn as a fine city hotel, is Boston's smallest luxury hotel. Across from Boston's historic commercial district, the hotel blends well with its neighbors. Part of the Blackstone Block, the city's oldest block dating to the late 1600s, the hotel incorporates two historic buildings in a predominantly modern structure. During construction, the developers and archaeologists uncovered remnants of a circa 1675 waterfront development. Glass walkways between the two buildings allow guests to peer down onto a narrow cobblestone passageway, one of the oldest in Boston. Business travelers appreciate its proximity to

Government Center and downtown; vacationers appreciate its proximity to Faneuil Hall and Quincy Market.

Guests enter the red brick building through a porte cochere and a circular cobblestone driveway. Luggage is taken directly to the guest rooms via a service elevator. Inside, the lobby combines traditional and contemporary elements to create the intimate feeling found in small private clubs and guest houses. For instance, a roaring fire and bowls of apples await guests in the winter. There isn't a typical registration counter, either; transactions are conducted discreetly from a mahogany desk.

A glass elevator connects the lobby with the hotel's multi-level, atrium-like restaurant, Seasons. Enclosed by glass and a stainless steel arched ceiling (sunglasses are given out at breakfast when it's necessary), Seasons offers an expansive view of Faneuil Hall Marketplace. The regional-American menu changes four times a year — with the seasons — and emphasizes native ingredients. Seasons's extensive wine list is exclusively American. Prices are reasonable for fine hotel dining: on our last visit, three courses were offered for $39.

Four color schemes and two types of furnishings are used in the guest rooms. Those in the new sections of the hotel are contemporary, while a more traditional approach (country French) has been taken in the historic Harkness Wing. We prefer rooms in the Harkness Wing, where the hallways zigzag and corners don't always form right angles. Many of these rooms have beamed ceilings; a few, surprisingly, have a working fireplace.

Most of the rooms have French windows opening onto small balconies with wrought-iron railings and flower boxes filled with seasonal plantings. Most suites have a Jacuzzi, many have oversize oval tubs, and all have VCRs and terrycloth robes. Other complimentary touches include a morning newspaper at the door as well as overnight shoeshine.

The Bostonian doesn't have a health club, but there is an excellent Nautilus facility — with great views of the city — just two blocks away. Six guest rooms have stationary bicycles in them, and at press time, the hotel was considering a fleet of movable exercise machines that could be delivered to guest rooms on request.

At press time, the hotel was undergoing an expansion, adding additional rooms in response to the tight hotel market in Boston.

The Ritz-Carlton Boston

15 Arlington Street
Boston, MA 02117
617-536-5700
800-241-3333
Fax: 617-536-9340

A timeless Boston tradition across from the Public Garden

General manager: Henri Boubee. **Accommodations:** 278 rooms, 48 suites. **Rates:** $260–$395 in rooms; $320–$415 in Club Rooms; $345–$2,000 in 1- and 2-bedroom suites; various packages, including one with tickets to the Boston Ballet's Nutcracker. **Parking:** $22 overnight, with in and out privileges. **Restaurants:** Open for all three meals and afternoon tea. **Added:** 9.7% tax. **Credit cards accepted:** All major ones. **Children:** No charge for 1 extra person in room. **Pets:** Smaller pets welcome. **Smoking:** Floors for nonsmokers. **Handicap access:** Yes. **Open:** Year-round.

➤ **From 1933 to 1946 (when the rooftop closed after hurricane damage) guests dined and danced under the stars to the likes of Benny Goodman, Tommy Dorsey, and Artie Shaw. The Roof reopened in 1993, reviving the spirit of the era with a seven-piece orchestra, fine dining, and magnificent Public Garden views. Inquire about seasonal "Night on the Roof" packages.**

"We are not merely surrounded by traditions, we have become one," boasts the Ritz-Carlton's promotional material. It's true. Guests who choose the Ritz appreciate its formal atmosphere and dress code, top-hatted doormen, and international renown. Inspired by the famed Ritz hotels of Europe, this 16-story hotel was built in 1927. An addition, which includes fifty-two condominiums, was completed in 1981. Inside the hotel, it is extremely difficult to distinguish between the two.

The new rooms certainly have the same careful detailing found in the original ones. But the newer bathrooms are roomier and modern; the old ones (refaced in Vermont marble) have their original porcelain fixtures. All the rooms are large, with windows that open, closets that lock, a safe, an honor bar, and umbrellas. Rooms are decorated with French provincial furnishings; suites are furnished with mahogany pieces.

Suites are the most handsome accommodations, with their elegant mirrored mantels (the Ritz has forty-two fireplaces) and fine antique breakfronts, desks, and sofas. Most have fine views, either of the Public Garden or the rooftops of fashionable Newbury Street. On the uppermost floors, exclusive Ritz-Carlton Club accommodations include private butler and concierge services. Club guests are welcome to relax in the Club Lounge and enjoy complimentary food and beverages.

The elevators are run by white-gloved operators, who keep track of the comings and goings of guests. One-third of the hotels 550 employees have been here for more than five years (some since the 1940s).

The second-floor Dining Room is formal (a jacket and tie required in this placed of hushed propriety), with tall mullioned windows overlooking the Public Garden. Continental cuisine is served under Chef Auguste Escoffier's influences. Dover sole, lobster au whiskey, and Chateaubriand are a few of the timeless offerings. This is one of the few restaurants that prepares Caesar salad at your table and it's a real treat. Newer, innovative dishes change seasonally. Tables are set with heavy silver and the hotels trademark cobalt blue goblets; a pianist accompanies dinner.

The Lounge (with no windows), a gathering place rather like a drawing room, is popular for tea. Tea at the Ritz, if you haven't heard, is a tradition enjoyed by generations of Bostonians and visitors. A harpist entertains here. On weekends, the Lounge hosts a jazz trio, a perfect complement to an after drink cordial.

On the ground floor, the Cafe is a less formal place for breakfast and lunch. In mid-1997 "celebrity chef" Mark Allen came on the scene offering creative Mediterranean cuisine with a California slant. Still, old standbys like chicken pot pie and lobster salad cannot be taken off the menu. It seems fresh and promising; it certainly has livened up the place. Stick to the classic rather than overly fancy dessert choices. The Bar, a popular meeting and lunch spot, has the look and feel of a private club, complete with rich paneling and a fireplace.

For families and children, the hotel offers strollers, cribs, coloring books in all the restaurants, and a Junior Presidential Suite outfitted with everything a child could want ($600 for up to five people). A Day of Social Savvy, an etiquette program for children aged 8 to 12, is occasionally offered.

A full range of health and fitness facilities, ice skates (to use on the pond in the Public Garden), and a chauffeured limousine (for morning appointments) round out the amenities of this full-service hotel. Guests also have complimentary access to the a nearby spa.

Cambridge

The Charles Hotel

One Bennett Street
Cambridge, MA 02138
617-864-1200
800-882-1818
Fax: 617-864-5715

> **Dazzling dining and a high-class hotel catering to Harvard VIPs**

General manager: Brian Fitzgerald. **Accommodations:** 252 rooms and 44 suites. **Rates (from April through June and from September through November):** $229–$309 in rooms; $429–$589 in suites; weekend packages. **Parking:** $16 overnight, with in and out privileges. **Restaurants:** Rialto open for dinner; Henrietta's Table open for all three meals. **Added:** 9.7% tax. **Credit cards accepted:** All major ones. **Children:** Welcome; free under 18. **Pets:** Accepted. **Smoking:** Three floors for nonsmokers. **Handicap access:** Yes. **Open:** Year-round.

➤ **The intimate Regattabar, popular among young professionals and jazz aficionados, attracts top national and international talent Tuesday through Saturday evenings. Jazz acts range from beboppers to traditional instrumentalists to Brazilian bossa novas.**

Built in 1985 of red brick to match Harvard's buildings and the sidewalks of Cambridge, the Charles caters largely to Harvard's visiting academics, benefactors, alumni, friends, and international VIPs. Its many large windows showcase river views, the university, and its own attractive courtyard. (Ask for a room above the 6th floor for the best vistas. Rates do not more expensive as you go higher.) With a late check-out time of 1:00 P.M., guests can enjoy the Harvard Square shops, restaurants, bookstores, and bustling street life that much longer.

Inside the hotel, walls are adorned with paintings of Cambridge and lovely quilts (there is a different pattern on each floor). The square, modern lines of the public rooms are set off nicely by New England country antiques.

Guest rooms are furnished with blond Shaker-style furniture. Triple sheeting, down quilts, terrycloth robes, slippers, and toiletries are luxurious. All rooms have three telephones, two cable TVs (one in the bathroom and one in an armoire), Bose Wave Radio/alarm clocks, and windows that open. The morning a newspaper is left outside your door.

Other amenities include a children's storyline on your phone and 24-hour room service, featuring an array of hors d'oeuvres, full dinners, and late snacks. (This is particularly appreciated by the hotels jetlagging international clientele.) Books can be delivered to your room from Words-worth Books in the Square. The concierge is helpful and knowledgeable.

The hotel's two restaurants have loyal followings other places can only aspire to. Nationally-renown chef Jody Adams and restaurateur Michela Larson are the creative forces behind the wildly successful Rialto. We've never talked to anyone who's regretted loosening their purse strings here. Make reservations early. The Euro-chic restaurant has drawn the highest accolades from the moment it opened in late 1994. The Mediterranean menu (which always features a highly creative vegetarian selection such as grilled asparagus and tomatoes on coarse polenta with morels and toasted walnut crumbs) changes with the season. It is always executed with utmost precision and flair, and features "intensely flavored, honest and straightforward [cooking], with respect for tradition, seasons, and local ingredients." The presentation is itself an art form, and service is, as you'd expect, professional yet friendly. Leave room for dessert! The breadth and depth of the wine list is impressive and the waitstaff adept at pairing food with drink. Even if you can't stay at the Charles, this is the one of two hotel restaurants worth seeking out.

For more casual dining, Henrietta's Table (opened in early 1995) is part farmer's market, part microbrewery, part New England country kitchen. The menu features hearty regional fare, emphasizing local farm produce. The dining room, with white wainscoting, old-fashioned cupboards, high beamed ceiling, and oak floors, resembles an open country kitchen. Dishes are well-priced and the whole experience represents a good value. The extensive Sunday brunch buffet ($40) is quite popular.

After all this fine dining, guests will enjoy complimentary use of the Wellbridge Health & Fitness Center, with a rooftop pool, Jacuzzi, sauna, cardiovascular equipment, and various weight machine systems. Offering a variety of fee structures, Le Pli Day Spa concentrates on beauty services, including facials, massages, body wraps, and a hair salon.

The Inn at Harvard

1201 Massachusetts Avenue
Cambridge, MA 02138
617-491-2222
800-458-5886
Fax: 617-491-6520
rcarbone@theinnatharvard

> **Part Italianate palazzo, part contemporary Georgian-style hotel**

General manager: Richard Carbone. **Accommodations:** 109 rooms, 4 suite. **Rates:** $199–$279 per room from April through November; $169–$199 mid-December to mid-March. Minimum stay: 3 nights during Harvard's commencement and some special event weekends. **Parking:** $20. Restaurant: Open for breakfast and dinner. **Added:** 9.7% tax. **Credit cards accepted:** All major ones. **Children:** Under age 18, free in parents room. **Pets:** Not accepted. **Smoking:** Third floor for nonsmokers. **Handicap access:** Yes. **Open:** Year-round.

➤ **The inn also owns the Harvard Manor House in Harvard Square and recently completely upgraded and renovated it. Inquire about rates. Both hotels are expertly managed by Doubletree Hotels.**

Just four short blocks east of Harvard Square, The Inn at Harvard is geared to and owned by Harvard University. But the inn appeals to anyone who appreciates understated elegance. Designed by Graham Gund Associates, the four-story brick building, like much of the Square, was inspired by the many Georgian Revival buildings on campus.

A dramatic common space, the Atrium, serves as the hotels living and dining room. By day the courtyard-like space is infused with soft, natural light from above; by night its peach-toned walls are romantically lit with candles and dim lamps. Bookcases, filled with literature you'd expect to find in a Harvard professors summer cottage (many volumes are published by Harvard University

Press), line one wall. The multihued walls are set off by handsome cherrywood moldings and arches.

Handsome cherrywood tables for four, some doubling as game tables, flank two sides of the room. In between are comfortable groupings of sofas, wingbacked chairs, and marble-topped tables. At meals, the tables are covered with white linen. For breakfast, an extensive European buffet is available in addition to Ö la carte items like Belgian waffles with fresh berries and oatmeal scones. The dinner menu features regional New England dishes such as roasted rack of lamb, poached salmon, grilled scallops with a warm bacon dressing, and Caesar salad. Vegetarian dishes are also popular.

In the guest rooms, the beds and armoires are carved from the same cherrywood found in the Atrium. All of them have large windows that open, a writing table, and original art. You'll appreciate the iron and ironing board and complimentary morning newspaper. The bathrooms, with night lights, are done in cool gray and white. Some rooms overlook the Old Cambridge Baptist Church, some have balconies facing Harvard Square, and others have French doors that open into the Atrium. Room service is available during meal times only.

The affiliations with Harvard are readily apparent: there is direct access to the university telephone system, and guests may eat lunch at the Faculty Club and charge it to their hotel bill. The hotel is also geared to business travelers; each room has a computer modem hookup and voice mail.

The Mary Prentiss Inn

6 Prentiss Street
Cambridge, MA 02140
617-661-2929
Fax: 617-661-5989
germno@aol.com

> **An eclectically furnished B&B**

Innkeepers: Jennifer and Nicholas Fandetti. **Accommodations:** 20 rooms and suites (all with private bath). **Rates:** $99–$159 per couple in winter and spring; $139–$229 in summer and fall. **Included:** Full breakfast. Minimum stay: 2 nights on some weekends. **Parking:** Available (and free) for 11 cars with reservation. Added: 9.7% tax. **Credit cards accepted:** All major ones. **Children:** Welcome; $25 each additional person in same room. **Pets:** Not accepted. **Smoking:** Not permitted. **Handicap access:** Yes. **Open:** Year-round.

➤ **Nearby you'll find one-of-a-kind boutiques and eateries that were once the hallmark of Harvard Square (now overly commercial with national shops).**

The Mary Prentiss Inn is located on a quiet residential street just off Massachusetts Avenue, a 10-minute walk from Harvard Square. Prior to 1990 when the building was converted in to a B&B, it had been a run-down former boarding house and a nursing home. Nicholas Fandetti's parents spent two years completely refurbishing the house, and in 1995 received a Historic Commission Preservation Award for their efforts.

Architecturally speaking, the house is a neoclassical Greek Revival beauty, complete with a front porch, fluted columns, and Ionic capitals. A two-story addition complements the main house and is connected by a second-story bridge that allows guests to use the same front door and appreciate the magnificent open, curved stairway.

Most of the stylish guest rooms are decorated with soothing fabrics and colorful chintzes. (One reader did write to complain about a particular two-room suite that combined striped wallpaper with floral designs.) All have a smattering of 19th-century antiques — perhaps a sleigh bed, cannonball post bed, Windsor chairs, or armoires. Some of the country-style furniture is intentionally "distressed," which gives it an antique look.

We prefer the two new rooms off the deck and guest rooms in the original 1843 house. The two newest rooms are designed like a coach house and have ten-foot ceilings, a working fireplace, and a whirlpool bath. French doors open onto the communal deck. This is a wonderful set-up in the summer except when you might have to close the curtains mid-day for privacy. Back in the main house, specifically we like the rooms with high ceilings and original wooden shutters.

Some rooms are more sunny than others, with a southerly exposure; some are darker and cozier. Beds are made with cotton linens, comforters, and lots of fluffy pillows. All the bathrooms and shower/tubs are tiled — many with period black and white tiles or Charlotte Forsythe's (Nicholas's mother) artsy designs. (Unfortunately the shower curtains are of the institutional plastic variety.) Modern conveniences include telephones, televisions, air conditioning, and a writing desk; most rooms have a refrigerator. The B&B has a fair number of twin-bedded rooms for parents and teenagers who are checking out Harvard University, right down the street.

A full breakfast and afternoon tea is served at individual tables in the small dining room, but if you're lucky you'll get one of the two tables in the conservatory.

In warm weather many guests prefer the walled outdoor deck, filled with fragrant potted herbs, container-grown vines, and colorful annuals. Because of its southerly exposure, the deck remains comfortably warm and sunny well into the autumn.

The only drawback we see concerns a substantiated report from a reader that service is less than perfect — an urgent phone message not delivered until the next day, for instance. As long as you're aware this may be the case and you prepare for it, you'll enjoy your stay.

Royal Sonesta Hotel

5 Cambridge Parkway
Cambridge, MA 02142
617-491-3600
Fax: 617-661-5956
800-766-3782

| **The best views of Boston** |

General manager: Alfred Groos. Accommodations: 371 rooms, 29 suites. Rates: $240–$270 in rooms; $335–$750 in 1-, 2-, and 3-bedroom suites; seasonal packages. Parking: $16 overnight, with in and out privileges. Restaurant: Open for all three meals. Added: 9.7% tax. Credit cards accepted: All major ones. Children: Under age 17 free in parents room. Pets: Not accepted. Smoking: Restricted in public places; 8 floors for nonsmokers. Handicap access: Yes. Open: Year-round.

➤ **The Sonesta makes an unusual effort to woo summer vacationers, especially families. Reasonable summer packages often include boat rides on the Charles River, the use of bicycles and Polaroid cameras (Polaroid's head-quarters is next door), and organized spa activities, not to mention all the ice cream you can eat.**

The Sonesta's location is both its beauty and its weakness. The beauty, of course, is the view: directly across the Charles River to Beacon Hill and the downtown high-rises and up the curve of the river along Back Bay. This is, moreover, one view in which guests can participate, strolling or jogging along the riverside promenade. The Museum of Science and MIT are within walking distance, and the Cambridgeside Galleria, the city's newest shopping mall, is just across the street. Still, the Sonesta is not in the thick of things like other hotels in Boston or Harvard Square. The green line of the subway, though, is just one block away. The hotel provides a courtesy van, which runs frequently from 7:00 A.M. to 10:00 P.M. daily, to Harvard Square and points of interest in Boston.

This particular Sonesta is the jewel of an international hotel chain based in Boston. Its two 200-room towers one built in the 1960s, the other in the 1980s are connected by a bright, attractive lobby and other public areas, including two restaurants and a bar. A spectacular pool with a retractable roof and outside sunning area is in the East Tower, which also houses a full compliment of fitness machines and full-service spa facilities.

The guest rooms in the old tower have been renovated to match those in the new one. While not particularly large, they are deftly decorated in soothing colors, and each holds a piece of art from the Sonestas contemporary collection. Downstairs the halls are enlivened with works by such artists as Andy Warhol, Jasper Johns, and Roy Lichtenstein. Many of the most interesting paintings and prints are by lesser known local artists.

Davio's, the hotel's dining room, is actually an offshoot of one of the city's prime Italian restaurants, specializing in dishes like pollo al ripieno (roast chicken, garlic, Bel Paese stuffing, and sherry tomato sauce). The decor is art deco and the view downriver. The indoor/outdoor Gallery Cafe and Patio, overlooking the Charles River, and surrounded by contemporary art, serves classic American fare.

Cape Cod
and the Islands

Best Bed-and-Breakfasts

Best Family Finds

Martha's Vineyard, Menemsha
Menemsha Inn and Cottages, 286
Provincetown
The Masthead Resort, 304
Truro
Kalmar Village, 312
Wellfleet
Cahoon Hollow Bed & Breakfast, 314
West Dennis
The Lighthouse Inn, 316

Best Gourmet Getaways

Brewster
Chillingsworth, 260
Martha's Vineyard, Edgartown
The Charlotte Inn, 276
Nantucket
The Wauwinet, 299

Best Grand Resorts

Chatham
Chatham Bars Inn, 264
Wequassett Inn, 266
Martha's Vineyard, Edgartown
The Harbor View Resort, 279
Nantucket
The Wauwinet, 299

Best Inns

Martha's Vineyard, Edgartown
The Charlotte Inn, 276
Martha's Vineyard, Gay Head
Outermost Inn, 284
Martha's Vineyard, West Tisbury
Lambert's Cove Country Inn, 291

Best Romantic Getaways

The most famous resort area in Massachusetts is, of course, Cape Cod, and the islands of Nantucket and Martha's Vineyard. The Cape is known for its beaches, (relatively) warm water, and quaint villages. Its charm is in small, delicate details: a spray of beachgrass anchored in the shifting sand, a tern nesting in the salt marsh, a mosaic of cranberries bobbing on the surface of a flooded bog. If tranquillity is what you're after, the trick — given the region's popularity and the two narrow bridges connecting it to the rest of Massachusetts — is to head to the Cape midweek to avoid traffic. If you come in July and August, try to avoid arriving on Friday afternoon or evening, when half of Boston seems to have the same idea.

Cape Cod's regional terminology can be confusing if you think in strict north-south terms. The Outer Cape, also known as the Lower Cape, is the top of the Cape, toward Provincetown. The Mid-Cape is self-explanatory. The Upper Cape is the area closest to mainland Massachusetts.

One logical way to explore is to head east on Route 6A, the scenic alternative to the Mid-Cape Highway (Route 6). Route 6A takes you past the colder waters of the less commercial bay side, the historic towns of **Sandwich, Barnstable, Yarmouthport,** and **Dennis.** On the south side, the heavily trafficked Route 28 links the resort towns of **Falmouth** and **Hyannis** to **Chatham,** a regal old resort village at the Cape's knobby elbow. The waters on this side are warmed by Nantucket Sound.

North of Orleans and on through the quiet villages of **Eastham, Truro,** and **Wellfleet,** the National Seashore beaches reign supreme. **Provincetown,** at the Cape's outer tip, is an old fishing port with a lively gay and straight summer scene as well as fine restaurants, art galleries, and shops that make it a year-round destination. In the summer, a daily ferry service links Provincetown directly with Boston.

Nantucket and **Martha's Vineyard** are reached by ferries from Woods Hole (near Falmouth) and Hyannis. Always popular in summertime, the island's high tourist season has extended in recent years to include September and October.

Barnstable

Beechwood

2839 Main Street (Route 6A)
Barnstable, MA 02630
508-362-6618
800-609-6618
Fax: 508-362-0298
bwdinn@virtualcapecod.com
www.virtualcapecod.com/market/beechwood/

| **A romantic, Victorian B&B** |

Innkeepers: Debbie and Ken Traugot. **Accommodations:** 6 doubles (all with private bath). **Rates:** $125–$160 per couple from May through October; $90–$130 off-season. **Included:** Full breakfast. **Minimum stay:** 2 nights on summer weekends. **Added:** 9.7% tax. **Credit cards accepted:** All major ones. **Children:** Over age 12 welcome; $20 additional person. **Pets:** Not accepted. **Smoking:** Not permitted indoors. **Handicap access:** No. **Open:** Year-round.

➤ **The wonderful wraparound porch, with rockers and a glider, is shaded by ancient copper and beech trees (hence the inn's name).**

Beechwood, a many-gabled, many-eaved Victorian summer home from the 1850s, has been meticulously restored with a sure decorator's touch. Each guest room has been created rather than merely furnished. For a quiet retreat or a romantic interlude, you won't be disappointed.

Debbie and Ken came onboard the former shipwright's house in 1994, infusing the inn with new energy. In warm weather there is plenty of outdoor space including the verandah and the expansive backyard with lovely gardens.

Although decorated in a high Victorian style, all guest rooms are light and airy. The Rose Room has a high, carved canopy bed, a fireplace, and floor-to-ceiling shuttered windows. The Marble Room has a brass bed, lace curtains, a garden view, and a marble fireplace. Both rooms have large bathrooms that combine modern convenience with antique elegance.

On the second floor, Eastlake has two double spoon-carved beds and stained glass windows. Soft light filters through Cottage, a room furnished with 1860s handpainted cottage furniture registered with the Smithsonian. The lavender walls here complement the colored panes of glass (a yellow-purple). The Lilac Room is country Victorian, with a king-size and single bed; its bath has a clawfoot tub and brass fixtures. The Garret Room, on the third floor, is our favorite, with steeply angled paneled walls and a half-moon window. Its bath, down a short flight of stairs, has a double sink and a black and white tile floor. In the summer, warm breezes stir the lace curtains next to a writing table. In case you couldn't tell, we highly recommend all the rooms. A few rooms are air-conditioned.

A full country breakfast is served at small tables in the dining room, complete with tin ceilings and tongue-and-groove pine paneling. After breakfast, you can play a game of badminton or head to the seven-mile-long barrier beach at Sandy Neck.

Charles Hinckley House

P.O. Box 723
Route 6A
Barnstable, MA 02630
508-362-9924
Fax: 508-362-8861

An authentically restored, gracious B&B

Innkeepers: Les and Miya Patrick. **Accommodations:** 3 rooms (all with private bath), 1 suite. **Rates:** $119–$149 per couple. **Included:** Full breakfast. **Minimum stay:** 2 nights on weekends. **Added:** 9.7% tax. **Credit cards accepted:** None. **Children:** Not accepted. **Pets:** Not accepted. **Smoking:** Not permitted. **Handicap access:** No. **Open:** Year-round.

➤   **Miya is a wonderfully talented cook and a highly sought-after caterer. Breakfast will be satisfying to both the eye and the palate.**

While other inns have added Jacuzzis, gas fireplaces, televisions, and air conditioning, the Charles Hinckley House has remained wonderfully authentic and true to its roots. But that doesn't mean it's stuck in the 18th century, either. Its restored rooms and hospitality harken to a simpler era, a quieter time. You can't help but appreciate it for encouraging you to slow down. Yes, it's on a busy road (like practically all B&Bs on this side of the Cape), but somehow the wildflower gardens provides an effective barrier to the world beyond.

The Patricks have been at this since the early 1970s. He restores old houses, she's in the catering business. The Hinckley House remains one of our all-time favorites, as appealing off-season as it is in the summer. The Federal house is very much a part of this quiet, history-proud side of Cape Cod.

There are two guest rooms upstairs, both with four-poster beds, quilts, and a fireplace. One has a small sitting room; one has just a tub. Another, in what was once the summer kitchen, has a private entrance. It's cozy, with a raised ceiling, a skylight, white brick walls, a hearth, and comfortable wing chairs as well as an antique brass bed. Done in yellow plaid, the library guest room off the living room is quite romantic.

The small country living room contains more magazines than you could read in a year. Love seats flank the fireplace, two armchairs sit before the front window, and soft music plays quietly in the background. Help yourself to a glass of sherry.

The full breakfast is no ordinary affair. It's a leisurely meal, taken course by course. First comes an urn of Colombian coffee or a pot of special tea, then warm pastries and a delicate fruit plate, perhaps of papaya and sweet raspberries. Then there's a choice of two entrées — perhaps black bean cakes with poached eggs or delicate pancakes with strawberry butter. The meal is served in the old tavernlike dining room at small, intimate tables set with well-worn heavy silverware.

Behind the house is a relaxing brick patio with a little fish pond. Perhaps you'll see daughter Erin and her new golden retriever puppy here.

Brewster

Chillingsworth

P.O. Box 1819
Route 6A
Brewster, MA 02631
508-896-3640
800-430-3640

| **Gourmet French cuisine and European rooms** |

Owners: Nitzi and Pat Rabin. **Accommodations:** 3 rooms (all with private bath). **Rates:** $95–$135 per couple. **Included:** Choice of full or Continental breakfast. **Minimum stay:** None. **Added:** 9.7% tax. **Credit cards accepted:** All major ones. **Children:** Not appropriate. **Pets:** Not accepted. **Smoking:** Not encouraged. **Handicap access:** No. **Open:** Mid-May through Thanksgiving.

➤ **On request, dinner can be served in the gazebo.**

Chillingsworth is widely renowned for its fine cuisine, but few people are aware that there are guest rooms tucked above the dining rooms. These are rented only to dining room patrons. The decor and sensibility of these rooms is as European as the cuisine is first-rate French. There's no doubt, however, that Chillingsworth is first and foremost a dining experience: most guests must pass through intimate dining rooms to reach the second-floor rooms. (You wouldn't want to check in after the first seating laden with packages and luggage.)

The building itself is more than 200 years old, the second oldest in Brewster. Located on scenic and historic Route 6A, the shaded house is set back from the road. The nicest room, the Stevenson room, also happens to be the largest and has its own entrance. It's filled with antiques (and cable television in a nod to the 20th century). The four-poster bed is outfitted with Ralph Lauren bedding. The Foster room is also large, with views of the back garden and gazebo. The Ten Eyck room, although small and without a view, is quite charming nonetheless. All rooms are air-conditioned.

Be sure not to fill up on the complimentary afternoon wine and cheese, served in a part of the dining room that feels rather like a salon-style living room. The seven-course dinner, served at a wonderfully relaxed pace, requires a healthy appetite. It surely won't disappoint you. On our last visit, the prix fixe dinner went like this: oysters and asparagus with spinach in a lemon butter sauce to start, followed by a potato and leek soup with crispy leeks, then a mixed green salad, then a cleansing sorbet. The main dish was seared salmon with orzo, leeks, tomatoes, peas, and a warm mushroom vinaigrette. A delicious apricot and peach soufflé and a cup of espresso rounded out the extravaganza.

For guests who don't want to eat that much, an à la carte bistro menu is offered in the evenings in the more casual greenhouse. À la carte luncheons are less formal but just as creative, including "hot soup of the chef's whim" and "chocolate delight of the moment."

Guests have access to the private bay beach just down the street, reached by a very quick walk. Just a half mile away, the Ocean Edge Resort also offers "executive club" memberships to Chillingsworth guests. This allows you access to tennis, a weight room, indoor and outdoor pools, and the ability to at least attempt getting reservations at their private golf course.

Chatham

The Captain's House Inn of Chatham

371 Old Harbor Road
Chatham, MA 02633
508-945-0127
800-315-0728
Fax: 508-945-0866
capthouse@capecod.net
www.captainshouseinn.com

> **A romantic, early American getaway**

Innkeepers: Jan and Dave McMaster. **Accommodations:** 16 rooms (all with private bath), 3 suites. **Rates:** $135–$325 per couple, May to early November; $125–$275 off-season. **Included:** Full breakfast. **Minimum stay:** 2 nights from June through October; 2 nights on weekends throughout the year. **Added:** 9.7% tax. **Credit cards accepted:** All major ones. **Children:** Over age 12 welcome. **Pets:** Not accepted. **Smoking:** Not permitted. **Handicap access:** No. **Open:** Year-round.

➤ **Guests staying in the Carriage House and Captain's Cottage often enter the inn through the back door and professional kitchen. It makes them feel as if they're staying at a friend's summer place.**

Dave and Jan, who purchased this venerable inn in 1993, have continued its fine tradition of providing guests with good service and warm accommodations. Assisting them in this vast undertaking is a fleet of young English and American women on a hotel management exchange program. They spend the summer overseeing the day-to-day aspects of running the inn, freeing the McMasters to enjoy the more pleasant aspects of innkeeping.

The 1839 Greek Revival house is the centerpiece of a nicely landscaped 2-acre spread. Behind the privacy hedge are broad lawns, ever-expanding perennial gardens, and plenty of places to sit under the shade of grand old trees.

The inn is primarily furnished with Early American pieces, complemented by period wallpaper, wide pumpkin pine floorboards, and Oriental carpets. Although there is only one common room, which also doubles as a waiting area when the breakfast tables are full, it sets the tone: elegant yet warm and welcoming.

Within the main inn one of our favorite rooms is actually one of the smallest: the Cambridge Room, in the rear of the house. It is bright and summery, with windows on three sides and an iron and brass bed. In addition to inn rooms, there are also guest rooms in an adjacent cottage and carriage house, which afford more privacy.

The restored Captain's Cottage, with the original barnboard entry, has three guest rooms. One room is very large (with low ceilings) and features hand-hewn beams, a fireplace, dark paneling, and a lacy white canopy bed with lots of pillows. Another interesting room, Hideaway, is almost split in half by a fireplace; it has low, sloping ceilings and plenty of character.

In 1997 three new luxury rooms were added in the "stables." Each features a whirlpool, TV, VCR, and four-poster canopy bed. The two-room suite (which rents for $325) boasts a fireplace in both the sitting room and bedroom.

The adjoining carriage house is tastefully furnished in modern country style; everything is first class here, too. Room 3, very spacious, has high, beamed ceilings and handsome wing chairs. Like the other carriage house rooms, it has wool carpeting. Throughout the complex, most of the rooms have four-posters or fishnet canopy beds; all beds are triple-sheeted. Bathrooms are tiled — even the shower ceilings — and towels are long and luxurious; the soap, extra thick. Each room has air conditioning and a phone jack.

A full breakfast is served at individual tables in the sunny conservatory-like dining room. Through floor-to-ceiling windows you can look out onto the gardens. In addition to three kinds of coffee, fruit, juices, bagels, raisin toast, and granola, you are also offered a hot entrée (or perhaps a choice of two). On our last visit, it went like this: savory salmon corn cakes, broiled tomato, fruit, and toasted cheese bread. But the goodies don't stop here: afternoon English tea with scones is also offered, as is a welcoming cup of hot chocolate or tea on arrival, and a cookie jar filled with chocolate chip cookies.

Chatham Bars Inn

Chatham, MA 02633
508-945-0096
800-527-4884
Fax: 508-945-5491
www.chathambarsinn.com

| A grand old seaside resort |

General manager: Christopher Diego. **Accommodations:** 40 inn rooms (all with private bath), 110 rooms in 26 cottages, 2 suites. **Rates:** $190–$320 per couple in rooms in season; $280–$675 for cottages. **Included:** No meals, but all meals are available. **Minimum stay:** 2 nights on weekends and holidays; 5 nights in July and August; flexible off-season. **Added:** 9.7% tax, 17% service charge added to food and beverage portion of the bill. **Credit cards accepted:** All major ones. **Children:** Under 5 free in parent's room; special summer program. **Pets:** Not accepted. **Smoking:** Nonsmoking rooms available. **Handicap access:** Yes. **Open:** Year-round.

➤ **A resident horticulturist gives informal talks about the inn's gardens — woodsy areas, a pond garden, a formal English garden, brilliant patches of annuals, and fragrant rose bushes.**

Built in 1914 as a hunting lodge by a wealthy Boston family, the historic oceanfront Chatham Bars Inn now is a full-service resort with fine dining, pampered service (there's a staff of 200 for 400 guests in season), and a variety of accommodations. As befitting a grand landmark of its stature, the Chatham Bars also offers a multitude of on-site activities, a full schedule of daytime sports, and evening entertainment. It's a popular destination for families and couples alike.

The shingled main hotel overlooks an expanse of the placid Pleasant Bay, a sandbar (Chatham Bar — the inn's namesake), and the mighty Atlantic Ocean beyond. You can take it all in from the rattan-furnished flagstone porch, a great place for the morning newspaper and coffee and for afternoon cocktails. The large, formal lobby exudes a style more closely associated with that of a small, luxury hotel than that of a seaside resort. Afternoon drinks are also served in the handsome library, off the airy and sophisticated living room.

There are plenty of dining rooms to suit your moods. The large, exquisite main dining room underwent a transformation in 1995. It now looks much as it did in 1914 — with original wall sconces, brass fixtures, and beautifully detailed ceilings. Entrées like grilled swordfish and roast fillet of beef are served with complementing salads and vegetables. The Tavern is cozy and publike, with a casual menu. The Beach House Grill offers light, informal lunches on the deck. Its beachside location can't be beat! During the summer, lavish buffets are hosted on Sundays, family barbecues on Mondays, and legendary waterside lobster and clambakes on Wednesdays. Picnic lunches can be arranged.

In the main inn, all of the rooms have been recently redecorated and have nicely restored bathrooms. About one-third also have a fireplace. All rooms in the main inn are air-conditioned and most are fairly spacious. Many of them have decks; a number are quite large. One- and two-bedroom cottages are connected to the main inn by pathways lit by authentic gas lanterns. Some waterside cottages have splendid views; others have a shared living room with a TV and fireplace. Since accommodations vary, when booking a room you may want to ask how recently a room has been renovated. You may also want to keep in mind that even the least expensive rooms allow guests access to all the inn's facilities. Or for a real splurge, ask for a description of the two master suites.

Life here can be very simple indeed. A private ocean beach, a heated oceanside pool, and the more remote outer sand bar (easily reached via the hotel's launch) all beckon. There are also four tennis courts, shuffleboard, croquet, and volleyball; several eighteen-hole courses are nearby; and bicycles can be rented. Just a third of a mile from one of Cape Cod's most historic villages, the hotel is close enough to, yet far enough from, the bustle of mid-summer crowds. (The inn offers a complimentary shuttle.)

The resort caters to families with movie nights, bingo nights, and, in the summer, with a complimentary, supervised "Beach Buddies" program for children aged 3½ and older. In addition to morning and afternoon sessions, the evening program includes a special children's dinner for a nominal fee.

Wequassett Inn

Pleasant Bay
Chatham, MA 02633
508-432-5400
800-225-7125
Fax: 508-432-1915
www.wequassett.com

A grand resort set on a tranquil cove

Managing partner: Mark Novota. **Accommodations:** 97 rooms (all with private bath), 6 suites, 1 cottage. **Rates:** $255–$360 per couple in rooms in July and August, $95–$315 off-season; $495 in suites in season, $200–$395 off-season. **Included:** No meals, but all meals are available; inquire about full American plan rates. **Minimum stay:** 2 nights on weekends in July and August. **Added:** 9.7% tax. **Credit cards accepted:** All major ones. **Children:** Welcome, under age 12 stay free in parent's room; $20 each additional adult. **Pets:** Not accepted. **Smoking:** Permitted. **Handicap access:** Yes. **Open:** Mid-April to mid-November.

➤ **One of the four all-weather tennis courts overlooks Pleasant Bay. A resident tennis pro, ranked #1 on the Cape, is on hand for lessons.**

Wequassett means "crescent on the water." This aptly named resort is a beautifully landscaped complex of 20 buildings on 22 acres, with views of both ocean and woods. In existence since 1944, the Wequassett prides itself on excellent service, nationally recognized cuisine, and gracious hospitality.

Each of the cape cottages, scattered among pine groves, have two, three, or four guest rooms. Most are near the water and have private decks and views of the sailboat-dotted cove. Rooms with water views cost about $75 more than those with a view of the wooded property. The decor is Early American, with easy chairs and simple knotty pine furniture. Some rooms are quite airy with cathedral ceilings. There are also some low-slung buildings, whose rooms have decks or sliding doors opening onto a grassy lawn and wooded walking trails.

Rose Cottage, at $495 a night (in season), can sleep five people in a master bedroom, a living room with a pullout sofa, and another bedroom with a twin bed. It has a full kitchen and three TVs, but only one bathroom.

The renowned restaurant, serving Continental cuisine, is housed in a restored 18th-century sea captain's house overlooking the bay.

You can also dine less formally on the garden terrace or poolside, at the bar and grill. The chef works wonders with fresh Atlantic seafood. On our last visit we sampled the sautéed crab cakes, a grilled mushroom and Brie salad, and a blackened seafood combination of shrimp, scallops, and swordfish in a corn tortilla. A jazz pianist entertains on summer evenings.

A large, heated swimming pool is perfectly situated: surrounded by salt water, it straddles the end of a long strip of sand that reaches out to Clam Point. From here you can swim and sun on the beach along Pleasant Bay or just take in the sunset. The Wequassett also offers boat rentals and sailing lessons. A health club with state-of-the-art equipment is next to the pool area.

While the concierge is particularly knowledgeable about the area, the whole staff of the Wequassett goes to great lengths to ensure a special holiday. For instance, the inn has a launch service that will take guests across the bay to Nauset Beach and pick them up again (for a small fee).

Dennis

Isaiah Hall B&B Inn

P. O. Box 1007
152 Whig Street
Dennis, MA 02638
508-385-9928
800-736-0160
Fax: 508-385-5879

A friendly, unpretentious, mid-Cape B&B

Innkeeper: Marie Brophy. **Accommodations:** 11 rooms (10 with private bath), 1 suite. **Rates:** $62–$112 per couple from mid-June to early September; $5 less off-season. **Included:** Continental breakfast. **Minimum stay:** 2–3 nights in season and on holidays and weekends (some flexibility). **Added:** 9.7% tax. **Credit cards accepted:** All major ones. **Children:** Over age 7 welcome; ages 7–12 free; $15 otherwise. **Pets:** Not accepted. **Smoking:** Not permitted. **Handicap access:** No. **Open:** April to mid-October.

➤ **The inn is a favorite of New York actors performing at the nearby playhouse.**

Homespun country comfortable describes this B&B, a Greek Revival farmhouse built in 1857. Once you find it (on a quiet residential road behind the Cape Playhouse), you'll probably return year after year. In the spring and summer, the grounds are a profusion of color, with lush perennial beds constantly in bloom. The presidential rocking chairs on the front porch or lawn chairs in the backyard are two good places to take it all in.

The living room is comfortable, with wing chairs, Oriental carpets, and a coal stove in front of the fireplace. The dining room, with an old-fashioned icebox and a hutch for crystal, feels homey. Breakfast is served at a long harvest table that seats twelve, and a smaller table in front of a picture window.

For those interested in history, Marie will eagerly tell stories of Isaiah Hall, the original builder and a barrelmaker who patented the original barrel for shipping cranberries, and Dorothy Gripp, who owned the house from 1948 to 1978. Small but important bits of their legacies remain: stenciled walls, a proofing (beehive) oven, and steep, narrow steps.

Wander through the inn's kitchen to the converted barn. The Great Room, with a cathedral ceiling and grand arched doorway, is furnished with wicker, knotty pine, rush mats, a woodstove, games, a TV, and a guest refrigerator. Notebooks are packed with information on nearby activities.

There are six guest rooms in the barn; four have small decks overlooking the grassy backyard. Most of the handmade beds — pineapple poster, spindle, and white iron — are covered with quilts. One room has a fireplace, and all have air conditioning.

Rooms in the main inn (two downstairs and three upstairs) are much less uniform. They may have queen-size or double mattresses, a hand-crocheted canopy, brass headboards, painted floorboards, or Oriental rugs.

Corporation Beach on Cape Cod Bay is a walkable half-mile away, but you'll have to get in your car or on your bicycle to reach Chapin Memorial Beach. One of the Cape's oldest cranberry bogs is practically at the back door.

Eastham

The Whalewalk Inn

220 Bridge Road
Eastham, MA 02642
508-255-0617
Fax: 508-240-0017
whalewalk@capecod.net
www.virtualcapecod.com/market/whalewalk

> **A sophisticated, first-rate
> B&B**

Innkeepers: Carolyn and Dick Smith. **Accommodations:** 11 rooms, 5 suites (all with private bath). **Rates:** $135–$210 per couple from late May to mid-October; $120–$270 off-season. **Included:** Full breakfast. **Minimum stay:** 2 nights in season and on all weekends; 3 nights on holidays. **Added:** 9.7% tax. **Credit cards accepted:** All major ones. **Children:** Over age 12 welcome; $30 extra per person. **Pets:** Not accepted. **Smoking:** Not permitted. **Handicap access:** Yes. **Open:** April through November.

➤ **The classic Cape saltbox, perhaps our favorite of the various accommodations, has been turned into an airy studio with a fireplace and private patio.**

Classic New England architecture, sophisticated but summery decor, and friendly innkeepers combine to make this a tranquil and romantic retreat. The inn is located on a quiet residential road, on three and a half acres of lawns and gardens. Even in the height of the season, it feels worlds away from the often-congested Cape.

The impressive 1830s whaling master's home, quintessentially Cape Cod, has been delightfully updated. When the Smiths purchased the inn in 1990, they set about completely refurbishing it, right down to the molding and trim. They excel both at the small details (bedside flowers and reading lights) and the big picture (we'd bet there isn't a guest who doesn't leave feeling rejuvenated).

The inn, decorated with a harmonious blend of European antiques and modern fabrics, has two sophisticated common rooms, both with working fireplaces. Like the rest of the inn, the rooms are light, breezy, and airy. In warm weather, most guests spend their time on the secluded brick patio surrounded by flowers. It's easy to pass a few hours here — at breakfast, reading, or enjoying an afternoon drink. In cooler weather Dick serves breakfast in the sunny dining room; Carolyn is responsible for substantial afternoon hors d'oeuvres. Guests can store drinks and snacks in the communal pantry refrigerator.

The guest rooms (most with fireplace) are certainly all individually styled, but they do have a few things in common: beautifully upholstered wing chairs, a few choice antiques, and area carpets over hardwood floors. Wallpaper, drapes, and pillow fabrics are all perfectly complementary. As for specifics, one deluxe room (it's next to the kitchen and you may hear breakfast preparations in the morning) has a king-size bed, sitting area, and a private entrance off the patio.

We like the five suites (all with fireplace) behind the main inn, located in a converted barn and a guest house. Each has a kitchen; one has a private deck. The west suite in the guest house has cathedral ceilings, a loft with twin beds, and a fireplace. A second bedroom can be connected to either of the suites in the guest house.

Guests can use the inn's bicycles and follow the nearby trails along the Cape Cod Rail Trail.

East Orleans

Nauset House Inn

P.O. Box 774
Beach Road
East Orleans, MA 02643
508-255-2195
www.virtualcapecod.com/market/nausethouse

| A comfortable B&B near Nauset Beach |

Innkeepers: Al and Diane Johnson and Cindy and John Vessella. **Accommodations:** 14 rooms (8 with private bath). **Rates:** $75–$128 per couple; $55 single. **Included:** Full breakfast. **Minimum stay:** 2 nights on weekends. **Added:** 9.7%

tax. **Credit cards accepted:** MasterCard, Visa, Discover. **Children:** Over age 12 welcome. **Pets:** Not accepted. **Smoking:** Not permitted. **Handicap access:** No. **Open:** April through October.

➤ **The delightfully unique conservatory was disassembled and brought here piece by piece from Greenwich, Connecticut, in 1907. Grapevines wind through the trelliswork, and white wicker sits amid the almost tropical plantings and flowers. The stained glass panels, made by Diane, are dramatic.**

Country casual and hospitable are terms that best describe this inn, an 1810 farmhouse owned and operated by the same family since 1983. One of the best things about this inn is its warm and knowledgeable innkeepers. But its location is choice, too: it's only a 10-minute walk to the spectacular Nauset Beach, a 7-mile-long barrier beach. The Cape Cod National Seashore, with many walking paths and bike trails, is a short car ride away.

The guest rooms, comfortably furnished with a mix of antiques, occupy three buildings. Our favorite is the cottage behind the inn; it's quite cozy and romantic. In the main house we also like the Rosebud Room. Set off the living room with a small deck overlooking the back patio, it is one of the most private rooms. Most of the rooms in the main house share baths (there are three guest rooms per bath), while those in the carriage house have private baths. One of the shared bathrooms, unfortunately, is next to the living room; some guests may feel awkward about this somewhat "public" arrangement. Two of the lovely carriage house rooms are much larger than the others.

The hands-on innkeepers, who pay great attention to details, are constantly improving the property, doing most of the work themselves. For instance, the ceiling borders in the guest rooms are hand-painted, not stenciled. The custom woodwork and tilework in the bathrooms are also their expert handiwork.

The large, comfy living room is a blend of styles. A handmade afghan is draped over the couch, a fireplace roars in the off-season, the glass-topped coffee table displays beach memorabilia collected by the hosts (sand, shells, and the like), and a collection of blue glass graces one window sill. There are lots of books, a game table, and another sitting area for relaxed conversation. It's the kind of room people aren't afraid to use. In fact, most people make the effort to return to the inn for the convivial wine (or cranberry juice) and cheese served every afternoon at 5:30 P.M.

Off the living room is a low-ceilinged dining room with a fireplace and brick floor. Breakfast is served at two long tables. The

BYOB bar is also set up in here. A sliding glass door provides easy access to the sunny brick patio, with lawn chairs and an ancient apple tree.

Falmouth

Mostly Hall

27 Main Street
Falmouth, MA 02540
508-548-3786
800-682-0565
Fax: 508-457-1572
mostlyhl@capecod.com
www.sunsol.com/mostlyhall

An elegant and friendly B&B

Innkeepers: Caroline and Jim Lloyd. **Accommodations:** 6 rooms (all with private bath). **Rates:** $110–$125 per couple, May through October; $85–$105 in the off-season. **Included:** Full breakfast. **Minimum stay:** 2 nights preferred in season and on weekends throughout the year. **Added:** 9.7% tax. **Credit cards accepted:** All major ones. **Children:** Over age 16. **Pets:** Not accepted. **Smoking:** Not permitted. **Handicap access:** No. **Open:** Mid-February through New Year's Day.

➤ **The enclosed widow's walk that caps the third floor is a retreat within a retreat. Sink into an upholstered easy chair, play a game of backgammon, watch TV, or let your mind wander out the ten windows that surround you.**

Mostly Hall combines the best of elegance and comfort. Its name comes from the distinct impression you get upon entering the house: it really is "mostly hall" — thirty-five feet worth! This stately house was Falmouth's first summer residence, built in 1849 for the New Orleans bride of a Yankee sea captain. Architecturally, it's a Greek Revival raised cottage. Fortunately, it's set back from the busy road and hidden behind a row of hedges, rhododendrons, and old trees that keep noise to a minimum and privacy to a maximum.

The tasteful country and traditional furnishings in the living/dining room are predominantly Victorian. It's an inviting room, with a marble fireplace, oriental carpets, love seats, and a decanter of complimentary sherry. Travel magazines and books, perhaps from Caroline and Jim's most recent winter destination, fill the coffee table. Ten-foot-high shuttered windows (the ceiling is thirteen feet) and a long oval table, where breakfast is served, dominate the room.

During warm weather, the morning meal, which may include cheese blintz muffins with blueberry sauce or an eggs Benedict soufflé, is served on the wide wraparound porch overlooking the deep back lawn and gazebo. (Jim is always hard at work on the gardens; they're lovely.) A selection of tea and hot water are available well into the evening. It's nice to come back from dinner and have a cup before bed.

A grand stairway leads to the second floor, where each of the large corner guest rooms has a sitting area with plenty of light and space for reading. All the rooms have four-poster, queen-size canopy beds, lovely antiques, shuttered windows, ceiling fans, and air conditioning. Some bathrooms are on the smallish side, and thus have a sink (a nice marble-topped one) outside the bathroom.

Across from the town green in the historic district, Mostly Hall is a convenient base for exploring Falmouth. It's a short drive or a healthy walk to the beach. Down the road a few miles is the vineyard to Martha's Vineyard. Complimentary bicycles are available for use on the Shining Sea bikeway just around the corner.

Hyannis

Captain Gosnold Village

230 Gosnold Street
Hyannis, MA 02601
508-775-9111
Fax: 508-775-8221

> **A low-key family find near the beach**

Manager: Jill Gulden. **Accommodations:** 51 cottages and studios. **Rates:** Mid-June to early September: $125-$260 for 4–6 people in cottages. **Included:** Kitchens in most units. **Minimum stay:** 2 nights in season in studios, 3 nights in cottages. **Added:** 9.7% tax. **Credit cards accepted:** MasterCard, Visa. **Children:** Welcome; $10 each extra person over age 5. **Pets:** Not accepted. **Smoking:** Permitted. **Handicap access:** No. **Open:** May to mid-October.

➤ **There is a heated swimming pool on the grounds, as well as horseshoes, badminton, basketball, shuffleboard, gas grills, and a playground; babysitters can be arranged.**

Between Main Street and the Sea Street Beach (a 10-minute walk in opposite directions), the gray shingle Captain Gosnold Village is a well-shaded complex — a great place for kids, those seeking privacy, and those who don't like eating out every night of a weeklong vacation. It's the kind of place where the inevitable sand tracked in from the beach won't be a problem.

The cottages and efficiencies have either a private deck or a patio with a picnic table. None are of the cracker-box variety that line the highways of Cape Cod. These are quite spacious by comparison. The knotty pine-paneled rooms have cottage-Colonial furnishings. Functional and tidy, they will comfortably hold extra people (except the one-room efficiencies). And for those chilly evenings at the beginning and end of the season, all units have heat. The newer cottages have as many as three bedrooms and can sleep up to fourteen people! With that in mind, the owners have installed three full baths and supplied three TVs for each. Linens, towels, and blankets are provided; beach towels are not.

The kitchens are fully equipped, down to lobster pots and corkscrews. In the largest units, the kitchen is separate from the living quarters. There is daily maid service except on Sundays. Lawns with scrub pines make a nice setting for a barbecue or picnic.

The Inn on Sea Street

358 Sea Street
Hyannis, MA 02601
508-775-8030
Fax: 508-771-0878
innonsea@capecod.net
www.capecod.net/innonsea

A good value near the beach

Innkeepers: Lois Nelson and J. B. Whitehead. **Accommodations:** 9 rooms (7 with private bath), 1 cottage. **Rates:** $78–$110 per couple in rooms; $125 for cottage. **Included:** Full breakfast. **Minimum stay:** None. **Added:** 9.7% tax. **Credit cards accepted:** All major ones. **Children:** Over age 16. **Pets:** Not accepted. **Smoking:** Not permitted. **Handicap access:** No. **Open:** April to mid-November.

➤ **Guests love the small, self-contained cottage that's delightfully summery and cool. It's pure white inside — white bedspread, white walls, white furniture — except for a gray-green pastel floor and a pin-striped sham.**

The Inn on Sea Street was the first B&B in town, and after all these years it still stands above the crowd. Lois and J.B. intentionally keep the prices reasonable because they prefer to give guests plenty of reasons to return again and again. And that they do! They are also especially accommodating; for instance, if you are taking the ferry to Nantucket, they may be able to give you a lift (as long as they're not serving breakfast or checking in a guest.) You may see J.B. tooling around in his 1931 Model A when it's not parked in front of the inn.

This small white Victorian inn exudes informality, even though there are choice antiques and Oriental rugs placed carefully throughout. On cool evenings, Lois and J.B. may light a fire in the comfortable living room, then discreetly disappear, turning the TV, games, and books over to the guests.

The private Garden Room, with its own entrance at the rear of the house, has a canopy bed and TV. A large guest room off the dining room has a lovely lace bedspread and private bath. Upstairs, two spectacular and spacious rooms receive good afternoon sun. They share a bathroom that has an old-fashioned bathtub and a black-and-white-checked floor. The third guest room upstairs has a private bath, reached via a private stairway — charming except, perhaps, in the middle of the night.

Across the street, the turn-of-the-century building has four more rooms and a wraparound porch with Adirondack chairs. These completely renovated rooms are decorated more uniformly with English country antiques, queen-size canopy beds, and TVs. We like the first-floor room the best, with its own private section of porch. Like the inn itself, it has a refrigerator for guests' use. In the morning, guests stroll across the street for breakfast. Most rooms are air conditioned.

Repeat visitors always ask if Lois and J.B. are still offering that great breakfast. Yes indeed. (One whiff from the kitchen gives it away!) Served at small, lace-covered antique tables or in the wicker-furnished sun room, the full breakfast is one of the best on the Cape. It always begins with homemade granola and something like mocha chocolate chip or rhubarb coffee cake, followed by an egg dish like "crab-scramble." You won't need lunch after a meal like this!

Martha's Vineyard

Martha's Vineyard is New England's largest island: ten miles wide and twenty miles long. It's blessed with plenty of breathing space for the bird watcher, beachcomber, and bicyclist. Most ferries put into Vineyard Haven, the island's largest year-round town. But most visitors head for Edgartown (a handsome old whaling port whose streets are lined with former captain's mansions and shops) or the vintage 1870s summer village of Oak Bluffs. It's far quieter up-island — in the tranquil fishing village of Menemsha, the pastoral area around Chilmark, and at the multi-hued cliffs at Gay Head. You can still get a sense of the island's rural and farming roots up here. Although you don't need a car to negotiate Vineyard Haven, Oak Bluffs, and Edgartown, you'll need one if you're staying up-island.

Martha's Vineyard, Edgartown

The Charlotte Inn

South Summer Street
Edgartown, MA 02539
508-627-4751
Fax: 508-627-4652

One of the most elegant, upscale inns in New England

Owners: Gery and Paula Conover. **General Manager:** Carol Read. **Accommodations:** 23 rooms and 2 suites (all with private bath). **Rates:** $295–$495 per couple in rooms in season; $495–$650 in suites. **Included:** Continental breakfast; dinner also served. **Minimum stay:** 2 nights on weekends unless there's a gap in reservations. **Added:** 9.7% tax. **Credit cards accepted:** All major ones.

Children: Not appropriate under age 14. **Pets:** Usually not accepted, but exceptions made. **Smoking:** Heavy smoking not permitted. **Handicap access:** No. **Open:** Year-round.

➤ **The very private carriage house, nestled among wisteria vines, has magnificent rooms with cathedral ceilings, fireplaces, English antiques, air conditioning, patios, and French doors. Many rooms overlook the oh-so-British brick courtyards.**

The most elegant place to stay on Martha's Vineyard (and one of the most exclusive in New England), the Charlotte Inn is a refined complex of buildings just steps from the center of Edgartown. The luxurious accommodations include rooms in an 1860s sea captain's home, a carriage house, a magnificently renovated garage, and a 1705 garden house. The buildings are impeccably furnished with fine art and antiques, and they're all connected by stunning gardens and lush, well-tended pathways. Owned by the Conovers since 1970, the inn exudes class, dignity, and a serious sense of itself and its mission.

Visitors are immediately taken with the art that occupies much of the ground floor: oil paintings, watercolors, and fine prints. Fresh flowers scent the air inside and out. Meticulous attention to detail is a trademark here — and it all begins when you sign in on the leather ledger.

It's not an understatement to say that each room is a work of art. Guest rooms brim with priceless furnishings, one-of-a-kind English antiques, and whimsical objets d'art. Every November the Conovers return to London in search of more antiques and accessories. Practically speaking, each guest room has down comforters and pillows, fluffy towels, and fancy tiled bathrooms. The rooms in the inn itself are a shade more formal than those in the other buildings.

The garden house, which has an informal TV parlor, also has outstanding formal gardens. A remarkable suite (a real treat) — situated over the old-fashioned garage that houses a couple of the inn's antique automobiles — it offers a separate living room with a Palladian window and a glimpse of the harbor.

A Continental breakfast is served outside on the lush terrace or in the bright, conservatory-like dining room. In season, L'Étoile serves dinner nightly, but only on weekends in the winter. The French cuisine by chef Michael Brisson is spectacular. Try any of the fresh game or seafood; nothing on the prix fixe menu will disappoint.

The Edgartown Inn

56 North Water Street
Edgartown, MA 02539
508-627-4794
www.vineyard.net/biz/edgartowninn

> A historic inn that's a good value

Manager: Sandi Hakala. **Accommodations:** 20 rooms (16 with private bath). **Rates:** $70–$180 per couple from late May to late September; $50–$120 off-season. **Included:** Full breakfast available for $7 per person. **Minimum stay:** 2 nights in season, but somewhat flexible. **Added:** 9.7% tax. **Credit cards accepted:** None. **Children:** Age 8 and over welcome. **Pets:** Not accepted. **Smoking:** Not permitted in common rooms; non-smoking rooms available. **Handicap access:** No. **Open:** April through October.

➤ **Built in the late 1700s the inn has hosted Daniel Webster and Nathaniel Hawthorne.**

The Edgartown Inn is perhaps the best value on the island. Smack in the middle of this former whaling captain's village, the inn is an unpretentious, well-maintained, homey hostelry.

Guest rooms are located in three buildings: the main inn, the garden house, and the barn. Some of the main inn rooms have harbor views and balconies; all are furnished simply and neatly, sometimes with period antiques. Bathrooms have been redone. The 12 rooms in the main inn are on the street, and if you are a light sleeper, you may prefer a room overlooking the garden courtyard. You'll also want to base your decision on the size of room you want (smaller rooms are less expensive), whether or not a harbor view is important, and whether you want a private bath. Sandi will steer you to a room that fits your requirements.

Garden house rooms, behind the inn, are quite spacious and have televisions. Most of the rooms in "La Barn" have shared baths.

The full breakfast, served at individual tables in a pine-paneled room or on the garden patio in warmer months, includes a choice of eggs any style or waffles or pancakes. It's preceded by coffee, the inn's signature coffee cake, and juice or steamed prunes. It's a bargain at $7 per person.

Although the garden patio is a tranquil place to relax, especially as an afternoon respite from the foot traffic in Edgartown, most guests sit on the front porch to people-watch.

The Harbor View Resort

P.O. Box 7
131 North Water Street
Edgartown, MA 02539
508-627-7000
800-225-6005
Fax: 508-627-8417

> **A full-service hotel
> overlooking a lighthouse**

Owner: Interstate Hotels Corporation. **General manager:** Dick McAulliffe. **Accommodations:** 124 rooms (all with private bath). **Rates:** Rooms: $210–$375 per couple in season, $85–$155 in winter; 1- and 2-bedroom suites: $375–$525 per couple in season, $175–$210 in winter. **Included:** All meals available. **Minimum stay:** 2 nights on weekends and holidays. **Added:** 9.7% tax. **Credit cards accepted:** All major ones. **Children:** Cribs and rollaways available; $20 per additional person in room. **Pets:** Not accepted. **Smoking:** Nonsmoking rooms available. **Handicap access:** Yes. **Open:** Year-round.

➤ **From the rocking chairs on the sweeping wraparound verandahs you can enjoy the ever-changing harbor view, which extends over to Chappaquiddick.**

The Harbor View Hotel, a 10-minute stroll from the center of Edgartown at the end of North Water Street, has a spectacular location. The prominent street is lined with grand 19th-century whaling captain's homes, long private piers, and stately elm trees. The hotel overlooks a windswept bluff from which Edgartown Lighthouse alerts mariners to the narrow stretch of water separating the harbor from Chappaquiddick Island. A Vineyard landmark since 1891, when tourism began to replace whaling as the island's principal commerce, the hotel underwent a $5.5 million renovation to celebrate its centennial in 1991.

The grand old four-story summer hotel has a lovely lobby, filled with wicker and upholstered chairs, needlepoint rugs, and a large stone hearth. In warm weather, though, you'll want to be in a rocking chair on the wide verandah.

Guest rooms are located in the shingled main hotel, the adjacent Governor Mayhew House, or in the Captain's Quarters. You can choose a variety of rooms from standard rooms to one- or two-bedroom suites. The latter, which have either a garden or water view, also have a spacious living room with sofa bed and a kitchen. Waterfront rooms in the main hotel generally cost about $100 more than those overlooking the grounds or the surrounding residential neighborhood.

All rooms have cable TV, telephone, and air conditioning; some have little balconies. Most are furnished with iron beds (some have two double beds), wicker furniture, armoires, and watercolors by local artists.

As expected, the hotel's Starbuck's restaurant features fine seafood. (We recommend sticking with the seafood, perhaps a mixed grill or a lobster.) The mood is elegant, with woven rugs covering hardwood floors, and tables set with linens. It's a particularly nice place for lunch, with items in the $7–$10 range.

The hotel's cozy bar, Breezes, serves a limited lighter menu, including a lobster roll and a pasta selection. Littleneck clams, oysters, and shrimp are available by the half dozen. Mahogany paneling, tile, and glass are in pleasant contrast to the otherwise breezy oceanside atmosphere.

Recreational facilities include two tennis courts, a private beach, and a centrally located swimming pool. Casual poolside dining is also possible.

The Interstate Hotels Corporation manages the property as well as the Kelley House in the center of town. Stop in at the Newes Pub at the Kelley House for a great selection of microbrews.

Tuscany Inn

22 North Water Street
Edgartown, MA 02539
508-627-5999
Fax: 508-627-6605
70632.3363@compuserve.com

A sophisticated B&B evocative of Tuscany

Innkeepers: Laura Sbrana and Rusty Scheuer. **Accommodations:** 8 rooms (all with private bath). **Rates:** $200–$325 per couple from mid-June to early September; $90–$245 off-season. **Included:** Full breakfast. **Minimum stay:** None. **Added:** 9.7% tax. **Credit cards accepted:** All major ones. **Children:** Over age 8 welcome. **Pets:** Not accepted. **Smoking:** Not permitted. **Handicap access:** No. **Open:** Mid-March through December.

➤ **Laura, a native of Tuscany, offers Northern Italian cooking classes most weekends in November, December, April, and early May.**

When this elegant B&B burst onto the lodging scene in 1993, it quickly catapulted to the highest echelon of places to stay. Laura and Rusty completely renovated the former sea captain's house, which had fallen into a sad state of disrepair. Those who stayed here when it was known as the Captain Fisher House would barely recognize it today — it is absolutely lovely.

Laura hails from Tuscany, and the atmosphere here conveys a distinctly refined sense of the Italian countryside. The entire inn is decorated with lush fabrics, overstuffed couches and chairs, and absolutely lovely objets d'art. (Laura has a magnificent flair for decorating, a flair she exercised in Taiwan — while Rusty worked for IBM, Laura was an interior decorator for a wealthy Chinese family.) There are two large living rooms and a cozy library in which to unwind amidst comfortable elegance. Although a sign indicates that everything is for sale, the truth is Laura has a difficult time parting with pieces she's collected.

The rooms are pricey but they have few competitors in New England in terms of flair. We're partial to the airy feel of room 3, with a canopy iron bed. Room 5 is top-of-the-line, with a king bed under the eaves and a whirlpool under a skylight. Even the two least expensive rooms, which are rather small, are decorated with the same finesse. You can rest assured that any room you choose will be a visual and aesthetic treat.

The breakfast room is open to the kitchen where Laura works her magic. We felt as if we were dining at a friend's villa. On our last visit, we enjoyed cappuccino (also available when you come in for the evening), fresh-squeezed juice, oh-so-light blueberry pancakes (dare we say, the best we've ever had), and fruit.

Since mid-1995 the inn has also housed a very good restaurant — La Cucina — that is operated by son Marco, who inherited his mother's talent and passion for cooking. Popular dishes include pappardelle, an herbed pasta with a four-mushroom sauce; rosemary marinated lamb chops; and filet mignon with Gorgonzola ravioli. Reserve a table inside or on the patio six nights a week from late May through September.

The Victorian Inn

24 South Water Street
Edgartown, MA 02539
508-627-4784
www.thevic.com

| An upscale B&B with Victorian decor |

Innkeepers: Stephen and Karyn Caliri. **Accommodations:** 14 rooms (all with private bath). **Rates:** $125–$265 per couple from late May to mid-October. **Included:** Full breakfast. **Minimum stay:** 2 nights on weekends in season. **Added:**

12% tax. **Credit cards accepted:** All major ones. **Children:** Age 8 and over welcome. **Pets:** Not accepted. **Smoking:** Permitted on porches only. **Handicap access:** No. **Open:** Year-round.

➤ **Across the street from the inn is the ancient "Pagoda Tree."**

Just a block from the harbor and a few blocks to the heart of shopping and dining, the Victorian Inn combines a great location with hospitable, hands-on innkeepers and guest rooms decorated with care.

Rooms at this former whaling captain's home are priced according to size and location; all are air-conditioned. For instance, the least expensive room is on the street side of the inn and has twin beds. We prefer the many rooms that open onto a balcony or porch with views of the garden or harbor (somewhat obstructed). Specifically, we like third-floor rooms with French doors that lead to balconies or sun decks; some have a view of distant Chappaquidick. (Of course, these are the most expensive.)

On the second floor is a lovely room with an antique carved headboard, hardwood floors covered with Oriental carpets, and a large, private covered porch that overlooks the garden patio. Couples traveling together might consider renting this and another room and sharing the porch. The only drawback to this room is the smallish size of the bathroom. Room 14 overlooks a lovely garden (maintained by the renowned Charlotte Inn, owner of the adjacent building) and a fountain that will lull you to sleep. One guest room boasts two balconies, each with a different exposure. Another, off a little hallway, has a very private feel. You can trust Stephen and Karyn to find the best room available to suit your needs and preferences.

A multi-course breakfast is served on the enclosed garden patio in warm weather or in a cozy dining room (set with tables for two or four) complete with chandelier, a working fireplace, and wainscoting. You'll always have two choices. On our most recent visit it was scrambled eggs with basil and feta or rum-banana pancakes. It's one of the better breakfasts on the island.

Martha's Vineyard, Gay Head

Outermost Inn

R.R. 1, P.O. Box 171
Lighthouse Road
Gay Head, MA 02535
508-645-3511
Fax: 508-645-3514
htaylor@vineyard.net
www.outermostinn.com

A low-key, stylish inn on the bluffs

Innkeepers: Jeanne and Hughie Taylor. **Accommodations:** 6 rooms and 1 suite (all with private bath). **Rates:** $250–$285 per couple in room, mid-June to mid-September; $190–$210 off-season. **Included:** Full breakfast. **Minimum stay:** 2 nights on weekends. **Added:** 5.7% tax. **Credit cards accepted:** All major ones. **Children:** Not appropriate under age 12. **Pets:** Not accepted. **Smoking:** Not permitted in guest rooms. **Handicap access:** No. **Open:** May to mid-October.

➤ **No discussion of the Outermost Inn is complete without noting that Hughie's brother is the singer James Taylor. A guitar, amplifier, xylophone, and keyboards sit in the living room, ready for a spontaneous visit. (J.T. occasionally drops in for dinner.) But remember that stargazing is frowned upon by protective islanders.**

Hughie and Jeanne built this two-story shingled and gabled family home in 1971 and splendidly converted it into The Outermost Inn in 1990. At the remote tip of the Vineyard, on a bluff overlooking Vineyard Sound and the Elizabeth Islands, the Taylors have taken full advantage of the rolling dunes, the unbroken views, the solitude, and the historic lighthouse. Thankfully, there's nothing to do in Gay Head except enjoy the peace and quiet, the multi-hued cliffs, and the beach. The inn's private beach at Pilot's Landing is a 5-minute walk away.

Even with what seems like a steady stream of visitors stopping in to check out the place, Jeanne never seems to lose her buoyant spirit and genuine friendliness. After settling you, she'll point out the wide, wraparound porch and the comfortable living room. Guests are welcome to mix a drink (BYOB) at the outdoor bar. It was made from an 18-foot-long tree felled especially for the inn by a lumberjack in Dalton, Massachusetts. Sunsets, by the way, are spectacular from here.

You may never want to leave the comfort and privacy of your room. Large picture windows, without the distraction of curtains, dominate. The guest rooms are named after the highly polished wood flooring: ash, bash (beech and ash), cherry, hickory, beech, or oak. The walls are white, the comforters are white, vases are filled with wildflowers, and the fabrics are natural, giving the rooms a stylishly cool sparkle. The Beech Room features a two-person Jacuzzi, and the Oak Room has a private deck. The two-room lighthouse suite boasts a private entrance and a deck that overlooks the lighthouse.

During warm weather, breakfast is served on the side porch. It might include fruit with frozen yogurt and Belgian waffles with fruit. With more than 20 acres of undeveloped land around the house, deer, rabbits, and other wildlife can be spotted darting through the scrub oaks and wild pear and bayberry bushes.

The Taylors also serve dinner in a simple dining room that accommodates only twenty-four diners. (The inn doesn't serve nightly and reservations are difficult to get, so you may wish to book a table when booking your room.) Prices range from $48 to $56 and include a salad, choice of appetizer (such as smoked bass chowder or crab cakes), and a baked stuffed seafood platter or grilled breast of duck.

Hughie offers sunset sails around the cliffs and a half-day jaunt on his 50-foot catamaran; ask him for details. He also sings on summer evenings at David's Island House, in Oak Bluffs.

Martha's Vineyard, Menemsha

Menemsha Inn and Cottages

P.O. Box 38B
Menemsha, MA 02552
508-645-2521
800-773-1466 in Massachusetts
www.vineyard.net/biz/menemshainn

> A quiet collection of up-island cottages and rooms

Hosts: Nancy and Richard Steves. **Accommodations:** 9 rooms (all with private bath), 6 suites, 12 cottages. **Rates:** $115–$170 per couple in rooms from mid-June to mid-September; $,1075–$1,475 per week in cottages. **Included:** Continental breakfast with rooms and suites. **Minimum stay:** 1 week in cottages (2 days off-season). **Added:** 9.7% tax. **Credit cards accepted:** No credit cards. **Children:** Welcome; cot or extra person, $15. **Pets:** Not accepted. **Smoking:** Permitted. **Handicap access:** No. **Open:** May through October.

➤ **Guests at Menemsha Inn and Cottages have access to nearby — and private — Lucy Vincent Beach (perhaps the island's finest) and Squibnocket Pond.**

There's a disarming simplicity to this weathered cluster, which consists of a gray shingle two-story building, an inn completed in 1989, and several cottages on 11 prime acres of Vineyard real estate. Far from the crowds, you can enjoy quiet sunset and water views and walk through a salt marsh down to the public Menemsha Beach.

The Steveses, who acquired the inn in 1984 (it had been owned by one family for the previous 37 years), have been methodically restoring the property. Cottages come fully equipped, and each is tastefully decorated. Some have a screened-in porch; others have a deck. None have a telephone, but all have a TV. Be forewarned: the Steveses have a firm policy against crowding four people into a one-bedroom cottage.

Almost all the inn rooms look out onto greenery and flowers and to a vista crowned by a body of water known as Menemsha Bite. Each suite has its own sitting room, a deck with a panoramic sunset view, carpeting, an overhead fan, and a small refrigerator. Half the rooms look directly to the water.

A Continental breakfast is served in a building that feels a bit like a greenhouse with cathedral ceilings. On a rainy day it is pleasant to read here, surrounded by local artwork.

An extra shower, for washing off seawater and beach sand, is available for guests after check-out time. The inn also has a tennis court.

Martha's Vineyard, North Tisbury

The Farmhouse

RFD Box 531
Vineyard Haven, MA 02568
508-693-5354
Fax: 508-693-5458

An authentic country farmhouse B&B

Hosts: Kathy and Volker Kaempfert. **Accommodations:** 5 rooms (3 with private bath). **Rates:** $85–$110 per couple in season. **Included:** Continental breakfast. **Minimum stay:** 2 nights on weekends. **Added:** 5.7% tax. **Credit cards accepted:** None. **Children:** Over age 12 welcome. **Pets:** Not accepted. **Smoking:** Not permitted. **Handicap access:** No. **Open:** May to mid-December.

➤ **The Red Cat Restaurant, one of the island's best, is right next door. Don't miss it.**

Located six miles from the Vineyard Haven ferry on State Road in North Tisbury, this is an authentic farmhouse dating to 1810, complete with original wide-pine floors throughout. The Kaempferts converted it into a bed-and-breakfast in 1982.

The charming and unpretentious guest rooms are decorated with family heirlooms. On the first floor, next to the front door, is the Blue room with twin beds and a marble-topped dresser. This corner room looks onto the front porch and shares a bathroom with the tiny Gray room in the rear of the house. All three rooms upstairs have private bathrooms. Maroon is large and features two primitive farmhouse bedsteads, while Green is a bit larger, with original built-in dressers and a cherry sideboard. Navy has an iron bed and a handmade trapezoid window in the dormer. Beds are dressed with comforter duvets.

Since the farmhouse sits just a few yards off State Road, you may wish to ask for a room in the back of the house if you're a particularly light sleeper.

Extending out into the lush backyard, a mahogany deck was built in 1997 around a large old tree and has become a popular gathering spot. On warm days it's nice to enjoy the light breakfast — blueberry muffins, juice, fruit, and coffee — out here. Otherwise, the living room, with details like original chair rails and beautiful 20-inch wide floorboards, makes a great alternative.

If you plan on eking out one last day at the beach before catching the ferry, you'll appreciate the private outdoor shower!

Martha's Vineyard, Oak Bluffs

The Oak House

Seaview Avenue
Box 299
Oak Bluffs, MA 02557
508-693-4187
Fax: 508-696-7385
www.vineyard.net/inns

A Victorian B&B filled with oak

Manager: Betsi Convery-Luce. **Accommodations:** 8 rooms and 2 suites (all with private bath). **Rates:** $140–$250 per couple from late June to early September; $100–$190 off-season. **Included:** Continental breakfast. **Minimum stay:** 3 nights on weekends in season; 2 nights otherwise. **Added:** 9.7% tax. **Credit cards accepted:** All major ones. **Children:** Over age 10. **Pets:** Not accepted. **Smoking:** Not permitted. **Handicap access:** No. **Open:** Mid-May to mid-October.

➤ **Betsi, a pastry chef trained at the Cordon Bleu in Paris and at Johnson and Wales in Rhode Island, prepares goodies for the breakfast buffet and an impressive Victorian tea. Be sure not to miss the four o'clock affair.**

You'll never see more oak under one roof than at the Oak House: ceilings, floors, paneling, and furniture are all oak. This is a wonderfully updated guest house in the gingerbread Queen Anne style for which Oak Bluffs is famous. Built by Massachusetts Governor William Claflin in 1876, the property was renovated in 1989. Most of the house is furnished with elegant antiques, but the glassed-in sun porch is full of white wicker. The view of Nantucket Sound stretches to Cape Cod.

All the large, airy rooms upstairs are furnished in different Victorian themes. Most rooms have an ocean view from a private balcony. Many bathrooms have turn-of-the-century fixtures and marble basins. The spacious Cottage City Room, with sloping eaves on the third floor, is one of the few rooms without a water view, but its more private location makes it a winner. The Tivoli Room is favored because of its little porch with an ocean view and its huge bathroom. Light sleepers should avoid the first-floor room, which receives a fair amount of noise from guests going up and down the stairs. The inn's brochure contains a color photograph of each of the rooms; you may want to send for it. All rooms have air conditioning, a TV, and telephone.

The Wesleyan Grove Camp Ground is just a few blocks away, as are the restaurants and shops of bustling Circuit Avenue. Ferries put right into the slip on Seaview Avenue, and a beach — not one of the Vineyard's best but fair by mainland standards — is right here, too. A guest refrigerator is located in the pantry.

Martha's Vineyard, Vineyard Haven

Thorncroft

P.O. Box 1022
460 Main Street
Vineyard Haven, MA 02568
508-693-3333
800-332-1236
Fax: 508-693-5419
kgb@tiac.net
www.thorncroft.com

> **A first-class romantic inn**

Innkeepers: Lynn and Karl Buder. **Accommodations:** 13 rooms (all with private bath), 1 cottage. **Rates:** $200–$450 per couple from mid-June to early September; $50 less in the off-season. **Included:** Full breakfast. **Minimum stay:** 3 nights on summer and holiday weekends; 2 nights during the week in summer. **Added:** 9.7% tax. **Credit cards accepted:** All major ones. **Children:** Over age 12. **Pets:** Not accepted. **Smoking:** Not permitted. **Handicap access:** Yes. **Open:** Year-round.

➤   **A private and romantic cottage, which measures 26 feet by 26 feet, is not for "the faint of heart." It features a fireplace, four-poster king bed, 1½ baths, two-person Jacuzzi set in a mirrored alcove, a long covered porch with hammock, and its own garage.**

One mile from town, the Thorncroft has an unassuming exterior that belies its elegant interior. Architecturally, it's a classic Craftsman bungalow with a dominant roof, carved shutters, and neo-Colonial details. Inside, it's comfortable and romantic. Outstanding service and consideration for your needs are of prime importance here. The Buders are professional innkeepers who know that many small details add up to one big impression. To that end they are always adding more amenities and implementing more services.

The Victorian reading parlor exudes the era in every detail, down to its rose-colored floral wallpaper. Select antiques, such as a wicker baby carriage, a platform rocker, a Victrola, and even vintage clothing, maximize the effect.

Each guest room has its own distinct personality — either early-20th-century or Colonial — and a host of modern amenities. All rooms are carpeted and soothingly decorated. No two are alike; some have a four-poster canopy bed, brass faucets, or an original clawfoot tub. Others might have a private entrance, a balcony, or a Jacuzzi. Almost all have a wood-burning fireplace. Bathrooms have hair dryers and plush robes. One of the loveliest rooms, with an exquisite Renaissance Victorian bedroom set, is tucked away near the sun room. It boasts a screened-in porch with a private 300-gallon hot tub. All rooms have a television, but in the main house guests use earphone headsets so as not to bother other guests.

Behind the main inn, the Carriage House (also centrally air-conditioned), has five large Colonial-style bedrooms. One has an outdoor hot tub ensconced in a private screened-in porch.

An elegant breakfast (sign up for one of two seatings) is served in the sun room or the formal dining room with soft lighting. The full menu changes daily, but always includes lots of fruit, and may include buttermilk pancakes with a blueberry honey sauce, burritos, or quiche. Guest may request that an expanded Continental breakfast be delivered to their room — a relaxing option if you want to linger over the newspaper (also delivered).

Thorncroft has an ample supply of beach chairs, towels, and blankets. And although the Buders have put together one of the most thorough island information booklets we've seen, you also have the opportunity to ask them about sightseeing during afternoon tea.

Martha's Vineyard, West Tisbury

Lambert's Cove Country Inn

R.R. 1, Box 422
Vineyard Haven, MA 02568
508-693-2298

A secluded inn with access to a private beach

Managers: Katherine and Louis Costabel. **Accommodations:** 15 rooms (all with private bath). **Rates:** $95–$175 per couple in high and shoulder seasons. **Included:** Full breakfast; dinner and Sunday brunch also served. **Minimum stay:** 3 nights in July and August, 2 nights in September, when making advance reservations. **Added:** 9.7% tax. **Credit cards accepted:** All major ones. **Chil-

dren: Welcome. **Pets:** Accepted off-season. **Smoking:** Not permitted. **Handicap access:** No. **Open:** Year-round.

➤ **Lambert's Cove Beach, a private, dune-backed stretch of fine white sand, is a 20-minute stroll down the road. The inn provides beach towels, parking, guest passes, and an outdoor shower for guests who use the beach after checking out.**

You approach Lambert's Cove on one of the island's prettiest roads, then turn onto a long wooded path. The 1790s farmhouse, which was converted into a country estate in the 1920s, sits amidst a 10-acre grove of pine trees with rambling English gardens and spacious lawns.

The low-beamed, spacious library is stocked with well-worn books and is comfortably furnished. There is also a separate TV room. French doors lead to the large deck, and beyond it to a grassy apple orchard, rock walls, a hammock, and a tennis court. The setting is idyllic.

Our favorite rooms are in the carriage house and barn. The carriage house, in a secluded grove, has two simple rooms with private screened porches. Another special room in the carriage house has its own little greenhouse, which has been converted into a sitting room. The Blue Room has a large private deck with sliding glass doors.

A few guest rooms in the main house share a comfortable second-floor sitting area and an outdoor porch overlooking the backyard. Among these, the Bridal Room has a canopy bed and fireplace. Two other rooms, which can be connected by a sitting room for couples traveling together, share a long deck with lawn chairs.

The unpretentious dining room currently has a good reputation. (BYOB; there is a guest refrigerator for chilling wine.) On our last visit we tried a rich torte consisting of three layers of cheese, pesto, and sun-dried tomatoes, which was followed with rainbow trout. Dessert selections lean toward the rich and chocolatey. A full breakfast is served on the deck in good weather.

You probably won't want to budge any farther than the beach or the shade of the catalpa tree, where wisteria vines bloom magnificently in the spring. But those who wish to explore will be rewarded by the unspoiled neighboring countryside.

Nantucket

Nantucket is half the size of the Vineyard, but it takes twice as long to get there. Most short-term visitors stay in the historic town of Nantucket, who's graceful clapboard and brick buildings date from its mid-19th-century prominence as the world's leading whaling port. It's preferable to get around the island on bike, which, once beyond the town's cobblestones, can take you to the beach and the village of Siasconset ('Sconset). The tourist season begins and ends with immensely popular events: the Daffodil Festival in April and a Christmas celebration in early December.

Cliffside Beach Club

P.O. Box 449
Jefferson Avenue
Nantucket, MA 02554
508-228-0618
Fax: 508-325-4735

| A sophisticated hostelry right on the beach |

Manager: Robert Currie. **Accommodations:** 22 rooms, two 3-bedroom apartments, 3 suites (all with private bath). **Rates** (late June to early September): $280–$450 per couple in rooms and studios, $550–$1,125 for apartments, suites, and cottages for 4-6 people; $25 per extra person. Off-season: $185–$335 per room or studio, $345–$550 per apartment and suite. **Included:** Continental breakfast; lunch and dinner also served. **Minimum stay:** 4 nights on summer weekends. **Added:** 9.7% tax, 5.3% service charge. **Credit cards accepted:** American Express. **Children:** Welcome. **Pets:** Not accepted. **Smoking:** Permitted. **Handicap access:** No. **Open:** Late May through mid-October.

➤ **There are only a few places like this in all New England, where nothing comes between you and the ocean except a private beach.**

A 15-minute walk from town, the Cliffside Beach Club is one of two beachside lodgings on Nantucket. The four acres of beachfront, with accommodations for a seventy guests, have been in Robert's family since 1958. Over the years, the family has prudently improved (but not overdeveloped) the property, with an eye toward maintaining its unpretentious atmosphere. It's all tasteful, blending harmoniously with the sun, surf, and sea that surround it.

Formerly a private club (with old-fashioned lockers and changing rooms) where members were granted private beach space, today the low-slung, weathered complex consists of the main building, a few freestanding cottages, and a series of connected rooms. Most have private decks on the beach and unobstructed views of the ocean.

The former clubhouse is now the lobby, with lovely quilts hanging from the rafters of the vaulted ceiling. Airy and bright, and filled with comfortable wicker groupings, the clubhouse looks out to a wooden verandah on the beach and to the sea beyond. Pick up a complimentary Continental breakfast and enjoy it here or take it to the beach.

The clubhouse and guest rooms are connected by a boardwalk over the sand. Nantucket craftspersons designed the elegantly simple furnishings and the walls are decorated with local art. Rooms are stylishly contemporary: cathedral ceilings, subtle lighting, simple upholstery, and quilts on the beds. It's all been designed with summer living in mind. The woodwork throughout is magnificent; much of it is custom-milled cedar. Other wood was reclaimed and recycled: 60-year-old beaded hemlock, for instance, was taken from the old Beach Club's changing rooms, and heart pine hails from Boston's old South Station.

Suite 131 is one of the most private accommodations; it also has the added bonus of sun on the deck throughout the day. A few rooms have kitchenettes; some rooms can be connected for families. All rooms have air conditioning and television. All the rooms are quite distinct, however, so ask the reservationist to describe them. You can't go wrong with any of the rooms.

There is a first-class fitness room on the premises, with plans for a new Jacuzzi, steam, and sauna room. Tennis courts are a 5-minute walk away. When you don't feel like walking into town or calling a cab, try the Cliffside's respected beachfront restaurant, operated by Robert's sister and nephews. The restaurant, like the rooms, faces the setting sun — on a clear night it doesn't get any better than this.

Corner House

P.O. Box 1828
49 Centre Street
Nantucket, MA 02554
508-228-1530
www.cornerhousenantucket.com

> **A historic B&B slightly off the beaten path**

Innkeepers: Sandy and John Knox-Johnston. **Accommodations:** 15 rooms and 2 suites (all with private bath). **Rates:** $100–$185 per couple from late June to late September; $65–$135 off-season. **Included:** Continental breakfast. **Minimum stay:** 3–4 nights in season and on spring and fall weekends (but do ask about 1- and 2-night openings). **Added:** 9.7% tax. **Credit cards accepted:** MasterCard, Visa. **Children:** No facilities for children under 8. **Pets:** Not accepted. **Smoking:** With discretion, but not in the guest rooms. **Handicap access:** No. **Open:** Year-round.

➤ **Be sure to be at the inn by 4:00 P.M. when tea is served. A tempting plate of lemon squares, scones, fruit breads, and sandwiches is set out on the sideboard with pots of tea and mulled cider in the cooler months.**

A range of accommodations is available within this cluster of houses just a couple of blocks from the center of town. Sandy has a background in historical restoration and renovation, so you can rest assured that the 1723 house is faithful to its origins. Even the hue of the paint on the walls is historically accurate. But what's refreshing about the Corner House is that it's not a museum showpiece. It's all very relaxed and comfortable.

Even though Sandy and John have been welcoming guests since 1981, their enthusiasm hasn't waned. Upon arrival, guests feel as if they have been anticipated since the day they made their reservations. The inn's talented staff shares this enthusiasm.

Most of the nine guest rooms in the main house have rough plaster walls and the original exposed beams. Uneven floors with wide planks are typical throughout the main house, as are 18th- and early-19th-century English and American antiques. All the rooms have fluffy towels, lots of pillows, down comforters, and bedside reading lamps. The Elderberry Room, although next to the kitchen, is a favorite with its canopy bed, fireplace, raspberry-colored walls, small television, and private entrance. Morning Glory, above the sun porch, has a little sitting room and a small bedroom.

Third-floor rooms are the least expensive because they are smaller, but we find them romantic and cozy. Lily (somewhat larger) is particularly nice, with a sunrise view of the harbor, exposed beams, and latched doors. The wide range of rates ensures that the house is often filled with guests of all ages. A number of rooms can accommodate three people. In the winter, only the main house remains open.

Swan's Nest is a newer post-and-beam building with four more rooms that are generally larger, each with a sitting area. They are still furnished with the same "Nantucket feel" — antiques, deep colors — as those in the main house. The guest rooms here each have a refrigerator and television and share a patio. Swan's Nest also has an apartment with beamed ceilings and lots of windows. There are also two additional rooms above Sandy and John's residence next door. One of them, Bandbox, is decorated with white lace curtains, white wood, deep blue walls, and a canopy bed; it has a very summery feel. The long harborview suite is cozy and not for the claustrophobic, with the bed at an angle under the eaves and windows. (It also has a wet bar and microwave.)

Guests may take their Continental breakfast in the living room of the main house, on the sun porch, or on the patio hidden from the road and rimmed with potted flowers. The living room and the original keeping room, with a hearth and nicely detailed paneling, are both comfortable places to relax.

Harbor House and Wharf Cottages

Nantucket, MA 02534
508-228-1500 (H. H.)
508-228-4620 (W. C.)
800-ISLANDS (reservations)
Fax: 508-228-7197

> **Sophisticated hotel and town house rooms, as well as harborside cottages**

Management: Interstate Hotel Corp. **Accommodations:** 112 Harbor Hotel rooms, 25 Wharf Cottages. **Rates:** $245–$285 per couple at the Harbor Hotel from June to early September, $115–$225 off-season; $295–$575 for 1-, 2-, and 3-bedroom Wharf Cottages in high season. **Included:** No meals. **Minimum stay:** 3 nights in July and August on weekends and holidays. **Added:** 9.7% tax. **Credit cards accepted:** All major ones. **Children:** Welcome; $20 each additional person in room. **Pets:** No dogs. **Smoking:** Permitted. **Handicap access:** Yes. **Open:** Harbor House, late April to early December; Wharf Cottages, late May to late September.

➤ **Inquire about off-season packages that offer substantial value.**

We have included these two distinct accommodations under one heading because they are owned and managed by the same company, and there is one central reservation number. Most importantly, though, both are first-rate properties providing exceptional accommodations.

The Harbor House, a large complex of buildings surrounding an 1880s summer hotel, offers a variety of luxurious rooms. It's located just a few blocks from the hustle and bustle of town on a quiet cul-de-sac. In the summer, the grounds are beautifully landscaped with bushes and flowers. A large swimming pool with a service bar is tucked between some of the units.

Guests choose among smart and sophisticated rooms in the main inn or in the gray shingled town houses. Ask for a garden-view room. Many town house rooms have two double beds, making it more economical for a family. The main inn has an attractive split-level lobby/living room decorated with antiques. It opens onto the Hearth dining room, elegant but comfortable with exposed beams and hardwood floors. Live entertainment, with dancing on summer weekends, is featured in the handsome turn-of-the-century lounge.

Wharf Cottages, right on the harbor, are a great choice for couples traveling together, families, or yachting folks who require a bit of firm footing for the night. Cottages are fully equipped, bright, and simply but tastefully furnished. You cant get any closer to the center of things than this.

Martin House Inn

P.O. Box 743
61 Centre Street
Nantucket, MA 02554
508-228-0678
martinn@nantucket.net
nantucket.net/lodging/martinn

A graciously elegant B&B

Innkeepers: Ceci and Channing Moore. **Accommodations:** 11 doubles (9 with private bath), 2 singles. **Rates:** $90–$160 per couple from mid-June to mid-October and holiday periods; $45–$55 single, shared bath; $65–$130 off-season. **Included:** Continental breakfast. **Minimum stay:** 3 nights preferred with advance reservations. **Added:** 9.7% tax. **Credit cards accepted:** All major ones. **Children:** Over age 5 welcome. **Pets:** Not accepted. **Smoking:** Not permitted. **Handicap access:** No. **Open:** Year-round.

➤ **Nantucket's streets are lined with cobblestones that originally served as ballast on English ships bound for the New World.**

This former 1803 sea captain's house, one of the most congenial guest houses in town, is run by hands-on residential owners. In a town like Nantucket, filled with dozens of lovely B&Bs, we look for places that have a personal touch, places where the front door doesn't feel like a revolving door. Although the house has taken in visitors since the 1920s, only recently has it taken them in with such style and grace.

Just a couple of blocks from the busiest part of town, the inn is well sited. Accommodations vary widely in price and layout, but all are airy and spacious, elegant without being stilted. Generally, guest rooms are traditionally furnished with period antiques, four-poster and canopy beds; a few have a working fireplace. Room 21 is particularly popular because of its canopy bed and private porch. Rooms on the third floor share two baths. One room can sleep four people.

The pretty living room (which opens onto the dining room) features window seats, a working fireplace, Oriental carpets over a hardwood floor, and plenty of armchairs from which to peruse local restaurants' menus. On lazy summer afternoons, it's easy to pretend you're an islander while napping on the hammock or lounging in white wicker on the side porch.

Because of the desire of most guests to get to the beach as early as possible, the Martin House, like most Nantucket guest houses, offers only a Continental breakfast. But few places present such a nice one. In the words of a guest who wrote to us, "The breakfast was delicious — terrific cranberry muffins, homemade granola, yogurt, juice, and fruit — all served at a lovely Queen Anne dining room table."

The Wauwinet

P.O. Box 2580
Nantucket, MA 02584
508-228-0145
800-426-8718
Fax: 508-228-6712
theinn@wauwinet.com
www.wauwinet.com

> **An oceanside retreat
> renowned for its
> breathtaking site, excellent
> service, and extensive
> amenities**

Innkeepers: Russ and Debbie Cleveland. **Accommodations:** 25 rooms (all with private bath), 5 cottages. **Rates:** Mid-June to mid-September: $280–$710 per couple in rooms, $540–$1,350 per cottage; off-season: $180–$570 and $300–$1,070, respectively. **Included:** Full breakfast and all recreational facilities; lunch and dinner also served. **Minimum stay:** 4 nights may be required in July and August (involving Friday and Saturday nights), and on holiday weekends. **Added:** 9.7% tax. **Credit cards accepted:** All major ones. **Children:** Welcome in family cottages. **Pets:** Not accepted. **Smoking:** Not permitted. **Handicap access:** Yes. **Open:** Mid-May through October.

➤   **In 1996, Topper's (the inn's famed restaurant) won the much coveted Grand Award from *Wine Spectator* magazine. This award is the magazine's highest honor and in 1996 only six restaurants world-wide were added to the existing membership. Put yourselves in Topper's hands, relax, and enjoy.**

The Wauwinet is, unquestionably, one of the best places to stay on the eastern seaboard. Period. It dates from the 1850s, but underwent a multimillion-dollar transformation in the mid-1980s. And it keeps getting better! (Is that possible?) Its location is the most isolated and dramatic of any inn on Nantucket, but you needn't have a car to get around. A jitney service runs to and from town throughout the day and evening. Guests walk out the front door to the quiet, beach-rimmed bay or out the back door to the dune-lined open Atlantic Ocean. The sun literally rises and sets on this place.

Understated elegance is the signature of the three-story seaside inn. The focal point of the public space is a broad porch that overlooks the broad lawn, which in turn stretches down to the beach. The library and living room are both brightly decorated in flowered chintz with *trompe l'oeil* touches, masses of fresh flowers, and bleached woods. Audubon prints, original paintings, folk art, and interesting antiques are everywhere, even in the hallways. There isn't an unsoothing corner in the place.

All the bedrooms are stunningly decorated and have a noteworthy antique or two, distinctive appointments, and luxurious bed linens. The bathrooms are magnificent, replete with plush towels and fine toiletries. Deluxe rooms have spectacular views of Nantucket Bay. Although cottage suites lack water views, they do have kitchens and fireplaces and can accommodate four to eight guests.

The inn's dining room, Topper's, is equally exceptional, and deserving of every accolade heaped on it. After a personal welcome, you'll settle into a leisurely three-hour dinner. The decor is sophisticated but relaxed. Chef Peter Wallace's menu is nouveau American, with an emphasis on seafood. On our last visit we indulged in the signature lobster and crab cakes with smoked corn, jalapeño olives, and mustard sauce (always a winner); melt-in-your-mouth tuna sashimi; a creamy wild mushroom risotto; grilled Atlantic salmon; and a savory seven-vegetable Napoleon. Request a dessert sampler: as it's brought out from the kitchen, it always receives a round of gasps from other diners. Even the most sophisticated diners can't help but be impressed.

The waitstaff is exemplary and solicitous but not overly so. And to top it off, the sunset views over the water — visible from many tables — are incredible. As of this writing, the absolutely excellent wine list had just topped 600 vintages; put yourself in the sommelier's hands. Breakfast may be enjoyed in your room, on the terrace, or in Topper's. Order as much from the menu as you'd like.

For those having lunch or dinner at Topper's, the inn offers a complimentary hour-long cruise from Straight Wharf to the restaurant and back again. At dinnertime, the voyage coincides with the setting sun.

As you might expect, the Wauwinet offers a number of small luxuries, and they are all complimentary. Our favorite is Russ's narrated 4-wheel-drive natural history excursion out to Great Point, which culminates with a glass of Chardonnay while watching anglers cast for bluefish. But the Wauwinet also hosts motor tours of Sconset in a vintage 1946 Ford Woodie wagon and bird-watching trips. You'll never have to leave the grounds if you don't want to, though. The inn has clay tennis courts, bicycles, croquet, beach chess, bocci, summer harbor cruises on a 28-foot boat, and sailing. There is also an intimate wine bar, an afternoon cheese and port reception, a full videocassette library (popcorn can be delivered with your movie), and nightly turndown service. As you can imagine, the staff-guest ratio is better than one-to-one. Trust us on this one; it really doesn't get any better than this.

Nantucket, Siasconset

The Summer House

P.O. Box 880
Siasconset, MA 02564
508-257-4577
Fax: 508-257-4590
smanolis@nantucket.net

| **An idyllic cottage hideaway** |

Host: Susan Manolis. **Accommodations:** 8 cottages. **Rates:** From mid-June to early September: $360–$425 per couple for a 1-bedroom, $500–$525 for a 2-bedroom; $175–$425 in the shoulder seasons; $50 each additional person. **Included:** Continental breakfast; dinner and lunch also served daily in July and August. **Minimum stay:** Requested at certain times. **Added:** 9.7% tax, 10% service. **Credit cards accepted:** All major ones. **Children:** Welcome. **Pets:** Not accepted. **Smoking:** Permitted. **Handicap access:** No. **Open:** Late April to late October.

➤ **The beachside pool, nestled between the cottages and ocean and surrounded by dune grass, can't be beat. In the summer, poolside lunches are served to the public under pink beach umbrellas and a large white tent.**

Rose-trellised cottages overlooking the ocean and undulating dune grass . . . little windows peeking out from behind a mass of honeysuckle vines . . . whitewashed interiors warmed by hand-painted borders and English country antiques. Its all here at the aptly named Summer House. The enchanting cottages, which are a mere sandal shuffle from the beach, embody the carefree essence of summer.

Built in the 1840s, the connected cottages range from simple studios with or without a fireplace to one- and two-bedroom units with or without a kitchen. (Actually, the two-bedroom cottages are freestanding, and thus most appropriate for families.) Most of the cozy rooms have a marble Jacuzzi tub. The Cagney cottage, a two-bedroom cottage named for the actor who stayed here in the 1930s, is L-shaped with a private garden sitting area looking toward the bluffs. From the smaller bedroom you can catch ocean glimpses. Although none of the cottages have expansive ocean views (they are small, antique cottages after all), the ocean remains the focal point of your stay. In our minds the true test of any cottage is how you feel after spending an entire rainy day inside it: we can assure you that should the weather turn grim, you'll feel rested and peaceful here.

A tray loaded with Continental goodies — a pot of coffee, fresh orange juice, filled or plain croissants, hard-boiled eggs, and muffins — can be brought to your cottage each morning. Sit back in your Adirondack chair, fold open the paper, and pour yourself a strong one. (If you don't request this tray, breakfast is usually taken on the covered porch or indoors by the fireplace in the autumn.) It doesn't get any better than this, unless of course, you've risen early to watch the sun rise in front of your cottage.

The inn's popular piano bar has been presided over by Sal Gioé since 1985. The inn's restaurant is under separate ownership; check with guests who may have recently dined there. Local watercolorist Bill Welch's paintings grace the walls.

'Sconset, as the locals refer to the little community of weathered, shingled, rose-covered cottages, has remained essentially unchanged since it was settled in 1675.

Provincetown

Hargood House

493 Commercial Street
Provincetown, MA 02657
508-487-9133
www.ptown.com/ptown/hargoodhouse

A bayfront apartment complex

Owners/managers: Ann Maguire and Harriet Gordon. **Accommodations:** 25 1-
and 2-bedroom apartments. **Rates:** $695–$1,395 weekly from late June to early
September; $72–$142 daily in off-season. **Included:** Kitchens in all apartments.
Minimum stay: 1 week in season; 2 nights off-season. **Added:** 8% tax. **Credit
cards accepted:** All major ones. **Children:** Welcome. **Pets:** Dogs accepted with
advance approval. **Smoking:** Permitted. **Handicap access:** No. **Open:** Year-
round.

➤   **Devoted guests know a good thing when they find one. If your schedule permits, make reservations well in advance. (A season ahead wouldn't
be a bad idea!)**

The Hargood House has long been considered the crown jewel of
Provincetown lodging. The former owners, who presided over the
property from 1960 to 1995, had developed a loyal clientele during
their tenure, and the current owners (who purchased the complex
in 1995) were among them! Although the Hargood House was a
wildly popular place to stay, it was admittedly in need of some
sprucing up. With zest and zeal, Harriet and Ann are nudging the
decor from the 1960s and 1970s into the next century, while still
retaining the same breezy seaside feeling that guests come for.

Longtime guests are thrilled about the changes (including phone service) and so are we.

This unique apartment complex, at water's edge in the quiet East End, is a short walk to the center of town, yet sufficiently far enough to avoid the bar-hopping bustle. The complex consists of five restored Cape houses, all beautifully landscaped with flowers and shrubs. Three of these guest houses are right on the harbor and bay beach, encircling a meticulously clipped lawn set with lounge chairs. (At low tide you can walk out quite a distance into the bay.) Two additional houses are located across the street. Although these rooms were completely overhauled in 1995, they are still our least favorite and have limited water views. Guests in these rooms can still use all the oceanside facilities, of course. Off-street parking is available for all guests. Ann and Harriet acquired an additional house with five units in 1997; inquire about its status.

The architecture capitalizes on the sun and sea: spacious decks and large windows are the norm. All the apartments are individually furnished, and Ann and Harriet have redecorated many of them. (Some are still a bit eccentrically appointed and designed, with cork or mirrors on the walls and ceiling, for instance.)

Each unit has a modern bath, individually controlled heating, and a complete kitchen. Some units have alcove beds, beamed or cathedral ceilings, fireplaces, and eat-in-kitchens; all have a sofa bed in the living room. All units have a private entrance. (The rate card notes the special features of each room in detail.) The Hargood House does have one freestanding house across the street, with a private sunning patio, a garden, and a fireplace in its living room.

The Masthead Resort

31-41 Commercial Street
P.O. Box 577
Provincetown, MA 02657
508-487-0523
800-395-5095
Fax: 508-487-9251
www.capecod.com/masthead

Waterfront cottages and apartments

Owners: The Ciluzzi family. **Accommodations:** 9 cottages, apartments, and efficiencies; 8 rooms (6 with private bath), 3 suites. **Rates:** $893–$1,668 weekly per couple in cottages and apartments in season; $79–$179 nightly per couple in rooms and efficiencies in season; inquire about off-season rates; cottages are rented nightly in the off-season. **Included:** Kitchen facilities. **Minimum stay:** Weekly from July to early September. **Added:** 8% tax. **Credit cards accepted:** All major ones. **Children:** Welcome; free 12 and under; $20 each additional person in room. **Pets:** Not accepted. **Smoking:** Permitted. **Handicap access:** No. **Open:** Year-round.

➤ **The resort is in the quiet West End, just a short walk to the end of Commercial Street where the Pilgrims first landed. Pack a picnic and walk along the stone breakwater that crosses the harbor to reach the Long Point Lighthouse at the absolute tip of the Cape.**

The Masthead, a snug complex of weathered and shingled buildings on the harbor, is equally well suited to families, groups, couples, and singles. Since it's located on the edge of town, a good 12-minute walk to the center, it's also peaceful and quiet. The buildings are all quite close together, separated by meticulously maintained gardens, blooming rose bushes, a closely clipped lawn, and white picket fences. A 450-foot boardwalk, lined with lounge chairs, separates the lawn from the beach and bay. At high tide you can swim from the boardwalk, and at low tide you can explore hundreds of yards into the bay.

Every cottage faces the water and has a large picture window. Many units are dark (but cozy) with knotty pine paneling. Although the predominantly early American furnishings are tasteful, many pieces are a bit dated. (To be fair, some have expensive antiques.) Each accommodation has its own quirky but charming characteristics. No two units are remotely the same, so ask the reservationist for a detailed description of cottages and apartments. Then narrow down your selection, and with that in hand, ask for even more detail.

Here are a few specifics about what is available to get you started in the right direction: cottage #35 is the largest, with two floors; cottage #39 is actually a two-story house; units #31A and #41A each have a private patio facing the bay; and studio #41R features a three-sided view. Except for the nondescript motel-style rooms (which have refrigerators), each of the apartments has a fully equipped kitchen, air conditioning, and television. For the off-season, each unit is individually heated.

Make reservations as early in the season as possible; this place has a devoted following. It has been in business since 1949 and has been operated by the same family since 1959.

Watermark Inn

603 Commercial Street
Provincetown, MA 02657
508-487-0165
800-734-0165 in Massachusetts
Fax: 508-487-2383

A contemporary retreat at water's edge

Owners: Kevin Shea and Judith Richland. **Accommodations:** 10 rooms and suites (all with private bath). **Rates:** $135–$290 per couple from July to early September; $880–$1,875 per week in season; $64–$145 nightly from November to late May. **Included:** 1 room with a full kitchen. **Minimum stay:** 7 nights preferred in July and August; 3–4 nights over holidays. **Added:** 8% tax. **Credit cards accepted:** All major ones. **Children:** Welcome, half the adult rate of $20–$40 per extra person. **Pets:** Not accepted. **Smoking:** Permitted. **Handicap access:** No. **Open:** Year-round.

➤ **The view of the Watermark Inn from Commercial Street is deceiving. The crushed-shell driveway, trellis, white picket fence, and gray clapboards fit right in with the traditional neighborhood construction. What you can't see immediately are the contemporary comforts and unobstructed ocean views.**

If unadulterated ocean views are what you're after, the Watermark is the place to be. At high tide the water laps at the lower deck. At low tide, a sandy private beach is exposed. From both the upper and lower decks guests can watch the sky change colors as the sun rises, listen to the sounds of the sea, and bask in the glow and warmth of a setting sun. The Watermark is in the quiet East End, a 15-minute walk into town. It's the kind of place where, once checked in, you'll be left to your own devices. Most guests seem content to relax on their decks sunbathing, reading, and snoozing during the day.

The owners of the Watermark have a design and architecture firm in Cambridge, Massachusetts, and they've put their skills to good use here. Many of the accommodations at this multi-gabled, two-story contemporary structure are suites with skylights and sliding glass doors. The second-floor suites (numbers 7, 8, 9, and 10 — with private decks) feature triangular windows in the gable, maximizing contact with the sun and sea. These units have a loft bed in addition to a separate bedroom. The widest panoramic views are from the two corner suites, numbers 7 and 10. The former faces west, toward the Provincetown pier and fishing boats; the latter faces east, toward the lights of Truro and Wellfleet. Suite 7 is the only one with a full kitchen.

All rooms have kitchenettes, modern tiled bathrooms, cable TV, sleek Scandinavian-style furniture, and white walls. Two of our favorites have a fireplace. Suite 3, the largest, has hardwood floors, a king-size bed, and twelve linear feet of glass opening onto the deck.

Suites 1 and 2 have no water view, while 5 and 6 have an oblique one. These, of course, are the less expensive rooms. But all of the rooms have access to the lower deck. Rooms can sleep four to six people.

The kitchenettes come with a toaster, coffeepot, small refrigerator, and sink — perfectly adequate for a Continental breakfast, chilling drinks, and preparing snacks.

White Horse Inn

500 Commercial Street
Provincetown, MA 02657
508-487-1790

| **A Bohemian guest house with eclectic studios** |

Innkeeper: Frank Schaefer. **Accommodations:** 12 rooms (2 with private bath), 6 studios. **Rates:** $50–$75 per couple in rooms, $125 per couple in apartments in season; $50–$75 off-season. **Included:** No meals served. **Minimum stay:** 3 nights in studios in season. **Added:** 8% tax. **Credit cards accepted:** None. **Children:** Welcome; small ones are free. **Pets:** Not accepted. **Smoking:** Permitted in moderation. **Handicap access:** No. **Open:** Year-round.

➤ **Frank has supported local artists since he arrived on the scene in the 1960s: more than 300 paintings hang throughout the house.**

The White Horse Inn embodies the true spirit of Provincetown: it's a bit Bohemian, artistically aware, and very casual. About half his clientele is European. In season, guests enjoy the town's main activities: sunning, sipping coffee at outdoor cafés, and people-watching. In the off-season, they enjoy tranquillity. Through it all, the stable presence of Frank Schaefer (who's been here since 1963) helps keep things grounded.

The facade of this 200-year-old captain's house in the quiet East End is classic — crisp and white, with blue shutters and a yellow door — but the interior is an eclectic surprise. The best accommodations are the studio apartments in a separate wing, where you'll find such treasures as Isabella Rossellini's writing table, Eugene ONeill's stained glass windows, woodcarvings that have been used as wallboard or door moldings, and a slab of marble from the Bank of Boston that's now a writing table (perfectly placed in front of a small window that peeks out onto the ocean). One studio has a sliding glass door that opens onto a private deck. Another has shingled walls, siding from an old barn, and other interesting odds and ends. Newly redone, apartment #2 is a bright loft space with good cross breeze; it sleeps three people.

Even Frank has a hard time describing his rooms: "Each is a work of art in progress, a piece of sculpture . . . one bathroom is postmodern nautical." You get the picture. Trust us: if you're adventurous, this place will appeal to you. Trust Frank to give you the best of what's available in your price range.

The rooms in the main house, with low ceilings and shellacked floors, are furnished with simple antiques and original artwork. Ten rooms share three baths. Room 14, in the back of the house, is larger with a private bath. A number of rooms are cozy singles; among these #21 overlooks the neighbor's lovely English garden. There are no special amenities or common space, just good value.

Frank doesn't offer breakfast because there are so many great little places in town for either a full meal or a cup of coffee. (Café Edwige is a personal favorite of his and ours.) However, he does have a backyard grill and a bike rack that guests can use. Directly across from the house is a path that leads right down to the water. The White Horse Inn is quite a find, folks.

Sandwich

Wingscorton Farm Inn

11 Wing Boulevard (off Route 6A)
East Sandwich, MA 02537
508-888-0534

A lovely 18th-century farmhouse

Innkeepers: Dick Loring and Sheila Weyers. **Accommodations:** 4 suites (all with private bath), 1 carriage house. **Rates:** $115–$150 per couple; $45 each additional person. **Included:** Full breakfast. **Minimum stay:** 2 nights on holidays. **Added:** 9.7% tax. **Credit cards accepted:** All major ones. **Children:** Welcome; $5 for cribs. **Pets:** Accepted; $10. **Smoking:** Permitted. **Handicap access:** No. **Open:** Year-round.

➤ **The farm raises free-range chickens and sells "farm fresh" eggs.**

For all those cynics who insist Cape Cod is overdeveloped, have we got a surprise for you. This delightful treasure, well hidden down a sandy road off Route 6A, is straight out of the 18th century. The white clapboard house and barn are situated on seven tranquil acres of lawns, vegetable and flower gardens, and orchards. (Only animal lovers need call — dogs, cats, chickens, and pygmy goats are plentiful.) The inn is also just a short walk from a private bayside ocean beach. It all adds up to a pleasant retreat during any season.

Low ceilings, fireplaces, brass lanterns, and rich wainscoting are all typical of a house dating to 1758. Plentiful common space includes a keeping room — said to boast the largest hearth in New England (unfortunately, it's only lit on special occasions) — furnished with Oriental carpets, a grand piano, and comfortable couches. Just beyond is a handsome, cozy library with a working fireplace flanked by wing chairs. As you might expect from a working farm, breakfast is served in a Colonial-style dining room and consists of food gathered from the gardens and animals.

Upstairs in the main house, each two-room suite consists of a large queen-bedded room and an attached smaller room with twin beds. All are appointed with simple, lovely antiques and perhaps a fishnet canopy four-poster bed or Shaker-style furniture. The Carriage House, a tastefully renovated two-story structure, includes modern amenities like a full kitchen, luxury bath, skylights, a woodstove, a private deck for sunbathing, and a beamed ceiling. It's perfect for those seeking more privacy, for longer stays, or for small families (since the living room has a sofa bed).

South Harwich

The House on the Hill

P.O. Box 51
968 Main Street (Route 28)
South Harwich, MA 02661
508-432-4321
www.virtualcapecod/market/houseonthehill/

> An old-fashioned guest
> house

Hosts: Carolyn and Allen Swanson. **Accommodations:** 3 rooms (all with private bath). **Rates:** $55–$65 per couple. **Included:** Continental breakfast. **Minimum stay:** None. **Added:** 9.7% tax. **Credit cards accepted:** None. **Children:** Welcome; $5–$10 additional. **Pets:** Not accepted. **Smoking:** In designated area. **Handicap access:** No. **Open:** Year-round.

> ➤ **The 1832 Federal farmhouse, on a little knoll on Route 28, has been in Allen's family since 1948, when he was 18. He and Carolyn moved back here in 1971 and began running it as a B&B in 1986.**

This is the kind of place we really appreciate — an unpretentious, quiet guest house that's affordable, neat, and run by honest, old-fashioned folks who care about giving their guests good value.

Built by the son of a sea captain, the house has many fine features. The keeping room, which doubles as the breakfast room, is the best part of the house. It's also the oldest, with a fireplace and beehive oven, wide pine wainscoting and floorboards, and original handwrought door latches. The Continental breakfast, served at one long country table, is simple, with juice, fruit, and breads.

The living room, with a beamed ceiling, original paneling, and a fireplace, is homey and comfortable. It also has a television. The bedrooms don't have the charm of the common rooms. Rather, they're furnished simply, in the acknowledgment that guests will be spending most of their time out and about.

On one side of the house is a nice deck with a gas grill, which guests are welcome to use. On the other side is a patio with lawn furniture, stone walls, and landscaped flower gardens.

South Yarmouth

Captain Farris House

308 Old Main Street
Bass River Village
South Yarmouth, MA 02665
508-760-2818
800-350-9477
Fax: 508-398-1262
www.captainfarriscapecod.com

A former sea captain's house

Innkeepers: Patricia and Stephen Bronstein. **Accommodations:** 4 rooms, 4 suites (all with private bath). **Rates:** $95–$140 per couple in rooms, $155–$185 in suites, in season. **Included:** Full breakfast. **Minimum stay:** 2 nights on weekends, 3 nights on holidays. **Added:** 9.7% tax. **Credit cards accepted:** All major ones. **Children:** Welcome. **Pets:** Not accepted. **Smoking:** Not permitted. **Handicap access:** No. **Open:** Year-round.

➤ **Less than a block from Route 28 but protected from the summertime hordes, the house is sequestered within a little-known, historic Quaker neighborhood.**

Travelers familiar with Cape Cod's overdeveloped Route 28 can scarcely believe us when we recommend this enticing place. But we do recommend it. After a period of renovation, during which the entire sea captain's house and adjacent building were gutted, the house opened to guests in 1994. Its central location makes it a good base for exploring the Cape.

The main house, furnished with flair, is filled with decorative arts and a harmonious blend of coolly contemporary pieces and warm colors and fabrics. Guest rooms (some of which are two-room suites with overstuffed chairs that you'll not want to rouse yourself from) are stylishly understated — even the walls have been artfully painted using subtle "washes" and ragging techniques. Although Room 3 doesn't have the best location, it has distinct furnishings indicative of the inn's style: a welded steel chair sits next to an antique armoir, and a large abstract iron sculpture sits at the foot of the bed, which is dressed with lots of fluffy pillows, fine linens, a down comforter, and a carved antique headboard. It works wonderfully. Because of the layout of the house, most rooms have a private feel; a few have private decks. Many rooms feature new fireplaces. The completely renovated bathrooms feature bright white tiles, wainscoting, oversize Jacuzzi tubs, thick white towels, and fine toiletries.

Although some guests never leave their rooms, some venture out to the expansive shaded lawn or the front porch rockers. The small front parlor is formal, its floor-to-ceiling windows dressed with elegant drapery, but not intimidating.

Breakfast is served at an oval table in the formal dining room, complete with chandelier, or in warm weather in the brick courtyard. Although the courtyard has been spruced up, there's no getting around the fact that the architect could have taken greater care in joining the buildings, thereby creating a more enticing patio. The focus, however, quickly turns to the food: abundant fruit plates, strong coffee, juice in cobalt blue goblets, and on our last visit, anything we wanted as a main dish.

Truro

Kalmar Village

Route 6A
P.O. Box 745
North Truro, MA 02652
508-487-0585
617-247-0211 (winter)
Fax: 508-487-5827
www.cyberrentals.com/MA/PrelTRUR.html

A tidy cottage-colony on the bay

Owners: The Prelack family. **Accommodations:** 36 1- and 2-bedroom cottages, 13 efficiencies, 3 motel rooms. **Rates:** $775–$1,595 weekly in cottages for 4 people, from July to early September (each additional person $60–$150 weekly); $435–$725 weekly for efficiencies; inquire about off-season rates.

Included: Full kitchens. **Minimum stay:** One week in cottages during peak summer. **Added:** 9.7% tax. **Credit cards accepted:** All major ones. **Children:** Welcome; cribs free. **Pets:** Not accepted. **Smoking:** Not encouraged, but permitted. **Handicap access:** No. **Open:** Mid-May to late October.

➤ **Provincetown, and the spit of sand beyond it, curl around to form a tranquil and sheltered bay. These cottages are well positioned to take full advantage of it.**

The shores of North Truro are lined, shingle to shingle, with cookie-cutter cottage colonies and two-story motels. But from the moment you set eyes on Kalmar Village, you realize it's a cut above the monotonous crackerboxes that surround it. In the same family since 1968, Kalmar is maintained with family pride.

The freshly painted black and white cottages, surrounded by white picket fences and lawns, look very much like a quaint little village — even the chimneys are painted with white with black tops. Paths connect the cottages and lead to the sandy bayside beach. Each cottage has its own little front yard, picnic table, grill, and lounge chairs. Many cottages surround the large freshwater pool; others have unobstructed ocean views, while some have oblique ones. The complex has 400 feet of bayside beach, but it's part of a long contiguous stretch so you can walk and walk. Families flock to Kalmar Village because there's plenty of space for kids to run around. Just across the road (Route 6A) loom the dramatic dunes of the pristine Cape Cod National Seashore.

Accommodations are neat, nicely furnished, spacious, and bright. Most have traditional, knotty pine interiors. Kitchens are fully equipped for cooking and dining. Linens and blankets are provided, as is daily housekeeping. (Units are heated for the chillier off-season months.) Four types of cottages are available, all of which comfortably sleep four people. Even the efficiencies can comfortably sleep four or five people. We like the newer three-room cottages, which can sleep six and are much bigger than the other cottages. Most of these have full water views and are thus more expensive. They're worth it if you're lucky enough to get one. A few other cottages, with a private porch, are also on the beach.

The Outer Cape draws visitors who want to be as close as possible to the sand, surf, and sea. The National Seashore is laced with walking and bicycling trails, as well as great places to fly a kite and sunbathe. Provincetown, just a 5-minute drive from North Truro, is filled with dozens of art galleries, fine restaurants, and one-of-a-kind shops.

Wellfleet

Cahoon Hollow Bed & Breakfast

Cahoon Hollow Road
P.O. Box 383
Wellfleet, MA 02667
508-349-6372

> **B&B rooms (and a house)
> off the beaten path**

Hosts: Bailey and Wally Ruckert. **Accommodations:** 2 suites (each with private bath). **Rates:** $95–$100 nightly at the B&B; $1,000 weekly from mid-June to mid-September, $750 off-season for the house. **Included:** Full breakfast with B&B rooms. **Minimum stay:** None for B&B rooms. **Added:** No tax to B&B rooms. **Credit cards accepted:** MasterCard, Visa. **Children:** Over age 6 welcome in B&B; $15 each additional person in B&B. **Pets:** Not accepted. **Smoking:** Not permitted. **Handicap access:** No. **Open:** Year-round.

➤ **Inquire about the rental house, down the road, that Bailey offers by the week for up to six people. It's a great place.**

After traveling around Scotland and staying in B&Bs, Bailey and Wally decided to open their home as a B&B in 1987. And although we don't usually include B&Bs that only have two rooms, we've made an exception in this case because of the unusual arrangement at Cahoon Hollow. The innkeepers live in separate accommodations, so you feel as if you have the 1842 Greek Revival house to yourself. It's an especially nice option for two couples traveling together.

The upstairs guest room is preferable for longer stays; it has a large bedroom and separate sitting room. The downstairs room features a fireplace and an extra little room with a daybed. Guests have access to a telephone and refrigerator. Two living rooms are comfortably elegant, stocked with plenty of reading material about the area. One has a television and fireplace. Bailey is a fiber artist and you'll see her handiwork throughout the house — in the form of baskets, rugs, pillows, and wall hangings.

As you drive up to the secluded house, you may be wondering how a garden so lush and grass so green could grow in such sandy conditions. Well, the house was built by a sea captain who traveled between Maine and Cape Cod, and on his return trips home, he used rich Maine soil as ballast for his ship. You'll enjoy the grounds from the shaded hammock. For exploring the area, Bailey has loaner bicycles.

The three-course breakfast, served at one table in the dining room or on the back patio surrounded by lush greenery, is a delight. On our last visit we enjoyed homemade yogurt and granola, popovers with honey butter, and a deep-dish custard French toast with beech plum jam. Other possibilities include rhubarb crumb cake and four-grain pancakes.

Even in the height of summer, Wellfleet is a wonderfully quiet old Cape Cod town, primarily inhabited by folks who rent houses or have their own summer homes here. There aren't as many nice B&Bs as there are people who want to stay in them, so reserve early if you can.

West Dennis

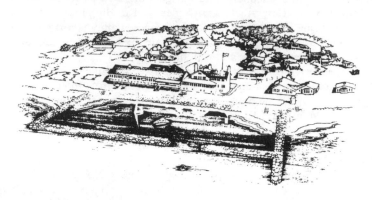

The Lighthouse Inn

P.O. Box 128
1 Lighthouse Inn Road
West Dennis, MA 02670
508-398-2244
Fax: 508-398-5658
www.lighthouseinn.com

An oceanfront family resort

Hosts: Greg and Patricia Stone. **Accommodations:** 61 rooms and cottages (all with private bath). **Rates:** $184–$224 B&B per couple in season; $134–$174 in May, June, September, and October. **Included:** Full breakfast, but packages vary with meal plan. **Minimum stay:** 2 nights on weekends in summer, 3 on holidays. **Added:** 9.7% tax. **Credit cards accepted:** MasterCard, Visa. **Children:** Welcome; $25–$50 per day depending on age, B&B. **Pets:** Not accepted. **Smoking:** Not permitted in dining room. **Handicap access:** Yes. **Open:** Mid-May to mid-October.

➤   **The Bass River Lighthouse, incorporated into the center section of the inn, was relit in 1989 after 75 years of disuse. Prior to that it served as a lighthouse from 1855 to 1880. Today it's the only privately owned and maintained lighthouse in the country.**

This is very much a family destination, and a full-service one at that. The Stone family has owned the place since 1938, and they added the last cottage back in 1956. As the oldest continually operated resort on the Cape, it remains charmingly old-fashioned while at the same time keeping up with modern conveniences.

Far enough from the congestion of Route 28, the inn occupies nine acres that abut the ever-popular West Dennis beach. Inn guests also have access to their own private beach on Nantucket Sound. Furthermore, the grassy grounds boast a tennis court, a pool, mini-golf, shuffleboard, basketball, and volleyball. A number of good golf courses are nearby.

The inn offers supervised activities in the morning for kids aged 3 and 4 and throughout the day for kids aged 5 and older. Among other things, there is sandcastle building, storytelling, arts and crafts, and kite flying. The Stone family's grandchildren host their own reception for kids, complete with entertainment. On Saturday night they throw a pizza party.

The airy, seaside dining room — with peaked ceilings, knotty pine paneling, and flags hanging from the rafters — overlooks the ocean. Dinners feature New England–style dishes such as chicken cutlets, Chatham scrod, and salmon pesto. On our last visit, we were delightfully surprised by the kitchen's quality. For breakfast you can begin with the cold buffet, then order a hot entrée off the menu. Lunch is served poolside or on the oceanside deck.

All of the modest but nicely maintained cottages have television, telephone, and a refrigerator. The two-, three-, and four-room cottages can sleep up to six people. The staff is always bustling about, making sure the cottages stay neat and tidy, the lawn manicured, and the flowerbeds weeded. On rainy days when you may want to spread out a bit more, the main lodge has plenty of games, books, a television, and comfortable living rooms furnished in a 1950s and 1960s style. Evening entertainment includes cabaret at the inn's Sand Bar.

West Falmouth

The Inn at West Falmouth

P.O. Box 1208
West Falmouth, MA 02574
508-540-7696
800-397-7696
Fax: 508-548-6974

A sophisticated country estate

Innkeeper: Karen Calvacca. **Accommodations:** 6 rooms (all with private bath). **Rates:** $175–$300 per couple from May through October; $145–$250 off-season. **Included:** Expanded Continental breakfast. **Minimum stay:** 2 nights. **Added:** 9.7% tax. **Credit cards accepted:** All major ones. **Children:** Over age 13 welcome. **Pets:** Not accepted. **Smoking:** Not permitted. **Handicap access:** No. **Open:** Year-round.

➤ **The house is situated on a hill and, as such, the ocean view from the back porch and some of the guest rooms is expansive.**

The three-story Inn at West Falmouth is an exquisitely restored 1900 Shingle-style home set high off the road. It enjoys a private and secluded setting. Stately and elegant, comfortable yet formal, it is reminiscent of an English country manor — with a twist of Italian villa.

The common rooms offer plenty of space. The living room, with a dominant pink granite fireplace, is perfectly balanced with a blend of contemporary and antique English and Chinese furniture. A screened-in porch, with hanging plants and wicker furniture, overlooks the pool and woods. A conservatory-garden room with stained glass windows leads out to the deck, pool, and a clay tennis court below the terraced backyard. The back deck and heated pool are landscaped with potted annuals and perennials. It's one of the most relaxing places we've found.

A collection of eclectic European antiques fills the guest rooms, the best of which have private balconies or arched windows. Most of the rooms have a fireplace and canopy bed. The rooms in the front of the house glow with morning light, while the other half have sunset water views. All have an oversize Jacuzzi. Bathrooms are particularly sumptuous with Italian marble.

An expanded Continental breakfast is served at individual tables.

Yarmouth Port

Wedgewood Inn

83 Main Street (Route 6A)
Yarmouth Port, MA 02675
508-362-5157
Fax: 508-362-5851

| A comfortably elegant and romantic B&B |

Innkeepers: Gerrie and Milt Graham. **Accommodations:** 5 suites and 4 rooms (all with private bath). **Rates:** $125–$175 per couple in season; $95–$135 from November through May. **Included:** Full breakfast. **Minimum stay:** None. **Added:** 9.7% tax. **Credit cards accepted:** All major ones. **Children:** Over age 10 welcome. **Pets:** Not accepted. **Smoking:** Not encouraged in common areas. **Handicap access:** No. **Open:** Year-round.

➤ **In 1997 the Graham's added new luxury rooms in the renovated barn behind the house. The historic post-and-beam structure now contains L-shaped suites with private decks, fireplaces, canopy beds, televisions, and telephones. There's also a great common room.**

The Wedgewood Inn was built for a Maritime lawyer in 1812, back when Yarmouth Port actually had a port. On historic and tranquil Route 6A, the house stands quite regal up on its grassy knoll, shaded by ancient trees. Lovely gardens encircle the house. This romantic and distinctive inn is appealing for its comfortable elegance.

The common room is small, serving as much like a pass-through area as a living room. But that's not a problem because the guest rooms are so comfortable, you'll not want to leave them. We like the four spacious rooms in the front of the house best. Two of these have a private screened-in porch; of these, Room 2 has bright afternoon light, and Room 1 has a daybed in a small sitting room. All the rooms are formally decorated with cherry wood pencil-post beds, quilts, Oriental carpets, and wing chairs. Most have a working fireplace and wide, hardwood floors, and all are air-conditioned. Most of the bathrooms are roomy, with clawfoot tubs, porcelain sinks, and antique fixtures. Rooms 5 and 6 are tucked away, with a more private feeling to them. Because of the fireplaces, the inn is as comfortable in the off-season as in the height of the summer.

You'll also find gracious service to match the 19th-century restoration and lovely furnishings. In between serving the dishes and pouring coffee, Milt is happy to help guests plan their day's schedule. On our last visit Milt offered a choice of herb scrambled eggs or French toast prepared by Gerrie. Small tables are set with flowers and fine china. The Graham's attention to details — which add up to create an inviting inn — is evidenced by wall sconces, a glowing chandelier, and period wallpapers and paintings.

One of the things we like best about the Wedgewood is that the innkeepers don't fuss over you, but they're helpful if you need them. Milt (a former FBI man) and Gerrie (a former schoolteacher) have been at this since 1983, and they're fully knowledgeable about the area. Route 6A is lined with antiques shops, a handful of fine restaurants, and historic homes. Afternoon tea is served for those taking a break from sightseeing and antiquing.

The Other Massachusetts

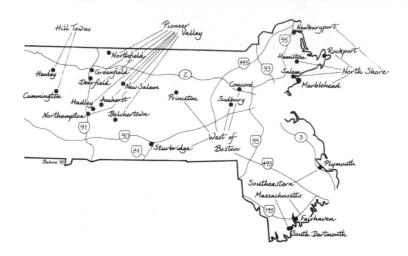

Berkshire Hilltowns

The North Shore

Pioneer Valley

Southeastern Massachusetts

West of Boston

Best Bed-and-Breakfasts

Best Small Hotels

Best Family Finds

Best Inns

Amherst
The Lord Jeffery Inn on the Common, 348
Concord
The Colonial Inn, 364
Deerfield
Deerfield Inn, 351
Rockport
Seaward Inn, 343

Best Romantic Getaways

Hamilton
The Miles River Country Inn, 331
Marblehead
The Harbor Light Inn, 333
Northfield
Northfield Country House, 358
Princeton
Fernside, 365
Rockport
Addison Choate, 337
Eden Pines Inn, 338

Best Rustic Retreat

Hawley
Stump Sprouts, 329

Half of the Bay State's residents live within the arc of Route 495, a highway that roughly defines Greater Boston. These people tend to play on Cape Cod Bay (the state's fastest-growing area) and the islands of Martha's Vineyard and Nantucket. Boston, the Cape, and the two islands also represent the Massachusetts that most visitors see. Which leaves the other two-thirds of the state relatively lightly populated and touristed. With the exception of the Berkshires, the state's westernmost hill country, this area lacks even a name, which is why we call it "the Other Massachusetts."

There are many different parts to the Other Massachusetts. Perhaps the most distinctive of them all is the North Shore, which begins less than twenty miles north of Boston and tacks and jibs thirty miles or so, along the ragged edge off Ipswich Bay to Newburyport, just below New Hampshire. Here the old seaports look much as they did in their heyday — for **Marblehead,** the decades just before the Revolution; for **Salem** and **Newburyport,** the Federal era; and for Gloucester, the late 19th century. Pleasant places to visit, these shore towns are great places to stay. In **Rockport** on Cape Ann, for instance, you can swim and walk the dramatic shore paths at Halibut Point, take an excursion boat out to watch whales, and hop a train into Boston.

A commuter rail also serves **Concord,** which is twenty miles west of Boston. This is yet another pleasant place to stay as well as tour Revolutionary and literary sites. Here you can rent a canoe and paddle on the Concord and Sudbury rivers and walk around or swim in Walden Pond, where the site of Henry David Thoreau's cabin in the woods has become an international literary shrine.

Concord is on Route 2, the more scenic of the two east-west highways that cross Massachusetts. It draws you into the Nashoba Valley and west through hills and country roads leading to forgotten old resort villages such as **Princeton** and Petersham, and on to gracious old Connecticut Valley towns like **Northfield** and **Deerfield** (known for its street lined with the dozen museum houses that form Historic Deerfield).

Continuing west, Route 2 becomes the Mohawk Trail, so named because it shadows an old Indian path along the Deerfield Valley, threading dramatically humped hills. These hills rise tier on tier and lend themselves, around Charlemont and **Hawley,** to both downhill and cross-country skiing.

The quick way back to Boston is, of course, the Massachusetts Turnpike, but there are other options, notably Route 9, the other old east-west high road, which follows rivers and ridges, inviting you to pause for a night or two at some of the fine old hill farms in towns like **Cummington.** Known for its poets, past and present, Cummington is also the former summer home of William Cullen Bryant, whose house is now a fascinating museum.

Continue east on Route 9 into **Northampton** and **Amherst,** the dining and shopping hubs of the Five College Area. The colleges — Amherst, Hampshire, Mount Holyoke, Smith, and the University of Massachusetts at Amherst — all offer art museums (in Northampton, Smith's Museum of Art is outstanding) and a full calendar of lectures, film, and live entertainment, much of it open to the public. Representing New England's largest concentration of students and faculty outside the Boston area, this old farmland also offers an unusual array of crafts shops, bookstores, and restaurants.

While it is at its liveliest during the academic year, this area is also delightful in summer, the season to take advantage of extensive hiking trails, bicycle paths, outdoor concerts, summer theater, and canoeing on the Connecticut River.

If you do take the Mass. Pike, be sure to stop in Springfield, the home of a cultural "quadrangle" of art, historical, and science museums as well as the Basketball Hall of Fame. Halfway back to Boston, another must stop is **Old Sturbridge Village**, New England's largest museum village, which re-creates the life of rural New England in the 1830s.

You can also detour into Worcester, the state's second city and the home of the superb Worcester Museum of Art and the Higgins Armory Museum (displaying more than one hundred suits of medieval armor).

Don't forget the southeastern corner of the state. The old whaling port of New Bedford is a great place to walk, shop, and dine, and the surrounding coastline is patched with good beaches. The quiet roads are good for biking. You can also spend a satisfying day walking the paths of Cuttyhunk Island, accessible by ferry from New Bedford.

BERKSHIRE HILLTOWNS

Cummington

Windfields Farm

154 Windsor Bush Road
Cummington, MA 01026
413-684-3786

> **A classic farmhouse built in 1830**

Hosts: Arnold and Carolyn Westwood. **Accommodations:** 2 rooms (with shared bath). **Rates:** $75 per couple, $50 single. Inquire about rates for two and three couples sharing winter weekends. **Included:** Full breakfast. **Minimum stay:** 2 nights on most weekends. **Added:** No tax required. **Credit cards accepted:** None. **Children:** Over age 12. **Pets:** Not allowed. **Smoking:** Not permitted in the house. **Handicap access:** No. **Open:** May through February.

➤ **A swimming pond, cross-country ski trails, Arnold's blueberry pancakes, Carolyn's maple syrup, and great conversation bring guests back again and again.**

Windfields offers many of life's true luxuries: a spring-fed pond in summer, cross-country skiing in winter, and bountiful breakfasts of eggs, maple syrup, jams, and berries, all produced on the premises. The Westwoods are particularly adept at making guests feel welcome, a skill Arnold honed in his former life as a Unitarian minister.

Although the farmhouse was built in 1830, it is a classic Federal design, with two 15-by-15-foot upstairs bedrooms. The rooms are homey, with floral wallpaper, wide-board floors, and braided rugs.

One is furnished in antiques, which include an exquisite early-19th-century canopy bed; the other is plainer but cheery and nearer the shared bath. The comfortable living room, with low beams and a stone hearth, is lined with books. Meals are served in a pleasant dining room, hung with original art.

The house is on an unpaved road not far from West Cummington, a village in the Hampshire hills. West of the Connecticut River valley, east of the Berkshires, this is high, rolling countryside, webbed with back roads leading to orchards, craft studios, and maple syrup producers.

Since the Westwoods bought Windfields in 1961, they have planted a sizable organic garden, built a sugar shack, added a solar wing to the house, and turned the pond into a sand-edged oasis, ideal for a summer dip. Music at Tanglewood and theater in Williamstown are just a pleasant drive away.

In winter Arnold and Carolyn open a kitchen to guests and offer "winter weekends" to a minimum of four people, who can cook their own lunch and dinner. Cross-country ski rentals and an assortment of trails are up the road. Windfields itself includes 200 explorable acres and adjoins the Audubon Society's 1,500-acre West Mountain Wildlife Sanctuary.

Hawley

Stump Sprouts

West Hill Road
West Hawley, MA 01339
413-339-4265

> The clapboard building stands on a 450-acre hilltop spread.

Hosts: Lloyd and Suzanne Crawford. **Accommodations:** 20-guest maximum.
Rates: $42 per person; $94–$119 per weekend with all meals included. $20 per

night, $69 per weekend on a cook-your-own basis. **Added:** 5.7% tax. **Credit cards accepted:** None. **Children:** Special rates. **Pets:** Not accepted. **Smoking:** Not permitted. **Handicap access:** No. **Open:** Year-round.

➤ **Guests are asked to bring sleeping bags, towels, and soap, but they are not roughing it — Stump Sprouts offers some rare luxuries.**

The Crawfords describe Stump Sprouts as a guest lodge and ski touring center, but it's really in a class of its own — a modern clapboard building that Lloyd built almost entirely himself from timbers standing on this 450-acre hilltop spread. From the lodge, you can see horses grazing immediately outside, tier upon tier of wooded hills in the distance, and, on a clear day, Mount Monadnock.

The lodge is well designed, built into a hill, with several levels. The guest rooms, which sleep from two to eight, are fitted with bunks made by Lloyd — some double, some tiered, some in lofts. The building has skylights and pleasing nooks, such as the cushioned reading or meditation loft over the skyroom. There is a fireplace, comfortable chairs, and sofas that Lloyd made, as well as lots of games. Sun streams in the stained glass windows.

Downstairs, a cheerful dining area is furnished with Lloyd's tables and benches. It opens onto a combination rock garden and terrace, which is also a good place to eat in nice weather.

The lodge is spotless and often decorated with fresh flowers. Special features include a phone, a freestanding wood-heated sauna and outdoor shower, badminton, volleyball, horseshoes, and croquet. The barn has also been nicely renovated as a dancing or meeting space with a "Dairy-Aire" room (the back of the barn, where the cows used to be) that has a cathedral ceiling, exposed timbers, and a balcony in the old silo.

The Crawfords themselves live across the road with their children in a tidy 1840s farmhouse with a touring center tacked onto it. In the winter, they groom 25 kilometers of trails that meander through the property. The trail system culminates at two thousand feet, on the summit of Lone Boulder Hill. Ski rentals and waxes are offered, along with hot drinks, in the touring center. Instruction is also available. For downhill skiing, Berkshire East is just seven miles away. This is one of the least-populated, least-known corners of Massachusetts, rich in waterfalls, bogs, and hiking trails, all of which Lloyd has carefully mapped for visitors. This can be a splendid spot for an informal wedding.

THE NORTH SHORE

Hamilton

The Miles River Country Inn

823 Bay Road
P.O. Box 149
Hamilton, MA 01936
978-468-7206
Fax: 978-468-3999
mrcipbc@tiac.net
www.milesriver.com

> **A country estate with gorgeous gardens**

Host: Gretel and Peter Clark. **Accommodations:** 1 suite, 7 rooms (5 with private bath, 4 with working fireplaces). Inquire about the cottage on the Essex marshes. **Rates:** June through October: $90 (for the small single) to $210 for the suite; double rooms are $110–$165. Off-season: $90–$145. **Included:** Full breakfast. **Minimum stay:** 2 days June through October. **Added:** 5.7% tax. **Credit cards accepted:** All major ones. **Children:** Welcome. **Pets:** Inquire when making reservations. **Handicap access:** No. **Smoking:** Not permitted. **Open:** Year-round.

➤ **The 24-room mansion with well-tended lawns is handy to both Boston and North Shore sights and beaches.**

Nowhere else in New England do you feel as much like an invited guest at a private country estate. While there are plenty of other mansions that have been turned into inns, nowhere else are the longtime owners of the estate your hosts. Despite its name, the

Miles River Country Inn is still very much the home of Gretel and Peter Clark, and it's an exceptional home, to say the least.

The 24-room mansion, dating from various periods between 1774 and the 1920s, is set among well-tended lawns and some quite extraordinary gardens, which stretch as far as the eye can see. There are 30 acres in all and you can walk on and on through a forest of Beech trees. No less than seven distinct gardens — including a "secret garden" with an iron gate — can be savored within steps of the house. In spring, thousands of daffodils blanket the banks of a pond; in the fall, the colors of the fields and river grasses turn deep rubies and golds; and what you see between both changes every month.

"I couldn't leave my gardens" is the reason Gretel Clark gives for opening her home to guests rather than putting it up for sale after her four children were grown. She needed an excuse, she explains, to hold on to such a large, elaborate place.

Four of the rooms are still named for the children to whom they belonged for many years. Liesl's room, the most expensive, has a view of the gardens, a working fireplace, a four-poster bed, and a bathroom with a clawfoot tub. Jock's room, which obviously belonged to a boy, also has a garden view, twin beds, and a bath. Heidi's room has a great old bed, a working fireplace, and a private bath and shower. The Lilac room is named for the bushes below its wall of windows, and the Hearthside Room, which can be rented as a single or a suite, opens onto a sitting room with a raised hearth. All the rooms have plenty of books, but Bryn's, on the third floor, has the most interesting collection. Bryn's is on the top floor, sharing a bathroom (assuming both rooms are taken) with The Nook. The claw-foot bathtub here, however, has the best view in the entire house. Family antiques are scattered through all the guest rooms and the artwork is both plentiful and exceptional.All the fireplaces in the rooms are, incidentally, pre-set for guests with real logs, not Duraflame ones.

All the common rooms are open to guests. All have working fireplaces, and a study is richly paneled with 19th-century wooden bedsteads from Brittany. Artwork reflects the Clarks' travels and extensive overseas sojourns in France, Germany, Norway, Chile (more than two years), and Nigeria (two years).

A full breakfast, frequently eggs from the resident hens and honey from Gretel's apiary, is served buffet-style either in the bright, glass-walled dining nook in the big country kitchen or on the flagstone terrace under a 90-year-old beech tree. Coffee is set out at 7:30 A.M. because, Gretel explains, guests get excited and want to get out and explore the grounds early in the morning. The lawns stretch down to the Miles River, a habitat for the great blue heron as well as countless varieties of ducks. You might also see beaver, otter, muskrat, and possum, or maybe a ringneck pheasant or a screech owl.

Hamilton, known for its Sunday afternoon polo games (at which the public is welcome), is one of the most aristocratic towns on Boston's North Shore. It's just 6 miles from the sand and dunes at magnificent Crane Beach and handy to the dozens of antiques shops between Essex and Rowley as well as to the shops and restaurants on Cape Ann. But you might not want to leave the lily pond or the Secret Garden, with its high hedge walls, fountain, and elaborate iron gate, or even the glassed-in porch, with its New Orleans iron filigree.

If you are flying into Boston, this is a great place to laze off your jet lag; it's little more than 20 miles from Logan Airport. Peter is currently a major energy developer in Latin America. Gretel, retired from the Massachusetts Department of Education, also speaks fluent Spanish as well as French and German. Obviously, this is a perfect setting for an (outdoor) bi- or trilingual wedding. Inquire about local birding, hiking, and bicycling possibilities.

Marblehead

The Harbor Light Inn

58 Washington Street
Marblehead, MA 01945
781-631-2186
Fax: 781-631-2216

Romantic rooms in Marblehead

Manager: Peter Conway. **Accommodations:** 20 rooms and suites (all with private bath). **Rates:** Rooms: $95–$155 per couple; suites: $169–$245. **Included:** Light breakfast and tea. **Minimum stay:** 2 nights on weekends, 3 nights on long weekends. **Added:** 5.7% tax. **Credit cards accepted:** All major ones. **Children:** Over age 5, by arrangement. **Pets:** Not accepted. **Smoking:** Discouraged. **Handicap access:** No. **Open:** Year-round.

➤ **The quiet and formal atmosphere is more that of a small hotel than a B&B. The setting is an old port where sailors (yachtsmen) still outnumber landlubbers.**

The inn comprises two square Federal houses, joined by a hallway, that abut a narrow, winding street in the heart of Marblehead's old downtown. (There's plenty of parking in the rear.) The living rooms are formal and elegant. The fireplaces are flanked by matching sofas, and Oriental rugs cover wall-to-wall carpeting, creating a hushed tone throughout. There's a small, nicely landscaped pool in the garden. For receptions and small meetings, there's also a conference room and dining room.

The high-ceilinged guest rooms and suites are quite luxurious. Eleven have working fireplaces, five have Jacuzzis; several have canopy beds, and all have interesting artwork. From the roof you can see the lighthouse and the harbor.

There's plenty to do in and around Marblehead. The immediate area is chock full of interesting shops and restaurants and the famous painting *The Spirit of '76* hangs in the town hall. Take a tour of the Jeremiah Lee Mansion or rent a sailing craft.

Newburyport

Clark Currier Inn

45 Green Street
Newburyport, MA 01950
978-465-8363

| An elegant B&B in a shipbuilder's mansion |

Innkeepers: Mary and Bob Nolan. **Accommodations:** 8 rooms (all with private bath). **Rates:** $95–$145 per couple. **Included:** Continental breakfast, afternoon tea. **Minimum stay:** 2 days on summer weekends. **Added:** 9.7%. **Credit cards accepted:** All major ones. **Children:** Welcome. **Pets:** Not accepted. **Smoking:** Not permitted inside. **Handicap access:** No. **Open:** Year-round.

➤ **The gazebo in the garden is a favorite photo stop for brides who have just been married in the Catholic church across the street.**

This classic three-story Federal home exudes the grace and hospitality of Newburyport at its height. When the house was built in 1803, this small seaport was the nation's fourth-largest city, and its houses — with decorative dentil moldings, Indian shutters, window seats, and elegant mantels — were treasure chests for the furnishings, china, and artwork acquired by the towns shipowners and mariners on their travels.

The Clark Currier Inn is a pleasant mix of formal and informal. The parlor, with elaborate woodwork and a Samuel McIntyre mantel, is furnished with wing chairs and appropriate antiques, but there is also a skylit sitting room with a TV, wicker furniture, and magazines just off the garden. The dining room, where a breakfast of muffins, fruit, and yogurt is served, is open to the pleasant kitchen. There is also a small, flowery garden with a gazebo — a pleasant place to sit.

The rooms vary. In the Clark Room, a canopy bed backs up to a graceful mantel, and there are window seats. In the Currier Room, the bed has high pencil posts, and there's a fireplace and enclosed porch. The Hale Room has a Franklin stove and a fine sleigh bed. The Merrimac Room is best for families.

Mary and Bob Nolan's daughter, Melissa, plays hostess to visiting children, introducing them to Missy the cat and the play structure out back.

From the inn it's a short walk to Market Square and the waterfront shops, theater, galleries, and the Custom House Museum. The Parker River National Wildlife Refuge, with nine miles of sandy ocean beach and nature trails, is also in town, as is 450-acre Maudsley State Park, on the Merrimac River. Newburyport is also a departure point for whale-watching excursions.

The Morrill Place Inn

209 High Street
Newburyport, MA 01950
978-462-2808

A friendly B&B in a beautiful home

Innkeepers: Rose Ann and Kristin Hunter. **Accommodations:** 9 rooms (5 private baths). **Rates:** $72–$95 double. **Included:** Continental breakfast, tea, tax. **Minimum stay:** None. **Credit cards accepted:** None. **Children:** Not appropriate. **Pets:** Welcome. **Smoking:** Not permitted. **Handicap access:** No. **Open:** Year-round.

➤ **Each room is different, and the antiques include substantial sleigh and canopy beds. A number of rooms have a third bed tucked in the corner.**

Morrill Place is one of many imposing mansions that line Newburyport's High Street. The classic three-story Federal house was built in 1806, in the era when this North Shore town ranked as the country's seventh-largest seaport. Newburyport has since weathered many ups and downs. The downs have prevented much physical change, and the most recent up has restored the early-19th-century look of the community. Now the old brick shops are filled with boutiques. Add to this the beach and beauty of the neighboring Parker River National Wildlife Refuge (one of the country's top birding destinations) and the whale-watching and fishing excursions available from the waterfront.

Newburyport is an undersung spot to spend a few days, and Morrill Place is both friendly and luxurious. The twenty-six rooms have been meticulously furnished with a liberal use of imagination as well as antiques — a mix of formality and fun. In the dining room, where guests eat breakfast on a long, lace-covered table, the hearth has been marbleized, and in an upstairs guest room the throw rug turns out to be a floor painting.

In contrast to the formal parlor and dining room, there is an inviting TV room upstairs. The library with its hearth and comfortable armchairs and the glassed-in winter porch also invite lingering.

Rose Ann Hunter, who has run a B&B in Newburyport since 1976, conducts seminars and lectures on the hospitality industry throughout the country. She is ably assisted by her daughter Kristin. Ask about murder mystery weekends and other special weekends. Rooms all have an extra bed in case two women who are here for a workshop want to share. The third-floor rooms — with lower ceilings and prices — are particularly geared to groups (shared baths).

Rockport

Addison Choate

49 Broadway
Rockport, MA 01966
978-546-7543
800-245-7543
Fax: 978-546-7543
www.cape-ann.com/addison-chaote

A relaxing B&B in the thick of things

Innkeepers: Knox and Shirley Johnson. **Accommodations:** 5 rooms (all with private bath), 3 suites. **Rates:** High season: $98–$125 for rooms; November through April: $85–$105; weekly rates for stable house suites; singles, $15 less; extra person, $10 more. **Included:** Buffet breakfast, afternoon tea. **Minimum stay:** 2 nights on summer and holiday weekends. **Added:** 9.7% tax. **Credit cards accepted:** MasterCard, Visa, Discover; checks preferred. **Children:** Over age 11. **Pets:** Not accepted. **Smoking:** Not permitted in the inn. **Handicap access:** No. **Open:** Year-round.

➤ **The shops, galleries, restaurants, and beach are all an easy walk from the Addison Choate's quiet garden and landscaped pool.**

In the heart of a lively resort village, this handsome Greek Revival house offers a deep garden with a landscaped swimming pool and rooms artfully decorated with a mix of antique and reproduction furnishings and original art.

Approaching the 1850s house from a side porch that brims with flowers all summer long, guests enter a pleasant dining room, a small living room with a fireplace, and a TV room that is comfortably furnished.

Shirley Johnson is a professional designer, and her sure touch is evident throughout. The third-floor Celebrations Suite has its own sitting room, a bed canopied in hand-tied netting, and a view of chimney pots and water. The stable house suites, situated behind the inn, have cathedral ceilings, full kitchens, a living room with a sofa bed, and loft bedrooms.

Breakfast, which features homemade granola and specially blended coffee, may be served in the dining room or on the porch overlooking the perennial garden, which Shirley actually brought with her from her former home. Because parking in Rockport in the summer is a problem, it's a luxury to be able to walk a few minutes to shops, restaurants, and the beach.

Eden Pines Inn

Eden Road
Rockport, MA 01966
978-546-2505
December to April:
c/o 8 Cakebread Drive
Sudbury, MA 01776

A B&B on the ocean

Innkeeper: Inge Sullivan. **Accommodations:** 7 rooms in inn. **Rates:** $100–$165 double, $25 per extra person; rates for suites in nearby Eden Point House available on request. **Included:** Buffet breakfast, tea, and setups. **Minimum stay:** 2 days in summer, 3 on holiday weekends. **Added:** 9.7% tax. **Credit cards accepted:** MasterCard, Visa. **Children:** Over age 12. **Pets:** Not accepted. **Smoking:** Restricted. **Handicap access:** No. **Open:** Mid-May to mid-November.

➤ **A rambling old oceanside mansion, Eden Pines Inn offers expansive rooms and ocean views.**

This airy Cape Ann mansion has fine ocean views. From all but one of the guest rooms and from both the pleasant living room and the large porch, fitted with comfortable wicker and bright fabrics, the view is an expanse of water broken only by a small offshore island with twin granite lighthouses. A brick patio and smooth rocks below invite you to sun and laze near the water, and two pebbly beaches are within walking distance.

Most of the large rooms have balconies. Room 6 has a canopy bed, a corner balcony, and a TV. All are decorated with flowered fabrics in soft colors and have quite splendid marble-lined bathrooms.

Breakfast usually includes yogurt, homemade muffins, cereal, and fresh fruit. It's served in the sun room, where theres a refrigerator for stowing drinks; cookies are set out here at "tea time" at 5:00 P.M.

The living room is a comfortable, inviting space with a fieldstone fireplace, bookcases, and a sand-colored rug.

It's a mile and a half to the village of Rockport and its many shops, galleries, and restaurants. June is a great time to come, before the crowds and during the chamber music festival.

You might inquire about the Eden Point House, up the road, which is also on the water. The house has four bedrooms, three and a half baths, a full kitchen, and a living room with a fireplace. It can be divided into two 2-bedroom suites.

Old Farm Inn

P.O. Box 2309
Rockport, MA 01966
978-546-3237
800-233-6828

> A B&B near and yet
> removed from resort bustle

Innkeepers: Bill and Susan Balzarini. **Accommodations:** 7 rooms (all with private bath), 2 suites, 1 cottage. **Rates:** $88–$130 double occupancy; less off-season. **Included:** Breakfast (except cottage). **Minimum stay:** 2 nights on weekends. **Added:** 9.7% tax. **Credit cards accepted:** MasterCard, Visa, American Express. **Children:** Five years and up. **Pets:** Not accepted. **Smoking:** Restricted. **Handicap access:** Possible. **Open:** Open May through late October.

➤ **A comfortable 18th-century inn, set in greenery, that is within walking distance of the smooth granite rocks and swimming holes at Halibut Point, the most dramatic promontory on Boston's North Shore.**

This 18th-century inn sits on five acres of gardens, meadow, and woods next to 54-acre Halibut Point State Park, a high granite headland with deep quarries to swim in and spectacular views up to the Maine coast. In the late 19th century, the Rockport Granite Company bought the property to house its workers, and in the early 1900s Antone Balzarini, an immigrant from northern Italy, rented it to raise dairy cows — and twelve children. It subsequently passed through several owners until 1964, when one of Antone's sons, John, along with his wife Mabel and son William, bought and restored the old farm, running it primarily as a restaurant. A few years ago Bill and his wife Susan began catering exclusively to houseguests.

The sitting rooms have low beams and are filled with comfortable, brightly upholstered couches and chairs and some interesting country antiques, including an unusual number of samplers. A light breakfast — yogurt, fruit, juice, cereal, coffee cake, and breads — is served in the sunny breakfast room, where sliding glass doors overlook the garden.

All the guest rooms have televisions and are furnished with flair and unusual care for the details that make a stay comfortable. The most romantic is the Captain Woodbury, with a star-pattern quilt on its canopy bed and an elegant settee. The Meadows and Sunshine rooms, both with queen-size and twin beds, the Garden Suite with two daybeds in a separate sitting room, and Fireside, a full housekeeping cottage with two large rooms upstairs, are all suited to families.

Sited several miles north of the village of Rockport, the setting is peaceful. Guests will want to walk the few minutes to the wooded paths that wind around deep old quarries and to headlands from which you can look out to sea. This is a romantic spot to come almost any time of year.

Bring a bicycle to pedal into Rockport — one of New England's most picturesque coastal towns, a low-key resort with an outstanding art association, dozens of shops and galleries, and some good restaurants (BYOB).

Rocky Shores Inn & Cottages

65 Eden Road
Rockport, MA 01966
978-546-2823
800-348-4003

> One of those unusual places that's good for families, singles, and couples

Innkeepers: Renate and Gunter Kostka. **Accommodations:** 11 rooms in the inn, 11 housekeeping cottages (two are 3-bedroom). **Rates:** $76–$117 per couple for rooms, $10 per extra person; $640–$825 per week for the cottages. **In-**

cluded: Room rates include breakfast; cottages do not. **Minimum stay:** 2 days in cottages. **Added:** 9.7% tax. **Credit cards accepted:** All major ones. **Children:** Small children welcome in the cottages. **Pets:** No. **Smoking:** Permitted. **Handicap access:** In cottages. **Open:** Mid-April through October.

➤ **A brown shingled mansion built by a wealthy Texan in 1905 overlooks the ocean from a hilltop, forming a centerpiece for this 3-acre compound. Renate and Gunter Kostka are originally from Berlin but acquired Rocky Shores in 1980, after living and working in the United States for many years.**

"We loved Rockport and wanted to live here," Renate explains. She shares her love and knowledge of the area and encourages guests to mingle in the living room and on the porch.

Guests in the main house meet over a full breakfast, which generally includes fresh fruit, yogurt, boiled eggs, and muffins. The most expensive guest room — a beauty — is spacious, with a balcony on which to savor the water view of Thacher Island and its twin granite lighthouses just off-shore. All the rooms are attractive, furnished in antiques and equipped with private baths and small TVs. Request one of the two cottages in the front with water views; the remainder are in the rear of the main house.

Rocky Shores is a few miles south of the village of Rockport, a location that has both distinct advantages and disadvantages in high season: on the one hand, you still have to face the challenge of trying to park in the village (bring or rent a bicycle), but on the other, you're just a 10-minute walk from Cape Hedge and pebble beaches.

Seaward Inn

Marmion Way
Rockport, MA 01966
978-546-3471

A small resort by the sea

Owners: Cameron family. **Accommodations:** 39 rooms (all with private bath), 10 cottages. **Rates:** $115–$195 per couple B&B; $20 per extra person in the room. **Minimum stay:** 2 nights on weekends. **Included:** Breakfast. **Added:** 9.7% tax. **Credit cards accepted:** MasterCard, Visa; checks preferred. **Children:** Welcome. **Pets:** Not accepted. **Smoking:** No. **Handicap access:** No. **Open:** April through October.

➤ **An old-fashioned, family-run inn on five landscaped oceanside acres**

With brown shingles and carefully tended landscaping, Seaward Inn seems very much a part of the granite ledge from which it overlooks Sandy Bay. The view follows guests into a glass-walled sun room that's filled with flowers, green plants, and comfortable chairs.

The gracious living room has Oriental rugs and its share of antiques. The three pine-walled dining rooms and less formal dining on the flagstone, glass-walled patio are open to the public.

The rooms, all with private bath, are divided between the main house, two waterside annexes, and assorted small cottages, some with fireplaces and/or kitchens. All of them have night lights and writing tables.

Behind the inn is a sheltered, spring-fed pond with a small sandy beach. A path winds along the shore and through tall blueberry bushes into small woods. Rustic benches stand along the way.

Guests can use the Rockport Country Club, and there is a 9-hole putting green on the grounds. Tennis, shore fishing, horseback riding, and bicycle rentals are also available. Old Garden Beach is a 5-minute walk down Marmion Way, and the village of Rockport, bustling with shops and galleries, is just a mile away.

Salem

Hawthorne Hotel on the Common

Salem, MA 01970
978-744-4080
800-SAY-STAY (729-7829)
Fax: 508-745-9842

A downtown hotel in an unusual town

Manager: Michael Garvin. **Accommodations:** 83 rooms, 6 suites. **Rates:** High season: $99–$162 per couple; $275 per suite; less mid-March through mid-July. **Added:** 9.7 % tax. **Credit cards accepted:** All major ones. **Children:** Family packages available. **Pets:** Accepted. **Smoking:** 40 percent of rooms are for nonsmokers. **Handicap access:** 1 room. **Open:** Year-round.

➤ **With intriguing museums, a variety of restaurants, and frequent commuter rail service to Boston, Salem is an appealing place to spend several days.**

This six-story, three-sided hotel was built by public subscription in the 1920s and has been totally renovated several times since. It is within walking distance of historic sights and museums, and since the Hawthorne is by far the tallest building around, most of the rooms have sweeping views of Salem.

The lobby ceiling is high, with fluted columns. Armchairs are grouped around coffee tables, and potted palms, Oriental rugs, and Chinese import vases add a dignified grace.

Three meals are served in Nathaniel's, the formal dining room, with such dinner specialties as chicken with walnut stuffing and mahogany duck. There's music on the ebony grand piano on Friday and Saturday evenings, and a brunch is served on Sunday. A moderately priced menu is available in the Tavern on the Green, a clubby, wood-paneled pub with leather chairs, nautical prints, and a large hearth.

The guest rooms have shrunk in number and expanded in size over the years. They are furnished in reproduction antiques with coordinated drapes and spreads, and all have a television. Guests have full access to the exercise room.

Salem is older than Boston and looks it. It still retains many graceful Federal homes from the early 19th century, when it prospered in its trade with India and the Orient. This era is vividly recalled by the thousands of exhibits in the Peabody Museum. The neighboring Essex Institute, which focuses on North Shore history, maintains a half-dozen historic houses, including several by the city's most famous architect, Samuel McIntyre.

The Peabody Essex Museum, New England's ultimate treasure chest of exotica, is within a few minute's walk, and the Salem Maritime National Historic Site is a short walk in the other direction.

The Salem Inn

7 Summer Street
Salem, MA 01970
978-741-0680
800-446-2995
Fax: 978-744-8924
saleminn@earthlink.net
www.salemweb.com/biz/saleminn

A historic inn in a historic town

Innkeepers: Dick and Diane Pabich. **Accommodations:** 22 rooms in the inn, 11 in the Curwen House. **Rates:** $99–$175, higher during Haunted Happenings. **Included:** Breakfast. **Minimum stay:** Some holiday weekends. **Added:** 9.7% tax. **Credit cards accepted:** All major ones. **Children:** Welcome, some family suites, cribs $15. **Handicap access:** No. **Smoking:** Restricted. **Open:** Year-round.

➤ The four-story brick town house was built in 1834.

Over the years Dick and Diane Pabich have turned a four-story brick double town house, built in 1834, into an appealing place to stay that's totally in keeping with its surroundings.

Just a short walk from most of Salem's museums, shops, and restaurants, the inn retains its townhouse feel. Just off the entry is a comfortable living room with a fireplace and an appropriate ancestor framed above it.

Guest rooms vary widely, from spacious bright doubles with working hearths (Duraflame logs) to top-floor family suites with cooking facilities to smaller rooms (some with fireplaces) with baths down the hall. Around the corner at 331 Essex Street, the Italianate Curwen House has been recently added to the inn. It has its own living room and a meeting room plus eleven guest rooms, seven with working fireplaces and three of these with two-person whirlpools and canopy beds. All rooms have cable TVs, phones and coffeemakers. Breakfast is served in the inn's restaurant, which has a garden patio.

PIONEER VALLEY

Amherst

Allen House Inn

599 Main Street
Amherst, MA 01002
413-253-5000
www.allenhouse.com

> **Ann's delicious breakfast might include stuffed French toast and homemade fruit sauces.**

Innkeepers: Alan and Ann Zieminski. **Accommodations:** 7 rooms (all private baths). **Rates:** $75–$135 per couple; $55–$115, December–March; from $45 for single. **Included:** Full breakfast, afternoon tea, 9.7% tax. **Minimum stay:** Only during school graduation weekends, foliage season. **Credit cards accepted:** All major ones. **Children:** Age 8 and over. **Pets:** Not accepted. **Smoking:** Restricted. **Handicap access:** No. **Open:** Year-round.

➤ **Peacock feathers in Chinese vases, ornate Victorian-style wallpaper on the ceilings as well as walls, and antimacassars on intricately carved chairs don't usually appeal to us — but the Allen House Inn does.**

This 1880s stick-style Queen Anne home (a painted lady in three shades of green plus straw and crimson) is a genuine period piece that's never really been on the market. The rush matting is as original to the house as the Eastlake fireplace mantels.

The walls of each of the five bedrooms (all with private baths) are covered in silk-screened copies of William Morris, Walter Crane, and Charles Eastlake papers, and all are furnished with appropriate antique beds and dressers bought locally. Rooms range in size from the back "scullery" to a large front room with three beds. All have ceiling fans and goose down comforters and pillows.

Alan Zieminski first became intrigued with the house while lodging here as a student, and he secured first option when it came up for sale. Ann Zieminski is a friendly hostess, and she is well known for her spectacular breakfasts, including Swedish pancakes, stuffed French toast, homemade fruit sauces, quiche, and fruit compotes. Breakfast is served at the dining room table, but all guests need not gather at the same time.

Allen House is down the street from the house in which Emily Dickinson penned her trenchant poems. Dickinson died in 1886, the year this house was built. You realize that Amherst in the 1880s — as it is today — was a very cultured, distinctive place. Inquire about the second house up the street, which Ann and Alan are in the process of restoring with the characteristic care.

The Lord Jeffery Inn on the Common

Amherst, MA 01002
413-253-2576
800-742-0358
Fax: 413-256-6152
lord jeffery@pinnacle inns.com

A college town inn and tavern

Manager: Michael Maderia. **Accommodations:** 50 rooms including 6 suites. **Rates:** $69–$124 per couple in rooms, $109–$168 in suites. **Included:** No meals but all are served. **Minimum stay:** None. **Added:** 9.7% tax. **Credit cards accepted:** All major ones. **Children:** Under age 12, free in parents room; over 12, $10; cots and cribs available. **Pets:** Only Seeing Eye dogs accepted. **Smoking:** Some guest rooms available for smokers. **Handicap access:** Yes. **Open:** Year-round.

➤ **On the edge of the Amherst College campus, the inn sits right beside the town common, where at any given time you may see students playing Frisbee, a political rally, or a pumpkin festival.**

The Lord Jeffery Inn remains a reliable standby in a culturally rich college town that receives a good number of year-round visitors. Built in 1926 in the Colonial Revival style, the Lord Jeff is a three-story whitewashed and red brick building with green shutters.

The ambience and service are more like that in a small hotel than a country inn and it serves as a frequent venue for functions, small group meetings, and weddings. At this writing we lament the loss of the old living room, which has been transformed into an intimate, high-end dining room. The large formal old dining room has, in turn, been converted to function space and Elijah Boltwood's Tavern has been redecorated to serve as the prime, blessedly informal, dining room for all three meals.

Over the past few years the guest rooms at the Lord Jeff have been redecorated, with new carpeting, wallpaper, prints, and Colonial furnishings. Request one with a balcony overlooking the garden courtyard. All have cable TV and a telephone. Suites have a connecting room with a convertible sofa bed. Room service is offered and the "breakfast inn bed" is reasonably priced.

We have manager Michael Maderia's word that by the time this guide appears, the lobby will be enhanced with more seating around its wood-burning hearth to compensate for the loss of the living room. In summer, common space includes seating in the garden and the line of green rockers along the porch, overlooking the common.

The bus (direct from Boston; via Springfield from New York) stops on the common and Amtrak's *Vermonter* from New York, with connections from Montreal, stops in town. A pleasant bike path also connects Northampton and Amherst, and there is also local bus service.

Belchertown

The Mucky Duck

38 Park Street	**Convenient to colleges and**
Belchertown, MA 01007	**a magnificent lake**
413-323-9657	
dukbb@aol.com	

Innkeepers: Richard and Annie Steiner. **Accommodations:** 3 rooms, private baths. **Rates:** $65–$85. **Included:** Full breakfast. **Minimum stay:** 2 night stay on 3-day holiday weekends. **Credit cards accepted:** Visa, MasterCard. **Children:** Age 12 and up. **Pets:** Not accepted. **Smoking:** Not permitted. **Handicap access:** No. **Open:** Year-round.

➤ **A sophisticated European-style B&B in an unexpected place**

"It's a smiling name," Annie Steiner replies when asked "Why mucky duck?"

Sited on the quiet side of Belchertown Common, this early-19th-century Greek Revival Gothic house is a smiling place to stay, as attractive inside as out. The exterior features a sharply peaked roof, a second-floor balcony, and an arched porch. Inside, it is tastefully and deftly decorated, filled with interesting art, antiques, and sun (no curtains).

Annie Steiner explains that she was born and bred in Belgium and is here because of her husband Richard's work, but she loves the B&B and delights in turning guests — who are usually here because of the nearby colleges — onto the little-known beauty of the Quabbin Reservoir, by far the state's largest lake.

In the two windows flanking the hearth are highlighted stained glass Annie has fashioned, and a carved oak armoir complements the hutch and sideboard in the adjacent dining room — both have been in Annie's family for two centuries. Oriental rugs, comfortable seating, and plenty of reading material make it all very inviting.

The largest guest room, the Aylesbury (the name of a white duck) is really a suite. The front bedroom behind the balcony is decorated all in white and Delft blur, and the bathroom features a refinished claw tub (with shower). The Wood Duck room, also upstairs, has wide pine floorboards and a king bed (that can be twins) and is decorated with colorful mementos the Steiners have collected in their travels. A shower has been tucked into one closet and the bath into another. The third room, the Mallard, is on the first floor, with a full-sized antique bed, hunter green walls, and a full bath.

Breakfast is Euorpean-style, with fresh fruit, a selection of cheeses, and the bread Annie bakes fresh every morning.

Deerfield

Deerfield Inn

81 Old Main Street
Deerfield, MA 01342-0305
413-774-5587
800-926-3865
Fax: 413-773-8712
DRinn@shaysnet.com

A historic inn at the center of Old Deerfield

Innkeepers: Karl and Jane Sabo. **Accommodations:** 23 rooms (all with private bath). **Rates:** $169–$242 per couple. **Included:** Tax, service, full breakfast. Lunch and dinner also served. **Minimum stay:** None. **Credit cards accepted:** All major cards. **Children:** Welcome. **Pets:** Not accepted. **Smoking:** Not permitted. **Handicap access:** Some rooms. **Open:** Year-round.

➤ **To simply visit Historic Deerfield by day, when its restored houses are filled with tourists, is to miss the real beauty of this village: its mile-long line of old homes silhouetted against fields. The inn is at the heart of the village.**

The Deerfield Inn sits on a broad street lined with 18th- and early-19th-century restored homes, more than a dozen of them open to the public. There is also a classic brick meeting house, Memorial Hall Museum (one of the country's oldest historical societies), and Deerfield Academy (one of the country's oldest boarding schools). Deerfield's early homes are impressive, silhouetted starkly against flat onion and tobacco fields.

The inn dates substantially from 1884. It was partially destroyed by fire in 1979, but most of its fine antiques were saved, and it has been faithfully rebuilt, albeit with modern conveniences such as air conditioning, wheelchair-accessible rooms, and an elevator. The Deerfield Inn is run quite professionally, more like a small hotel than a classic country inn.

Eleven of the guest rooms are on the second floor of the inn, with the remainder in the 1982 south wing, connected by a covered walkway. Most of them have twin or queen-size beds or a pullout sofa, which makes them good for a family. Many have four-poster beds with canopies and are well lit with three-way lamps. Room 141, in the front of the main inn, is a large corner room that's bright and sunny in the morning. Guests recently spent an eventful night with a ghostlike presence in Room 148. The fabrics throughout replicate those used in the Federal era.

The spacious living room is furnished with Chippendale and wing chairs, sofas, and period sketches. The large, formal dining room contains delicate chandeliers, antique mirrors, and mahogany tables. The menu on a given night might include Maine crab cakes with haricots verts, carrot strings, shredded cabbage, and couscous and New York Strip served over roast garlic mashed potatoes. The lunch offerings are equally substantial and may include a fresh seafood casserole or homemade manicotti. Breakfast is sometimes served buffet-style, with table service for coffee. The menu includes cinnamon French toast, sausage, bacon, an egg dish, and hash browns. An informal café and cafeteria are downstairs, serving the many tourists who want a quick bite to eat between house tours.

Greenfield

The Brandt House

29 Highland Avenue
Greenfield, MA 01302
413-774-3329
800-235-3329
Fax: 413-772-2908
brandt@crocker.com
www.brandt-house.com

> **A sixteen-room Georgian revival house**

Innkeeper: Phoebe Compton. **Accommodations:** 8 rooms, all private baths. **Rates:** $110–$175, May–October; slightly less off-season; corporate rates: $65–$105. **Included:** Full breakfast weekends, hearty Continental breakfast on weekdays. **Minimum stay:** None. **Added:** 9.7% tax. **Credit cards accepted:** All major ones. **Children:** Inquire when making reservations. **Pets:** Inquire when making reservations. **Smoking:** Not permitted. **Handicap access:** No. **Open:** Year-round.

➤ **A relaxing getaway handy to Old Deerfield and the five-college area**

This 16-room Georgian revival mansion is set on more than three acres in the Highlands section of Greenfield, handy to an extensive park along a ridge that overlooks the Connecticut River.

The common rooms include a comfortable living room that is spacious and tasteful; a garden-view dining room; a broad, wicker-furnished porch and patio; a game room with a full-size pool table; and an upstairs sun room. There's also a well-equipped guest closet stocked with everything you may need.

The guest rooms vary widely in size but most are sunny and there's central air conditioning. Rooms 9 and 1 both have a working fireplace, and all guest rooms are furnished with antiques and bright florals. The top floor harbors a two-room suite. All rooms have phones and TVs.

We like everything about this place except the prices. The lowest in-season rate for a regular traveler is $110; that's midweek for the same small third-floor room (shared bath) for which a "corporate" traveler pays $65. And the large, king-bedded room with fireplace for which tourists pay $175 costs a "corporate traveler" only $105 (admittedly it's $20 extra for a second person).

Hadley

Clark Tavern Inn

98 Bay Road
Hadley, MA 01035
413-586-1900
MRCallhn@aol.com
www.bbonline.com/ma/clarktavern/index.html

> 18th-century taverns were
> never this comfortable

Hosts: Ruth and Michael Callahan. **Accommodations:** 3 rooms, private baths. **Rates:** $100–$105 for smaller room, $115–$135 for rooms with working fireplaces. **Included:** A very full breakfast. **Credit cards accepted:** All major ones. **Children:** Age 12 and over. **Pets:** Not accepted. **Smoking:** Smoking allowed on patio. **Handicap access:** No. **Open:** Year-round.

➤ **Enthusiastic, skilled young hosts offer an entrée to this naturally and culturally rich area.**

This classic 1740 tavern stood on the other side of the Connecticut River until 1961, when it was slated for demolition to make way for I-91. Luckily two Hadley residents undertook the cost of moving and restoring the house, which retains its "King's Lumber" panels, wide pine floors and much original detailing. The best news here, however, is the hospitality. Ruth Callahan, a nurse, and her husband Michael, a physician's assistant, are obviously both adept at ministering to the public.

"It's so good to be able to make people feel great, not just better," Michael comments.

The three rooms are each meticulously but not fussily furnished. The "fireplace room" has both a canopy bed and working fireplace. All rooms have private baths and plenty of reading and relaxing space. Breakfast is served either on the large screened porch, overlooking the extensive garden (with swimming pool), or in the Keeping Room, also overlooking the garden. The sound of birds, audible inside as well as from the porch, is so constant that you might think this is one of those soothing tapes. It isn't.

The Callahans furnish detailed printed information about local attractions and are themselves a fund of local knowledge, happy to lend advice on dining, walking, biking, and entertainment. A guest's refrigerator is well stocked.

New Salem

Bullard Farm

89 Elm Street
North New Salem, MA 01364
978-544-6959

| An inn with an authentic country feel |

Innkeeper: Janet Kraft. **Accommodations:** 4 rooms. **Rates:** $75 for double, $65 single. **Included:** Full breakfast. **Minimum stay:** No. **Credit cards accepted:** MasterCard, Visa. **Children:** Welcome. **Pets:** Not accepted. **Smoking:** Not permitted. **Handicap access:** No. **Open:** Year-round.

➤ **This vintage 1792 farmhouse, just a mile from Quabbin Reservoir, has been in Janet Krafts' family for many generations, and visitors are welcomed like members of the family.**

If you must have a private bath, Laura Ashely wallpaper, and mints on your turndown, this isn't the place for you. But if you appreciate the authentic feel of a country bedroom with a comfortable bed and windows overlooking fields (the house is set among 400 acres), then this is a good place to know about — especially if you like to bicycle quiet roads down to forgotten towns like New Salem village. An eerily quiet cluster of white clapboard buildings, New Salem includes a large antiquarian bookstore (a former schoolhouse) at its heart. Concerts are also regularly orchestrated in the old meeting house.

Bear's Den, a spectacular waterfall and swimming hole, is within walking distance of the house and, a mile away, a gate to Quabbin Reservoir accesses walking trails on which you're likely to spot eagles or wild turkeys.

Bullard Farm offers four large and comfortable guest rooms with period furniture and two shared baths. We return regularly and always leave refreshed and wishing we had more time. We never stay long enough, in fact, to figure out how the living rooms and dining rooms (there are two of each) all fit together. Often, after taking a wrong turn, we would spot a book we had wanted to read, sit down with it, and become so comfortable and absorbed that we forget where we were headed.

Breakfasts are full, and if you come during blueberry season, you will most likely be loaded down with berries to go. Janet delights in turning guests on to birding, bicycling, hiking, and otherwise appreciating this little known corner of the state. Amherst, with its college and university, is just a half hour away. Some perfectly good restaurants are only minutes in several directions. Groups are accommodated (both day and nights) in the small conference space at the rear of the inn.

Northampton

Hotel Northampton

36 King Street
Northampton, MA 01060
413-584-3100
Fax: 413-585-0210
www.hotelnorthampton.com

A historic hotel in a college town

General manager: Mansour Ghalibaf. **Accommodations:** 70 rooms, 6 suites. **Rates:** $89–$195 per couple; suites: $135–$325; packages available. **Included:** Continental breakfast; lunch and dinner also served. **Minimum stay:** 3 nights on graduation weekends. **Added:** 9.7% tax. **Credit cards accepted:** All major ones. **Children:** Welcome; free. **Pets:** Not accepted. **Smoking:** Some guest rooms. **Handicap access:** 2 rooms in rear of the hotel. **Open:** Year-round.

➤ **Northampton is the home of Smith College and the hub of an area that probably boasts the country's highest ratio of college students and faculty to regular residents. The town is known for the quality as well as quantity of its galleries and restaurants.**

After years of restoration and renovation of its 1926 building, the classic Hotel Northampton (a member of the Historic Hotels of America) once again claims its place as the centerpiece of lively Northampton.

The lobby is grand, with plants, rich carpeting, and comfortable chairs in front of an ever-present crackling fire. The glassed-in porch, with yet more greenery and brick, is a good place for morning coffee and the newspaper, a snack, or a quiet conversation. Group functions are often held here, so you may find yourself sharing the lobby with a wedding party, prom, or reunion.

Two elevators take you to the guest rooms, some of which are fairly standard, furnished in reproduction antiques. Some king-size canopy beds are available. The suites, which we recommend highly, feature Laura Ashley fabrics and wicker accents; some have Jacuzzis and balconies and terraces that overlook King Street. All the rooms have a telephone, radio, and TV, and there is ample free parking behind the building. Guests may use the YMCA, about a mile and a half away.

Your dining choices are many. Our favorite is the Coolidge Park Café, a lively meeting place for residents and students. The prices are moderate, and the fare varies from traditional to vegetarian dishes. In warm weather, the café crowd spills out onto the terrace, under the shade of old trees. You may also enjoy Wiggins Tavern, an authentic 18th-century tavern that was incorporated into the hotel when it was built, featuring a low-beamed dining room with a large hearth and traditional menu.

The Salt Box

153 Elm Street
Northampton, MA 01060
413 -584-1790

| **A small college town B&B** |

Innkeeper: Carol Melin. **Accommodations:** 3 rooms. **Rates:** $100–$130 double, $85–$115 single. **Included:** Full breakfast. **Credit cards accepted:** Visa, MasterCard, American Express, Discover. **Minimum stay:** 2 nights on weekends, 3 nights on holiday weekends. **Children:** Not appropriate for small children. **Pets:** Not accepted. **Smoking:** Not permitted. **Handicap access:**Yes. **Open:** Year-round.

➤ **A decorator's delight.**

Sited right across from the Smith College campus, with its inviting botanical gardens and exceptional art museum, Carol and Craig Melin's 18th-century house makes a great base from which to explore the Five College area.

A mural greets guests in the entry hall, and the parlor, though small, has a working fireplace and an air that's both comfortable and gracious; beyond is a cheery breakfast room. The three guest rooms are decorated with verve. Ground-floor Timothy's Orchard has its own entrance and patio (good for smokers). But the two rooms that impressed us are The Sabbatical (a suite with a queen-bedded room, full bath, efficiency kitchen and sitting area — and numerous tea cups) and Hester's Retreat, with a four-poster queen, an alcove with an extra daybed, and a bath with a two-person whirlpool tub. While it isn't fussy, the decorating is unusually imaginative and the general feel of the place, very welcoming. Park your car in back and walk to shops, restaurants and museums.

Breakfast, which usually includes fresh-squeezed juices, coffee, and baked goods, is served buffet style.

Northfield

Northfield Country House

R.R. 1
P.O. Box 79A
School Street
Northfield, MA 01360
413-498-2692
800-498-2692

| **A gracious country home in an old river town** |

Innkeeper: Andrea Dale. **Accommodations:** 7 rooms (5 with private baths). **Rates:** $50–$90 per couple. **Included:** Full breakfast. **Minimum stay:** None. **Added:** 5.7% tax. **Credit cards accepted:** MasterCard, Visa. **Children:** Over age 9. **Pets:** Not accepted. **Smoking:** Limited. **Handicap access:** No. **Open:** Year-round.

➤ **Nineteenth-century grace pervades this rural house and town in a quiet corner of New England, where Massachusetts, Vermont, and New Hampshire meet.**

In the summer this inn, though alluring in any season, is blessed with massive pink hydrangeas. Guests gather around the pool or relax in wicker rockers on the porch. The views from both are stunning and solitary.

The Northfield Country House was built high on the wooded ridge above the village of Northfield in 1901 as a country home for a prominent Boston family. The cherry paneling in the dining room dates from 1850, and the feeling downstairs is almost baronial, for there is a grand piano, Oriental rugs, and luxurious reading nooks. A porch overlooking the gardens and a landscaped pool are other common spaces.

Up a rather grand stairway, the guest rooms feature high brass bedsteads and color-coordinated walls, furniture, and sheets. The three larger rooms have working fireplaces. The two cheery singles are every bit as inviting and a real bargain; they also have the makings of a family suite.

In the evening, guests can congregate by the fireplace, with its inscription, "Love warms the heart as fire the hearth." Two big sofas face the fire.

The Country House serves a full breakfast of pancakes or eggs along with fruit, homemade muffins, and juice.

Northfield is a handsome old Connecticut River valley town just south of New Hampshire. Today, most guests are visiting the Northfield–Mount Hermon School or enjoying the hiking, riding, and cross-country ski trails at Northfield Mountain. This is also a prime base for biking on the byways of the valley and canoeing the Connecticut River. Andrea Dale is an unusually helpful, naturally hospitable, and locally knowledgeable host.

SOUTHEASTERN MASSACHUSETTS

Fairhaven

Edgewater Bed & Breakfast

2 Oxford Street
Fairhaven, MA 02719
508-997-5512
kprof@aol.com
www.rixsan.com/edgewater/

A friendly haven

Innkeeper: Cathy Reed. **Accommodations:** 5 rooms including 2 suites. **Rates:** $70–$90 per couple; $65–85 single. **Included:** Full breakfast. **Minimum stay:** On holiday weekends. **Added:** 9.4% tax. **Credit cards accepted:** All major ones. **Children:** Over age 5. **Pets:** Not accepted. **Smoking:** Not permitted. **Handicap access:** No. **Open:** Year-round.

➤ **The rambling house dates in part to the 1760s.**

The Acushnet River seemingly surrounds this house, moving so quickly by its many windows that you actually feel afloat.

A rambling 1880s home with the best views to be had of New Bedford — which is across the Acushnet River — this is an unusually relaxing, welcoming B&B, thanks in good measure to the personality of its host, Cathy Reed.

Hidden away at the tip of Poverty Point, the house dates in part to the 1760s, when it was a store. The feel today is very spacious and gracious, with a handsome sunken living room and a formal dining room in which guests breakfast on just-baked muffins and juice.

Each of the five guest rooms has a private bath and a small TV. Our favorite is the Captain's Suite, with a sitting room and working fireplace and water views on three sides. Another bright room has water views and a clawfoot tub. The Joshua Slocum Suite (good for families) is in the 1760 part of the house with a private entrance and deck, and a sitting room and kitchenette. Rooms in the oldest part of the house are nicely furnished but lack views. Thanks to a brand-new seawall and extensive landscaping, there are, however, now plenty of places to enjoy the water views outside as well as from the common rooms.

Cathy Reed, a college professor, enjoys chatting with guests and offers helpful advice on local restaurants and the local sights to see, as well as the beaches and byways of this very special area.

Plymouth

Foxglove Cottage

101 Sandwich Road
Plymouth, MA 02360
800-479-4746
Fax: 508-747-7622
www.foxglove-cottage.com

> **Peace and comfort, minutes from downtown Plymouth**

Innkeepers: Michael and Charlie Cowan. **Accommodations:** 3 double rooms with private baths. **Rates:** $75–$90. **Included:** Full breakfast. **Minimum stay:** 2 nights on high-season weekends. **Credit cards accepted:** Discover. **Children:** Age 12 and older. **Pets:** Not accepted. **Smoking:** Not permitted. **Handicap access:** No. **Open:** year-round.

Michael and her husband Charlie lived in this 1820 Cape-style home for some years before their own experiences in European B&Bs inspired them to host visitors themselves. Just a few miles from heavily touristed downtown Plymouth, the cottage is on a quiet road lined with old homes, where there's an out-in-the-country feel. It's surrounded by 40 acres of fields and woods and sits behind a flower-bordered lawn.

Michael collects 19th-century porcelain and early Victorian antiques, which add to the ambiance, without overpowering. The B&B is small but conveys a sense of space and peace.

The three upstairs guest rooms all have private baths, working fireplaces, and reading and sitting areas. The downstairs common room also has a fireplace and is furnished in bright print and Victorian oak; it includes a TV and VCR for guests.

Breakfast is full — maybe waffles with bananas and maple syrup or a sausage, egg, and cheese casserole. It's served either in the formal dining room or on the deck.

South Dartmouth

Salt Marsh Farm

322 Smith Neck Road
South Dartmouth, MA 02748
508-992-0980
saltmarshF@ad.com

A 200-year-old farmhouse B&B

Hosts: Sally and Larry Brownell. **Accommodations:** 2 rooms (with private bath). **Rates:** $70–$90 per couple, including tax. **Included:** Full breakfast and afternoon tea. **Minimum stay:** 2 nights, in-season and holiday weekends. **Credit cards accepted:** MasterCard, Visa. **Children:** Any age as long as family takes both rooms. **Pets:** Not accepted. **Smoking:** Not permitted. **Handicap access:** No. **Open:** Year-round.

➤ **Out the back door are more than 90 acres of hayfields, pastures, woodlands, and wetlands. A trail winds back into the salt marsh. Bicycles are available for guests; you can also take the bikes down to the otherwise private town beach.**

In a relatively unexplored corner of the southeastern part of the state, a real treat awaits those in search of a quiet weekend. Salt Marsh Farm, a hip-roofed Colonial that dates from 1727, has been in Sally's family since World War II. Sally and Larry spent summers here until they moved in in 1987.

The two guest rooms are small but each is very inviting. On our last visit we chose the yellow room with its maple bed, old prints, and hand-stitched samplers. A pitcher of ice water and fresh flowers welcomed us and we curled up with a local history book (there's an amazing amount of very local history here) from a shelf full of such books in the living room.

Guests can order almost anything they want for breakfast, including a fire in the fireplace. Dishes range from multigrain pancakes to eggs any style (fresh from the hen house on summer and fall mornings). Blueberry muffins made with yogurt are a trademark. The organic gardens yield melons, all sorts of berries, herbs for the eggs, and tomatoes that are served stuffed and baked. During the harvest season, Larry can usually be found selling his vegetables and flowers at his roadside stand.

Quiet roads web this area, leading to beaches, shore walks, and interesting small villages. This is, in other words, ideal bicycling country and your hosts have maps already marked with appropriate routes — which they are happy to discuss. On the other hand, you might want to just walk back through the fields. Afternoon tea and complimentary sherry are served by the fire in the living room.

WEST OF BOSTON

Concord

The Colonial Inn

48 Monument Square
Concord, MA 01742
508-369-9200
800-370-9200
Fax: 508-369-2170

An inn in a historic village

Innkeeper: Jurgen Demisch. **Accommodations:** 49 rooms, 4 suites. **Rates:** April through October: $109–$169 per couple, $10 per extra person; November through March: $99–$135 per couple; packages available. **Included:** Breakfast with most packages. **Minimum stay:** None. **Added:** 9.7% tax. **Credit cards accepted:** Most major ones. **Children:** Welcome; 12 and under stay free. **Pets:** Not accepted. **Smoking:** Some rooms available for nonsmokers. **Handicap access:** No. **Open:** Year-round.

➤ **The Colonial Inn has evolved from the 18th to the 20th century and, like Concord itself, has remained surprisingly authentic and lively.**

This rambling gray clapboard building — its various parts dating from 1716 to 1961 — sits on Concord's green, serving all the functions of a traditional inn. On foliage weekends it literally swarms with tourists and on quiet weekdays civic groups and businesspeople meet in the Merchants Row Dining Room, which also takes bus groups in stride.

So if you are looking for a quiet retreat from the world, this isn't it. But if you enjoy being in the middle of a historic village — in its still-lively centerpiece — this is as well-managed and comfortable place as any.

Afternoon high tea is served in the café, and a variety of live music, from folk to jazz, is featured in the Liberty Lounge and Village Forge Lounge. Sunday brunch is another specialty of the house, and you can always enjoy such fare as roast beef and chicken pie.

The Colonial Inn is an alternative to Boston for those who would sooner approach the city by train than car. The depot, a pleasant walk up Main Street, is served by frequent commuter service o Cambridge and Boston. Guests can, of course, also walk to Concord's historic and literary sites, and Lexington is just down the road.

The guest rooms in the main inn are furnished with antiques, in keeping with their low ceilings and wide floorboards. The thirty-two rooms in the air-conditioned Prescott Wing, the newest section, are also gradually acquiring antique pieces, quilts, hooked rugs, and flowery wallpaper. All the units have TVs and phones. The two suites in "The Cottage" each have two rooms and, when available, are an ideal solution for families.

Concord has many historic and literary shrines to visit, but you can also rent a canoe and paddle down the river. Nearby, Walden Pond is a great place to walk and to swim, especially on a warm summer evening.

Princeton

Fernside

162 Mountain Road
P.O. Box 303
Princeton, MA 015411
978-464-2741
800-545-2741
Fax: 978-464-2065
fernside@msn.com

A romantic getaway that's nearer than you think

Innkeepers: Jocleyn and Richard Morrison. **Accommodations:** 6 rooms. **Rates:** $105–$135, Sunday through Thursday; $125–$155, Friday and Saturday. **Included:** Full breakfast. **Minimum stay:** Peak weekends. **Added:** 5.7% tax. **Credit cards accepted:** American Express, Visa, MasterCard. **Children:** Not appropriate under age 12. **Pets:** Not welcomed by resident golden retriever and two resident cats. **Smoking:** Not permitted. **Handicap access:** Yes. **Open:** Year-round.

➤ **Around the turn of the century, the town of Princetown boasted no less than 13 hotels and it's easy to understand why.**

Some 55 miles west of Boston, this is real country with some amazing views — including Boston — from the flanks and top of the state's second highest mountain, Mount Wachusett, and from the windows and deck of Fernisde.

The last and one of the most unusual of the more than a dozen summer hotels that had operated in Princeton in the late 19th century, Fernside is an 1830s house to which wings and porches were added in the 1890s by "The Girls' Vacation House Association" of Boston. For the next hundred years it served as a subsidized vacation retreat for working girls, most of them shop girls who would otherwise not have been able to escape the city heat.

Happily, when it came up for sale in 1994, the inn was purchased by local residents Jocelyn and Richard Morrison, a couple as eager to honor its past memories as to create new ones. Lovingly, painstakingly, they have renovated the old place from top to bottom. The ground floor, aside from a couple of handicapped accessible suites, retains its several spacious common rooms, all now tastefully decorated with plenty of comfortable seating around its several hearths.

Upstairs, the many small rooms have been reduced to just the original four, each luxuriously large and graced with canopy beds and elegant furnishings. Some rooms have working fireplaces and long views east to Boston. Our bath matched the spaciousness of the room and offered a separate shower and a deep soaking tub on a pedestal with a fern beside it. Other touches included bottled spring water, soaps, and a bouquet of flowers.

Guests should try to arrive in time for sunset, which can be savored from the porch with a glass of wine. Several local restaurants offer serious dinner options and in the morning it's not a bad idea to walk a ways up or down Mountain Road (one fellow guest followed a path half way up Wachusett) to work up an appetite for the sumptuous multi-course breakfast.

It's not difficult to spend a day or two in Princeton and the surrounding countryside — this is great poke-around country, good for antiquing and swimming holes. And if you don't want to hike Mount Wachusett, you can drive to the top, which is a favorite vantage point for hawk watching in the fall. A nearby Audubon sanctuary also offers pleasant walks. In winter, Mount Wachusett is a major alpine ski area and lower reaches of the mountain are webbed with cross-country trails.

Sturbridge

Publick House Historic Inn
Colonel Ebenezer Crafts Inn
Chamberlain House
Country Lodge

P.O. Box 187
Sturbridge, MA 01566
508-347-3313
800-PUBLICK
Fax: 508-347-1246

> **An inn complex with something for everybody**

Manager: David Lane. **Accommodations:** Publick House: 18 rooms, 4 suites. Crafts Inn: 7 rooms, 1 suite. Chamberlain House: 1 room, 4 suites. Country Lodge: 91 rooms, 4 suites. **Rates:** $74–$135 per room, $114–$155 per suite; $114–$135 per room, $155 per suite in the Colonel Ebenezer Crafts Inn; $59–$89 per room, $85–$130 per suite in the Country Lodge motel (less January–June); MAP available. **Included:** Breakfast in Crafts Inn rates; all meals available. **Minimum stay:** None. **Added:** 9.7% tax. **Credit cards accepted:** All major ones. **Children:** Free under age 17. **Pets:** Accepted in the Country Lodge. **Smoking:** Some rooms for smokers. **Handicap access:** Some rooms. **Open:** Year-round.

➤ **Within a mile of the junction of I-84 and the Massachusetts Turnpike, the Publick House is a natural stop between Boston and New York. With**

Old Sturbridge Village just down the road, it has also become a destination, extending the atmosphere found at the museum village.

The Publick House is one of New England's landmark lodging places. Built in 1771, it has expanded over the years, its dining rooms spilling through the stables and on into the barn. Guests can now stay upstairs in the old house or next door at the Chamberlain House. They can also drive five minutes to the top of Fiske Hill, to the peace and solitude of the Colonel Ebenezer Crafts Inn, another 18th-century house named for the founder of the Publick House.

The Publick House has been lucky. Meticulously restored in the 1930s, it has been ably managed, first by Treadway and now by Restaurant Associates.

While some four hundred patrons can sit down to dine at once (and usually do on weekends), the waitresses are notably helpful. The meals are prepared with pride — from the morning "Cockscrow" (a $4.50 special of fruit, gooey sweet rolls or memorable muffins, and coffee) to the evening Yankee pot roast or lobster pie. Because the dining rooms are all relatively small and genuinely distinctive — like the Tap Room (with a huge open hearth), the Barn (with tables in the old stalls), or Paige Hall (a 1780s barn) — the ambience is surprisingly intimate. If you want to escape the 18th century and moderately high prices, you can walk down to Charlie Brown's Steak House. Another part of the complex, it is recognized as one of the best dining deals in Sturbridge.

But you can't get the complete sense of what this amazing complex is about unless you actually stay here. The Colonel Ebenezer Crafts Inn is the standout: an elegant Federal clapboard home with exquisitely paneled rooms and a secret panel that once concealed runaway slaves. The rates include a Continental breakfast, afternoon tea and sherry, and use of the private pool. Guests can also use the tennis court at the Publick House and the local golf course. The high point of the Crafts Inn is its living room, so comfortable and spacious — the one ingredient missing at the Publick House itself. The rooms in the Country Lodge (formerly the Orchard Inn) are mostly standard motel units, with TVs, air conditioning, and an outdoor pool.

The guest rooms in all three of the older buildings are furnished with antiques, including four-poster and canopy beds and wing chairs. Guests can walk out to the pool or rent bicycles at the office.

In all, the Publick House property includes 60 acres, a good percentage of it forested (many lodge rooms overlook woods). At the core of the old village center (not the motel and shopping strip on

Route 20, near the entrance to Old Sturbridge Village), the inn invites guests to step out and stroll through a slice of genuine New England landscape. It's worth noting that during the bleakest months of the year (January to March), the Publick House offers Yankee Winter Weekends, which include plenty of 18th-century-style feasting and entertainment as well as admission to the museum village.

Sudbury

Longfellow's Wayside Inn

Wayside Inn Road
Sudbury, MA 01776
508-443-1776
Fax: 508-443-8041
innkeeper@wayside.org
www.wayside.org

An inn can't be much more historic

Innkeeper: R. Purrington. **Accommodations:** 10 rooms (all with private bath). **Rates:** $82.70–$144.80 per couple; single: $72.40–$116.28. **Included:** Breakfast and tax; all meals served. **Minimum stay:** None. **Credit cards accepted:** All major ones. **Children:** Welcome. **Pets:** Stalls for horses. **Smoking:** Not permitted. **Handicap access:** No. **Open:** Year-round.

➤ **Longfellow's Wayside Inn is a mid-18th-century tavern that's a popular restaurant and sightseeing attraction not far west of Boston. It's also one of the most reasonably priced and interesting places to stay in the greater Boston area — a rural roost from which to explore the city.**

Billed as America's oldest operating inn, this tavern was first licensed at the beginning of the 18th century. It was so creaky by

1861, when Henry Wadsworth Longfellow visited on weekends, that he dubbed it Hobgoblin Hall. The poet grouped a half-dozen characters around the hearth and gave each a story to tell, like Chaucer and his Canterbury pilgrims. The most popular poem from these Tales of a Wayside Inn is still the landlord's: "Listen my children and you shall hear / Of the midnight ride of Paul Revere."

In the 1920s, Henry Ford not only restored the inn but acquired the surrounding acres as a fitting frame for the picture. He filled the inn first with antiques from his own home, then patiently hunted up its original furnishings. He also funded a highway by-pass to protect the building from the traffic he had helped to generate. Around the inn he assembled an assortment of other early Yankee buildings: the red schoolhouse Mary and her little lamb attended, a general store, a gristmill, and the Martha and Mary Chapel (the latter two built from scratch).

Be prepared to find parts of the inn maintained as a museum and expect weddings on weekends and bus tours at lunchtime. The low-beamed dining room is always busy. The dinner menu features Colonial-era cocktails and traditional fare, including Yankee pot roast and Boston baked schrod with a cheese sauce.

The second-floor guest rooms are separated from the bustle of the rest of the inn by heavy fire doors flanking a wide hall. Although relatively small, all the rooms include a sitting area, and most have writing desks and a respectable antique bureau. They are brightened with small print spreads and drapes, Oriental rugs, and some amazing mementos, such as a framed letter written by Longfellow in 1879. Guests can also enjoy the upstairs parlor and, when its not in use, the graceful upstairs ballroom installed by Colonel Ezekiel Howe in 1800.

The Berkshires

Best Bed-and-Breakfasts

Best Gourmet Getaways

Best Inns

Best Romantic Getaways

Best Spa

The most logical way to explore the Berkshires, in the western part of Massachusetts, is via Route 7. This essay will take you south from Williamstown to Sheffield.

Williamstown, encircled by mountains in the state's northwesternmost corner, is a college town that's known for its two fine art museums (the Clark Art Institute and the Williams College Museum of Art) as well as the highly regarded Williamstown Theater Festival, in the summer. This is North Berkshire, a region of steep, isolated valleys cut by rushing rivers and divided by Mount Greylock, the highest mountain in Massachusetts.

For your first detour, you may wish to head east to North Adams, a former mill town, then south to one of the two roads leading to the peak of Mount Greylock. Head south to Pittsfield to visit the Hancock Shaker Village, a magnificent open-air village and museum where the Shaker religious community lived from 1781 to 1960. Note, in particular, the Round Stone Barn, a masterpiece of functionalism. In Pittsfield stop at Canoe Meadow, one of two wildlife sanctuaries in western Massachusetts supported by the Massachusetts Audubon Society. (The other is Pleasant Valley, farther south in Lenox.)

From Pittsfield, the mountains soften into hills and the valleys widen and are punctuated with mansions, all built as summer "cottages" before the era of income taxes. Joseph Choate, the original owner of Naumkeag, a Stockbridge cottage with splendid gardens, endeared himself to his fellow townspeople by managing to reverse an income tax law passed by Congress in 1894.

In **Lenox,** dozens of these cottages survive, a number as inns. One estate, named Tanglewood by Nathaniel Hawthorne, is the summer home of the Boston Symphony Orchestra; another, designed and built by Edith Wharton, serves as a backdrop for performances of Shakespeare. A number of other summer concert series, not to mention opera, ballet, and theater, are staged here in Central and South Berkshire. Of particular note is the Jacob's Pillow Dance festival, founded in 1933. Mark Morris, Merce Cunningham, Agnes de Mille, and Bill T. Jones have honed and polished new works here.

The museums in the area include the definitive collection of Norman Rockwell canvases and prints at the new Norman Rockwell Museum in **Stockbridge,** the town he made famous. It still epitomizes the spirit of small-town America (except when traffic jams the town in August and during foliage season). Chesterwood, the studio of Daniel Chester French (who carved the seated Lincoln at the Lincoln Memorial in Washington, D.C.), is worth a morning of your time. Stroll through gardens and along nature trails and visit his studio. **Lee** and **West Stockbridge** are quieter towns close to Lenox.

As you move south to Great Barrington and on to the Connecticut border, the pace slackens. **Great Barrington** is a delightful town with many fine restaurants. Sheffield is a quietly gracious old antiques center, and **New Marlborough** is a refreshingly sleepy village. On the nearby back roads you'll find an old-fashioned general store in Monterey, a good picnic spot at Bartholomew's Cobble, and a cool waterfall at Bash Bish Falls.

Great Barrington

Baldwin Hill Farm B&B

121 Baldwin Hill Road N/S
Great Barrington, MA 01230
413-528-4092
888-528-4092
Fax: 413-528-6365

A hilltop B&B with expansive views

Hosts: Priscilla and Richard Burdsall. **Accommodations:** 4 rooms (2 with private bath). **Rates:** June–November: $85–$100 per couple; off-season: $75–$90. **Included:** Full breakfast menu and afternoon snack. **Minimum stay:** 2 nights on seasonal weekends. **Added:** 5.7% tax. **Credit cards accepted:** MasterCard, Visa. **Children:** Over age 10 welcome. **Pets:** Not accepted. **Smoking:** Not permitted. **Handicap access:** No. **Open:** Year-round.

➤ **In the winter, the Burdsalls groom cross-country trails with their snowmobiles. They also direct guests to the finest viewing points in the area as well as the best routes for biking and walking.**

On a hilltop overlooking hundreds of acres of woodland in the Berkshires, this Victorian farmhouse offers peace and quiet and a chance to reflect on the simpler things in life. It's been important for the Burdsalls not to break up the farm and sell off parcels to developers. To that end, much of their five hundred acres is farmed by neighbors. Three-hundred-and-sixty-degree views have been preserved and, with all this undeveloped land, you may even hear a few coyotes at night.

Relax in the wicker furniture on the screened porch and enjoy the constant breeze that prevails on the hilltop. It can get cool up here even in the summertime. Two small living rooms are filled with a large hearth, a piano, picture windows affording expansive views, area rugs, fresh flower arrangements, and jam-packed bookcases. Most of the antiques and paintings have been passed down through the generations, for the house has been in Richard's family since 1910, when it was his grandfather's summer home.

The guest rooms are lovely in their simplicity. The Bay Window Room is appropriately named for the views from the two chairs tucked in the curve of a bay window. The Balcony Room accesses a second-floor porch, from which you can enjoy the view under the shade of the magnificent catalpa tree. Long robes and large towels hang in each room and there are washbasins to lessen the pressure on the bath by the two rooms that share.

Breakfast is served at one table, and guests are asked to circle their breakfast choices on a menu before they retire for the evening. Choose among many styles of eggs, pancakes, French toast, or old-fashioned creamed dried beef.

The property is beautifully landscaped with perennial gardens and a heated pool, all set well back from the road. Deer, geese, and turkeys are frequently seen nibbling vegetation.

Littlejohn Manor

One Newsboy Monument Ln.
Great Barrington, MA 01230
413-528-2882

The best breakfast and afternoon tea in the Berkshires

Hosts: Herb Littlejohn and Paul DuFour. **Accommodations:** 4 rooms (share 2 baths). **Rates:** $75–$90 per couple in season; otherwise $65–$90. **Included:** Full breakfast, afternoon tea. **Minimum stay:** 2 nights on summer weekends. **Added:** 9.7% tax. **Credit cards accepted:** None. **Children:** No facilities for young children. **Pets:** Not accepted. **Smoking:** Permitted. **Handicap access:** No. **Open:** Year-round.

➤ **Paul and Herb are both very involved in the community and enjoy talking with guests. Their combined years of experience have produced a style of hospitality that is warm, elegant, and generous.**

Littlejohn sits handsomely off the road just behind the Newsboy Monument on the outskirts of town. Dating from around 1830, this charming pale yellow clapboard home and its spacious, cultivated grounds show all the signs of the care and attention Herb and Paul have invested in it since 1984.

The Manor and its grounds was one of the few properties in Great Barrington hit by a freak tornado in May of 1995, but recovery has been equally dramatic, resulting in some major refurbishing.

Warmth and Victorian charm are reflected in the carpeted guest rooms upstairs, furnished with the hosts' personal treasures and eye-catching wallpapers. One guest room has a fireplace and one is particularly large, with a king-size bed and a brushed velvet couch; the other three rooms are smaller but equally attractive.

A small guest parlor on the first floor has a color TV, a fireplace, mustard-colored love seats, and a variety of collectibles. Adding to the warmth are the resident Maine coon cats, Robin Hood and Maid Marian.

A full English breakfast, skillfully prepared by Paul, is served in the formal, carpeted dining room with elegant service and accessories. Eggs to order, homemade English muffin breads, real English bangers, potatoes, and broiled tomatoes might be on the menu. In keeping with the British flavor, a high tea is set out in the afternoons with offerings both homegrown and homemade, such as scones, rhubarb jam, and shortbread.

Flower and herb beds, nurtured by Paul, provide a rich array of colors and fragrances. Paul is happy to take guests through the gardens and share tidbits of information and lore about many of the plantings. He uses the herbs and flowers as essential ingredients in his own herbal vinegars, oils, and potpourris (all of which may be purchased for a reasonable price). Beyond the grounds are expansive views of the nearby hills and fields. Paul is a justice of the peace, and the gardens are a popular wedding setting.

The Windflower Inn

684 So. Egremont Road
Great Barrington, MA 01230
413-528-2720
800-992-1993
Fax: 413-528-5147
windflowr@windflowerinn.com
www.windflowerinn.com

A family-run country inn

Innkeepers: Claudia and John Ryan. **Accommodations:** 13 rooms (all with private bath). **Rates:** $100–$170. **Included:** Breakfast and tea. **Minimum stay:** 2 nights on weekends; 3 nights on July and August weekends. **Added:** 9.7% tax. **Credit card accepted:** American Express. **Children:** In parent's room: $25 under age 10. **Pets:** Not accepted. **Smoking:** Restricted. **Handicap access:** No. **Open:** Year-round.

➤ **Claudia Ryan is the chef and her husband John tends the berries, herbs, and vegetables from his garden. Claudia's parents, Barbara and Gerald, are longtime innkeepers who lend their skills wherever needed.**

The Windflower Inn, a turn-of-the-century gentleman's retreat, is run by two generations of the same family who have operated it since 1981.

The white clapboard inn with gables, black shutters, and a wrap-around porch, across from a country club, exudes comfort. There is plenty of common space, including a reading room and a screened porch. Afternoon tea and homemade cookies are set out for guests.

The bedrooms and baths are large and bright, all individually decorated, some with canopy beds and six with fireplaces. Check out the deep clawfoot tub in Room 5 and the four-poster and big stone hearth in Room 12. Another particularly nice room has a private entrance and a large fireplace. Room 1, with a fireplace, could sleep a family of five — as long as the children aren't fully grown!

In the summer, guests can enjoy the inn's swimming pool, bordered with perennial gardens, and golf and tennis at the country club.

For many years the Windflower was widely known for its dinners (the dining room was open to the public) and dinner can still be arranged for groups off-season. Now, however, Claudia pours her vast culinary skills into breakfast preparation.

Lee

Applegate

R.R. 1, Box 576
279 West Park Street
Lee, MA 01238
413-243-4451
800-691-9012
Fax: 413-243-4451
applegate@taconic.net
www.applegateinn.com

> **An alternative to the bustle of Lenox**

Innkeepers: Nancy and Rick Cannata. **Accommodations:** 6 rooms (all with private bath). **Rates** (vary between weekdays and weekends as well as the season): from $85 on a weekday in November to $225 for Rooms 1 and 2 on a summer weekend. **Included:** Continental candlelight breakfast, wine and cheese, brandy and chocolates. **Minimum stay:** 2 to 3 nights on summer, fall, and holiday weekends. **Added:** 9.7% tax. **Credit cards accepted:** MasterCard, Visa. **Children:** Over age 12. **Pets:** Not accepted. **Smoking:** Not permitted. **Handicap access:** No. **Open:** Year-round.

> ➤ **Rick and Nancy, both retired from the airline industry, have created a delightful place to stay put.**

Don't be put off by the apparent pretension of the portico at Applegate or by the wrought iron fence that delineates the front of the six acres. The mansion was built by a New York doctor in the 1920s, but today's owners, who purchased the house in 1990, are quite down to earth, and so is the mood of the refined house.

The downstairs is spacious, beginning with the foyer and opening into the living room. Wine and cheese are served here in the afternoon. Classical recordings usually fill the air, except when someone is playing the piano. The bookshelves and fireplace mantel are filled with family photographs and pictures of past guests. A separate game/TV room has a TV, VCR, a small game table, and film library.

In warm weather the manicured lawns are a natural extension of the house; the grounds include a pool, a croquet area, and stone walls. A screened porch with a slate floor and wicker furniture extends the length of the house.

The most expensive guest room measures 39 by 18 feet and boasts its own steam shower with two shower heads, a fireplace, four-poster bed, nice sitting area, and Early American reproduction furniture. Room 2 has a queen-size four-poster bed dressed in white lace and peach colored walls decorated with cherubs. Room 3 is simple, with a nice sleigh bed and fireplace. Room 4 is furnished with white wicker and white iron. The sheer white French voile curtains in Room 5 infuse the room with a glow; the ethereal effect is furthered by the canopy. Though the smallest, Room 6 is one of our favorites, tucked in the back of the house under the eaves. Green floral wallpaper and a massive bedstead dominate the room but there is still room for two wing chairs, inviting a couple to sit and read or talk.

The breakfast menu is announced with the aid of a pig figurine holding a chalkboard. On our last visit, there was an outstanding array of baked goods. Guests have their own refrigerator for storing picnic items.

Nancy is a trove of information about local restaurants, and guests can thumb through restaurant reviews by previous guests. The couple also help plan local itineraries and offer bicycles for guest use.

Lenox

Amadeus

15 Cliffwood Street
Lenox, MA 01240
413-637-4770
800-205-4770
info@amadeushouse.com
www.amadeushouse.com

Low key and friendly

Innkeepers: Marty Gottron and John Felton. **Accommodations:** 8 rooms (only 5 in November–April). **Rates:** Late June to Labor Day: $90–$155 on weekends, $70–$110 in midweek; $15 extra per person in room; $1,200 per week for the Beethoven suite during Tangleowod Season. Spring and fall: $80–$130 per couple on weekends; $65–$110 in midweek; $140–$190 for Beethoven suite. November to mid-May: $75–$115 per couple on weekends; $65–$90 in midweek; $100–$145 for Beethoven suite. Inquire about winter packages. **Included:** Full breakfast and tea. **Minimum Stay:** During Tangleowod season, 4 nights for big rooms, 3 nights for smaller; otherwise 2 nights on weekends. **Added:** 9.7% tax. **Credit cards accepted:** Visa, MasterCard, American Express. **Children:** Over age 6. **Pets:** Not accepted. **Smoking:** Not permitted. **Handicapped access:** No. **Open:** Year-round.

➤ **Music is the theme.**

Nicely situated on a quiet side street within walking distance of Lenox shops and restaurants, this large, late-19th-century house is an unusually comfortable, low-key B&B.

John and Marty explain that they have four types of accommodations. Bach, Brahms, and Mozart are extra-large rooms, each with a private bath, queen-size bed, and sitting area. Our favorite is Mozart, a first-floor room that's large and a soothing green, and handsomely furnished in antiques. The high bird's-eye maple fourposter leaves plenty of space for a comfortable sitting area in front of the woodstove. A bust of Mozart presides over the mantel and there's much to read both by and about the composer.

Upstairs are Bersntein and Copland, both medium-size rooms with private baths, and Schubert and Sibelius (available May through October), each with two twin beds that can easily be converted to a king, share a bath. The Beethoven Suite, on the third floor (it's air-conditioned), is really an apartment with two bedrooms, a kitchen, sitting area and bath, and rents by the week or month.

We like the feel of this place — the colors of the walls and the unpretentious but attractive furnishings. Guests are invited to select from a collection of several hundred compact discs, pick up a book or magazine from the library, or play a game at a table in the dining room. Breakfast is as full as you like it or don't like, beginning with freshly squeezed orange juice and Marty's just-made muffins and including something hot, maybe John's no-cal yogurt pancakes. The dining room adjoins the kitchen and guests and hosts tend to talk.

John and Marty both grew up in Ohio and have spent much of their lives working with words. John was a reporter for many years, serving as deputy foreign editor for National Public Radio before settling into innkeeping. Marty continues to freelance as an editor for a variety of prominent publications. Amadeus, it's worth noting, is one of a half-dozen inns to take full advantage of the number of spa services available in Lenox, combining its low November–mid-May rates for two people with packages that include a massage, facial, or similar service. We gave a Lenox spa weekend for a birthday, that way getting to share the present.

Lenox is one place that's as enjoyable "off-season" as on. There's plenty of local cross-country and downhill skiing and the restaurants seem even better without the summer rush.

Blantyre

P.O. Box 995
Lenox, MA 01240
413-637-3556
Fax: 413-637-4282
hide@blantyre.com
www.blantyre.com

| A grand country house with outstanding service and cuisine |

Proprietress: Ann Fitzpatrick. **Managing director:** Roderick Anderson. **Accommodations:** 23 rooms divided between the main house, carriage house, and three cottages (all with private bath). **Rates:** $235–$650 per couple; $50 for additional person in room. **Included:** Continental breakfast, lunch and dinner also served. **Minimum stay:** 2 nights on weekends. **Added:** 9.7% tax, 10% service charge. **Credit cards accepted:** All major ones. **Children:** Children under 12 discouraged. **Pets:** Not accepted. **Smoking:** Cigars not permitted in the dining room. **Handicap access:** Yes. **Open:** May through October.

➤ **Blantyre was the first American hotel to win the coveted International Welcome Award from Relais et Chateaux.**

Exquisite, romantic, courteous. A member of Relais et Chateaux Hotels, Blantyre ranks right up there with the best of the world's smallest hotels.

Built in 1902 as a summer retreat, Blantyre is a magnificent Tudor mansion intended to re-create an ancestral home in Scotland — a mass of turrets, gargoyles, and carved friezes. By 1980, when the Fitzpatricks of the Red Lion Inn in Stockbridge purchased it, Blantyre Castle (as it was called) had degenerated into a rather dark, shabby place. But the Fitzpatricks spent an entire year refitting it in royal style and simplified its name to lower its profile. One of the most surprising facets of Blantyre is that the atmosphere isn't snobbish, but rather genteel, discreet, and friendly.

An ornate hobby horse created for the space (the sole playful touch in an otherwise formal setting) graces the front lobby. The hall is baronial, with a stone hearth, ornate paneling, and an antelope head. A brighter, graceful music room, with a piano and a harp, has crystal chandeliers, sofas covered in petit-point, and velvet chairs. Exquisite flower arrangements enhance the public rooms.

The main dining room has dark paneling hung with portraits and a tapestry. Dinner, by reservation only, is $70 per person. Before eating, take time to have a drink and listen to the harpist. It's really difficult to say what shines brightest at Blantyre, the level of professional service or the quality of the decor.

The guest rooms are impeccably furnished with antiques. Some rooms have four-poster beds, fireplaces, and upholstered sofas and chairs. The twelve rooms in the carriage house, some of which are split-level lofts, are more contemporary, but they're still decorated with the same attention to detail and quality. There are also four more rooms in several small cottages on the property. In all the rooms, bathroom amenities are outstanding.

The mansion has four fine Har-Tru tennis courts (whites required), a swimming pool with hot tub and sauna, and competition croquet on its 85 acres. Professional tennis and croquet instructors are on hand, and a massage therapist is available with 24 hours notice.

Canyon Ranch in the Berkshires

Bellefontaine
165 Kemble Street
Lenox, MA 01240
413-637-4100
800-742-9000 or 800-326-7080
Fax: 413-637-0057
www.canyonranch.com

> The ultimate spa in a grand mansion

Director: Mary Ellen St. John. **Accommodations:** 120 rooms and suites. **Rates:** From $1,430 per person, double occupancy, for a three-night package; many packages available. **Included:** All meals; use of the spa and resort facilities, fitness classes, sports activities, airport transfers, gratuities and a selection of services based on length of stay. **Minimum stay:** 3 nights. **Added:** 9.7% tax, 18% service charge. **Credit cards accepted:** MasterCard, Visa, American Express, and Discover. **Children:** Over age 14. **Pets:** Not accepted. **Smoking:** Not permitted. **Handicap access:** Some rooms. **Open:** Year-round.

➤ **Day guests can take advantage of the spa facilities for a fee. The staff has honed its skills at the original Canyon Ranch, in Arizona. If it's in your price range, there's no place better.**

Ask spa-goers where Canyon Ranch is and they will quickly reply: Tucson, Arizona. Billing itself as "the first major coed health and fitness resort to open year-round in the Northeast," Canyon Ranch has been in the Berkshires since the fall of 1989.

The centerpiece of this 120-acre luxurious complex is one of the grandest of Lenox's 1890s cottages. Bellefontaine was built of marble and brick to resemble Louis XVI's Petit Trianon, and its vast rooms, which include a dining room, library, and Health and Healing Center, are richly detailed.

The 120-room inn itself is a separate new clapboard building designed along traditional New England lines. Behind the mansion, it's connected by all-weather, glass-enclosed walkways. These also connect with the spa facilities: exercise rooms, pools, lockers, a gymnasium, indoor track, indoor racquetball and tennis courts, and more. Of course, there are also spa and massage and treatment rooms as well as a wide variety of programs — from smoking cessation and stress reduction to myriad combinations of exercise and nutrition. The staff-to-guest ratio is nearly three to one.

The Gables Inn

103 Walker Street (Route 183)
Lenox, MA 01240
413-637-3416
800-382-9401

An innlike B&B with an indoor pool and tennis in the garden

Owners: Frank and Mary Newton. **Accommodations:** 18 rooms (all private bath), 3 suites. **Rates:** $90–$210 per couple, May through October; otherwise $80–$160 per couple. **Included:** Continental breakfast. **Minimum stay:** 3 nights in July and August; 2 nights in October; 2 nights on holiday weekends. **Added:** 9.7% tax. **Credit cards accepted:** All major ones. **Children:** Over age 12. **Pets:** Not permitted. **Smoking:** No cigars. **Handicap access:** No. **Open:** Year-round.

➤ **Novelist Edith Wharton lived in this Queen Anne–style "cottage" while waiting for the Mount to be built. In the restored octagonal library she wrote short stories.**

Built in 1885, when Lenox vied with Newport and Bar Harbor as a fashionable summer resort, the Gables is a classic Queen Anne house originally known as Pine Acres.

All the graceful guest rooms are air-conditioned; some have fireplaces. One of the most popular rooms is the richly colored Jockey Suite, on the first floor. It has a big picture window overlooking the tennis court, a large-screen TV with two sofas facing it, a private entrance, and a canopy brass bed tucked into a niche. The Wharton Wing, with the bold Teddy Room and the plush Edith Room, is quite popular. The guest room named for Wharton is one of the inn's best, with a four-poster canopy bed, a patterned carpet, and a plum-colored sofa next to the fireplace. Frank says he was inspired by inns he's known in Charleston and Savannah.

Two front parlors are decorated in comfortable Victorian style, with wall-to-wall carpeting covered by Oriental carpets. The full breakfast, served from a sideboard, consists mainly of assorted breads and special cakes, pancakes, and waffles. Eat at one of the half-dozen little round tables in front of a window or be more social and dine at the long formal table. The glass-covered, skirted tables are set with crystal, china, and Gables Inn mugs. (Though sympathetic to the problem, we were rather put off by the signs suggesting we not linger over breakfast for an inordinate amount of time.)

The Gables offers some remarkable facilities for an inn its size, including a well-maintained tennis court (Frank has rackets) and a solar-heated swimming pool in a greenhouse-like structure. A back deck, where you can read the paper or have a drink, overlooks the garden. A brick patio by the pool has plenty of lounge chairs.

Garden Gables

141 Main Street
Lenox, MA 01240
413-637-0193
gardeninn@aol.com
wwwgardengables.com

> **A delightful B&B that's
> constantly upgraded**

Innkeepers: Mario and Lynn Mekinda. **Accommodations:** 18 rooms (all with private bath). **Rates:** $90–$225 per couple in Tanglewood and foliage seasons; otherwise $70–$170 per couple; weekly and monthly rates available. **Included:** Full breakfast. **Minimum stay:** 3 nights on weekends in July and August and holidays; 2 nights in June, September, and October. **Added:** 9.7% tax. **Credit cards accepted:** All major ones. **Children:** Not appropriate. **Pets:** Not accepted. **Smoking:** Not permitted in bedrooms. **Handicap access:** Some rooms. **Open:** Year-round.

➤ **Well back from the main road and one mile from Tanglewood, Garden Gables' five acres are wooded, with many gardens and flowering trees. The inn has perhaps the longest pool (72 feet) in western Massachusetts. It's crystal clear, deep (cold toward the bottom!), and has a nicely landscaped deck.**

Mario and Lynn Mekinda, an energetic Canadian couple, have transformed an old Lenox lodging standby into a very special place, enhancing the original beauty and integrity of the house, which dates in part to 1780. The two sitting rooms, on either side of the front door, have low ceilings and a fresh, bright look, like the rest of the house. The larger and brighter of the two has a Steinway baby grand piano, a TV, and a VCR. The other has comfortable love seats and a fireplace. Some guest rooms have whirlpool tubs, fireplaces, cable TV with VCRs, private porches and canopy beds, and all have in-room telephones and answering machines, as well as air conditioning with individual thermostats.

When guests arrive, they are offered lemonade and shown the kitchen, where they should feel free to use the refrigerator.

There isn't a room that we wouldn't be delighted to spend the night in; seven rooms have working fireplaces. One of our favorites is the room in the back of the house (which dates from 1908) with a canopy bed and its own deck. Attesting to the comfortable nature of the place, many of the rooms are taken for long stretches of time. The smaller rooms are less expensive but have been given the same fresh makeover. All are air-conditioned.Two rooms built over a screened porch have fireplaces and canopy beds. Four suites in the garden cottages have cathedral ceilings, queen canopy beds, and sitting areas.

A buffet breakfast featuring freshly baked muffins, buttery croissants, fresh fruit, yogurts, and eggs as well as cereals can be enjoyed at large tables that overlook well-kept gardens. Tea and coffee are available all day. The inn has a strong following, with many guests booking a year in advance for the July and August Tanglewood season.

Walker House

64 Walker Street
Lenox, MA 01240
413-637-1271
800-235-3098
Fax: 413-637-2387
phoudek@vgernet.net
www.regionnet.com/colberk/walkerhouse.html

A B&B for cat and music lovers

Innkeepers: Peggy and Richard Houdek. **Accommodations:** 8 rooms (all with private bath). **Rates:** $80–$190 per couple in June through October, otherwise $70–$120 per couple. **Included:** Expanded Continental breakfast. **Minimum stay:** 3 nights on summer weekends; 2 nights, all other weekends. **Added:** 9.7% tax. **Credit cards accepted:** None. **Children:** Over age 12. **Pets:** Welcome by arrangement. **Smoking:** Not permitted. **Handicap access:** No. **Open:** Year-round.

➤ **The sound of music fills the house throughout the day. Your first introduction to the role of music here is the doorbell, which announces guests to the tune of Beethoven's Ninth Symphony's *Ode to Joy*.**

The atmosphere and the decor here reflect the creative vitality and friendliness of longtime hosts Peggy and Richard Houdek. In 1980 they left California and their careers in the arts (she was the editor of *Performing Arts* magazine and is a trained opera singer; he was an arts administrator and music critic) to run their own business in musically rich Lenox. This is one of our favorite places to stay in western New England.

The house itself, in the center of Lenox, is a handsome Federal landmark built in 1804. Downstairs, the library is not only lined with books and recordings but doubles as a screening room with surround sound for films, opera, and TV specials. The overall decor of the inn is a harmonious blend of antiques, contemporary art, personal treasures, and lush greenery. Several cats, having found their way to Walker House, have become permanent and dearly loved residents.

Breakfast is served in the dining room or, in nice weather, on the verandah. Long and wide and thoroughly inviting, the verandah is filled with comfortable wicker furniture and lush plants; it overlooks three acres of beautifully landscaped and wooded grounds.

The spacious bedrooms, each named for a composer, are furnished with antiques. Verdi has lime green floral wallpaper, white wicker, and two iron and brass double beds; it gets good afternoon sun. Handel is a large and airy front room with a large bath, fireplace, and canopy brass bed. Another favorite is Chopin, decorated in pastels with a canopy bed. Next to the front door, Beethoven's room has nice wood floors, a fainting couch, and a king-size bed with creaky springs. Puccini has a private little side porch. The smallest, Debussy, is down a narrow hallway.

In addition to running the inn, Peggy and Richard are involved in the community's cultural events, and they produce three or four recitals a year for their guests and the public. These concerts give unknown artists the chance to perform and, of course, keep the Houdeks in touch with the world of music, their greatest love.

New Marlborough

The Old Inn on the Green/Gedney Farm

New Marlborough, MA 01230
413-229-7924
800-286-3139
Fax: 413-229-8421
brad@oldinn.com
www.oldinn.com

> Exceptional cuisine and two
> room types: classic Colonial
> and Mediterranean-style

Innkeepers: Leslie Miller and Brad Wagstaff. **Manager:** Mike Smith. **Accommodations:** The Old Inn: 6 rooms (all with private bath); Gedney Farm: 6 rooms (all with private bath), 5 suites. **Rates:** $160–$175 per couple in the Old Inn, $175–$285 at Gedney Farm; $40 per extra person in room; winter and spring packages. **Included:** Expanded Continental breakfast; a prix fixe dinner is offered on Saturdays; à la carte dinner served nightly except Saturdays; lunch also served; dining room closed Monday through Wednesday from November through June. **Minimum stay:** 2 nights on summer and fall weekends. **Added:** 5.7% tax, 10% service charge. **Credit cards accepted:** All major ones. **Children:** Welcome. **Pets:** Not accepted. **Smoking:** Restricted. **Handicap access:** No. **Open:** Year-round.

➤ **Some bathrooms at Gedney Farm have a glass roof, so that when soaking in a whirlpool tub by candlelight, you can see the interior beams of the barn.**

The Old Inn on the Green, a circa 1760, double-porch tavern, served as a classic village inn through the 1920s. It was resurrected and deftly restored by Brad and Leslie in the mid-1970s and today stands as the centerpiece of the wonderfully sleepy and tranquil village. Gedney Farm (Brad's second acquisition, just down the road) is a completely renovated Normandy-style barn whose rooms have wood-burning fireplaces and/or whirlpool baths.

Authenticity is the unspoken but proud theme at the Old Inn. Guest rooms have minimalist period furniture, an occasional throw rug, simple white plaster walls with stenciling or pastel trim, and unfinished wide floorboards. In 1996, private baths were added to the Old Inn guest rooms and the second-floor porch was partitioned to give a few rooms private access. It's lovely to sit with a book or a glass of wine overlooking the quiet town green and out to the mountains beyond.

Gedney Farm, a turn-of-the-century Jersey cow barn, is a nice complement to the Old Inn. Brad transformed it by gutting it and building elegantly simple rooms. They have a hint of luxury (in the form of deep whirlpool baths and wood-burning fireplaces) as well as a hint of Spartan farmhouse comfort (like well-worn overstuffed armchairs). Architectural details were painstakingly preserved and incorporated into the interior common areas (decorated with Turkish kilims and tapestry-upholstered chairs) and second-floor rooms.

Guest room furnishings may include iron canopy beds, slightly battered country antiques, and simple floor-to-ceiling drapery. The plaster walls are sparingly adorned. Only one guest room has a fireplace as well as a whirlpool; you'll have to book early for it. (The more expensive suites, of course, have both.) Although the two least-expensive rooms lack lofty ceilings (like the second-floor rooms), a fireplace, or a whirlpool, they are lovely, bright corner rooms. There is also a loft suite, with a private entrance. If you opt for a whirlpool instead of a fireplace, you can still enjoy the fireplace in the long hallway that connects the rooms.

Breakfast is served in the restored horse barn next door. Help yourself to muffins and more unusual baked treats (Leslie does most of the baking from the aromatic first-floor bakery), fruit, coffee, and juice, and sit down to a table set with white linen and heavy silver. If you're lucky, you'll get one of the tables in front of the fireplace. A bistro-style lunch is served on the patio courtyard here, looking out onto the fields.

The romantic dining rooms at the Old Inn are relaxing and the cuisine exceptional and creative. On our last late summer visit the room was warmed by the fireplaces and lit by flickering candlelight (from the wall sconces, on the table, and above in the wrought-iron chandeliers). Impeccably presented and prepared dishes included a yellow tomato and arugula soup with lobster and saffron and a wild mushroom tart for starters, and, among a wide choice of entrées, roasted shrimp with scallop mousse, linguini cake, shredded spinach and lemongrass coulis, and sautéed veal loin steak with black bean salad and red wine jus. Make sure to leave room for crème brûlée or a warm fruit tart.

South Lee

Historic Merrell Inn

1565 Pleasant Street
South Lee, MA 01260
413-243-1794
800-243-1794
Fax: 413-243-2669
merey@ben.net
www.merrell-Inn.com

> An authentic stagecoach tavern is now a hospitable B&B

Innkeepers: Pam Hurst and Chuck and Faith Reynolds. **Accommodations:** 9 rooms (all with private bath). **Rates:** Summer and fall weekends and holidays:$135–$165 per couple; weekdays: $95–$115; less off-season. **Included:** Full breakfast. **Minimum stay:** 3 nights in summer; 2 nights on weekends. **Added:** 5.7% tax. **Credit cards accepted:** MasterCard, Visa. **Children:** $15 extra. **Pets:** Not accepted. **Smoking:** Not permitted. **Handicap access:** No. **Open:** Year-round.

➤ **Stepping into the Merrell Inn is stepping back into the early 19th century.**

The brick landmark on Route 102, a stagecoach stop during much of the 19th century, was constructed in 1794. In 1837 the third floor, a ballroom, was added. The inn was empty for seventy-five years before Chuck and Faith purchased it in 1981, and they spent years bringing it up to its present condition. Many of the historic features have been preserved, including the original cooking fireplace, the beehive oven in the parlor, and the false wood graining in the dining room.

For breakfast, choose from omelettes, scrambled eggs and sausage, pancakes, French toast, and cereal. Seconds and additional entrées are always available and cheerfully given at no extra charge. The Colonial-era dining room, in which a fire glows even for one guest, boasts the country's only complete birdcage circular

Colonial bar that survives intact in its original location. Today, the bar serves as a check-in desk.

The cozy parlor, with matching wing chairs and a love seat in front of the fireplace, has Oriental carpets and hardwood floors. It's particularly romantic in the evening, when the candlebeam lighting and sconces shed a flickering light. This room is closed to guests after 10:00 P.M. since some of the guest rooms are right next to it. There is also a television room.

The guest rooms are unusually romantic, finished in lovely wallpapers, with swags and valances on the windows and Oriental carpets, all of which highlight the fine architectural details and historically accurate colors. The nicest rooms, in our opinion, are the larger ones on the first floor. The small rooms in the rear of the house originally accommodated the stagecoach drivers. Most of the rooms have a canopy bed, telephone, and fine bedding. In winter a two-night stay is required for the rooms with working fireplaces. The inn is located right on the main road, but the 12- to 18-inch-thick walls seem to do their job. In the summer, air conditioners in the front room obscure noise.

Behind the inn two well-tended acres extend to the quiet Housatonic. Two trees support a hammock, and there are plenty of lounge chairs around the lawns, arbor, Victorian gardens, screened gazebo, and tea house. In winter the inn's fireplaces and cozy common rooms are also unusually appealing.

Stockbridge

Red Lion Inn

Stockbridge, MA 01262
413-298-5545
Fax: 413-298-5130

| A historic inn, the centerpiece of a very special village |

Owners: The Fitzpatrick family. **Accommodations:** 111 rooms (some with shared bath). **Rates:** $115–$165 per couple for rooms; $185–$245 for two rooms, shared baths; $185–$355 for suites. **Included:** No meals but all are served. **Minimum stay:** 2 nights on July and August weekends. **Added:** 9.7% tax. **Credit cards accepted:** All major ones. **Children:** Free with parents; cot charge: $20. **Pets:** Not accepted. **Smoking:** Restricted. **Handicap access:** 2 rooms. **Open:** Year-round.

➤ **Summer guests enjoy the pool, walk up the street to productions at the Berkshire Playhouse, or climb up Laurel Hill to take in the view from a stone seat designed by Daniel Chester French. In the winter, when the prices drop, there is cross-country and downhill skiing nearby.**

This is the most famous inn in the Berkshires, immortalized in a portrait of Main Street, Stockbridge, by Norman Rockwell. The rambling white clapboard beauty was built in 1897, after fire destroyed an expanded version of the tavern that had stood on this spot since 1773.

Back in 1968 the landmark was sagging, and there were rumors of tearing it down and replacing it with a gas station, but Jack and Jane Fitzpatrick bought it. While setting up their Country Curtains business in its ample extremities, they brought the inn back to life, and both businesses have prospered spectacularly.

There isn't a musty or dusty corner in the entire place, and the curtains are still showcased in a back-of-the-building shop. Guest rooms run an unusually wide gamut — from spacious honeymoon suites to small, old-fashioned rooms with shared baths. Even the least expensive rooms are carefully furnished with real and reproduction antiques and bright prints. Most have color TV, and all have air conditioning and phones.

There are some truly splendid rooms, like Room 102, with a canopy bed covered with a Waverly print made expressly for the inn, a marble-topped bureau, and a comfortable sitting area with a

Victorian sofa. Rooms 442 and 240 have painted country furniture and old-fashioned baths with modern fixtures. The bathrooms in fifteen or so rooms have recently been redone with a slew of marble. The newest rooms are in nearby village houses, ranging from vintage houses to the old Stockbridge firehouse (the former fireman's quarters are now a honeymoon suite).

Guests enter the Red Lion from an inviting verandah, with an ample supply of flowers and rockers in the warm months. The low-ceilinged lobby is large and comfortable, usually with an elaborate flower arrangement in the center and a crackling fire in the parlor. A red velvet curtain divides this area from the formal Victorian dining room, decorated in shades of red. An informal lunch is served in the cozy, paneled Widow Bingham's Tavern. There is a formal check-in area and an old-fashioned cage elevator. The common areas and hallways are a visual treat.

The main dining room, popular throughout the region, specializes in traditional dinner favorites such as filet mignon and filet of sole, with some interesting variations like sirloin of venison and chicken stuffed with garlic and herb boursin. All the public rooms serve as meeting spots for South Berkshire.

Given the size of the inn, the constant bustle simply adds to its charm. Groups predominate in the off-season. The Red Lion is always a welcoming place, with the same air of quality and comfort found in fine city hotels.

West Stockbridge

The Williamsville Inn

Route 41
West Stockbridge, MA 01266
413-274-6118
Fax: 413-274-3539

A country inn on a back
road

Innkeepers: Gail and Kathleen Ryan. **Accommodations:** 16 rooms (all with private bath). **Rates:** $140–$185 per couple in season; otherwise $120–$165. **Included:** Full breakfast; dinner ($30–$50 per person) also served. **Minimum stay:** 3 nights on summer and 2 nights on holiday weekends. **Added:** 9.7% tax. **Credit cards accepted:** Major credit cards. **Children:** Accepted. **Pets:** Not

accepted. **Smoking:** Not permitted in dining rooms. **Handicap access:** No.
Open: Year-round.

➤ **In the summer, when the inn holds a regional sculpture show, the
property is dotted with whimsical and serious objets d'art.**

The mother-daughter team of Kathleen and Gail Ryan purchased
the Williamsville Inn, originally an 18th-century farmhouse, in
1990. On a rural road south of West Stockbridge, it is old-fashioned
but nicely renovated.

Ten acres of well-tended flower and vegetable gardens, a swimming pool, a swing hanging from an old elm, croquet, horseshoes,
badminton, and volleyball should be enough to occupy most
guests. For the more adventurous, there is a clay tennis court. The
Ryans have a range of activities planned throughout the year.

The inn is renowned for its elegant country cuisine. (Be forewarned, however, the dining room closes Tuesdays in high season).
A large and varied summer menu might include such appetizers as
shrimp and corn chowder and Monterey chèvre on a black olive
crouton, and among the entrées are shrimp and oriental vegetables
wrapped in sesame scallion crêpes served with orange honey soy
glaze and tenderloin of beef with red wine sauce and portobella
mushrooms.

Wide pine floorboards run throughout the inn and are covered
with braided rugs. Fireplaces warm the already cozy pub and the
comfortable living room. The guest rooms are upstairs. Two cozy
rooms on the third floor are tucked under the eaves with a double
and twin bed. Each room has been freshly painted and papered and
outfitted with four-poster and canopy beds. A few of the rooms
have a fireplace.

The rooms in the former barn aren't as spiffy and polished as
those in the main house but they have new brass beds and woodstoves.

This is, incidentally, a beautiful place for a wedding.

Williamstown

Field Farm Guest House

554 Sloan Road
Williamstown, MA 01267
413-458-3135

| An intriguing country
estate

Managers: Trustees of Reservations staff. **Accommodations:** 5 rooms (all with private bath). **Rates:** $100 per couple, $15 each extra person. **Included:** Full breakfast. **Minimum stay:** None. **Added:** 9.7% tax. **Credit cards accepted:** MasterCard, Visa, Discover. **Children:** Welcome. **Pets:** Not accepted. **Smoking:** Not permitted. **Handicap access:** No. **Open:** Year-round.

➤   **Views of Mount Greylock and the Taconic Range, well-marked walking trails, and a spring-fed pond stocked with carp and goldfish are good diversions. With any luck you'll see deer, wild turkey, coyote, fox, raccoon, heron, and migrating osprey. This is a special place for quiet and meditation.**

Field Farm is one of around 80 properties owned by the Trustees of Reservations, a Massachusetts land conservation organization established in 1891 and dedicated to preserving properties of exceptional scenic, historical, and ecological significance. Indeed, Field Farm is a rare bird! The estate encompasses 296 acres of corn and hay fields and country woodlands that have been farmed continuously since the founding of Williamstown. Recently, the guest house has become a destination in and of itself.

Field Farm is a genuine period piece, which you sense as soon as you walk in. The 1948 house and 1950s furnishings you see today, down to the complete set of dishes and glassware in the kitchen, were left when Lawrence and Eleanore Bloedel donated the property in 1984. In addition to being an avid art collector, Lawrence Bloedel was a librarian at Williams College, and his personal collection of more than 2,000 volumes fills the bookshelves.

The main house was designed in 1948 by Edward Goodell in the American Modern style. No expense was spared in creating the visible and invisible eccentricities of the house; the parquet cork floors downstairs, for instance, are warmed by a sophisticated series of copper pipes. Built to house the Bloedels' art collection, the walls are long and flat with rounded corners. Large picture windows and recessed lighting in the living and dining rooms highlight the artwork and heighten the sense of space. The living room has a modern, rather Spartan feel.

The only guest room on the first floor has a queen and two twin beds. Upstairs, the master bedroom has an enormous balcony, three twin beds, and a glass-fronted fireplace with bird tiles. The East Room, facing Mount Greylock, has two twin beds and a private balcony. The North Room also has a balcony, a fireplace with hand-painted butterfly tiles, a queen bed, and a mirrored dressing table with lingerie drawers. The bathrooms are from the 1940s, with fine porcelain fixtures.

On the grounds you may enjoy gardens, a tennis court, a kidney-shaped swimming pool that's eight feet deep, and sculptures. You'll also want to explore the Folly, designed in 1965 by Ulrich Franzen, who was influenced by the Shingle-style architecture of the 1880s.

River Bend Farm

643 Simonds Road
Williamstown, MA 01267
413-458-3121

An authentic Colonial B&B

Innkeepers: Judy and Dave Loomis. **Accommodations:** 4 rooms (sharing 2 baths). **Rates:** $80 per couple, $65 single. **Included:** Expanded Continental breakfast. **Minimum stay:** None. **Added:** 9.7% tax. **Credit cards accepted:** None. **Children:** Welcome. **Pets:** Not accepted. **Smoking:** Not permitted in guest rooms. **Handicap access:** No. **Open:** April–October.

➤ **It's said that bread for Revolutionary soldiers at the Battle of Bennington was baked here.**

A real timepiece, this authentic 1770 Georgian home is the embodiment of Colonial life, and the town's history unfolded under its roof. The most intriguing and dominant feature of the house is the central chimney, which serves five fireplaces, two bake ovens, and a smoking chamber in the attic. The chimney is 13 feet thick at its base, and considerably narrower at the top. You can see it from almost every room.

Each guest room reflects careful, scholarly restoration. The bed in the first-floor room has blocks underneath to level it (the floorboards are wavy). The bulging and slanting walls, which follow the line of the fireplace, are most noticeable in this room. Old-fashioned lighting fixtures, latch doors, low ceilings, and exposed original wallpaper lend authenticity. One bathroom has an antique clawfoot tub; the other, downstairs, has a shower and shelves filled with old glass bottles, antique pottery, and jugs.

The comfortable living room, once a tavern, now displays a collection of pewter and old muskets. If you look hard enough, you may find a 16-inch floorboard or two. The law in those days required that all 16-inchers had to go to the king to help build ships, but a few were snuck in as testament to the solid construction by Colonel Benjamin Simonds.

The front rooms, by the way, are covered with plaster, which was more expensive and more prestigious, while the rear rooms simply have plank walls.

A substantial Continental breakfast is served in front of the hearth. The copper-and-tin-lined sink and 14-inch-wide floorboards confound your sense of time. Even the granola is ladled out of a crock into speckled Bennington pottery.

On occasion, the entire house may be rented to one group of people (ten maximum). It's a wonderful retreat for family and college reunions.

New Hampshire

Dixville Notch

White Mountains
&
North Woods

Franconia

North Conway

Waterville
Valley

Hanover

Central & Lakes

Sunapee

Henniker

Portsmouth

Peterborough

Southern
New Hampshire

Southern New Hampshire

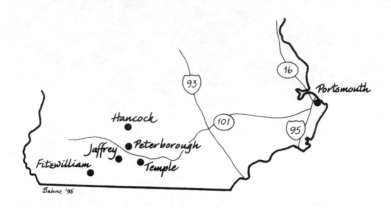

Best Bed-and-Breakfasts

Fitzwilliam
  Amos A. Parker House, 409
  Hannah Davis House, 410
Jaffrey
  The Benjamin Prescott Inn, 413
Peterborough
  Apple Gate Bed and Breakfast, 415

Best City Stop

Portsmouth
  The Inn at Strawbery Banke, 416

Best Inns

Hancock
  The Hancock Inn, 412
Temple
  The Birchwood Inn, 417

Best Romantic Getaways

Fitzwilliam
  Amos A. Parker House, 409
  Hannah Davis House, 410

In southern New Hampshire, there are a scattering of fine places to stay near the short seacoast and in the Monadnock region, New Hampshire's southwestern roll of hills.

Portsmouth, on the coast, is a gracious old city that has preserved its history in the form of aristocratic houses, a mid-19th-century market area filled with shops and restaurants, and a 10-acre museum village called Strawbery Banke. There is free summer entertainment, including theater, in Prescott Park, right on the river. There is also swimming just downriver, along New Hampshire's short but sandy bit of shore.

The hilly southwestern region of New Hampshire is a high granite island unto itself. The state's recent economic boom region lies just to the east, and I-89 skirts it to the north. Its landmark is the lone mountain that has given its name to all similar monadnocks throughout the world — Mount Monadnock — which is said to be one of the most frequently climbed of the world's mountains, right up there after Fuji. It towers above picture-perfect white clapboard villages like **Jaffrey** and Fitzwilliam, and is visible from other little villages, such as **Hancock,** Peterborough, and **Temple.**

Fitzwilliam in particular is known for its many antiques shops and for the Rhododendron State Forest, a preserve with rare wild rhododendrons growing to unusual heights (they bloom early in July). In the summer you can cool off in Laurel Lake.

Peterborough, the home of one of the regions only alpine ski areas (Temple Mountain), one of New England's oldest summer theaters, and the country's only marionette theater devoted to opera, is the shopping and dining hub of the region. The area's wooded roads and small towns also attract bicyclists, and in winter its high, wooded trails can offer superb cross-country skiing. Little more than an hour from Boston but well off the highways to New York and points south, the Monadnock region offers some exceptional places to stay at prices well below those in most touristed areas.

Fitzwilliam

Amos A. Parker House

Route 119
P.O. Box 202
Fitzwilliam, NH 03447
603-585-6540

| An elegant but homey B&B in the Monadnock region |

Innkeeper: Freda B. Houpt. **Accommodations:** 2 rooms (with private bath), 2 suites. **Rates:** $80–$90 per couple. **Included:** Full breakfast. **Minimum stay:** 2 nights during peak foliage season. **Added:** 8% tax. **Credit cards accepted:** None. **Children:** Over age 9. **Pets:** Not accepted. **Smoking:** Restricted. **Handicap access:** No. **Open:** Year-round.

➤ **Freda Houpt is an enthusiastic transplant from the Midwest, where she lived on a farm as well as in Chicago. She loves the way New Hamp-**

shire's Monadnock region manages to combine genuine country with urban amenities — fine art, music, and theater.

This gray clapboard 18th-century home, which combines formal
elegance and homey comfort, sits squarely on Route 119, a major
country road but one that gets little traffic after dark. Its back
rooms overlook a spectacular, acre-deep formal garden with a lily
pond that extends to a marsh and the woods beyond.

The formal rooms in the house retain their original paneling and
hearths. The dining room is especially gracious; you'll look forward
to Freda's breakfast creations. (For dinner, the Fitzwilliam Inn, in
the center of the village, is a dependable, moderately priced option.)

There is plenty of space to relax. Besides the formal parlor,
there's a light-filled reading room with a deck overlooking the garden and an inviting, open-beamed barn room with a deep couch
and ample reading material.

The one downstairs guest room is a romantic little suite with its
own fireplace and a kitchenette. Upstairs, one room has a four-
poster bed and woodburning fireplace; another has a bed that can
be either king or twin, with a woodburning fireplace; and a suite
features unusual wall murals deftly painted by local artists and has
a sitting room overlooking the garden. All rooms are furnished
with flair and care.

The gardens at the Amos Parker are exceptional. Half perennial,
half annual, the flowers change constantly from spring through fall
(there are literally hundreds of them — irises of every hue, heleni-
ums, larkspurs, lilies, dahlias, foxgloves, and on and on). Birds, too,
frequently figure in this unusual landscape: occasionally blue her-
ons and even eagles appear.

Hannah Davis House

Route 119
186 Depot Road
Fitzwilliam, NH 03447
603-585-3344

| A romantic B&B |

Innkeepers: Kaye and Mike Terpstra. **Accommodations:** 3 rooms (all with pri-
vate bath), 3 suites. **Rates:** $60–$85 per room; $105–115 for suites. **Included:**
Full breakfast. **Minimum stay:** 2 nights on a few weekends. **Added:** 8% tax.
Credit cards accepted: MasterCard, Discover, Visa. **Children:** Welcome. **Pets:**

Not accepted. **Smoking:** Not permitted. **Handicap access:** No. **Open:** Year-round.

➤ **Kaye and Mike renovated the house to its original condition and opened it as a bed-and-breakfast in 1990. Earlier, they ran an old country store in southern New Hampshire.**

The Hannah Davis House has bountiful breakfasts, romantic rooms, unobtrusive hosts, and a separate, loft-style carriage house. In the heart of the Monadnock region, the 1820 Federal house is just a stones throw from the classic village green.

The light and airy house has little common space, but it is the kind of place where you may not want to leave your cozy room. (There is a television in the small sitting room for guests who want to catch the news.) Whichever country-style guest room you choose, you'll enjoy velvety smooth, natural woodwork, pumpkin pine floors, latch doors, and thoughtful touches like a cachet of soaking grains by the tub.

One of the most desirable rooms is the two-room suite, with two fireplaces and a sofa bed. It's a large, bright corner room with a separate entrance and fieldstone porch. Hannah's room is the smallest, overlooking the backyard. Canopy and Chauncey's rooms are both bright and large; Chauncey's room has a fireplace and Canopy, a pencil-post canopy bed. "Popovers" is the largest room, with a fireplace and its own deck.

In another part of the rambling house, the loft is the most private room, with its own entrance.

In the former carriage shed, the bed in the two-level room overlooks a sitting room with wing back chairs and a fireplace. Exposed beams and cathedral ceilings with white walls create a slightly rustic but contemporary feel.

From the kitchen, three sets of French doors lead to a long screened porch overlooking the gardens. Guests tend to gather around the table in the open kitchen, and Kaye talks to guests while she's cooking. When the house is full, the adjacent dining room (with impressive wainscoting) is also used. Breakfast is served at an antique pine table covered with pressed linens. A typical menu includes all of the following: granola and applesauce, pumpkin bread, cinnamon-raisin bread, stuffed French toast (peaches-and-cream-filled slices of sourdough bread, topped with strawberry and blueberry sauce), scrambled eggs, and green beans from the garden.

Hancock

The Hancock Inn

33 Main Street
P.O. Box 96
Hancock, N.H. 03449
603-525-3318
800-525-1789
Outside NH: 800-525-1789
Fax: 603-525-9301
www.hancockinn.com

Dinner is served by waiters in 18th-century dress

Innkeepers: Linda and Joe Johnston. **Accommodations:** 11 rooms (all with private bath). **Rates:** $106–$172 per couple. **Included:** Breakfast. **Minimum stay:** 2 nights some weekends in summer and fall. **Added:** 8% tax, 10% service. **Credit cards accepted:** All major ones. **Children:** Not appropriate under age 12. **Pets:** Not accepted. **Smoking:** Not permitted. **Handicap access:** No. **Open:** Year-round.

➤ **The oldest inn in continuous operation in New Hampshire**

Built in 1789, this pillared inn is the state's oldest, yet looks like a 19th-century structure, thanks to two-story pillars and a mansard roof. It sits in the center of a picture-perfect village with Norway Pond shimmering just up the street. In the past few years Linda and Joe Johnston have breathed new life into the old place, sponge-painting the dining room cranberry and cheering the common room with murals.

Historic stencils are one of the prides of the inn, which was host to three well-known early-19th-century primitive wall artists. One guest room is decorated on all four sides with a mural fresco by Rufus Porter; another is decorated by Moses Eaton. Cheaper than wallpaper in the 1820s, the old stencils hold up remarkably well. The best example by Eaton is in a linen closet; the Johnstons have reproduced it in one room. All rooms have private baths, phones, and cassette players with classical music cassettes. Cable TVs are hidden under quilted cozies. Some rooms have gas fireplaces.

Wide pine floors, braided rugs, antiques, and hand-sewn quilts are in keeping with the inn's historic status. The old tavern is now a common room in which guests can gather to play checkers on an antique board. The old dining room is open for dinner, specializing in traditional American fare like Shaker Cranberry Pot Roast ($14.95) and Down East Maine Crab cakes ($14.50).

Jaffrey

The Benjamin Prescott Inn

Route 124 East
Jaffrey, NH 03452
603-532-6637
Fax: 603-532-6637

A stately 1850s country house

Innkeepers: Jan and Barry Miller. **Accommodations:** 10 rooms and suites (all with private bath). **Rates:** $65–$85 per room, $90–$130 per suite; $15 per extra person. **Included:** Full breakfast. **Minimum stay:** 2 nights on a few weekends. **Added:** 8% tax. **Credit cards accepted:** Major credit cards. **Children:** Not appropriate for children under 10. **Pets:** Not accepted. **Smoking:** Restricted. **Handicap access:** No. **Open:** Year-round.

➤ **The Monadnock region, with its quiet back roads connecting classic villages, is fast becoming known as a haven for bicyclists.**

This stately 1850s house sits back from Route 124 a few miles east of Jaffrey. It has a real country feeling, especially if you are lucky enough to have booked the third-floor suite, which sleeps at least four. Glass doors and a private porch overlook classic farm fields that roll to the horizon.

The guest rooms, many with wall-to-wall carpeting, have been decorated with care. All are furnished with antiques and are comfortable without being cluttered. The bathrooms have been updated except for a few metal shower stalls, which are in good condition. Colonel Prescott's room gets the morning sun; Elder Eldad's room is quite large; John Adams's Attic has pine floors and a skylight in the sitting room. To reach one room in the back of the house, you walk through a private corridor that doubles as the bathroom (it's very private back there). Light sleepers should avoid the room on the first floor at the bottom of the stairs.

The third-floor room arrangement is especially suited to couples traveling together or a family with older children. The front room includes built-in sleeping alcoves under the eaves as well as a pencil-post king-size bed. The rear room, with a view beyond the deck, has a sitting area and a wet bar and microwave oven as well as a queen-size bed. The bathroom is divided into three spaces to facilitate sharing. In a connected building are two guest rooms that share their own living room.

Breakfast is hearty enough to fuel the bicycling expeditions that the hosts encourage. On our last visit, it consisted of a pitcher of coffee, peach and strawberry breads, and blueberry pancakes. Jan has a repertoire of eighteen kinds of bread and thirteen entrées.

Peterborough

Apple Gate Bed and Breakfast

Route 123 South
199 Upland Farm Road
Peterborough, NH 03458
603-924-6543

A small, hospitable B&B

Hosts: Dianne and Ken Legenhausen. **Accommodations:** 4 rooms (all with private bath). **Rates:** $60–$75 per couple. **Included:** Full breakfast. **Minimum stay:** 2 nights on some weekends. **Added:** 8% tax. **Credit cards accepted:** Visa, MasterCard. **Children:** Over age 12. **Pets:** Not accepted. **Smoking:** Not permitted. **Handicap access:** No. **Open:** Year-round.

➤ **The house sits across the street from 90 acres of apple orchards with a little white picket fence and gate (hence its name) in front.**

Just south of Peterborough in the Mount Monadnock region is Apple Gate, an unassuming 1832 Colonial house with a wraparound porch. The innkeepers, once a teacher and a police officer from Long Island, have created a warm and homey atmosphere.

The apple theme is carried indoors, but it's not oppressive. Most of the dozens of breakfast dishes rely on apples, too. Some items you might sample are baked apples with spinach pie, French toast with sautéed apples, or baked apple pancakes. Breakfast is served at one long table, and on cool mornings a fire might be laid in the dining room.

The Legenhausens purchased the property in 1990 and proceeded to update the bathrooms and put in new windows. Cortland and Granny Smith are large and sunny corner guest rooms; Granny

Smith's private bath is on the first floor, but bathrobes are provided. Crispin is in the back of the house, down a long, narrow hallway; it has two twin beds. McIntosh is small, accommodating a three-quarter-size bed. Guests can relax in two small, comfortable living rooms (with low ceilings, typical of the period) and have full use of a refrigerator.

Peterborough, the delightful town that inspired Thornton Wilder's *Our Town*, boasts the "first tax-supported Free Public Library in the world." Apple Gate is just up the road from the Sharon Arts Center, which showcases paintings, sculpture, furniture, and local handcrafts.

Portsmouth

The Inn at Strawbery Banke

314 Court Street
Portsmouth, NH 03801
603-436-7242
800-428-3933

| A simple B&B in town

Innkeeper: Sarah Glover O'Donnell. **Accommodations:** 7 rooms (all with private bath). **Rates:** $75–$105 double; $20 for third person in room. **Included:** Full breakfast. **Minimum stay:** 2 nights on holiday and college weekends. **Added:** 8% tax. **Credit cards accepted:** All major ones. **Children:** Over age 10. **Pets:** Not accepted. **Smoking:** Not permitted. **Handicap access:** No. **Open:** Year-round.

➤ **The Strawbery Banke museum is just around the corner, on Marcy Street, as is Prescott Park, which is on the river and is known for its flower gardens and a summer festival of free theater and music. The Children's Museum of Portsmouth is just a bit farther down Marcy Street. It's also a short walk to Market Square, the city's picturesque old commercial center.**

Portsmouth is one of New England's most picturesque old ports, and the Inn at Strawbery Banke is well positioned for exploring the town on foot. Sarah, the innkeeper since 1990, is very helpful. The early-19th-century clapboard house adjoins Strawbery Banke, the 35-building museum spanning three centuries. It's also a short stroll in one direction from the river and in the other from the city's many shops and restaurants. This is a real luxury in a town in which parking can be a problem (off-street parking for guests is provided).

We like the feel of the guest rooms, especially those in the older part of the house, with wide pine slanting floors, stenciling, and Indian shutters. One has a brass bed and antique cherry dresser. The blue room is a personal favorite. Most of the rooms have newer baths; request one that does. Air conditioning is a recent, welcome addition.

There is a common room upstairs as well as down — nothing fancy but with lots of books and games. The only TV is in the living room. The breakfast room is unusually cheery, with skylights brightening things up. Fresh fruit, cereal, meats, sourdough pancakes, quiche, crêpes, and fresh breads and muffins are all served for breakfast.

Temple

The Birchwood Inn

Route 45
Temple, NH 03084
603-878-3285
www.virtualcities.com

> A homey, relaxing country inn in a quiet town

Innkeepers: Bill and Judy Wolfe. **Accommodations:** 7 rooms (5 with private bath). **Rates:** $60–$70 per couple in season; less off-season. **Included:** Full breakfast; dinner also served. **Minimum stay:** 3 nights on Columbus Day weekend. **Added:** 8% tax. **Payment:** No credit cards. **Children:** Over age 10; $10 extra in same room. **Pets:** Not accepted. **Smoking:** Restricted. **Handicap access:** 1 room. **Open:** Year-round except 2 weeks in April, 1 week in November.

➤ **Temple Mountain, a fine family ski area with extensive snowmaking and a cross-country ski network, is just three miles up the road. In the summer, this is great country for aimless touring, music, hiking, antiques, and shopping.**

Built as an inn around 1775, this brick building with a frame addition sits in the center of a picture-perfect village in the Monadnock region. Birds chirping in the late afternoon, rockers on the front porch, and lilacs and birches all contribute to the serenity of this quiet corner of a quiet town green. Inside, lovers of country inns will not be disappointed.

Judy and Bill Wolfe, enthusiastic hosts who have owned the inn since 1980, have restored the fine 1825 Rufus Porter murals on the dining room wall. There's a cheery tavern room (with a BYOB bar) with a stenciled floor, red glass, local crafts, toy trains, and tables set up for checkers and chess. In the parlor there's a television as well as a square Steinway grand piano from 1878; many other antique instruments hang on the walls.

Each guest room has its own theme (the Seashore Room, Music Studio, Library, Editorial Room), carried out in wallpaper and antique furnishings. Braided oval rugs cover the wide floorboards, and each room has a TV. All the rooms are on the second floor except one.

Dinner entrées, posted on the blackboard, may include roast duckling, filet mignon, lamb chops, or fresh fish. Bill is the chef, and Judy bakes the breads and desserts. In addition to the intimate main dining room, a smaller dining room can hold up to twelve people for a private party.

Central
New Hampshire
and the Lakes

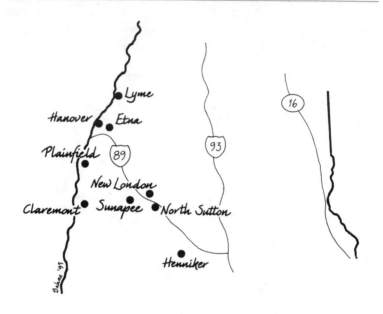

Best Bed-and-Breakfasts

Claremont
  Goddard Mansion, 424
North Sutton
  Follansbee Inn, 435

Best Inns

Etna
  Moose Mountain Lodge, 425
Hanover
  The Hanover Inn, 427
Henniker
  Colby Hill Inn, 428
  The Meetinghouse Inn and Restaurant, 430
Sunapee
  Dexter's Inn and Tennis Club, 439

Best Family Find

Lyme
  Loch Lyme Lodge and Cottages, 432

Best Gourmet Getaway

Plainfield
  Home Hill Country Inn, 437

Central New Hampshire is defined principally by its lakes, so most of the recommended hostelries are on the water. There are also a few fine places to stay on the region's western boundary, in the Connecticut River valley.

From southern New Hampshire, head up I-93 and west on I-89 through the lake-dotted region and eventually across the Connecticut River. In less than two hours from Boston you are in the lovely old college town of **New London,** also known for its ski mountain, King Ridge. Next comes the exit for Route 11, which plunges downhill for four miles to the resort village of **Sunapee.** In the summer, Lake Sunapee is the center of outdoor activity, and in winter, Mount Sunapee is a popular ski area. In the southeastern corner of this region, the college town of **Henniker** (the world's only Henniker) has distinctive shopping, dining, and lodging options. Nearby are the little lakeside towns of **North Sutton** and Canaan.

East of I-93 we pretty much bypass New Hampshire's largest lake, Lake Winnipesaukee. Its shores and waters are limited to property owners, condominium developments, and cottages and motels, none of which we recommend. But don't overlook Mirror Lake, next door to Winnipesaukee. Its pristine shoreline and wooded trails are a welcome respite.

Continue west on Route 11, from the western lakes region, through interesting old towns like **Claremont** to the Connecticut River. Turn north on Route 5 and follow it a few miles to the covered bridge and, just beyond, to Cornish, the summer home of the 19th-century sculptor Augustus Saint-Gaudens. The artist's house, now a National Historic Site, is the setting for outdoor concerts on summer weekends.

Take Route 5 north, along the Connecticut River, to **Hanover** and Dartmouth College. About six miles east, away from the river and off the beaten path, is **Etna.** This stretch of the Upper Valley — which also includes **Lyme,** Orford, and Haverhill — is distinguished by many handsome 18th-century homes, reminders of the era when residents considered forming a state of their own (to have been called New Connecticut).

Claremont

Goddard Mansion

25 Hillstead Road
Claremont, NH 03743
603-543-0603
800-736-0603
Fax: 603-543-0001

| An 18-room Victorian B&B |

Host: Debbie Albee. **Accommodations:** 10 rooms (3 with private bath), 1 suite. **Rates:** $65–$125 per couple. **Included:** Expanded Continental breakfast. **Minimum stay:** 2 nights on foliage weekends and some holidays. **Added:** 8% tax. **Credit cards accepted:** All major ones. **Children:** Cribs available. **Pets:** Not accepted. **Smoking:** Not permitted. **Handicap access:** No. **Open:** Year-round.

➤ **Outside, a screened porch offers refuge against mosquitoes on warm, quiet summer nights. The porch wraps around the side of the house under the porticos. From here you can walk through gardens to the tea house.**

Built from 1903 to 1905 for Frank Maynard, an affluent industrialist, the 18-room, Shingle-style mansion sits on an expansive lawn in the quiet town of Claremont. A bed-and-breakfast since the fall of 1986, its location makes it a good base for exploring this section of the Connecticut River valley and the Lake Sunapee region.

Outdoor areas for relaxing and first-floor common rooms are plentiful and varied. The living room is semi-formal, with a piano and a cushioned window seat. The library has a more intimate and welcoming feel; there's also a TV room. A fully operational, restored 1939 Wurlitzer is ready to be used. Upstairs is a little sitting room with a daybed and a long window seat affording nice views of the mountains.

The guest rooms are all different. The French Country Room has a canopy bed and an old armoire. Joy's Room, at the end of the hall, has a nice view of the distant mountains. The bridal suite has a four-poster canopy. The whimsical Cloud Room is papered in an artistic rendering of white puffy clouds against a light blue sky. Another room is particularly well suited to families; a double, two twins, and a crib are tucked under the eaves in one corner of the house. (It's also air-conditioned.) Ask Debbie about the newer king-bedded room.

Debbie enjoys sitting and talking with guests over breakfast in the dining room lit by a Tiffany lamp. A bountiful buffet of wholesome foods is provided as well as a large selection of teas and a rich blend of coffee. Goddard Mansion is a relaxing, low-key retreat.

Etna

Moose Mountain Lodge

P.O. Box 272
Moose Mountain Highway
Etna, NH 03750
603-643-3529
Fax: 603-643-4119
meeze@aol.com

A comfortably rustic all-season mountain retreat

Innkeepers: Kay and Peter Shumway. **Accommodations:** 12 rooms (shared baths). **Rates:** $60 per person B&B, $80 per person MAP in summer, $90 with three meals in winter; 10% discount for 3 nights or more. **Included:** Varies with season and meal plan. **Minimum stay:** 2 nights on weekends. **Added:** 8% tax. **Credit cards accepted:** MasterCard, Visa. **Children:** Over age 5 welcome. **Pets:** Not accepted. **Smoking:** Not permitted. **Handicap access:** No. **Open:** June through October, late December to late March.

➤ **Skiing enthusiasts, Kay and Peter encourage their guests to explore the cross-country ski trails on the property. Two staff members also provide expert skiing tips.**

Moose Mountain Lodge is at the top of a hill so steep that in the winter Kay and Peter Shumway sometimes meet guests at the lower parking lot and take them up the rest of the way in their four-wheel-drive vehicle. The views from the lodge are spectacular. Though it is only seven miles from Hanover and Dartmouth College, it is secluded and offers a sense of robust mountain living. It's not for everyone, but those who like it, really like it.

Moose Mountain is primarily a ski lodge, but it is also wonderful in the summertime. Just a few steps form the front door you'll find a swimming pond and hiking trails that connect to the Appalachian Trail. A porch extends the full length of the building and, at 1,600 feet, overlooks miles and miles of New Hampshire and Vermont hills and mountains. Some guests set off for the hills, others are content to sit here for hours, reading and gazing out at the spectacular scenery.

In fall and winter, the big sitting room just off the porch is particularly inviting and cozy. It has lots of windows and red corduroy window seats as well as a massive stone fireplace. Upstairs, the guest rooms are small but attractive, with spruce log beds that Kay made herself and has dressed with Martex bedspreads. All the rooms share immaculate baths.

The lodge was built from the stones and logs cleared from the hills to create ski trails. Upstairs and down, the walls are dark pine. It is the kind of place where you feel you can put your feet up and not worry about ruining an heirloom. At the same time, the inn is very attractive. In short, Moose Mountain epitomizes the rustic mountain lodge we've all dreamed of finding.

Kay, we should mention, is justly famed as a cook. Innkeepers since 1975, Kay and Peter still welcome each guest with enthusiasm and genuine interest. They obviously enjoy their work and sharing the beauty of their special roost.

Hanover

The Hanover Inn

Hanover, NH 03755
603-643-4300
800-443-7024
Fax: 603-646-3744
hanover.inn@dartmouth.edu

| A full-service hotel in a college town |

General manager: Matthew Marshall. **Accommodations:** 92 rooms and suites. **Rates:** $207–$287 per couple. **Included:** All meals are available. **Minimum stay:** None. **Added:** 8% tax. **Credit cards accepted:** All major ones. **Children:** Welcome, free in same room as parent's. **Pets:** Small ones accepted. **Smoking:** Floors available for nonsmokers. **Handicap access:** Yes. **Open:** Year-round.

➤ **Guests can use the college's indoor pool, tennis courts, and golf club. Some of the inn's patrons are affiliated with Dartmouth; others come to explore the upper Connecticut River valley.**

This four-story neo-Georgian landmark, an extension of Dartmouth College, faces Baker Library across a magnificent green. It is right next to Hopkins Center, a modern arts complex where art exhibitions, concerts, plays, films, and lectures are held throughout the year.

On bright summer days, the terrace is crowded with both visitors and residents enjoying a light lunch or late afternoon drink. The white rockers on the long porch are quite popular. In cooler weather, a sitting room with clawfoot sofas and floral-patterned armchairs invite lounging by the fire. It's all quite refined and elegant without being stuffy. Gilt mirrors and delicate brass wall lamps ornament the rooms and leatherbound books line the shelves.

Each of the guest rooms in the two wings of the inn is individually decorated, painted in pastel colors or papered with flower prints. Some have canopy beds with eiderdown quilts and armchairs; others have large antique desks. You may want to request a "junior suite" with all these features, a view of the campus, and a sitting area. Many of the rooms were enlarged and reconfigured recently without losing their graceful moldings and millwork. Window treatments and bedding continues to be upgraded.

Dining options range from the casual, contemporary Ivy Grill, offering primarily American cuisine cooked over an open flame (the menu changes often), to the formal Edwardian decor of the Daniel Webster Room, where more traditional New England and classical dishes are featured. The Daniel Webster, it should be noted, is the area's only four-diamond eatery.

Henniker

Colby Hill Inn

P.O. Box 778
Henniker, NH 03242
603-428-3281
800-531-0330
Fax: 603-428-9218
bpsne@colbyhillinn.com
www.colbyhillinn.com

> **A college village inn**

Innkeepers: Ellie and John Day, and Laurel Day Mack. **Accommodations:** 16 rooms (all with private bath). **Rates:** $85–$165 per couple. **Included:** Full breakfast; dinner also available. **Minimum stay:** 2 to 3 days on some weekends. **Added:** 8% tax, 10% service charge. **Credit cards accepted:** All major ones. **Children:** Over age 7 welcome. **Pets:** Not accepted. **Smoking:** Not permitted. **Handicap access:** No. **Open:** Year-round.

➤ **Residents are proud that this is the only Henniker in the world. On the Conticook River, this former mill village is the home of New England College, Pat's Peak Ski Area, and some interesting shops.**

On the fringe of the small college town of Henniker, this 200-year-old farmhouse has had an up-and-down history as an inn. It has been turned around nicely by Ellie, John, and Laurel Day since the family purchased it in 1990. You will no doubt be greeted by dogs Bertha and Delilah, Great Dane and retriever mixes.

All the guest rooms are furnished with homey antiques. Most have Oriental and hooked rugs and walls covered with flowery print paper. Those in the main house are generally more elaborate than those in the carriage house. Most feature queen-size canopy beds and several have twin beds; four have working fireplaces. All have private phone lines with data ports and central air conditioning. We like Room 3, a large corner room with a wood-burning stove. Repeat guests often request rooms that overlook the gardens.

A comfortable living room with a woodstove and a TV room with games offer guests their own space even during dinner hours. The rooms are chock-a-block with collectibles (a dollhouse and an old Victrola, for instance), although not oppressively so. In the summer the five-acre property is dotted with lawn chairs for reading, a pool, and croquet and badminton courts. In winter, activities turn toward the skating rink.

In the evening, the two dining rooms are the focal points of the inn, their paneling glowing in the candlelight. The dinner menu ranges from tournedos Oscar to eggplant roulade, but the signature dish is "chicken Colby Hill," which is boneless breast of chicken stuffed with lobster, leeks, and boursin. At breakfast time, light pours in through a glass-paneled wall, and guests watch birds at the barnyard feeders. It's a tranquil setting. Breakfast always includes a choice of eggs or something like pancakes or French toast. Throughout the day classical music fills the air.

Henniker is handy to I-89 and the central lakes area as well as to the Monadnock Region. The Days are happy to help guests plan their day's explorations.

The Meetinghouse Inn and Restaurant

35 Flanders Road
Henniker, NH 03242
603-428-3228
meetinghouse@conknet.com
www.conknet.com

> **An inn with delightful perks and quirks**

Innkeepers: June and Bill Davis, Cheryl Davis Bakke and Peter Bakke. **Accommodations:** 4 rooms (all with private bath), 2 suites. **Rates:** $65–$105. **Included:** Breakfast. **Added:** 8% tax. **Credit cards accepted:** All major ones. **Children:** Welcome; one 2-room suite for families. **Pets:** Not accepted. **Smoking:** Not permitted. **Handicap access:** No. **Open:** Year-round.

➤ **There's a friendly feel to this inn, but guests are not pressured to mingle.**

On snowy winter weekends, the Meeting House is very much an extension of Pat's Peak, the family ski area just across the road. Midweek in winter is quiet. And after the ski season the atmosphere is very much that of an out-of-the-way country inn — one with a highly unusual and very popular dining room in its 200-year-old dairy barn. In the summer, the inn's front arbor is a profusion of flowers and herbs.

Common space is limited but well compensated for by the quality of the guest rooms. They are charming, immaculate, and furnished imaginatively with family antiques — a chest here, a coverlet there. The linens are high quality and turned down for you in the evening. Each room is thoughtfully outfitted with books, magazines, and a few games; all are air-conditioned. Room 3 is a large suite that can accommodate a family (with the aid of a daybed), complete with refrigerator and stove. With the windows open you can hear the river from here. Room 2 is tiny (and only $65) but cozy, with all the fine features of the other rooms. Room 4, a two-room suite, is a great value for four people. Room 6 is the only room that is reached from inside the inn; it's quite cozy and comfy.

Breakfast, prepared by June, arrives at your guest room door in a basket. Each room has a place to dine; you'll only end up eating breakfast in bed if you want to. For folks who wish to keep to themselves, this arrangement is very appealing.

The barn, with lofty ceilings, deep booths, and twinkling lights, makes a great dining room and, like the inn, is furnished with antiques. The walls are hung with dozens of plastic bags filled with sand that patrons have sent from all over the world. We've never seen anything like it.

Peter is a self-taught chef and cooks for the joy of it. He prepares hearty New England–style signature dishes like filet mignon with cassis and individual servings of beef Wellington. Other popular choices include lobster in a cream Marsala and brandied seafood beurre blanc. The salad dressings are homemade.

Between the inn and the restaurant, a "solar recreation area" includes a large sauna and a hot tub (the temperature is lowered in summer). It is rented privately by the hour ($25). The hosts, innkeepers since 1981, are adept at suggesting nearby swimming, shopping, sailing, and bicycling possibilities. Henniker is handy to both the interstate and some of the most scenic back roads in central and southern New Hampshire.

Lyme

Loch Lyme Lodge and Cottages

Route 10 (70 Orford Road)
Lyme, NH 03768
603-795-2141
800-423-2141

| **A family retreat with cabins on a pond** |

Proprietors: Judy and Paul Barker. **Accommodations:** 4 rooms (with shared baths), 26 cabins (1 to 4 bedrooms). **Rates:** $94–$116 per couple, MAP, from mid-June to early September; $48–$70 B&B off-season; in-season B&B rates also available; $315–$675 weekly in cabins without meals (meals are available for an additional charge). **Included:** Varies with the meal plan. **Minimum stay:** Weekly in cabins with kitchens; 2 nights on some weekends. **Added:** 8% tax. **Credit cards accepted:** None. **Children:** Welcome; $18–$26 per child ages 5– 15. **Pets:** Well-trained pets accepted in cabins. **Smoking:** Not encouraged. **Handicap access:** No. **Open:** Main lodge, year-round; cabins, May through September.

➤ **Children will find plenty to do — hills to roll down, fields to play in, swimming, tennis, and games. Babysitting is available so that parents may enjoy the peaceful atmosphere.**

On a hillside opposite a sparkling pond in the upper Connecticut River Valley, Loch Lyme Lodge and Cottages offers moderately priced accommodations with or without cooking facilities. It is presided over by Paul and Judy Barker and their children — the latest generation of the family to run this lodge, which has been in operation since 1917. This delightfully old-fashioned rustic retreat offers a wide range of activities. Guests come for fresh air, starry nights, and family fun. If this is your first introduction to Loch Lyme, call the inn and they will put you in touch with a former guest who can tell you about the Loch Lyme experience.

Loch Lyme is a friendly, homey place, with cabins designed to be lived in and hearty, nutritious meals served in the vintage 1784 farmhouse. One of the main attractions is a private lakefront beach, with large white chairs, a sandy swimming area, a float, and a squadron of rowboats and canoes. Two clay tennis courts and a recreation cabin, with croquet, badminton, volleyball, and other sporting equipment, provide other diversions.

Dotted over a hillside, the brown shingle cabins are pleasantly private. Families who want to make their own meals can choose a housekeeping cabin with one to four bedrooms, a bath, a living room with a fireplace, a kitchen or kitchenette, and a porch. Some of them are just a step above camping. Try to get a cabin facing the lawn; those in the thick of the woods don't get much light. Lakefront cabins are reserved years in advance, so don't get your hopes up.

Most cabins have one or two bedrooms (one has four), a living room, porch, and bath and housekeeping service. There are also rooms in the main lodge, but in summer the cabins are more enjoyable. The bed-and-breakfast rate includes a full breakfast until 9:00 A.M., then self-service until 10:00 A.M.

Hearty New England meals, emphasizing fresh fruit and vegetables, are served in the main lodge except on Sunday evenings, when there is a popular lakefront buffet with casseroles, cold meats and cheeses, and fruit. While there is not a specific children's menu, dishes are prepared with little ones in mind.

Guests can bring bicycles; the relatively flat road running up the valley is perfect for cycling. Just ten miles from Hanover and Dartmouth College and near many small towns, the area is filled with activity, from cultural events to hiking to church suppers.

New London

Twin Lake Village

21 Twin Lake Villa Road
New London, NH 03257
603-526-6460
Fax: 603-526-2439

| **A low-profile, old-shoe family resort** |

Innkeepers: Jan Kidder and family. **Accommodations:** 25 rooms in the Villa and 6 apartments, 14 houses with 27 bedrooms. **Rates:** $325–$640 per person per week (generally, from Saturday to Saturday). **Included:** All meals. **Minimum stay:** 1 week, unless space available. **Added:** 8% tax; 15% gratuity suggested. **Credit cards accepted:** None. **Children:** Special rates. **Pets:** Leashed dogs accepted in the cottages, $10 per reservation. **Smoking:** Not permitted in dining room. **Handicap access:** Yes. **Open:** Full service late June to Labor Day; several cottages available earlier as housekeeping rentals.

➤ **Guests can play all the golf they want on the par 3 course, and they can also take advantage of the clay tennis courts, the rowboats, sailboats, canoes, and kayaks.**

Opened by Henry Kidder in 1897, this wonderfully old-fashioned resort is still managed by three generations of Kidders. It accommodates 150 or so guests between the rambling white clapboard "Villa" and the Victorian houses (hence the "Village") scattered among the surrounding trees. The setting is impressive.

A 9-hole golf course stretches from the Villa down to the dock and beach on Little Sunapee Lake, a relatively quiet, little-developed area. The resort itself keeps such a low profile that many residents of New London don't know it exists.

The focus here is on families, many of whom have been coming for generations. There's a supervised playhouse for children ages two to five and a program of weekly activities that will keep older youngsters busy. The organized program also includes golf and tennis tournaments, evening bingo, and a picnic supper at Mount Kearsarge. There's a thick activity book for kids and "those young at heart."

The rooms are simple, with knotty pine walls and wicker and old desks and beds that were here before they were considered antiques. All but three rooms have private baths.

Meals are served in the large, fairly formal dining room, and the menu is surprisingly large, too. For lunch you can have juice or soup, a choice of entrée (on the day we stopped by, the choices ranged from pork and chicken stir fry to corned beef and cabbage to chef salad with vegetables), salads, and desserts such as fruit, raspberry Jell-O, or blueberry crumb cake with lemon sauce.

The beauty of the setting aside, the appeal of this place is the camaraderie between hosts, guests, and the friendly young staff. You can be as active as you like or you can rock away the week on the Villa's endless porch (you won't be alone) in what is probably New England's largest surviving lineup of rockers.

North Sutton

Follansbee Inn

Route 114
P.O. Box 92
North Sutton, NH 03260
603-927-4221
800-626-4221
follansbeeinn@conknet.com
www.follansbeeinn.com

| A friendly lakeside inn |

Innkeepers: Dick and Sandy Reilein. **Accommodations:** 23 rooms (11 with private bath). **Rates:** $75–$105 per couple, $25 per extra person. **Included:** Full breakfast. **Minimum stay:** 2 days on peak weekends. **Added:** 8% tax. **Credit cards accepted:** MasterCard, Visa. **Children:** Over age 10 welcome. **Pets:** Not accepted. **Smoking:** Not permitted. **Handicap access:** No. **Open:** Year-round except for certain weeks in November and April.

➤ **Many guests like to walk, jog, or bike (the inn has several bicycles for guests) on the three-mile shore drive around the lake.**

This distinctive lakeside summer inn, with white clapboard and green trim, is a good spot for year-round relaxing. Sandy and Dick Reilein, with their son, Matthew, have run this landmark with enthusiasm since 1985. The inn is the heart of the early-19th-century village of North Sutton. It's a quiet, non-commercial area and a convenient base for exploring — just 90 miles from Boston and a few miles off I-89.

Kezar Lake is literally a few steps away. The inn has a private dock on the lake with a canoe, rowboat, windsurfer, and paddle-boat. The small island on the lake is a nice place for a picnic, while the beach at Wadleigh State Park is just down the way.

In the winter there's ice fishing on the lake, downhill skiing at nearby Ragged Mountain and Mount Sunapee, and cross-country skiing from the inn (the trails around the lake are great) or at a touring center in New London.

The rooms upstairs, divided by wide central halls stocked with books, are individually furnished and very tidy. If you don't mind sharing a bath, the third-floor rooms are a steal.

Downstairs, the ample common areas have fireplaces and plenty of reading material. There is a big porch with wicker and rocking chairs — a great place to while away a rainy afternoon.

Breakfast always includes homemade granola, fresh fruit, and a hot dish. When there are more than 10 guests in the house, they help themselves from the kitchen and sit together. It's quite homey, friendly, and relaxing. Otherwise, there is table service.

Plainfield

Home Hill Country Inn

River Road
Plainfield, NH 03781
603-675-6165
Fax: 603-675-5220
homehill@msn.com

A romantic spot with fine French cuisine

Innkeepers: Victoria and Stephane de Roure. **Accommodations:** 7 rooms (all with private bath), 1 suite. **Rates:** $125–$175 per couple. **Included:** Continental breakfast; dinner also served except Mondays and Tuesdays. **Minimum stay:** 2 nights on a few weekends. **Added:** 8% tax. **Credit cards accepted:** All major ones. **Children:** Over age 10 welcome. **Pets:** Not accepted. **Smoking:** Restricted. **Handicap access:** No. **Open:** Year-round.

➤ **One of the best things about this inn is that it's small yet roomy — you feel as though you own the place. Come for the well-respected French cuisine, elegantly simple guest rooms, and supreme peace and quiet.**

Home Hill sits all alone, at the end of a 3½-mile rural road on 25 acres next to the Connecticut River. On the grounds are a clay tennis court, a lap pool near the woods, miles of well-maintained cross-country ski trails, and a private 3-hole golf course. Just a few miles off the interstate, the inn feels remote but is quite easily reached.

This is one of the magnificent, four-square 1820s mansions spaced along the Connecticut River in the Upper Valley. In the 1890s, many of the houses here were bought by prominent artists and their wealthy patrons, and the town remains one of the most elegant in the area. Home Hill was restored and opened as an inn in 1983 and purchased by the de Roures in 1996.

The inn is known for it's food. The prix fixe menu is $34 for a four-course meal, not including coffee and dessert. Nightly selections include four or five appetizers and entrées. The menu features fresh seafood, grilled poultry, local vegetables, and game.

The table settings are elegant in each of the three small dining rooms, which have hardwood floors and Oriental carpets, candelights, and a fireplace. There is an extensive wine list and an intimate little library-bar for cocktails before dinner and cognac afterward. In warm weather there is outside dining (by advance reservation) on the brick patio, which is lit with torches.

Dining isn't the only thing this place is about though. The guest rooms in the main inn are delightfully simple, with stenciled walls and quilts. We particularly like the master bedroom suite and the Sunset room, aptly named for the view at twilight. The renovated carriage house offers three rooms that are more modern (they have tasteful wall-to-wall carpeting, for instance) and furnished with country antiques. Guests share a living room. The two-bedroom pool house is rented only in the summer.

Home Hill is nicely situated both for skiing (at Mount Ascutney, just across the river in Vermont) and aimless country wandering. The Augustus Saint-Gaudens National Historic Site is just down the road.

Sunapee

Dexter's Inn and Tennis Club

Stagecoach Road
Sunapee, NH 03782
603-763-5571
800-232-5571
www.innbook.com/dexters.html

A country inn with a tennis pro

Innkeepers: Michael and Holly Durfor. **Accommodations:** 17 rooms (all with private bath); Holly House cottage. **Rates:** $135–$175 per couple MAP; off-season B&B rates; tennis packages. **Included:** Breakfast and dinner. **Minimum stay:** 2 nights on weekends. **Added:** 8% tax, 15% service charge. **Credit cards accepted:** MasterCard, Visa, Discover. **Children:** Welcome, special rates. **Smoking:** Restricted. **Pets:** Permitted in annex; $10 daily charge. **Handicap access:** Yes. **Open:** May through October.

➤ **The screened porch, with comfortable wicker furniture and an expansive view, is the kind of place you can sit for hours.**

Dexter's is a standout, as great for family reunions and tennis players as it is for those who just want to get away from it all. The big yellow clapboard house sits on a steep back road and commands a sweeping view of the lake and mountains. It is shaded by mature trees and backed by a stretch of flowers and a lawn with a nicely hedged pool. The three tennis courts are the stuff of tournaments, and the food is another point of pride.

The main house was built in 1801 and restored in the 1930s by an adviser to President Hoover. It has been in the same family since 1969 and run by Michael and Holly since 1984.

A formal living room has upholstered chairs and sofas around the hearth and some five hundred books. The large, pine-paneled "cocktail lounge" is the other gathering space, with tables and plenty of games. It's all quite comfortable and unpretentious, the way inns were meant to be.

Many of the guest rooms are large and bright, with flowered wallpaper, modern furniture, and some antiques. Some are shaped oddly, and the halls zigzag to conform with the building. Room 12, in the annex across the road, is a favorite, with a four-poster bed and a view.

Holly Cottage, accommodating up to six people (with or without meals), includes a living room with a fireplace as well as a kitchen and two bedrooms. A five-course dinner can be served here on request.

The dining room is a small, sunny room on the other side of the house, with a view over the lake. As for the food, Dexter's doesn't hire "chefs," they hire "cooks." The breakfast cook, in fact, has been here 30 years. The food isn't fancy, but it is consistently good. For breakfast, you'll have a choice of eggs any style, pancakes, and sides of bacon or sausage, toast or muffins. We recommend the eggs Benedict. As for dinner, there is always a choice of eight or so entrées. On weekends, the poached salmon is practically de riguer.

Usually about half the guests play tennis, and the inn retains a full-time tennis pro. (In foul weather, guests can use indoor courts in nearby New London.) But there is plenty to do in this low-key region: summer theater in New London, golf, boating and swimming on Lake Sunapee, and hiking on Mount Sunapee (you can take a ski lift to the top) and Mount Kearsarge (an 1870s scenic road climbs three-fourths of the way up). There are also some outstanding crafts and antiques shops salted along back roads.

Northern
New Hampshire and the
White Mountains

Best Bed-and-Breakfasts

Best Inns

Best Family Finds

Pinkham Notch
Appalachian Mountain Club — Pinkham Notch Visitor Center
and High Hut System, 478
Waterville Valley
Waterville Valley Resort, 482
Whitefield
The Spalding Inn, 484

Best Gourmet Getaways

Dixville Notch
The Balsams Grand Resort Hotel, 454
Jackson
The Wentworth Resort Hotel, 469

Best Grand Resorts

Bretton Woods
The Mount Washington Hotel and Resort, 451
Dixville Notch
The Balsams Grand Resort Hotel, 454

Best Romantic Getaways

Bartlett
The Notchland Inn, 447
Bethlehem
Adair, 449
Franconia Area
Bungay Jar Bed and Breakfast, 459

New Hampshire is known chiefly for its White Mountains, the
highest peaks in New England, and more than half of the state's
lodging places cluster in the few resort villages in the 751,000-acre
White Mountain National Forest.

To reach the mountains from southern New Hampshire, take
the Spaulding Turnpike north from the Portsmouth rotary until it
peters out into Route 16, a country highway that offers some delightful detours. Two possibilities are a two-mile drive into Tam-
worth, a beautiful old village with a summer theater and a view of

Mount Chocorua, and a jaunt into **Eaton Center,** a picturesque village on Crystal Lake near tiny **Snowville.**

New Hampshire's biggest resort town is **North Conway,** a skiing and climbing center that has more than its share of outlet stores. To be within reach, but away from the crowds, consider staying in Intervale. In many guidebooks, this part of the White Mountains is called the Eastern Slope. Mount Washington, New England's highest mountain, towers just north of town. You can approach it by continuing north on Route 16, past the lovely mountain village of **Jackson** (be sure to stop) and through steep-walled **Pinkham Notch.** You might want to drive up the Auto Road (or ride up in one of the vans) to the summit; it's a memorable experience, whatever the weather. You can also stop at the Appalachian Mountain Club's headquarters and ask about hiking trails, guided expeditions, and the ever-changing weather conditions on the summit.

Route 16 meets Route 2 above Pinkham Notch; if you enjoy exploring, you might turn east along the Androscoggin River and follow it through Shelburne and into Maine (see the Bethel section of the Maine itinerary). Or turn down Route 113 through Evans Notch, following this beautiful byway south all the way back to Conway. You can also turn west on Route 2/16, continuing north on Route 16 as it follows the Androscoggin River to Errol; it's just a short drive east on Route 26 to the Balsams, a grand old resort hotel in **Dixville Notch.**

From Boston there is a quick way into the White Mountains: I-93. In about two hours you are at Squam Lake (the real Golden Pond) and at the exit for **Waterville Valley,** one of New Hampshire's largest ski resorts. Waterville Valley offers all the facilities of a condominium-based summer resort and stages a summer arts festival. Just up the road, Loon Mountain vies for attention as a prominent ski and year-round destination.

A bit farther north on I-93 you can cut over to Conway on the Kancamagus Highway, a 37-mile wilderness road through the national forest, or you can continue north through Franconia Notch (**Bartlett**), another spectacular mountain pass offering a number of places to walk or hike. Its most famous attraction is the stony-faced profile known as the "Old Man of the Mountain." The venerable resort villages of **Franconia** and **Sugar Hill** are nestled in a hidden valley beyond the Notch. This area is known as the Western Slope.

Beyond Franconia Notch, I-93 snakes west through the Ammonoosuc Valley into Vermont (see the Northeast Kingdom in the Vermont itinerary). We suggest you turn east on Route 3, through the national forest to Twin Mountain. You might want to continue north on Route 3 to **Bethlehem,** with its late-19th- and early-20th-century homes, and to the old resort town of **Whitefield.** You will certainly want to turn south on Route 302 to visit **Bretton Woods,** a small settlement built around the grand Mount Washington Hotel and Resort, set in turn against the western flank of Mount Washington. The cog railway, in business since the 1860s, climbs to the summit (you can also hike). Route 302 continues south through Crawford Notch to North Conway.

Bartlett

The Notchland Inn

Harts Location S.R.
Bartlett, NH 03802
603-374-6131
800-866-6131
Fax: 603-374-6168
notchland@aol.com
www.notchland.com

> Each guest room at this
> mountain inn has a
> fireplace

Innkeepers: Ed Butler and Les Schoof. **Assistant:** Kath Harris. **Accommodations:** 7 rooms and 5 suites (all with private bath). **Rates:** $175–$220 per couple MAP; $30–$40 more during foliage and holidays; $50 less per couple for B&B. **Included:** Varies with the meal plan. **Minimum stay:** 2 nights on weekends; 2–3 nights during holidays and foliage. **Added:** 8% tax, 15% gratuity. **Credit cards accepted:** All major ones. **Children:** Over age 12 welcome. **Pets:** Not accepted. **Smoking:** Not permitted. **Handicap access:** No. **Open:** Year-round.

➤ In the winter, you can don your swimsuit, bundle yourself in winter outerwear, and traipse along a snowy path to the wood-fired outdoor hot tub. There's nothing quite like having snowflakes fall around you while

you're soaking up to your neck in hot water. By day, you can ice skate on the adjacent pond.

This 1862 granite and timber English manor house stands at the entrance to Crawford Notch, one of the more spectacular natural spots in New England, surrounded by sheer mountain walls. Guests gravitate to the inn to explore its 400 acres, nestled within the White Mountain National Forest, or to curl up next to one of more than a dozen fireplaces. Ed and Les, who hail from New York City, purchased the inn in late 1993 and have been garnering praise from guests ever since. They see themselves as stewards rather than owners of this idyllic property.

The inn has plenty of comfortable common space: an Arts and Crafts–style front parlor (designed by Gustav Stickley, a founder of the movement) with paneling, tin ceiling, fireplace, and hardwood floors; a large music room with another fireplace, game boards, and a piano; a small sun room filled with plants and wicker; and a library.

All the guest rooms are quite large, and suites can accommodate a third person comfortably. Each is outfitted with antique furnishings, designer floral fabrics, bedside reading lamps, and quilts. There isn't an undesirable room in the inn. Even the smallest room, Zealand, has a fresh feel to it, with white walls and forest green trim. In the back wing of the house, a two-room suite can comfortably accommodate a family. The latest guest room addition is a spectacular suite featuring a private Jacuzzi tub and deck overlooking the gardens and mountains.

On the first floor, we like Carrigain (which boasts two small private balconies) and the original master bedroom, Franconia (a large, canopy-bedded corner room). Crawford is perhaps the most requested room: it has plush wall-to-wall carpeting, a king-size bed, and a settee that you can sink into and soak up the mountain views. Generally, rooms in the front of the house have the best views and plenty of sunshine streaming in through casement windows. Non-city folks, though, might be bothered by road noise — cars and trucks tend to move through the mountain pass at high speeds.

Next to the main house is a former two-story schoolhouse. Each of the two suites is decorated in a country-lodge motif. One has a nice little deck, perfect for stargazing; the other has a telescope.

The dining room overlooks lovely gardens and a spring-fed pond, which has a gazebo and a wood-fired hot tub on its banks. A five-course dinner is served promptly at 7:00 P.M. To help you make up your mind about which soup, appetizer, and dessert to choose, Les or Ed brings the evening's choices to your table on a cart. On our last visit, entrée choices included blackened swordfish, chicken roulade, and pork tenderloins. For breakfast you have a choice of eggs any style or French toast or pancakes served a number of ways.

Two of the area's best swimming holes and 8,000 feet of frontage on Saco River are on the inn's property across the road. From here, the Davis Path, one of the oldest trails in the country, leads all the way to the top of Mount Washington. Nearby is a 100-kilometer cross-country system and Alpine skiing. The Notchland is also home to a couple of llamas, miniature horses, and a Burmese mountain dog, Coco, which Les received as a gift when he left the American Ballet Theatre as general manager to come to Notchland.

This is a great place to come midweek in the winter; if you come for 3 or 4 nights, the price is very reasonable and you won't have to wait in line at the ski resorts. You may even have the hot tub all to yourself.

Bethlehem

Adair

80 Guider Lane
Bethlehem, NH 03574
603-444-2600
888-444-2600
Fax: 603-444-4823
adair@connriver.net

A romantic and luxurious hilltop mansion

Innkeeper: Nancy, Pat, and Hardy Banfield. **Accommodations:** 7 rooms and 2 suites (all with private bath). **Rates:** $135–$155 per couple in rooms; $185–$220 in suites. **Included:** Full breakfast. **Minimum stay:** 2 nights during foliage. **Added:** 8% tax. **Credit cards accepted:** All major ones. **Children:** Expected to be well behaved. **Pets:** Not accepted; boarding facilities nearby. **Smoking:** Restricted. **Handicap access:** No. **Open:** Year-round.

➤ **In the winter you can cut your own holiday tree from a nearby farm, cross-country ski out the front door, and snowshoe at the 1,200-acre Rocks Estate right down the road.**

It's difficult to say what's more impressive here: the grounds, the architecture, the public spaces, or the first-class amenities and elegant touches. Shortly after you drive onto the 200-acre estate (designed by the Olmsted firm), passing fieldstone walls and a small pond, you'll see the knoll-top manse.

The house was built in 1927 by Frank Hogan, a nationally famous trial lawyer, as a wedding present for his daughter Dorothy Adair. When she passed away in 1992, Nancy's parents, Pat and Hardy, purchased the property and converted it into an inn. Since the Banfields are only the second family to own it, the estate has retained much of its original essence.

Guest rooms are on the second and third floors of the 10,000-square-foot mansion. All of them feel quite luxurious, with wall-to-wall carpeting, restored or renovated bathrooms, bedside reading lights, automatic closet lights, and reproduction furnishings. Many have Vermont Castings gas fireplaces. Lindt chocolates, fine toiletries, triple sheeting, and thick white towels are standard in each room. Lafayette and Waterford (quite bright) are the larger second-floor rooms, while Dalton and Huntington (a bright corner room) have views of Mount Washington. Dalton is just one of the favorites. The Kinsman suite, with fireplace, is very private. By the way, even the two smallest rooms at Adair are quite comfortable, even roomy, in comparison to other inns.

A breakfast menu and a list of overnight guests is posted in the formal entryway. Breakfast is served at 8:30 A.M. at tables of two and four. The inn's signature hot popovers are preceded by delicious homemade granola from the sideboard and a martini glass filled with fresh fruit. On our last visit, the breakfast entrée was "egg blossoms," a cheese and egg soufflé in a phyllo crust. In warm weather, enjoy your last morning cup of coffee and the Sunday paper on the slate patio. It overlooks the back lawn and gardens, a water garden, gazebo (which was originally a swimming pool), and all-weather tennis court.

The elegant living room, warmed by a fire in the winter, extends the width of the house. Sculpted area carpets cover most of the light wood floors. The basement Tap Room feels baronial yet cozy with its slate floor, granite walls, billiards table, Oriental carpets, VCR, and comfy sofas. The honor bar is fully stocked; just sign a chit.

Try not to miss afternoon tea, served from four to five o'clock in antique china cups and on deliberately mismatched plates. Offerings might include delicate slices of banana bread, cheesecake, and fruit, along with Harney and Sons tea (hot and cold).

Tim-Bir Alley, a locally renowned restaurant, serves dinner Wednesday through Saturday in-season. By all means, dine here; you will not be disappointed. You might try hot-and-sour wild mushroom soup, followed by salmon with a sunflower seed crust and sundried tomato vinaigrette. Leave room for an apple and pecan tart with brandy caramel sauce. A three-course dinner will run you about $26 per person without beverage.

Perched on the northern edge of the White Mountain National Forest, Bethlehem and the inn are right off I-93, an easy 2½-hour shot north of Boston.

Bretton Woods

The Mount Washington Hotel and Resort

Route 302
Bretton Woods, NH 03575
603-278-1000
800-258-0330
Fax: 603-278-8838

| An exemplary grand resort |

Manager: Robert Clement. **Accommodations:** 194 rooms and 3 suites in the Grand Hotel; 50 rooms at The Bretton Woods Motor Inn; 31 rooms and 3 suites at The Bretton Arms Country Inn; 55 town homes at Bretton Woods. **Rates** (packages available): Grand Hotel: $185–$445 per couple MAP (suites $565–$799 per couple MAP). Motor Inn: $70–$129 EP. Bretton Arms: $90–$189 per couple EP. Town homes: $129–$369 EP. **Included:** Breakfast and dinner with Grand Hotel rates. **Minimum stay:** 2 nights in town homes (3 on holidays), 2 nights on all other properties during holidays. **Added:** 8% tax on all properties, 8% gratuity to Grand Hotel rates. **Credit cards accepted:** All major ones. **Children:** Free under age 4 in the hotel; special rates for older children. **Pets:** Not accepted. **Smoking:** Restricted. **Handicap access:** Yes. **Open:** Hotel, mid-May to mid-October; all other accommodations open year-round.

➤ **The Mount Washington Hotel and Resort, built in 1902, was the sight of the 1944 Bretton Woods International Monetary Conference, which established the International Monetary Fund and the international gold standard. In 1991, after this historic property was put on the FDIC auction block, a small group of local investors purchased it. They've done a laudable job refurbishing the place and restoring its reputation.**

Your first view of The Mount Washington Hotel and Resort may very well take your breath away — a mammoth white palace with a bright red roof backed by New England's most majestic mountains. Surely there are only a handful of places more dramatically sited.

The splendid lobby, with tall columns and a baronial hearth, can accommodate a hundred people without seeming the least bit crowded. Some guests (who shall remain nameless) have been known to spend half their waking hours in a wicker chair on the vast wraparound verandah. Views of the Presidential Mountains at sunset are unparalleled.

Other guests, of course, come for the recreational opportunities. Instead of offering free, unlimited access to sporting facilities, the hotel has adopted a pay-as-you-play approach for golf, tennis, horseback riding, and carriage rides. Alternately, there are many lodging and sporting packages available. There are 12 red clay tennis courts, 9-hole and 18-hole PGA golf courses (designed by Donald Ross), an 18-hole putting green, and indoor and outdoor pools. Joggers and mountain bikers use marked trails. (Bicycles may be rented.) For a nominal fee, there is also a fully supervised program for children aged 5 to 12.

At any given time, there may be a chamber group, a jazz trio, or a pianist performing somewhere in the common areas. In fact, you may even dance to a six-piece band between courses in the main dining room at dinnertime. The Cave Lounge, a lively place to have a drink, also offers nightly entertainment.

All the guest rooms have recently been refurbished. Decor and furnishings are simple, functional, and comfortable. The rooms vary in size and view, of course, some with door-size windows and sweeping views of the mountains. There are at least two dozen well-priced family suites at the Grand Hotel. Guests at the Bretton Arms, Motor Inn, and town homes can use all the Grand Hotel's facilities.

Guests can dine at any of the resort's seven dining options. The Arms is a restored Victorian-era inn with an intimate dining room. Modern guest rooms at the Motor Inn have private balconies; Darby's, a rustic, family-style restaurant is located here. Both

Stickney's and Fabyan's, an authentically restored railroad depot, offer casual lunches.

Everything about The Mount Washington is grand in manner as well as size. A dinner jacket is required in the main dining room, where guests choose from New England–style dishes; the menu changes nightly. The professional waitstaff is friendly and efficient. Crystal chandeliers reflect the stained glass in the octagonal main dining room, designed so that no guest feels slighted by sitting in a corner. Breakfast consists of two sumptuous buffets, one hot and one cold, brimming with everything you could possibly want.

In winter the Grand Hotel closes, but the Motor Inn (with an indoor pool, sauna, and Jacuzzi) and the condominiums represent some of the best ski bargains in New England. The Bretton Arms caters more to couples and cross-country skiers, since the stables are turned into a ski touring center. The nearby Bretton Woods Ski Area offers thirty-two trails, with a vertical drop of 1,500 feet and dependable conditions. The 100-kilometer network of cross-country trails here is considered one of the best in the East.

And although you need never leave the property, you might want to know that the Cog Railway to the summit of Mount Washington is just 7 miles away.

Dixville Notch

The Balsams Grand Resort Hotel

Dixville Notch, NH 03576
603-255-3400
800-255-0800 in New Hampshire
800-255-0600 in the United States
and Canada
Fax: 603-255-4221
thebalsams@aol.com
www.thebalsams.com

> **The grandest of New England's grand hotels**

Owners: Stephen Barba and Warren Pearson. **Accommodations:** 209 rooms (all with private bath), 7 suites. **Rates:** $250–$450 per couple in summer, FAP; $200–$340 per couple in winter, MAP; ski packages available; healthy discounts for multiple-night stays. **Included:** All meals in summer, full breakfast and dinner in winter; all facilities and programs. **Minimum stay:** 4 nights involving Friday or Saturday nights in July and August when booking more than 10 days in advance. **Added:** 8% tax; 15% service charge except in July and August. **Credit cards accepted:** All major ones. **Children:** $7 multiplied by their age (minimum $28) per day when staying in same room with two adults. **Pets:** Not accepted. **Smoking:** Nonsmoking sections in lounges and base lodge. **Handicap access:** Yes. **Open:** Late December through March, late May to mid-October.

➤ **Remember that when you come to The Balsams, your room rate gives you complete access to all the fabulous facilities for no additional charge. Take advantage of them.**

Grandeur isn't a word we use lightly. But the word describes The Balsams, a 216-room, multi-towered hotel set on 15,000 stunning acres — above Lake Gloriette and beneath sheer, fir-clad peaks. There's a certain sense of timelessness here.

Summer guests play golf on either the 18-hole panorama course (designed by Donald Ross) or a 9-hole course. They also swim, play tennis (on six hard and clay courts), mountain bike, canoe, fly fish for rainbow trout, and hike. Volleyball, horseshoes, bocce, shuffleboard, and croquet are favored pastimes. The Balsams has its own map of 29 hikes of varying degrees of difficulty as well as a natural history handbook. (These trails are used for mountain biking and climbing, too.) Children will enjoy the elaborate playground. In summer, there's a supervised daily program for kids aged 3 through 13, which includes hikes, games, arts and crafts, swimming, and boating. All these facilities are included in the one price you pay when checking in.

In the winter, days can be spent skiing, either downhill at the hotel's own ski hill (thirteen trails) or cross-country on 76 kilometers of high-elevation, dependably snow-covered groomed trails that wind up through balsam firs to frozen ponds and vistas. There is also lighted ice skating, snowboarding, and showshoeing. Again, take all the advantage you want of the activities for no additional fees.

In the evening, men don jackets and ladies dress. Even the children — of whom there are always a number — seem to sense what's expected in this opulent world of intricately carved teak, ginger jars, potted palms, and endless carpeting. Youngsters find their way (via an ornate, vintage 1912 Otis elevator) to the library, which has tiers of books and piles of puzzles, and some never make it back to the pool tables, TV, or game rooms. For adults, there is music in La Cave and in the Wilderness Lounge, off the lobby. But that's just the prelude.

Promptly at 6:00 P.M., the leaded glass doors of the dining room slide open and guests head to their assigned table, complete with 11 pieces of silverware at each table setting. The table d'hôte menu is extensive; order as much of it as you like. There are seven range chefs in the kitchen, one for each entrée on the nightly menu. In order to get a good look at the evening's choices, samples of each dish on the menu — appetizers through desserts — are displayed on a two-tiered table. If it happens to be Saturday night in the winter, an elaborate buffet covers long, linen-clad tables in the center of the many-pillared, 8,500-square-foot dining room. Chef Phil Learned has been the Director of Food Service since 1966 and is a partner at the hotel, so you can imagine that he has a vested interest in high standards and consistency.

The Balsams is one of the few surviving grand hotels to distinguish between the "social season" and periods when it caters to groups. From the Fourth of July through Labor Day weekend, no groups (except family reunions) are accepted. Conventions and other groups are scheduled from fall through spring.

Oh yes, about the guest rooms. The best rooms in the house are huge and circular, with at least six windows. (The hotel is ingeniously heated, using sawdust from nearby lumber mills.) The less expensive rooms are smaller, with limited views. Over the last few years most of the rooms have been totally renovated, from the plumbing to the windows, and redecorated with flower-patterned wallpaper. The closets remain deep and large, and the windows are still curtained in organdy, the better to let in the amazing view. Many rooms can be connected to create family suites, sometimes a whole family wing.

Most guests agree: the best thing about The Balsams is its staff, which numbers more than four hundred for about four hundred guests. At meal times they get to know your likes and dislikes, and throughout your stay they'll be there to ask how your skiing is coming along or if you had fun showshoeing.

Eaton Center

Rockhouse Mountain Farm Inn

Eaton Center, NH 03832
603-447-2880

A family retreat on a country farm near Conway

Innkeepers: The Edge family. **Accommodations:** 15 rooms (some with shared baths), 3 bunkrooms for children. **Rates:** $104–$120 per couple. **Included:** Full breakfast and dinner. **Minimum stay:** Negotiable. **Added:** 8% tax. **Credit cards accepted:** None. **Children:** $28–$40, depending on age, when occupying parent's room. **Pets:** Not encouraged, but exceptions are made. **Smoking:** Not permitted. **Handicap access:** No. **Open:** Mid-June to late October.

➤ **The homemade meals are hearty. Dinner is served family-style by candlelight and is designed to help guests get acquainted. Breakfast is casual, with adults and children coming down to eat whenever they are ready.**

Rockhouse Mountain Farm is definitely a family place. The Edge family offers hayrides, Saco River canoe trips, and barbecues, as well as plenty of space to play along the private lake beach (with rowboats and canoes) or in the woods and meadows on the 450-acre farm. The farm animals are an integral part of the experience here. Many of the barnyard animals — chickens, peacocks, geese, and kittens — do indeed spill out of the barn and into the yard. Others, like the horses, llamas, and pigs, remain corraled.

The Edge family has been running the farm as an inn since 1946. The staff consists mostly of family friends and college students, some of them former guests. The informal atmosphere puts both parents and kids at ease. There is also an effort to let parents have some time to themselves. Adults gather for happy hour — BYOB — under the big maple tree in the front yard. Children eat dinner in a separate dining room and at night can sleep in girl's or boy's bunkrooms.

The rooms are clean and comfortable. Perhaps surprisingly, there are fine paintings and antiques throughout the informal farmhouse. Some of the furniture was brought from Wales years ago by the family.

Be sure to make reservations, because although the house can accommodate 40 to 45 people, many loyal guests come back year after year. Family reunions are a specialty.

Franconia Area

Blanche's B&B

Easton Valley Road (Route 116)
Franconia, NH 03580
603-823-7061
shannon@ncia.net

A warm and welcoming B&B

Host: Brenda Shannon. **Accommodations:** 3 rooms (1 with private bath). **Rates:** $65–$95 per couple. **Included:** Full breakfast. **Minimum stay:** 2 nights may be required during busy periods. **Added:** 8% tax. **Credit cards accepted:** All major ones. **Children:** $20; cribs available for $5. **Pets:** Not accepted, but nearby kennels are recommended. **Smoking:** Not permitted. **Handicap access:** No. **Open:** Year-round.

➤ **The B&B is located on Easton Valley Road (Route 116), a delightful rural road that follows the valley floor, passing farms and mountain scenery.**

Although with each edition we recommend fewer and fewer places with shared baths, we can't help but include Blanche's, an 1887 farmhouse with whimsical decor and genuine hospitality. Brenda has been at this since the mid-1980s, creating a warm, simple, and enchanting retreat.

Brenda is a decorative painter, responsible for all the marbled, ragged, stenciled, and stippled walls, as well as the creative floor coverings and painted furniture. She operates her Kinsman Ridge Design studio from the B&B. The farmhouse retains its original dignity but is also full of fanciful details like gold stars twinkling on the ceiling.

One of our favorite rooms, Wild Rose, is next to the front door. (Noise isn't really a problem because the B&B is so small.) Although it is the most spacious room, its bathroom is tiny. Second-floor rooms are tucked under the eaves. Lilac, a corner room, has a queen-size iron bed with feather comforter. Another room is well-suited to a family, with a twin bed tucked into an alcove.

A sunny breakfast room is the setting for good conversations, partially fueled, perhaps, by the warmth of the woodstove and good tea and coffee. The bountiful meal includes a bowl of mixed fruit drizzled with maple yogurt, scones or popovers, and a soufflé, omelet, or "raised" waffles.

French doors lead to a comfortable living room, complete with wood-burning fireplace and stenciled hardwood floors. A deck overlooks the backyard.

In case you're wondering, Blanche was the family dog, who is no longer with us except in spirit.

Bungay Jar Bed and Breakfast

Easton Valley Road (Route 116)
Franconia, NH 03580
603-823-7775
Fax: 603-444-2919
www.bungayjar.com

A quirky B&B with beautiful gardens

Owner: Kate Kerivan. **Accommodations:** 8 rooms (6 with private bath), 1 cottage. **Rates:** $75–$150 per couple, $85–$225 during foliage; $145 daily ($195 in foliage) or $650 weekly ($895 during foliage) for the cottage. **Included:** Full breakfast. **Minimum stay:** 2 nights may be required July through October, and over holidays. **Added:** 8% tax. **Credit cards accepted:** All major ones. **Children:** Not appropriate under age 5. **Pets:** Not accepted. **Smoking:** Not permitted. **Handicap access:** No. **Open:** Year-round.

➤ **Plum Cottage, down the road in Franconia Village, is available from July through October. Landscaped in an "English Cottage" style, the cottage features a fireplace, whirlpool, dining room/solarium, loft, fully equipped kitchen, and separate bedroom and study.**

This charming house, built from an 18th-century post-and-beam barn, is much larger than it appears from the front. Wander down the lusciously landscaped and terraced backyard and look back up at the four stories.

The vista from the back side of the house is a treasure, enjoyable from a number of little balconies. The view overlooks the Kinsman Range of the White Mountains and the clearing where Kate has worked her magic as a landscape architect. The backyard is filled with trellises, vines, pathways, perennials, potted plants, a water garden, and a whiskey barrel or two filled with water plants and goldfish. In 1997, Kate, winner of prestigious awards for her gardens, opened a garden shop in a wooded glen; she also dispenses free advice.

Inside, the two-story hayloft features an intimate and eclectically furnished living room with a massive hearth. You may find son Kyle, a couple of cats, and a couple of large poodles enjoying the fireplace, too. Plenty of plants, books, and an assortment of antiques create a warm and inviting space. Speaking of warmth, there's a small two-person sauna off the second floor. Guests dart from the sauna to a small balcony to cool off (even in the dead of winter).

Each guest room is different from any others we've seen. The Rose suite features a private sitting area that looks down onto the living room. The long and narrow Cinnamon room boasts mountain views, a six-foot soaking bathtub, and a small balcony beyond the French doors. On the ground floor, with a private patio that opens directly onto the garden, is the cheerful Garden Suite, which features a gas fireplace, two-person Jacuzzi, and kitchen and dining area. It's quite private — perfect for longer stays.

Heading up to the third floor, with exposed brick and hand-hewn beams, a collection of toys and lightning rods have been incorporated into the staircase. The small but romantic Hobbit room has a little balcony and mountain views. Its shower makes you feel as if you're in the woods: the slanted roof is, in essence, one large skylight. The sleigh bed is perfectly positioned under another skylight.

The Stargazer room, perhaps our favorite, has two large skylights over the bed. On a clear night, you'll count stars (both real and stenciled) instead of sheep as you fall asleep. But before you do, enjoy the twig furniture, an antique gas fireplace, and a clawfoot tub — under two additional skylights in the main part of the room.

Breakfast can be taken to any of the little porches or enjoyed in the small dining areas off the living room. The full breakfast buffet might include fruit salad, popovers, oatmeal, and French toast garnished with edible flowers from the garden. Throughout the day, a large selection of tea is set out, yours for the steeping. Create your own tea party in the garden.

There are many definitions of bungay (pronounced bun-gee with a hard g). One is an unusual springtime wind that moves up through Easton Valley, rhythmically shaking everything in its path.

The Franconia Inn

Easton Valley Road (Route 116)
Franconia, NH 03580
603-823-5542
800-473-5299
Fax: 603-823-8078
infor@franconiainn.com
www.franconiainn.com

> **A large country inn with many facilities**

Innkeepers: Richard and Alec Morris. **Accommodations:** 29 rooms and 3 suites (all with private bath). **Rates:** $130–$225 per couple, MAP; B&B and EP rates and packages also available. **Included:** Full breakfast and dinner, but more limited meal plans are available. **Minimum stay:** 2 or 3 nights on selected weekends. **Added:** 8% tax, 15% to food and beverage portion of the bill. **Credit cards accepted:** All major ones. **Children:** Ages 6-11, $5 extra; 12 and older, $10. **Pets:** Not accepted. **Smoking:** Restricted to bar. **Handicap access:** No. **Open:** Year-round.

➤ **In fine weather, it's hard to imagine a more tranquil place. And in foul weather, the inn's ample common space is welcoming, much of it paneled in oak and warmed by crackling hearths. The basement houses a lounge, movie room, and a children's game room.**

The Franconia Inn offers a variety of resort activities in a quiet valley, a spectacular corner of the White Mountains that seems delightfully stuck in a 1950s time warp. What is not stuck in a time warp, however, is the quality of the rooms and facilities. These have been constantly maintained and upgraded by the Morris brothers, who acquired the inn in 1981.

The imposing, three-story white frame inn was built in the 1930s. It is located in the broad, magnificent Easton Valley, a quiet byway just west of Franconia Notch. (There *is* a small grass strip airport across the street.) Even if you don't climb Mount Lafayette, you can always enjoy the magnificent view of it from the inn.

In addition to some of New England's most spectacular hiking, area activities include biking (use of 12-speed mountain bikes are complimentary), swimming in the outdoor pool, golf at a nearby 9-hole course, tennis on four courts, lounging in the Jacuzzi, gliding from the airport across the road, and horseback riding from the inn's own stables. Trail rides are offered on portions of the 60-kilometer network that the inn maintains for cross-country skiing. In winter, sleigh rides are also available, and ice skates can be rented for use on the town rink. Cannon Mountain's ski trails are just five miles away.

The rooms range in size and price from cozy to spacious, and ten have an additional single bed to accommodate a third person. They are all decorated with Laura Ashley prints, canopy beds, and down comforters and quilts. The rooms on the top floor are pine-paneled; most are freshly carpeted. One suite includes a living room with a woodstove, a daybed, and a kitchen; another has a Jacuzzi. Ask for a corner room or a room on the back side of the hotel with a mountain view. The inn also owns a nearby motel annex; be sure to request a room at the main inn, though.

The spacious, country-elegant dining room offers candlelight dining. Stick to the simpler choices at dinner and if you're staying more than one night (which we recommend you do), we suggest you try nearby area restaurants. There is also a children's menu. A small dining room, used off-season and for private parties, has a fireplace.

The Hilltop Inn

Main Street
Sugar Hill, NH 03585
603-823-5695
800-770-5695
Fax: 603-823-5518
bp@hilltopinn.com
www.hilltopinn.com

> **A homespun B&B in a quiet village**

Innkeepers: Meri and Mike Hern. **Accommodations:** 6 rooms and suites (all with private bath), 1 cottage. **Rates:** $70–$110 per couple in rooms, $200 in cottage; more during foliage. **Included:** Full breakfast. **Minimum stay:** 2 nights on summer weekends, during foliage, and over major holidays. **Added:** 8% tax. **Credit cards accepted:** MasterCard, Visa. **Children:** Additional $15–$25 in parent's room. **Pets:** Accepted; $10 extra. **Smoking:** Permitted in the living room in bad weather; otherwise, not permitted. **Handicap access:** No. **Open:** Year-round.

➤ **The inn also rents a two-bedroom cottage with full kitchen and fireplace in the living room, which is great for longer stays and those seeking more privacy.**

Some inns appear suddenly — fully decorated, complete with Laura Ashley wallpaper, wing chairs, fluffy pillows, and bedside mints. Others, like Hilltop, evolve over the years according to their own dictates. Hilltop offers a refreshingly sincere respite rather than an overly commercial or formulaic one.

The Herns have been tinkering with Hilltop since 1985, and it keeps getting better and better. After such a long tenure in the hospitality business, many innkeepers grow tired. But the Herns continue to add many small touches that add up to big, lasting impressions. They haven't jumped headstrong into the latest innkeeping fads. They have become very astute at knowing when to leave guests to themselves and when to attend to them.

Guests enjoy a small front parlor, filled with just the right balance of memorabilia, quilted pillows, and antiques, as well as a

Vermont Castings gas stove. If guests gather around the VCR for communal movie-watching (the video library includes about 400 movies), Meri has been known to pop a big bowl of popcorn.

The inn has a full liquor license and a very reasonably priced and well-chosen wine list. Summertime guests often take wine and cheese to the large deck hung with bird feeders or the small front porch overlooking the lovely garden and evening sunsets. The hummingbirds that flock to hanging flower baskets are a constant source of entertainment. Midweek in the winter, when there are only a couple of guests in the house, Meri and Mike often leave wine and cheese in front of the stove and disappear.

Guest rooms range from unusually small to unusually large. All have comfortable antiques, flannel sheets and electric blankets in the winter, handmade quilts, candles that are meant to be used, bubble bath, overhead fans, and telephones. Most of the artwork that graces the walls has been done by guests and local artists. Room 6, a favorite, is hidden away in the rear of the house. It's large but cozy, with a brick chimney running up the middle of it. Note the stenciled hardwood floors. Even the smallest room, with stenciled furniture, features the same attention to detail found elsewhere. A few rooms can accommodate a third or fourth person. Children of any age are welcome, and the Herns have baskets of toys at the ready for different age groups.

A breakfast buffet is served from 8:30 to 9:30 A.M. at individual tables in the dining room, dotted with a collection of weathervanes. The buffet includes plenty of fresh fruit, homemade muffins, eggs, cheese, yogurt, French toast, and granola. You might wish to enjoy your coffee on one of the rocking chairs set in front of the wood-burning stove.

The house is in the sleepy, picturesque village of Sugar Hill, contentedly off the tourist path. In summer, you can walk up to the historical society museum and cheese shop, then down Lovers Lane; Franconia Notch is just 10 minutes away. In winter, there's cross-country skiing on the grounds as well as an extensive network of trails nearby. Hilltop has printed lists with detailed information on area hikes and restaurant suggestions.

Sunset Hill House

Sunset Hill Road
Sugar Hill, NH 03585
603-823-5522
800-786-4455
Fax: 603-823-5738

> **A hilltop, hotel-style country inn with a pool**

Innkeepers: Michael and Tricia Coyle and family. **Accommodations:** 30 rooms (all with private bath). **Rates:** $90–$215 per couple; golf, ski, and midweek packages are available; MAP rates during foliage. **Included:** Full breakfast; MAP rates also available. **Minimum stay:** 2 nights on some holidays and during foliage. **Added:** 8% tax. **Credit cards accepted:** All major ones. **Children:** Under 10 may stay in parent's room for an additional $20 B&B, $35 MAP. **Pets:** Not accepted. **Smoking:** Not permitted. **Handicap access:** No. **Open:** Year-round.

➤ **For two weeks in the middle of June, the Fields of Lupine Festival draws guests to this quiet corner. Scheduled activities include garden and studio tours, teas, photo stops, and inn tours.**

First things first, the inn straddles a 1,700-foot ridge, with spectacular sunset views of the Kinsman, Presidential, and Franconia mountain ranges.

The hotel you see standing today was actually the annex to the original historic grand hotel built in 1882. Michael Coyle purchased the inn at a foreclosure auction in 1993 and subsequently invested a substantial amount of capital and an equivalent dose of faith to transform it from stem to stern.

The three connected common rooms in the front of the inn are bright and airy, each with a fireplace. There is plenty of room for guests to spread out. Outdoors in the summertime, guests gather around the attractive, heated swimming pool that faces the mountains. Poolside lunches are served on weekends in the summer. Some guests come to play golf on the 9-hole (par 33) course across the street; others come for great mountain biking and hiking. In the winter, you can cross-country ski and snowshoe from the back door, or take a horse-drawn sleigh ride over the golf course across the street, or ice skate on the pond. Several downhill skiing areas are nearby.

The guest rooms are spiffy and somewhat spartanly furnished. You will not find any teddy bears gracing the beds here. To that Michael says, "People go away to get away from their 'do-dads.' They don't want me to replace their 'do-dads' with my 'do-dads.'" All guest rooms have new bathroom fixtures and polished hardwood floors. They are similarly decorated in coordinated Waverly fabrics and patterns; beds are covered with floral down comforters. Many have bay windows with window seats; some have a fireplace or Jacuzzi. Odd-numbered rooms have mountain views.

Each of the four dining rooms feature large picture windows that bring the expansive mountain view indoors. The full breakfast includes scones, muffins, fruit, and, perhaps, French toast stuffed with cream cheese and fruit or an omelet of your choice. If there is a large group in the inn on Sunday, the kitchen will set out an extensive buffet. On our last visit, the dining room setting was elegant, the service friendly, but the evening meal was inconsistent. We recommend you stick to the simpler offerings for dinner, which never failed; among the winners that evening were spinach salad with roasted sweet potatoes, seafood bisque, trout, and apple strudel. The inn also offers a more informal menu in the tavern.

Jackson

Carter Notch Inn

Carter Notch Road
P.O. Box 269
Jackson, NH 03846
603-383-9630
800-794-9434
www.journeysnorth.com/mwv/carter

> **A completely renovated B&B on a lovely loop road**

Innkeepers: Jim and Lynda Dunwell. **Accommodations:** 7 rooms (5 with private bath). **Rates:** $59–$109 per couple with private bath. **Included:** Full breakfast. **Minimum stay:** 2 nights on winter weekends and some holiday weekends. **Added:** 8% tax, 10% service charge during peak periods. **Credit cards accepted:** All major ones. **Children:** Welcome; $15 per additional person in same room. **Pets:** Not accepted. **Smoking:** Not permitted. **Handicap access:** No. **Open:** Year-round.

➤ **The hosts have lived in Jackson and operated other B&Bs in town since the mid-1970s. They can direct you to all the right spots.**

If you're looking for a small, moderately priced place to stay while hiking or skiing in the White Mountains, look no further. On a picturesque country road above the village, the B&B is also within walking distance of Jackson Falls, a popular swimming and picnicking spot. The mountain view from the front porch is lovely. There is a great golf course across the street, which in the winter hosts the largest network of cross-country trails in the Northeast.

The turn-of-the-century Shingle-style cottage originally belonged to the owners of the historic Eagle Mountain House next door. When the hotel was converted into condos, the Carter Notch house was used as staff housing and fell into a state of disrepair. The Dunwells purchased it in 1995 and renovated it from top to bottom. They installed central air conditioning but left the old-fashioned dumbwaiter and elevator intact.

The living room, with wall-to-wall carpeting and a fireplace, is comfortable, but summertime guests will spend most of their time on the front wraparound porch. Its views, and the white wicker rockers, invite leisurely afternoon lounging. Guests have access to a large refrigerator in the kitchen, so they can store snacks and drinks.

The bright and fresh guest rooms have shiny painted floors and simple, painted furniture. We're partial to the large room (#2) with two beds and two bay windows looking toward Eagle Mountain House and golf course. The blue room (#5), with a bay window overlooking the golf course, is also very pleasant. A couple of rooms can handle a family of four. As of our last visit, two dormered rooms on the third floor shared one bath, but Jim had plans to convert them into the most luxurious rooms in the inn (both with private bath). With a lot of elbow grease (Jim plans to do most of the work himself), the renovated rooms eventually will have fireplaces and Jacuzzis.

In addition to the outdoor hot tub and deck, reached from a glassed-in atrium area, guests have access to the health club, tennis courts, and swimming pool at the Eagle Mountain Hotel.

At breakfast, cold items are laid out on the sideboard. Jim cooks and serves hot dishes like Grand Marnier or apricot cheese French toast and whole wheat apple blueberry pancakes.

The Wentworth Resort Hotel

Box M
Jackson, NH 03846
603-383-9700
800-637-0013
Fax: 603-383-4265
wentwort@nxi.com
www.thewentworth.com

> A gourmet getaway in the
> heart of the village

Owner/General Manager: Fritz Koeppel. **Accommodations:** 58 rooms and suites (all with private bath) in the summer, 45 in the winter; approximately 20 condominiums in the rental pool at any given time. **Hotel Rates:** $159–$249 per couple, MAP, in summer; $48 less per couple, B&B, in summer; surcharge for rooms with Jacuzzi and/or fireplace. **Condominium Rates:** $175–$250 for a 2-bedroom; $225–$300 for a 3-bedroom; weekly rates also available; excellent midweek packages. **Included:** Full à la carte breakfast and dinner for hotel rooms. **Minimum stay:** 2 nights on some weekends in hotel; 2 nights at all times in condos. **Added:** 8% tax. **Credit cards accepted:** All major ones. **Children:** Welcome; free under 12; $10, over age 12 in same room with parents. **Pets:** Not accepted. **Smoking:** Permitted. **Handicap access:** Yes. **Open:** Year-round.

➤ **If anyone has the credentials to turn this place into a first-class establishment, it's Fritz Koeppel. The Swiss-educated hotelier has garnered experience at the Four Seasons and Ritz hotels around the U.S. and at Banff Springs Hotel in the Canadian Rockies.**

The 1869 grand hotel has hosted travelers continuously except for a fourteen-year period in the 1970s and early 1980s when it was boarded up. In the 1980s a condominium development company purchased the complex of 37 buildings and promptly tore down 30 of them. They rebuilt the golf course, condos, and rejuvenated the old hotel before selling. Fritz Koeppel purchased the inn in 1990, has made significant improvements, and still has ambitious plans.

The three-story hotel and nearby buildings are smartly dressed with green and white awnings. The nicely lit exterior is inviting, especially on a winter evening. In warm weather the front porch is draped with hanging flower baskets and window boxes. From the front porch you can enjoy morning coffee and the newspaper or an afternoon cocktail from a comfortable wicker chair. (Unfortunately, most of the chairs look onto the driveway.) A photographic history of the property is displayed under the porticos. The large lobby, with hardwood floors and overstuffed chairs, is particularly comfortable, especially if you nab one of the couches in front of the fireplace. A small convivial lounge and multi-paned billiards room overlook the back porch.

Head and shoulders above the regular hotel rooms are the specialty suites with Jacuzzi and fireplace. It is well worth it to splurge on these. Of the suites, Thornycroft is the pièce de résistance: The luxuriously outfitted suite boasts highly polished birch floors, a fireplace, and king canopy bed. The marble bathroom with Jacuzzi has its own wet bar and fireplace. Suite 404, with a Jacuzzi, gas fireplace, and stereo in the bathroom, is another particularly romantic retreat.

In the main hotel, if you can't get a suite, you'll definitely want to ask for a second-floor nonsmoking room in the front of the hotel. These are generally larger and brighter, with bay windows. Most guest rooms have been renovated with hotel-style reproduction French Provincial furnishings, upholstered chairs, and cable television. Bathrooms have all new fixtures, but not much artwork on the walls to warm them as of our last visit. Unfortunately, the boxed-in air ducts that lower some ceilings are a casualty of central air conditioning installed a few years ago. The main hotel rooms see a lot of foot traffic and some show signs of wear, but if you take advantage of midweek specials (which include dinner), the lower price more than compensates.

As for the food, it is outstanding, without qualification. Guests on the meal plan can choose anything off the à la carte breakfast and dinner menus. In the evening, the dining room is elegant without being stuffy; the tables are set with hurricane lamps and classic silverware. Service is well informed and nicely paced. Chef Jim Davis has presided magnificently over the kitchen since 1995. One recent meal started with a delicate but terrifically flavorful mushroom tart, followed by a poached pear and walnut salad, and seared salmon roulade. Presentation is artful. A chocolate torte drizzled with a passion fruit coulis was topped off with flavorful cappuccino. The wine list currently tops 300 bottles and gets better all the time (although it's already quite good).

The Wentworth serves as the management agency for adjacent condos. The two- and three-bedroom condominiums, many of which are on the golf course, are spacious and well suited to families. Inquire about golf packages.

Other resort facilities include clay tennis courts and a swimming pool. In case you didn't know, Jackson is a cross-country-skiing mecca in the winter, with over 150 kilometers of groomed trails.

Whitneys' Inn at Jackson

Route 16B
P.O. Box 822
Jackson, NH 03846
603-383-8916
800-677-5737
Fax: 603-383-6886
whitneyinn@aol.com
www.mountwashingtonvalley.com/whitneysinn

A family-oriented ski lodge

Manager: David Linne. **Accommodations:** 19 rooms (all with private bath), 2 cottages, 8 family suites. **Non-winter Rates:** $110–$156 per couple MAP; $70–$116 B&B; $120–$156 per cottage and suites for up to 4 people B&B. **Winter Rates:** $116–$170 per couple MAP; $76–$130 per couple B&B; $150–$174 per cottage and suites for up to 4 people B&B. **Included:** Varies with meal plan. **Minimum stay:** 2 nights on peak foliage weekends and during school vacations. **Added:** 8% tax, 10–15% service charge. **Credit cards accepted:** All major ones. **Children:** In summer, kids stay and eat free when parents rent family suites; in winter, $10–$28 extra. **Pets:** Accepted in cottages. **Smoking:** Not permitted in dining room; some nonsmoking rooms available. **Handicap access:** No. **Open:** Year-round.

➤   Year-round, Whitneys' caters to children (note the summer rate structure) — with a great barn recreation room and a separate dinner seating at 5:30 P.M. A movie follows so that parents can dine alone if they wish.

Whitneys' has a solid place in the history of New England skiing. In the early 1930s, it was one of the first farmhouses to welcome skiers and one of the first to install a motorized cable to tug them up the hill. Over the years, both the mountain and farmhouse grew in popularity. In the 1950s, Bill and Betty Whitney (Betty still lives next door) developed the larger peak out back, now known as Black Mountain. The vertical drop is 1,200 feet; it has twenty trails and four lifts, including a triple chair.

In summer, Whitneys' is popular with families, who take advantage of the sandy beach and paddle boats at the pond across the road. A short walk uphill yields a spectacular view of the whole Presidential Mountain Range. The rambling farmhouse is, in fact, surrounded by mountains.

The guest rooms are for the most part modest but comfortable. Request one of the corner rooms or roomy doubles with great views. In the unassuming, paneled chalet next door, the functional rooms have kitchenettes and can sleep four. These rooms (dubbed family suites) are a great bargain for families from late March to early September: depending on what meal plan their parents are on, children eat for free. For more privacy, we particularly like the two 2-bedroom cottages next to the main inn.

The pleasant dining room features a fireplace and big picture windows. The fare includes sumptuous breakfasts and a generous choice of evening entrées, including charbroiled sirloin and roast duckling, or the fish, veal, and pasta specialties of the evening. As you'd expect, there's a separate children's menu. Many guests plan their summer stays around the weekly Wednesday evening lobster bakes by the pond.

There's plenty of common space here: a comfortable living room, an enclosed flagstone patio that serves as a lounge, and the Shovel Handle Pub — the setting for wintertime slopeside lunches and aprés-ski drinks.

Black Mountain (under separate ownership) has a well-equipped nursery where infants and tots can play while their parents ski downhill or on the East's most extensive and scenic cross-country trail system — 140 kilometers meandering over golf courses, through the woods, and around the picturesque village of Jackson.

Jefferson

The Jefferson Inn

Route 2
Jefferson, NH 03583
603-586-7998
800-729-7908
Fax: 603-586-7808

Suitable for families as well as couples

Innkeepers: Marla Mason and Don Garretson. **Accommodations:** 9 rooms and 2 suites (all with private bath). **Rates:** $70–$90 per couple; $110–$140 in suites for a family of 4 to 5. **Included:** Full breakfast. **Minimum stay:** None. **Added:** 8% tax. **Credit cards accepted:** All major ones. **Children:** All ages welcome. **Pets:** Not accepted. **Smoking:** Not permitted. **Handicap access:** No. **Open:** Year-round except in April and November.

➤ **North of the northern edge of the White Mountains, the inn looks across an expansive meadow to Franconia Notch and the Presidential Mountain Range.**

Marla and Don purchased the late-19th-century inn in late 1994 and proceeded to carve out bathrooms for every room, move doorways, and change hallway configurations. Rich cherry, walnut, and pine floors were sanded and polished to a high luster.

On warm summer days, breezes waft through the house, set on a knoll above Route 2. Those concerned about road noise — primarily in the summer when the windows are open — might want to request a room in the back of the house. Even light sleepers make an exception for the Tower Room, a large and bright room in the front of the house with a sitting area tucked into the turret.

A favorite room is "New England," a large third-floor room with an oak spindle bed and window seats facing Mount Starr King. We also like Shadwell, a quiet room in the back of the house with antiques and navy wallpaper. Roses is a corner room with a sleigh bed. Shaker embodies simplicity with its four-poster bed and hand-crafted furniture. Two cheery and cozy suites can accommodate a family of four or five quite comfortably. (This is one inn where children of all ages are not only welcome, but there are accommodations well suited to them.) These family suites are somewhat set off from the rest of the rooms. Books about Jefferson are tucked into each guest room.

Guests sign up for a breakfast seating at 7:00, 8:00, or 9:00 A.M. A full breakfast, which might very well hold you over until dinnertime, is served on china in the countrified dining room overlooking active bird feeders. A substantial fruit plate might be followed by fluffy blueberry yogurt pancakes or an egg dish like baked crab scramble. Signature dishes include an apple cheddar breakfast bake with granola and Danish aebelskivers (ask for a definition).

On our last visit, a tangy cranberry pie and afternoon tea were offered in the two comfortable living rooms beyond the reception desk.

Although many people think the New Hampshire border stops at the White Mountains, there's more to do and see up here than you might think. Across the street is a great swimming hole with a sandy beach and floating dock, and, in winter, a skating rink with a warming hut. Two hiking trails begin at the inn, while more hiking, fishing, golfing, and biking are within 20 minutes of the Jefferson. You can reach Sunday River in 45 minutes, while Wildcat and Cannon are only 30 minutes away.

North Conway

Buttonwood Inn

Mount Surprise Road
P.O. Box 1817
North Conway, NH 03860
603-356-2625
800-258-2625
Fax: 603-356-3140
button_w@moose.ncia.net
www.buttonwoodinn.com

Seclusion off the beaten path

Innkeepers: Claudia and Peter Needham. **Accommodations:** 9 rooms (5 with private bath). **Rates:** $85–$150 per couple in season; $60–$130 off-season. **Included:** Full breakfast. **Minimum stay:** 2 nights on weekends in season. **Added:** 8% tax. **Credit cards accepted:** All major ones. **Children:** Well-behaved ones welcome. **Pets:** Not accepted. **Smoking:** Permitted on porch only. **Handicap access:** No. **Open:** Year-round.

➤ **On Saturday evenings in January and February, Claudia and Peter offer four-course candlelight dinners to guests.**

The Buttonwood Inn is a welcome oasis at the end of a dead end road off the highly trafficked route through North Conway. The inn is set on five wooded acres, with another dozen or so acres of adjacent woodlands, all of which is great for hiking. (In the winter, the trails lead to 65 kilometers of groomed cross-country ski trails.) With welcoming innkeepers who are always thinking of their guest's needs (like providing day packs for hikers) without being overbearing, the inn is head and shoulders above all others in town.

The original part of the Cape-style farmhouse dates to 1820. As for the guest rooms, room 2 is a personal favorite, with a large mural of the house, barn, and property. We also particularly like room 1, newly redone with a gas fireplace and a view of the backyard pool. Room 3 has also been recently redone with hardwood floors and area carpets. Families are welcome here; one two-bedroom suite works particularly well and is right off the game room, which has a television.

Breakfasts, taken at individual tables, are good and filling. You'll always have a choice between eggs any style or the daily special, perhaps Belgian waffles with warm cranberry-apple compote or ham and cheese strata with melon salsa and cornsticks.

There is plenty of common space. We particularly appreciate the front porch rockers, which are even kept out in the winter. Downstairs is a much enjoyed game room with a large fieldstone fireplace; it is warm and cozy in the winter, and cool in the summer.

In the backyard, old barn foundations have been transformed into lovely gardens and a sitting area. They also provided a colorful backdrop for the 20-by-40-foot pool. On the grounds, you can always try your hand at horse shoes and badminton. As for other diversions, downhill skiing at Mount Cranmore is about a mile away and the outlet shops are omnipresent. The Needhams can also arrange for a sleigh ride at one of two locations.

Pinkham Notch

Appalachian Mountain Club — Pinkham Notch Visitor Center and High Hut System

Pinkham Notch Visitor Center
Route 16
P.O. Box 298
Gorham, NH 03581
603-466-2727
Fax: 603-466-2822
www.outdoors.org

Hiker's havens

Huts manager: Chris Thayer. **Accommodations:** 35-room Joe Dodge Lodge at Pinkham Notch Visitor Center; 8 high huts with a variety of rooms, 6- to 23-person dorms. **Rates** (less for members, without meals): Joe Dodge Lodge: $47 per adult. High huts: From $62 per adult. **Included:** Breakfast, dinner, and tax. **Credit cards accepted:** MasterCard, Visa. **Children:** Special rates. **Pets:** Not allowed. **Smoking:** Not permitted. **Handicap access:** Yes. **Open:** Pinkham Notch Visitor Center, year-round; season for high huts varies.

➤ **Hike New England's highest mountains and dine with fellow hikers from around the world.**

The Appalachian Mountain Club was founded in 1876 to blaze and map hiking trails through the White Mountains. A few decades later, when logging operations scarred these slopes, outraged club members were instrumental in establishing the White Mountain National Forest. Gradually the club's scope widened to include feeding and sheltering hikers in its Pinkham Notch base camp and in maintaining a chain of eight high huts, a days hike apart, in the Presidential Range.

Huts in name only, the high-altitude hostelries are comfortable if spartan. Our favorite is Mizpah Spring, at 3,800 feet, just below treeline on the southern flank of Mount Clinton. You reach it by hiking up from Crawford Notch; the next morning, you can continue up to the summit of Mount Washington. The hut is nicely designed, nestled on the flank of Mount Clinton. Classic French railroad posters brighten the walls, and books in the corner library date from the 1890s. Its eight bunk rooms each accommodate at least six hikers on tiered bunks. As in all the huts, lavatories are segregated by sex; and do bring a flashlight — there is no electricity.

Lonesome Lake Hut, the southernmost in the chain, is a popular family destination because it's just 1.7 miles up from Franconia Notch. As the name implies, there is a lake here, good for swimming and canoeing. Greenleaf Hut, at 4,200 feet, is at treeline above Eagle Lake. Galehead and Zealand huts are smaller, each holding just 36 people and conveying an off-the-beaten-trail feeling. Carter Notch lies in a divide between two high mountains and is easily reached; there is even a shortcut via the Wildcat Mountain Gondola, then an easy walk along a ridge trail (another good one for less hardy hikers). Madison Spring Hut, the oldest, has the most rugged setting, nestled above the sheer walls of Madison Gulf and below the summit of Mount Adams. Lakes-of-the-Clouds Hut is the highest, the largest (housing up to ninety), and the most boisterous. Well above treeline on Mount Washington, at 5,050 feet, it is popular with groups.

At all the huts, the atmosphere is friendly and the food plentiful. Hikers from the world over trade stories, play games, and participate in guided walks offered by resident naturalists.

Pinkham Notch Visitor Center is a comfortable complex at the eastern base of Mount Washington. Guests eat at long tables in the dining room, which has a dramatic view of Wildcat Mountain. Slide shows and lectures are held frequently after dinner. The rooms in neighboring Joe Dodge Lodge have two, three, or four bunks; the lodge also has a living room with sofas and a hearth. A few family rooms have a double bed and three bunks. There is one bathroom to a hall.

Throughout the year, special programs are offered at Pinkham Notch. They include workshops on photography, nature drawing, bird-watching, botany, and history as well as camping, backpacking, rock climbing, canoeing, snowshoeing, and cross-country skiing.

Pinkham Notch Visitor Center and the huts put the best hiking in New England within reach of those without cars. The Concord Trailways bus from Boston stops at Pinkham, and an AMC van shuttles back and forth at regular intervals all day between Pinkham (near the eastern base of Mount Washington) and the Crawford Depot, the AMC's information center near the trailheads to the western flank of Mount Washington and the rest of the Presidential Range.

Snowville

Snowvillage Inn

Snowville, NH 03849
603-447-2818
800-447-4345
Fax: 603-447-5268
snowvill@nxi.com
www.snowvillageinn.com

> **An off-the-beaten path country inn**

Innkeepers: Kevin and Barbara Flynn. **Accommodations:** 18 rooms (all with private bath). **Rates:** $129–$219 per couple, MAP; B&B rates $30 less per couple. **Included:** Breakfast and dinner. **Minimum stay:** 2 nights on weekends and during foliage season, 3 nights on holiday weekends. **Added:** 8% tax, 15% service. **Credit cards accepted:** All major ones. **Children:** Over age 6 welcome. **Pets:** Not accepted. **Smoking:** Restricted. **Handicap access:** No. **Open:** Year-round.

➤ **The views of the Presidential Mountain Range from the porch are spectacular, and the gardens have won awards.**

The red shingle house sits high up a back road, above the picturesque lakeside village of Eaton Center. Both the village and inn feel far away from it all, even though they're just a short drive from the Mount Washington Valley.

The Flynns, who are raising two young children here, purchased the inn in 1994. They hail from East Hampton on Long Island where they ran an 8-room B&B.

The inn consists of three buildings, with six rooms in the main house, eight in the barn, and four in the newer chimney house. In the main house, the Robert Frost Room is perhaps the most popular. It has a marvelous view of the mountains from the bed. Both large guest rooms above the dining room have the feel of a Swiss chalet. They are reached through the dining room or via the side porch. One project the Flynn's wish to tackle is upgrading the 1950s-style pink bathrooms.

Guest rooms in the carriage barn are paneled in knotty pine. Ask for Steinbeck or Hemingway, two of the larger rooms. Some of the inn's least-expensive and smallest rooms are on the south side, with sloping ceilings. (Even the small rooms are comfortable though.) The two-story, lodge-like living room is lined with books. Each of the rooms in the newly constructed Chimney House has a fireplace, quilts, whitewashed walls, new bathrooms, and New England country decor. The handsome common area boasts a large fireplace.

Guests have cocktails and hors d'oeuvres on the screened porch in summer, and by the fireplace in the beamed living room in winter. Come wintertime, the hammocks and Adirondack chairs (scattered about the property) are put away and the sauna is in constant use.

The chalet-style dining room serves wholesome dinners by candlelight. Our most recent meal consisted of homemade oatmeal rolls, Mediterranean fish soup, tasty grilled shrimp with roasted red pepper purée, and apple pie à la mode. Vegetarian meals are also available. If you request a window table, dine early so that you're less likely to face another couple at the table right next to yours.

In summer there is swimming in Crystal Lake (just down the road), a variety of lawn games, and wooded hiking trails from the inn.

In winter there are 13 kilometers of groomed cross-country trails on the property; rentals, lessons, and guided tours are available at the inn. The closest downhill skiing is at King Pine; more well-known Wildcat, Attitash, and Mount Cranmore are a half-hour's drive.

Waterville Valley

Waterville Valley Resort

Waterville Valley, NH 03215
603-726-4193
800-GO-VALLEY (468-2553)
Fax: 603-726-7000
infor@waterville.com
www.waterville.com

> **New Hampshire's largest
> year-round vacation village**

Owner: Booth Creek Ski Holdings. **Accommodations:** For 2,500 guests in hotel rooms and condominium units. **Rates:** From $49 per person double occupancy for "Summer Unlimited" packages; from $59 in the winter. **Included:** Use of all facilities. **Minimum stay:** 2-3 nights during holidays. **Added:** 8% tax, plus resort fee of 11%. **Credit cards accepted:** All major ones. **Children:** Free in parent's room. **Pets:** Not accepted. **Smoking:** Some lodges offer rooms for nonsmokers. **Handicap access:** Yes, in Snowy Owl. **Open:** Year-round.

➤ **Most guests stay on the "Winter Unlimited" and "Summer Unlimited" packages, which include access to practically all the resort has to offer.**

Waterville Valley has been a resort area since the middle of the 19th century. The valley itself is a 10-mile cul-de-sac cut by one of New England's many rivers and encircled by majestic mountains, many of them more than 4,000 feet high.

The Town Square, a restaurant and shopping complex, occupies the center of the valley. Within walking distance is an excellent athletic club with two indoor pools and courts for racquet sports, and an ice arena as well as a pond that's good for summer boating and sunbathing. A sports dome features a 28-foot climbing wall.

The winter centerpiece of the valley is 4,004-foot Mount Tecumseh, a ski mountain with 50 slopes and trails and 12 lifts, including a high-speed detachable quad and three triple chair lifts. There are also 105 kilometers of cross-country trails; snowshoers have their own trails, too. Waterville Valley offers a strong Skiwee program and a supervised children's program in the winter along with some of New England's most reasonably priced condo-ski weeks (and the condos are a shade above the norm).

In the summer, there is a supervised day program for children aged 3 to 12 and organized activities for children aged 8 and older. "Base Camp" offers maps, equipment, and guided naturalist tours for every season and sport; mountain adventuring and orienteering is popular. There's also a 9-hole golf course, 18 clay tennis courts, in-line skating, extensive mountain biking trails, and horseback riding. The Town Square is the backdrop for a lively music festival all summer.

Many of Waterville Valley's condominium units are in distinctive condo hotels, most with game areas and indoor pools. The Golden Eagle Lodge, with 143 suites, is a 1990s version of an 1890s grand hotel, patterned after an Adirondack lodge. Request one of the many tower suites with 360-degree views of the mountains. Even the least expensive units, however, are exquisite in design and detail.

The Snowy Owl is another striking building with a three-story fieldstone fireplace and a cupola in which you can sit and contemplate the stars or mountains. The garden-level lounge, with a sunken hearth, is removed from the game rooms, which have table tennis and electronic games. Of course there are indoor and outdoor pools. Half of the 80 rooms have a whirlpool. Breakfast and afternoon wine and cheese are included in the rates.

The Valley Inn and Tavern is also worth special mention. It has a fine dining room and a superb indoor-outdoor pool, the kind that is warm enough in winter to enjoy at night, under the stars. This full-service hotel has town house rooms, parlors, and master suites.

There are currently nine or ten dining options to suit all tastes, ranging from the Coffee Emporium to a pizza joint to the romantic Valley Inn.

Whitefield

The Spalding Inn

Mountain View Road
Whitefield, NH 03598
603-837-2572
800-368-8439
Fax: 603-837-3062
www.nettx.com/spalding

> **A rejuvenated resort for families as well as couples**

Owners/operators: Diane and April Cockrell and Michael Flinder. **Accommodations:** 36 rooms and 6 cottages (all with private bath). **Rates:** $150–$180 per couple, MAP; $99–$129 per couple, B&B; $150 for family of four in 2-room suites, B&B; $195 for a family of 4, MAP. **Included:** Full breakfast and dinner; lunch also served. **Minimum stay:** None. **Added:** 8% tax, 15% service added to dinner portion of the bill. **Credit cards accepted:** All major ones. **Children:** Welcome; under age 12 free; over age 12, add $20 each child to family suite rates. **Pets:** Accepted in cottages. **Smoking:** Not permitted. **Handicap access:** Yes. **Open:** Late May through October.

➤ **Because of the wide variety of room types, the inn is equally nice for a quiet retreat or a family reunion. Family suites, two connected rooms with separate bathrooms, represent a great value.**

The Spalding Inn continues, slowly but steadily, to reclaim its status as a value-oriented New Hampshire destination. It offers all the sports — either on the premises or nearby — anyone could want, economical family suites, and wonderfully expansive views.

In 1991 Diane purchased the 200-acre property, which had languished for years under mismanagement and neglect. Things have been looking up ever since. Her mission is to cast away the inn's outdated aspects (like the jacket-and-tie requirement for dinner) while maintaining the inn's precious attributes (like old-fashioned hospitality and graciousness). She's succeeding in creating a place to put your body and mind back on track.

There are plenty of quiet nooks for enjoying a conversation or a good book. The informal and charming common areas include the main living room with a large fireplace, a library, card room, enclosed porch, and outdoor terraces. The artwork of Diane's daughter Terri graces the long corridors. A wide verandah looks toward the White Mountains in the distance and perennial gardens and orchards in the foreground.

The inn can hold one hundred people in the spiffy rooms and cottages, all furnished with simple antiques. Each room has a telephone and either two twins or a king-size bed covered with a handmade quilt. The corner rooms, numbers 29 and 30, at the end of the hall in the main inn, have sitting areas both inside and outside. Each cottage has a living room with a wood-burning fireplace, a service bar, and one or more bedrooms.

Carriage House rooms are the loveliest — very spacious and more romantic. Ask for a completely refurbished one, with fresh wallpaper, polished wood floors, and newly painted furniture.

Choose anything on the breakfast menu, including fruit, cereal, homemade muffins, eggs any style, pancakes, and sausage. Informal poolside lunches are served on the weekends. As for dinner, we recommend you plan to eat here once and see if the blend of Continental and old-fashioned New England cooking appeals to you. Rotating chefs come from a variety of culinary schools and some are more adept than others. A choice of three entrées is always offered. The service is friendly. Children's menus are available. The occasional lobster bakes and steak roasts around the pool are popular, and every Friday evening there is a lobster boil.

The highly regarded Weathervane Theatre (just down the road) is a big draw, and the inn offers very attractive theater packages, as well as family and golf packages.

Sporting facilities include four well-kept clay tennis courts (a tennis pro is on call), a large heated swimming pool, croquet and other lawn games, an 18-hole pitch 'n' putt golf course, and four excellent 18-hole courses nearby. Volleyball, shuffleboard, and a children's play area are popular.

As you approach the inn from one direction, you'll pass a huge decrepit yellow building, the former Mountain View Hotel. It stands as an arresting reminder of the area's heyday and prosperity. Those seeking a step back in time will be thankful that the Spalding Inn has survived.

Rhode Island

Best Bed-and-Breakfasts

Narragansett
  The Richards, 494
Newport
  Cliffside Inn, 495
  Elm Tree Cottage, 497
  The Francis Malbone House, 499
  Hydrangea House, 501
  Ivy Lodge, 502
  The Melville House, 504

Best Grand Resort

Weekapaug
  Weekapaug Inn, 509

Best Romantic Getaways

Newport
  Cliffside Inn, 495
  Elm Tree Cottage, 497
  The Francis Malbone House, 499

Newport, Newport, Newport — that's all most tourists see when they visit Rhode Island, but the Ocean State has much more to offer than the venerable seaport's glittering mansions and pricey waterfront shops. The South County shoreline has a string of what many consider to be the finest ocean beaches in the Northeast. The capital, Providence, is richly endowed with well-preserved 18th- and 19th-century buildings. And tranquil Block Island, 12 miles out to sea, is a Victorian jewel, still largely untouched by the commercial world.

Rhode Island's southern seacoast is known by locals as South County. Some 20 miles of public and private beach are the prime attraction here. There are barrier beaches, protecting a line of salt ponds that are the home of wild waterfowl and fish. Trustom Pond, Kimball Refuge, and the Great Swamp State Management Area are some of the wildlife sanctuaries worth visiting in the area. In **Narragansett,** a condominium-shopping complex overlooks Narragansett Beach, a favorite of surfers. South Kingstown has fine, unspoiled beaches, but parking for nonresidents can cost as much as $20.

The township of Westerly, on the Connecticut border, includes Watch Hill and Weekapaug. Watch Hill, a famous society watering hole of the early 1900s that has retained much of its gentility, has a charming waterfront arcade of small shops and a historic flying horse carousel. **Weekapaug,** less pretentious but with a more exclusive cottage colony, has an unspoiled, private shorefront. Between the two lies Misquamicut, a strip of family amusements and a state beach. A waterslide, roller-skating rink, and miniature golf course are among its attractions.

The second largest city in New England, **Providence** was founded in the 1600s by Roger Williams, a religious refugee from Massachusetts. Many fine 18th-century houses have been preserved in the College Hill and Benefit Street neighborhoods, on the east side. Beautifully restored Victorian houses dot the Broadway and Armory districts, on the west side. Although only a few houses are open to the public, the Providence Preservation Society sponsors walking tours.

The city's small downtown suffered an economic depression after its heyday in the early 1900s. Today, however, its lovely collection of vintage public buildings has been joined by some flashy new additions, and the Capitol Center project is pumping new life into the area.

Rhode Island's capital is also the home of Brown University and the Rhode Island School of Design as well as the nationally celebrated Trinity Square Repertory Company. Fancy shopping areas can be found in the Arcade (an 1828 Greek Revival building that was the country's first enclosed shopping mall), at Davol Square Marketplace (a former rubber factory complex), and along South Main Street (the center of Providence's shipping industry in the 17th and 18th centuries).

Newport has it all — nightlife, boutiques, fine restaurants, museums, mansions, yachting, ocean views, and swimming, as well as traffic and parking problems. The restored mansions of the Gilded Age robber barons are the undisputed stars of Newport. You may tour nearly a dozen of these carefully restored white elephants, relics of the time before income taxes were levied. Hammersmith Farm, the Auchincloss family estate that was used as a summer retreat by John F. Kennedy during his presidency, is also open for tours; its gardens are particularly lovely in the spring.

Newport's Colonial harborfront has been dwarfed by the tourist industry, but fine examples of 17th- and 18th-century architecture still exist. Hunter House Museum and Trinity Church are two of the best. Cliff Walk is a 3½-mile public park that wends its way between the backs of the Bellevue Avenue mansions and the ocean. The Walk and Ocean Drive, along the south coast, are two of Newport's most scenic public waterfront areas. Middletown, Newport's less ostentatious neighbor to the north, has good beaches (Sachuest is the most popular) and two notable historic restorations: Prescott Farm, the scene of a Revolutionary War skirmish, and Whitehall, the residence of British philosopher George Berkeley.

East of Newport, on the other side of the Sakonnet River, is a little strip of land, perhaps the least explored in Rhode Island. This narrow peninsula of farmland, crisscrossed by rock walls, affords lovely views of the water. Explore the tiny villages of Tiverton Four Corners and **Little Compton,** boasting the Sakonnet Vineyards and an active fishing harbor at the end of the point.

Block Island, less than 20 square miles in size, is reached by ferry from Galilee, Newport, and Providence or by air from Westerly. Largely residential, it attracts people who enjoy the quiet summer pleasures of swimming, sailing, fishing, and bird-watching. Mammoth, gently aging hotels have been island landmarks since the late 1800s. Excellent beaches line the island's east coast, where the sand is fine and white and the clear blue water breaks into a moderate surf. A scenic spot is Mohegan Bluffs, 150-foot clay cliffs on the south coast. Extensive conservation areas are open to the public, including Rodman's Hollow and the Maze. Old Harbor, the island's central village, has shops that are mostly of the postcard and T-shirt variety. A tiny movie theater and a handful of casual nightclubs provide the only nightlife, but there are several good restaurants.

Little Compton

The Roost

Sakonnet Vineyards
Little Compton, RI 02837
401-635-8486 (vineyard)
Fax: 401-635-2101
www.sakonnetwine.com

A small B&B associated with a winery

Manager: Jen Charleson. **Accommodations:** 3 rooms (all with private bath). **Rates:** $65–$80 per couple. **Included:** Continental breakfast. **Minimum stay:** 2 nights on weekends in the summer. **Added:** 7% tax. **Credit cards accepted:** MasterCard, Visa. **Children:** Over age 12 welcome. **Pets:** Not accepted. **Smoking:** Not permitted. **Handicap access:** No. **Open:** Year-round.

➤ **The vineyard is open for tours and tastings and has developed quite a following among Boston restauranteurs. Guests are encouraged to stroll amidst the grapevines and wander over to the reservoir for a picnic.**

You'll barely notice this little farmhouse at the vineyard's entrance. But it is a welcome retreat, for this undiscovered peninsula is well worth exploring and there is no other recommended place to stay in the area. This isn't a drop-in kind of place; reservations must be made through the vineyard. Nor is it the kind of place where the innkeepers are hovering over guests; it's for independent folks who want a good inexpensive place to rest their heads.

The small living room (perfect for two people) is comfortable, with magazines and cable TV. It opens onto a breakfast nook, which is just large enough to accommodate a trestle table. A Continental breakfast of muffins or scones and fruit is offered here.

The guest rooms are clustered at the top of the stairs on the second floor. They're crisp, somewhat urbane, and small. The blue room has a pickled floor, midnight blue walls, shuttered windows, a down comforter, and tiled shower. The beige room, in the front of the house, has a trundle bed; its bathroom is brightened by a skylight. The smaller gray room in the back of the house has two day beds; its bath is across the hall. Fine toiletries and nice bedding complete the picture.

The surrounding flat terrain, dotted with farm stands and rock walls, is a lovely place to bicycle. Six miles down the road is a working harbor.

Narragansett

The Richards

144 Gibson Avenue
Narragansett, RI 02882
401-789-7746
Fax: 401-783-1791

A restful hideaway made of stone

Hosts: Nancy and Steven Richard. **Accommodations:** 3 rooms (2 with private bath), 1 suite. **Rates:** $80–$125 per couple, $160 for 4 in suite. **Included:** Full breakfast. **Minimum stay:** 2 nights on weekends, 3 on holidays. **Added:** 5% tax. **Credit cards accepted:** None. **Children:** Over age 12 welcome. **Pets:** Not accepted. **Smoking:** Not permitted. **Handicap access:** No. **Open:** Year-round.

➤ **Nancy and Steven are personable and friendly without being intrusive. We immediately felt as if we were old friends visiting for the weekend.**

Many people overlook Narragansett, but once you discover The Richards, we bet you'll go out of your way to stay here. This formidable stone house, built in 1884 for the prominent Joseph P. Hazard family, is on the National Register of Historic Places. Secluded behind tall stands of trees, you approach it via a semicircular gravel driveway.

Ten-foot ceilings downstairs and 9-foot ones upstairs create a lofty sense of space. The dark entrance area opens to a grand hall, from which you can look up to the second-floor guest rooms or walk out to the grounds. The living room feels like an intimate club, with linen drapes, French doors, a fireplace, and a large, comfortable couch.

The guest rooms — each with a fireplace, down comforter, and thick towels — are decorated with a sure designer's touch. The rose room, with an old-fashioned bathroom, has a king-size bed and opens onto the yard. The 2-room lavender Hydrangea room, with a canopy bed and a couple of wicker chairs, has large, deep windows draped with swags and valances. If you are traveling as a foursome, inquire about the former maid's quarters, which have been converted into a nice two-bedroom suite with an adjoining bathroom.

Breakfast, served at the long mahogany table at 8:45 A.M., might feature baked apples, blueberry blintzes, a soufflé, or French toast made with Portuguese bread. After breakfast, take a 10-minute walk along a private way down to the rocky coast; there are plenty of relatively undiscovered beaches nearby. On property, Nancy recently added a fish pond and lots of new plantings, creating an even more lovely place to read a book.

Newport

In the past few years, the B&Bs we recommended have all continued to improve themselves in substantial ways. So, although the prices in Newport seem quite high, you actually get a lot for your money here, unlike some other resort towns in New England. Newport in the summertime is very crowded, so if you have flexibility in planning a getaway, consider coming midweek or better yet, in the off-season. There are hundreds and hundreds of beds in Newport, but we believe the following B&Bs are head and shoulders above the rest.

Cliffside Inn

2 Seaview Avenue
Newport, RI 02840
401-847-1811
800-845-1811
Fax: 401-848-5850
cliff@wsii.com
www.cliffsideinn.com

| A luxuriously romantic Victorian B&B |

Manager: Stephan Nicolas. **Accommodations:** 8 rooms (all with private bath) and 5 suites. **Rates:** $175–$325 per couple from May through December; lower in the off-season. **Included:** Full breakfast. **Minimum stay:** 2 nights on weekends. **Added:** 12% tax. **Credit cards accepted:** All major ones. **Children:** Over age 13 welcome. **Pets:** Not accepted. **Smoking:** Not permitted. **Handicap access:** No. **Open:** Year-round.

➤ **You won't want to miss the afternoon Victorian tea. Possible treats include savory spinach or crab wrapped in phyllo dough, finger sandwiches, scones, and raspberry tartlettes or lemon petit fours.**

The architecture and decor at Cliffside is high Victorian, but the pampering is pure 1990s: fireplaces and Jacuzzis have been added to most guest rooms. The decorators have struck a good balance between ornate antiques, elegant Victorian bric-a-brac, and light billowing fabrics.

This Victorian cottage was built as a summer getaway for Maryland's governor in 1880. It was later owned by Beatrice Pastorius Turner of Philadelphia, a famous portrait artist who spent her summers here. Beatrice painted more than 1,000 self-portraits from her home, more than 100 of which are on display at the inn. Located on a quiet residential side street about a mile from the center of town, the house is also a 5-minute walk from the famed Cliff Walk and First Beach. (Beach towels are provided.)

The combination living and dining room is dominated by a large mirror over an ornately carved mantel and fireplace. Many large self portraits of the reclusive Turner watch over the pink and green room. A full breakfast is served at two communal tables or on individual tables on the front porch when weather permits. Choices might include eggs Benedict, crêpes, or stuffed French toast. From 7:00 A.M. to 9:00 A.M. you can enjoy coffee, tea, and juice in the privacy of your room; all you have to do is ask one of the bustling staff members.

As for the rooms, all boast an extensive lineup of amenities: air conditioning, a telephone, a television with VCR (and a stash of movies), a basket of fruit, flowers, turndown service complete with sweet treats, triple sheeting, and plush bathrobes. Bay windows flood the house with light and illuminate the floral wallpaper and Laura Ashley fabrics.

Specifically, we like Attic, a contemporary room with skylights, a cathedral ceiling, and a whirlpool tub. The Miss Beatrice Room, one of the largest, has a black marble fireplace, an antique Lincoln-style bed, a large bathroom, and an overstuffed sofa under the bay window. The least-expensive room is also quite nice: The Library is small and cozy, with six different patterns of wallpaper!

The Governor's Suite (the most expensive room) boasts a double-faced fireplace that can be seen from the four-poster king bed as well as the Jacuzzi. The deluxe cherry- and oak-paneled bathroom has an antique double porcelain sink and a rare Victorian brass shower. The next most expensive room is the Tower Suite, a two-story room topped with an octagonal cathedral ceiling and cupola tower.

In 1996 two new suites were carved out of the Seaview Cottage. Of these we prefer the Atlantic suite, with skylights, cathedral ceiling, Jacuzzi, and a native stone fireplace.

Elm Tree Cottage

336 Gibbs Avenue
Newport, RI 02840
401-849-1610
888-ELM-TREE
Fax: 401-849-2084
elmtreebnb@aol.com
www.elmtreebnb.com

**High-style B&B rooms in a
transformed mansion**

Innkeepers: Priscilla and Tom Malone. **Accommodations:** 5 rooms (all with private bath), 1 suite. **Rates:** $165–$325 per couple from May through October; $145–$225 off-season. **Included:** Full breakfast. **Minimum stay:** 2 nights on weekends, 3 nights on holidays and weekends from June through October. **Added:** 12% tax. **Credit cards accepted:** All major ones. **Children:** Over age 14 welcome. **Pets:** Not accepted. **Smoking:** Not permitted. **Handicap access:** No. **Open:** Year-round except Christmas and January.

➤ **Both Malones have backgrounds in the fine arts — one in wood-working and painting, the other in stained glass. They have a design studio and glass-making studio in the basement.**

Designed by William Ralph Emerson in 1882 for the daughter of a famed Unitarian clergyman, this Shingle-style mansion is typical of Newport's magnificent summer cottages. It's on a quiet residential street just two blocks from the Cliff Walk and a mile from the center of town. The backyard is landscaped with lovely gardens, a pergola, and a little fieldstone bench nestled into a stone wall.

The interior, loaded with Queen Anne and Colonial Revival details, is quite spacious, to say the least. The living room is large enough for both an upright and a grand piano and for two formal sitting areas. Framed family photos of the Malones' three daughters are placed throughout. There's also a smaller, less formal sun room comfortably decorated with natural wicker and plants. A paneled and mirrored pub, said to resemble the cabin of the original owner's 1930s yacht, features complimentary bar setups.

The atmosphere in each guest room has been consciously and deliberately created. Decorating at Elm Tree is, in fact, an art that's referred to as "construction." Priscilla can't sit still; she is constantly making new window treatments or perfecting a vision she has for a room. Each guest room has plush wall-to-wall carpeting and air conditioning; most have fireplaces. Thoughtful touches include fresh flowers, wine glasses, and bottled water on silver trays.

Our favorite guest room, the first-floor Library Room, is richly designed in an English hunt theme. It overlooks the garden through large windows. When we last stayed here there were ten pillows on the bed! (This is one place where you'll appreciate turndown service.) Another favorite is the smaller Harriman Room, with a fireplace and striped-and-paisley burgundy wallpaper. The Windsor Suite, which measures 39 by 20 feet, is very formal, with a carved Louis XV style headboard on the king-size bed, two sitting areas, and a bathroom outfitted in crystal. Easton has a regal feel, with gold and burgundy tones and a puffy down comforter. Most of the rooms are corner rooms, so they receive good cross breezes and light.

A candlelit breakfast is served in the formal dining room where intimate tables are set with lace and linen. The entrée (there's a choice on weekends) may be something like herb scrambled eggs with chateau potatoes and heart-shaped toast or French toast soufflé with whipped maple cream.

The Francis Malbone House

392 Thames Street
Newport, RI 02840
401-846-0392
800-846-0392
Fax: 401-848-5956
www.malbone.com

| **Centrally located elegance** |

Manager: Will Dewey. **Assistant manager:** Mary Francis Mahaffey. **Accommodations:** 16 rooms (all with private bath), 2 suites. **Rates:** $165–$325 per couple from May through October; $135–$225 off-season. **Included:** Full breakfast. **Minimum stay:** 2 nights on weekends in season. **Added:** 12% tax. **Credit cards accepted:** All major ones. **Children:** Over age 12. **Pets:** Not accepted. **Smoking:** Not permitted. **Handicap access:** Yes. **Open:** Year-round.

➤ **Strong evidence suggests that Colonel Malbone had an underground tunnel built from the shoreline to the house so that he could avoid paying duty on much of his merchandise.**

Built in 1760 for a wealthy shipping merchant and used as a storehouse for British gold during the Revolutionary War, this yellow Colonial brick mansion sits right on busy Thames Street. (Most of the guest rooms are well shielded from the sidewalk noise.) Its proximity to the harbor makes it an ideal base for walking tours of the city. Although the house looks imposing and is listed on the National Historic Register, it's quite welcoming. Since Francis Malbone feels more like a small luxury hotel than a B&B, those who shy away from more intimate B&Bs will appreciate the atmosphere here.

One of the most architecturally and historically significant houses in Newport, the mansion is attributed to architect Peter Harrison, who also designed the old Touro Synagogue. The 13,000-square-foot mansion has high ceilings, spacious rooms, and elegant furnishings. The period details have been superbly restored, and the integrity of the original interior colors has been retrieved through extensive research. Three common rooms on the first floor — furnished with comfortable upholstered furniture — provide plenty of space to stretch out. One of the living rooms has a TV; they each have a fireplace.

In late 1995 the inn constructed one of the most "sensitively" designed additions we've encountered. It's absolutely wonderful. Nine new luxury rooms surround a tranquil courtyard, the perfect respite from Newport bustle. (If you're a light sleeper, request one of these rooms.) Rooms are linked by an interior brick walkway and the hallway is lined with Portuguese tiles. French doors open onto the courtyard complete with columns, winding wisteria, Adirondack chairs, and a bubbling fountain. Of these new guest rooms (all with king-size bed, fireplace, television, and Jacuzzi), we prefer the room on the ground floor with immediate courtyard access.

The guest rooms in the original house, six of which have working fireplaces, are furnished with high four-poster beds topped with puffy white comforters, crisp bedding, and lots of pillows. White molding provides a modern accent to the warm Colonial furnishings and wall hangings. The Counting House suite — one very long room — features a four-poster king-size bed, a sitting area with foldout couch, a dining table, and a two-person Jacuzzi. It has its own private entrance onto Thames Street.

A bountiful breakfast is served in the domed dining room. Guests may be served quiche, pumpkin waffles, or eggs Benedict in addition to a selection of fruit and baked goods. In the afternoon cakes and pastries are offered. Throughout the day, "colossal" cookies and lemon squares are set out for guests; they tend to disappear quickly. The hospitable staff is adept at making guests feel at home. Stephanie Walmsley, who greets guests from the kitchen in the evening, acts as a concierge; she knows Newport quite well.

Hydrangea House

16 Bellevue Avenue
Newport, RI 02840
401-846-4435
800-945-4667
Fax: 401-846-4435
bandbinn@ids.net
www.bestinns.net/usa/ri/hydr.html

An artsy, European-style B&B

Hosts: Grant Edmondson and Dennis Blair. **Accommodations:** 5 rooms (all with private bath), 1 suite. **Rates:** $89–$139 per couple from May through October. **Included:** Full breakfast. **Minimum stay:** 2 nights on weekends, 3 nights on event and holiday weekends. **Added:** 12% tax. **Credit cards accepted:** Master-Card, Visa. **Children:** Welcome. **Pets:** Not accepted. **Smoking:** Not permitted. **Handicap access:** No. **Open:** Year-round.

➤ **Note this offer: from November through April (excluding Christmas week), check in Sunday through Wednesday and stay a second night for free.**

The Hydrangea House, with a striking deep purple exterior, resembles a small European pension with hospitable and welcoming hosts. Located in Newport's "walking district," the house is a convenient oasis from the hordes that descend on the area in the summer. Flower boxes brighten the windowsills, and the namesake hydrangea plants bloom profusely (in season) at the rear of the house.

The B&B has an artsy feel to it, with yellow-veined faux marble in the hallways. In 1997 Grant and Dennis added the magnificent Hydrangea Suite, which will surely illicit a round of oohs and aahs when you enter. It's spacious but handsome and cozy, with colors of forest green and plush fabrics. A fireplace is visible from both the two-person Jacuzzi and the half-canopy king bed. (There is also a steam shower.)

The other guest rooms are also individually furnished with stylish antiques that Grant and Dennis acquired from their former antique business. (They have owned Hydrangea House since 1988.) One bright bedroom, with coordinated floral wallpaper, bedspread, and drapes, has a writing table and comfy upholstered chairs. This large room is one of our favorites, although it is in the front of the house. Even though the drapes muffle the street noise, non-city dwellers may still wish to request another room. Another favorite room is actually the least expensive; it's a bit dark but very cozy.

A full breakfast is served on the quiet, flower-filled rear deck, or in the dining room cum art gallery on the first floor. Offerings include an egg entrée or something sweet, perhaps raspberry pancakes with fruit salad. You can always have Dennis's homemade granola and a house-blend coffee.

The B&B has two very different, very comfortable common areas. The street-level living room is elegant but inviting, genteel and subdued. The refined mood is set with fine fabrics and upholstery, fanciful antiques, rose carpeting, and crown molding. Although you can hear street noise from here, you feel quite insulated from it. The living room is particularly inviting at night: You'll get the feeling you're staying in a friend's sophisticated flat for a couple of days. In the winter a fire is set here and afternoon tea is served.

In the summer, the back porch is partially enclosed with latticework and essentially functions as another room. It has two sitting areas with iron patio furniture, worn Oriental carpets, and a refrigerator stocked with complimentary beverages.

The scale and price of rooms at the Hydrangea House is refreshing for Newport.

Ivy Lodge

12 Clay Street
Newport, RI 02840
401-849-6865
800-834-6865

| **A romantic B&B mansion just off Bellevue Avenue** |

Hosts: Maggie and Terry Moy. **Accommodations:** 6 rooms (all with private bath) and 1 family suite. **Rates:** $135–$185 per couple May through December; $200 for four in the family suite. **Included:** Full breakfast. **Minimum stay:** 2 nights on most weekends, 3 nights on holidays and during festivals. **Added:** 12% tax. **Credit cards accepted:** All major ones. **Children:** Welcome. **Pets:** Not accepted. **Smoking:** Restricted. **Handicap access:** No. **Open:** Year-round.

➤ **Most of the guest rooms are quite spacious, especially the Turret Room, which features a king-size bed, a sitting area tucked into the turret, and a large bathroom across the hall with a soaking tub.**

The inn has an absolutely exquisite 33-foot-high, oak-paneled entry hall designed by Stanford White, complete with a brick fireplace that glows on cool afternoons. The open foyer is impressive, with rich oak ceilings, paneling, and 365 spindle balusters. On a quiet, tree-lined street, this 1880s Queen Anne Victorian is nicely positioned between the beach, mansions, and downtown.

The particularly spacious drawing room has a baby grand piano and comfortable, elegant furnishings. A smaller sitting room has upholstered wicker chairs. In warm weather you can relax on the wraparound porch, with afternoon snacks, next to the 100-year-old Japanese maple.

There isn't a guest room we would hesitate to recommend. They are all comfortably furnished, brightly decorated, and nicely maintained by a diligent staff. The Ivy Room, so called because of the ivy wall-paper, can connect with Turret to accommodate two couples or a family. Rooms 1 and 2, each with a long window seat, share an outdoor balcony. One of the smallest (and least expensive) rooms is also one of our favorites: it has a lovely bedstead and mantel. It is hidden away on the first floor, and although its bathroom (with Jacuzzi) is across the hall, robes are provided. A cozy but bright two-room suite, perfect for families, is tucked up under the eaves on the third floor. One other third-floor room has two double beds.

The Moys, who have owned the house since 1987, and their staff know how to impress with breakfasts. A buffet is set up at one long mahogany dining table and always features a hot entrée, like blueberry blintzes or popovers with peaches and Romanoff sauce. You can also have your fill of fruit, croissants, special breakfast cakes, and assorted muffins. Maggie is a former social worker who still likes "doing good for people." Indeed, that includes making sure people leave feeling quite relaxed and refreshed.

The Melville House

39 Clarke Street
Newport, RI 02840
401-847-0640
Fax: 401-847-0956
innkeeper@ids.net

> **A good value in the heart of Colonial Newport**

Innkeepers: Vincent DeRico and David Horan. **Accommodations:** 7 rooms (5 with private bath). **Rates:** $110–$145 per couple from May through October; $85–$110 off-season, except $165 for the wintertime suite. **Included:** Full breakfast. **Minimum stay:** 2 nights on summer weekends, 3 on holidays. **Added:** 12% tax. **Credit cards accepted:** All major ones. **Children:** Welcome, but rooms are too small for an extra bed. **Pets:** Not accepted. **Smoking:** Not permitted. **Handicap access:** No. **Open:** Year-round.

➤   **From November to April, the innkeepers convert two guest rooms into one suite. The lucky guests receive champagne on arrival, after-dinner drinks, and breakfast in bed. Or they can dine leisurely, at whatever time they want, on almost whatever they want, in front of their own fireplace.**

Newport has a strong Colonial history, so it seems only fitting to include a bed-and-breakfast that recaptures this period. Furthermore, it's the most reasonably priced recommended lodging in Newport. Vincent and David, who purchased the Melville House in 1993, come from careers in the hospitality and restaurant business. Whenever we visit the Melville House, we appreciate anew its unpretentious atmosphere, especially in comparison to some of its fussier neighbors.

The circa-1750 house sits right on the gas-lit street. Upon entering, you'll be offered biscotti (or some treat baked by David) and tea or sherry, depending on the time of day and season. In the winter the innkeepers often have a hearty soup simmering on the stove. The small country living room is quite homey, with a couch and rocking chair flanking the fireplace. The living room, which houses an interesting collection of antique household appliances, opens onto the bright yellow breakfast room. The buffet breakfast always features the inn's granola and might include Rhode Island Johnny cakes and Yankee cornbread, followed by a hot entrée.

The low ceilings of this historic house lend the guest rooms a cozy feel. Fortunately, central air conditioning keeps the place cool in the summer. Guest rooms are small (remember, this is a Colonial house) and furnished comfortably with solid Colonial and Early American pieces. The hodgepodge of period furnishings — bureaus, chests, pineapple-post beds, braided rugs, muted floral wallpapers, and lacy curtains — all work quite nicely. The bathrooms are small but they've been nicely updated. Two couples traveling together often rent the rooms that share a bath. Primitive-style murals decorate the hallways.

Located in the quiet, downtown historic district, the Melville House is just a 2-minute walk to the Brick Marketplace and the waterfront. Another big plus: it's also only a minute to Newport's best restaurant. Vincent can tell you all about it; it happens to be his favorite too. Vincent's a gardener and has done an impressive job with the postage-stamp-size yard.

Vanderbilt Hall

P.O. Box 840
41 Mary Street
Newport, RI 02840
401-846-6200
888-VAN-HALL
Fax: 401-846-0701

A mansion house hotel

General manager: Lewis Kiesler. **Accommodations:** 45 rooms (all with private bath), 5 suites. **Rates:** $195–$395 per couple in rooms, $395–$650 per week. **Included:** All meals are served. **Minimum stay:** None. **Added:** 12% tax, 8% service. **Credit cards accepted:** All major ones. **Children:** Over age 13 welcome. **Pets:** Not accepted. **Smoking:** Not permitted. **Handicap access:** Yes. **Open:** Year-round.

➤ **The billiards room, complete with fireplace and leather chairs, is reminiscent of grand country hotels. Some will want to enjoy brandy and a cigar here.**

Opened in the summer of 1997, this turn-of-the-century property immediately elevated the already high standard of quality and service of the lodging scene in Newport. Located just blocks from the waterfront in the "Historic Hill District," the distinctive, four-story manse was built in 1909 in memory of Cornelius Vanderbilt and given to the town thereafter.

The grand house is formal yet inviting; its elegant public rooms have high ceilings, original paneling, polished hardwood floors, deep-seated furniture, and fireplaces. A piano takes center stage in the music room. There are plenty of nooks for reading. On the ground floor is an indoor heated pool, sauna, steam room, and fitness room; some spa treatments are offered. The brick courtyard, complete with an herb greenhouse, is a quiet place to sit. And you'll also want to head up to the small roof deck to get a glimpse of the town and harbor.

All the guest rooms have some elements in common: tasteful period furnishings, a few eclectic objects, fine Frette linens, luxurious toiletries, and thick cotton robes. Many rooms have views of the ocean or the Trinity Church steeple. Some are decorated with themes — tennis or polo, art deco or world traveler, Victorian or Regency. Some bathrooms have whirlpools and towel warmers. The rooms in the older part of the house have higher ceilings than the newer wing.

Rooms fall into five categories: house, state, studio, executive study, and suites. "House" rooms are the smallest (we like the topiary theme in #7), while "executive studies" have been designed with the business traveler in mind. The two-floor Lighthouse room features a spiral staircase that leads up to a work area with dedicated fax line. "State" rooms are more plush while "studios" are particularly spacious (we liked the high ceilings in #14).

Since the hotel had only been open for a few days when we visited, we chose not to dine there and judge them so quickly. (To be fair, it takes a little while to work out the bugs and kinks.) At its inception, the restaurant served two- and three-course prix-fixe lunches for $17.50 and $24.50, respectively, and five-course dinners for $50 per person. You'll want to check the menu to see what's cooking and ask your fellow travelers if they've dined there. The richly paneled dining rooms are graciously set with Wedgewood china and Rosenthal crystal. All indications on our initial visit led us to believe the kitchen, service, and ambiance would be as accomplished as the rest of the hotel.

Providence

The Old Court

144 Benefit Street
Providence, RI 02903
401-751-2002
401-351-0747
Fax: 401-272-4830
reserve@oldcourt.com
www.oldcourt.com

A tasteful B&B in a historic neighborhood

Manager: David Dolbashian. **Accommodations:** 10 rooms (all with private bath), 1 suite. **Rates:** $115–$135 per couple from March to mid-November; $85–$115 off-season. **Included:** Full breakfast. **Minimum stay:** 2 or 3 nights on event weekends. **Added:** 12% tax. **Credit cards accepted:** MasterCard, Visa. **Children:** Over age 12 welcome; $20 for a cot. **Pets:** Not accepted. **Smoking:** Not permitted. **Handicap access:** No. **Open:** Year-round.

➤   **The Old Court is in a quiet, historic neighborhood just minutes from the Rhode Island School of Design and Brown University and just down the hill from the city's business and shopping district.**

The Old Court is far and away the nicest place to stay in Providence. Built in 1863 as an Episcopal church rectory, the three-story brick building was gutted in 1986 and remodeled with Victorian styling. Twelve-foot ceilings and Italian architectural detailing coexist with such modern conveniences as coffee percolators, air conditioning, and in-room televisions and phones.

The noticeable lack of common space doesn't seem to be a problem for most of the guests, who spend much of their time around the city rather than at the inn. Breakfast is served at a large mahogany table or smaller bistro tables.

The guest rooms, with hardwood floors and Oriental carpets, are well appointed, typically with antiques like Chippendale clocks or Eastlake furniture. Most of the rooms are quite spacious, though two of our favorites are on the smaller side. One is decorated in a country style; the other is on the first floor, with a brass bed and old stove. The modern bathrooms are tiled in gray and white. Two suites have wet bars.

Across the street, a tastefully furnished first-floor brownstone apartment is perfect for families with older children, couples traveling together, or for longer stays. It has two bedrooms, a modern kitchen, a living room, and access to a shaded backyard brick patio.

Weekapaug

Weekapaug Inn

25 Spring Avenue
Weekapaug, RI 02891
401-322-0301

> A grand old resort with a
> mile-long private beach

Owners: Jim and DeeDee Buffum. **Accommodations:** 55 rooms (most with private bath), 10 rooms "on the bridge" (share 2 baths). **Rates:** $330–$350 per couple. **Included:** All meals. **Minimum stay:** 2 nights. **Added:** 12% tax, gratuity additional. **Credit cards accepted:** No credit cards. **Children:** Welcome; rates from $40–$85 nightly depending on age and location. **Pets:** Not accepted. **Smoking:** Not permitted indoors. **Handicap access:** No. **Open:** Mid-June to early September; open for a few weeks prior and after that for special functions.

➤ **There are very few family places like this remaining on coastal New England. There are no TVs or phones in the rooms, but there are plenty of lawn chairs from which you can settle into a good book.**

Although Weekapaug is one of the least-known old-fashioned family resorts in New England, it is certainly still one of the best. The location of this weathered gray building is lovely — on a spit of land surrounded by the sea and sheltered by a breakwater. It offers all of the facilities of a complete resort (tennis, boating, sailing, windsurfing, lawn bowling, croquet, shuffleboard, and ocean swimming), plus good food and a lack of pretension. The guest rooms, though small and evocative of grandmother's house rather than your city cousin, are immaculate.

There are some "family rooms" that adjoin and other "family rooms" that are actually large, one-room suites with a pullout couch and space for a crib. Generally, rooms have simple white curtains and maple furnishings. We try to avoid ground-floor rooms, which have more exposed plumbing pipes than second-floor rooms. (Remember, though, that this is an old summer hotel, and all the bathrooms recall earlier days.) Corner rooms are not as spacious as some other rooms, but they are brighter. And if you want a water view (which faces due east), you will not get the benefit of southwesterly breezes.

The old-fashioned common rooms offer enough space so that even when the inn is full (with a maximum of 90 guests), the place does not feel crowded. The paneled Pond Room is an informal gathering area where guests mix their own drinks (BYOB) before dinner and relax in front of the fire overlooking the water. The Sea Room, a large living room, is used for bridge, bingo, and an occasional movie. It is encircled by a spacious wooden porch that faces the pond, sea, and breakwater. A wraparound deck, with plenty of rockers, faces the ocean.

The food is very good, although it stops short of gourmet. Seats are assigned for the length of your stay, so a nice rapport develops between you and your college-age server. (They're a close knit, enthusiastic bunch.) At breakfast, guests can have as much off the menu as they want. Lunch is a beautifully presented buffet with two main choices: Maine crab cakes and Greek-style pizza on our last visit. Box lunches are available with prior notice.

Bill Wolf has been the chef since the late 1980s, so there's a nice consistency in the kitchen. At dinnertime (jackets are requested for men), Bill offers dishes that appeal to a variety of palates, young and old, refined and not so. Perhaps offerings will include grilled salmon or filet mignon, or baked stuffed lobster, or seared sea scallops over bok choy with a Thai dressing. There are always about 10 choices, so you should have no problem finding something to suit you. Lobster is served every Friday, and on Thursdays there is an informal barbecue on the back lawn. On Sundays the buffet is more elaborate, while supper is lighter than usual. Deserts are homespun.

There are supervised morning and evening children's programs, which might include nature trips, arts and crafts, movies, and storytelling. Babysitters are also available. (Children who are old enough can sleep in the rooms on "the bridge.") Two public golf courses are close by, and a splendid, mile-long unpopulated beach is just a short walk away. In early June and late September, the resort caters to family gatherings and weddings.

The resort has been in the Buffum family since it was built by Jim's great grandfather in 1899. In late 1996, Jim and DeeDee bought out the other family members, so it should be easier for changes to be implemented.

Vermont

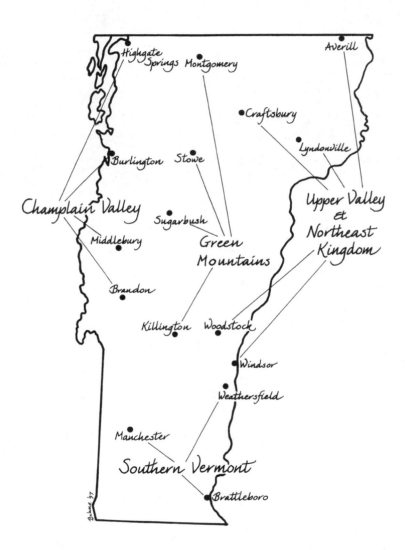

Highgate Springs Montgomery

Averill

Craftsbury

Lyndonville

Burlington Stowe

Champlain Valley

Upper Valley & Northeast Kingdom

Sugarbush

Middlebury

Green Mountains

Brandon

Killington Woodstock

Windsor

Weathersfield

Manchester

Southern Vermont

Brattleboro

B. Wise '97

Southern Vermont

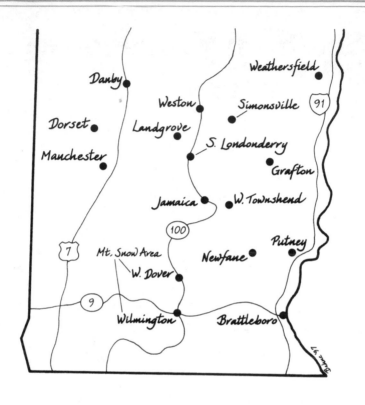

Best Bed-and-Breakfasts

Best Family Finds

Best Gourmet Getaways

Best Grand Resort

Manchester
The Equinox, 536

Best Inns

Danby
Silas Griffith Inn, 525
Grafton
The Old Tavern at Grafton, 529

Best Romantic Getaways

Manchester
The Inn at Ormsby Hill, 538
The Reluctant Panther, 541
Mount Snow Area
The Inn at Sawmill Farm, 543
Trails End, A Country Inn, 545

Vermont is one state that defies an attempt to outline itineraries. Every Green Mountain community offers something of interest, and there are any number of scenic ways of getting from one village to the next. What you do in Vermont is pick a place — ideally, several places — to stay and then poke around the surrounding countryside, exploring back roads that go in all directions.

Vermont is also difficult to break into regions. The Champlain Valley is on the west and the Connecticut Valley on the east, but nowhere are you out of sight of mountains, and everywhere you find the steepled white churches, general stores, farmland, and country inns for which Vermont is known.

Interstate highways play little part in exploring Vermont. True, I-91 snakes up the eastern edge, a conduit for visitors from the south, and I-93 and I-89 usher in flatlanders from the west. But Route 100, a twisty old two-lane road that follows the spine of the Green Mountains right up the middle of the state, remains its principal connector.

Having said all this, we'll divide the Green Mountain State into regions and suggest some ways of getting around.

Brattleboro, at the confluence of the Connecticut and West rivers in the southeastern corner of the state, is a funky, friendly red brick town, a great place to stop for lunch and some shopping. It's the gateway to the West River valley, with the classic white clapboard towns of **Newfane, West Townshend** — both with outstanding village commons — and **Jamaica,** all strung like pearls along Route 30.

Don't miss **Putney,** known for its scholars and craftspeople and as the hometown of Basketville. It's north of Brattleboro on Route 5, and you can cut back over to Route 30 on a narrow, paved back road over the hills and down through a covered bridge, coming out just south of Newfane.

The conventional route west from Brattleboro to the **Mount Snow area** and Bennington is Route 9, the Molly Stark Trail; it's a fine but heavily trafficked and touristed road that passes Marlboro, the site of a famous summer concert series. If you take this route, be sure to pull out at the designated area west of Marlboro, to enjoy the dramatic multistate view from the top of Hogback Mountain, and to stroll around Wilmington (at the junction of Routes 9 and 100), a picturesque resort town and trading center.

The alternate way from Newfane to West Dover (Mount Snow) is west from Route 30 (turn on the West Dumerston Road) over an exceptional back road that follows the Rock River through Williamsville and South Newfane (a tiny gem of a village). The road takes you over steep hills and down to Route 100 in the Deerfield Valley, which is dominated by Mount Snow and Haystack, two ski resorts with 18-hole golf courses. While the nine miles north to Mount Snow are lined with motels, shops, restaurants, and condominiums, the scenery changes abruptly just north of the entrance to Mt. Snow. Here Route 100 becomes a wooded byway for the eight miles it takes to join Route 30 in East Jamaica.

Routes 30 and 100 part again not many miles farther north, the former continuing west past Stratton Mountain (one of Vermont's most sophisticated ski resorts) and on to **Manchester,** known for its shopping and its fine summer arts center. Manchester Village is one of New England's most elegant summer resorts, with its marble sidewalks, golf courses, a grand hotel, and Hildene, a fabulous mansion built by Robert Todd Lincoln, the son of the president.

From Manchester you can head north on Route 7 to the handsome old community of **Dorset** (known for its summer theater) and continue through this wide valley to Wallingford. Or you can turn east again, quickly climbing into the Green Mountains on Route 11, passing Big Bromley Ski Area (which maintains an Alpine Slide in warm weather). Take Route 11 north at Peru on the Landgrove

Road, a scenic byway. This passes the Hapgood Recreation Area (a great summer swimming spot) and continues through the village of **Landgrove** on the way back to join Route 100 in Weston (just 12 miles north of where it left Route 30).

Weston is one of Vermont's most famous villages, complete with an oval common, a bandstand, one of the country's oldest and best summer playhouses, and the state's most famous general store (it was the first to turn itself into a nostalgia outlet, complete with mail-order catalogue). You can take a pleasant road east (maybe detouring a mile to **Simonsville**) for 11 miles to Chester, a proud old town with a fine historical society and art guild and excursion trains connecting it with both Bellows Falls and Ludlow. Seven miles south is **Grafton,** an exquisite village that has been called Vermont's Cinderella. A decaying derelict as late as the early 1960s, the entire village — including its inn and cheese company — have been restored by a private foundation. Of course, you can also reach Grafton by driving 9 miles up Route 35 from Townshend.

Drive north from Chester, or from Weston, or west through Cuttingsville from Wallingford and you come to Ludlow, a former mill town (the picturesque mill has been converted to condominiums). It has a major ski resort, Okemo, rising from its heart. East of Ludlow you pass through the former mill village of Proctorsville, on through river valleys that gradually widen into rich farmland around **Weathersfield.** North from Ludlow, Route 100 follows a chain of lakes all the way to Plymouth, where a small white clapboard village has been preserved, complete with cheese factory, because it was the boyhood home of Calvin Coolidge.

Brattleboro

Latchis Hotel

50 Main Street
Brattleboro, VT 05301
802-254-6300
www.brattleboro.com/latchis

An Art Deco downtown hotel

Innkeeper: Elizabeth Latchis. **Accommodations:** 30 rooms, 3 suites. **Rates:** $67–$110 per couple per room; $140 for deluxe suite; off-season: $62–$95 per room, $120 per suite. **Included:** Continental breakfast. **Minimum stay:** None. **Added:** 9% tax. **Credit cards accepted:** All major ones. **Children:** No charge under age 12. **Pets:** Not accepted. **Smoking:** Restricted. **Handicap access:** No. **Open:** Year-round.

➤ **The air-conditioned rooms are cheerfully furnished with a mix of Art Deco and country pieces.**

The Latchis Hotel is the antithesis of the classic Vermont country inn, and Brattleboro is no clapboard village. But both the Latchis and Brattleboro hold considerable charm for those who can appreciate a 1930s Art Deco hotel built to serve a red brick town. The wonder is that the hotel has been restored and the town retains its unusual vitality.

The hotel was built by Peter Latchis, whose father, Demetrius, emigrated from Greece in 1901. It has been restored with loving care by his grandson and his wife, from its terrazzo floors and chrome fixtures to its ornate movie theater.

Don't be put off by the exterior. Rooms are all nicely furnished, equipped with TVs and coffeemakers. Those to request are on the second and third floors (there's an elevator), with views down Main Street and across to Wantastiquet Mountain, just the other side of the Connecticut River.

Brattleboro, at the confluence of the Connecticut and West rivers in the southeastern corner of Vermont, offers an unusual number of restaurants and shops, ranging from Sam's Army & Navy (two floors of two buildings, right across from the hotel) to crafts and alternative bookstores and boutiques.

In its bowels the hotel harbors the Windham Brewery, a small brewery with a growing reputation, and the attractive Latchis

Grille, decorated with paintings of Brattleboro and serving entrées like seafood quesadilla and grilled, marinated lamb chops; there's also a café menu with reasonably priced offerings like fried calamari Gloria and Louisiana meatloaf.

Fresh muffins are delivered to guest rooms at 8:00 A.M.

Naulakha

c/o Landmark Trust
RR1, Box 510
Brattleboro, VT 05301
802-254-6868 for inquiries
For reservations: 011-44-1628-825-925
Fax: 011-44-1628-825-471

> **Spend a week in Rudyard Kipling's Vermont home**

Director: David Tansey. **Accommodations:** 4 rooms. **Rates:** $1,200–$2,000 per week for the house; $250–$265 per night off-season. Note: rates are tied to the British pound and so fluctuate with the exchange rate. **Minimum stay:** 3 nights. **Included:** Full use of house and 55 acres; no tax. **Credit cards accepted:** MasterCard, Visa. **Children:** Welcome; cribs available. **Pets:** Permitted. **Smoking:** Restricted. **Handicap access:** No. **Open:** Year-round.

➤   **"Naulakha" is an Indian word meaning great treasure.**

In 1893 Rudyard Kipling, still in his twenties but already widely recognized as a writer, built this long, arc-like shingle mansion on the shoulder of a hill near Brattleboro. In his uncluttered library — with a view across the Connecticut River Valley to Mount Monadnock — he wrote *Jungle Book, Captains Courageous,* and *Just So Stories.*

The house has been meticulously restored by the Landmark Trust, an English nonprofit foundation that maintains more than 150 historic properties as moderately priced rental properties in Great Britain. This is Landmark's first project in America, and it is very impressive. With the exception of modern appliances, the house looks much as it did during the three years in which Kipling lived and wrote here. More than half the furnishings — including a third-floor pool table — actually belonged to the Kiplings.

Rudyard Kipling built Naulakha (meaning "great treasure") to be a secluded retreat in which he could write in peace. You may notice that while the house is filled with light from its many windows, the ground-floor sills are unusually high above the ground, designed to foil snooping reporters. Kipling came to this southeastern corner of Vermont to be near his wife Caroline's family, but it was a court case against his brother-in-law that blew his cover and forced him to leave Brattleboro — and America.

While Kipling's fame continued to increase, even its subsequent owners seemed to forget about Naulakha. It remained in the Cabot family from 1903 until the Landmark Trust purchased it in 1992 and renovated it from top to bottom — with far more care and scholarship than a commercial contractor could have done.

Even if Kipling hadn't lived here, this would be a glorious spot for a large family or four couples to rent for a week — it has three stories, long and narrow, the better to maximize the light and view. The four bedrooms are spacious and comfortable. The plumbing is new but fixtures are original; you can steep in the same deep tub in which Kipling wrote of "luxuriously parboiling."

The property is set among its own 55 acres and there is plenty to do in this cultured corner of Vermont: music festivals, crafts studios and galleries, horseback riding, canoeing, and more. Needless to say, however, the house itself is the big attraction here. There is simply nowhere else in the world that you can curl up with the Jungle books on a sofa by a fire, only a few feet from where they were written.

Danby

Silas Griffith Inn

R.R. 1
P.O. Box 66F
Danby, VT 05739
802-293-5567
800-545-1509
Fax: 802-93-5559

> **A country inn in an**
> **elaborate mansion**

Innkeepers: Lois and Paul Dansereau. **Accommodations:** 17 rooms (14 with private bath). **Rates:** $87–$107 per couple; off-season: $72–$92 per couple; family packages. **Included:** Full breakfast, afternoon tea; dinner also served (MAP rates available). **Minimum stay:** 2 nights on holiday weekends. **Added:** 9% tax. **Credit cards accepted:** MasterCard, Visa. **Children:** Under age 10, free; 11 and older, $15; not appropriate at dinner. **Smoking:** Not permitted indoors. **Pets:** Not accepted. **Handicap access:** No. **Open:** Year-round except early December and April.

➤ **"My aim was to make it comfortable," says Lois Dansereau. "There are a lot of Victorian inns with stained glass windows, and too many are too stiff."**

Danby is a small village, not the kind of place where you would expect to find one of the grandest mansions in all of Vermont. The inn is near the old domain of the lumber baron Silas Griffith. Now called the Green Mountain National Forest, it's the new domain of hikers and cross-country skiers. Lois and Paul are avid hikers and share useful information about area trails.

Built in 1891, this very Victorian house has exceptional detailing: handcarved cherry woodwork, stained glass, embossed tin ceilings, marble sinks, and unusual touches, like the sliding door designed to resemble a moon gate. This door opens onto a TV and game room. There's also a spacious, inviting, carpeted "great room" with deep sofas, a big hearth, and shelves and shelves of books. Rockers fill the shaded front porch.

The emphasis on comfort and hominess is evident in the guest rooms, right down to a bowl of apples on arrival. One favorite is #16, with a huge bed made specifically for the room. Another is #15, with a circular bay window, tin ceiling, and beautiful fireplace. Although #14 is small, it has a lovely marble sink in the room and a tiny balcony. The house has nine rooms and the rehabbed carriage house eight more; all are nicely fitted with antiques. Bath robes are provided for the rooms with shared bath. Carriage house rooms are furnished in a simple country style, all with wall-to-wall carpeting.

Meals are served in the carriage house dining room, decorated with what Lois describes as "thirty years' worth of gadgets." It has a fireplace and a bar. The menu, which always includes meat, fowl, and fish entrées, might feature a sun-dried tomato and onion tart, a fresh pea salad with greens and wild honey dressing, a choice of baked scrod or beef bourguignon, and a hot fudge sundae cake with vanilla ice cream.

Breakfast specialties include a variety of pancakes and almond French toast made from challah bread. A favorite selection is ginger pancakes with fresh peaches.

In summer, guests can swim in the pool or in nearby Emerald Lake. It's also just two miles to the Appalachian Trail and twelve miles to the galleries, shops, and outlets of Manchester. In winter, there's cross-country skiing in the national forest and downhill skiing at six fairly close slopes.

Dorset

Cornucopia of Dorset

P.O. Box 307
Routc 30
Dorset, VT 05251
802-867-5751
Fax: 802-867-5753
corncop@vermontel.com
www.cornucopiaofdorset.com

> **A small, romantic B&B**

Innkeepers: Linda and Bill Ley. **Accommodations:** 4 rooms (all with private bath), 1 suite. **Rates:** $115–$225 per couple in season. **Included:** Full breakfast. **Minimum stay:** Required at certain times. **Added:** 9% tax. **Credit cards accepted:** MasterCard, Visa. **Children:** Over age 16 welcome. **Pets:** Not accepted. **Smoking:** Not permitted. **Handicap access:** No. **Open:** Year-round.

➤ **The Owl's Head cottage behind the inn is the most romantic accommodation. The spacious two-floor cottage, with its own fully equipped kitchen, features a living room with cathedral ceiling, a loft bedroom with skylights, a wood-burning fireplace, and a private deck.**

Linda and Bill Ley pamper their guests and their guests love it. Here are just a few of the ways. On arrival you are offered a glass of champagne that can be enjoyed in your room or the living room. Bill and Linda make dinner recommendations and reservations for guests. When you've decided where you'll be having dinner, they leave a miniature copy of the menu in your room. They offer to bring a coffee or tea tray to your room in the morning. They request that you let them know what time you'd like breakfast so that it may be cooked to order. They provide turn-down service with fancy chocolates. And they'll light the oil lamp in your room.

The white clapboard building has a hideaway feel to it, even though it's right on Route 30. The backyard features a sheltered marble patio. Adirondack chairs are placed around the manicured lawns and extensive gardens, so there are plenty of places to relax in privacy. Linda and Bill take great pride in creating an atmosphere guests thoroughly enjoy.

The entire first floor is given over to common space, including a sun room, with a wall of windows, white sectional couches (please, don't leave the newspaper here lest the ink turn the white couch gray), and a television with VCR (there are plenty of movies on hand). In addition, there are two more small living rooms with fireplaces. Kitt, the sweet inn dog, will even win over cat lovers.

On a recent stay, breakfast was served at one long table and included freshly squeezed juice, an artful fruit and yogurt course, and baked eggs and smoked bacon in maple toast "nests" with hollandaise.

As for the guest rooms, there are four spacious chambers in the completely renovated, turn-of-the-century house. Scallop is a corner room with a wood-burning fireplace, fishnet canopy bed, and a large bathroom. Green Peak is a deep corner room with garden views, pencil-post bed, and a gas fireplace. Dorset Hill, too, has a gas fireplace and overlooks the lush backyard. All have sitting areas, air conditioning, and a quilt or down comforter, depending on the season. Fine toiletries, plush robes, and oversized towels are a few of the standard niceties.

Dorset, a sleepy old resort village, is quintessentially Vermont. It still has a town ordinance that requires houses on the village green to be painted white with green trim and shutters. Vinyl siding is outlawed. The sidewalks are of marble quarried in town at the country's first marble quarry. (The quarry is now a popular swimming hole.) In town you'll also find the acclaimed Dorset Playhouse, a golf course, a fashionable *and* historic general store, a marble church, and a dance center. The Southern Vermont Art Center is nearby.

Grafton

The Old Tavern at Grafton

Grafton, VT 05146
802-843-2231
800-843-1801
Fax: 802-843-2245
info@oldtavern.com
www.old-tavern.com

A historic, elegant country inn

Innkeeper: Kevin O'Donnell. **Accommodations:** 66 rooms (in the inn and 6 houses, one honeymoon cottage). **Rates:** Rooms: $105–$260 per couple; houses: $500–$710 per couple. **Included:** Breakfast buffet and tea; lunch and dinner served. **Minimum stay:** 2 nights on October weekends. **Added:** 9% tax. **Credit cards accepted:** MasterCard, Visa. **Children:** Under age 8, only in 3 houses. **Pets:** Not accepted; horses stabled. **Smoking:** Restricted. **Handicap access:** Yes. **Open:** Year-round except Christmas and April.

➤ **You can see most of Grafton from a rocking chair on the Old Tavern's porch, but the village grows as you walk . . . and walk.**

The Old Tavern at Grafton, on the main street of this jewel-like town, is a gracious old stagecoach inn. Built in 1801, it became one of the most popular stops on the route between Boston and Montreal. In those days, it numbered many dignitaries and literary figures — Teddy Roosevelt, Rudyard Kipling, Emerson, and Thoreau — among its guests. A visit to the old barn, now a rustic lounge, brings the inn's history to life. Wonderful old pictures of guests in long dresses and tails, stepping out of horse-drawn coaches and Model Ts, line the upstairs walls.

Most of Grafton's houses were for sale — cheap — in the 1940s and 1950s. A New York financier, long a summer resident, established the Windham Foundation. Incorporated in 1963, it set about buying up the town, ultimately restoring it to its pre–Civil War glory.

The inn, appropriately elegant, offers spacious and handsomely furnished guest rooms, many with canopy beds. It also has several restored houses, with full kitchens, available for full or partial rental. Some of the houses are in town, but a few are tucked away in the surrounding woods, offering privacy and a spectacular view.

The dining room is open for three meals a day; in the summer, lunch in the Garden Room is a treat.

The pleasures of the inn (and the town) include a lazy afternoon by the swimming pond followed by a round of tennis, long walks, a ski tour through pristine woods, and sitting on the porch under a clear sky. The Windham Foundation displays before-and-after photographs of the restored homes and buildings. The inn has its own stables and cross-country skiing center. Golf is nearby, and downhill skiing is reasonably close by.

Jamaica

Three Mountain Inn

PO Box 180
Jamaica, VT 05343
802-874-4140
Fax: 802-874-4745

Fine dining in a Vermont village

Innkeepers: Charles and Elaine Murray. **Accommodations:** 10 rooms in the main house, 6 in Robinson House; 1 cottage. **Rates:** $130–$195 per couple MAP, $200–$230 in suite; 5-day ski packages. **Included:** Breakfast and dinner. **Minimum stay:** 2 days on weekends and in peak seasons. **Added:** 9% tax, 15% gratuity. **Credit cards accepted:** All major ones. **Children:** Possible; special rates. **Pets:** Not accepted. **Smoking:** Restricted. **Handicap access:** No. **Open:** December through March and mid-May through mid-November.

➤ **This 1790s inn, with comfortable rooms, superb food, and a pool, is close to one of Vermont's most scenic swimming holes.**

This 1790s inn on Route 30 is in the middle of a classic white clapboard village. You enter through an inviting little pub and step into a living room with wide-planked pine floors and a comfortable couch that faces a large 18th-century hearth, complete with a beehive oven. The two small dining rooms, one of which doubles as a library, have their original fireplaces; it's easy to imagine, especially by candlelight, that you are in a Colonial tavern. The menus, which change frequently and offer a choice, feature Elaine Murray's soups, breads, and desserts. House specialties include fresh trout, chicken paprikas, and eggplant Parmesan. Hot apple oatmeal is a popular start to breakfast.

The guest rooms have been individually decorated and stenciled, and are filled with framed needlework, locally made country furniture, and candlewick spreads; all have private baths. One has a king-size four-poster bed, two have working fireplaces, and a suite in the neighboring Robinson House offers a fireplace and a view of the flowery gardens.

With a classic white clapboard, green-shuttered Congregational church down the street and space for meetings and receptions (up to 40 people), the inn lends itself to weddings as well as honeymooning.

For downhill skiing, Stratton is ten minutes up the road. Antiquing, hiking, biking, and fishing are summer pastimes. Best of all is Jamaica State Park, within walking distance, where skiers use the old railroad bed in winter. In addition to the inn's nicely landscaped pool, swimmers frequent Salmon Hole or walk the mile and a half to Hamilton Falls, where water cascades through three distinct pools.

Landgrove

The Landgrove Inn

R.R.D. Box 215
Landgrove, VT 05148
802-824-6673
800-669-8466

A family secret

Innkeepers: Kathy and Jay Snyder. **Accommodations:** 16 rooms (all with private bath). **Rates:** $85–$120 per couple; midweek specials. **Included:** Full breakfast; dinner available. **Minimum stay:** 2 nights on winter weekends. **Credit cards accepted:** All major ones. **Children:** Age 5 and under, $5; others, $20. **Pets:** Not accepted. **Smoking:** Not permitted. **Handicap access:** No. **Open:** December 15 through March, Memorial Day through October 20.

➤ **Landgrove seems miles from everywhere, but it isn't. It's just somewhere you won't want to leave.**

This red, mostly clapboard inn is sequestered down a birch-lined dirt road in the Green Mountain National Forest. The building rambles on and on, back and around, beginning with the original house built in 1820 and ending with the newest portion, added in 1976. The low, connected buildings have been a Snyder family operation since the early 1960s, and families will feel very much at home here.

Billed as a country resort, the facilities include all-weather tennis courts, a heated pool, a trout pond, carriage rides, and croquet and lawn games.

Behind barn doors lies the heart of the inn: the huge, timbered Rafter Room lounge (with a full bar), where you must sample the supine couch near the hearth, which seats twelve. The room also offers games and books, a big-screen TV with VCR, and plenty of comfy chairs.

All rooms are stenciled and traditionally decorated, but couples will prefer those in the old homestead (more antiques, new bathrooms). Families may prefer the newer wing.

The wood-beamed dining room has recently been expanded with a windowed wall overlooking the garden. Dinner, served Thursday through Sunday, is by candlelight, with a choice of four entrées prepared by a well-respected local chef.

While Weston, with its shops and theater, is just 4 miles away, and Landgrove is convenient to much of southern Vermont, the village and inn feel so removed from it all that you may not want to budge. In winter, you can enjoy the 10-mile cross-country trail system from the inn into the national forest; sleigh rides are also offered. Alpine skiing is 6 miles away at Bromley or 20 miles away at Stratton; skating and snowshoeing are just outside. It's easy to earn that soak in the hot tub.

Manchester

Over the past half-dozen years this proud old resort has been transformed into Vermont's shopping mecca. More than 100 top brand outlet stores and specialty shops have opened within walking distance of each other. A summer resort since the Civil War, Manchester already had an unusual number of bed-and-breakfasts and inns, most notably the white-columned, tower-topped, 180-room Equinox, Vermont's only survivng grand hotel. The attractions have historically been golf, summer theater (in nearby Dorset), music, art, polo, and hiking the trails on Mount Equinox, a lone member of the Taconic Range that thrusts up 3,825 feet above Manchester Village on the western side of town. Just east of town, moreover, the Green Mountain ski resorts of Bromley and Stratton are winter draws. Busy in summer and especially fall, Manchester is a little-recognized winter bargain, just far enough away from the mountains to have to entice visitors with off-season prices. Yet it offers the same fine dining, lodging, and shopping that it does at other times in the year, as well as good downhill and cross-country skiing.

1811 House

Manchester Village, VT 05254
802-362-1811
800-432-1811
Fax: 802-362-2443
stay1811@vermontel.com

| Museum-quality furnishings and house |

Innkeepers: Bruce and Marnie Duff. **Accommodations:** 14 rooms (all with private bath). **Rates:** $110–$200 per couple. **Included:** Full breakfast. **Minimum stay:** 2 nights on weekends and 3 on holidays. **Added:** 9% tax. **Credit cards accepted:** All major ones. **Children:** Over age 16 welcome. **Pets:** Not accepted. **Smoking:** Not permitted. **Handicap access:** No. **Open:** Year-round.

➤ From the sweeping lawns in the backyard there are absolutely lovely views of lush gardens (thank Bruce for these), golf fairways, a little pond, and the mountains beyond. During warm weather you'll enjoy the view from a shaded hammock or an easy chair.

This elegant New England frame house, built in the 1770s, has been an inn since 1811 (except for the 30 years it was the home of Mary Lincoln Isham, a granddaughter of President Lincoln). Over the years it has been expertly and authentically restored. In fact, stepping inside is like stepping back in time. Since the Duffs purchased it in 1990, complete with furnishings et al., they have maintained its integrity while adding modern comforts such as central air conditioning. A B&B this lovely could easily be stuffy and uncomfortable, but it isn't.

Common space is plentiful. The two front parlors, each with a fireplace, are formally decorated but comfortable: vintage paintings, Oriental rugs on top of hardwood floors, period furnishings, and wainscoting. One, with a television and built-in bookcases, functions more like a library. In the other, guests can pour through area menus while sipping a glass of sherry and complimentary afternoon snacks. The basement houses an informal game room with Ping-Pong, billiards, and a television with a VCR.

An intimate, beamed tavern with a polished bar, fireplace, dart board, and small tables is known for its collection of 54 single-malt Scotch whiskeys. Bruce and Marnie, whose Scottish coat of arms hangs above the bar, take turns as bartender and get to know guests here. There is a little porch off the pub so that you can take in the expansive backyard view, rain or shine.

A full breakfast, which may include eggs Benedict or buttermilk pancakes with maple syrup, is served in the formal dining room at three tables or at tables for two in the pub. On our last visit, the aroma of Marnie's chocolate chip cookies filled the inn in the afternoon.

The guest rooms, filled with predominantly American and English antique period appointments, fall into three price categories ($110, $160, and $200). The most expensive rooms have wood-burning fireplaces and four-poster canopy beds; half are located in an adjacent building and have modern bathrooms. Our favorite of these adjacent rooms encompasses all of the second floor, with a peaked ceiling and leather chairs flanking the fireplace.

Back in the main inn, the Robinson Room has a marble shower stall and a private porch that overlooks three acres of English gardens, a golf course, and the mountains. The Jeremiah French Suite includes a beautiful sitting room.

More moderately priced rooms are also outfitted with original oil paintings, antiques, and old clawfoot tubs. Of these, Burr, Orvis, and Skinner have mountain views. All rooms have comfy seating and reading lights. Not surprisingly, the two least-expensive rooms are the smallest; of these, we prefer the Hidden Room.

The 1811 House is across the street from the Equinox Hotel and is within walking distance of shops and restaurants, a real plus when traffic comes to a crawl.

The Equinox

Route 7A
Manchester Village, VT 05253
802-362-1595
802-362-4700
800-362-4747 in the U.S.
Fax: 802-362-1595
www.Equinoxresort.com

> **A grand old resort with a spa and mountain views**

Manager: S. Lee Bowden. **Accommodations:** 136 rooms and 47 suites. **Rates:** $169–$309 per couple in rooms; $379–$899 in suites; $669 per night (up to 6 people) in town houses; less off-season; packages available. **Included:** Spa use. No meals, but all meals are available. Many packages available. **Minimum stay:** 2 nights on holiday weekends. **Added:** 9% tax, $2.50 per night gratuity; fitness center, tennis, golf fees. **Credit cards accepted:** All major ones. **Children:** Under 12, free in parent's room; over 12, $30 extra. **Pets:** Not accepted. **Smoking:** Some rooms available for smokers. **Handicap access:** Some rooms. **Open:** Year-round.

➤ **Summer sports include tennis, championship golf, and swimming in both indoor and outdoor pools. Mountain bikes, canoeing, horseback riding, and fly-fishing are available nearby. In winter, downhill skiing is west of Manchester, at Bromley and Stratton mountains, and cross-country trails begin from the resort's touring center.**

One of Vermont's oldest and certainly its grandest hotel, the Equinox is still evolving. The vast, many-columned, square-towered inn has had its ups and downs over the last 225 years. It was closed in the 1970s, reopened in the mid-1980s after a $20 million restoration, and is now enjoying an infusion of British funds and taste (Guinness Enterprises).

The exterior is an impressive structure, with hundreds of windows and twice as many green shutters. It has a commanding presence even at the foot of an equally commanding Mount Equinox. The front porches are filled with rockers; it's a nice place for an afternoon drink, overlooking sidewalks paved with marble (if you dont mind the passing cars). Inside, the handsome common spaces have a luxurious feel to them.

Most of the rooms are large by today's standards, with long, many-paned windows overlooking the surrounding mountains (ask for a room in the rear of the hotel) or the elegant white church and shops of Manchester Village (front rooms). Views from many of the side rooms are blocked by trees. Rooms that end with "37" have the most impressive views, but you'll have to pay for it. The recent renovation, which stripped the building to its wooden bones, has left the rooms with a solid but spare feel; they are furnished with standard reproduction pine bedsteads, armoires, wing and rocking chairs, and phones and TVs.

Each one-, two-, and three-bedroom town house unit has a fully equipped kitchen, porch, mountain views, and a fireplace. Top-floor units are much brighter; not all units have a view. In the small, ultra-luxurious Charles Orvis Inn next door, each suite has a cherry-paneled kitchen, oak floors, gas fireplace, and a separate living and bedroom. Common rooms include a handsome bar, billiards room, and a private marble patio. The level of service offered is referred to as "pampering." Orvis guests have access to all the hotel's facilities and room service. As you might imagine, the house is often booked for corporate getaways.

Both hotel dining rooms are open to the public but, given the unusual number of dining options nearby, they are rarely crowded. The Marsh Tavern, the actual 18th-century tavern from which the hotel has grown, is a dimly lit space with a large hearth and a menu featuring English specialties such as beef Wellington and trifle. The main dining room is elegant, with a vaulted ceiling and bow windows at one end. Breakfast, served in the tavern, is bountiful and intriguing, featuring Vermont and Scottish specialties.

In addition to the Anglo-influenced menu, the new backers have installed new plumbing, added pictures and antiques in the rooms, and renovated the hotel's vintage 1927 18-hole golf course.

Individual guests, moreover, seem better served than they were a few years ago. While groups still constitute roughly 50 percent of the patrons, vacationers will find an attentive staff, including a concierge, ready to suggest nearby dining and outlet shopping and to map bike routes. The Equinox Fitness Center offers an indoor lap pool, exercise facilities and classes, and spa facilities. A 12-acre pond within easy walking distance of the hotel is stocked with trout. Inquire about special programs ranging from falconry to driving Range Rovers off-road, ecologically. The resort also maintains miles of hiking trails on Mount Equinox for hiking and cross-country skiing and offers family-geared nature programs.

The Inn at Ormsby Hill

R.R. 2, P.O. Box 3264
Route 7A
Manchester, VT 05255
802-362-1163
800-670-2841
Fax: 802-362-5176
ormsby@vermontel.com
www.ormsbyhill.com

> **A luxurious B&B with outstanding breakfasts**

Innkeepers: Chris and Ted Sprague. **Accommodations:** 10 rooms (all with private bath). **Rates:** $140–$235 per couple on weekends and holidays; $110–$180 midweek. **Included:** Full breakfast. **Minimum stay:** 2 nights on weekends. **Added:** 9% tax. **Credit cards accepted:** All major ones. **Children:** Over age 10 welcome. **Pets:** Not accepted. **Smoking:** Not permitted indoors. **Handicap access:** Yes. **Open:** Year-round.

➤ **Chris and Ted offer supper to guests until 9:30 P.M. on Friday evenings ($20 per couple). Perhaps it will be pasta or stew simmering on the stove when you arrive. In any event, you'll feel like you're coming home for the weekend. On Saturdays, don't pass up the single-seating, single-entrée meal ($65 per couple). Chris's reputation as an outstanding chef is well deserved.**

The singlemost important thing that sets Ormsby Hill apart from other inns is that Chris and Ted care about attention to detail. Yes, of course, other innkeepers (especially Best Places's innkeepers) care, too; but Chris and Ted *really* care.

Two miles west of town on scenic Route 7A, Ormsby Hill is a refreshing alternative to the bustle of Manchester's in-town inns. When this dynamic-duo innkeeping team purchased the inn in mid-1995, they immediately carved five new luxurious guest rooms from the undeveloped wing. But they also upgraded the original five guest rooms. We don't hesitate recommending every room. (Besides, they all come with a little yellow rubber ducky for the whirlpool and a plate of fancy homemade cookies that melt in your mouth.)

Let's start with the newer rooms. Each has a gas fireplace (ingeniously placed so as to be visible from both the bed and whirlpool), a canopy bed, and is richly decorated with Waverly wallpapers and fine bedding. Robes are plush. We particularly like the private feel of the Ethan Allen and Gideon Ormsby rooms. If you're tired of "foofy" rooms, you'll appreciate these sophisticated handsome rooms.

Of the original five rooms, our favorite guest room is off the gathering room. The "library room" is large but very cozy and features a fireplace, a canopy bed, and a whirlpool. The room oozes history; the hand-hewn beams and original volumes that line the bookshelves date to the late 1800s. The Taft room is the largest and features a dramatic vaulted dome ceiling. At press time, Chris and Ted had plans to upgrade the least-expensive turret room into a very desirable space indeed.

There is plenty of comfortable common space, filled with antiques and country furniture. The more formal front parlor and comfy gathering room have low ceilings, creating a warm atmosphere enhanced by both the dominant hearth (there are nine wood-burning fireplaces in the house and gas fireplaces in the newer guest rooms) and the innkeeper's hospitality. On the second floor is a small room with cable TV and help-yourself soft drinks.

Chris calls herself "a frustrated dinner chef" — she used to cook dinner seven nights a week at their previous inn — and when you sit down to one of her multi-course breakfasts, you'll know why. Breakfast, one of the ten best in New England, is served at 9:00 A.M. in a dramatic, spectacularly sunny, glassed-in dining room conservatory. On busy mornings a buffet is set out at 8:00 A.M. and the entrée served at 9:00 A.M. Recent dishes included bacon and egg risotto, basil scrambled eggs on portobello mushrooms, and ricotta cheese pies. To top it off, a New England–style dessert such as warm gingerbread with ice cream finishes the meal. (Does that sound like anything you've ever been served for breakfast? Guests love it!)

One of the special attractions of this late-18th-century restored manor house is the private flagstone terrace and the back porch, complete with hammock.

Manchester Highlands Inn

P.O. Box 41
Manchester, VT 05254
802-362-1793
800-273-1793
Fax: 802-362-4565
relax@highlandsinn.com
www.highlandsinn.com

> **A family find in the middle of Manchester**

Innkeepers: Patricia and Robert Eichorn. **Accommodations:** 15 rooms (all with private bath). **Rates:** $95–$125 per couple, $10 more in foliage season; off-season packages. **Included:** Full breakfast, afternoon tea. **Minimum stay:** 2 days on weekends and holidays. **Added:** 9% tax. **Credit cards accepted:** MasterCard, Visa, American Express. **Children:** Welcome. **Pets:** Not accepted. **Smoking:** Not permitted. **Handicap access:** One room. **Open:** Year-round.

> ➤ **Patricia and Robert Eichorn call their Victorian inn "Manchester's best-kept secret."**

This big, turreted Victorian house stands on a quiet side street — a short walk uphill from Manchester's outlet strip on one side and a comfortable stroll from the village proper on the other. Somehow, though, it manages to convey an away-from-it-all feel, especially in summer when guests can make full use of the back porch and the lawn with its pool.

Guest rooms are divided between the main house and the carriage house and the two are connected by the "Tunnel," an underground corridor decorated with guest graffiti. Rooms in the main house have a few more angles and some elegant detailing (the Turret and Tower rooms are especially fine) but all are decorated with family antiques. The carriage house is reserved for families.

Humphrey, the Maine coon cat, usually greets visitors, escorting them into the comfortable living room. There's also a wicker-filled sun room and an honor-system bar. A basement-level TV room — with a VCR, a library of movies, and a fireplace — and the Remedy Room, with its dart board, are linked (via the "Tunnel") to a game room with a Ping-Pong table, a sitting area with games, and a wood-burning stove beneath the carriage house.

The full breakfast might include morning-glory muffins and maybe lemon soufflé pancakes or a cheddar soufflé. Patricia and

Robert are adept at advising guests on restaurants, shops, and sights.

The Reluctant Panther

West Road
P.O. Box 678
Manchester, VT 05254
802-362-2568
800-822-2331
Fax: 802-362-2586
panther@sover.net
www.reluctantpanther.com

A sophisticated inn with fine dining

Innkeepers: Robert and Maye Bachofen. **Accommodations:** 12 rooms (all with private bath), 6 suites. **Rates:** $168–$288 per couple, MAP; higher during foliage and some holiday weekends. **Included:** Full breakfast and dinner. **Minimum stay:** 2 nights during foliage and Christmas, 3 nights on holiday weekends. **Added:** 9% tax and 15% service charge. **Credit cards accepted:** All major ones. **Children:** Over age 14 welcome. **Pets:** Not accepted. **Smoking:** Not permitted. **Handicap access:** No. **Open:** Year-round; dining room closed some nights.

➤ **In 1997 the Panther added the luxury Garden Suite, which was well worth the money. The two-room suite, with terra cotta and marble floors, features a massive bedstead, a gas fireplace visible both from the double Jacuzzi and bed, and a separate sitting room with another fireplace. It also has its own marble terrace.**

With a mauve exterior, yellow shutters, and a stretching purple panther as its logo, The Reluctant Panther immediately distinguishes itself as a different sort of country inn. In fact, the three-story house, which dates back to the mid-1800s and became an inn in the 1950s, feels more like a small luxury hotel. Robert and Maye

(Robert hails from the Plaza in New York City) purchased the inn in 1989.

It's a refined place, a place where guests come seeking privacy. The innkeepers have struck a good balance between accommodating guests with fine service and leaving them be. Upon entering the marble foyer, your gaze settles on a gas fireplace glowing in the dining room. Except for a sweet and small marble patio in the rear of the house, the inn's sole common space is a small living room, which doubles as a full-service bar.

There are various room types, from rooms with a private bath across the hall to deluxe suites with a Jacuzzi and wood-burning fireplace or woodstove. All are decorated with soothing color schemes, plush fabrics, and goose down comforters.

In the main inn, Room G is sunny, cheerful, and large. Room J, furnished with lovely oak pieces, is spacious enough to comfortably spend a few days. Room B has a very country feel to it. And while Room D is small, it's worth it just to see the wallpaper, made by a 27-step process. All rooms have air conditioning, a television and phone, good reading lights, a complimentary half-bottle of wine on arrival, and nightly turndown service.

The Mary Porter House, adjacent to the inn, has four large luxury suites that feel very private. They are furnished traditionally with four-poster beds and floral wallpapers. Of these, the Mark Skinner Suite has two fireplaces — one in the large bathroom and one in the bedroom.

Dining is an elegant and soothing affair. Tables are set with white linen, silver, crystal, flowers, and candles; we particularly like sitting at tables in the lush "greenhouse" area. Service is well paced and the dishes beautifully presented. Breakfast is simpler, but includes a warm entrée.

In 1997 Robert stepped in as chef (inquire whether or not he has hired an outside chef). On our last visit, dinner began simply: a warm artichoke in a citrus buerre blanc, followed by a creamy broccoli soup. Creative energies were concentrated on the entrées, which were exceptional: salmon on a bed of mixed-color peppers and capers with polenta, and a spicy shrimp and scallop curry with bananas and toasted almonds and wild rice. We barely had room for a tasty pear tarte and linzer torte.

For $15 per person per day, guests have access to the Equinox Hotel's health club and spa.

Mount Snow Area

The Inn at Sawmill Farm

P.O. Box 367
Mount Snow Valley and Route 100
West Dover, VT 05356
802-464-8131
800-493-1133
Fax: 802-464-1130

| An elegant inn with fine food |

Innkeepers: Brill, Ione, and Rodney Williams. **Accommodations:** 10 rooms (all with private bath), 10 cottage suites. **Rates:** $320–$425 per couple; $85 for extra person in room. **Included:** Breakfast and dinner. **Minimum stay:** 2 days on a weekend. **Added:** 9% tax, 15% gratuity. **Credit cards accepted:** All major ones. **Children:** Over age 10. **Pets:** Not accepted. **Smoking:** Restricted. **Handicap access:** No. **Open:** Closed April through mid-May.

➤ **The Inn at Sawmill Farm figures in everyone's list of Vermont's top inns.**

The Inn at Sawmill Farm is elegant, from the meticulously trimmed lawns to the polished copper plates. Bring tweeds and cashmeres for kicking about the countryside, whites for tennis, a dinner jacket for after six, and a hefty checkbook.

Inside the main house, wide stairs lead up to a lobby, where a grandfather clock stands behind a glistening baby grand piano. There are several sitting areas, from the main living room, where cocktails are served by the fire, to a small reading loft lined with books. In all the rooms, country touches like healthy plants, raw wooden walls and beams, dried flowers, log fires, and period furniture are artfully blended with the elegant interiors.

The spacious guest rooms have canopy beds, fireplaces, wall-to-wall carpeting, roomy closets, and handsome antiques. The suites and rooms in the cottages have their own living rooms and fireplaces.

Two dining rooms open off the main lobby. One, with a sloping glass roof and a profusion of plants, is light and airy. The other — dark, rich, and intimate — is perfect for a romantic dinner. The tables are set with goblets, slender candles, and flowers. The restaurant, known for its Continental cuisine, enjoys a reputation that often makes reservations necessary weeks in advance. You might dine on fresh sautéed foie gras with caramelized apple and vale glace, followed by breast of pheasant with forestier sauce. The wine cellar of 36,000 bottles complements the menu.

In the summer, guests can have drinks by the pool, fish in the two trout ponds, or play tennis on secluded courts. In winter, a day of downhill skiing at Mount Snow or cross-country on nearby trails can be followed by skating on the pond, then cocktails by the fire. Fall offers glorious long walks in the woods surrounding the inn.

Misty Mountain Lodge

326 Stowe Hill Road
Wilmington, VT 05363
802-464-3961

A friendly lodge for families and groups

Innkeepers: Elizabeth and Lensey (Buzz) Cole. **Accommodations:** 8 rooms (4 private, 4 shared baths). **Rates:** In summer: $57–$85 per couple B&B; in foliage and ski season: $62–$110 B&B; packages available; inquire about ski packages. **Included:** Full breakfast; dinner by reservation is $20, $8 for children aged 2 to 12. **Minimum stay:** None. **Added:** 9% tax. **Credit cards accepted:** American Express, Discover, MasterCard, Visa. **Children:** $20–$48, ages 2-12; $15 for crib. **Pets:** Not accepted. **Smoking:** Not permitted. **Handicap access:** Some rooms. **Open:** Year-round.

➤ **This sprawling Vermont farmhouse has been the Cole family's home for generations, and their photographs decorate the walls, the piano, and the desk. This is, in fact, one of the last inns in Vermont run by Vermonters.**

Misty Mountain offers excellent value and a homey atmosphere, making it ideal for families, single travelers, and anyone seeking a reasonably priced and friendly lodge in this area. Guests always receive a warm welcome, and the house is designed to be lived in, with a comfortably furnished living room, and a choice of accommodations, ranging from simple, old-fashioned rooms with shared bath to newly renovated rooms with air conditioning, TV, and whirlpool tub. All rooms overlook the mountains. Bountiful meals are served family-style, and after-dinner sing-alongs in the living room are common.

"I don't want anyone to be surprised," Buzz cautions. What he means is that this is a real country home. The living room — with a roaring fire, an old-fashioned rocker, a sofa and chairs with embroidered pillows, and a piano — is the heart of the inn. Everyone gathers to play cards, read, sit, and chat, and magazines cover the coffee table. Guests will also find a good selection of board games and books as well as a TV.

The Coles prepare and serve two meals a day. There's a big country breakfast of juice, hot and cold cereals, eggs, toast, and bacon and always an option of maybe homemade wheat pancakes one day and French toast the next. Dinner is equally bountiful: a main dish (perhaps roast beef or baked chicken), seasonal vegetables, bread, potatoes, salad, and dessert. Dishes are prepared with local farm produce; the muffins, cakes, and pies are homemade. Meals are served at several long tables in the large, beamed dining room.

The inn commands an unbroken view of the Mount Snow Valley and the steeples of Wilmington. The 150 acres of trails and fields invite hiking and skiing.

Trail's End, A Country Inn

5 Trail's End Lane
Wilmington, VT 05363
802-464-2727
800-859-2585
www.sover.net/~dvalncws/trailsend.html

A romantic inn for skiers

Innkeepers: Debby and Kevin Stephens. **Accommodations:** 13 rooms, 2 suites (all with private bath). **Rates:** May to September: $105–$155 per couple; November to April: $115–$185. **Included:** Full breakfast and afternoon refreshments. **Minimum stay:** 3 nights on holiday weekends; 2 nights on weekends; inquire about special packages. **Added:** 9% tax, 15% service charge. **Credit cards accepted:** All major ones. **Children:** $30 extra. **Pets:** Not accepted. **Smoking:** Permitted. **Handicap access:** No. **Open:** Year-round except late April and early May.

➤ **This whimsically designed, deftly decorated ski lodge is unusually appealing year-round.**

Hidden up a wooded road, this is one of the most appealing inns in the Deerfield Valley, four miles from Mount Snow. The public spaces are unusual.

The large living area has a sloping full-length solar window framed by dozens of hanging plants, a beamed cathedral ceiling, and an enormous central fieldstone fireplace. Long sofas built into the wall and stuffed magazine racks make it a central gathering place.

The dining area, too, is unusual, with large round pine tables and "the bar," lined with wooden booths. There's another balcony-level sitting room with a TV as well as a recreation room with board games and bumper pool, as well as a VCR and a library of movies.

The guest rooms are all individually decorated and come in all sizes, including suites with fireplaces and whirlpool tubs; four rooms also have fireplaces.

In summer, you may not want to stir far from the heated pool and trout pond, the gardens, clay tennis court, and nature trails. With access to your own fridge, you don't have to budge for lunch.

The aroma of baking bread and simmering soup fills the house each afternoon. On the weekends of the Marlboro Music Festival, four-course Saturday dinners ($16.50) are served in the dining room, which has antique kerosene lamps on each of the round tables. Guests are invited to bring wine to accompany the meal.

In the summer, the English flower gardens around the pool are lovely. Private nooks and arbors, surrounded by acres of open meadows and deep cool woods, are idyllic places to escape for a walk. The wooded trails that start at the lodge lure explorers in every season.

Newfane

The Four Columns Inn

P.O. Box 278
Newfane, VT 05345
802-365-7713
800-787-6633
frcolinn@sove.net
www.fourcolumnsinn.com

> **Formal dining in a famous village**

Innkeepers: Pamela and Gorty Baldwin. **Accommodations:** 10 rooms (all with private bath), 5 suites. **Rates:** $110–$195 per couple B&B, $25 for extra person in room; foliage season: $210–$295 per couple MAP. **Included:** Depends on meal plan. **Minimum stay:** 2 nights on some weekends and holidays. **Added:** 9% tax. **Credit cards accepted:** All major ones. **Children:** Welcome. **Pets:** Accepted with permission. **Smoking:** Not permitted. **Handicap access:** No. **Open:** Year-round.

➤ **The Four Columns is probably as well known in Manhattan as it is in Vermont.**

Facing one of Vermont's most famous classic commons, the Four Columns has the facade of an antebellum mansion. The Baldwins preside over the inn, giving it a warmth and informality that is frequently lacking in famous culinary retreats.

The restaurant, which is open to the public, is in the beamed barn. It has a huge brick fireplace and is appropriately set for candlelight dining. Chef Gregory stayed on when inn ownership changed a couple years ago and continues to earn kudos from guests and critics. The wide choice of entrées might include New England–style bouillabaisse ($25) and breast of squab with onion compote, Napa cabbage, and foi gras ($27).

Most of the guest rooms are in the old mansion and a connecting wing. They are snug, bright, and furnished with antiques. The top-floor suite has access to the great little porch above the four columns, overlooking the common. Suites have gas fireplaces and several rooms have Jacuzzis. The former parlor of the mansion is a rather gloomy but palatial suite with a canopy bed and Jacuzzi.

Pam and Gorty have added a small sitting space for guests off the pub, with a TV and reading space. There is a pool in the back and a path through the woods and up a hill. The inn's own 158 acres have trails for hiking. A surprising number of shops are tucked in and around Newfane. Across Route 30, up a road marked Dead End, an old cemetery with an obelisk marks the resting place of Sir Isaac Newton (Newton is a common local name). Winter visitors can ski on nearby thrown-up roads (Vermont roads that are no longer maintained for traffic) or drive the half hour to Stratton Mountain and Mount Snow.

West River Lodge

R.R. 1, Box 693
Newfane, VT 05345
802-365-7745

A classic country inn and a horseman's haven

Innkeepers: Gill and Jack Winner. **Accommodations:** 8 rooms (2 connecting, 2 with private bath). **Rates:** $77–$88 per couple B&B, $116–$130 per couple MAP; ask for single and triple, weekly, off-season, and midweek rates. **Included:** Full country breakfast; dinner in MAP rates; lunch served on request. **Minimum stay:** 2 days on weekends and in foliage season. **Added:** 9% tax. **Credit cards accepted:** Visa, MasterCard. **Children:** Welcome. **Pets:** Not accepted. **Smoking:** Restricted. **Handicap access:** No. **Open:** Year-round.

➤ **Riding is a big draw. The trails are extensive, and you can bring your own mount, take a lesson, or join an all-day ride. Carriage driving is another option.**

West River Lodge is a white 1840s farmhouse next to a big red barn, surrounded by farmland and circled by hills. In the 1930s it was a well-known riding school and since then has catered to horse lovers, doing so exclusively through the 1970s until Gill (pronounced Jill, short for Gillian) and Jack Winner, former college professors, bought it in 1983.

Both riders and nonriders can enjoy the isolation of this place, actually just a mile or two off busy Route 30. If you happen by on a Sunday you cant miss the turn: it's at the Newfane Flea Market, the biggest in southern Vermont. Jack is an active antiques dealer and can point guests toward the best shops in this antiques-rich area.

The swimming hole is just across the field in the river and, in winter, the surrounding fields and bridle trails invite cross-country skiing. Downhill skiing is just down the road at Maple Valley (one of Vermont's few surviving family ski hills) or a half-hour's drive up Route 30, at Stratton.

The rooms are cheerful, unpretentious, and country comfortable. The meals, served at the long dining room table, are what Gill describes as country cooking with a Welsh accent, to match her own. Special weekends range from art workshops to "centered riding clinics" in the spring and fall. This is also the kind of place that's particularly suited to small family reunions and weddings, as well as to single travelers who do not like to eat alone.

Putney

Hickory Ridge House

R.F.D. 3
P.O. Box 1410
Hickory Ridge Road
Putney, VT 05346
802-387-5709
800-380-9218

> A classic country B&B

Innkeepers: Jacquie Walker and Steve Anderson. **Accommodations:** 7 rooms (3 with private bath). **Rates:** $50–$85 per couple with shared bath, $85–$95 with private bath, $18 per extra person. **Included:** Full breakfast. **Minimum stay:** 2 nights on holiday weekends. **Added:** 9% tax. **Credit cards accepted:** All major ones. **Children:** Welcome. **Pets:** Not accepted. **Smoking:** Not permitted. **Handicap access:** 1 first-floor room with fireplace. **Open:** Year-round.

> ➤ **One ground-floor room with a fireplace offers easy access and a bathroom designed for disabled guests.**

Hickory Ridge House, a mellow brick Federal country manor built on a southern Vermont hillside in 1808, is a rare beauty and a real discovery. The ceilings are high, and the old small-paned windows fill the house with bright light. The rooms are painted pumpkin, rose, blue, and other period colors.

The house is set in twelve acres of rolling meadow near the village of Putney — a community known for its private school and college as well as a summer music festival and diverse craftspeople.

Guests enter from the side, across a deck that brims with flowers in summer and is set up for sunning and relaxing. Note the National Register of Historic Places plaque on the wall. Steve can greet you in German, Russian, or French, for both he and Jacquie have led full and interesting lives, including college teaching, chimney sweeping, social services, and extensive travel. The house is well stocked with books, its walls hung with original art.

Upstairs rooms are airy and comfortable, furnished with carefully chosen country antiques. The blue room has a sleigh bed, and the headboard for the bed in the lemon room has been fancifully fashioned from a choir stall. All four original Federal bedrooms (our favorites, without question) are large, each with a Rumford fireplace. All three smaller rooms in a renovated late 1800s wing have both a double and single bed. The only TV is in the casual upstairs sitting room.

The house is not cluttered: just enough pieces of furniture and just enough special touches give it unusual charm. At Christmas a big tree with 300 lights is placed in front of the Palladian window in the broad, upstairs hall.

Breakfast features muffins, breads, pastries and eggs from a flock of resident chickens. Two highly rated restaurants are just over the hill in Newfane and nearer still, the Putney Inn is justly famed. Nearby Brattleboro is also a good dining and shopping town.

Its an easy 5-minute walk to the swimming hole and there is fishing and canoeing in the Connecticut River, two miles away. Putney Mountain with its short trail to incredibly long views, is a short drive. In the winter, cross-country ski trails begin right at the back door, doubling as lovely walks the rest of the year. Crawford, a lively black lab, is happy to guide guests around. Hickory Ridge House is a lovely spot for weddings.

Simonsville

Rowell's Inn

Simonsville
R.R.1
P.O. Box 267-D
Chester, VT 05143
802-875-3658
800-728-0842
Fax: 802-875-3680

> **Striking, both inside and out**

Innkeepers: Beth and Lee Davis. **Accommodations:** 5 rooms (all with private bath). **Rates:** $160–$175 per couple. **Minimum stay:** 2 nights on weekends. **Included:** Breakfast, afternoon tea, and dinner. **Added:** 9% tax, 15% gratuity. **Credit cards accepted:** MasterCard, Visa. **Children:** Over age 12. **Pets:** Not accepted. **Smoking:** Restricted. **Handicap access:** No. **Open:** Year-round except April.

➤ **The distinctive architecture of this old stage stop is still a traffic stopper and both decor and dining here are special.**

Simonsville, a cluster of homes between Weston and Chester, is the unlikely site of Rowell's Inn. This distinguished red brick building has a third-floor porch with an arched ceiling and a gabled roof, part of its Federal heritage. A plaque to the left of the solid wooden door announces its place on the National Register of Historic Places.

Built as a stagecoach stop by Major Edward Simon, the inn has served the public off and on since 1820 — as a post office and general store as well as an inn.

A Mr. Rowell, who procured the inn in 1900, added the elegant tin ceiling in the sitting room and the cherry and maple floorboards. By the time Beth and Lee Davis found it, the old landmark had lapsed into disrepair. The couple from the Midwest restored it from top to bottom, adding their own Americana, ranging from a vintage Coca-Cola machine to a 1960s 12-passenger airport limo that still runs. The old-fashioned parlor is richly furnished with upholstered sofas and antique tables, but we prefer the Sun Room with its wooden booth and gaming tables, the fireplace and view of the garden, and the Tavern Room with its soda fountain stools and Vermont-brewed beer.

Each bedroom is different, but they all have sinks, thick quilts, and hooked rugs. The corner room, with a brass double bed and stone fireplace, is particularly pleasing. The two third-floor rooms, carved out of the old ballroom, are the largest and most grand, each with a double and single bed.

Although self-taught, Beth has earned top ratings for her five-course dinners. On a summer night the menu included a mushroom strudel, herb garlic soup, medallions of pork, and peach cobbler. Specialties of the house range from her signature applesauce (according to family legend, she is related to Johnny Appleseed) and oatmeal pie at breakfast to fiddlehead fern soup, a far-from-bland boiled dinner, and Vermont cheddar cheese pie. The dining room is small but elegant.

Beth and Lee Davis are both easy, helpful hosts who know the area well and are delighted to help guests plan their stay.

South Londonderry

The Three Clock Inn

Middletown Road
South Londonderry, VT 05148
802-824-6327
Fax: 802-824-4115

Fine food in southern Vermont

Innkeepers: Marcie and Serge Roche. **Accommodations:** 2 rooms (both with private bath). **Rates:** $85–$110 per couple. **Included:** Breakfast. **Minimum stay:** 2 days on busy weekends. **Added:** 9% tax. **Credit cards accepted:** Visa, MasterCard. **Children:** Welcome. **Pets:** Not accepted. **Smoking:** Not permitted. **Handicap access:** No. **Open:** Year-round except November and April (open Thanksgiving).

➤ **This white clapboard inn is a little gem tucked up on a hilly back street in the tiny crossroads village of South Londonderry.**

Established under a previous, longtime owner, this inn preserves its reputation for exceptional dining under present owner Serge Roche, former head chef for New York–based Restaurant Associates.

The focal points of the inn are unquestionably the country-elegant, low-beamed dining rooms with their vanilla walls, white tablecloths, and glowing candles and hearths. In the summer there are also tables on the flowery porch.

The menu changes seasonally but might include sea bass in a potato and zucchini crust, fettucini with wild mushrooms, or braised rabbit. A $35 menu — including any appetizer, entrée, and dessert on the menu — is offered. There are over 150 classic and boutique wines to choose from. The dining room closes Monday nights.

While the rooms are not what this place is about, the rooms are pleasant — one has a fireplace and the other is really a two-room suite. There is a sitting area with fireplace upstairs. Rates include a full breakfast.

Weathersfield

The Inn at Weathersfield

Route 106
P.O. Box 165
Weathersfield, VT 05151
802-263-9217
800-477-4828 outside Vermont
Fax: 802-263-9219

Exceptional dining in a traditional inn

Innkeepers: Mary and Terry Carter. **Accommodations:** 10 rooms (all with private bath), 2 suites. **Rates:** $175–$225 per couple; $5 additional for use of guest room fireplace. **Included:** Full breakfast and dinner. **Minimum stay:** 2 nights on weekends, 3 nights on some holidays. **Added:** 9% tax, 17% service charge. **Credit cards accepted:** All major ones. **Children:** Over age 8. **Pets:** Not permitted. **Smoking:** Not permitted indoors. **Handicap access:** No. **Open:** Year-round.

➤ **On any given night Mary and her family-like staff light seven dozen candles — in the wrought-iron dining room chandeliers, in the living room sconces, in the Colonial keeping room, and in the guest rooms. The atmosphere propels you back 200 years.**

The Inn at Weathersfield is a dignified, 18th-century mansion set on 21 acres. It is distinguished from other inns primarily by exceptional cuisine served in a romantic setting. But the inn also features many rooms furnished with lovely family antiques and unpretentious innkeepers. It stands at the end of a tree-lined drive off a hilly country road in the village of Perkinsville, not far from the Connecticut River.

Dinner is the focal point of any stay. Of the several dining spaces, request a table in the carriage house, with a low, dark, beamed ceiling, and a dominant stone fireplace. The bookshelves here are lined with Terry's grandmother's wedding gifts: beautiful engraved silver and elaborate china servings. (The display prompted us to ask, "Who *was* this woman?" Answer: The daughter of the founder of Bailey's ice cream.) Intimate tables are set with starched linens and fresh flowers. Tom McDermott entertains on the piano. If you can't stay here, the five-course dinner to outside guests is $34.95 per person; don't pass it up.

A recent summer meal started with duck liver pâté. Chef Michael McNamara's classical cooking emphasizes light sauces that let the flavor of the food shine through. We chose the brie in a flaky puff pastry, followed by a crisp mixed salad and a refreshing sorbet with champagne. From comments overhead in the dining room, entrées as varied as grilled angus sirloin au poivre were just as well executed as salmon Wellington with a basil cream sauce. Michael makes a few desserts himself, including a luscious sour cream blueberry pie with a pecan crumble crust. The wine cellar wins deserved awards.

We were given a choice at breakfast of eggs any style or pancakes. At breakfast you may be treated, as we were on a recent visit, to a native Vermont storyteller who reads his own work, tells tales, or recites Robert Frost's poetry.

Weddings are held here almost every weekend from April through the summer and on some weekends in March and November. So, if you want to stay here, you'll have to plan on a midweek stay or a winter weekend. (Again, try to eat here if you stay somewhere else.)

Guest rooms are named after romance novels and are decorated accordingly. Each has its own style and mood. Eight rooms have working fireplaces and a couple of rooms have private balconies with a view of Hawk's Mountain. In the older part of the house, with creaking and uneven floorboards, the premier accommodation is Tara, a large corner room with four-poster bed. Guest rooms in the new 1980s post-and-beam wing tend to be smaller, with more of a country feel. It's best to ask for a complete description when booking. A few bathrooms have quite a low overhead.

Horse-drawn sleigh and carriage rides and snowshoes are available. Downstairs in the inn is a Finnish sauna and a rowing machine.

Weston

The Colonial House

P.O. Box 138 R.B.
Weston, VT 05161
802-824-6286
800-639-5033
Fax: 802-824-3934

| Homey but with better- |
| than-home cooking |

Innkeepers: John and Betty Nunnikhoven. **Accommodations:** 15 rooms (9 with private bath). **Rates:** $60–$84 per couple in fall and winter, $50–$74 in spring and summer. **Included:** Full breakfast. **Minimum stay:** 2 nights on weekends; 3 nights on holiday weekends. **Added:** 9% tax. **Credit cards accepted:** All major ones. **Children:** Special rates for ages 4 to 12. **Pets:** Not accepted. **Smoking:** Restricted. **Handicap access:** No. **Open:** Year-round.

➤   **Given the smells from the kitchen and the atmosphere in the common room, you'll want to sit right down and relax.**

"Families should have a nice place to come to," observes John Nunnikhoven. His Colonial House is a long red building — an old inn with a dining room wing and motel units rambling off behind — which looks as natural as the connected farmhouses and barns for which Vermont is famous.

John and Betty are from Iowa. One summer (now years ago) they drove east, looking for the source of a special variety of tobacco that had found its way to the family from the Vermont Country Store in Weston. Camping that night at Hapgood Pond, they vowed to move to Vermont. It took a dozen years, but the Nunnikhovens have now been in Weston long enough to build up a strong following.

The check-in counter is at the door of the kitchen, because that's where you'll usually find Betty, baking bread for supper or breakfast or goodies for afternoon tea. The room is walled in barnboard, with dried flowers hanging from the rafters and comfortable chairs grouped around the woodstove here and in the adjoining greenhouse-like sun room.

The guest rooms are clean and comfortable, varying in size and shape depending on whether they are in the inn or motel wing. Off by itself is a recreation room with a Ping-Pong table, games, and books.

Breakfast is important here. In the morning John presides over the cheerful dining room, whipping up pancakes (a different kind every day) and omelettes, served with fresh breads and coffee cakes. Betty is the wizard behind dinner: hearty down-home fare such as New England pork roast, Cornish game hen stuffed with herbs and apples, or scallops basil. All meals come with a green salad, fresh vegetables, and homemade breads and desserts like caramel honey flan or grasshopper pie; but bring your own wine. Dinner is served most nights in the summer and winter but may not be available in the off-seasons. Ask when you make your reservation.

In the winter you can step right out the back door onto cross-country ski trails that stretch for 150 miles. Alpine skiers can choose from nearby Okemo, Bromley, and Stratton mountains. In the summer you can walk the mile-plus into Weston, known for its summer theater, shops, and for Weston Priory. Or take to the hills in a variety of directions. The best swimming is still in Hapgood Pond.

The Wilder Homestead Inn

25 Lawrence Hill Road
Weston, VT 05161
802-824-8172

The waterfall lulls you to sleep

Innkeepers: Peggy and Roy Varner. **Accommodations:** 7 rooms (5 with private bath). **Rates:** $60–$70 for shared bath, $80–$105 per couple with private bath; highest rates are October 1–20, Christmas week, and winter weekends. **Included:** Full breakfast. **Minimum stay:** None. **Added:** 9% tax. **Credit cards accepted:** MasterCard, Visa. **Children:** Over age 6; ages 6–10, $25 extra. **Pets:** Not accepted. **Smoking:** Not permitted. **Handicap access:** No. **Open:** Year-round.

➤ **Weston is a place to spend the night, not just the day.**

This classic Federal brick mansion was built in 1827 by Judge Wilder. Just around the corner from Weston's famous green and within walking distance of shops, restaurants, and summer theater, it's tucked away on a quiet side street across from a small waterfall.

The heart of the inn is the long trestle table in the sunny old dining room, in front of the huge old hearth. Guests tend to linger over breakfast, which usually includes eggs and country sausage, Lumberjack Mush, butter biscuits and jams, and pancakes with maple syrup.

"People want to talk to us and to each other," innkeeper Peggy Varner observes, noting that this social give-and-take is something she enjoys and encourages.

The guest rooms are all furnished with country-elegant antiques, like canopy beds, and small decanters of sherry appear around bedtime. The two front bedrooms are particularly elegant, with small fireplaces and original stencils by Moses Eaton. The snug third-floor rooms under the eaves (sharing a bath) are good for single travelers.

Downstairs is a choice of sitting rooms with a TV, a piano, and games. Roy's "1827 Craft Shoppe," near the entrance, features goods that are hard to find elsewhere, such as window sticks and Vermont Flamingos.

Peggy and Roy Varner totally renovated the homestead before hanging out their shingle in 1986. They are thoroughly familiar with the area's hiking, biking, and skiing options. Weston is best known for its highly professional summer theater, chamber music concerts, and the Vermont Country Store, a famous source of gadgets and sensible clothing. There's also some good swimming and cross-country and downhill skiing in the neighborhood.

West Townshend

Windham Hill Inn

West Townshend, VT 05359
802-874-4080
800-944-4080
Fax: 802-874-4702
windham@sover.net
www.windhamhill.com

| **Hilltop hospitality** |

Innkeepers: Grigs and Pat Markham. **Accommodations:** 21 rooms and suites (all with private bath). **Rates:** $195–$295 per couple; $60 for extra person in room. **Included:** Breakfast and dinner. **Minimum stay:** 2 nights on weekends. **Added:** 9% tax, 15% service charge. **Credit cards accepted:** All major ones. **Children:** Not appropriate. **Pets:** Not accepted. **Smoking:** Not permitted. **Handicap access:** Some rooms. **Open:** Year-round except April.

➤ **Days begin with a hearty country breakfast and end with a superb, five-course candlelit dinner.**

At the end of a hilltop road, on a secluded 160 acres, this vintage 1825 farmhouse looks down the West River valley.

We have watched this inn evolve over the past twenty years and must say that its common rooms are now superb, beautifully and thoughtfully redesigned by innkeepers Grigs and Pat Markham. And the food, we understand, has never been better.

The check-in desk now doubles as an inviting bar. Guests can find privacy and plenty to read in one of three common rooms, ranging from formal parlors to a many-windowed music room with a grand piano and choice of board games.

The expanded dining room is a beauty, complete with a hearth and windows overlooking the pond. Tables are set for two or four, and those who prefer to dine at a common table still can, in the adjacent, original dining room. On a summer day, the five-course menu offered three appetizers — including a savory Napoleon pastry with duck ragout and sun-dried cherry-rhubarb compote — a choice of four entrées — including mustard seed-encrusted lamb loin, grilled with rosemary merlot sauce — and fantasy desserts like strawberry-rhubarb soufflé.

The inn is centrally air-conditioned and some rooms have private porches and/or fireplaces or woodstoves. The most expensive rooms also feature a Jacuzzi, soaking tub, or large window seat. Canopy and reproduction beds are graced with locally made stuffed animals. You might want to request a room in the "White Barn," overlooking the valley.

The West River valley is known for unusually handsome villages, like nearby Townshend and Newfane. It offers good antiquing and hiking and is within easy striking distance of summer theater and music. Skiing at both Stratton and Mount Snow is a half-hour's drive, and the inn maintains its own cross-country trail system and offers rentals and lessons. The grounds include a swimming pool and tennis court. Inquire about special packages.

Green Mountains

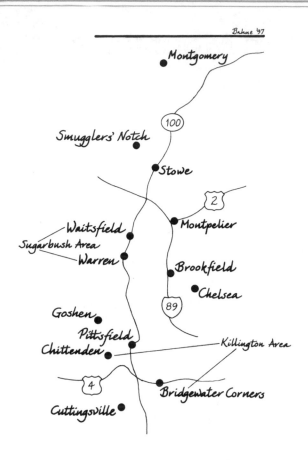

Best Family Finds

Cuttingsville
Maple Crest Farm, 572
Pittsfield
Hawk North, Ltd, 581
Stowe
The Golden Eagle Resort and Motor Inn, 586

Best Gourmet Getaways

Chelsea
Shire Inn, 570
Killington Area
The October Country Inn, 577
Tulip Tree, 578
Stowe
Edson Hill Manor and Ten Acres Lodge, 584
Sugarbush Area
Millbrook Inn, 596

Best Inns

Montgomery Village
Black Lantern Inn, 579
Stowe
Green Mountain Inn, 588
Sugarbush Area
Inn at Mad River Barn, 593

Best Romantic Getaways

Killington Area
Tulip Tree Inn, 578
Stowe
Edson Hill Manor and Ten Acres Lodge, 584
Stowehof Inn, 589
Sugarbush
The Inn at the Round Barn, 595

The Green Mountains run the entire length of the state, from Massachusetts to Canada: 162 miles as the crow flies, but 270 miles as the hiker trudges over the Long Trail and 211 miles as Route 100 runs right up the spine of Vermont, hugging the eastern base of the range.

The Green Mountains effectively divide the state in two. They also form a region in their own right, one with its share of valley farms but characterized chiefly by wooded mountains and a string of resort villages. They have evolved around more than a dozen ski resorts and now offer golf and other sports, theater, fine dining, and shopping in summer as well as winter.

The largest of these is **Killington,** the largest ski complex in New England: six mountains with 155 slopes and trails boasting the most extensive snowmaking in the world. Neighboring Pico is older, far smaller, and geared to families. Lodging for 11,000 visitors within twenty miles of these resorts includes hundreds of condos as well as dozens of inns, resorts, lodges, and B&Bs.

Killington and Pico are in Sherburne Pass on Route 4, the sole major east-west road in all of central and northern Vermont. Two more scenic roads — Route 73 from Rochester to Brandon through the Brandon Gap and Route 125 from Hancock to East Middlebury through the Middlebury Gap — are also great ways to cross the mountains; for adventurous drivers there are the more tortuous, less-traveled Appalachian (between Waitsfield and Bristol) and Lincoln (between Warren and Bristol) gaps, not to mention the Roxbury Gap, east of the Mad River Valley. The highest and most famous of all these high mountain passes is, of course, Smugglers' Notch, on Route 108 north of Stowe.

North of Killington, Route 100 follows the spine of the Green Mountains through valleys that alternately widen, as in Rochester, and narrow, as in Granville Gulch. The resort area here is the Mad River or **Sugarbush Valley** (it's known as both). The old logging and farming villages of Warren and Waitsfield have been transformed in recent decades, evolving a new look and way of life spawned by the ski areas — Mad River Glen and Sugarbush — just as the earlier villages took shape around their greens. But from Route 100 it all seems deceptively quiet. Lodging for some 6,000 visitors is squirreled away, mostly in condominiums clustered in the woods or off the Sugarbush access road. This valley is known as a major soaring center; it also offers golf, tennis, polo, theater, and an exceptional choice of dining.

From the Sugarbush Valley, Route 100 continues north, crossing I-89 at Waterbury, the gateway to **Stowe,** the state's most famous resort village. While its no longer the state's largest ski area, Stowe remains the ski capital of the East in spirit and New England's most beautiful summer mountain resort as well. Stowe is positioned at the foot of Mount Mansfield, the highest mountain in the state, which is accessible in summer by road as well as gondola.

A five-mile traffic-free Recreation Path runs through meadows, inviting walkers or bicyclists. It parallels Mountain Road, which is lined with shops and lodges as it connects the village with the mountain. The village also offers plenty of golf, tennis, live entertainment, and fine dining.

The obvious route north from Stowe is over **Smugglers' Notch** (closed from December to May), by Smugglers' Notch Resort and into the less touristed, gently rolling Lamoile Valley, with classic old villages like **Montgomery.** East is Jay Peak, the northernmost of the Green Mountains, with magnificent views north across Lake Memphremagog into Canada and back down the Green Mountain range (Jay's summit is accessible by aerial tramway).

Brookfield

Green Trails Inn

Brookfield, VT 05036
802-276-3412
800-243-3412
Greentraios@quest-net.com

| Inn by a mountain pond

Innkeepers: Sue and Mark Erwin. **Accommodations:** 14 rooms (8 with private bath). **Rates:** $79–$130 per couple. **Included:** Breakfast. **Minimum stay:** None. **Added:** 9% tax, 15% gratuity. **Credit cards accepted:** MasterCard, Visa. **Children:** Over age 10. **Pets:** Not accepted. **Smoking:** Not permitted. **Handicap access:** No. **Open:** Year-round.

➤ **While the horses are long gone, the green trails are still good for summer hiking, and forty kilometers are maintained in winter for cross-country skiing (equipment can be rented) and snowshoeing. In winter there's also sleigh riding at a nearby farm and skating (bring your own) on Sunset Lake.**

Brookfield is a cluster of white wooden houses at a crossroads by Sunset Lake — really a pond, but so deep its bridge has to float on pontoons.

The unusual name and shape of the inn is explained by its history. Green Trails began as an informal scattering of rooms in houses owned by friends and relatives of Jessie Fiske, a Brookfield native who became one of the first female professors at Rutgers University. The rooms were rented in summer to her students and friends, who came to ride horseback and to "botanize" with Miss Fiske.

The rooms in the present inn are divided between the 1830s inn and the neighboring 1790s "Guest House." The entire first floor of the inn is common space: a large, informal dining area is combined with sitting space around a big stone hearth. There is also a more formal dining room and a parlor with a big fish tank in one corner.

In a previous life Mark raised fish and repaired antique clocks, which range from a handsome grandfather to a striking 19th-century Anglo-American piece (Mark can explain). Clocks don't strike in the parlor of the Guest House because its within earshot of the inn's two most luxurious rooms: the Stencil Room (which retains floor-to-ceiling stenciling from the early 1800s and also offers a whirlpool tub) and a fireplace suite, also with a jacuzzi.

The formal dining room is also filled with clocks (Mark tells us there are between 40 and 50 clocks throughout the house). Guests tend to congregate in the less formal breakfast room with its sitting area around a stone fireplace. Breakfast can include baked omelettes, buttermilk waffles, fruit, homemade granola, yogurt, cold cereal, and homemade muffins or scones; with it comes a string of possible exercise options.

In the summer there's swimming from the small beach, just across the road on the lake. A canoe is available to guests, and the network of hard-packed dirt roads invites bicycling and walking. Allis State Park, across the bridge, also offers some good hiking, and its observation tower commands a view of four states. Lawn games like croquet and horseshoes are also offered, and there's fishing, too, from the nation's only wooden floating bridge.

Chelsea

Shire Inn

Main Street
P.O. Box 37
Chelsea, VT 05038
802-685-3031
800-441-6908
shireinn@sover.net
www.innbook.com/shire.html

> **An elegant inn where meals are a point of pride**

Innkeepers: Jay and Karen Keller. **Accommodations:** 6 rooms (all with private bath), four with working fireplaces. **Rates:** $140–$185 MAP, $95–$125 B&B. Less weekdays and for more than 3 days. **Included:** Breakfast and tea; MAP rates include five-course candlelit dinner. **Added:** 9% tax, 15% gratuity; $25 surcharge during fall and holiday seasons. **Minimum stay:** 2 nights on weekends, fall and holidays; $20 surcharge for one-night stays during these periods. **Credit cards accepted:** MasterCard, Visa, Discover. **Children:** Age 7 and older. **Pets:** Not accepted. **Smoking:** Permitted on the porch only. **Handicap access:** Some rooms. **Open:** Year-round.

➤ **Jay and Karen like to share their enthusiasm for exploring the local web of high farm roads with splendid mountain views.**

Chelsea has been hailed as one of the few remaining bastions of "Vermont character." Far enough from ski areas, colleges and other flatlander enclaves to retain its genuine rural quality, it's a beautiful village with a courthouse, steepled church, and two commons surrounded by handsome public buildings and Federal-era homes — one of them now the Shire Inn.

Built in 1832 of Vermont brick, the inn is elegant, from its graceful curving staircase and formal parlor to its lawns. The sunny parlor is furnished in a mix of antiques. Jay likes to point out the priceless 16th-century French version of a highboy that has found its way into the family. Ceilings and windows are high, the floorboards are exceptionally wide, and the room is filled with the chatter of a pair of parakeets.

The four larger guest rooms with fireplaces are so special that we can't imagine coming all this way not to spend the night in one. The Windsor Room, the former master bedroom, has a canopy bed and lovely feel, as does the Essex room (in yellow and green); antique quilts are scattered throughout the rooms. Jay and Karen are zealots when it comes to 100 percent cotton sheets, all perfectly ironed.

Meals are a point of pride with the innkeepers. Karen has been honored by the James Beard Foundation for her culinary skills. A country breakfast features muffins and scones, a choice of omelettes, or French toast. A five-course dinner, served by candlelight, might begin with a three-layer vegetable terrine followed by a pear sorbet, then chicken Wellington or veal Sicilian or a vegetable ravioli with basil sauce, followed by a salad and an irresistible dessert. Wine is served.

While it feels a hundred miles from everywhere, Chelsea is actually a short, scenic ride from the Connecticut River valley on one hand and the Stowe and Sugarbush valleys on the other. We always leave this special place feeling far more relaxed than when we arrived.

Cuttingsville

Maple Crest Farm

Box 120
Cuttingsville, VT 05738
802-492-3367

A vintage B&B on a working farm

Innkeepers: The Smiths. **Accommodations:** 6 rooms (some shared baths), 2 apartments. **Rates:** 2 apartments: $75 per couple; rooms: $50 per couple. **Included:** Full breakfast with rooms. **Minimum stay:** 2 nights requested. **Added:** 9% tax. **Credit cards accepted:** None. **Children:** Welcome in the apartments. **Pets:** Not accepted. **Smoking:** Restricted. **Handicap access:** No. **Open:** Year-round except January.

➤ **The Smiths are famous for their maple sugaring, done in their sugar house at the very top of the hill. Breakfast is as hearty and authentic as one would expect on a working farm. Winter offers spectacular cross-country skiing.**

High on a hill with a commanding view of stone walls and grazing land, this white brick house, built in 1808, has been in the Smith family for five generations. The views are great from any of the rooms, and the secluded setting on a typical Vermont backroad adds even more to the farm's beauty and charm. This is a gem of a B&B in a small hilltop village. Flower and vegetable gardens surround the house and a patio, where guests can relax.

The antiques aren't here to create an effect; they have been in the family for generations. The living room and downstairs parlor have Oriental and braided rugs, a Victrola and upright piano, old town ledgers, and pots of flowering violets. The house smells pleasantly old and is full of character.

The downstairs guest room, with a private half bath, is perfect for those who have difficulty with stairs. Upstairs is a wonderful sitting area shared by the three bedrooms. The old beds are short, and the antique dresser tops hold little boudoir accessories found in country life magazines. There also a modern two-bedroom apartment on the second floor that can be reserved by the week or weekend. Inquire about quilting weekends. This is also a popular place for small weddings.

Goshen

Blueberry Hill Inn

State Road 34
Goshen, VT 05733
802-247-6735
800-448-0707
Fax: 802-247-3983
info@blueberryhillinn.com
www.blueberryhillinn.com

> **A secluded cross-country ski mecca**

Owner: Tony Clark. **Accommodations:** 12 rooms (all with private bath). **Rates:** $240 per couple from mid-December through March and mid-September to mid-October; $190 per couple the rest of the year; $40 less per couple B&B. **Included:** Full breakfast and dinner. **Minimum stay:** 2 nights on weekends. **Added:** 9% tax, 15% service. **Credit cards accepted:** MasterCard, Visa. **Children:** Welcome; age 4 to 12 charged $44.50–$60 when in same room with parents. **Pets:** Not accepted. **Smoking:** Not permitted. **Handicap access:** Yes. **Open:** Year-round.

➤ **The cottage next door, complete with loft, sleeps a family of five comfortably.**

Guests may originally be drawn to Blueberry Hill because of the natural surroundings and wealth of outdoor activities. Once here, they quickly see that the meals are also very good and the atmosphere comfortable. In the winter the big draw is cross-country skiing on 75 miles of groomed trails; Blueberry Hill boasts the highest amount of groomed trails in the state. Snowshoeing is also growing in popularity. In the summer there's mountain biking, hiking for all levels of ability, all sorts of activities on nearby Lake Dunmore, and fishing.

Five miles down a state-maintained dirt road, Blueberry Hill stands alone in its splendor, nestled in the 13,000-acre Green Mountain National Forest. Atop a hill bursting with high bush blueberries, this 1813 farmhouse is a classic and unpretentious country inn.

The living rooms are comfortable, with the requisite fieldstone fireplace and creaking and uneven floors. Some guests gather in the greenhouse or outside, next to the spring fed pond. In the summer, use an inner tube to float lazily for hours. In the winter, a hole is cut in the ice so that you can jump in from the European-style sauna.

Chocolate chip cookies, coffee, and leftover desserts are available throughout the day from the pantry. The communal dining room is special: dried herbs and colorful flowers hang from the low rafters and a large hearth dominates the room. The pre-dinner cheese board tends to bring everyone together before the meal is served family-style at two long tables. The night of our arrival, the five-course dinner included shrimp tarts, crisp greens, roasted leg of lamb with squash and fruited couscous, and English scone short-cake with blueberries. (We've heard Tony makes a great soufflé, but we haven't had it yet.) A single entrée is served, but dietary conditions can be accommodated with advance notice.

As for the guest rooms in the main inn, the most popular of the four upstairs rooms is Romance, a corner room with expansive views and good afternoon light. We prefer the more countryish rooms off the lush greenhouse. (It stays vibrantly green even when the hill is covered in a blanket of snow.) Of the rooms in the back wing with peaked ceilings, we prefer the more spacious corner rooms. Three others are good for families, with an additional set of twin beds in the loft.

Killington Area

Cortina Inn

Route 4
Killington, VT 05751
802-773-3333
800-451-6108
Fax: 775-6948
cortina@aol.com
www.cortinainn.com

A full-service mini-resort

Innkeepers: Bob and Breda Harnish. **Accommodations:** 91 rooms, 6 suites. **Rates:** $95–$135 B&B, summer; $139–$179, winter; inquire about multi-day packages. **Included:** Breakfast. **Added:** 9% tax. **Credit cards accepted:** All major ones. **Minimum stay:** None. **Children:** Supervised programs; free in parent's room. **Pets:** By reservation in certain rooms. **Smoking:** Restricted in dining room but not tavern. **Handicap access:** 5 rooms. **Open:** Year-round.

➤ **A mix of qualities you don't expect to find in one place.**

Over the past twenty years, Bob and Breda Harnish have turned a roadside motor inn into an unusual small resort. Facilities include a health center, eight tennis courts, and an extensive network of trails for hiking, mountain biking, and skiing. Fly-fishing lessons, tennis clinics, and horseback riding are also offered, along with naturalist-led walking excursions.

As longtime owner Bob Harnish explains, the Cortina Inn is an unusual mix of things. On the one hand it accepts tour groups, and on the other it offers one of the most sophisticated menus and some of the most luxurious rooms in Vermont. It also caters to families with its sports facilities and programs and services like supervised dining and evening activities for kids so that parents can dine in style and get off to the theater.

Guests enter a dramatic, two-story lobby with plenty of places to sit around a circular hearth and an art gallery along the upper level. A second Centre Court Lobby, with a massive fieldstone fireplace and grand piano, serves as a gathering space for rooms in the east wing and as a setting for afternoon tea. Rooms vary substantially. Most in the old wing have two double beds; king-size beds prevail in the new wing. All the rooms have balconies, but request one on the back rather than the front (facing the parking lot and Route 4). A dozen of the luxurious rooms have fireplaces, and six have whirlpool tubs.

The fitness center includes an indoor pool, hot tub, saunas, and exercise machines, and a masseuse is on the premises.

The dining room, Zola's Grille, is soothingly decorated with dark green flowered walls and mauve linens. The moderately priced menu is imaginative enough to include homemade game sausage and Vermont goat cheese ravioli, and moderately priced entrées include fresh pasta with tossed vegetables and apple-smoked salmon.

In winter, the Alpine trails at Killington and Pico are just minutes away.

The October Country Inn

Upper Road
P.O. Box 66
Bridgewater Corners, VT 05035
802-672-3412
800-648-8421
ocie@vermontel.com
www.vermontel.com/~ocl/

An exceptionally hospitable country inn

Innkeepers: Richard Sims and Patrick Runkel. **Accommodations:** 10 rooms (8 with private bath). **Rates:** $125–$156 per couple MAP; $45 for each extra person in room; $25 per child aged 5–12; single rate, 20% less; weekend and midweek packages; inquire about B&B rates. **Included:** Breakfast and dinner. **Minimum stay:** 2 days on peak weekends. **Added:** 9% tax, 10% gratuity. **Credit cards accepted:** All major ones. **Children:** Welcome; no charge for children aged 5 and younger; $25 MAP for ages 5 through 12. **Pets:** Not accepted. **Smoking:** Not permitted. **Handicap access:** No. **Open:** Year-round except early November and early April.

➤ **Handy to Woodstock, Killington, and much of central and southern Vermont, this comfortable inn has exotic menus and a hilltop pool; guests feel unusually welcome.**

Just off busy Route 4 at one of its busiest junctions (Route 100A), the October Country Inn is tucked up a back road, seemingly a million miles from anywhere. Walk out the back door and up the terraced hill, up through the gardens and past the swimming pool, up and up for a sweeping view of steep valleys and the Green Mountains.

Painted oxblood red and retaining its plain lines, the old farmhouse has been opened up inside to create both airy spaces and cozy corners. The living room has inviting books, magazines, games, and places to sit around the hearth and potbellied stove as well as at the big round table in the dining room. In a second large, cheery dining room, guests gather at long tables for memorable meals — which can be Greek, Hungarian, Chinese, Mexican, Italian, or, occasionally, American. Candlelit dinners include homemade breads, cakes, home-grown vegetables, and splendid desserts.

Breakfasts are equally ambitious, geared to the cyclists at the inn when the skiers aren't here (Killington's Northeast Passage lifts are just five miles away).

The guest rooms vary in size and decor but not in the care with which they are decorated.

More than the decor, even more than the food, what guests remember about this place is the warmth of its hosts. Richard and Patrick do their utmost to introduce you to the full beauty and possibilities of the area. Woodstock, with its many restaurants and shops, is eight miles to the east, Killington's gondola is a little farther the other way, and the Calvin Coolidge Homestead is just down Route 100A, which continues on through Ludlow to the marvelous summer playhouse in Weston. Your hosts are theater buffs who offer packages featuring summer theater at Killington and Weston; they are also familiar with the current productions at the White River Theater Festival, the Dartmouth Summer Repertory, and the Dorset Playhouse. Consider the five-day midweek rates; this inn is ideally situated for exploring much of what's most beautiful in central and southern Vermont.

Tulip Tree Inn

Chittenden Dam Road
Chittenden, VT 05737
802-483-6213
800-707-0017
ttinn@innsover.net
www.tuliptreeinn.com

Backwoods pampering

Innkeepers: Ed and Rosemary McDowell. **Accommodations:** 8 rooms (all with private bath). **Rates:** $120–$289 per couple. **Included:** Breakfast and dinner. **Minimum stay:** 2 days on weekends, 3 on holidays. **Added:** 9% tax, 15% service charge. **Credit cards accepted:** MasterCard, Visa. **Children:** Not appropriate. **Pets:** Not accepted. **Smoking:** Not permitted. **Handicap access:** No. **Open:** Year-round except April and most of May.

➤ **Five-course candlelit dinners are served at a common table, and guests are encouraged to mingle.**

This luxurious home was built by William S. Barstow, a businessman who was one of Thomas Edison's collaborators and who was canny enough to sell his holdings for $40 million and retire here before the Great Depression.

It's the kind of place you feel pretty savvy yourself about finding. Although it's not far from Killington, it is definitely in its own hill-town world and caters to cross-country skiers in winter. In the summer there is swimming, canoeing, and fishing in Chittenden Reservoir, just down the road.

All of the rooms are attractive, but you may want to request one of the five with a Jacuzzi or one of those with a fireplace. Cocktails are served in the library/tap room, and dinner is a four-course, candlelit event.

Montgomery Village

Black Lantern Inn

Route 118
Montgomery Village, VT 05470
802-326-4507
800-255-8661
Fax: 802-326-4077

> **About as far north as you can get in Vermont, with fine dining and lodging**

Innkeepers: Rita and Allan Kalsmith. **Accommodations:** 10 rooms (all with private bath), 6 suites. **Rates:** $60–$75 per person MAP; $85 per person MAP in suite; $85–$125 B&B; less off-season. **Included:** Depends on meal plan; inquire about EP and ski week rates. **Added:** 9% tax, 13% gratuity. **Credit cards accepted:** All major ones. **Minimum stay:** None. **Children:** Welcome; half price. **Pets:** Not accepted. **Smoking:** Not permitted in dining room. **Handicap access:** No. **Open:** Year-round.

> ➤ **If the Black Lantern were in a resort village, it would cost twice as much. It's handy to nothing but exceptional downhill and cross-country skiing.**

This white-pillared brick inn was built in 1803 in the middle of town as a stage stop. No longer on any main route to anywhere, it is for couples who share a love of fine food and scenery far from busy resorts.

In winter, the ski trails at Jay Peak are just up Route 118, and some of the most reliable cross-country skiing in the East can be found in Hazen's Notch, visible from the inn's backyard. Montgomery Village itself is unusually picturesque and boasts seven covered bridges.

The inn offers a nice little pub and a gathering space warmed by a soapstone woodstove. The low-beamed dining room is intimate, with just seven round and oval tables, and the "Continental cuisine" is served by candlelight. Lamb Margarite is a specialty.

The guest rooms upstairs are small but sweet, not overly frilly but furnished with taste and comfortable antiques. There are also two suites (one three-bedroom with a fireplace) in the main inn and four more with fireplaces, sitting rooms, and whirlpool baths next door in the Burdett House.

Montpelier

The Inn at Montpelier

147 Main Street
Montpelier, VT 05602
802-223-2727
Fax: 802-223-0722

Sleep like a senator

Innkeepers: Maureen and Bill Russell, Heather and Patrick Henry. **Accommodations:** 12 rooms (all with private bath), 7 suites. **Rates:** $89–$155 per couple. **Included:** Continental breakfast. **Minimum stay:** None. **Added:** 9% tax. **Credit cards accepted:** All major ones. **Children:** $10 per person; no cribs or cots. **Pets:** Not accepted. **Smoking:** Not permitted. **Handicap access:** No. **Open:** Year-round.

➤ **A Continental breakfast is set out early each morning in the guest pantries in each house. It includes homemade granola as well as muffins, cereals, juice, and toast.**

Montpelier's wonderful 1870s Pavilion Hotel is now the Vermont Museum, but this minute capitol has another exceptional lodging place. The Inn at Montpelier, not far up Main Street from the state buildings and museum, is composed of two imposing Federal mansions, standing side by side.

A wide, columned verandah and large, 1880s sash windows have been added to the yellow brick Lamb-Langdon-Baird House, built in 1818. Inside, guests find a parlor with a marble fireplace and sofas covered in dark red chintz. There's also a small tap room, a formal dining room, and a game room.

Nine rooms are upstairs. Number 1 has a fireplace as well as a four-poster bed, a dressing alcove, and an inviting space for writing and reading. Ten more rooms are next door, in the vintage 1807 white clapboard house; all have been furnished with care. Six have fireplaces, and all have cable TV.

Pittsfield

Hawk North, Ltd.

Route 100
P.O. Box 529
Pittsfield, VT 05762
802-746-8911
800-832-8007
Fax: 802-746-8424

> **Luxurious condominiums off the beaten path**

Owner/manager: Tom Paino. **Accommodations:** 25 2- to 5-bedroom homes. **Rates:** $175–$405 per night, depending on season; off-season packages. **Minimum stay:** 2 nights. **Added:** 9% tax, 7% service charge. **Credit cards accepted:** All major ones. **Children:** Welcome. **Pets:** Not accepted. **Smoking:** Permitted in some homes. **Handicap access:** No. **Open:** Year-round.

➤ **The ultimate in privacy and luxury, condo-style**

Hawk homes have become synonymous with complete privacy and expansive views. They began to appear on this central Vermont hillside in the 1960s, all designed by Robert Williams to maximize their views and well built with massive fieldstone hearths and shake roofs.

No longer related to Hawk Mountain Resort (a later variation on this theme), Hawk North still offers some true resort amenities: tennis and swimming ponds on the property, and maid service, a stocked refrigerator, and catered meals can also be arranged.

Guests check in at the office, at the junction of Routes 100 and 107, then find their way farther up Route 100 onto the expansive property, comprising several former farms. The houses are widely scattered, out of sight of one another and everything else except the valley views. Each home is individually owned and the decor varies, but all offer spacious living/dining rooms, full kitchens, and spacious bedrooms. Some have saunas and/or hot tubs.

In winter, skiers can choose between cross-country at Blueberry Hill in Goshen or Mountain Meadows at Killington, or downhill skiing at Killington, Sugarbush, and the Middlebury Ski Bowl.

Smugglers' Notch

Smugglers' Notch Resort

Smugglers Notch, VT 05464
802-644-8851
800-451-8752 in the U.S. and Canada
Fax: 802-644-2713
smuggs@smuggs.com
www.smuggs.com

> **A mountain geared to week-long family stays**

President: Bob Mulcahy. **Accommodations:** 415 condominium units. **Rates:** Winter: $89–$105 per adult per day for 5-night, 5-day Club Smugglers Program; $75–$89 per child (age 17 and under); 5-night family special studio (2 adults, 2 children) from $1,560. Summer: from $289 per person for 5 days; family special (2 adults, 2 children) $899–$1,359. Packages are available for 2-, 3-, 5-, and 7-night stays. **Included:** Lifts, lessons, activities, summer programs for children and adults, all facilities. **Added:** 9% tax. **Credit cards accepted:** All major ones. **Minimum stay:** 2 nights on weekends. **Pets:** Not accepted. **Handicap access:** Yes. **Open:** Year-round.

➤ **Smugglers' Notch began as a ski area, but it has evolved into a condo-based resort dedicated to keeping families busy for five days at a time, in summer as well as ski season.**

This forest of condominiums is clustered around a ski area just north of Smugglers' Notch. While it all began as a ski village, the skiing has now been upstaged by a year-round program of family-oriented activities.

You can stay here for just a night or two, but it doesn't make sense, any more than it does to come alone. Smugglers' is for families who stay at least a weekend and preferably for five days. That's how the programs and packages are set up.

The ski mountain is 3,640-foot-high Madonna, but the condominium village is clustered at the bottom of Morse Mountain (2,250 feet), from which guests can get to the resort's other trails.

The condos range from studios to five-bedroom units in a variety of shapes. Most have fireplaces, balconies, telephones, TVs, and washers and dryers, and many have mountain views. You might want to request the newest, nicely designed units with whirlpool baths. All the units are clustered in a way that puts the ski trails and other facilities within an easy walk.

Activities include year-round tennis, swimming, and horseback riding; in both winter and summer the Alice's Wonderland nursery, for newborns and tots, is particularly impressive, as is the program for teens. All the summer rates include a supervised childrens camp with riding, movies, hikes, fishing, and games. Water options include a family lap pool, a turtle slide (geared to children up to age three), a giant rapid river ride (a 300-foot-long tube ride ending in a splash pool), and the Little Smugglers' Lagoon — a whimsical pool with a cave, disappearing fountains, a tunnel, and a lazy current you can float down.

Rum Runners' Hideaway, a freshwater lake, offers swimming, fishing, boating, picnics, and shoreline activities.

Winter and summer alike, the programs include activities every day. In winter the focus is on skiing (cross-country as well as downhill), and something is scheduled for every evening. On Thursdays, for instance, it's Showtime in winter; in summer it's the night for a Vermont Country Fair, complete with fried dough, games, craftspeople, and pony rides. Notchview Park has a climbing wall, croquet court, swimming pools, family bbq court, volleyball court, and a small children's wishing well (you have to see it to believe it).

Stowe

Edson Hill Manor and Ten Acres Lodge

1500 Edson Hill Road
Stowe, VT 05672
802-253-7371
800-621-0284
Fax: 635-2694

| This inn is about as romantic as an inn can be |

Innkeepers: Jane and Eric Lande. **Accommodations:** 9 rooms in the manor, 16 in the carriage houses at Edson Hill. At Ten Acres: 8 rooms upstairs in the Lodge; 8 in Hill House and two cottages. **Rates:** Summer: $55–$85 per person B&B; $75–$105 per person MAP; 3-day, 5-day, and 7-day-weekend packages available; more in foliage season and winter, less in spring and after foliage. **Included:** Varies with meal plan. **Minimum stay:** 5 nights in holiday weeks. **Added:** 9% tax, 15% service charge. **Credit cards accepted:** All major ones. **Children:** Under age 4 free; special rates for older youngsters. **Pets:** Not accepted. **Smoking:** Permitted only in certain rooms. **Handicap access:** Some rooms. **Open:** Year-round.

➤   **Few inns in New England are characterized by such genuine opulence, inside and out.**

A part of and yet apart from Stowe, on 225 very private acres, Edson Hill Manor sits at the end of a road high on the northern flank of the valley. The brick and wood structure has a high pitched and gabled roof. The living room is probably the most luxurious in Stowe: it is pine-paneled, hung with unusually fine art, and furnished with Oriental rugs, antiques, couches, and chairs covered in needlepoint. The dining room is surprisingly small, overlooking landscaped lawns. The menu changes constantly but consistently earns rave reviews.

Each of the guest rooms in the manor is a fanciful blend of papers, fabrics, and furnishings, and most of the bathrooms have hand-painted designs. The rooms in the carriage house are more subdued and spacious, with fireplaces and books, knotty pine walls, wing chairs, desks, and reproduction antiques.

The terrace and landscaped lawns invite you to stroll outside in summer, and in winter, 25 kilometers of cross-country trails are maintained. Guided trail rides are offered year-round, and carriage rides in the summer.

Edson Hill is one of the best places to eat in Stowe and, now that Jane and Eric Lande have acquired Ten Acres Lodge, that venerable inn too has regained its old reputation for fine dining. Our menu on a summer night at Ten Acres included spicy Maine crab cakes with warm cucumber salad and a mustard dill sauce and salmon Wellington. Chef Matt Delos supervises the kitchens at both inns, and MAP guests at either enjoy reciprocal dining privileges.

The two establishments, however, remain very different. Ten Acres is an 1840s farmhouse that has been one of Stowe's more distinguished inns for more than forty years. Its property (10 acres) features a small pool and tennis courts.

Ten Acres is across the valley from Edson Hill, less removed from tourist traffic but by the same token handier to shops, the Recreation Path, and the trails and views at nearby Trapp Family Lodge.

We prefer rooms in the manor at Edson Hill to those in the Lodge, but the spacious units, each with a fireplace, in the Hill House at Ten Acres are preferable to the Carriage House rooms at Edson Hill. The two cottages at Ten Acres (one with two and the other with three bedrooms) both have fireplaces and are delightfully furnished. Artwork in both common and guest rooms throughout both properties is outstanding.

The Golden Eagle Resort

Mountain Road
Stowe, VT 05672
802-253-4811
800-626-1010
Fax: 802-253-2561
stoweagle@aol.com
www.stoweagle.com

A family-run resort in Stowe

General manager: Neil Van Dyke. **Accommodations:** 71 rooms, 20 apartments and chalets. **Rates:** $79–$169 for rooms, $169–$239 per unit for suites and chalets in summer; packages available. **Included:** Children's program, facilities; breakfast and dinner served. **Minimum stay:** 2-day minimum some weekends; some multi-day stays during holiday periods. **Added:** 9% tax. **Credit cards accepted:** All major ones. **Children:** Under age 12 free; special programs. **Smoking:** Rooms available for smokers. **Pets:** Not allowed. **Handicap access:** 3 rooms (there are also rooms designed specifically for the hearing impaired). **Open:** Year-round.

➤   **This motel has evolved into a full-service resort, with dining rooms, pools, a complimentary children's program, and units geared to families.**

Family owned and operated, this resort began as a twelve-unit motel in 1963 and has evolved through two generations into a sprawling, 80-acre landscaped complex with two restaurants serving dinner, three swimming pools, hiking and nature trails, a fitness center, two stocked trout ponds, and a supervised children's program. Despite its size, the inn seems to pay attention to each guest's needs, a quality of caring.

The check-in desk is adjacent to the pleasantly paneled coffee shop, where breakfast is served. The Library Lounge, upstairs in the fitness center, is large and comfortable and has board games, books, and a big-screen TV. The center also includes an indoor pool, a whirlpool, and sauna as well as exercise machines. Massages are offered.

An unusually extensive program for children is available on certain nights in winter as well as throughout July and August; it includes arts and crafts, short hikes, and evening movies. There's also a game room and a playground, complete with jungle gym and playhouse.

All the rooms have cable TV, air conditioning, coffeemakers and direct-dial phones; some have kitchenettes. Mini-suites have fireplaces and whirlpools; one-bedroom suites have cathedral ceilings, brick hearths, and full kitchens. There are also two- and three-bedroom apartments as well as chalets.

Guests breakfast in the cheerful Coffee Shop and can dine at the Partridge Inn across the road, where the specialty is seafood. Both convey a sense of being privately, enthusiastically managed rather than the impersonal atmosphere you might expect from a resort this size.

The Golden Eagle is near the bottom of Route 108, better known as "the mountain road." It's an easy stroll to Stowe Village along the Recreation Path, a well-designed jogging and biking road. You can also rent a bike and follow the Rec Path much of the way up the mountain; in winter, a shuttle bus provides access to the ski slopes and touring centers. Since the resort offers comlimentary pickup at both the bus and train in Waterbury (Vermont Transit and Amtrak's *Vermonter*), and will also meet arriving guests at Burlington airport, this is one Vermont resort that is genuinely accessible without a car.

Green Mountain Inn

Route 100
P.O. Box 60
Stowe, VT 05672
802-253-7301
800-445-6629
Fax: 802-253-5096
grnmtinn@aol.com
www.greenmountaininn.com

> A historic inn at the core of Vermont's number one resort

Innkeeper/manager: Patty Clark. **Accommodations:** 39 inn rooms, 15 annex rooms, 10 clubhouse rooms, 8 millhouse rooms. **Rates:** $89–$259 per couple EP, more for a unit with kitchen. **Included:** Use of pool, fitness center. **Minimum stay:** 2-night minimum in peak season weekends. **Added:** 9% tax. **Credit cards accepted:** All major ones. **Children:** Under age 12, free. **Pets:** Accepted. **Smoking:** Some rooms for smokers. **Handicap access:** Some rooms. **Open:** Year-round.

> ➤ **The Green Mountain Inn is large, complete, and ideal for those who want to be in the thick of the resort village hustle and bustle.**

At the corner of Route 100 and Mountain Road in the heart of the village sits the Green Mountain Inn, dating from 1833.

Since a complete restoration in the late 1980s, the inn exudes grace. The first floor has many sitting areas, a bar and living room with fireplaces, a library with a chess set, Oriental rugs, and fine antiques reminiscent of old New England. There are guest rooms on both the second and third floors; the rambling second floor has more character and some nice sitting areas. The rooms are all decorated with reproduction antiques; the queen-size beds have canopies. Deluxe Clubhouse rooms have kitchen facilities and the most luxurious rooms of all are in the new Mill House — each with a gas fireplace, canopy bed, and Jacuzzi — which are set in landscaped grounds behind the inn.

The Main Street Dining Room serves breakfast and dinner (seasonally). The Whip Bar downstairs, with old photographs leading guests toward the bar, offers a less formal atmosphere and a twelve-page menu. Antique buggy whips and riding crops, a marble floor, a brick hearth, and brass fixtures contribute to the atmosphere. Meals may also be served on the patio, which leads to the pool.

Beyond the pool is the Stowe Athletic Club, disguised as an old red barn. Its ammenities, complimentary to guests, include a whirlpool, sauna, steam room, Nautilus, rowing machines, treadmills, free weights, Stairmaster, and exercise classes. Massage and tanning are available at an added charge.

Nine clubhouse rooms above the health club have canopy beds, gas fireplaces, Jacuzzis, stenciling, cathedral ceilings, and views of the pool and gardens. Annex rooms, accessible directly from the parking lot and overlooking the pool, are also unusually spacious and nicely decorated. Note the unusually bold, brilliant Stowe watercolors by Walton Blodgett scattered through the inn.

Stowehof Inn

Edson Hill Road
P.O. Box 1108
Stowe, VT 05672
802-253-9722
800-932-7136
Fax: 802-253-7513

| Vermont's most fanciful inn

Owners: Peter and Tim Bartholomew. **Accommodations:** 46 rooms (all with private bath). **Rates:** $138–$240 per couple B&B; $75–$130 B&B, off-season; add $22 per person for MAP; inquire about many special packages. **Included:** Depends on meal plan.. **Minimum stay:** No set policy. **Added:** 9% tax, 15% gratuity. **Credit cards accepted:** All major ones. **Children:** Under age 13, free; crib is exta. **Pets:** Not accepted. **Smoking:** Some guest rooms for smokers; not permitted in dining room. **Handicap access:** No. **Open:** Year-round.

➤ **Whimsy, fine food, and good service combine to give Stowehof a loyal following.**

Stowehof is unique, almost eccentric. The sod-roofed porte cochere is supported by two giant maple trees. Twinkling white lights and a heavy lavender door greet guests before the bellhop does. Inside, hand-planed wide floorboards begin to convey the feeling of an unusual European hotel.

The multilevel living room has three areas: one has a sunken fireplace, one a huge glass pane affording mountain views, and the third an imaginative alcove. These nooks and corners (with more downstairs in the lounge) are decorated with peculiar antiques and artifacts. Game tables suit every mood, and an almost life-size king, queen, and jack of hearts are painted on the wall. The common room furnishings are modest, but the taproom resembles a Tyrolean bar, with barrel chairs, a red rug, and beer steins on the shelves. A replica of the interior of an old Vermont covered bridge is another imaginative architectural touch.

The second and third floors are accessible via an antique Otis elevator. A second-floor game room has a pool table and space to put up your feet.

Each guest room has been individually designed and furnished; frankly, we like some far more than others. You might inquire about the particular decor of your room when you book it. Some have mirrors for walls; some have an extra Murphy bed; some have Chippendale desks or Queen Anne chairs. The deluxe rooms have dressing and sitting rooms and mirrored doors. Fireplaces and honeymoon suites are also available. The demi-suites have fireplaces and kitchenettes. All the rooms have an adjoining balcony or patio, but the nicest views are found in the back, toward the birches, fields, and mountains.

The chef creates American cuisine with a stress on local produce. The menu changes with the seasons, but you can count on exotic dishes such as venison breast stuffed with broccoli and Vermont cheddar cheese and roast quail with a wild rice stuffing. Elaborate desserts are a specialty. The inn is a winner of the *Wine Spectator* award of excellence. The elegant dining room is less flamboyantly decorated than the rest of the inn. In summer you can also dine on lighter fare on the terrace, and in winter, by the fire in the Tap Room.

The facilities include an attractive heated pool, four tennis courts, a sauna, and sleigh rides in the winter. Golf, tennis, and horseback riding packages are available in summer.

Topnotch at Stowe Resort and Spa

P.O. Box 1458
Stowe, VT 05672
802-253-8585
800-451-8686
Fax: 802-253-9263
topnotch@sover.net
www.topnotch-resort.com/spa

The height of luxury at the base of Vermont's highest mountain

General Manager: Robert Boyle. **Accommodations:** 77 rooms, 13 suites, 17 2- and 3-bedroom town houses. **Rates:** $140–$310 EP per couple per standard room; inquire about suites and condominiums. Spa and tennis packages offered, except during Christmas holidays. **Included:** Use of pool, coed sauna, and whirlpool; cross-country trails. **Minimum stay:** 6 nights at Christmas, 2 nights on some winter weekends. **Added:** 9% tax. **Credit cards accepted:** All major ones. **Children:** Welcome. **Pets:** Accommodated in hotel. **Smoking:** Smoking and nonsmoking rooms; not permitted in restaurant. **Handicap access:** Some rooms. **Open:** Year-round.

➤ **Topnotch offers an exceptional winter spa package: morning skiing, afternoon exercise and spa services, plus a diet program.**

You know you are in an unusual place from the moment you enter the stone-walled lobby, with its 12-foot-high windows and panoramic view.

Each guest room has been individually decorated with carefully selected furniture, antiques, and art. Most of the views are of Stowe's ski mountains and forests. The extras include a private library, TV, imported perfumed soaps and bath gels, and ice delivered every afternoon. Personal sewing kits, plush towels, a radio, and a direct-dial phone complete the picture.

The candlelit, formal dining room has an intimate, rich feel to it. Varied and expensive menus, vintage wines, and sumptuous desserts are de rigueur. A spa menu is also available. Breakfast can be served in your room, and lunch can be taken on the terrace (enclosed by lush foliage in summertime), where the 17-foot statue *Acrobats* is mounted. Tea is served each afternoon in the living room. In the bar, decorated with farm kitchen memorabilia, sofas and chairs are grouped around the fireplace.

Topnotch also includes a full-service spa, with exercise rooms, a beautiful pool, and a waterfall for tired muscles in one of the Jacuzzis. There are also steam and sauna rooms and a range of spa services (seaweed body wraps, mineral and salt hydrotherapy treatments).

An equestrian center and cross-country ski touring center are on the premises, and the facilities include an outdoor pool and indoor and outdoor tennis. Alpine skiing at Mount Mansfield is up the road, and Topnotch's cross-country trails tie into Stowe's extensive network. Bicycles can be rented here.

Sugarbush Area

The Guest House at Knoll Farm

Box 179
Bragg Hill Road
Waitsfield, VT 05673
802-496-3939

A farm for adults who want to tune in

Innkeeper: Ann Day. **Accommodations:** 4 rooms (all with shared baths). **Rates:** $100 per couple; 5- and 7-day rates. **Included:** Full breakfast, dinner. **Added:** 9% tax. **Credit cards accepted:** None. **Children:** Over age 12. **Pets:** Not accepted. **Smoking:** Not permitted. **Handicap access:** No. **Open:** May through October.

➤ **Set high above the Mad River Valley on 150 acres of pasture and woods, this farmhouse offers unusual peace and beauty.**

Ann Day, a locally respected poet and photographer, has acquired a strong following since she began taking in guests in 1957. The bright, comfortable guest rooms have expansive views and both the common room and music room (with a player piano and pump organ) are well stocked with good books and magazines.

Many guests get in a long walk up through the meadows before breakfast, which is ample and served in a flower-filled room with a view of the pond. Dinner is family-style and features farm-grown food.

Outdoors, gardening and general farm chores await visitors so inclined. The pond is good for swimming and rowboating.

The classic red barn houses horses, a pig, a flock of chickens, and dogs and cats. A small herd of Scottish Highland cattle graze nearby.

This is not the kind of place to stop for just one night. The idea is to get into the rhythm of farm life and simple country living as it has been practiced on this hillside since 1803. Ann, an ardent naturalist, frequently leads nature hikes and guests tend to find their own favorite walks through this spectacular hilltop spread. Ask about the special workshops, ranging from an intensive course in Spanish to poetry workshops and the annual barn reading.

Inn at Mad River Barn

R.R. 1
P.O. Box 88
Waitsfield, VT 05673
802-496-3310
800-631-0466

A vintage ski lodge that's a summer find

Innkeeper: Betsy Pratt. **Accommodations:** 15 rooms (all with private bath). **Rates:** Winter: $60–$80 per couple, B&B; $130, MAP. Summer (B&B): $60 per room in the Barn, $65 in the annex; $85 on weekends and in foliage season; $10 less midweek. Group rates offered. **Included:** Breakfast; dinner added in winter. **Minimum stay:** Rarely. **Added:** 9% tax. **Credit cards accepted:** Master-Card, Visa. **Children:** Welcome. **Pets:** Not accepted. **Smoking:** Permitted. **Handicap access:** No. **Open:** Year-round.

➤ **This is the kind of ski area and ski lodge you thought had vanished decades ago, geared to active guests year-round.**

Mad River Barn preserves the rich, warm atmosphere of a 1940s ski lodge (it opened in 1948, the same time as Mad River Glen, the neighboring ski area). Betsy Pratt is the primary owner and manager of both and she's very much here, answering the phone, waiting up for late arrivals, and, in summer, rising early to cook breakfast.

The Barn houses a large game room, a lounge with a fireplace and a full bar, a restaurant, and many comfortable deep chairs. The bar, in particular, is simply wonderful — it comes alive with skiers warming themselves by the fire. Furnished in the rustic, historic decor of the Green Mountains, the room features antlers over the fireplace and antique skis on the walls. A huge sundeck off the lounge is good for breakfast and gazing across the expansive back lawn up into the birches. The dining room is another special space, filled with mismatched oak tables and original American art of the 1930s.

The pine-paneled guest rooms in the Barn are unusually large, permitting an extra cot or two without crowding and making it a good spot for families. The rooms are simply but nicely furnished, and the beds have quilts that Betsy has made herself. The annex, a small farmhouse dating from 1820, has been remodeled to provide deluxe rooms, each with a sauna, a TV, and a kitchenette.

Up the slope behind the Barn and past a grove of birches is a swimming pool, secluded in an idyllic meadow. The gardens are nicely landscaped with white perennials and conifers making this, incidentally, a great setting for wedding receptions.

Food is taken seriously here, and while the chefs vary from year to year, meals here can usually rival those elsewhere in this resort valley, which is known for its dining as well as its skiing. Mad River Glen is a challenging ski area that is favored by many Vermonters and a number of New England's best skiers.

There are also 60 kilometers of old logging roads that unfold from the surrounding meadows to make cross-country and hiking or mountain biking trails. One downhill trail runs right to the lodge. In the summer, when the lodge is strictly B&B, the valley offers theater and an unusual choice of sports, including gliding and horseback riding.

The Inn at the Round Barn

R.R. Box 247
East Warren Road
Waitsfield, VT 05673
802-496-2276
Fax: 802-496-8832
roundbarn@madriver.com
www.innattheroundbarn.com

A plush farmhouse with a lap pool in its round barn

Innkeepers: Annemarie Simko Defrest. **Accommodations:** 11 double rooms (all with private bath). **Rates:** $115–$205 per couple; more on holidays and foliage. **Included:** Full breakfast, afternoon snacks. **Minimum stay:** 2 nights on weekends, foliage season. **Added:** 9% tax. **Credit cards accepted:** All major ones. **Children:** Over age 15. **Pets:** Not accepted. **Smoking:** Not permitted. **Handicap access:** No. **Open:** Year-round.

➤ **Weddings of up to two hundred people are a specialty.**

The Joslin Round Barn is one of only a dozen round barns left in Vermont, and visitors have always stopped to admire it. Set on 85 acres, mostly fields that stretch back into the hills, it is on the East Warren Road on the quiet side of the Mad River Valley, away from the ski area and the traffic on Route 100.

The Simko family has painstakingly restored both the barn and the farmhouse, now a B&B. Downstairs, the rooms are unusually gracious without being stuffy. There's a living room with books and a fireplace and a bright, wicker-filled sun porch, the scene of elegant breakfasts that guests tend to linger over. Some guest rooms have canopy beds and Jacuzzis; others have spool or Victorian beds and standard bathrooms.

The Simkos previous life was the flower business (which their sons continue), and the house is filled with buds and greenery. There's a greenhouse behind the barn, and you can swim into it from the 58-foot lap pool that's been created in the bottom of the barn. The top two floors of the barn are now the Green Mountain Cultural Center, the site of frequent concerts, plays, exhibits, and receptions.

Outside there are manmade ponds, one fifteen feet deep for swimming, as well as trails that are tracked and marked in winter for cross-country skiing. The major ski mountains in the valley are Sugarbush and Mad River Glen. In the summer, there is a choice of summer theater, tennis, and golf, not to mention soaring and horseback riding. In spring and summer, a series of workshops, from cooking classes to painting and photography, are also held in the barn.

Millbrook Inn

Route 17
R.F.D. Box 62
Waitsfield, VT 05673
802-496-2405
800-477-2809
Fax: 802-496-9735
millbrkinn@aol.com
www.bbonline.com/vt/milbrook/

Fine food in a small, informal inn

Innkeepers: Joan and Thom Gorman. **Accommodations:** 7 rooms (all with with private bath, all queen-size except one twin). **Rates:** $60–$70 per person MAP in winter; ski week, childrens rates; $49 per person MAP or $34 B&B in summer. **Included:** Depends on meal plan. **Minimum stay:** 2 nights on selected weekends. **Added:** 9% ta9. **Credit cards accepted:** All major ones. **Children:** Over age 6. **Pets:** Accepted with approval in summer and fall. **Smoking:** Not permitted. **Handicap access:** No. **Open:** Except April, May, and from late October to early December.

➤ **Good value and warm hospitality characterize this pleasant, casual inn.**

You don't notice the dining room at first. You enter through the warming room (heated by a woodstove in winter); beyond are two attractive living rooms that invite you to sit down.

But Millbrook's heart is the dining room, well known locally for an extensive, moderately priced menu featuring fresh ingredients grown nearby and Indian dishes, a vestige of Thom Gorman's days in the Peace Corps. It seats just twenty-six people, but it feels spacious, and French doors open to the garden. Joan is the hostess, waitress, and baker.

The menu usually includes a choice of pasta dishes, fish, Vermont lamb in some guise, and Indian entrées such as chicken Brahmapuri (boneless breast of chicken cooked in a rich, spicy, village-style curry). Beef crusted with a crushed five-peppercorn mixture and served with homemade fettuccini is another specialty. The desserts are all homemade and sinful, and there is always anadama bread.

The first-floor guest room, the Willow Tree Room, has a queen-size and a smaller sleigh bed, floor-to-ceiling bookcases, and a private bath. The other bedrooms are upstairs: the Rose Room has a slanted ceiling stenciled with American folk art and furnished in bright hand-painted furniture; and the Jack Dana Room is a bright sunny room with a brass, queen-size bed. The Waterfall Room is named for the style of its bed and matching dresser; the Henry Perkins Room, named for the inn's founder, is a large sunny room with a log cabin quilt on its queen-size bed; and the Shell Room, for the shape of the headboard, matching dresser, and mirror. The spacious Wedding Ring Room has antique pine furniture.

A ski lodge since 1948 (Mad River Glen and Sugarbush are just up the road), Millbrook has become a true country inn under the Gormans' nurturing since 1979. In winter there is extensive cross-country as well as Alpine skiing, and in summer the Mad River/Sugarbush Valley, a lively resort center, offers theater, horseback riding, gliding, hiking, and much more. In summer, breakfast is served in the garden, overlooking the pond.

The Champlain Valley

Best Bed-and-Breakfasts

Best Family Finds

Best Gourmet Getaways

Best Resort

Best Inns

Best Romantic Getaways

Addison
Whitford House, A Country Inn, 604
Brandon
Lilac Inn, 608
Middlebury
Swift House Inn, 614
Shelburne
The Inn at Shelburne Farms, 619

Enclosed on the west by Lake Champlain and on the east by the Green Mountains, this rolling, mostly pastoral region has a feel of its own. Its bounded by Route 4 (a limited-access highway here) on the south, the Canadian border on the north, and crossed by Route 7, the old north-south highway that is beautiful in spots but bogs down into a commercial strip around Rutland and Burlington.

Rutland, the second-largest city in Vermont — population 18,435, a medium-size suburb in most states — is the business and shopping center for the Lower Champlain Valley and makes a good lunch or dinner stop. Just north of town, Proctor is the site of the Vermont Marble exhibition.

Lake Champlain itself flows contrarily north, looking like a river until it widens above Chimney Point, ultimately emptying after a hundred miles or so into Canada's Richelieu River. The largest lake in the East, it's one of the most beautiful in the country, with views of the Adirondacks as well as the Green Mountains.

The heart of the Champlain Valley is the rolling orchard and dairy country of Addison County. Its hub is **Middlebury,** the home of prestigious Middlebury College and a number of restaurants and shops that cluster around Otter Creek Falls. Don't miss the State Craft Center at Frog Hollow.

You may also make the justifiably popular excursion in the Middlebury area through apple country around Shoreham to Larrabees Point and across the lake on a small cable ferry (franchised by the Vermont legislature in 1799) to Fort Ticonderoga. Lake excursions are also offered from Teachout's General Store (vintage 1836) on the Vermont shore.

Vergennes, midway between Middlebury and Burlington, is the smallest city (population 2,300) in the United States and the home of the Lake Champlain Maritime Museum on Basin Harbor.

Burlington, Vermont's biggest city with a population of under 40,000, is a lively college town with grand views across Lake

Champlain. Just south of town in **Shelburne** is the Shelburne Museum, a magnificent collection of Americana amassed by Electra Havemeyer Webb, whose family built New England's grandest lakeside estate. The central mansion is now an inn, and the grounds are used in summer for Mozart concerts.

North of Burlington the highway heads for Montreal, but the byway (Route 2) leads across a long causeway right out onto Lake Champlain and its three largest islands: Grand Isle, **North Hero,** and Isle la Motte. This is beautiful, relaxed, surprisingly little frequented summer country. It is rolling farmland, but with small golf courses, marinas, beaches, and views across the lake to the high mountains on either shore. In winter, when the lake is frozen and windswept and humans are few and far between, it's pristine and almost ghostly.

Addison

Whitford House, A Country Inn

Grandey Road (off Route 22A)
RR 1, Box 1490
Vergennes, VT 05491
802-758-2704
800-746-2704
Fax: 802-758-2089

An elegantly comfortable farmhouse B&B like no other

Innkeepers: Barbara and Bruce Carson. **Accommodations:** 2 rooms (both with private bath), 2 suites. **Rates:** $90–$110 per couple for rooms, $150 for suite; $15 more during foliage. **Included:** Full breakfast. **Minimum stay:** None. **Added:** 9% tax. **Credit cards accepted:** None. **Children:** Welcome. **Pets:** Dogs sometimes accepted. **Smoking:** Not permitted. **Handicap access:** No. **Open:** Year-round.

➤ **It's difficult to describe these views without using superlatives that could sound exaggerated. Trust us: if you appreciate uninterrupted rolling meadows, cornfields, and mountains, you won't want to leave.**

When you first come upon the Whitford House, located a few miles off scenic Route 22A and down a country dirt road, you'll feel like you stumbled onto a little secret. The guest cottage, coupled with the common space in the main house, catapults the sophisticated

Whitford house onto the short list of great New England hideaways. In the days when so many bed-and-breakfasts feel commercial, the Whitford House falls into the category of a welcoming country home.

The cottage is separated from the main house by a trellis and brick walkway. Like the common rooms in the farmhouse, the cottage is elegantly furnished with a stylish mix of country antiques and contemporary pieces. Kilims and hand-woven wool carpets cover pine floors, while the bathroom boasts radiant heat beneath the slate floor.

The master suite features a separate sitting room, peaked ceilings, and floor-to-ceiling windows that face the mountains. French doors lead from the king-bedded room into the sitting room. It's all quite dramatic. The first-floor guest room is a cozy corner room, shaded by the front porch, with barnboard walls in its private bathroom.

The "slate room" is as dramatic a living room as we've seen in a long time. It's rustically elegant with wrought-iron chandeliers, a baby grand piano in front of multi-paned glass windows, a floor-to-ceiling stone hearth, and an open stairway leading up to the second floor. (Though not used by guests, it is architecturally striking.) Many of the fine modern paintings around the house were created by the Carsons' daughter Katie. And since the they hail from Arizona, you'll notice some Southwestern accents.

The Carson's make a great breakfast, which might consist of granola, zucchini bread, scalloped apples, and frittatas. It's served at one long harvest table in the simple Colonial-style dining room. Guests often gather in the library room for morning coffee, where unobstructed picture windows let in plenty of light and mountain views. Shelves are lined with books, the mission chairs are comfy, and in cool weather, the fire is lit.

The pantry is always open for guests. Barbara is known for her spicy ginger cookies and for working hard to please guests. On our last visit the Carsons offered lunch to us and to guests who were checking in early. We get the distinct impression that's just the way they are.

Just beyond the cornfields is Dead Creek, along a north-south flyway for blue heron and geese, among other birds you'll see. Sheep and beagles also make their home here. This is prime bicycling country, and the Carsons have loaner bikes available.

Alburg

Thomas Mott Homestead

Box 149B, R.F.D. 2
Blue Rock Road on Lake Champlain
Alburg, VT 05440
802-796-3736
800-348-0843 (outside Vermont)
Fax: 802-796-3736
www.go-native.com/inns/0162.html

A lakeside B&B

Innkeeper: Pat Schallert. **Accommodations:** 5 rooms (all with private bath).
Rates: $75–$95 per couple, $10 per extra person. **Included:** Full breakfast.
Added: 9% tax. **Credit cards accepted:** All major ones. **Children:** Over age 6.
Pets: Not accepted. **Smoking:** Not permitted. **Handicap access:** No. **Open:**
Year-round.

➤ **Pat Schallert seems to genuinely care about his guests and shares
with them his understanding of all there is to see and do in this seemingly
quiet byway.**

This vintage 1838 farmhouse is right on the shore of Lake Champlain, overlooking some of the highest mountains in Vermont. You
may just want to sit on the porch or in the gazebo and take in the
amazing view. Or you can hop into a canoe and paddle around Ransom's Bay.

Each guest room is different, and two are so exceptional that
regulars tend to schedule their trips around their availability —
Ransom's Rest, with a fireplace and balcony, and the downstairs
Corner Suite, with a lake view and dressing room. All guest rooms
look onto the lake and are brightly, carefully furnished with quilts
and antiques.

While the common space includes a living room with a fireplace and a glassed-in porch, the center of the house is the kitchen and adjacent dining room. The freezer is stocked with Ben & Jerry's ice cream (help yourself; chilled glass dishes are provided). The old tailors table is set each morning for a breakfast so elaborate that you make your selections the day before: quiche, French toast, and an array of omelettes are usual, with plenty of fresh fruit, juice, and local maple syrup.

In his previous life Pat Schallert was a wine importer and distributor in California (note the collection of books on wine and cookbooks near the stairway).

From mid-July through August, the Royal Lipizzan horses perform in a meadow down the road. Otherwise there is boating (from a new 40-foot-long dock), bicycling, swimming, fishing, antiquing, and whatever else you desire to slow down and tune into this exceptionally beautiful corner of New England. The grounds of the Thomas Mott Homestead are a great place just to play horseshoes or watch birds at the ubiquitous feeders. Pat always has a flock of baby quails you can feed.

Fall foliage is every bit as beautiful here as in more touristed parts of Vermont. In winter you can cross-country ski on the frozen lake or on 40 miles of nearby trails. Any time of year, this is also a good stop en route to Montreal, roughly an hour's drive to the north.

Brandon

Lilac Inn

53 Park Street
Brandon, VT 05733
802-247-5463
Fax: 802-247-5499
lilacinn@sover.net
www.lilacinn.com

This 10,000-square-foot mansion hosts many weddings

Innkeepers: Melanie and Michael Shane. **Accommodations:** 9 rooms (all with private bath). **Rates:** $110–$175 per couple; higher during foliage; multiple-night discounts. **Included:** Full breakfast; dinner also served for $36.50 per person. **Minimum stay:** 2 nights during foliage. **Added:** 9% tax. **Credit cards accepted:** All major ones. **Children:** Welcome. **Pets:** Not accepted. **Smoking:** Not permitted. **Handicap access:** Yes. **Open:** Year-round.

➤ **Michael and Melanie are good public citizens; they created a local scholarship fund and host free public concerts and readings in the grand ballroom on winter weekends.**

Even the most casual passerby can't help but notice the grand 1909 mansion a couple of blocks from the village green. In mid-1991 Michael and Melanie — he a contractor from southern California, she an architect and interior designer from Long Island — began the painstaking two-year-long job of restoring and renovating the spacious house.

The Georgian Revival mansion, in a distinguished historic district, has ample indoor and outdoor common space, including a wide front verandah decked with wicker furniture. A formal garden and brick patio sit nestled between the two rear wings of the house. A putting green, gazebo, and formal gardens are the focus of the backyard. The living room is small but inviting with a fireplace and floor-to-ceiling bookcases. Guests may lounge in the handsome bar, or at overstuffed chairs in front of the fireplace.

Wide hallways, high ceilings, and a grand staircase infused with light lead to second-floor guest rooms. Room 7, a large corner room overlooking the cobblestone courtyard, has a tall, four-poster pine bed and fireplace. Room 2 is also a favorite, a bright corner room with a wrought-iron bed. Room 1, an enormous suite, features a two-person Jacuzzi and a fireplace. The most inexpensive room, number 9, is smaller, without much of a view.

All rooms have luxurious bathrooms with deep, clawfoot tubs with hand-held European shower heads and a chunk of milled soap. Each has a bedside reading lamp and a hidden television. Most have area carpets over refurbished oak floors and ceiling fans.

A full country breakfast is served in the bright and handsome dining room, which is paneled in oak and overlooks the courtyard. Michael cooks breakfast and Sunday brunch, which begins with a fruit plate, muffins, and excellent cappuccino. He can prepare almost anything you'd want; just ask. Dinner is offered Wednesday through Saturday throughout the year, with the exception of Easter to Mother's Day (when it's offered by special arrangement).

The property is well suited to weddings of up to 250 people and the Shanes host many. In fact, so many weddings are held here that "average travelers" often cannot get a room on weekends when a wedding party reserves the whole place. If you are passing through New England during the wedding season, plan to stay here on a weekday. There are glossy, coffee table bride books in the living room; framed wedding photos and many of Melanie's handmade wedding dolls are displayed throughout the first floor. Melanie also designs and bakes wedding cakes — it's a natural extension of her training as an architect.

Three affectionate cats and three pugs are very much a part of the household, greeting guests at breakfast and at check-in. One cat is even bold enough to wander into your room if you've left the door ajar.

Burlington

Willard Street Inn

349 South Willard Street
Burlington, VT 05491
802-561-8710]
800-577-8712
Fax: 802-651-8714

> **A beautifully preserved inn built in the late 1880s**

Innkeeper: Gordon and Beverly Watson. **Accommodations:** 15 guest rooms (10 with private baths, 2 with adjoining shared bath). **Rates:** $75–$200 per couple. **Included:** Breakast and tea. **Minimum stay:** 2 days on holiday season. **Added:** 9% tax. **Credit cards accepted:** MasterCard, American Express, Visa, Discover. **Children:** Welcome. **Pets:** Not accepted. **Smoking:** Not permitted. **Handicap access:** No. **Open:** Year-round.

Finally, a place to stay that amplifies the charm of Burlington. Vermont's financial, educational, medical, and cultural center, Burlington boomed in the late 19th century as a lumbering port and much of its waterfront, walkable downtown — and the mansions on "the Hill" above the downtown, overlooking Lake Champlain — date from this period.

The Willard Street Inn was built in the late 1880s in The Hill section by Charles Woodhouse, a prominent businessman and Vermont Senator. Incorporating both Queen Anne and Colonial-Georgian Revival style, it's a brick mansion with marble detailing, a slate roof, and a marble exterior staircase descending to elaborate gardens below. Inside, high ceilings, intricate moldings, and wood floors have all been beautifully preserved. Guests enter a spacious, cherry-paneled foyer and are drawn to the solarium with its green and white tiles and walls of multi-pained windows overlooking Lake Champlain. Probably the most inviting breakfast room in all of Burlington, it's filled with flowering plants as well as light and the scent of freshly ground coffee and of still-warm muffins. Breakfast also includes fresh fruit, granola, and a hot dish that changes each day.

The adjoining parlor has a marble hearth, grand piano, and a comfortable couch and armchairs, but it's the solarium we keep returning to, especially in winter when the woodstove glows near the sofa and the floors contast with the snow outside.

Just converted to a B&B in 1996, the Willard Street Inn offers 15 rooms — ranging from the master bedroom to former maids' rooms, some of which have lake and some street views. All are crisply, tastefully furnished in antiques and well-chosen fabrics; most walls are papered. Request one of the front rooms overlooking the lake; those on the second floor are truly handsome and some of the more reasonably priced third-floor rooms have an even better view.

Innkeeper Beverly Watson also operates two of Burlington's most popular restaurants: the informal Whitecaps in the Burlington Boathouse and Isabel's, which is housed in a restored mill building also down by Lake Champlain. Inquire about occasional culinary workshops at the inn.

Within easy walking distance of the University of Vermont and Champlain College, and of the downtown shops and restaurants along Church Street, the Willard Street Inn is a logical roost from which to explore much of this fascinating city.

Highgate Springs

The Tyler Place on Lake Champlain

Box 100
Highgate Springs, VT 05460
802-868-4000
Fax: 802-868-7602

A family resort on Lake Champlain

Owners: The Tyler family. **Accommodations:** 23 suites, 27 cottages. **Rates:** $114–$183 per adult, $67–$78 per child in season; less in May, June, and September. **Included:** All meals and sports. **Minimum stay:** 1 week in July and August. **Added:** 9% tax, 10% service charge. **Credit cards accepted:** Master-Card, Visa, Discover. **Children:** Special programs, rates. **Pets:** Not accepted. **Smoking:** Restricted to your room. **Handicap access:** Some rooms. **Open:** Late May to mid-September.

➤ **Tyler Place has great programs designed for kids aged 2½ to 16 — plus facilities and care for newborns and toddlers. It's perhaps the best such program in New England.**

For more than sixty years, the Tyler Place has developed its own version of a family vacation. At this 165-acre spread on Lake Champlain, kids lead wonderful lives of their own while their parents enjoy numerous sports or activities and still have afternoons with the children. At dinner, parents and children regroup with their peers, frequently forming close friendships in the course of a week that are renewed in subsequent years. The capacity is about fifty families (two hundred guests of all ages).

Tennis, sailing, windsurfing, canoeing, mountain biking, boating, kayaking, fishing, swimming in the indoor and outdoor heated pools, and many other sports are included. Golf is nearby. There are children's programs for seven age groups, from infants to teens, under capable leadership. Intriguing sports activities, instruction, and entertainment are offered from breakfast through lunch and again in the evening.

Families who wish to eat breakfast together can gather in an optional breakfast room anytime between 7:30 and 9:30 A.M.; then the children are off to their programs. Even infants are cared for; if you prefer to bring your own parents helper rather than hire one from the resort, that can be arranged.

The Tyler Place, with buildings scattered over 25 acres, looks like an upgraded summer cottage colony. The cheerful, simple, but hardly rustic cottages (each with two to four bedrooms) are all on or near the lake. Most have a fireplace in the living room. The 1820 farmhouse, the 1890 Victorian guest house, and a modern inn all have a number of doubles, suites, and studios. All of the accommodations feature air-conditioned rooms and separate rooms for parents. All the rooms have been recently redecorated; some have a porch or screened-in deck.

Dining and leisurely cocktails (at the inn, with glimpses of the lake) can be with other couples at large tables or alone. Low-key entertainment takes the form of DJs, square dances, Monte Carlo nights, and specialty parties. Informal daytime activities include weekly get-acquainted punch parties, tennis round-robins, mountain bike tours, and guest-staff volleyball and softball games.

Reservations are on a weekly, Saturday-to-Saturday basis during the peak season; there is a no-tipping policy. A visit in May, June, or September costs far less and is becoming increasingly popular with parents of young children. (Children's prices vary with age; there is no charge for children under 18 months.)

A wide variety of food is served to meet the tastes of all ages, and in recent years it has been getting rave reviews. Ask for the resort's brochure; it's very complete and detailed.

Middlebury Area

Cornwall Orchards Bed & Breakfast

Route 30 in Cornwall
RD 4, Box 428
Middlebury, VT 05753
802-462-2272
www.virtualcities.com/ons/vt/m/vtm/7702.htm

> **A pristine farmhouse B&B**

Hosts: Juliet and Bob Gerlin. **Accommodations:** 5 rooms (all with private bath). **Rates:** $80 per couple. **Included:** Full breakfast. **Minimum stay:** None. **Added:** 9% tax. **Credit cards accepted:** None. **Children:** Welcome. **Pets:** Not accepted. **Smoking:** Not permitted. **Handicap access:** No. **Open:** Year-round.

➤ **Middlebury is a lively college town with more than seventy shops, including the Vermont State Craft Center (a short walk from the inn) — alone worth the trip. But just a couple of miles out of town lie expansive farms, rolling fields, and quiet country roads.**

Just three miles from downtown Middlebury, this 1783 farmhouse is a welcome addition to Middlebury's lodging scene. Juliet (originally from England) and Bob lived in Connecticut for 27 years before moving to the area in 1994. They spent their first year completely renovating the place before opening it as a B&B in mid-1995. Guest rooms are fresh and furnished simply and tastefully.

We're not sure how to explain it, but . . . the farmhouse just feels right when you open the front door. Yes, there are jackets hanging on a pegged coat rack and you walk right into a lovely kitchen. It feels homey, but you don't feel as if you're invading someone's private space. (You feel as if, perhaps, you've come home.) Wide pine floors are beautifully refinished, the walls are white, and some beams are exposed. It's quite refreshing.

The guest rooms are nicely spread throughout the house. Gov is the largest corner room, off the living room, and looks towards the Adirondack Mountains. Normally, we'd be concerned about recommending a guest room off the living room, but not here — it's nice and quiet. Guest rooms are unadorned. Down comforters and simple white curtains billowing with the breeze are evocative of country life. Bathrooms are sparkling white with new fixtures and wainscoting.

The comfortable living room is furnished with farmhouse antiques and Oriental carpets; the working fireplace is warming. This opens onto the breakfast room, which in turn looks out toward the Adirondacks. Juliet uses Vermont products for her full breakfasts, including farm-fresh eggs from her next door neighbor. From the back deck, you can enjoy the view with a glass of wine or beer. On our last visit, the Gerlins were talking about clearing some trees to open up the view.

Swift House Inn

25 Stewart Lane (off Route 7)
Middlebury, VT 05753
802-388-9925
Fax: 802-388-9927

A romantic inn with a country feel

Innkeepers: John Nelson and Karla Nelson-Loura. **Accommodations:** 21 rooms (all with private bath). **Rates:** $85–$155 per couple. **Included:** Expanded Continental breakfast; full breakfast available for $5 additional; dinner also served. **Minimum stay:** None. **Added:** 9% tax. **Credit cards accepted:** All major ones. **Children:** Under age 13, free; others, $15 in parent's room. **Smoking:** 3 rooms for nonsmokers; restricted indoors. **Pets:** Not accepted. **Handicap access:** Yes. **Open:** Year-round.

➤ **The dining room also offers a lighter, less expensive café menu that's quite popular.**

This three-building complex, tucked away on a side street in downtown Middlebury, has acquired a reputation as one of the best inns in Vermont. Extensive lawns and formal gardens add to the beauty of the place.

The main house, a Federal beauty built in 1815 by local legislator Samuel Swift, was remodeled with Victorian features in 1875 by Governor John Stewart. The legislator's grandson married the governor's daughter, who lived to be one hundred and ten — in this house — thus keeping it in the same family until 1982.

John and his late wife Andrea acquired the Swift House in 1985 and two years later added the adjacent 1902 Gatehouse, on the corner of Route 7. They did a first-rate job of converting the neighboring Carriage House into luxury suites. Gatehouse rooms (less desirable but by no means undesirable) share a living room, while each of the Carriage House rooms has its own sitting area with a fireplace. At the Carriage House, the large bathrooms have Jacuzzis, plush robes, and coffeepots. Turndown service is available. There is a sauna in this building for all guests to use.

Guest rooms in the main inn are furnished with antiques and fine reproductions. Nine guest rooms have marble fireplaces, most have TVs, and all have air conditioning and phones. Some of our favorites include the Governor's and Emma Willard rooms (both corner rooms with a fireplace and a whirlpool) and the Swift room (with private terrace and large bathroom).

The sitting rooms in the Swift House are elegant yet comfortable. A small bar and screened porch are particularly inviting.

The dining room is richly paneled in cherry wood, complementing the formally set tables. Request a dinner table in the library or on the enclosed porch. The dinner menu, which changes weekly, usually includes a half-dozen entrées from focaccia to rack of lamb. It always features Vermont-fresh products. On our last visit we sampled a crisp brie and tomato tart followed by a vegetarian delight: peppers and eggplant stuffed with ratatouille and various rices. Crème brûlée seemed to be the dessert of choice among the diners the night we were there. And to top it off, the cappuccino was perfect! Although the wine list has deservedly garnered awards, wines available by the glass are limited and on the small side.

For those of you who like to lounge around in the morning, room service at breakfast time is offered. We were offered eggs any style, cooked to order.

North Hero Island

North Hero House

Route 2, Champlain Islands
North Hero, Vermont 05474
802-372-4732
888-525-3644
Fax: 802-372-4732
www.members.aol.com/nhhlake/

> **A fine old Lake Champlain inn reborn**

Owner: Walt Blasberg. **Accommodations:** 9 rooms in the inn (open year-round), 15 in three lakeside buildings (open summer and fall only). **Rates:** Weekends, Memorial Day to mid-October: $110–$235 B&B; $160–$285 MAP; off-season: $79–$179 B&B, $129–$225 MAP; ask about packages. **Included:** Varies with meal plan. **Minimum stay:** 2 nights on some weekends. **Added:** 9% tax. **Credit cards accepted:** Visa, Mastercard. **Children:** 5 and under, free; ages 5–12, $5 B&B, $12 MAP. **Pets:** Not accepted. **Smoking:** Not permitted. **Handicap access:** Yes. **Open:** Year-round.

➤ **Lakeside rooms and fine dining**

This century-year-old summer hotel has a new lease on life thanks to New York investment manager Walt Blasberg, who pumped almost $1 million into the landmark in 1997.

North Hero House isn't a grand hotel, just a clapbboard inn in the center of an appealing lakeside village that you pass through in a minute. That's unless you stop. Then you are hooked because North Hero, you discover, is a very special place.

The inn is now a prim gray with black shutters and masses of red geraniums. The lobby is small and low-beamed and you tend to continue walking back, looking for more. What you find is a dark, inviting pub and a small library. Beyond there's a large, elegant dining room and beyond it a table-filled solarium. Obviously this is a big place in the Champlain Islands to eat.

Upstairs are nine rooms, ranging from fairly standard back rooms to the Captain's Suite with its porch, canopy bed, and double jacuzzi. All rooms have custom-made featherbed mattresses and private baths. Each room has its own color theme, fresh papers and fabrics complementing the antiques.

Frankly, however, we would prefer to stay across the road in one of the units overlooking the lake. Here you not only have the expansive view — miles across Lake Champlain to the Green Mountains — but the sound of water lapping you to sleep.

The dining room does indeed enjoy a fine reputation. On a typical night you migt begin with a crab cake with garlic aioli and dine on a wide range of entrées, from chicken pot pie ($10.95) to rack of lamb with a Dijon pinenut crust ($17.25). Of course the Friday night lobster buffet on the beach is a such an honored tradition that no new manager would think of breaking it.

There's a long, grassy dock area (Champlain steamers once used it) and a sandy beach and canoes, kayaks, pedal and power boats are available. Cycling is particularly popular on the quieter roads in the Champlain Islands, especially on nearby Isle La Motte. In summer the Royal Lipizzan Stallions perform a few miles up the road and in Fall this is as beautiful a spot as anywhere in Vermont. Inquire about off-season pacakges. There's cross-country skiing and ice fishing on the lake.

Shore Acres Inn and Restaurant

Box 3, R.R. 1
North Hero Island, VT 05474
802-372-8722

| An attractive, innlike motel with sweeping views of Lake Champlain

Managers: Mike and Susan Tranby. **Accommodations:** 19 motel units, 4 annex rooms. **Rates:** $77.50– $135 per couple. **Included:** No meals, but breakfast and dinner available; lunch served in summer. **Minimum stay:** None. **Added:** 9% tax. **Credit cards accepted:** MasterCard, Visa. **Children:** Welcome. **Pets:** Extra charge. **Smoking:** Permitted in rooms. **Handicap access:** No. **Open:** Motel units, early May through late October; annex is year-round on a B&B basis.

➤ **Thanks to unstinting efforts by Mike and Susan Tranby, this long-established landmark is as much of an inn as a motel can be. In fact, it combines some of the best of both species: the privacy of the individual**

units and an unusually attractive dining room with a large fieldstone hearth and space to simply sit as well as to dine.

The lawn sweeps down to the shore and the views — from the motel units and from the attractive dining room — sweep across Lake Champlain to Mount Mansfield and its flanking mountains.

Most rooms are in crisp-looking motel units set way back from Route 2, near the edge of the water. Most sleep two people and are airy and clean, with carefully chosen prints and furnishings that create an almost homey atmosphere. Each has a TV but no phone. Four rooms are in the annex, set back in the middle of the property. These are less desirable in summer since they are not on the lake, but they are cozy in winter — when they are the only rooms open.

The dinner menu ($12–$20) ranges from a vegetarian dish to broiled loin lamb chops. The chocolate pie is famous. All three meals are served in July and August. Breakfast and dinner are served through foliage season and then on weekends until New Year's.

Thirty miles north of Burlington and sixty miles south of Montreal, North Hero is not only a town but also one of the three linked Champlain islands, a thin land chain that stretches south from Canada. Surprisingly quiet and still agricultural, this little-known northwestern corner of the state is a great place to bicycle, fish, swim, play golf, or simply laze about in a lawn chair. From mid-July through August, the Royal Lipizzan stallions perform in a meadow just up the road.

Shelburne

The Inn at Shelburne Farms

Shelburne Farms
Shelburne, VT 05482
802-985-8498
Fax: 802-985-8123

A romantic mansion retreat on a working farm

Manager: Karen Polihronakis. **Accommodations:** 24 rooms (17 with private bath). **Rates:** $95–$260 per couple in summer and fall. **Included:** All meals available. **Minimum stay:** 2 nights on weekends. **Added:** 9% tax, 15% gratuity. **Credit cards accepted:** All major ones. **Children:** Welcome. **Pets:** Not accepted. **Smoking:** Not permitted. **Handicap access:** No. **Open:** Mid-May to mid-October.

➤ **The inn has been referred to as an "incomparable American landmark," which is highly apropos. The estate's resources, of which the inn is just one "attraction," revitalize the mind and spirit.**

We consider this one of the very best of the best places to stay in New England. Shelburne Farms offers more than just a magnificent country mansion and exceptional dining. The 1,400-acre estate and working farm, perched magnificently on the edge of Lake Champlain, is a testimony to creative land planning and use. Operations include an environmental education center for schoolchildren, a Brown Swiss dairy herd, a bread bakery, a cheddar cheesemaking operation, an organic garden, woodworking shops, and woodlands managed for firewood and lumber.

The estate and farm were established in 1886 by William Seward Webb and his wife Lila Vanderbilt Webb, who embarked on an ambitious agricultural experiment: a sustainable model farm using modern farming equipment and practices. By the turn of the century, the farm was renowned throughout the country. Today, their creative land management practices continue to serve as a conservation model. You can learn about the fascinating history of Shelburne Farms in great detail through the complimentary guided tour of the property and an excellent slide show.

The estate, designed by America's preeminent landscape artist Frederick Law Olmsted, is criss-crossed with walking paths, lovely spots for picnics, and marvelous views of the lake, pastures, and mountains beyond. Don't miss the vista from Lone Tree Hill. There aren't many places left where you'll find such peace and quiet.

The brick-over-wood Queen Anne mansion is handsome and elegant, with grand common rooms. Quite remarkably, though, it's comfortably unstuffy. In fact, it's quite easy to feel as if you're a friend of the Vanderbilts or Webbs, just up for the weekend. Ancestral portraits hang on the walls, fires crackle in the massive fireplaces (which supply the only heat for the house), and the library piano is yours to play.

On a warm evening you may want to linger outside on one of the two grand porches, sipping a drink, gazing beyond the formal gardens to the sun setting on Lake Champlain. Or play a game of billiards in the billiards room, furnished with Jacobean-style furniture. In cooler weather, enjoy a before-dinner drink or after-dinner dessert in front of one of the many fireplaces. The library, with more than six thousand volumes, is particularly cozy.

The mansion evolved as the Vanderbilt family grew, and rooms were built with certain guests in mind. The most spectacular rooms belonged to the most important family members. Among our favorite bedrooms are Webb (with William Henry Vanderbilt's furniture), Overlook (huge, with a curved wall of windows looking toward the lake), South (with a turret and magnificent view of the lake), and White. Of the moderate rooms, we like Lilac, Louis XVI, Empire, and the Pink Room. Some rooms are quite spartan and small; these were intended for servants or friends of the children. (These rooms represent a great value since, for a moderate price, you still get the run of the mansion and grounds.) Bathrooms are all original.

Meals, though not included in the room rate, are a real value. Dinner is as good as you'll find in New York's finest restaurants, at a fraction of the cost. The dining room is elegant without being pretentious: tables are set with china, linen, and original Chippendale chairs. Walls are covered in silk damask and the floor is tiled in marble. The service is polished, knowledgeable, and friendly, and the wine list is extensive and extremely well priced. If it's a special occasion, ask for table 5 in the corner; otherwise, a window seat is perfect.

Much of the food served is grown on the farm. For breakfast, try something with maple syrup, cheddar cheese, or farm fresh eggs. Picnic lunches are always available.

Vergennes

Basin Harbor Club

Vergennes, VT 05491
802-475-2311
800-622-4000 outside Vermont
Fax: 802-475-2545
res@basinharbor.com
www.basinharbor.com

A grand old resort on Lake Champlain, ideal for families and reunions

---

Owners: Pennie and Bob Beach and family. **Accommodations:** 136 cottages and rooms. **Rates:** $198–$238 per couple in season in rooms, FAP; $262–$370 in cottages, FAP; B&B rates in spring and fall; plenty of packages. **Included:** All meals, full children's program, recreational facilities. **Minimum stay:** Peak weekends and holidays. **Added:** 9% ta9, 15% service charge. **Credit cards accepted:** Visa, MasterCard. **Children:** Special programs. **Smoking:** In some accommodations. **Pets:** Small pets accepted. **Handicap access:** 7 cottages. **Open:** Mid-May to mid-October.

➤ **In the large formal dining room, where an introductory card announces formally attired guests, guests are treated to a spectacular view of the gardens and lake as they dine on New England–style cuisine.**

The Beach family — Great Aunt Ardelia Beach to be precise — began taking in summer boarders at the farm in 1886. Although farming ceased in the 1950s, today's fourth generation would do their ancestors proud. The Beaches have kept up with the times, upgrading facilities and accommodations, while maintaining the friendly spirit.

The cottages are all quite spiffy, bright with a soothing upscale country feel, and designed to harmonize with the natural surroundings. They are decorated with simple but lovely furnishings and contemporary fabrics. Bathrooms are newly tiled and well lit. No two are alike. Some of the cottages are tucked away under pine trees. The private decks and the woods make them feel remarkably secluded. Some are right on the lake; others overlook the golf course, tennis courts, pool, or gardens. Some have screened porches or white picket fences. Roughly half have fireplaces, with wood provided daily. All the cottages have a phone and a refrigerator and/or a wet bar.

You will never lack for things to keep you busy here: a Geoffrey Cornish–designed golf course, driving range (the well-known golf pro specializes in teaching young people), golf schools for children, women, and families, five tennis courts, and swimming in the lake and pool. The lake, the nation's sixth largest, has 600 miles of shoreline and is more than 120 miles long. The harbormaster has a vast array of water vehicles, including a 40-foot cruiser. Canoes, row boats, paddleboats, windsurfers, and small motor boats can be rented by the hour; you can water-ski, sail, and fish to your hearts content. And if that's not enough, you can rent bicycles, jog or walk the trails, or go bird watching. There's also a fully equipped fitness center. A variety of activities abound for older youngsters, while children enjoy the supervised playground. A sheltered cove with a sandy beach serves as the base for water sports.

Of course, you can spend the entire time lounging in an Adirondack by the lake or on the deck of your cottage. Or sit on the inn's porch, filled with potted and hanging flowers, overlooking the lake. The point is, you can do one thing while others in your family do their own thing.

A lavish lunch buffet and afternoon cocktails are served in the Ranger Room overlooking the pool. The rustic Red Mill, next to the air strip, offers snacks and a casual retreat for families and those who don't want to dress up for dinner. Picnics, if the maître d' is informed the night before, are a snap.

The dining room dinner menu always features eight entrées (such as Vermont cob smoked ham with maple glaze and Madeira sauce or baked halibut with shrimp butter). On our last visit there were also three appetizers, four soups, two salads, and a dozen desserts. The restaurant features an extensive and moderately priced wine list as well as nightly specials. Chef David Merrill, who has worked at the Basin Harbor Club in one capacity or another since the mid-1970s, has been head chef since 1993.

The Basin Harbor Club also hosts weekly activities, including family picnics on Tuesdays (hayrides, music, and a marshmallow roast), lobster dinner at the Red Mill on Wednesdays, a theme night on Thursdays, and a Friday lobster bake on the lake.

The Lake Champlain Maritime Museum, an 1818 stone schoolhouse, houses a full-scale replica of a Revolutionary War gunboat and details 150 years of boat travel on the lake — from ice boats to birch-bark canoes to other small crafts. The resort also boasts its own private airstrip.

Perhaps best of all, this 700-acre lakeside retreat is large enough to absorb a full house of 300 guests even in high season; you probably won't feel overrun by other guests.

Upper Valley and
Northeast Kingdom

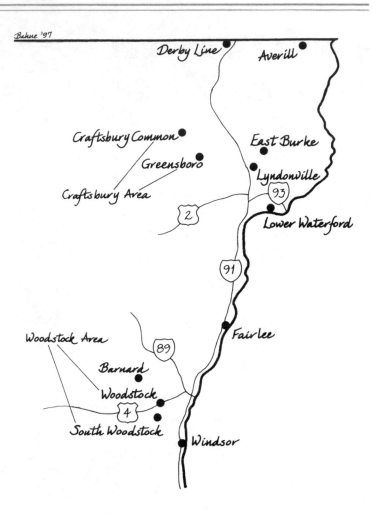

Bahne '97

Derby Line

Averill

Craftsbury Common

East Burke

Greensboro

Lyndonville

Craftsbury Area

93

2

Lower Waterford

91

Woodstock Area

89

Fairlee

Barnard

Woodstock

4

South Woodstock

Windsor

Best Family Finds

Averill
  Quimby Country Lodge and Cottages, 628
Craftsbury
  The Craftsbury Outdoor Center, 634
  The Highland Lodge, 636
Fairlee
  Silver Maple Lodge, 642
Lyndonville
  Wildflower Inn, 645

Best Inns

Woodstock
  Kedron Valley Inn, 651
  Woodstock Inn & Resort, 653

Best Gourmet Getaways

Barnard
  Twin Farms, 631
Craftsbury
  The Inn on the Common, 637
Windsor
  Juniper Hill Inn, 647
Woodstock
  Jackson House, 649

Best Romantic Getaways

Barnard
  Twin Farms, 631
Lower Waterford
  Rabbit Hill Inn, 643
Woodstock
  Jackson House, 649

Unlike New Hampshire, Vermont is far wider at the top than the bottom. So it is in central and northern Vermont, that the swaths of hill and valley on either side of the Green Mountains are broader than in southern Vermont.

On the eastern side of the state, the Connecticut River valley becomes a distinctive region around Windsor. Today this area is called the Upper Valley and includes the river towns in both New Hampshire and Vermont, extending west along the Ottauquechee River valley to include the aristocratic old village of Woodstock.

Three major highways I-89, I-91, and Route 4 all cross in the old railroad center of White River Junction. As you follow Route 4 west along the Ottauquechee, be sure to note dramatic Quechee Gorge (there's a viewing spot) and the village of Quechee, a former mill town reborn as a resort community. **Woodstock,** 14 miles west of White River, has been the shire town of Windsor County since the 1790s and it ranks among the prettiest towns in America. The Billings Farm & Museum here re-creates farm life in the 1890s, and the Dana House is one of New England's most interesting historical museums. Woodstock is also a place to walk — along the extensive nature trails at the Vermont Institute of Natural Science and up the paths on Mount Tom, the hill that rises from the middle of town and commands a panoramic view of the valley. This area is also laced with bridle paths. In South Woodstock horses outnumber cars, and New England's leading commercial stable offers inn-to-inn as well as standard trail rides.

In the Upper Valley, the rich bottomland along the Connecticut River was settled early on, and in the late 18th century it looked as though this area was to be a state all its own, with Hanover, New Hampshire, the home of Dartmouth College, as the capital. Hanover, with the Hood Art Museum and Hopkins Center entertainment complex, remains the cultural center for the Upper Valley. Don't miss the Montshire Museum of Science, just across the river in Norwich. Displays geared to all ages run through the natural and theoretical sciences, and special exhibitions extend to art forms.

The Upper Valley extends north along the Connecticut well beyond the picturesque Thetfords and the town of **Fairlee,** where two lakes, Fairlee and Morey, offer resort facilities. I-91 follows the Connecticut River north, shadowing old Route 5, a scenic road beloved by bicyclists.

Above the oxbow in Newbury you enter the Northeast Kingdom, a name coined by the late Senator George Aikin. It refers to Vermont's three northeasternmost counties, still the state's most rural and, some believe, most beautiful corner. The sole ski resort here is low-key Burke Mountain, in **East Burke.** Generally, the Northeast Kingdom is an open, gently rolling land of humped hills and farmland spotted with lakes, old resort communities like Greensboro and Lake Willoughby, dramatically walled by two mountains.

The Northeast Kingdom is also known for its beautiful hill towns, most notably **Craftsbury Common,** a proud old white clapboard community gathered around an oversize common on a high plateau. Here farm roads follow ridges and fields roll away like waves to the Green Mountains in the distance. This is great mountain biking country, and in winter it's one of the most dependable places in New England for cross-country skiing.

This northeastern corner of Vermont also harbors fine old Connecticut River villages such as **Lower Waterford** and Peacham with views extending across the valley to New Hampshire's White Mountains. Farther north, in the little-populated North Country, towns dwindle into gores and wilderness lakes offer good fishing.

Averill

Quimby Country Lodge and Cottages

P.O. Box 20
Averill, VT 05901
802-822-5533

A remote, century-old family resort

Manager: Joan Binns. **Accommodations:** 20 housekeeping cottages (studios to 4-bedrooms). **Rates** (mid-June to late August): $105–$133 per adult, $48–$58 for ages 3–8, $62–$75 for ages 9–16; discounts for weekly stays and in the off-season. **Included:** All meals and facilities. **Minimum stay:** None, but rates are higher for less than a week. **Added:** 9% tax, 12% service charge in season. **Credit cards accepted:** None. **Children:** Special rates and programs. **Pets:** Accepted. **Smoking:** Restricted. **Handicap access:** No. **Open:** Early May to mid-October.

➤ **Quimby, which boasts 650 acres and 2 lakes, also bills itself as a way of life — indeed, once a Quimby kid, always a Quimby kid. Generations have been coming to this remote camp, "far removed from the pressures of the outside world." True enough; there's good reason to start the tradition if you haven't yet.**

After long and careful thought, we can't think of another place like this in New England — and we mean this as an unreserved compliment. From the moment you begin driving down the long, rutted dirt road that hugs one of the lakes, you sense that you've entered a place apart.

Quimby Country began in 1894 as a fishing lodge and evolved into a family-oriented resort under the proprietorship of Hortense Quimby, attracting a loyal following in the process. On Miss Quimby's death, a group of regulars bought it and hired a manager, Joan Binns. That was some thirty-odd years ago. Joan laughs, "It's got to be the most non-profit for-profit corporation in the country!" It was here that Governor Aiken is said to have coined "Northeast Kingdom."

The main lodge, with stone hearth and wraparound porch, is furnished with rattan and twig furniture, braided rugs, lots of old books on the shelves, and children's games, crayons, and books. The blackboard near the check-in desk lists cabin occupants by first name and age (ages are disclosed only for the children!), so that when the kids get to know one another, they know how to find each other later.

Recently, Quimby sold most of its acreage to the Vermont Land Trust to raise capital funds to improve the property. To that end, Joan has embarked on a five-year plan to upgrade the cottages with this goal: The regulars should not know anything has changed. Truth be told, Joan has leveled floors and then some, and is slightly disappointed that regulars haven't noticed! The cottages are quite homey, with space for one to eight guests. Each has a Franklin stove and a porch with a lake view.

To one long-time guest who inquired with faux incredulity, "Don't you have a clock that works in this place?" Joan commented, "No. It's today." Take this as a commentary on the philosophy at Quimby rather than the fact that things don't work. The things that need to work do work.

Meals are served in the central dining room on highly polished wood tables with fresh flowers. Long-time guests remember the food well — high-quality selections and lots of it. Regularly scheduled dinners include a Saturday evening prime rib and seafood dinner. Friday's dinner is a lakeside lobster cookout. Picnic lunches are available for those who request them.

In season, there are at most 65 guests for a staff of 28 or so. A couple of counselors organize children's activities, but participation is optional. Rest assured that kids are happy campers here, well before the Wednesday overnight down by the lake (complete with s'mores). Sailboats, sailboards, rowboats, kayaks, and canoes are all available, and there are tennis and basketball courts. Forest Lake is out the front door and the 1,200-acre Averill Lake is a five-minute walk away. A network of trails criss-cross the property. Landlocked salmon, smallmouth bass, and trout will keep anglers busy. The early foliage season draws people canny enough to experience the season's beauty at its best.

Down on the lake, Nevin Brugger Hall (named for a magician revered at Quimby) is a lifesaver on rainy days and a focal point for the resort every day. It's the spot for evening square dances, theatricals, and magic shows as well as Ping-Pong, karakoe, and storytelling.

Barnard

Twin Farms

Barnard, VT 05031
802-234-9999
800-Twin Farms (894-6327)
Fax: 802-234-9990

| In a class that matches its prices |

Innkeerpers: Beverly and Shaun Matthews. **Accommodations:** 4 suites in the main house, 2 suites in one cottage, 8 freestanding cottages. **Rates:** $800–$1,500 per night; the entire property: $14,500 per night. **Included:** All meals, tea, use of all facilities, open bar. **Minimum stay:** 2 nights on weekends, 3 nights on holidays. **Added:** 9% tax, 15% service. **Credit cards accepted:** All major ones. **Children:** Not appropriate. **Pets:** Not accepted. **Smoking:** Not permitted. **Handicap access:** Yes. **Open:** Closed in April.

➤ **Twin Farms is dedicated to offering "peaceful and understated elegance while upholding a tradition of graceful hospitality for those guests tired of ostentation."**

Twin Farms offers luxury several levels above that of any other place to stay in this book — hence in New England. The 300-acre compound with its staff of 50 cater to no more than 28 guests at a time. But that's only the beginning. Every room in the main house and widely scattered cottages has been designed and decorated with superlative skill and detailing. Several spaces qualify as works of art in their own right as well as harboring museum-quality pieces and paintings. Add to this every conceivable comfort and totally appropriate landscaping.

We didn't believe a single night anywhere could be worth $1,500. Now that we have seen "The Studio," the cottage that fetches that fee, we're not so sure. As in all the cottages, almost everything you see — from the freeform staircase to the chandelier with wrought-iron tendrils and silver spheres — has been custom-made to complement specific works of art, perhaps the Frank Stella over the fireplace or the David Hockney over the bed. The combined effect is truly amazing. Guests enter through a stone porch and are confronted by a two-story window overlooking a wooded hill. Huge French windows open onto a deck with a view of marshland and a deep copper tub (nothing as nuvo as a Jacuzzi) is tucked into a windowed corner of the bathroom.

Each of the cottages is totally different, each devoted to a theme. "Perch" features the dark green paneling of a fantasy fishing lodge; Orchard Cottage, set among old apple trees, is vaguely Oriental or Scandinavian — with ceilings of woven ash, hand-carved granite fireplaces, and woodwork that borders on sculpted art. Meadow Cottage is the supreme fantasy, its clapboard exterior masking a sultan's daydream, its ceiling deftly mimicking (in plaster) a striped tent, and its intricate terra cotta floors covered in rich Persian rugs and mosaic tiling (by a local craftsman) that has to be seen to be believed. Only the four rooms in the main house are traditional New England in decor and even these go a shade beyond what you can anticipate.

Obviously there's a story here. It begins with two 18th-century farmhouses (hence "Twin Farms") that became a second home in the 1920s for Sinclair Lewis — who satirized the materialism of American life in novels like *Babbit* — and his journalist wife Dorothy Thompson. In the 1970s it was acquired by Laila and Thurston Twig-Smith, Honolulu residents whose fortune is newspaper-based. In the early 1990s they were just about to sell the property when they happened to spend a few days at The Point, a similarly luxurious retreat on Upper Saranac Lake. Not a family to do anything by halves, the Twig-Smiths have invested $26 million in the property to date. Those inspired interiors are the work of Jed Johnson of New York, arguably the country's leading interior designer when he was killed in the infamous TWA crash off of Long Island in 1996.

"The Twigg-Smith's had a huge American art collection," explains innkeeper Beverly Matthews, gesturing to a Milton Avery on a wall of the two-story-window central living room in the main house. Again this is a room that you could steep in for several hours, then move to the second living room and game room for another few.

Across an iron foot bridge is the "Pub" with its Wurlitzer juke box, big-screen TV, pool table, and bar. Of course there is a fully equipped exercise room with a Japanese *Furo* (soaking tub), a swimming pond, a stocked fishing pond with canoes and rowboats, tennis courts, miles of hiking and cross-country trails, and in winter the alpine ski trails (for many years this was the private Sonnenberg Ski Resort) are served by a single chairlift.

We haven't mentioned food because we didn't sample any, but we assume it's up to the rest of the operation. Head chef Neil Wiggesworth is the former chef at The Point. Guests are not forced to mingle in any way but cocktails are served in the living room before dinner.

Craftsbury Area

The Craftsbury Outdoor Center

P.O. Box 31
Craftsbury Common, VT 05827
802-586-2514
800-729-7751
Fax: 802-586-7768
crafts@sover.net
www.craftsbury.com

> **A sports resort geared to active guests of all ages**

Owners: The Spring family. **Accommodations:** 2 lodge buildings with dorm-style lodging (shared baths, 3 rooms with private baths); 2 efficiency apartments; 3 lakeside housekeeping cottages. **Rates:** $73–$104 single; $125–$220 per couple; packages and family rates available. **Included:** All meals, sports facilities. **Minimum stay:** None. **Added:** 9% tax. **Credit cards accepted:** MasterCard, Visa. **Children:** Ages 13–17, 25% off; 6–12, half price; under 6, free. **Pets:** Not accepted. **Smoking:** Not permitted. **Handicap access:** No. **Open:** Year-round; dining room closed in April and November.

➤ **In some ways, The Craftsbury Outdoor Center is the exact opposite of a traditional resort. Instead of remaining within its confines, guests ski, bike, or run through the surrounding farmscape.**

Craftsbury Center offers plenty of exercise and delicious, wholesome food in an unbeatable Vermont setting. It's not a resort in the usual sense. The accommodations are Spartan, and sports are taken seriously. Most guests come here either to try a sport or to hone their skills in one. During the summer it may be sculling, mountain biking, walking, or running; in winter it is definitely cross-country skiing.

Founded in 1977, the Craftsbury Outdoor Center is a mile or so from Craftsbury Common, one of the most beautiful towns in Vermont's rural and rolling Northeast Kingdom. It occupies the site of a former boys' boarding school, with 140 acres overlooking Lake Hosmer. Initially, its highly structured programs catered to serious athletes: scullers, long-distance runners, competitive cross-country skiers. But gradually it has widened its scope to appeal to guests of all ages and shapes, anyone up for a healthy dose of physical activity and natural beauty.

The setting is remarkably well suited to mountain biking, walking, and running, since the Center sits squarely in the midst of a 200-mile maze of unmarked farm roads in the kind of high, open farm country that gives you a sense of being on top of the world. Grassy, cross-country ski trails also radiate from the center, an ideal introduction to off-road biking. You can bring your own bike or rent one and set out on your own, but the specialty of the house is guided tours — which not only eliminate the distinct possibility of getting lost but also offer instruction and encouragement. Tours include lunch, usually by a swimming hole.

In the winter, this is one of the few places in New England where you can almost always count on snow. With its 1,000-foot elevation, carefully laid and groomed trail system, and unusually reliable snowfall, Craftsbury Center is likely to have snow cover if there's any to be found in New England. It grooms 105 kilometers of trails, through woods and over open fields.

Most of the guest rooms are in one of two former dorms, and in one there's a living room — it's comfortable and well stocked with books, but nothing even bordering on fancy. If you want to take advantage of all the Center offers except its accommodations, that's possible too. Lodging in Craftsbury itself is surprisingly plentiful, from Margaret Ramdell's comfortable Craftsbury Bed & Breakfast down the road to the posh Inn on the Common.

Meals at Craftsbury Center, served buffet-style in a dining hall across the road, are both relentlessly healthful and delicious. Lunch may consist of two kinds of whole-wheat pizza and a home-grown salad, homemade bread pudding, and maple-flavored yogurt, washed down with the best milk (local) you've ever tasted.

Craftsbury Outdoor Center appeals to an unusually broad spectrum of people. While it's a place families or couples can enjoy without joining a particular program, it's also good for single men or women who want to be part of a group and for single parents who want to get away with a child and learn or perfect a sport together.

The Highland Lodge

R.R. 1
P.O. Box 1290
Greensboro, VT 05841
802-533-26478
Fax: 802-533-7494
HLodge@connriver.net
www.pbpub.com/vermont/hiland.htm

A family resort by a lake
with excellent cross-
country skiing

Innkeepers: Wilhelmina and David Smith. **Accommodations:** 11 rooms (all with private bath), 10 cottages; in winter, only 4 cottages. **Rates:** $190-$230 per couple in the lodge; $112.50–$115 per couple in the cottages; children's rates. **Included:** Breakfast and dinner and gratuity; all facilities, including cross-country skiing; lunch also served. **Credit cards accepted:** MasterCard, Visa. **Added:** 9% tax. **Children:** Welcome. **Pets:** Not accepted. **Smoking:** Restricted. **Handicap access:** 1 cottage. **Open:** Christmas to mid-March, Memorial Day to Columbus Day.

➤ **More than forty miles of groomed cross-country ski trails through maple groves and pine forests start at the lodge's touring center, which provides equipment rentals, instruction, and tours. The trails connect with the Craftsbury Center system, good for a leisurely day's trek through Vermont's most beautiful farm country.**

The Highland Lodge is an old-fashioned white clapboard inn overlooking Caspian Lake. It has evolved from a handsome farmhouse, and its long wooden porch is hung with flowers and lined with rockers in summer. The cottages are salted along the hillside above a rural road. They overlook an expansive field filled with wildflowers, sloping to woods and a lake. The inn has been owned and managed by the Smith family for two generations.

The public rooms are all furnished comfortably. A living room with fireplace, a sunny sitting room with a baby grand piano and clawfoot chairs, and a library with desks and cozy armchairs allow guests to mingle or find a quiet corner.

Guests have a choice of spacious, comfortably furnished rooms in the main house; each one is different. In summer, with open windows and short white curtains blowing in the breeze, these rooms have an airy appeal. The cottages each have a porch, living room, and one to three bedrooms, but no housekeeping facilities.

Three meals — with the emphasis on fresh fruits and vegetables and careful seasonings — are served in the large, attractive dining room. In summer, lunch and dinner are served outdoors.

Depending on the season, guests can ski, hike, bicycle, swim, play golf, or drive over the backroads to picturesque rural towns. In summer, the paths through the Barr Hill Nature Preserve invite exploration, and the nearby 9-hole Mountain View Club is one of the oldest and most scenic golf courses in the state.

The inn's beach house, with a fireplace and grills, is the focal point of the summer activities on pristine Caspian Lake. Swimming in the clear waters, sunbathing on the float, sailing, boating, and canoeing are all popular. There is also a clay tennis court, and in June, September, and early October, anglers can find salmon, lake trout, rainbow trout, and perch.

Depending on the season and the demand, the inn organizes activities for children. Youngsters will also find swings, a play area, and a well-equipped playroom, the base for a supervised program. Babysitters are available if requested in advance.

The Inn on the Common

Craftsbury Common, VT 05827
802-586-9619
800-521-2233
Fax: 802-586-2249

| A regal lodging |

Innkeepers: Michael and Penny Schmitt. **Accommodations:** 14 rooms (all with private bath), 2 suites. **Rates:** $200–$270 per couple; packages available. **Included:** Breakfast and dinner. **Minimum stay:** 2 nights during Christmas and foliage season. **Added:** 9% tax, 15% service charge. **Credit cards accepted:** MasterCard, Visa. **Children:** Special rates. **Pets:** With prior approval, $15 extra. **Smoking:** No Smoking in dining room. **Handicap access:** No. **Open:** Year-round.

➤   **Exquisite rooms and fine dining in a quintessential Vermont village.**

The most elegant lodging in the Northeast Kingdom, this inn has been operated by the Schmitts since 1973. Every appointment, every subtle detail — from the formal gardens to the elaborate table settings — has been arranged with precision.

The guest rooms have four-poster or brass beds, handmade quilts, original art, and hooked rugs or wall-to-wall carpeting. Long plush robes hang in the deep closets; thick towels, soaps, and sewing articles are found in the tiled bathrooms.

Each bedroom has been decorated individually in a particular color scheme. The deluxe rooms have sitting areas, and most have a fireplace or stove. The North Annex, a house with five guest rooms on the common itself, includes one room with a kitchenette, one with a fireplace, and one with a woodstove. The South Annex, across the road, has its own living room with fireplace and TV.

Dignified family portraits preside over the evening feast in the formal dining room. Three enormous windows and a sliding door open onto well-tended formal gardens; the 15-acre grounds include an English croquet court and a clay tennis court set far behind beds of perennials. There's also a small, landscaped pool.

Guests gather in the library for the cocktail hour (wine and bar drinks are not complementary), when they are encouraged to mingle before sitting down to dine around shared tables on delectable dishes. The menu changes nightly but might include a peppercorn and pistachio pâté with maple mustard as an appetizer and a choice of three entrées, such as sautéed rack of lamb with roast garlic demi-glace, pheasant breast with pineapple salsa and monterey jack cheese and baked salmon with olives, sundried tomatoes, artichokes and fresh dill (a vegetarian entrée is always available on request). Dessert might be a choice between flourless chocolate cake à la mode and chocolate swirl cheese cake.

Wine is Michael Schmitt's particular passion and his cellar is selective as well as large (243 labels on our last visit). Inquire about wine-tasting weekends.

Breakfast is another production. You might want to take a long morning walk to work up an appetite after the previous night's feast. Omelettes are the specialty of the morning and they come with about everything you can conceive.

Depending on the season, guests are encouraged to use the rowing, mountain biking facilities, or the network of cross-country ski trails radiating from nearby Craftsbury Outdoor Center where conditions are so reliable, January through mid-March, that guests are told they can reclaim their deposit if nature doesn't cooperate.

Derby Line

Birchwood B&B

48 Main Street
P.O. Box 550
Derby Line, VT 05830
802-873-9104
Fax: 802-873-9121
birchwd@together.net

> **A lovely small B&B**

Hosts: Betty and Dick Fletcher. **Accommodations:** 3 rooms (all with private bath). **Rates:** $65–$70 per couple. **Included:** Full breakfast. **Minimum stay:** None. **Added:** 9% tax. **Credit cards accepted:** None. **Children:** Welcome if older. **Pets:** Not accepted. **Smoking:** Not permitted. **Handicap access:** No. **Open:** Year-round.

➤ **Betty and Dick "work both sides of the border" so they're a good source of information — whether you're exploring the Northeast Kingdom, Vermont's last pristine frontier, or heading into Canada where U.S. dollars go further. They can arrange sleigh rides, direct you to skiing at Jay Peak, or show you where there's maple sugaring.**

Straddling the border of Quebec and northernmost Vermont, this small and elegant bed-and-breakfast offers spotless rooms for a very good price. Dick and Betty (who owns an antique shop in town) moved here in the early 1990s, spent a year renovating the house from top to bottom, and opened it as a B&B in 1994. The Fletchers claim to be "retired."

The 1920 house has a formally decorated living room that is quite comfortable, not at all fussy. The fireplace is frequently lit in the winter. Through a set of French doors, is one long table around which guests gather for a candlelit breakfast. The day we visited, Betty and Dick served homemade breads, fruit, and an "enhanced" French toast. Betty also serves paper thin crêpes topped with berries and maple syrup. Fresh flowers grace the dining room as well as the guest rooms.

For our purposes we'll identify the guest rooms as small, medium, and large. All are quite lovely, immaculate, and outfitted with crisp linens, fluffy towels, and firm mattresses. The smallest room served as the former maid's quarters and has a marble topped bureau, hooked throw rugs, and a pineapple post bed. The medium-sized room features maple furnishings and a fishnet canopy bed, while the largest room in the rear of the house has twins. All have been decorated with care and taste.

Guests frequently join the Fletchers in the casual family room (with TV) off the dining room. The backyard is small but lush and the house is on a quiet residential street.

East Burke

Mountain View Creamery

Darling Hill Road
P.O. Box 355
East Burke, VT 05832
802-626-9924
innmtnvu@plainfield.com

> Some of the most breathtaking views in New England

Owner: Marilyn Pastore. **Manager:** Laurelie Welch. **Accommodations:** 10 rooms (all with private bath). **Rates:** $95–$175 per couple; reduced for stays longer than 2 nights. **Included:** Full breakfast. **Minimum stay:** None. **Added:** 9% tax. **Credit cards accepted:** MasterCard, Visa. **Children:** Welcome. **Pets:** Not accepted. **Smoking:** Not permitted. **Handicap access:** No. **Open:** Year-round.

➤ **The adjacent yellow farmhouse is well suited to longer stays. It rents for $1,500 weekly in season ($1,200 off-season) and can accommodate six people. It features two bedrooms, a bathroom with Jacuzzi, a well-proportioned living room with fireplace, and a full kitchen.**

This 440-acre hilltop estate occupies one of the most spectacular natural settings in New England. We can easily imagine whiling away a couple of lazy summer days on the property — strolling among the restored barns, sipping a cranberry spritzer or sun tea surrounded by a profusion of perennial gardens, reading amidst the deafening quiet, watching puffy cloud formations develop overhead, and strolling through rolling meadows. Fall foliage and winter wonderlands also provide a great backdrop for this property.

In 1883 Elmer Darling began construction on this farm and creamery, which would eventually supply his New York City Fifth Avenue Hotel with meat and dairy products. At one time, the landmark barn housed 100 Jersey cows and the creamery churned out 600 pounds of butter monthly and 70 pounds of cheese daily. Today the "gentleman's" farm raises its own produce, turkeys, pheasants, and egg-laying chickens. The Morgan horse barn is just as elegant as it once was and the longtime caretaker's horses now run in the paddocks.

The creamery, a brick Georgian Colonial, has been transformed into a 10-room inn that serves dinner Thursday through Sunday year-round. The centerpiece of Darling's Restaurant is an old Stewart stove, around which lovely tables are set. Walls are brick, the ceiling of pressed tin, and the tables candlelit. The cuisine is simple but sophisticated for these parts: rainbow trout with almond stuffing, fettucine with pan-roasted chicken filet, or pork medallions sautéed with mustard and ginger sauce for $11–$19 per entrée.

Breakfast might include a vegetable frittata or cinnamon swirl French toast with walnuts. There is always a buffet of fruit, yogurt, muffins, and cereals.

Choose your room according to the sun: half get full morning sun, the other half afternoon. Since the windows are smallish, rooms can be dark in the morning. In any event, the rooms have fresh floral or striped wallpapers, quilts, one or two sitting chairs, and stripped wooden floors. Farmhouse antiques fill most of the simple but lovely guest rooms. Many have twin beds; some rooms can be connected for couples or families traveling together. Dorset is a particularly bright corner room if you don't need a shower (it has a tub); we also like Sheffield.

As for the common space, there is one living room with the trademark painted cement floors (this was a creamery!) and a country farmhouse feel.

On the property are herb and lettuce gardens, draught horses and ponies, roosters and pheasants, a sugar shack, and wagon or sleigh rides. This property and similarly large tracts of adjacent land boast hundreds of trails open to non-mechanized trails — it's a great place to cross-country ski (trails are groomed but not tracked), hike, or ride mountain bikes.

Fairlee

Silver Maple Lodge

R.R. 1, Box 8
South Main Street
Fairlee, VT 05045
802-333-4326
800-666-1946

**Good value and genuine
hospitality**

Innkeepers: Scott and Sharon Wright. **Accommodations:** 8 rooms (6 with private bath), 7 cottage units. **Rates:** $54–$79 per couple; $6 per extra person in room (cots available); third day free off-season. **Included:** Light breakfast. **Minimum stay:** None. **Added:** 9% tax. **Credit cards accepted:** All major ones. **Children:** Welcome. **Pets:** Accepted in cottages. **Smoking:** Permitted in cottages. **Handicap access:** Some rooms. **Open:** Year-round.

➤ **Scott, a sixth-generation Vermonter, grew up on a farm in nearby Tunbridge, and he knows the kind of Vermont hospitality he wants to extend.**

This distinctive 1880 Vermont house has steep gables and a big, screened wraparound porch with plenty of Adirondack chairs. It was in the 1920s that its previous owners, Elmer and Della Batchelder, began taking in overnight guests who stopped in Fairlee, a Connecticut River town with two large lakes. Eventually they added a few cottages.

Scott and Sharon Wright are an energetic, friendly young couple who obviously enjoy their guests. Over the past few years they have renovated the house bit by bit, adding a fireplace here and exposing beams there, tile bathrooms everywhere, and air conditioning. The two newest cottage units are beauties; both with fireplaces, one with a kitchenette. Still, they don't want to fancy up the old place too much. The Wrights pride themselves on offering spotlessly clean, comfortable rooms (and Sharon's baking) at reasonable prices. The couple is also happy to share their love and knowledge of the Upper Valley with guests.

There is only one drawback to this place: I-91 slices through a nearby meadow. The house, however, is set back from the traffic noises on Route 5 and is far enough from the highway to be out of earshot.

Guests can rent ten-speeds and canoes and take advantage of the inn's ballooning package: two days of lodging, breakfast, and a champagne hot-air balloon flight from the nearby Post Mills Airport.

Lower Waterford

The Rabbit Hill Inn

Route 18
Lower Waterford, VT 05848
802-748-5168
800-762-8669
Fax: 802-748-8342
Rabbit.Hill.Inn@connriver.net
www.RabbitHillInn.com

As romantic and pampering as an inn can be

Innkeepers: Leslie and Brian Mulcahy. **Accommodations:** 15 rooms (all with private bath), 5 suites. **Rates:** $189–$279 per couple; $10 more during foliage; less off-season. **Included:** Full breakfast and dinner. **Minimum stay:** 2 nights on weekends, 3 nights on most holidays. **Added:** 9% tax, 15% service. **Credit cards accepted:** All major ones. **Children:** Over age 12 welcome. **Pets:** Not accepted. **Smoking:** Not permitted. **Handicap access:** Yes. **Open:** Year-round except early April and early November.

➤ **Leslie and Brian, intent on making guests feel completely at ease, view innkeeping as a theatrical event. They are the stagehands and provide the stage: the right atmosphere, music, and food. Rabbit Hill provides an oasis for couples celebrating honeymoons, anniversaries, and special events.**

The Rabbit Hill Inn is both a peaceful retreat and a convenient base for exploring northern Vermont and New Hampshire. But come for the romance of it all, for the five-course, candlelit meals, and for all the little surprises too numerous to detail (and better left for you to discover). Besides, surprises are rare in these times of all-disclosing web pages. Personal attention and whimsy are hallmarks of Rabbit Hill.

Once a popular stop on the trader's route between Canada and Boston, the main inn is a pillared Greek Revival building with an attached carriage house topped by a gabled roof. Between here and the tavern are five outdoor porches for relaxing! The public space inside includes a parlor with Federal decor where afternoon tea is served, a fireplaced living room with an addictive antique jigsaw puzzle, a convivial pub with darts and checkers, and a well-stocked VCR den.

The guest rooms (dubbed "fantasy chambers" here) are constantly upgraded and fussed over. They are meticulously furnished around a theme, such as music and Victoriana. Special touches include homemade candy, robes, rose petals on the turned-down bed, soothing music, and candles lit when you return to your room after dinner. Amenities are first-class. The premier accommodation is the loft; ask for a detailed description. The four newest rooms and suites have fireplaces, Jacuzzis, and private porches. Rooms off the hallway near the office are smaller and less expensive, though still desirable.

The candlelit dining rooms are intimate. Elegant place settings, artistic presentations, and an inconspicuous musician add to the effect. On our last visit, the relaxing two-hour dinner (open to the public by reservation) consisted of salmon dill ceviche with melon, papaya, and grapes, followed by the inn's ever-changing but signature Caesar salad. A braised chicken breast surrounded by a melange of vegetables was topped off by a Kaluha crème caramel with a chocolate biscotti. Chef Rusell Stannard has adeptly presided over the kitchen since 1989.

Breakfast is almost as elaborate as dinner. Serve yourself from a bountiful and artistically presented buffet of juices and granola, fruits, muffins, and breads. Then choose from two main dishes, perhaps maple walnut whole wheat pancakes with bacon.

The inn maintains its own cross-country trails, and downhill skiing is just 25 miles away. In warm weather the inn has canoes for use on the nearby Connecticut River, a golf membership, and lawn games. There is also swimming and fishing in a freshwater pond. Leslie is a ready source of information on the area. A stroll through this village of nine homes reveals a 150-year-old post office and a library that still operates on the honor system.

Lyndonville

Wildflower Inn

Darling Hill Road
Lyndonville, VT 05851
802-626-8310
800-627-8310
Fax: 802-626-3039
nekingdom@aol.com
www.pbpub.com/wldflwr.htm

A first-rate family destination

Innkeepers: Jim and Mary O'Reilly. **Accommodations:** 3 inn rooms (with shared bath), 10 rooms in the carriage house (with private bath), 10 suites. **Rates:** $95–$220 per couple B&B; slightly higher during foliage and holidays, less off-season; special rates for children. **Included:** Breakfast. **Minimum stay:** 2 nights on weekends. **Added:** 9% tax. **Credit cards accepted:** MasterCard, Visa. **Children:** Welcome. **Pets:** Not accepted. **Smoking:** Not permitted. **Handicap access:** Some rooms. **Open:** Year-round.

➤ **This hilltop retreat has gorgeous 360-degree views. Although it's geared to families, couples will appreciate it too.**

This nicely landscaped farmhouse estate dates from 1796 and, like the other homesteads along this dramatic ridge, was absorbed into a gentleman's estate around the turn of the century. There are few other inns so dramatically sited.

Jim and Mary O'Reilly have five boys and three girls, so children are especially welcome here. There are plenty of animals — a petting barn with horses, sheep, a calf, rabbit, donkey, and pony — as well as cats and a dog. Horse-drawn sleigh and wagon rides are also offered; weekly pony rides are particularly popular. Children's activities are scheduled every morning from 9:30–11:30; babysitters are available on request. There is also a new teen rec center. In the winter a lighted skating rink and the sledding hill are well-used.

Adult spaces include an attractive parlor and a library stocked with games and the kind of books you really want to read. Off by itself is a TV room. There's also a little gift shop, a sauna, spa room, and landscaped pool. Tea, served every afternoon, features cheese made in nearby Cabot and homemade snacks. You might want to enjoy a before-dinner drink at one of the tables underneath the trellis facing the spectacular sunsets — a most relaxing spot!

Most rooms in the post-and-beam carriage house are just right for families, each with a private entrance and a number of beds and bunks. Some have kitchen and all are skylit and have porches. Off by itself, a former one-room schoolhouse is now a honeymoon retreat, with a view of the valley and a two-person Jacuzzi. The other premium romantic accommodations include "Upper Meadow" and "Grand Meadow" with expansive views. Couples with and without children will feel right at home here. Three new family suites were added for the 1998 season.

At breakfast, the preferred tables are out on the glassed-in sun porch, overlooking Lyndonville down in the valley and the mountains beyond. You help yourself to coffee or tea, granola, cereals, and fruit. Then comes a hot dish: fresh eggs, bacon, muffins, and pancakes.

A family-style dinner is served from 5:00–6:30 P.M.; it's served when you sit down so that small children won't fidget. At 7:00, adults begin to filter in, ordering off the menu. On our last visit we enjoyed a hearty chicken vegetable soup, followed by a large serving of yellow fin tuna. It was by no means gourmet, but it was very good. Be sure to save room for dessert.

Jim and the staff are delighted to help you explore this corner of Vermont, the least-populated corner of the state. The inn itself has more than 550 acres on Darling Hill, and guests are welcome to stroll or cross-country ski. Neighboring Burke Mountain offers both downhill and cross-country skiing in winter and, in summer, an unusual toll road to its summit. The view from Burke's slopes is across Willoughby Lake, a narrow sheet of water walled by two abrupt mountains. Willoughby is beloved by windsurfers and sailors (there's always a breeze) and surrounded by a public forest webbed with trails. In any season, this is blessedly undeveloped country worth exploring on bike, skis, or foot. Although this beautiful inn has clearly defined itself as a family find in recent years, it tends to be a couple's find at times — such as foliage season, when school is in session.

Windsor

Juniper Hill Inn

RR 1, Box 79
Windsor, VT 05089
802-674-4273
800-359-2541
innkeepers@juniperhill.com
www.juniperhill.com

> **A romantic retreat with a view**

Innkeepers: Rob and Susanne Pearl. **Accommodations:** 16 rooms (all with private bath). **Rates:** $90–$150. **Included:** Breakfast, use of 18-speed bikes. **Credit cards accepted:** MasterCard, Visa, Discover. **Added:** 9% tax, 15% gratuity on dinner. **Children:** Not appropriate under 12. **Pets:** Not accepted. **Smoking:** Not permitted. **Handicap access:** No. **Open:** All months except first three weeks in April.

➤ **A grand, turn-of-the-century mansion set on a hill above the Connecticut River with a view of Mt. Ascutney.**

Few New England inns combine a feel of such spaciousness and warmth. Your first sense is of grandeur as you travel up the long, winding driveway to the Georgian-style mansion and then enter the palatial living room. When you cross the room and look out the door, you see a sweep of lawn, a pond, and the mountains.

Then Rob Pearl will show you to a guest room that's an artful mix of fabrics, wallpapers, and antiques, with all the right touches: bed lights, maybe an extra chair or writing desk, and probably a fireplace (nine of the sixteen rooms have working hearths).

Teddy Roosevelt, we were told, once spent the night in the comfortable room we occupied, one of two set off in a quiet wing of the house, beyond a second living room (with TV). A classic "gentleman's library" features leather chairs, an unusual hearth, plenty of books, and the only guest phone.

Breakfast and dinner are served in the wine-colored dining room, which has long windows and an ornate hearth. Less than a dozen well-spaced tables are white-clothed, garnished with fresh flowers. The dinner ($27–$29 prix fixe) menu, which changes nightly, will feature a selection of entrées like roast French rack of lamb, poached salmon with dill sauce, and ginger lemon chicken. Dessert might be Swedish crème topped with fresh fruit. Breakfast is full. Susanne Pearl does most of the cooking.

The inn is a place you could contentedly spend entire days, straying only as far as the pool and neighboring walking trails. But the immediate surroundings are unusually interesting, and the Pearls do their best to convey this to guests. Windsor is styled as Vermont's birthplace (in the Old Constitution House in 1777), and the American Precision Museum is cited as the birthplace of the "American system" of manufacturing.

In Cornish, New Hampshire, just across the covered bridge (which is said to be the longest in America) from Windsor, is the Saint Gaudens National Historic Site, home of the famous 19th-century sculptor. It's a fascinating place to visit, and Sunday concerts are held in its extensive gardens in the summer.

Guests are welcome to use the inn's 18-speed bikes to explore a mapped loop of the valley; they can also paddle down the river to savor the amazing view of the covered bridge — set against Mount Ascutney. In winter this is a ski mountain, offering both Alpine and cross-country trails.

In the 1940s, the woman engineer who first developed ski trails on Mt. Ascutney lived at Juniper Hill, using it as an office for her construction company and combination inn/fine restaurant for the mountain's first skiers. This house has had such a varied history that we could fill another few pages. It's history is printed in a small book, just one of many touches found in every guest room.

Woodstock Area

Jackson House

37 Route 4 West
Woodstock, VT 05091
802-457-2065
800-448-1890
Fax: 802-457-9290
posadajh@aol.com
www.jacksonhouse.com

**A romantic B&B with
magnificent gardens**

Innkeepers: Juan and Gloria Florin and Matt and Jennifer Barba. **Accommodations:** 11 rooms (all with private bath), 6 suites. **Rates:** $170 per couple, $240 for suites. **Included:** Full breakfast and champagne and hors d'oeuvres. **Minimum stay:** 2 days on weekends. **Added:** 9% tax. **Credit cards accepted:** MasterCard, Visa. **Children:** Over age 14. **Pets:** Not accepted. **Smoking:** Not permitted. **Handicap access:** Yes. **Open:** Year-round.

➤ **Staying at the Jackson House is like being part of an elegant house party, and many guests who meet for the first time at breakfast find themselves going out together that evening.**

This 1890s clapboard house was lovingly renovated, from the polished oak, cherry, and walnut floors to the gleaming copper roof. Each room is furnished with carefully chosen fabrics and antiques. The exquisite gardens are a symphony of colors.

Some houses are just lucky! When the Jackson House changed hands in 1996, almost all the exquisite furniture and furnishings of its previous owners remained and were enhanced by the new additions — four new suites and an elegant dining room (open to the public).

Chef Brendan Nolan, formerly sous chef of Boston's Four Seasons dining room, presides over a kitchen producing appetizers such as feuillete of white asparagus (oyster mushrooms and black truffles, Madeira and chervil), entrées like grilled filet of beef with wild mushroom strudel, rösti potato, aspargus and red wine, and sesame-crusted tuna medallions and lobster in lemongrass soy broth, quiona pilaf, and bok choy. The menu is à la carte or $48 prix fixe for five courses. The dining room is a newly created pleasant space with many windows overlooking the garden.

The Jackson House is in West Woodstock, a gathering of houses along the old Route 4. The verandah is lined with rocking chairs and hung with plants, and in back the 3-acre garden includes a small pond, formal gardens, and a stream complete with moon bridge.

Breakfast is served at a round table in the dining room, a cheerful space that opens onto the library and parlor, all flawlessly and formally furnished. Here guests gather again for hors d'oeuvres and champagne before dinner.

Each guest room has a theme. The centerpiece for the first-floor Josephine Tasher Bonaparte Room, for instance, is a stunning French Empire sleigh bed, and every detail complements it. The Mary Todd Lincoln Room is Victorian. The two rooms on the third floor are "one-room suites" with marble-walled bathrooms and French doors opening onto decks overlooking the garden. The new suites echo the decor of the old and feature either French doors opening onto the gardens or garden views, as well as gas fireplaces and elaborate plumbing (therm-massage or Jacuzzis tubs).

All the rooms are air-conditioned, but the only TV is in the spa — an attractive basement-level steam room with exercise equipment, including a Nordic Track and a weight center.

Woodstock is a great town for walkers. There are trails up Mount Tom and Mount Peg as well as around the extensive grounds of the Vermont Institute of Natural Science. In winter there's also skiing at Suicide Six and Killington; cross-country trails are right in town. From May through October the Billings Farm & Museum is open, and Woodstock is a shopping town year-round.

Kedron Valley Inn

Route 106
South Woodstock, VT 05071
802-457-1473
800-836-1193
Fax: 802-457-4469

> **A country inn with good food and outstanding horseback riding**

Innkeepers: Max and Merrily Comins. **Accommodations:** 26 rooms: 13 in the main house, 7 in the Tavern, others in the "log cabin." **Rates:** $120–$195 per couple B&B; Jacuzzi suites: $215. Less midweek in May and June, more during foliage season and Christmas vacation. **Included:** Varies with plan. **Minimum stay:** 2 nights on most weekends. **Added:** 9% tax, 15% gratuity. **Credit cards accepted:** All major ones. **Children:** No charge except for food. **Pets:** Accepted. **Smoking:** Restricted. **Handicap access:** Some rooms. **Open:** Year-round except April and 1 week in November.

➤ **This is the kind of Vermont country inn you picture in your imagination, plus New England's best riding facilities.**

This brick inn and adjacent tavern have formed the center of South Woodstock, one of Vermont's most affluent and picturesque villages, since the 1820s. Horses actually outnumber cars here, and the surrounding hills are webbed with trails — to which inn guests have access on mounts from the Kedron Valley Stables, next to the inn.

The inn itself is a luxurious retreat. The rooms have been carefully decorated; all have antique quilts. Fourteen rooms have fireplaces; six others have woodstoves. The most spacious rooms are in the old tavern, but those in the main house, while varying in size, have their own charm. The "log cabin" was built by the previous owners as a motel annex, but even here the rooms are large, deftly furnished with antiques, and have fireplaces.

There are several dining rooms and a large, pubby bar with a baby grand piano. The menu changes frequently and usually offers a half-dozen entrées that might range from vegetarian Wellington (oven-roasted vegetables layered with Portabello mushroom and chèvre, baked and topped with plum tomatoes; $16.50) to roast rack of lamb ($24). Year-round there's air-conditioned or fireside dining on the enclosed garden patio. The pond out back has two sand beaches, one for adults only.

The riding offered by Kedron Valley Stables is outstanding. This is the place for riders to hone their skills with weekend clinics, trail rides, or inn-to-inn treks. Tennis and golf are also easily accessible, and guests are encouraged to take advantage of the local walks outlined for them. In the winter there's downhill skiing at Killington or Suicide Six and plenty of cross-country trails. Horse-drawn sleigh rides are a specialty.

Woodstock Inn & Resort

14 The Green
Woodstock, VT 05091
802-457-1100
800-448-7900
Fax: 802-457-6699
Woodstock.Resort@connriver.net
www.woodstock.com

**One of New England's
premier resorts**

Manager: Tom List. **Accommodations:** 134 rooms, 7 suites, 3 cottages. **Rates:** $155–$315 per couple, third person $20; suite rates available on request; many packages. **Included:** Sports center use, skiing, and more, depending on package. **Minimum stay:** None. **Added:** 9% tax; add $53 per day for breakfast and dinner. **Credit cards accepted:** All major ones. **Children:** Age 14 and under, free in parent's room. **Pets:** Only in the Justin Morgan House. **Smoking:** Permitted in some guest rooms. **Handicap access:** Some rooms. **Open:** Year-round.

➤ **Golf is important here. The course is one of the country's oldest, with carts, a pro shop, and a putting green. Ask about special golf packages. Croquet is increasingly popular, and special clinics are offered.**

The Woodstock Inn is set respectfully back from Woodstock's oval green, within easy walking distance of the town's museum and shops. The inn offers the facilities of a complete resort: an 18-hole golf course, 12 tennis courts, paddle tennis courts, a pool in summer, and both an alpine ski hill and an extensive ski touring center in winter. It is owned by one of the world's most famous hoteliers, Laurance Rockefeller, who lives in the Billings mansion on the other side of town.

Memory of the turreted 19th-century Woodstock Inn that was knocked down in the 1960s to make way for this less lovable, more efficient model, are finally fading and certainly the dining room remains the most popular meeting spot in town, and draws guests from all over the world. The resort unquestionably ranks among the half-dozen best places to stay in New England.

The inn is pleasantly old fashion in the amount of common space it offers. In addition to the lobby, with its huge stone hearth, there is also a library, a sunny sitting room (where there's a grand piano and afternoon tea is served), and a lower-level lounge that looks like a posh men's club.

As the older guest rooms are renovated, built-in bookcases and darker colors, reproduction antiques and many special touches are added. Those in the new wing are exquisite if not very large. Many have fireplaces and several have porches. Throughout, the rooms are bright and country elegant. The suites are tastefully luxurious.

The formal dining room features New England and Continental cuisine. The menu changes frequently but might include roast rack of lamb or roasted free-range chicken with lobster medallions. In the pleasant Eagle Café you can dine on pretty much the same menu or have a salad or sandwich instead. A children's menu is available all day.

The resort is catering increasingly to families, offering a program of supervised early dining in the Eagle Café, then a movie during dinner while parents relax in the formal dining room. A second-floor game room features video machines and there are several family-geared packages.

In summer there's also a pool banked with flowers. In winter you can ski at Suicide Six, one of the country's oldest ski areas (also part of the resort). It has a 650-foot vertical drop, snowmaking, two chairlifts, a J-bar, a modern lodge, and a reputation for its challenging skiing despite its size. The cross-country center uses the golfers pro shop and 60 miles of trails, including trails that meander around Pogue Pond and past a warming hut, up to the top of Mount Tom — for a splendid view of the Ottauquechee Valley. Sleigh rides are another winter feature.

The property includes a separate two-story Sports Center complete with fitness machines, saunas, an indoor pool, a whirlpool, steam room, two tennis courts, two squash courts, and two racquetball courts.

Buses disgorge lunch patrons and business groups of up to three hundred that may fill the inn during the off-season, but this is primarily a place for families and couples. Except during foliage season and school vacation periods, it offers a number of packages, and skiing at Suicide Six is included in the price of a room in winter.

What's What

Activities and Facilities

A cross reference of accommodation types and special interests

Croquet

Connecticut
Under Mountain Inn, 19
Maine
Asticou Inn, 166
Black Point Inn, 85
The Bradley Inn, 115
The Claremont, 170
The Lodge at Moosehead, 198
Nannau-Seaside Bed & Breakfast, 144
Manor House, 142
Sparhawk Resort, 77
Massachusetts
Blantyre, 384
Chatham Bars Inn, 264
Lambert's Cove Country Inn, 291
The Lighthouse Inn, 316
The Wauwinet, 299
Wequassett Inn, 266
New Hampshire
The Balsams Grand Resort Hotel, 454
Dexter's Inn and Tennis Club, 439
The Franconia Inn, 461
Loch Lyme Lodge and Cottages, 432
The Mount Washington Hotel and Resort, 451
The Spalding Inn, 484
Rhode Island
Weekapaug Inn, 509

Gardens

Connecticut
Boulders Inn on Lake Waramaug, 15
Copper Beech Inn, 37
Manor House, 17
The Mayflower Inn, 23
Merrywood Bed & Breakfast, 21
Maine
Asticou Inn, 166
Black Point Inn, 85
Bradley Inn, 115
Breakwater 1904, 139
Bufflehead Cove, 60
Captain Lord Mansion, 61
Castine Inn, 155
Field Farm Guest House, 400
Harbourside Inn, 167
Manor House, 142
Nannau-Seaside Bed & Breakfast, 144
Massachusetts
Chatham Bars Inn, 264
Charles Hinckley House, 259
The Charlotte Inn, 276
Isaiah Hall B&B Inn, 267
Lambert's Cove Country Inn, 291
Littlejohn Manor, 378
The Miles River Country Inn, 331
Mostly Hall, 272
The Summer House, 301
The Wauwinet, 299
Wequassett Inn, 266
The Whalewalk Inn, 269
The Windflower Inn, 380
New Hampshire
Amos A. Parker House, 410
The Balsams Grand Resort Hotel, 454
Bungay Jar Bed and Breakfast, 459
Colby Hill Inn, 428
The Hilltop Inn, 463
The Notchland Inn, 447
Snowvillage Inn, 480

Rhode Island
  Elm Tree Cottage, 497
Vermont
  Basin Harbor Club, 621
  Cornucopia of Dorset, 527
  1811 House, 534
  The Inn at Shelburne Farms, 619
  Inn on the Common, 637
  Jackson House, 649
  Rabbit Hill Inn, 643
  Silas Griffith Inn, 525
  Swift House Inn, 614
  Trail's End, A Country Inn, 545
  The Tyler Place on Lake Champlain, 611

Golf

Maine
  Bethel Inn, 186
  Black Point Inn, 85
  The Cliff House, 74
  Spruce Point Inn, 102
Massachusetts
  Chatham Bars Inn, 264
  The Windflower Inn, 380
New Hampshire
  The Balsams Grand Resort Hotel, 454
  Carter Notch Inn, 467
  Home Hill Country Inn, 437
  The Mount Washington Hotel and Resort, 451
  The Spalding Inn, 484
  Sunset Hill House, 465
  Waterville Valley Resort, 482
  The Wentworth Resort Hotel, 469
Vermont
  Basin Harbor Club, 621
  1811 House, 534
  The Equinox, 536
  Highland Lodge, 636
  Woodstock Inn & Resort, 653

Gourmet Getaways

Grand Resorts

Maine
  The Asticou, 166
  Bethel Inn, 186
  Black Point Inn, 85
  The Claremont, 170
  The Colony Hotel, 63
  Inn by the Sea, 81
  Sparhawk, 77
  Spruce Point Inn, 102
Massachusetts
  Chatham Bars Inn, 264
  The Lighthouse Inn, 316
  The Wauwinet, 299
  Wequassett Inn, 266
New Hampshire
  The Balsams Grand Resort Hotel, 454
  The Mount Washington Hotel and Resort, 451
  The Spalding Inn, 484
Rhode Island
  Weekapaug Inn, 509
Vermont
  Basin Harbor Club, 621
  Edson Hill Manor, 584
  The Equinox, 536
  Topnotch at Stowe Resort and Spa, 591
  Woodstock Inn & Resort, 653

Horseback Riding

Maine
  The Birches, 205
  Telemark Inn, 188
New Hampshire
  The Franconia Inn, 461
  The Mount Washington Hotel and Resort, 451
  Waterville Valley Resort, 482
Vermont
  Edson Hill Manor, 584
  Hawk North, Ltd., 581
  Hickory Ridge House, 550

Island Getaways

Spa Facilities

Rustic Retreats

Tennis

Weddings

The Basics

A cross reference for families, groups, solo travelers, those with handicaps, and those with pets.

Family Finds

Connecticut
The Homestead Inn (New Milford), 13
Madison Beach Hotel, 39
Maine
Albonegon Inn, 98
Bald Mountain Camps, 203
Bear Spring Camps, 202
Bethel Inn & Country Club, 186
The Birches, 205
Dockside Guest Quarters, 89
Hiram Blake Camp, 164
Inn by the Sea, 81
Kawanhee Inn, 211
Migis Lodge, 207
Oakland House, 153
Pleasant Bay Bed & Breakfast, 137
Quisisana, 190
Telemark Inn, 188
Massachusetts
Baldwin Hill Farm B&B, 377
Boston Harbor Hotel at Rowes Wharf, 224
The Charles Hotel, 243
Chatham Bars Inn, 264
The Eliot, 228
The Four Seasons, 233
Harbor House and Wharf Cottages, 296
Hotel Meridien, 235
Kalmar Village, 312
The Lighthouse Inn, 316
The Masthead Resort, 304
Menemsha Inn and Cottages, 286
Old Farm Inn, 340
The Ritz-Carlton Boston, 241
Rocky Shores Inn & Cottages, 341
Royal Sonesta Hotel, 249

Groups

(as in friends, not business meetings)

Solo Travelers Feel Welcome

Handicap-Accessible Guest Rooms

Pets Welcome with Permission

Connecticut
  Bishopgate Inn, 35
  The Inn at Chester, 34
Maine
  Asticou Inn, 166
  Bethel Inn & Country Club, 186
  The Birches, 205
  The Colony Hotel, 63
  Driftwood Inn and Cottages, 57
  The Herbert Hotel, 200
  Hiram Blake Camp, 164
  Inn by the Sea, 81
  Kawanhee Inn, 211
  Pomegranate Inn, 82
  Portland Regency, 84
  Tootsie's Bed and Breakfast, 165
Massachusetts
  The Brandt House, 353
  Boston Harbor Hotel at Rowes Wharf, 224
  The Charles Hotel, 243
  The Charlotte Inn, 276
  The Eliot, 228
  Fairmont Copley Plaza Hotel, 231
  The Four Seasons, 233
  Hargood House, 303
  Hotel Meridien, 235
  Lambert's Cove Country Inn, 291
  Longfellow's Wayside Inn, 369
  The Morrill Place Inn, 336
  Publick House, 367
  The Ritz-Carlton Boston, 241
  Walker House, 391
  Wingscorton Farm Inn, 308
New Hampshire
  Dexter's Inn and Tennis Club, 439
  The Hanover Inn, 427
  The Hilltop Inn, 463
  Loch Lyme Lodge and Cottages, 432
  The Spalding Inn, 484
  Twin Lake Village, 434
  Whitneys' Inn at Jackson, 472

Recommended Guidebooks

Outdoor Recreation Guides

In the past few years, a number of outdoor soft-adventure guides have cropped up. Mountain biking has boomed more than any other sport perhaps. Countryman Press publishes an extensive selection of bicycling guides, including *25 Bicycle Tours on Cape Cod and the Islands* and *25 Mountain Bike Tours in Massachusetts*. *25 Bicycle Tours in Vermont* is written by the founder of the country's biggest touring company (Vermont Bicycle Touring). This classic guide to the best biking routes in the state helped popularize Vermont as a biking mecca.

In-Line Skate New England (Countryman Press) details the best 101 tours you can take around the six-state region.

Countryman Press publishes a series of state-by-state guides to rewarding hikes for all ages and ability levels. Among the titles are *50 Hikes in the Maine Mountains, 50 Hikes in Vermont, 50 Hikes in the White Mountains, 50 More Hikes in New Hampshire, 50 Hikes in Connecticut, 50 Hikes in Southern and Coastal Maine,* and *50 Hikes in Massachusetts*. More than a half-million of these guides are in print! Each hike is designed as a day's outing, rich in historical and natural lore and easy to follow. *Country Walks Near Boston* (Appalachian Mountain Club) is a very readable and useful guide to 20 walks in the areas surrounding New England's largest city.

If you're interested in more of a naturalist approach to hiking, look for Countryman Press's *Walks and Rambles on Cape Cod and the Islands* and *Walks and Rambles in Rhode Island*. These thorough guides include carefully described walks on beaches, woods, rocky ravines, and waterfalls in every corner of the state. *Country Walks in Connecticut* (Appalachian Mountain Club) includes 41 hikes around the state and is geared to residents of nearby urban areas.

Sea kayaking is a relatively inexpensive and easy sport that offers access to New England's coast and islands. The Appalachian

Mountain Club publishes *Sea Kayaking Along the New England Coast*. Revered standbys include the excellent *Appalachian Mountain Club Trail Guides* published by the Appalachian Mountain Club. These handy pocket guides cover thousands of miles of hiking and canoeing routes in New England. Canoeing remains a traditional, favorite way to explore the region's riverways. Good companions to the AMC guides are Countryman Press's *Canoe Camping Vermont & New Hampshire Rivers* and *Canoeing Massachusetts, Rhode Island and Connecticut*. These books detail all the possibilities and include information about where to find rentals, lessons, and guided expeditions.

As for fly fishing, which has really caught on in New England, we recommend *Fishing Vermont's Streams and Lakes* (Countryman Press).

Specialty-Interest New England Guides

Moving on to less physically challenging interests, Sloan's *Green Guide to Antiquing in New England* (Globe Pequot) is the most respected guide to the region's antiques stores. *Open Houses in New England* (Yankee Books) covers more than 600 homes in the six-state region; it is thorough and well written. The *Smithsonian Guide to Historic America: Northern New England* and the *Smithsonian Guide to Historic America: Southern New England* (Stewart, Tabori & Chang) feature lavish photography, historical paintings, engravings, and maps — making them excellent guides to New England's towns, historical homes, and politically, militarily, and culturally significant locales. *Special Museums of the Northeast: A Guide to Uncommon Collections from Maine to Washington, D.C.* (Globe Pequot) will give you a good overview of 144 small but fascinating museums covering a vast array of subjects, such as locks, soups, computers, antique toys, baseball, photography, dogs, and on and on.

Regional Guides

Anything written by Richard and Nancy Woodworth or Betsy Wittemann and Nancy Webster Woodworth (all published by Wood Pond Press) is worth picking up. They are excellent researchers and writers; descriptions are detailed and extensive. Specifically they write *Weekending in New England*, *Waterside Escapes*, *Getaways for Gourmets in the Northeast*, and *Inn Spots & Special Places*.

Webster and Woodworth's *Restaurants of New England, A Guide to Good Eating* is the only book that seriously tackles the ins and outs of dining throughout the six-state region. This book does for restaurants what Best Places does for lodging.

State-by-State Guides

As for state guides, we're obviously partial to the Explorer's Guides published by Countryman Press. The series includes a guide to Vermont, Maine, New Hampshire, Cape Cod and the Islands, Massachusetts (beyond Boston and Cape Cod), Connecticut, and Rhode Island. The travel specialists at Boston's famed Globe Corner Bookstore have said they are "New England's best guide series." (With all due modesty, the authors of several of these guides agree.) Each book details impartial descriptions of more than five hundred places to stay in all corners of the state and in all price ranges as well as places to "eat" and "dine." Special care has been given to suggesting things you can do with children, and bargains have been highlighted.

A History of Vermont (Mountain Press) is a lively, nicely illustrated companion to driving in the Green Mountain State. This is the only visitor-geared, once-over-lightly Vermont history available. *A Roadside Geology of Vermont and New Hampshire* (also by Mountain Press) explores the geology you might otherwise bypass! This is a wonderful book for the nongeologist and part of the Roadside Geology Guide series.

The *Compass Guide to Maine* (Fodor's) is lavishly produced with color photos, paintings, and sketches. The writing is sharp and the historical anecdotes and cultural material keenly researched. It's sprinkled with literary extracts and topical essays.

Boston Guides

One of the best of its kind, the *A.I.A. Guide to Boston* (Globe Pequot) gives an extensive architectural view of Boston through numerous, well-described tours that bring the city to life. Photographs are used extensively, and the maps are clear. *Blue Laws, Brahmins, and Breakdown Lanes* (Globe Pequot) is a humorous and enlightening guide to phrases and words that Bostonians use frequently and that visitors might not fully comprehend. *The Boston Globe Historic Walks in Cambridge* and the *Boston Globe Historic Walks in Old Boston* (both by Globe Pequot) are two first-class, comprehensive guides to walking tours through the history of old Boston and Cambridge. Clear maps and an excellent narrative make both these books a good choice if you like to stretch your legs and explore.

In and Out of Boston With (or Without) Children (Globe Pequot) has been very popular since its inception in 1966. The focus is on fun and exploration, though there are sections on food and lodging. There is also a list of 151 things to do and see for free. Meanwhile, if you're looking for bargains in Boston, you'll find them in *Mr. Cheap's Boston*. For the thrifty and frugal-minded, this is a delightful and helpful guide to reasonably priced places to eat and shop in Greater Boston.

The most useful restaurant resource is the annual *Zagat Boston Restaurant Survey*, conceived and executed differently from most restaurant guides. Instead of one person's opinion on a particular restaurant, this survey employs thousands of people — people who eat out an average of 3.6 times a week — to provide the factual information and evaluation of each establishment. It's quite reliable and a good read.

Index

Best Places Report

Authors of the Best Places to Stay series travel extensively in their research to find the best places for all budgets, styles, and interests. However, if we've missed an establishment that you find worthy, please write to us with your suggestion. Detailed information about the service, food, setting, and nearby activities or sights is most important. Finally, let us know how you heard about the place and how long you've been going there.

Send suggestions to:

> The Harvard Common Press
> Best Places to Stay Suggestions
> 535 Albany Street
> Boston, Massachusetts 02118

NAME OF HOTEL_____

TELEPHONE_____

ADDRESS_____

_____ ZIP _____

DESCRIPTION_____

_____

_____

_____

_____

_____

_____

YOUR NAME_____

TELEPHONE_____

ADDRESS_____

_____ ZIP _____

Best Places Report

Authors of the Best Places to Stay series travel extensively in their research to find the best places for all budgets, styles, and interests. However, if we've missed an establishment that you find worthy, please write to us with your suggestion. Detailed information about the service, food, setting, and nearby activities or sights is most important. Finally, let us know how you heard about the place and how long you've been going there.

Send suggestions to:

The Harvard Common Press
Best Places to Stay Suggestions
535 Albany Street
Boston, Massachusetts 02118

NAME OF HOTEL_____

TELEPHONE_____

ADDRESS_____

_____ ZIP _____

DESCRIPTION_____

_____

_____

_____

_____

_____

_____

YOUR NAME_____

TELEPHONE_____

ADDRESS_____

_____ ZIP _____

Best Places Report

Authors of the Best Places to Stay series travel extensively in their research to find the best places for all budgets, styles, and interests. However, if we've missed an establishment that you find worthy, please write to us with your suggestion. Detailed information about the service, food, setting, and nearby activities or sights is most important. Finally, let us know how you heard about the place and how long you've been going there.

Send suggestions to:

> The Harvard Common Press
> Best Places to Stay Suggestions
> 535 Albany Street
> Boston, Massachusetts 02118

NAME OF HOTEL_____

TELEPHONE_____

ADDRESS_____

_____ ZIP _____

DESCRIPTION_____

_____

_____

_____

_____

_____

_____

YOUR NAME_____

TELEPHONE_____

ADDRESS_____

_____ ZIP _____

Best Places Report

Authors of the Best Places to Stay series travel extensively in their research to find the best places for all budgets, styles, and interests. However, if we've missed an establishment that you find worthy, please write to us with your suggestion. Detailed information about the service, food, setting, and nearby activities or sights is most important. Finally, let us know how you heard about the place and how long you've been going there.

Send suggestions to:

> The Harvard Common Press
> Best Places to Stay Suggestions
> 535 Albany Street
> Boston, Massachusetts 02118

NAME OF HOTEL _____

TELEPHONE _____

ADDRESS _____

_____ ZIP _____

DESCRIPTION _____

_____

_____

_____

_____

_____

_____

_____

YOUR NAME _____

TELEPHONE _____

ADDRESS _____

_____ ZIP _____

Best Places Report

Authors of the Best Places to Stay series travel extensively in their research to find the best places for all budgets, styles, and interests. However, if we've missed an establishment that you find worthy, please write to us with your suggestion. Detailed information about the service, food, setting, and nearby activities or sights is most important. Finally, let us know how you heard about the place and how long you've been going there.

Send suggestions to:

> The Harvard Common Press
> Best Places to Stay Suggestions
> 535 Albany Street
> Boston, Massachusetts 02118

NAME OF HOTEL _____

TELEPHONE _____

ADDRESS _____

_____ ZIP _____

DESCRIPTION _____

_____

_____

_____

_____

_____

_____

YOUR NAME _____

TELEPHONE _____

ADDRESS _____

_____ ZIP _____

Best Places Report

Authors of the Best Places to Stay series travel extensively in their research to find the best places for all budgets, styles, and interests. However, if we've missed an establishment that you find worthy, please write to us with your suggestion. Detailed information about the service, food, setting, and nearby activities or sights is most important. Finally, let us know how you heard about the place and how long you've been going there.

Send suggestions to:

> The Harvard Common Press
> Best Places to Stay Suggestions
> 535 Albany Street
> Boston, Massachusetts 02118

NAME OF HOTEL_____

TELEPHONE_____

ADDRESS_____

_____ ZIP _____

DESCRIPTION_____

_____

_____

_____

_____

_____

_____

YOUR NAME_____

TELEPHONE_____

ADDRESS_____

_____ ZIP _____

Best Places Report

Authors of the Best Places to Stay series travel extensively in their research to find the best places for all budgets, styles, and interests. However, if we've missed an establishment that you find worthy, please write to us with your suggestion. Detailed information about the service, food, setting, and nearby activities or sights is most important. Finally, let us know how you heard about the place and how long you've been going there.

Send suggestions to:

> The Harvard Common Press
> Best Places to Stay Suggestions
> 535 Albany Street
> Boston, Massachusetts 02118

NAME OF HOTEL_____

TELEPHONE_____

ADDRESS_____

_____ ZIP _____

DESCRIPTION_____

_____

_____

_____

_____

_____

_____

YOUR NAME_____

TELEPHONE_____

ADDRESS_____

_____ ZIP _____